Individuals as
Producers of Their Development
A Life-Span Perspective

Individuals as Producers of Their Development
A Life-Span Perspective

EDITED BY

RICHARD M. LERNER

*Center for Advanced Study
in the Behavioral Sciences
Stanford, California
and
College of Human Development
The Pennsylvania State University
University Park, Pennsylvania*

NANCY A. BUSCH-ROSSNAGEL

*Human Development and Family Studies
Colorado State University
Fort Collins, Colorado*

With a Foreword by
ORVILLE G. BRIM, JR.

1981

ACADEMIC PRESS
A Subsidiary of Harcourt Brace Jovanovich, Publishers
New York   London   Toronto   Sydney   San Francisco

ACADEMIC PRESS, INC.
111 Fifth Avenue, New York, New York 10003

United Kingdom Edition published by
ACADEMIC PRESS, INC. (LONDON) LTD.
24/28 Oval Road, London NW1 7DX

Library of Congress Cataloging in Publication Data
Main entry under title:

Individuals as producers of their development.

    Includes bibliographies and indexes.
    1. Developmental psychology. 2. Social systems.
3. Personality and situation. I. Lerner, Richard M.
II. Busch-Rossnagel, Nancy A. [DNLM: 1. Human develop-
ment. BF 713 I39]
BF713.I53   155.2'5   81-3672
ISBN 0-12-444550-0   AACR2

Contents

6

Adolescents and Young Adults as Producers of Their Development   155
NORMA HAAN

7

Making It: The Dialectics of Middle Age   183
DEAN RODEHEAVER AND NANCY DATAN

8

Proactive and Reactive Aspects of Constructivism:
Growth and Aging in Life-Span Perspective   197
GISELA LABOUVIE-VIEF

9

The Role of Temperament in the Contributions of
Individuals to Their Development   231
ALEXANDER THOMAS AND STELLA CHESS

List of Contributors

Numbers in parentheses indicate the pages on which the authors' contributions begin.

JAY BELSKY (87), College of Human Development, The Pennsylvania State University, University Park, Pennsylvania 16802

NANCY A. BUSCH-ROSSNAGEL (1, 281), Human Development and Family Studies, Colorado State University, Fort Collins, Colorado 80523

STELLA CHESS (231), Department of Psychiatry, New York University Medical Center, New York, New York 10016

NANCY DATAN (183), Department of Psychology, West Virginia University, Morgantown, West Virginia 26506

GRETA G. FEIN (257), University of Michigan School of Public Health, Ann Arbor, Michigan 48109

NORMA HAAN (155), Institute of Human Development, University of California, Berkeley, Berkeley, California 94720

JANELL I. HANEY (349), Program in Special Education, University of Pittsburgh, Pittsburgh, Pennsylvania 15260

SARA HARKNESS (69), Graduate School of Education, Harvard University, Cambridge, Massachusetts 02138

RUSSELL T. JONES (349), Department of Clinical Psychology, University of Pittsburgh, Pittsburgh, Pennsylvania 15260

GISELA LABOUVIE-VIEF (197), Department of Psychology, Wayne State University, Detroit, Michigan 48202

RICHARD M. LERNER (1), College of Human Development, The Pennsylvania State University, University Park, Pennsylvania 16802

LYNN S. LIBEN (117), Department of Psychology, University of Pittsburgh, Pittsburgh, Pennsylvania 15260

JOHN A. MEACHAM (447), The Boys Town Center for the Study of Youth Development, The Catholic University of America, Washington, D.C. 20064

CAROL A. NOWAK (389), College of Human Development, The Pennsylvania State University, Altoona Campus, Altoona, Pennsylvania 16603

DEAN RODEHEAVER (183), Department of Psychology, West Virginia University, Morgantown, West Virginia 26506

GWENDOLYN T. SORELL (389), Division of Individual and Family Studies, College of Human Development, The Pennsylvania State University, University Park, Pennsylvania 16802

CHARLES M. SUPER (69), Graduate School of Education, Harvard University, Cambridge, Massachusetts 02138

ALEXANDER THOMAS (231), Department of Psychiatry, New York University Medical Center, New York, New York 10016

ETHEL TOBACH (37), Department of Animal Behavior, The American Museum of Natural History, New York, New York 10024

WILLIAM J. TOLAN (87), Department of Human Development and Family Studies, Cornell University, Ithaca, New York 14853

JUDITH WORELL (313), Department of Educational Psychology and Counseling, University of Kentucky, Lexington, Kentucky 40506

Foreword

In this unique volume, the editors and authors take us beyond the familiar study of humans trying to create an environment in which food is plentiful, life is safe, children are warm and comfortable, and water is abundant. A very different matter is under review by these scholars: how individuals strive to alter and re-create the environment so as to facilitate and induce a desired change in themselves.

What is it that makes this volume so interesting and provocative and important? The idea that organisms act to create environments to elicit responses from themselves is not new. The plan for getting oneself into the right situation to help one become something else, something more than he or she is today, is exemplified by hanging "Think" signs at strategic points in one's home and work place, and joining some of the thousands of organized groups devoted to helping one become a different person. What is new and powerful about this book is that it is the first major work dealing in broad perspective with the idea, and placing the idea firmly in the theory of life-span development.

Behind this idea, to be sure, is the view that the organism is dynamic, powered by curiosity, growth, expansion, and a drive toward mastery over itself and its world; and also by the development during the first 2 years of life of a sense of self as a distinctive being, and the construction of images of future selves that are different from what one is now. Behind the idea is also the view that organisms are open to change, are much more malleable than heretofore thought, and that the consequences of early experience and biological endowment are transformed by later experience.

Even though it is the case that in the early months of life biology paces the infant's development and there is little mastery over the environment—although as we know the baby does manipulate the caretakers—the fact is that very soon the infant, fragile though it still may be, is at work creating a variety of future selves that are only dimly seen for now. Is it reaching too far to imagine that children may seek to influence and thus create parental responses that give them the space and resources to work upon and grow toward these images of their future selves?

As adults we have concepts of ideal selves to which we aspire; real but future selves that we think we can become; abandoned selves (one survey of 200 corporate executives discovered that more than half had wanted to become professional athletes, believed still that they could have been professional athletes, and viewed it as a lost self); and of course negative or rejected selves, something to be avoided. Beyond gratification of simple, basic needs, a person has a concept of him- or herself in the future, has a vision of the years ahead, some image of the possible real self as well as the ideal self. One's striving to create an environment in the present that will contribute to a recreation of one's self for the future is the idea that guides this book.

The person is not alone in working on his or her own development. The society in which one lives, the social institutions that constitute the society, aid in efforts to master and alter the environment for development. In science there is a rapidly growing technology of physical and behavioral change that can be drawn upon, ranging from organ transplants and genetic surgery to behavior therapy and behavior modification and community intervention. The biological and psychological sciences have advanced from being studies of the constraints on human development to being the sources of enhancement and liberation of human development. Moreover, there has been an unprecedented emergence of many social groups, thousands of national groups, designed to provide social support to those who are seeking to change themselves. Mastering one's environment to enhance one's own development requires in most instances the anchoring of new identities in a social support system, and these national groups provide this resource.

Throughout this volume the subject is humanity and the concern is with the species rather than with individual differences. Certainly there may be individual differences in degree of mastery of, and re-creation of, the environment because of individually endowed or acquired differences, but the idea refers to the main thrust of the human animal, not an occasional remarkable human being.

In these essays are references to the human animal seeking and changing and creating its habitat into more optimal conditions, that have helped this animal change over 2 million years and more. It may be, as the editors say, that in the species there is evolution for plasticity. I like to think also of the primordial ooze itself, of DNA programmed in its own right to seek to create an environment for evolving into something that it is not yet but can be; molecules dreaming away, so to speak, about how they will remake the universe.

ORVILLE G. BRIM, JR.
New York City

Preface

A major conceptual change, if not a paradigm shift, has occurred among many of today's social scientists. Spurred by theoretical and empirical developments in life-span developmental psychology and in life-course sociology, many scientists have altered the focus of their work. Instead of dealing exclusively with ideas derived from either mechanistic or organismic paradigms, many have included a concern with contextually derived and contextually sensitive conceptions (see Baltes, 1979). This new focus has led to the evolution of a new perspective about human development. Brim and Kagan (1980) have summarized the status of this alteration in focus by noting that this

> conception of human development . . . differs from most Western contemporary thought on the subject. The view that emerges . . . is that humans have a capacity for change across the entire life span. It questions the traditional idea that the experiences of the early years, which have a demonstrated contemporaneous effect, necessarily constrain the characteristics of adolescence and adulthood . . . there are important growth changes across the life span from birth to death, many individuals retain a great capacity for change, and the consequences of the events of early childhood are continually transformed by later experiences, making the course of human development more open than many have believed [p. 1].

The perspective embodied in the view described by Brim and Kagan has led to a new concern with issues of relationships between evolution and ontogeny, of life-course constancy and change, of human plasticity, and of the role the developing person plays in his or her own development. These issues are linked by the idea that reciprocally deterministic, dynamic interactions between individuals and the multiple contexts within which they live characterize human development. Thus, all these issues arise out of common appreciation of the basic role of the changing context in developmental change. This appreciation is reflected in the growing commitment among scientists to expand disciplinary expertise by an understanding of the relationships among levels of analysis and, as such, to create a broadened interdisciplinary knowledge base. The series of *Life-Span Developmental Psychology* volumes, the annual *Life-Span Development and Behavior* volumes (Baltes, 1978; Baltes & Brim, 1979, 1980), the recent, edited volume by Burgess and Huston (1979), and the Brim and Kagan (1980) volume are all products and producers of this growing knowledge base.

The present volume grew out of another instance of this intellectual orientation. In 1978, Lerner and Spanier edited *Child Influences on Marital and Family Interaction: A Life-Span Perspective*, a book exploring the contribution of the child to the behavior and development of the people and roles found within the family. The basic idea behind this volume was that, by affecting their parents and their spousal relationship, as well as by influencing others in the familial network, children provided a basis of feedback to themselves. By influencing those who influence them, children were, in this way, thought to be producers of their own development.

The present volume further assesses the usefulness of viewing the individual as an active contributor to his or her development. However, in several ways this volume is a significant extension of the Lerner and Spanier one. First, the breadth of organism–environment reciprocities is extended beyond those involved with the child and family. On the one hand, this extension involves a consideration of the role of evolutionary biological processes; on the other, it pertains to the broader ecology of human development—the social network lying outside the family, and the physical environmental contexts of development. Second, person–context reciprocities linked to variables that may play their greatest role in the extrafamilial context are considered. Variables such as physical attractiveness, race, and physical handicap are examples of those discussed in this regard. Finally, because of the greater scope of our analysis, we may examine a potentially greater data base in a search for documentation of the presence and role of dynamic person–context interactions.

References

Baltes, P. B. (Ed.) *Life-span development and behavior* (Vol. 1). New York: Academic Press, 1978.
Baltes, P. B. On the potential and limits of child development: Life-span developmental

perspectives. *Newsletter of the Society for Research in Child Development*, 1979 (Summer), 1–4.

Baltes, P. B., & Brim, O. G., Jr. (Eds.) *Life-span development and behavior* (Vol. 2). New York: Academic Press, 1979.

Baltes, P. B., & Brim, O. G., Jr. (Eds.) *Life-span development and behavior* (Vol. 3). New York: Academic Press, 1980.

Brim, O. G. Jr., & Kagan, J. Constancy and change: A view of the issues. In O. G. Brim, Jr., & J. Kagan (Eds.), *Constancy and change in human development*. Cambridge, Massachusetts: Harvard University Press, 1980.

Burgess, R. L., & Huston, T. L. (Eds.) *Social exchange in developing relationships*. New York: Academic Press, 1979.

Lerner, R. M., & Spanier, G. B. (Eds.) *Child Influence on marital and family interactions: A life-span perspective*. New York: Academic Press, 1978.

Acknowledgments

There are several people whose contributions were most significant in making this book a reality. First and foremost, we owe a great debt of gratitude to the authors of the chapters in this volume. Their expertise, cooperation, patience, and professionalism did much to facilitate our tasks. We are also greatly indebted to Orville G. Brim, Jr., whose encouragement and support was a great help. His kindness in writing a foreword to this volume is also greatly appreciated. Much of the senior editor's work on this volume was done while at the Center for Advanced Study in the Behavioral Sciences. He is grateful for financial support provided by National Institute of Mental Health Grant No. 5-T32-MH14581-05 and by the John D. and Catherine T. MacArthur Foundation, and for the assistance of the Center's staff. Colleagues at Penn State—Lynn S. Liben, David F. Hultsch, and, especially, Paul B. Baltes and John R. Nesselroade (to whom this book is dedicated)—provided both personal and intellectual support. Finally, and not at all least, we thank Becky Gorsuch and Kathie Hooven for their many, many hours of typing and secretarial assistance.

RICHARD M. LERNER
NANCY A. BUSCH-ROSSNAGEL

1

Individuals as Producers of Their Development: Conceptual and Empirical Bases[1]

Introduction: Conceptual Trends in the Study of Human Development in the 1970s

The disciplines involved in the study of human development themselves undergo developmental change (Hartup, 1978; Riegel, 1972). In developmental psychology, the decades preceding 1970–1979 were characterized by a movement away from the descriptive and normative study of human development (Sears, 1975) to a primary focus on process and explanation (Bronfenbrenner, 1963; Looft, 1972). Philosophical and theoretical essays (McCandless & Spiker, 1956; Spiker & McCandless, 1954) illustrated this trend by involving calls for studies of developmental processes and mechanisms, especially ones involving learning (Lipsitt, personal communication, 1979). In addition, the theoretical and editorial work of Harris (1956, 1957) furthered the concern with process and explanation, instead of with descriptive, normative work. Characterizing the emphases

[1]This chapter was partially prepared while the first author was a Fellow at the Center for Advanced Study in the Behavioral Sciences. He is grateful for financial support provided by the National Institute of Mental Health (Grant #5-T32-MH14581-05) and by the John D. and Catherine T. MacArthur Foundation. An earlier version of this chapter was presented at the Center for Advanced Study in the Behavioral Sciences while the first author was a participant at its 1979 Summer Institute on Morality and Moral Development.

1

by 1970, Mussen (1970) noted, "The major contemporary empirical and theoretical emphases in the field of developmental psychology, however, seem to be on explanations of the psychological changes that occur, the mechanisms and processes accounting for growth and development [p. vii]."

The 1970s saw an increasingly more abstract concern with the study of development. Two interrelated themes emerged. First, there occurred a renewed appreciation of the metatheoretical, or paradigmatic, bases of developmental theories (Overton & Reese, 1973; Reese & Overton, 1970). Second, there was a trend toward the multidisciplinary, life-span study of human development.

THE ROLE OF PARADIGMS OF HUMAN DEVELOPMENT

In the 1970s, discussions occurred concerning how the "family of theories" (Reese & Overton, 1970) derived from the organismic and the mechanistic world view, respectively, were associated with different ideas about the nature and nurture bases of development (Overton, 1973), with different stances in regard to an array of key conceptual issues of development (e.g., the quality, openness, and continuity of change [Looft, 1973], with contrasting methodologies for studying development (Overton & Reese, 1973), and, ultimately, with alternative truth criteria for establishing the "facts" of development (Overton & Reese, 1973; Reese & Overton, 1970).

This focus on the philosophical bases of developmental theory, method, and data led to considering the use of still other paradigms in the study of development (e.g., Riegel, 1973). In part, this concern occurred as a consequence of interest in integrating assumptions associated with prototypic organismic- and mechanistic-derived theories (Looft, 1973). For instance, Riegel (1973, 1975, 1976a, 1976b) attempted to formulate a paradigm of development including both the active organism focus in organicism and the active environment focus in mechanism. In addition, however, interest in continual, reciprocal *relations* between active organism and active context (and not in either element per se), and concern with these relations as they existed on all phenomenal levels of analysis, was a basis of proposing a dialectical (Riegel, 1975, 1976a), transactional (Sameroff, 1975), or relational (Looft, 1973) model of human development.

Contrary to assumptions associated with the other paradigms of human development, Riegel's (1975, 1976a, 1976b) view emphasized the continual conflict among inner–biological, individual–psychological, outer–physical, and sociocultural levels of analysis; he assumed that constant changes among the multiple, reciprocally related levels of analysis were involved in development (Overton, 1978). Thus, his dialectical model can be seen as derived from the paradigm that Pepper (1942) labeled as *contextualism* (Hultsch & Hickey, 1978; Lerner, Skinner, & Sorell, 1980).

The dialectical model, as summarized by Riegel (1976a), involves a commitment to the study of "ceaseless flux," of actions and changes, and to a concern with short-term (e.g., situational) changes, long-term (e.g., individual and cultural) changes, and, *especially*, to the interrelation between the two. Thus, ceaseless, interrelated changes are the core ideas in the paradigm promoted by Riegel. These ideas are also basic to the contextual paradigm of Pepper (1942). From this view "every behavior and incident in the world is a historic event" and "change and novelty are accepted as fundamental [Hultsch & Hickey, 1978, p. 79]." The basic facts of existence are "complexes or contexts [Pepper, 1942, p. 142]," where "The real historic event, the event in its actuality, is when it is going on *now*, the dynamic dramatic active event [p. 232]," and where "the relations involved in a historic event are inexhaustible, and a set of contextualistic categories does not so much determine the nature of our world as lead one to appreciate fair samples of the world's events [p. 237]." Thus, constant change of the "now" (the event) and the total interrelation of this event are the basic ideas of Pepper's contextual paradigm. Riegel's (1975, 1976a, 1976b) ideas, then, along with those of Pepper (1942), promoted interest in the developmental implications of active organisms being engaged in relations with their active context.

In summary, from this perspective, developmental changes occur as a consequence of reciprocal (bidirectional) relations between the active organism and the active context. Just as the context changes the individual, the individual changes the context. As such, by acting to change sources of their own development, by being both a product and a producer of their contexts, individuals effect their own development (Riegel, 1976a; also see Schneirla, 1957). Moreover, because the context is seen as a multilevel one—having interrelated biological, sociocultural, physical–environmental, and historical components—Riegel's ideas meshed with the second theme that can be identified as emerging in the study of human development in the 1970s. That is, by stressing that there was change across life, and that it involved variables from several levels of analysis, Riegel's ideas were compatible with a multidisciplinary, life-span view of human development.

THE MULTIDISCIPLINARY, LIFE-SPAN STUDY OF HUMAN DEVELOPMENT

Developmental psychology is not the only scientific discipline concerned with the study of human development. Family and life-course sociologists, developmental and evolutionary biologists, comparative psychologists, physicians, and economists are also concerned with human development (e.g., see Riley, 1979). Human development, or more accurately child development, was often studied in the first several decades of this century within university institutes (e.g., at Iowa, Minnesota, and Berkeley) designed to be multidisciplinary; however, this pluralistic perspective began to erode by the 1950s, and was replaced by a unidisciplinary, psychological view of development (Lipsitt, 1979; Palermo, 1980; personal communications). Indeed, some reviewers (e.g., Hartup, 1978), have thus noted that relative disciplinary isolation characterized developmental research in the 2 decades prior to the 1970s. However, the years following this time were marked by renewed calls for interdisciplinary integration (e.g., Brim & Kagan, 1980; Bronfenbrenner, 1977; Burgess & Huston, 1979; Hill & Mattessich, 1979; Lerner & Spanier, 1978; Petrinovich, 1979; Riley, 1979; Wilson, 1975). The bases for these calls were primarily conceptual. Although it is possible to present these bases from multiple disciplinary foci (e.g., from a life course sociological perspective; Brim, 1966, 1968; Riley, 1979), emphasis on changes in the developmental psychological analysis of human development is a useful representative case.

Attempts to use a unidimensional biological model of growth, based on an idealistic, genetic–maturational (organismic) paradigm, to account for data sets pertinent to the adult and aged years were not completely successful (Baltes, Reese, & Lipsitt, 1980; Baltes & Schaie, 1973). Viewed from the perspective of this organismic conception, the adult and aged years were necessarily seen as periods of decline. However, all data sets pertinent to age changes (e.g., in regard to intellectual performance) during these periods were not consistent with such a unidirectional format for change. In summarizing the implications of this work for the understanding of the human life course, Brim and Kagan (1980) note that "humans have a capacity for change across the entire life span . . . there are important growth changes across the life span from birth to death, many individuals retain a great capacity for change, and the consequences of the events of early childhood are continually transformed by later experiences, making the course of human development more open than many have believed [p. 1]."

Accordingly, increasingly greater interindividual differences in intraindividual change were evident in many data sets (Baltes, 1979a; Baltes & Schaie, 1974, 1976; Schaie, Labouvie, & Buech, 1973). On the basis of such data, Brim and Kagan (1980) conclude that "growth is more individualistic than was thought, and it is difficult to find general patterns [p. 13]." Variables associated with membership in particular birth cohorts and/or with normative and non-normative events occurring at particular times of measurement appeared to account for more of the variance in behavior change processes with respect to adult intellectual development than did age-associated influences (Baltes *et al.*, 1980). Data sets pertinent to the child (Baltes, Baltes, & Reinert, 1970) and the adolescent (Nesselroade & Baltes, 1974) that considered these cohort and time effects also confirmed their saliency in developmental change. Conceptualizations useful for understanding the role of these non-age-related variables in development were induced (e.g., Baltes, Cornelius, & Nesselroade, 1977).

As a consequence of this empirical and conceptual activity, the point of view labeled "life-span developmental psychology" or the "life-span view of human development" (Baltes, 1979a,b; Baltes *et al.*, 1980) became crystallized. The emerging nature of this orientation has become clear over the course of several conferences (Baltes & Schaie, 1973; Datan & Ginsberg, 1975; Datan & Reese, 1977; Goulet & Baltes, 1970; Nesselroade & Reese, 1973), the initiation of publication of an annual volume devoted to life-span development (Baltes, 1978; Baltes & Brim, 1979), and the publication of numerous empirical and theoretical papers (Baltes *et al.*, 1980). From this perspective, the potential for developmental change is seen to be present across all of life; the human life course is held to be potentially multidirectional and necessarily multidimensional (Baltes, 1979b; Baltes & Nesselroade, 1973; Baltes *et al.*, 1980). In addition, the sources of the potentially continual changes across life are seen to involve both the inner–biological and outer–ecological levels of the context within which the organism is embedded. Indeed, although an orientation *to* the study of development and not a specific theory *of* development (Baltes, 1979b), it is clear that life-span developmentalists are disposed to a reciprocal model of organism–context relations. As Baltes (1979b) has indicated:

> Life-span developmental psychologists emphasize *contextualistic–dialectic* paradigms of development (Datan & Reese, 1977; Lerner, Skinner, & Sorell, 1980; Riegel, 1976a) rather than the use of "mechanistic" or "organismic" ones more typical of child development work. There are two primary rationales for this preference. One is, of course, evident also in current child development work. As development unfolds, it becomes more and more apparent that individuals act on the environment and produce novel behavior outcomes, thereby making the active and selective nature of human beings of paramount importance. Furthermore, the recognition of the interplay between age-graded, history-graded, and non-normative life events suggests a contextualistic and dialectical conception of development. This dialectic is further accentuated by the fact that individual development is the reflection of multiple forces which are not always in synergism, or convergence, nor do they always permit the delineation of a specific set of endstates [p. 2].

In summary, the development of life-span developmental psychology in the 1970s has led to a multidisciplinary view of human development, one suggesting that individual changes across life are both a product and a producer of the multiple levels of context within which the person is embedded.

Three points about the present status of this view are important to note. First, to study the complex interrelations among organism and context, life-span developmentalists (e.g., Baltes, 1968; Schaie, 1965) promote the use of particular research designs and methodologies (e.g., sequential designs, multivariate statistics, cohort analysis). Second, they seek both methodological and substantive collaboration with scholars from disciplines whose units of analysis have traditionally been other than individual–psychological, or personological, ones. For example, the work of life-course sociologists has been important in advancing life-span developmental psychology (e.g., Brim, 1966, 1968; Brim & Kagan, 1980; Brim & Ryff, 1980; Elder, 1974, 1979; Riley, 1978, 1979). Third, however, these methodological and multidisciplinary activities are undertaken primarily for conceptual reasons. If contextual influences were not seen as crucial for understanding individual development, neither methods for their assessment in relation to the individual, nor information about the character of these levels of analysis, would be necessary.

Accordingly, the life-span view promotes a model of development we have seen described as a contextual (Pepper, 1942) or a dialectic (Riegel, 1975, 1976a, 1976b) one. In so doing, it sees individuals as both products and producers of the context that provides a basis for their development. As such, individuals may be seen as producers of their development.

THE PLAN OF THIS BOOK AND
THE GOALS OF THIS CHAPTER

To summarize the preceding discussion, we may note that

1. After decades of increasing interest in developmental theory, further conceptual elaboration resulted in a more abstract plane of discussion, one that acknowledged the role of paradigms and therefore the philosophical bases of theories.
2. Empirically based scientific developments have been associated with the elaboration of a multidisciplinary, life-span view of human development.
3. Because of these developments, the 1970s involved
   a. a concern with a contextual–dialectic model of development, and
   b. a concern with the idea that individuals, in action with their changing context, can provide a basis of their own development.

The purpose of this book is to explore the conceptual, methodological, and empirical implications of the idea that individuals are producers of their development. The use of this concept both at specific portions of the life span and for selected processes across the life span will be considered. Moreover, as a contextual perspective does not imply any one theoretical perspective (Baltes, 1979b; Looft, 1973), and as a life-span view of human development promotes theoretical pluralism in the service of the potential use of multiple perspectives in the understanding of behavior change processes (Baltes *et al.*, 1980), diverse theoretical perspectives will be represented in the succeeding chapters. Cognitive developmental (Liben, Chapter 5; Labouvie-Vief, Chapter 8; and Fein, Chapter 10), cognitive social learning (Worell, Chapter 12; Jones & Haney, Chapter 13), and psychodynamic (Haan, Chapter 6; and Rodeheaver & Datan, Chapter 7) orientations are represented. In addition, conceptions derived from contextual (Tobach, Chapter 2; Super & Harkness, Chapter 3; Thomas & Chess, Chapter 9; Busch-Rossnagel, Chapter 11; and Sorell & Nowak, Chapter 14), dialectic (Meacham, Chapter 15), and human ecological (Belsky & Tolan, Chapter 4) perspectives are forwarded. This pluralism of theoretical perspective is enhanced by the inclusion of chapters by authors trained in the psychological subdisciplines of clinical, comparative, developmental, and anthropological psychology and the disciplines of special education, cultural anthropology, and psychiatry.

The chapters that are provided offer an analysis of the evolutionary biological and cultural bases of the phenomena involved in organism–context reciprocities (Tobach, Chapter 2, and Super and Harkness, Chapter 3). The Tobach and Super and Harkness chapters combine with the present one to offer a conceptual foundation for viewing individuals as possessing processes that contribute to their development, both within specific portions of life and across ontogeny.

Accordingly, these initial chapters are followed by ones that evaluate the "individuals as producers" notion within successive portions of life: infancy (Belsky & Tolan, Chapter 4), childhood (Liben, Chapter 5), adolescence and young adulthood (Haan, Chapter 6), adulthood (Rodeheaver & Datan, Chapter 7), and in the aged years (Labouvie-Vief, Chapter 8). In turn, these chapters are followed by ones that consider variables and/or processes which, across life, may provide a basis for the person's contribution to his or her own development. The roles of temperament (Thomas & Chess, Chapter 9), characteristics of the physical setting of development (Fein, Chapter 10), physical handicaps (Busch-Rossnagel, Chapter 11), sex (Worell, Chapter 12), race (Jones & Haney, Chapter 13) and physical attractiveness (Sorell & Nowak, Chapter 14) are discussed. A final chapter (Chapter 15), by Meacham, provides a historical analysis of the political, economic, and scientific contexts of the central idea of this volume: Active individuals engage their active world in providing a basis for their development.

Thus, the multidisciplinary knowledge base suggested by both contextualism and the life-span view of human development is represented in this book, and the goal of the remainder of the present chapter is to elaborate these bases. The idea that individuals are producers of their development, when derived from a contextualistic, life-span view, rests on ideas that have bases in several disciplines. Accordingly, the next section of this chapter discusses the assumptions upon which the contextual–dialectic model, advanced by Pepper (1942) and Riegel (1975, 1976a, 1976b), is based. The relevance of these assumptions to ideas important to several disciplines will be suggested. Specifically, their implications for understanding evolutionary and ontogenetic change in a unified framework will be suggested. Conceptual and empirical support for these ideas will be indicated. Finally, illustrations of the potential empirical use of a contextual life-span model of human development will be suggested.

Assumptions of a Contextual–Dialectic Paradigm

Over the course of its history, knowledge about psychological development has been advanced most notably by research derived from either an organismic or mechanistic paradigm (Baltes, 1979b; Overton & Reese, 1973; Reese & Overton, 1970). Although contributions derived from the two paradigms have remained relatively unintegrated (Kuhn, 1978), both paradigms nevertheless share some common assumptions (cf. Kaufmann, 1968). These assumptions pertain to the views that: (*a*) the universe is uniform and permanent; and (*b*) that the laws to be discovered about the development of organisms are all absolute ones, whether they involve variables lying inside the organism (for example, arising as a product of its nature) or outside the organism (for example, in its nurture). Although sampling and technological limitations lead science to be able to generate only probabilistic laws, these probabilistic statements are regarded as unbiased estimates of absolute ones (Hempel, 1966).

Alternatively, however, a contextual–dialectic paradigm assumes (*a*) *constant change* of all levels of analysis; and (*b*) *embeddedness* of each level with all others, that changes in one promote changes in all. The assumption of constant change denotes that there is no complete uniformity or constancy. Rather than change being a to-be-explained phenomenon, a perturbation in a stable system, change is a given (Overton, 1978); thus, the task of the scientist is to describe, explain, and optimize the parameters and trajectory of processes (i.e., variables that show time-related changes in their quantity and/or quality).

The second assumption of contextualism–dialecticalism is thus raised. It stresses the interrelation of all levels of analysis. Because phenomena are not seen as static, but rather as change processes, and any change process occurs within a similarly (i.e., constantly) changing world (of processes), any target change must be conceptualized in the context of the other changes within which it is embedded. Thus, change will constantly continue as a consequence of this embeddedness.

IMPLICATIONS OF EMBEDDEDNESS AND CONSTANT CHANGE

Conceptualizations of human development derived from the contextual–dialectic paradigm speak of the joining of multiple change processes (e.g., see Lerner, 1978, 1979; Meacham, 1976, 1977; Riegel, 1975). Whereas a personological explanation of human development is therefore seen as quite limited from this perspective (Baltes, *et al.*, 1980), this view does not mean *only* that the individual's ontogeny must be understood as linked to his or her family and society. In addition, it means that the inner and outer syntheses that compose the human condition have to be integrated as well; biological and cultural change, or in other words biocultural, historical, or evolutionary changes, must be understood (Baltes, *et al.*, 1980; Lerner, 1978; Lewontin & Levins, in press; Schneirla, 1959; Tobach & Schneirla, 1968).

Thus, the idea of embeddedness, that any level of analysis is reciprocally related to all others, leads to the idea that human biology is both a producer *and* a product of social and cultural change. This view contrasts with those of other scholars who, in writing about the relation between biological and social change, stress either that the former is primarily the unidirectional shaper of the latter (Wilson, 1975) or that the two are relatively independent (Campbell, 1975). The present position is that any level of analysis may be understood in the context of the distal biocultural and more proximal ontogenetic changes of which it is a part (Tobach, 1978), and that the idea of "one level in isolation" as the "prime mover" of change is not a useful one. Conceptual and empirical support for these interpretations of the implications of embeddedness will be discussed in the next section.

First, however, it is important to note that embeddedness, in relation to the constant change assumption of contextualism, leads to another key idea about the character of human development. If change on multiple, interrelated levels of analysis characterizes the human life span, then neither specific ontogenetic end states (Baltes, 1979b) nor totally uniform features of development at any portion of ontogeny characterize the life course. Instead the human life span is characterized by the *potential* for plasticity (i.e., intraindividual change; Baltes & Baltes, 1979; Schneirla, 1957; Tobach & Schneirla, 1968), as well as by the potential for interindividual differences in such change. Conceptual and empirical support for this view will also be presented in a succeeding section.

In summary the contextual–dialectic assumptions of constant change and embeddedness lead to ideas stressing both the plastic and social natures of biological and psychological developments. These ideas have strong implications for our understanding of evolution, of ontogeny, and thus of organism–environment relations. Although, as will be demonstrated, the concepts of constant change and of embeddedness are inextricably related, it is useful to review separately lines of evidence and arguments in support of each. Following the order used above, we begin by specifying support for the ideas associated with the embeddedness notion.

Bases of the Social Nature of Human Development

Concepts and data sets derived from both evolutionary and ontogenetic perspectives support the view that human development is an outcome of interdependent biological, psychological, and sociocultural changes. This support includes ideas about the meaning of adaptation, about the nature of the environment to which organisms adapt, about hominid evolution, and about individual and group interdependencies.

THE MEANING OF ADAPTATION

The concept of development has strong biological roots (Harris, 1957). Development has often been defined as progressive, adaptive changes in an organism or living system (e.g., see Schneirla, 1957). From this view, the processes defining development are those involving adaptation, and the function of adaptation is to meet the demands of the environment. That is, an organism's survival depends on its being able to meet the demands of its context. This context is made up of physical phenomena and, in ecologically prototypic milieus (Tobach & Schneirla, 1968), other organisms and the products of other organisms (i.e., physical and abstract products associated with other organisms, or simply social objects; Lewis & Feiring, 1978). Indeed, the idea that biological adaptation is a social relational phenomeon is found in Sahlins' (1978) definition of adaptation as the maximization of social life chances.

Moreover, as Tobach & Schneirla (1968) point out, until the transitions from inorganic to organic life are better understood, it is fair to conclude that no form of life, as far as we know, comes into existence independent of other life. No animal lives in total isolation from its conspecifics across its entire life span.

Thus, the concept of development, drawing on its biological foundation, indicates a necessary link between adaptation and social functioning. Other links between biological and social life exist.

THE NATURE OF THE ENVIRONMENT

Information about the nature of the environment, or context, to which organisms adapt also provides evidence for the embeddedness of biological and social functioning. Richard Lewontin, one of the world's leading population geneticists, believes that just as many social scientists have an oversimplified view of genes and their contribution to behavior (Lewontin, 1976; Lewontin & Levins, in press), many biologists do not adequately understand one half of what he contends should be their unit of analysis: the organism–environment relation. Lewontin and Levins state that "evolutionary theory is concerned with the relations and changing relations of organisms and environments," and has as "its fundamental dichotomy . . . organism and environment." However, they note that to biologists the organism is "active, richly described and changing," but the environment is poorly understood, and thus viewed globally; they believe it is typically "delineated superficially and treated as fixed [p. 69]."

As such, Lewontin and Levins indicate several aspects of the environment that must be understood to adequately appraise the details of what are dynamic organism–environment relations. In so doing they provide information of use to both biological and social scientists. Lewontin and Levins (in press) note that:

> As a preliminary analysis, the separation of organism and environment or of physical and biological factors of the environment . . . have proved useful. But they eventually become obstacles to further understanding: the division of the world into mutually exclusive categories may be logically satisfying but in scientific activity there seem to be no non-trivial classifications that are really mutually exclusive. Eventually their interpenetration becomes a primary concern of further research. It is in this sense that dialectics rejects the excluded middle [p. 71].

In contrast to a model in which an organism is seen as inserted into an *already given* environment, Lewontin and Levins (in press) note several aspects of an organism–environment interpenetration model. These include

1. *Organisms select their environments:* Organisms actively respond to environmental signals so as to find favorable habitats (milieus). Lewontin and Levins note that the selection of environments by organisms is generally adaptive, in that it brings them into contact with more favorable conditions than would random movement. However, environmental selection is not the seeking of optimal conditions. What is optimal depends on the changing state of the organism and on its developmental history. In addition, different organismic processes often have different requirements for optimality; as such, individuals often select milieus that compromise among conflicting needs. Finally, environmental selection with respect to one dimension carries with it other dimensions, due to environmental correlations; these correlates become factors in selection.

2. *Organisms modify their environments:* They do this by consuming and depleting resources, by excreting waste products, and by leaving evidence of their presence in a setting (which may serve to attract predators and parasites). These effects are often nonadaptive (Lewontin & Levins, in press).

3. *Organisms transform the statistical structure of their environments:* They do this by changing the presence and predictability of features of their milieu.

4. *Organisms define their environments, determining what aspects are relevant and which environmental variations can be combined or ignored.*

5. *Organisms respond to their environments:* Any aspect of the environment that stimulates the organism does so through multiple pathways

and, as such, the responses to the environment are the result of a network of mutually interdependent interactions (cf. Kuo, 1967).

6. Finally, as a way of summarizing the points mentioned, Lewontin and Levins (in press) note that *the reciprocal interaction of organism and environment takes place through several pathways that link the individual and evolutionary time scales:* Here, Lewontin and Levins (in press) note that, because organisms actively select those environments in which they can survive and reproduce, each organism determines the environment to which it is exposed. On an ontogenetic level, this activity determines what environmental impacts the organism will respond to. On an evolutionary level, this activity determines the environments to which the organism adapts, and thus, the kind of selection it experiences. In these ways, the organism is a producer of its own ontogenetic and evolutionary history.

Consistent with a contextual viewpoint, however, Lewontin and Levins (in press) note that the environment acts differently on different genotypes. In some environments, different genotypes may lead to virtually identical phenotypes, whereas, in other environments, that same array of genotypes would lead to a diverse assortment of phenotypes. However, in common or normative environments, "there is less variation among the responses of different genotypes than in unusual or extreme environments [Lewontin & Levins, in press]." In moderately atypical environments, the differences among genotypes may be enhanced. Unfortunately, however, in very extreme or atypical environments, for example, as may occur in times of rapid social change, uniformity (or stereotypy) of response typically occurs. When it does, then, to use Lewontin and Levins' (in press) phrase, it is "commonly lethal." In other words, evolutionary theory needs to take into account this double impact of the environment: The environment, as a developmental stimulus, helps to create the variability that the environment, as "Darwinian filter" (Lewontin & Levins, in press), selects. Thus, these relations between organism and environment underscore the evolutionary salience of plasticity (as opposed to stereotypy or uniformity) of response. We will return to the importance of plasticity in what follows.

To summarize the present argument, however, we should note that, given Lewontin and Levins' depiction of the environment, it is not possible to construe it as static surroundings. To Lewontin and Levins (in press), "It is also a way of life; the activity of the organism sets the stage for its own evolution [p. 78]." Lewontin and Levins see this strong interaction between what an organism does and what happens to it over its life span to be especially important in understanding human evolution. To quote Lewontin and Levins (in press): "The labor process by which the human ancestors modified natural objects to make them suitable for human use was itself the unique feature of the way of life that directed selection on the hand, larynx, and brain in a positive feedback that transformed the species, its environment, and its mode of interaction with nature [p. 78]."

Lewontin and Levins' concluding point thus leads us directly to the next line of evidence that supports the view that links between evolutionary and ontogenetic change are, in great part, social ones.

HOMINID EVOLUTION

The social nature of human development is supported also by current anthropological reasoning, the gist of which is as follows: Humans have been selected for social dependency. The course and context of evolution was such that it was more adaptive to act in concert, with the group, than in isolation.

Masters (1978), an anthropologist, notes that early hominids were hunters. These ancestors evolved from herbivorous primates under the pressure of climatic changes that caused African forest to be replaced with savannah. Our large brains, he speculates (Masters, 1978, p. 98), may be the (naturally selected) *result* of cooperation among early hominids and hence, in an evolutionary sense, a social organ. Indeed, he believes that with such evolvement the "central problem" in anthropological analysis, that of the origin of society, may be solved. Washburn (1961), another anthropologist, appears to agree. He notes that the relative defenselessness of early man (lack of fighting teeth, nails, or horns), coupled with the dangers of living on the open African savannah, made group living and cooperation *essential for survival* (Hogan, Johnson, & Emler, 1978; Washburn, 1961).

In short, the basis of human evolution appears to have involved social processes. Moreover, not only does human evolution implicate social relations, but, to return to our first point about the link between adaptation and social functioning, we may note that one simple way of defining evolution is as a type of continuous adaptation over time (Wispé & Thompson, 1976). Of course, implied in this definition is that the history of organisms' adapting is one of adjustments to something, some environmental context impinging on or pressing the organisms. Organisms cannot remain static by this implication; they must change, or have the ability to change, because another implication of this definition is that the "thing" that presses them, that context, does not exert isomorphic, unchanging presses over time.

These implications are made progressively more explicit in other definitions of evolution. Thus, stressing the mechanisms involved in the process by which evolution occurs, Campbell (1975) defines it as blind variation and systematic selective retention, and Dobzhansky (1973) depicts it as the creative response of living matter to its environment. Similarly, Hogan, et al. (1978) indicate that "development is a never-ending process of trying to adjust internal conditions to external demands (that is, to adapt). These adjustments are necessary because the environment as well as the person is continually changing. But since change is the only certainty, any accommodation made will only be temporary [p. 5]."

However, as noted, in the human development literature, human evolution has been labeled as biocultural change and the animal comparative literature (e.g., Tobach, 1978; Tobach & Schneirla, 1968) speaks of the adaptation of organisms at all psychological levels as involving social functioning. What these latter perspectives about evolution and adaptive functioning offer is not a set of ideas contradicting the conceptions of evolution offered by Wispé and Thompson (1976), Campbell (1975), Hogan, *et al.* (1978) and Dobzhansky (1973). Rather, they serve to clarify the character of the context to which organisms adapt. They indicate that the environment, the context, is largely a social one.

The point, then, is that biological adaptation means social adaptation, or, in other words, the adaptive changes that have comprised human evolution are, in a unified sense, both biological and social. Indeed, *biological is social* from this view.

INDIVIDUAL AND GROUP INTERDEPENDENCIES

Several points may now be raised about the nature of the individual and its social context, and of the development of their interrelations.

1. Processes linking the person to the group have been selected for in evolution. But, given the present dynamically interactive view, these processes do not exist preformed or innate in the newborn (cf. Lerner, 1978, 1979). Accordingly it is the job of human developmentalists to understand what processes, across ontogeny, link the individual to its context. Reinforcement processes, cognitive developmental processes, and social relational processes, such as attachment and dependency, may *all* be involved.

2. Because of the link between individual adaptation and social functioning, the group is necessary for the individual's survival. For example, Hogan, *et al.* (1978) point out that "social living is the key to man's evolutionary success [p. 3]," and, in regard to behavioral functioning (to them largely *moral* functioning), they note that if the societal "rules are ignored, social living is impossible. If a person seriously does not care about the survival of his or her culture, then that person would not be immoral in an absolute sense—but that person would be either criminal or insane [p. 3]." Thus, from this view, personal survival depends on supporting, at least in part, the social context within which one is embedded.

3. However, a third point is raised, one which changes our focus from embeddedness to constant change, and to the concept of plasticity. Just

as the individual needs the group, the group needs the individual, and a singular individual at that. The individual is necessary for the group's survival (e.g., to populate it and perpetuate the techniques it has used for survival). That is, as Brim and Kagan (1980) have put the issue, "Society must transform the raw material of individual biology into persons suitable for the activities and requirements of society [p. 19]."

For example, Hogan, *et al.* (1978) point out that, "the process of transmitting culture across human generations is fundamental to human survival [p. 6]" although "the rules are important not in themselves but because they serve to legitimize, sanction and promote certain behaviors that are essential to the operation and survival of culture [p. 4]." Thus, the "tendencies toward ritualization, codification, and organization make social living predictable and more efficient [p. 6]." Simply, these rules enhance the adaptiveness of social functioning. Similarly, Baumrind (1978) has suggested that "The function of social rules, whether conventional or moral, is to coordinate the individual's immediate prudential or hedonistic aims with (1) his or her longer-range interests; and (2) the interests, shorter- and longer-range, of his or her primary group and impersonal collective [p. 66]." Accordingly, she notes that social–moral: "sanctions, then, are simply metaconventions that the human species has evolved in adapting to and mastering its environment. When conditions of long-range survival change, then moral sanctions change with them. Moral principles and their development, like other social rules and their development, arise from concrete cultural–historical conditions [p. 69]." Similarly, Hogan *et al.* (1978) note that a major evolutionary component of the sociocultural context is "a set of child-rearing practices that serves to transmit whatever technological wisdom the group has evolved, together with the values necessary to apply that wisdom effectively. Thus we have a feedback loop consisting of environmental demands, the cultural resources developed in response to these demands, and child-rearing practices which provide for cultural transmission and development of the character type best suited to the environmental demands [pp. 6–7]."

But, there is another, essential feature to the link between the individual and his or her social context. As noted by both Hogan, *et al.* and by Baumrind, it is clear that the context changes. If the rules of a social group represent a specification of the content of the exchanges people and their institutions must make with their context for adaptation to occur (i.e., maintenance and perpetuation, or reproduction), then both person and group must "institutionalize" plasticity as well as stability. Hogan, *et al.* (1978) make this point by noting that: "the moral rules that make social living possible only tell us what kinds of behavior were necessary for survival in the past; they may not be valid for the future. Moreover, the conditions under which any social group lives may change. Thus cultures must always be open to the possibilities for change and innovation [p. 3]."

Thus, consideration of the implications of embeddedness leads to a consideration of plasticity. Conversely, in now turning to plasticity, we will see that it leads back to a recognition of the idea of embeddedness.

Bases of Plasticity in Human Development

As with the bases of the social nature of human development, there are several bases of support for the idea that plasticity is a key feature of human ontogenetic and biocultural change. These bases pertain to ideas linking intergenerational relations and biocultural change, ideas in evolutionary biology and comparative psychology about the different functional progressions characteristic of species at different psychological levels, or evolutionary grades, and ideas in theoretical physics about the second law of thermodynamics.

INTERGENERATIONAL RELATIONS AND BIOCULTURAL CHANGE

The last point raised in our discussion of the implications of embeddedness led to our discussion of plasticity. By amplifying that point we may see how the social nature of human development provides a basis of plasticity. Sociologists and various human developmentalists point out that plasticity is needed on both a macro and a micro level of analysis (e.g., Bengtson & Troll, 1978; Haan, Chapter 6 this volume; Riley, 1979). Haan (Chapter 6, this volume) notes that, although individuals may be inextricably linked to the group, they strive to see themselves as individuals, and John Clausen (cited in Brim & Kagan, 1980) observes that "the natural state of the person is to be in the process of becoming something different while in many respects remaining the same [p. 17]" (e.g., like himself or herself in earlier developmental periods and like others in his or her group).

Sociologically, such an orientation—one counter to complete social molding (Hartup, 1978)—must occur if individuals and their society are to be maximally adaptative. An individual member of a new birth cohort enters a social system composed of already existing cohorts. If all a person could or would do is replicate the behaviors that were adaptive for that older cohort, then, given a changed context, that person would not be adaptive (cf. Riley, 1978). The social context has an investment in the individual. They need members of the new cohort to maintain the society and to perpetuate it. Accordingly, it would be necessary to promote, foster, and tolerate variation from the existing context's behavioral repertoire.

But, however, the older cohort will not "permit" too much variability from its orientation, or else their "generational stake" (Bengtson & Kuypers, 1971; Bengtson & Troll, 1978) would be diminished significantly. However, the new cohort will rarely, if ever, completely overthrow the inculcation orientation of the older cohorts, because:

1. They have their own "generational stake" in the older cohort—they may need them for the production of certain goods or for the presence of certain skills they themselves do not have.
2. There is much in the older cohort's repertoire that still remains functional (i.e., that shows cross-cohort adaptive significance).
3. There is meaning (e.g., valuation, placed on these others).
4. There are empathic, attachment, or dependency processes that may be engaged in intergenerational relations.

In summary, avoiding complete social mold, individuals maintain their individual plasticity, which enhances their adaptiveness and that of their context. Thus, there is a "dialectic" between individual (I) and group (G) processes:

1. I's goals $=$ G's goals (because of the social nature of individual behavior).
2. I's goals $\neq$ (differ from) G's goals (because I wants to see self as an individual; Haan, Chapter 6 this volume).
3. In supporting I's individuality, or potential for individuality (i.e., plasticity), G's goals—of maintenance *and* of perpetuation—will be served (i.e., there will be a population of Is who are plastic enough to meet potentially new contextual demands); thus, it is again the case that;
4. I's goals $=$ G's goals.

In addition, we may note that individuals are responsive to (belong to) multiple groups (the social context is not unidimensional). Although the social context is integrated (e.g., interdependent) it is also differentiated. Thus, in a sense, each individual may be unique by virtue of his or her being a "composite" of those reciprocal relations maintained toward an array of segments of the social context. As such, individuals' views of themselves as unique may, in this way, be quite veridical. They will therefore make a distinct, or variable, contribution to the society, and in this way, enhance the overall context's level of plasticity.

Brent (1978) has made a compatible point:

A dialectical relationship exists between the tendency toward specialization of each individual member of an organismic collective during the course of individual development (e.g., ontogenesis) and the tendency toward adaptation of the organismic collective-as-a-whole to a shifting set of environmental opportunities and constraints during the course of its development (e.g., phylogenesis). The general principle is this: As each individual within an organismic collective becomes increasingly more specialized in the unique niche which he/she occupies in the collective, the collective-as-a-whole becomes increasingly more flexible in its ability to adapt to its changing environment. Put in other terms: *The specialization of individuals within an organismic collective is the concrete realization at the micro-structural level of differentiation of the organismic collective-as-a-whole at the macrostructural level* [p. 23].

Moreover, Brent points out that social context maintenance and perpetuation depend on intergenerational relations that involve the continuation of past adaptation strategies along with the promotion of plasticity, especially in the newer cohorts. He argues that:

Each organismic collective in order to survive and prosper must fulfill three kinds of functions simultaneously. First, it must maximize the efficiency with which it fulfills those functions essential to its maintenance and survival as an entity under some existing set of environmental conditions. Second, it must maximize the facility with which it can maintain its own stability in the face of changes in these environmental conditions. And, third, it must at the same time maintain the ability to expand into new environmental niches as the opportunity for such expansions arise [pp. 24–25].

and indicates that the biocultural "solution" to this problem involves a situation wherein: "Each phylogenetically younger structural cohort embeds all of the older cohorts in a layer of protective environment which allows the older to continue to function in a stable and 'traditional' manner while permitting the organism, i.e., collective-as-a-whole, to expand into new environmental niches in which the older cohorts, by themselves, could never survive or function . . . [pp. 27–28]."

In summary, a focus on the biocultural changes involving the flow of birth cohorts indicates the necessary role of plasticity at both individual and group levels of analysis. In the next section, information derived from evolutionary biology, and comparative and developmental psychology indicates also that phylogenetic and ontogenetic change is in the direction of increasingly greater plasticity.

PSYCHOLOGICAL LEVELS AND FUNCTIONAL ORDERS

Interest in the nature of species' evolutionary changes, in interspecies differences in species' evolutionary changes, and in providing criteria for discriminating among species levels has led evolutionary biologists and comparative psychologists to study the concept of *anagenesis* (Yarczower & Hazlett, 1977). Although not an uncontroversial idea (Capitanio & Leger, 1979; Yarczower & Yarczower, 1979), most scientists agree that "anagenesis refers to the evolution of increased complexity in some trait [Capitanio & Leger, 1979, p. 876]." For example, Dobzhansky, Ayala, Stebbings, and Valentine (1977) note that "Anagenetic episodes commonly create organisms with novel characters and abilities beyond those of their ancestors [p. 236]," or simply that anagenesis is an "evolutionary advance or change." Similarly, Jerison (1978) notes that an evolutionary analysis of progress from earlier to later species "is called 'anagenetic' and is about progressive evolution," and indicates that in such an analysis "the objective is to identify grades in evolution . . . [pp. 1–2]."

Thus, an anagenetic (evolutionary) advance would place a species at a different evolutionary grade (Gould, 1976), and location of a species at a different grade would mark interspecies differences in evolutionary changes (i.e., anagenesis; Dobzhansky, *et al.*, 1977; Jerison, 1978).

However, it is clear that an advance in complexity is often difficult to identify (e.g., what specific structural and behavioral criteria need to be met; cf. Capitanio & Leger, 1979)? This is especially true when human social behavior is involved (Yarczower & Hazlett, 1977; Yarczower & Yarczower, 1979; also see Sampson, 1977). However, Schneirla (1957, 1959; Tobach & Schneirla, 1968), among others (e.g., Birch & Lefford, 1963; Sherrington, 1951; Tobach, 1978) have provided a useful framework.

Schneirla (1957) proposes the use of a behavioral *stereotypy–plasticity continuum* to differentiate the levels of complexity representative of different species. Stereotyped behavior shows a high correspondence between sensory input and motor output. It is "sense dominated" (Hebb, 1949) behavior. There is little intraindividual change across time within situations. Plastic behavior shows considerable response variability given invariant sensory input. There is intraindividual change across time within situations (cf. Baltes & Baltes, 1979). Moreover, Schneirla indicates that this continuum must be understood along with two other key concepts: *psychological levels* and *functional orders.*

Organisms at higher psychological levels are those whose most ontogenetically advanced level of functioning shows considerable plasticity. Their initial ontogenetic periods will show "sense dominated" behavior. However, after relatively long developmental period in comparison to organisms more stereotyped in their final functional level (Hebb, 1949; Schneirla, 1957), they will progress to this plastic level. Presumably, these characteristics of progression through their functional order are based on the greater association–sensory fibers ratio (the A/S Ratio: Hebb, 1949) representative of the level; thus there is a longer time necessarily involved in the organization of this structure (Lerner, 1976).

Organisms at lower psychological levels are those whose functional order is characterized by a more stereotyped final form. However, presumably because they have less structure to organize (they have a lower

A/S Ratio), they reach this last point in their functional order relatively sooner in their ontogeny than do organisms at higher psychological levels (Lerner, 1976).

Thus, Schneirla's (1957) ideas have relevance for both the phylogenetic and the ontogenetic changes of humans. Human evolution should be characterizable by progressively greater potentials for plasticity. In turn, however, although evolution has led to the presence of this potential, its basis, in structure, requires organization over the course of ontogeny. As such, normative patterns of human ontogeny should be characterizable by the progressively greater presence of plasticity. There are data supporting these ideas.

In evolutionary biology, Lewontin and Levins (in press) provide evidence for the link between anagenesis, complexity, plasticity, and what they term "coupling–uncoupling" phenomena. Lewontin and Levins (in press) cite Hegel's warning "that the organism is made up of arms, legs, head and trunk only as it passes under the knife of the anatomist," and note "the intricate interdependence of the parts of the body . . . permit survival when they function well, but in pathological conditions produce pervasive disaster [p. 79]." However, such interdependence of parts is neither phylogenetically nor ontogenetically static. Relations among parts change over the course of evolution; often this involves the rapid evolution of some characteristics, or "traits," and the relative constancy of others. In other words, whereas various aspects of an organism may be bound together as traits if they are either units of development or selection, they may lose their cohesion and evolve independently if the direction of selection is altered (Lewontin & Levins, in press).

Indeed, there are several aspects of adaptation that suggest that tight integration of traits, or in Lewontin and Levins' terms, coupling, is disadvantageous. First, a given characteristic may be subject to alternative selection pressures. If the optimal states of the characteristic under the separate pressures are not vastly different, then adaptation would be best served by a "compromise in which the part in question is determined by" all the presses. Second, the uncoupling of traits is advantageous "as the number of interacting variables and the intensity of their interaction increases [pp. 83–84]"; this is the case because, in the face of these increases, it becomes increasingly difficult for selective pressures to increase fitness. Thus, species with very tight coupling will be unable to adapt as readily as those in which the different components that increase fitness are more autonomous. Third, the more strongly coupled and interdependent the traits of an organism are, the more pervasive is the damage done to an organism when some stressor overwhelms a particular trait.

Accordingly, what has occurred over the course of evolution is that the advantages of coordinated functioning and mutual regulation have come to oppose the disadvantages of excessive constraint and hence vulnerability, and that, at least at the human level, organisms may have the capacity to successively couple and uncouple traits. Ontogenetically, then, it may be that the most adaptive organisms are those which have the potential to develop the capacity to couple and uncouple traits as the context demands. We may suggest, then, that the direction of evolution at the human level has been to move toward providing the substrate for the coupling–uncoupling of traits. This is what may be involved in anagenesis. That is, if higher evolutionary grades are defined as being more complex, and if greater complexity means greater plasticity, a key instance of plasticity would be the capability to couple, uncouple, and couple anew—either through recoupling or with ontogenetically unique couplings. This facility should become progressively established across ontogeny, as the physiological substrate of the psychological level of analysis becomes organized.

Again, then, we reach the view that evolutionary and ontogenetic progression involves progressive change toward greater plasticity of functioning. The view that such progressions characterize the human psychological level is supported by still other lines of evidence.

Birch and Lefford (1963) note that the essential evolutionary strategy in the emergence of the mammalian nervous system from lower forms "has been the development of mechanisms for improved interaction among the separate sensory modalities [p. 3]." In turn, currently evolved organisms can be differentiated on the basis of their structural capability for plasticity at their highest functional order. They note that "as one ascends in the vertebrate series from fish to man the unimodal sensory control of behavior comes to be superseded by multimodal and intersensory control mechanisms [p. 3]." Similarly, Sherrington (1951) indicated that: "The naive would have expected evolution in its course to have supplied us with more various sense organs for ampler perception of the world . . . The policy has rather been to bring by the nervous system the so-called 'five' into closer touch with one another . . . A central clearing house of sense has grown up . . . Not new senses, but better liaison between old senses is what the developing nervous system has in this respect stood for [pp. 287–289]."

In turn, with regard to human ontogeny, Schneirla's (1957) ideas find support in Birch and Lefford's (1963) study of intersensory integration in 5- to 11-year-old children. Information received by the younger children through one sense modality (visual, haptic, or kinesthetic) was not directly transduced to another. Rather, intersensory integrative ability showed a negatively accelerated increase across this age span, indicating that the presence of intermodal equivalence is a developmental phenomenon. Not only did Abravanel (1968) replicate these findings with children ranging in age from 3.3 to 14.2 years, but he found that covarying with these increments in perceptual plasticity was an increase in the child's activity in exploration of the stimulus. In addition, more differentiated motor behavior developed, as fine finger movements replaced the use of the less effective palms.

This role of the organism's own activity in the development of its own plasticity has been identified in other human data sets reported by Piaget (1961; Piaget & Inhelder, 1956) and by Birch and Lefford (1967). In addition, experimental research with animals (Held & Hein, 1963) confirms this role of the organism's activity. Litter mate kittens were or were not allowed to make motor adjustments as they traversed a circular route. Those animals making the active motor adjustments later performed better on a visual cliff apparatus than did the restricted animals.

Thus, the idea that human plasticity is a developmental phenomenon, advanced by Schneirla (1957), as well as by Hebb (1949), Piaget (1961; Piaget & Inhelder, 1956), Bühler (1928), and Baldwin (1897) finds empirical support. In addition, support for the notion that the organism itself actively provides a basis of this progression is evident.

Finally, whereas this evidence about the role of plasticity in human evolutionary and ontogenetic change, as well as that pertinent to plasticity in intergenerational relations and biocultural change mentioned earlier, supports a contextual model of human development, it also indicates the presence of *universal* structural changes. The present contextual view of human development does not lead to the view that there are *no* universal features of development. Although the "characteristics of given historical periods make individual change more or less likely [Brim & Kagan, 1980, p. 16]," a universal structural process, involving increasingly greater plasticity of function as a consequence of continuing integration of structure, appears to characterize the human species' evolution and ontogeny.

However, this *structural* progression, while invariantly subserving the *function* of adaptation (Birch & Lefford, 1963; Brent, 1978a; Dobzhansky, et al., 1977; Schneirla, 1957), still does not provide a basis for asserting that there are totally uniform features of development. Structure has a *content*. And because content may be expected to show both cohort and time-related variation (Baltes, 1979b; Baltes, et al., 1980; Hogan, et al., 1978), a contextual view of development, stressing the *relation* between structure and content, would emphasize the uniqueness that characterizes the human life course. Simply, the same content embedded in a different structure, or a different content embedded in the same structure, would have different implications for the individual–psychological functioning of the person (Liben, Chapter 5, this volume; Schneirla, 1957).

In summary, although progression toward plasticity may be universal, a contextual view of this progression contrasts with other universal structural views (e.g., an organismic one) in its stress on the importance of the structure–content relation. Moreover, a final line of evidence that may be presented about the role of plasticity in human ontogeny not only also emphasizes a contextually based, universal structural progression, but in so doing, indicates the need to understand plasticity by reference to the concept of embeddedness. This line of evidence is derived from the discipline of physics.

ILYA PRIGOGINE AND
THE SECOND LAW OF THERMODYNAMICS

The development of humans—be the level of analysis biological, psychological, or social—is sometimes defined, and more often is described, as involving *orthogenetic* change (Werner, 1957). According to Werner (1957), orthogenesis is a general, descriptive principle of development. It indicates that, whenever development occurs, it proceeds from a state of globility, or lack of differentiation, to a state of differentiation, integration, and hierarchic organization.

This progression need not pertain only to structure. Typically, functional progressions toward increasingly greater behavioral differentiation and integration characterize the life course (Brent, 1978b; Lerner, 1979; Werner, 1957). In fact, as discussed in the previous section, the changes noted by Abravanel (1968) and by Piaget and Inhelder (1956), involving more actively differentiated and integrated search strategies of stimulus objects in perceptual tasks, can be described as orthogenetic. Thus, structural and functional orthogenetic progressions, providing a basis of and behaviorally demonstrating, respectively, development toward greater plasticity, characterize the human life span. However, this orthogenetic principle of human development, which appears to have wide empirical and theoretical applicability (Brent, 1977, 1978a; Freud, 1954; Piaget, 1960), seems to introduce a problem when one considers the nature of changes that are presumed to characterize the physical world.

The second law of thermodynamics states that as physical systems change they move toward greater disorganization and lack of integration. These changes are accompanied by an increase in *entropy*. Thus, as described by Brent (1978b), the second law of thermodynamics indicates that "every physical process will result in a net decrease in the amount of order (hence, a net increase in the amount of disorder) in the universe as a whole" and therefore "every physical process will result in an irreversible increase in the amount of entropy in the universe as a whole over time [p. 374]."

However, both Prigogine, a chemist, and Brent (1978b), who has provided a useful discussion of the former's work for social scientists, note that biological systems change in accordance with the orthogenetic principle. In other words, they are characterized by a local decrease in entropy, or *negentropy*.

A major problem is thus introduced: Are the human developmental data about orthogenesis in opposition to the second law of thermodynamics? Or, are human developmental laws not those that apply to the natural, physical world? Prigogine (1971) has presented this problem as follows:

> The idea of evolution emerges in the science of the nineteenth century in two conflicting ways:
>
> (a) In thermodynamics the second law is formulated . . . the law of progressive disorganization, of the destruction of existing structures. Since its formulation, this law appears to most physicists as one of the greatest achievements of theoretical physics, as one of the cornerstones of our understanding of the physical world . . .
>
> (b) On the contrary, in biology and sociology the idea of evolution is closely associated with an increase in organization with the creation of more and more complex structures . . .
>
> The extension of the thermodynamical concept of evolution to the world as a whole leads to the idea that "structure" existed mainly in some far distant past, in a kind of "golden age." Since then the world has been dissolving in a progressive chaos . . .
>
> The biological concept of evolution points in exactly the opposite direction [pp. 1–2].

Prigogine's great achievement, for which he was awarded a Nobel Prize in 1977, was in the steps he and his colleagues made toward the solution of this paradox (Prigogine, 1978; Prigogine, Allen, & Herman, 1977). Prigogine demonstrated that *both* physical and biological systems followed the second law. Both can move to greater negentropy, but only by draining continually wider, broader areas outside of the local system of their organization which, as a consequence, increases the total entropy in the universe as a whole. Physical and biological systems increase their organization and energy by depleting an increasingly greater area around them of its organization and energy. Within the negentropic system there is increasingly greater local organization; but outside of the system there is greater and greater entropy.

Brent (1978b) describes the situation as follows:

> In terms of a classical biological metaphor we can say that each locally developing system achieves an increase in structural order and complexity only by 'ingesting,' 'digesting,' and 'assimilating' relatively low entropy (i.e., orderly) structures from its surrounding environment, and by 'excreting' back into that environment 'waste products' which are higher in entropy (i.e., in disorderliness) than those which it initially ingested . . . Since the transport processes themselves are entropy producing, they tend to be in dialectical opposition to, hence placing limits upon, the negative entropy available for local structural maintenance itself, at that level of organization . . .
>
> The transcendence of this inherent limitation appears to come with the emergence of each more complex level of organization, for the constituent parts of that new structure are then able, by virtue of their participation (i.e., coop-

eration) in that more complex organization to exploit an ever-wider and deeper range of environments as both resources and 'dumping grounds' . . . the limitation imposed upon exploitive capacity of any given structure by these thermodynamic constraints may therefore be valid only for any particular level of organizational complexity. With increasing complexity an increasing range of environments becomes available for such exploitation. Indeed, one might speculate that it is for this reason that increasing individual and social complexity has proven to be the course which biological adaptation has followed [pp. 377–379].

Thus, from this view, a system at any level of analysis moves in the direction of increasingly greater plasticity (or orthogenesis) and this involves an increasingly greater integration of the system and its context. In other words, an organism's plasticity develops as a consequence of its embeddedness in its context and, in turn, the relations between the biological and physical components of the context may be understood as involving biocultural and ontogenetic progressions toward greater plasticity. Prigogine (1971, 1978; Prigogine, *et al.*, 1977) provides a mathematical basis and empirical support for the idea that the developing individual is necessarily linked to a concomitantly evolving physical and social context across life; and, as a consequence of this linkage, the individual both influences and is influenced by the context, and as such is a producer of his or her own development.

Conclusions and Future Directions

This chapter has presented key features of a conceptualization of development derived from a contextual paradigm: plasticity, the social nature of human development, and the role of individuals as producers of their development. Yet, despite the multidisciplinary conceptual and empirical support for these ideas, it is appropriate to characterize this presentation as more of a prospectus for theory building than as a detailing of the particulars of a finished system. It is more of a promise about the potential of interdisciplinary integration, than an instance of its realized assets. To fulfill the promise traditional intra- and interdisciplinary boundaries will have to be stepped over. New research questions will have to be addressed. Some examples may be offered.

1. *The study of temperament.* Results from the New York Longitudinal Study (NYLS; Thomas, Chess, Birch, Hertzig, & Korn, 1963; Thomas *et al.*, 1968, 1970) have indicated that particular types of individual differences in temperament, or behavioral style, are differentially associated with adaptive psychosocial functioning. For example, low rhythmicity of biological functions, high activity levels, high distractibility, low response thresholds, and high intensity reactions represent a cluster of character-

istics that have been found to place samples of both handicapped children (e.g., mentally retarded children or children born with multiple physical handicaps as a result of maternal rubella) and nonhandicapped children "at risk" for behavioral and emotional problems (see Thomas & Chess, 1977). Alternatively, similarly handicapped children, and nonhandicapped children, who either have none of these temperamental characteristics and/or have high rhythmicity and moderate activity, threshold, intensity, and distractibility levels, have fewer problem behaviors. Data from samples other than the NYLS, collected by the Thomas group (Korn, Chess, & Fernandez, 1978; Thomas & Chess, 1977) and others (Sameroff, 1978), confirm the linkages between differential temperamental repertoires and contrasting psychosocial developments, again among children having various categories of handicap and among nonhandicapped children.

However, both Thomas and Chess (1977, Chapter 9, this volume) and J. Lerner (1980) believe that adaptive psychological and social functioning does not derive directly from the nature of the child's characteristics of temperamental individuality per se. Rather, if a child's characteristics of individuality match (or "fit") the demands of a particular setting, adaptive outcomes in that setting will accrue. Those children whose characteristics match most of the settings within which they exist should show evidence of the most adaptive behavioral development. In turn, of course, mismatched children, whose characteristics are incongruent with one or most settings, should show alternative developmental outcomes.

These authors have thus proposed a person–context "goodness of fit" model for adaptive development. Just as a child brings his or her characteristics of individuality to a particular social setting, there are demands placed on the child by virtue of the social and physical components of the setting. The child's individuality, in differentially meeting these demands, provides a basis of the feedback he or she gets from the socializing environment.

For example, teachers and parents may have relatively individual and distinct expectations about behaviors desired in their students and children, respectively. Teachers may want students who show little distractibility, as they would not want attention diverted from the lesson by the activity of other children in the classroom. Parents, however, might desire their children to be moderately distractible, for example, when they require their child to move from television watching to dinner or to bed. Children whose behavioral individuality was either generally distractible or generally not distractible would thus differentially meet the demands of these two contexts. Problems of adaptation to school or to home might thus develop as a consequence of a child's lack of match (or "goodness of fit") in either or both settings.

Thomas and Chess (1977) and their associates (e.g., Korn, 1978) have speculated about how their data are congruent with this relational model.

The NYLS sample is a white, middle-class one. Such social contexts may have fairly generalizable views about desirable behavioral styles for children. If so, then a child with a particular repertoire (e.g., one that has been labeled as difficult; Thomas & Chess, 1977), is only "at risk" insofar as his or her arhythmicity, negative mood, and high intensity reactions are not congruent with such demands. However, in another context, having alternative appraisals of such attributes, the "at risk" status would change. Korn (1978) and Gannon (1978) have presented data indicating that in lower class Puerto Rican settings these "difficult" attributes are not only not undesirable but may be highly regarded; in turn, they indicate that, as compared to white middle-class samples, there is less association of such attributes with negative psychosocial development. Sameroff (1978) provides similar data in regard to social class and race differences in the implications of a "difficult" temperament.

A more direct test of the goodness-of-fit model was conducted by J. Lerner (1980). She examined the role of congruence between temperamental attributes and school demands for psychosocial adjustment in young adolescents. Junior high school students were assessed with regard to their temperamental attributes. The demands of the school–social and the school–academic contexts in regard to the temperamental attributes were also assessed. In addition, for each of the two contexts, both *actual* and *perceived* demands were assessed. Finally, as indices of personal and social adjustment, measures of grade point average, perceived academic and social competence, positive and negative peer relations, general self-esteem, academic self-esteem, social self-esteem, and overall peer relations were obtained for all subjects.

Results indicated that those subjects whose temperamental attributes were *least* discrepant from the demands of the two contexts had scores on the measures used to index adjustment that were indicative of better adjustment than was the case for those subjects whose temperamental attributes were *most* discrepant from the demands. Moreover, consistent with the view that the person plays an active role in his or her own development, the results also indicated that the discrepancy scores for the *perceived* contexts had more import for prediction than did those for the *actual* contexts.

In summary, current theory and research in temperament support a contextual view of the role of individuals in their own personal and interpersonal development. In so doing, a relational, person–context match variable is suggested as useful. Indeed, by focusing on the array of matches–mismatches that exist across several of the contexts within which people are embedded, a study of the "relations of relations" (Looft, 1973; Riegel, 1973, 1975) may be made. Such a study would allow for testing whether those people who show appropriate plasticity, or flexibility, for example, in the coupling–uncoupling of attributes in their temperament repertoire to meet the context-specific demands imposed on them, are in fact the most adaptive (cf. Lewontin & Levins, in press; Schneirla, 1957).

2. *Sex differences in personality and social behavior.* Sex differences in personality and social behavior development also can be assessed by a perspective that is based on the contextual concepts we have been emphasizing. Given current changes in the sociocultural context (e.g., increased cost of living, difficulty in maintaining a middle-class life style—ownership of a median priced home—with a single, median income, the increased age of marriage among more highly educated women, the increased delay in age of first pregnancy, and the greater likelihood of professional men marrying professional women; U.S. Bureau of the Census, 1978), important individual–psychological changes may be expected. Assessments of self-esteem, self-concept, and vocational role ideology should reveal biocultural changes in that both males and females of more recent birth cohorts are moving away from conformity with traditional sex-role stereotypes (Block, 1973; Lerner, Sorell, & Brackney, in press). To meet the demands of the changing sociocultural context more successfully, personal functioning should move toward normative possession of a repertoire of self-appraisals and behaviors that are more flexible.

A behavioral repertoire that shows high commitment only to the behaviors traditionally associated with one gender may be seen as involving unidimensional role stereotypy. A repertoire that shows high commitment to the behaviors traditionally associated with both males and females (a repertoire that has been at times labeled "androgynous"; e.g., Bem, 1975) may also be seen to involve role stereotypy, but here along two dimensions. Neither of these two types of repertoires should be as functional as one that involves facile alternation or synthesis of any behavior necessary to meet the demands of the social context. Again, the potential adaptive significance of a coupling–uncoupling mechanism is suggested. Currently, given the history in Western culture of dichotomizing roles on the basis of sex (cf. Block, 1973), such flexible repertoires could be characterized as egalitarian.

Thus, if role flexibility rather than role stereotypy represents a behavioral repertoire better meeting the demands of the social context, the development of role flexibility should covary with increases in scores on independent measures of adaptive functioning (Bem, 1975, 1979; Block, 1973; Spence & Helmreich, 1979).

However, if role flexibility involves little or no behavioral commitment to traditional psychosocial role prescriptions, it would not afford a basis for optimal functioning. As already discussed, one must be flexible enough to meet the adaptational demands that may impinge uniquely on a person as an individual and as a member of a particular birth cohort; but, part of adaption to one's context also involves coordination with the presses imposed from older cohorts. Thus, embedded in a context with older cohorts, and given the presses for collective adaptation as well as individual specialization (Brent, 1978a), an inverted-U function between degree of nontraditionality in psychological–behavioral repertoire and adaptiveness should be seen. Complete traditionality or nontraditionality should be associated with the lowest scores on an index of adaptive functioning; a middle-range score on traditionality should be associated with highest scores for adaptive functioning.

Furthermore, as cohort flow proceeds, and thus as formerly younger cohorts now become older ones, then, given the continuation of current historical trends, newer cohorts are likely to be pressed to make coordinations with a social context having more cohorts closer to the egalitarian end of a nonegalitarian–egalitarian dimension. Thus, although the apex of the inverted-U function may remain at the same point of the Y axis of a graphic display, it should, with cohort flow, and social change, move progressively along the X axis toward the egalitarian end of the dimension.

3. *Sex differences in spatial cognition.* An example of contextual-based research that combines interest in sex differences with explanatory intervention research, here in the area of cognitive functioning, may also be offered. Sex differences in spatial cognition and perception are among the best documented ones in the developmental literature (Liben, Patterson, & Newcombe, in press; Wittig & Petersen, 1979). Explanations of these differences range from those stressing native neurohormonal mechanisms to those emphasizing socialization differences (Wittig & Petersen, 1979). Although interventions designed to ameliorate the sex differences are not numerous, those that have been presented are, understandably and appropriately, derived from the perspective of a favored theoretical view.

However, from a contextual perspective emphasizing the potential for plasticity—based on the individual's embeddedness, and developing as a consequence of his or her own activity—another approach might be suggested. The processes involved in a behavior's development need not be the targets of intervention in a strategy aimed at modifying that behavior. As discussed earlier, there are data, in both the human and animal developmental literatures (Abravanel, 1968; Birch & Lefford, 1963, 1967; Held & Hein, 1963), indicating that when active and differentiated–integrated (i.e., orthogenetically organized) motor activities are used in conjunction with exploration of an object, better perceptual performance is seen. Whether or not differential histories of active, orthogenetically organized exploratory activities characterize males and females manifesting the typical sex-specific behaviors, an intervention involving a change in previously existing behaviors to ones more active and orthogenetically organized should enhance cognitive–perceptual performance.

4. *Behavioral functioning in the aged.* Other types of explanatory or intervention research can also be conducted from a contextual perspective. In an attempt to optimize the behavioral functioning of the institution-

alized elderly, an emphasis on the role of the organism in its own development might lead one to combine the strategies that operant researchers have used for changing the setting of nursing home residents (Baltes & Barton, 1977, 1979; Baltes, Burgess, & Stewart, 1979), with other strategies that promote the individual's activity. Whereas a mechanist perspective might emphasize a main effect for the changed context, and an organismic orientation might emphasize the main effect for the person (and perhaps little or no effect for the context; Cumming & Henry, 1961), a contextual view would emphasize the interaction effect. The contextualist would predict that, in those conditions wherein both individual and setting were engaged in active transactions, maximum optimization would occur.

A more general point of this last illustration is that contextually based intervention rests on a view of human development that stresses the existence of a potential for change after the early years of life, and that such change can be enhanced by facilitating individuals actively to engage their contexts. These optimistic beliefs run counter to more pessimistic ones associated with views of human development stressing that constancy (or developmental fixity) is established early in life and/or that the individual is a passive recipient of either genetically or environmentally determining influences. Characterizing such views, Brim and Kagan (1980) have noted that:

> The belief that early experiences create lasting characteristics, like the belief in biological and genetic determinism, makes it possible to assume that attempts to improve the course of human development after early childhood are wasted and without consequence. If society believes that it is all over by the third year of life, it can deal harshly with many people in later life because nothing more can be done, and social programs designed to educate, redirect, reverse, or eliminate unwanted human characteristics cannot be justified. Policies of racial, ethnic, and sex discrimination, incarceration rather than rehabilitation of criminals, ignoring urban and rural poverty, and isolation of the elderly have found shelter in the belief in the determinism of the early years of life [p. 21].

In summary, as a consequence of their embeddedness and plasticity, individuals may contribute to their own behavior change processes. Fruitful research questions can be formulated on the basis of ideas associated with this perspective. However, as we have emphasized, such questions have not been frequently answered in the research literature. As such, the major contemporary contribution of a contextual perspective is to suggest ways that current theoretical questions and empirical literatures can be better integrated or extended. Such a contribution is the major goal of the succeeding chapters.

Acknowledgments

Thanks are expressed to colleagues at the Center for Advanced Study in the Behavioral Sciences and to fellow participants in the Center's 1979 Summer Institute on Morality and Moral Development for their helpful comments and stimulating discussions. Both authors thank Paul B. Baltes, Jay Belsky, Sandor B. Brent, Orville G. Brim, Jr., Anne Colby, Roger A. Dixon, David L. Featherman, Richard Goldberg, David F. Hultsch, Jerome Kagan, Richard C. Lewontin, Lynn S. Liben, Lewis P. Lipsitt, Michael Lougee, David S. Palermo, and Michele Philibert for their comments about earlier versions of the present chapter.

References

Abravanel, E. The development of intersensory patterning with regard to selected spatial dimensions. *Monographs of the Society for Research in Child Development*, 1968, *33* (2, No. 118).

Baldwin, J. M. *Mental development in the child and the race.* New York: Macmillan, 1897.

Baltes, M. M., & Barton, E. M. New approaches toward aging: A case for the operant model. *Educational Gerontology: An International Quarterly*, 1977, *2*, 383–405.

Baltes, M. M., & Barton, E. M. Behavioral analysis of aging: A review of the operant model and research. *International Journal of Behavior Development*, 1979.

Baltes, M. M., Burgess, R. L., & Stewart, R. B. *Independence and dependence in nursing home residents: An operant ecological study.* Unpublished manuscript, The Pennsylvania State University, 1979.

Baltes, P. B. Longitudinal and cross-sectional sequences in the study of age and generation effects. *Human Development*, 1968, *11*, 145–171.

Baltes, P. B. (Ed.). *Life-span development and behavior* (Vol. 1). New York: Academic Press, 1978.

Baltes, P. B. Life-span developmental psychology: Some converging observations on history and theory. In P. B. Baltes & O. G. Brim, Jr. (Eds.), *Life-span development and behavior* (Vol. 2). New York: Academic Press, 1979. (a)

Baltes, P. B. On the potential and limits of child development: Life-span developmental perspectives. *Newsletter of the Society for Research in Child Development*, 1979 (Summer), 1–4. (b)

Baltes, P. B., & Baltes, M. M. *Plasticity and variability in psychological aging: Methodological and theoretical issues.* In Department of Gerontology, Institute of Neuropsychopharmacology, Free University of Berlin: Symposium contribution to appear in "Methodological considerations in determining the effects of aging on the CNS." Berlin, West Germany: July 5–7, 1979.

Baltes, P. B., Baltes, M. M., & Reinert, G. The relationship between time of measurement and age in cognitive development of children: An application of cross-sectional sequences. *Human Development*, 1970, *13*, 258–268.

Baltes, P. B., & Brim, O. (Eds.). *Life-span development and behavior* (Vol. 2). New York: Academic Press, 1979.

Baltes, P. B., Cornelius, S. W., & Nesselroade, J. R. Cohort effects in behavioral development: Theoretical and methodological perspectives. In W. A. Collins (Ed.), *Minnesota symposia on child psychology* (Vol. II). New York: Crowell, 1977.

Baltes, P. B., & Nesselroade, J. R. The developmental analysis of individual differences on multiple measures. In J. R. Nesselroade & H. W. Reese (Eds.), *Life-span developmental psychology: Methodological issues.* New York: Academic Press, 1973.

Baltes, P. B., Reese, H. W., & Lipsitt, L. P. Life-span developmental psychology. *Annual Review of Psychology,* 1980, *31,* 65–110.

Baltes, P. B., & Schaie, K. W. (Eds.). *Life-span developmental psychology: Personality and socialization.* New York: Academic Press, 1973.

Baltes, P. B., & Schaie, K. W. The myth of the twilight years. *Psychology Today,* 1974, *7,* 35–40.

Baltes, P. B., & Schaie, K. W. On the plasticity of intelligence in adulthood and old age: Where Horn and Donaldson fail. *American Psychologist,* 1976, *31,* 720–725.

Baumrind, D. A dialectical materialist's perspective on knowing social reality. *New Directions for Child Development,* 1978, *1*(2), 61–82.

Bem, S. L. Sex role adaptability: One consequence of psychological androgyny. *Journal of Personality and Social Psychology,* 1975, *31,* 634–643.

Bem, S. L. Theory and measurement of androgyny: A reply to the Pedhazur-Tentenbaum and Locksley-Colten critiques. *Journal of Personality and Social Psychology,* 1979, *37,* 1047–1054.

Bengtson, V. L., & Kuypers, J. A. Generational differences and the developmental stake. *Aging and Human Development,* 1971, *2,* 249–260.

Bengtson, V. L., & Troll, L. Youth and their parents: Feedback and intergenerational influence in socialization. In R. M. Lerner & G. B. Spanier (Eds.), *Child influences on marital and family interaction: A life-span perspective.* New York: Academic Press, 1978.

Birch, H. G., & Lefford, A. Intersensory development in children. *Monographs of the Society for Research in Child Development,* 1963, *28* (5, Serial No. 89).

Birch, H. G., & Lefford, A. Visual differentiation, intersensory integration, and voluntary motor control. *Monographs of the Society for Research in Child Development,* 1967, *32,* (2, No. 110).

Block, J. H. Conceptions of sex roles: Some cross-cultural and longitudinal perspectives. *American Psychologist,* 1973, *28,* 512–526.

Brent, S. B. *Order, entropy, and the formal development of psychological structures.* Unpublished manuscript, Wayne State University, Detroit, 1977.

Brent, S. B. Individual specialization, collective adaptation and rate of environment change. *Human Development,* 1978, *21,* 21–33. (a)

Brent, S. B. Prigogine's model for self-organization in nonequilibrium systems: Its relevance for developmental psychology. *Human Development,* 1978, *21,* 374–397. (b)

Brim, O. G., Jr., & Wheeler, S. *Socialization after childhood: Two essays.* New York: Wiley, 1966.

Brim, O. G., Jr. Adult socialization. In J. A. Clausen (Ed.), *Socialization and society.* Boston: Little, Brown, 1968.

Brim, O. G., Jr., & Kagan, J. Constancy and change: A view of the issues. In O. G. Brim, Jr. & J. Kagan (Eds.), *Constancy and change in human development.* Cambridge, Mass.: Harvard University Press, 1980.

Brim, O. G., Jr., & Ryff, C. D. On the properties of life events. In P. B. Baltes & O. G. Brim, Jr. (Eds.), *Life-span development and behavior* (Vol. 3). New York: Academic Press, 1980.

Bronfenbrenner, U. Development theory in transition. In H. W. Stevenson (Ed.), *Child psychology. Sixty-second yearbook of the National Society for the Study of Education, Part I.* Chicago: University of Chicago Press, 1963.

Bronfenbrenner, U. Toward an experimental ecology of human development. *American Psychologist,* 1977, *32,* 513–531.

Bühler, C. *Kindheit und Jugend.* Leipzig: S. Herzel, 1928.

Burgess, R. L., & Huston, T. L. (Eds.). *Social exchange in developing relationships.* New York: Academic Press, 1979.

Campbell, D. T. On the conflicts between biological and social evolution and between psychology and moral tradition. *American Psychologist,* 1975, *30,* 1103–1126.

Capitanio, J. P., & Leger, D. W. Evolutionary scales lack utility: A reply to Yarczower and Hazlett. *Psychological Bulletin,* 1979, *86,* 876–879.

Cumming, E., & Henry, W. E. *Growing old.* New York: Basic Books, 1961.

Datan, N., & Ginsberg, L. H. (Eds.). *Life-span developmental psychology: Normative life crises.* New York: Academic Press, 1975.

Datan, N., & Reese, H. W. (Eds.). *Life-span developmental psychology: Dialectical perspectives on experimental psychology.* New York: Academic Press, 1977.

Dobzhansky, T. Ethics and values in biology and cultural evolution. *Zygon,* 1973, *8,* 261–281.

Dobzhansky, T., Ayala, F. J., Stebbings, G. L., & Valentine, J. W. *Evolution.* San Francisco: Freeman, 1977.

Elder, G. H., Jr. *Children of the Great Depression.* Chicago: University of Chicago Press, 1974.

Elder, G. H., Jr. Historical change in life patterns and personality. In P. B. Baltes & O. G. Brim (Eds.), *Life-span development and behavior* (Vol. 2). New York: Academic Press, 1979.

Freud, S. *Collected works, standard edition.* London: Hogarth Press, 1954.

Gannon, P. *Behavioral problems and temperament in middle-class and Puerto Rican five year old boys.* Unpublished Master's thesis. Hunter College of the City University of New York, 1978.

Gould, S. J. Grades and clades revisited. In R. B. Masterton, W. Hodos, & H. Jerison (Eds.), *Evolution, brain and behavior: Persistent problems.* Hillsdale, N.J.: Erlbaum, 1976.

Goulet, L. R., & Baltes, P. B. (Eds.). *Life-span developmental psychology: Research & theory.* New York: Academic Press, 1970.

Harris, D. B. *Child psychology and the concept of development.* Presidential address to the Division of Developmental Psychology, American Psychological Association, September 3, 1956. (Reprinted in D. S. Palermo & L. P. Lipsitt (Eds.), *Research readings in child psychology.* New York: Holt, Rinehart & Winston, 1963.

Harris, D. B. (Ed.). *The concept of development.* Minneapolis: University of Minnesota Press, 1957.

Hartup, W. W. Perspectives on child and family interaction: Past, present, and future. In R. M. Lerner & G. B. Spanier (Eds.), *Child influences on marital and family interaction: A life-span perspective.* New York: Academic Press, 1978.

Hebb, D. O. *The organization of behavior.* New York: Wiley, 1949.

Held, R., & Hein, A. V. Movement-produced stimulation in the development of visually guided behavior. *Journal of Comparative and Physiological Psychology,* 1963, *56,* 872–876.

Hempel, C. G. *Philosophy of natural science.* Englewood Cliffs, N.J.: Prentice-Hall, 1966.

Hill, R., & Mattessich, P. Family development theory and life-span development. In P. B. Baltes & O. G. Brim, Jr., (Eds.), *Life-span development and behavior* (Vol. 2). New York: Academic Press, 1979.

Hogan, R., Johnson, J. A., & Emler, N. P. A socioanalytic theory of moral development. *New Directions for Child Development,* 1978, *1*(2), 1–18.

Hultsch, D. F., & Hickey, T. External validity in the study of human development: Theoretical and methodological issues. *Human Development,* 1978, *21,* 76–91.

Jerison, H. J. *Smart dinosaurs and comparative psychology.* Paper presented at the meeting of the American Psychological Association, Toronto, Canada, August, 1978.

Kaufmann, H. *Introduction to the study of human behavior.* Philadelphia: Saunders, 1968.

Korn, S. J. *Temperament, vulnerability, and behavior.* Paper presented at the Louisville Temperament Conference, Louisville, Kentucky, September 1978.

Korn, S. J., Chess, S., & Fernandez, P. The impact of children's physical handicaps on marital quality and family interaction. In R. M. Lerner & G. B. Spanier (Eds.), *Child influences on marital and family interaction: A life-span perspective.* New York: Academic Press, 1978.

Kuhn, D. Mechanisms of cognitive and social development: One psychology or two? *Human Development,* 1978, *21,* 92–118.

Kuo, Z. Y. *The dynamics of behavior development.* New York: Random House, 1967.

Lerner, J. V. *The role of congruence between temperament and school demands in schoolchildren's academic performance, personal adjustment, and social relations.* Unpublished doctoral dissertation, The Pennsylvania State University, 1980.

Lerner, R. M. *Concepts and theories of human development.* Reading, Mass.: Addison-Wesley, 1976.

Lerner, R. M. Nature, nurture, and dynamic interactionism. *Human Development,* 1978, *21,* 1–20.

Lerner, R. M. A dynamic interactional concept of individual and social relationship development. In R. L. Burgess & T. L. Huston (Eds.), *Social exchange in developing relationships.* New York: Academic Press, 1979.

Lerner, R. M., Skinner, E. A., & Sorell, G. T. Methodological implications of contextual–dialectic theories of development. *Human Development,* 1980, *23,* 225–235.

Lerner, R. M., Sorell, G. T., & Brackney, B. E. Sex differences in self-concept and self-esteem of late adolescents: A time-lag analysis. *Sex Roles,* in press.

Lerner, R. M., & Spanier, G. B. (Eds.). *Child influences on marital and family interaction: A life-span perspective.* New York: Academic Press, 1978.

Lewis, M., & Feiring, C. The child's social world. In R. M. Lerner & G. B. Spanier (Eds.), *Child influences on marital and family interaction: A life-span perspective.* New York: Academic Press, 1978.

Lewontin, R. C. The fallacy of biological determinism. *The Sciences,* 1976, *16,* 6–10.

Lewontin, R. C., & Levins, R. Evolution. *Encyclopedia Einaudi* (Vol. 5), in press.

Liben, L. S., Patterson, A. H., & Newcombe, N. (Eds.), *Spatial representation and behavior across the life span.* New York: Academic Press, in press.

Looft, W. R. The evolution of developmental psychology: A comparison of handbooks. *Human Development,* 1972, *15,* 187–201.

Looft, W. R. Socialization and personality throughout the life-span: An examination of contemporary psychological approaches. In P. B. Baltes & K. W. Schaie (Eds.), *Life-span developmental psychology: Personality and socialization.* New York: Academic Press, 1973.

Masters, R. D. Jean-Jacques is alive and well: Rousseau and contemporary sociobiology. *Daedalus,* 1978, *107,* 93–105.

McCandless, B. R., & Spiker, C. C. Experimental research in child psychology. *Child Development,* 1956, *27,* 78–80.

Meacham, J. A. Continuing the dialogue: Dialectics and remembering. *Human Development,* 1976, *19,* 304–309.

Meacham, J. A. A transactional model of remembering. In N. Datan & H. W. Reese (Eds.), *Life-span developmental psychology: Dialectical perspectives on experimental research.* New York: Academic Press, 1977.

Mussen, P. H. (Ed.). *Carmichael's manual of child psychology* (3rd ed.). New York: Wiley, 1970.

Nesselroade, J. R., & Baltes, P. B. Adolescent personality development and historical change: 1970–1972. *Monographs of the Society for Research in Child Development,* 1974, *39*(1, Serial No. 154).

Nesselroade, J. R., & Reese, H. W. (Eds.). *Life-span developmental psychology: Methodological issues.* New York: Academic Press, 1973.

Overton, W. F. On the assumptive base of the nature–nurture controversy: Additive versus interactive conceptions. *Human Development,* 1973, *16,* 74–89.

Overton, W. F. Klaus Riegel: Theoretical contribution to concepts of stability and change. *Human Development,* 1978, *21,* 360–363.

Overton, W. F., & Reese, H. W. Models of development: Methodological implications. In J. R. Nesselroade & H. W. Reese (Eds.), *Life-span developmental psychology: Methodological issues.* New York: Academic Press, 1973.

Pepper, S. C. *World hypotheses: A study in evidence.* Berkeley: University of California Press, 1942.

Petrinovich, L. Probabilistic functionalism: A conception of research method. *American Psychologist,* 1979, *34,* 373–390.

Piaget, J. *The psychology of intelligence.* Totoway: Littlefield & Adams, 1960.

Piaget, J. *Les mecanismes perceptifs.* Paris: Presses Unitversitaries de France, 1961.

Piaget, J., & Inhelder, B. *The child's conception of space.* London: Routledge, 1956.

Prigogine, I. Interpretations of life and mind. In A. Greene (Ed.), *Essays around the problem of reduction.* New York: Humanities Press, 1971.

Prigogine, I. Time, structure, and fluctuation. *Science,* 1978, *201,* 777–785.

Prigogine, I., Allen, P. M., & Herman, R. The evolution of complexity and the laws of nature. In E. Laszlo & J. Bierman (Eds.), *Goals for mankind* (Vol. 1). New York: Pergamon, 1977.

Reese, H. W., & Overton, W. F. Models of development and theories of development. In L. R. Goulet & P. B. Baltes (Eds.), *Life-span developmental psychology: Research and theory.* New York: Academic Press, 1970.

Riegel, K. F. The influence of economic and political ideology upon the development of developmental psychology. *Psychological Bulletin,* 1972, *78,* 129–141.

Riegel, K. R. Developmental psychology and society: Some historical and ethical considerations. In J. R. Nesselroade & H. W. Reese (Eds.), *Life-span developmental psychology: Methodological issues.* New York: Academic Press, 1973.

Riegel, K. F. Toward a dialectical theory of development. *Human Development,* 1975, *18,* 50–64.

Riegel, K. F. The dialectics of human development. *American Psychologist,* 1976, *31,* 689–700. (a)

Riegel, K. F. From traits and equilibrium toward developmental dialectics. In W. Arnold (Ed.), *Nebraska Symposium on Motivation.* Lincoln: University of Nebraska Press, 1976. (b)

Riley, M. W. Aging, social change, and the power of ideas. *Daedalus,* 1978, Fall, 39–52.

Riley, M. W. (Ed.). *Aging from birth to death.* Washington, D.C.: American Association for the Advancement of Science, 1979.

Sahlins, M. D. The use and abuse of biology. In A. L. Caplan (Ed.), *The sociobiology debate.* New York: Harper & Row, 1978.

Sameroff, A. J. *Differences in infant temperament in relation to maternal mental illness and race.* Paper presented at the Louisville Temperament Conference, Louisville, Kentucky, September, 1978.

Sameroff, A. Transactional models in early social relations. *Human Development,* 1975, *18,* 65–79.

Schaie, K. W. A general model for the study of developmental problems. *Psychological Bulletin,* 1965, *64,* 92–107.

Schaie, K. W., Labouvie, G. V., & Buech, B. V. Generational and cohort-specific differences in adult cognitive functioning: A 14-year study of independent samples. *Developmental Psychology,* 1973, *9,* 151–166.

Schneirla, T. C. The concept of development in comparative psychology. In D. B. Harris (Ed.), *The concept of development.* Minneapolis: University of Minnesota Press, 1957.

Schneirla, T. C. An evolutionary and developmental theory of biphasic processes underlying approach and withdrawal. In M. R. Jones (Ed.), *Nebraska Symposium on Motivation.* Lincoln: University of Nebraska Press, 1959.

Sears, R. R. Your ancients revisited: A history of child development. In E. M. Hetherington (Ed.), *Review of child development research* (Vol. 5). Chicago: The University of Chicago Press, 1975.

Sherrington, C. S. *Man on his nature.* New York: Cambridge University Press, 1951.

Spence, J. T., & Helmreich, R. L. The many faces of androgyny: A reply to Locksley and Colten. *Journal of Personality and Social Psychology*, 1979, *37*, 1032–1046.

Spiker, C. C., & McCandless, B. R. The concept of intelligence and the philosophy of science. *Psychological Review*, 1954, *61*, 255–266.

Thomas, A., & Chess, S. *Temperament and development*. New York: Brunner/Mazel, 1977.

Thomas, A., Chess, S., & Birch, H. G. *Temperament and behavior disorders in children*. New York: New York University Press, 1968.

Thomas, A., Chess, S., & Birch, H. G. The origin of personality. *Scientific American*, 1970, *223*, 102–109.

Thomas, A., Chess, S., Birch, H. G., Hertzig, M. E., & Korn, S. *Behavioral individuality in early childhood*. New York: New York University Press, 1963.

Tobach, E. The methodology of sociobiology from the viewpoint of a comparative psychologist. In A. L. Caplan (Ed.), *The sociobiology debate*. New York: Harper & Row, 1978.

Tobach, E., & Schneirla, T. C. The biopsychology of social behavior of animals. In R. E. Cooke & S. Levin (Eds.), *Biologic basis of pediatric practice*. New York: McGraw-Hill, 1968.

U.S. Bureau of the Census. *Statistical Abstract of the United States: 1978*. (99th Edition). Washington, D.C., 1978.

Washburn, S. L. (Ed.). *Social life of early man*. New York: Wenner-Gren Foundation for Anthropological Research, 1961.

Werner, H. The concept of development from a comparative and organismic point of view. In D. B. Harris (Ed.), *The concept of development*. Minneapolis: University of Minnesota Press, 1957.

Wilson, E. O. *Sociobiology: The new synthesis*. Cambridge, Mass.: Harvard University Press, 1975.

Wispé, L. G., & Thompson, J. N., Jr. The war between the words: Biological versus social evolution and some selected issues. *American Psychologist*, 1976, *31*, 341–347.

Wittig, M. A., & Petersen, A. C. (Eds.). *Sex-related differences in cognitive functioning*. New York: Academic Press, 1979.

Yarczower, M., & Hazlett, L. Evolutionary scales and anagenesis. *Psychological Bulletin*, 1977, *84*, 1088–1097.

Yarczower, M., & Yarczower, B. S. In defense of anagenesis, grades, and evolutionary scales. *Psychological Bulletin*, 1979, *86*, 880–884.

ETHEL TOBACH

2

Evolutionary Aspects of the Activity of the Organism and Its Development

> There is an *ensemble* of vital phenomena
> presented by each organism in the course
> of its growth, development, and decay;
> and there is an *ensemble* of vital
> phenomena presented by the organic
> world as a whole. Neither of these can be
> properly dealt with apart from the other.
> . . . What interpretation we put on the
> facts of structure and function in each
> living body, depends entirely on our
> conception of the mode in which living
> bodies in general have originated
> [SPENCER, 1866, p. 331].

Why Discuss Development in an Evolutionary Context?

SOME HISTORY ABOUT THE CONCEPTS OF EVOLUTION AND DEVELOPMENT

Most of the usual answers to the question posed can be assigned to one of two categories: (*a*) to understand evolutionary processes; or (*b*) to understand developmental processes. Both types of answers are derived from the interconnectedness of development and evolution, as indicated by Spencer, one of the earliest consciously evolutionist philosophers. Depending on the specific question asked, each is seen as having explanatory power for the other. The history of the two terms has been variously discussed (Carniero, 1972; Gould, 1977) but the consonance of their meaning and history is always deemed most significant.

Etymologically, the words evolve and develop have similar roots: *evolve* is derived from *volvere*, 'to roll', and *e*, meaning 'out'; *develop* is also derived from *volvere*, 'to roll', but the prefex *de* signifies 'from'. Their interchangeability is evident in the definitions in *Webster's Unabridged Dictionary*. Evolve, as a transitive verb, is given as the first meaning: to unfold, to open out, to *develop* gradually; as an untransitive verb, the first meaning is "to *develop* gradually"; develop as an intransitive verb is given

37

a second meaning of "to become larger, fuller, better, etc., grow, *evolve* [italics added]."

This closeness of meaning was evident from the earliest of Spencer's writings. Although we owe to him one of the most insightful expositions of the relationship between the two, his distinction between them is not helpful. In *The Principles of Biology* he says, "In ordinary speech, Development is often used as synonymous with Growth. It hence seems needful to say, that Development as here and hereafter used, means *increase of structure*, and not *increase* of bulk. It may be added, that the word Evolution, comprehending Growth as well as Development, is to be reserved for occasions when both are implied [P. 133]."

In formulating his *First Principles*, which would explain *all* phenomena, "inorganic, organic and super-organic [Spencer, 1880, p. iv,]," he proposed that the primary premise underlying all phenomena was the relationship between matter and motion.

> The law we seek, therefore, must be the law of *the continuous redistribution of matter and motion*. Absolute rest and permanence do not exist. Every object, no less than the aggregate of all objects, undergoes from instant to instant some alteration of state. . . . And the question to be answered is: What dynamic principle, true of the metamorphosis as a whole and in its details, expresses these everchanging relations [p. 240]?

This statement may be seen to epitomize his philosophy. Despite the use of the word "dynamic," he was a mechanical materialist in that he thought that matter and motion were fixed and limited; thus, it was only in their "redistribution" that one could see *change*. However, change was fundamental, as is evident in his use of "metamorphosis." This redistributional principle had a corollary: Something had to be there before metamorphosis as well as after it.

> Be it a single object or the whole universe, any account which begins with it in a concrete form, or leaves off with it in a concrete form, is incomplete; since there remains an era of its knowable existence undescribed and unexplained . . . (T)he (ET change) sphere of knowledge is co-extensive . . . with all modes of the unknowable that can affect consciousness. Hence, wherever we now find being so conditioned as to act on our senses, there arise the questions, How came it to be thus conditioned? and How will it cease to be thus conditioned? . . .(I)t (ET change) must have had an antecedent existence under this sensible form, and will have a subsequent existence under this sensible form. These preceding and succeeding existences under sensible forms are possible subjects of knowledge; and knowledge has obviously not reached its limits until it has united the past, present and future histories into a whole [p. 241].

In his formulation of the historical aspect of change, he saw the first principle of evolution as one that applied to both the thing (or individual) and the entire universe (the species or other superordinate levels) [Tobach, 1976]. Logically, however, growth and development related to the individual. In his usage of development and evolution, one sees a glimmer of the concept of levels of organization. This is clearer in his description of his response to Von Baer.

As a footnote to the following statement, Spencer (1880) discusses his indebtedness to Von Baer: "Pursuing an idea which Harvey set afloat, it has been shown by Wolff and Von Baer that during its *evolution* each organism passes from a state of homogeneity to a state of heterogeneity [pp. 291–292; italics added]." His footnote on Von Baer follows:

> It was in 1852 that I became acquainted with Von Baer's expression of his general principle. . . . It is true that in "Social Statics" (Part IV, Paragraphs 12–16), written before meeting with Von Baer's formula, the *development* of an individual organism and the development of the social organism[1] are described as alike consisting in advance from simplicity to complexity, and from independent like parts to mutually dependent unlike parts . . . But though admitting of extension to other super-organic phenomena, this statement was too special to admit of extension to inorganic phenomena. The great aid rendered by Von Baer's formula arose from its higher generality; since, only when organic transformations had been expressed in the most general terms, was the way opened for seeing what they had in common with inorganic transformations. The conviction that this process of change gone through by each *evolving* organism, is a process gone through by all things, found its first coherent statement in an essay on "Progress: Its Law and Cause;" which I published in the *Westminister Review* for April, 1857 [p. 292; italics added].

He believed that it was in the evolution (and dissolution) of phenomena and the *history* of that evolution (and one might add *development* for the individual) that the explanatory principles of all phenomena were to be sought.

THE SYNTHETIC THEORY OF
EVOLUTION AND DEVELOPMENT

Since Spencer's time, the formulation of a "synthetic" theory of Evolution (Dobzhansky, 1955; Fisher, 1930; Haldane, 1932; Huxley, 1942) and the discoveries in the field of genetics have tied the concept of evolution and development together, but in a significantly altered relationship. That relationship rests on the assumption that evolution is primarily an expression of genetic processes and, accordingly, that development is the expression of genetic processes in the individual (Dobzhansky, 1955b). This view of the primacy of genetic processes in determining development and evolution would seem to provide a rationale for the study of development within an evolutionary context. The narrowness of such a view has been

---

[1] Compare T. C. Schneirla, 1970, Part V, about levels of social organization.

discussed at length (Caplan, 1978; Sahlins, 1976; Tobach, 1972), but its relevance to development is particularly critical.

Although genetic change in evolution is undeniable, the emphasis on genetics as the ultimate determinant is problematical. Differences in the genetic structure of different populations and generations are not to be gainsaid; neither are the differences in characteristics or developmental patterns. The emphasis is problematical, however, because it denies the significance of other processes involved in bringing about the differences in structure and function. It ignores the inseparable interconnectedness of genetic processes with ecological change and with the activities of the individual; all these processes are interpenetrating and causal.

In regard to the genes themselves, it overemphasizes genetic structure and underemphasizes cytoplasmic and other factors. For example, the virus, which at one stage is a configuration of DNA molecules (a genetic structure) is not alive, that is, it is not capable of metabolism, replication, or mutation (Eigen, 1971). Once the genetic structure is in a functional relationship with cellular structures, that is, when it is in a living cell, it is alive and functioning (Lwoff, 1966).

DEVELOPMENT SHOULD BE STUDIED IN AN EVOLUTIONARY CONTEXT

Insights about Development Derive from Evolutionary Processes

If one rejects genetic determinism as a narrow view of evolution and development, however, is there any other basis for discussing development in an evolutionary context? The answer to this question is in part derived from the insights of Spencer, and his emphasis on the *historical* approach to phenomena. The history of the individual is written in the special circumstances of its conception and development. These circumstances derive from the life of the group of animals into which it is born. The special circumstances of the life of the group or species evolved through many interconnected processes, including the function of genetic processes under particular conditions.

One special circumstance is true of all animals, whether they are produced through sexual or asexual reproduction. The individual, from its conception, is part of a social process that immediately relates it to its conspecifics. Therefore, any analysis of developmental phenomena must be within the context of the relationship between the developmental environment and the social organization into which the young individual enters. The characteristics of such relationships vary significantly depending on the level of organization and integration of the individual and species involved (Tobach & Schneirla, 1968). Because sexual reproduction is patently a social process it will not be discussed further here. The presence of the "daughter" cells, or the "bud" or the "colonial organism," which results immediately from asexual reproduction, brings about a relationship between or among the individuals (Freese & Freese, 1977). In the case of the asexually reproducing amoeba, the presence of other cells is conducive to growth and development. If the number of cells in the medium or culture is too low, the colony will not prosper. Social facilitation on this level of organization is primarily through the biochemical products of a sufficient number of conspecifics.

Social facilitation is a continuum throughout all the phyletic levels: For all organisms at all stages of development there is a level of effects produced by conspecifics that is salutory for growth, development, and maturation. The optimum will vary with different phyletic levels, and will vary as to the energy system through which the effects are expressed. That the biochemical level of organization is probably ubiquitous in the animal world is likely, as chemoception is apparently not only involved in monitoring environmental change but may also have tonic effects on growth and development (Tobach, 1977). The studies of an airborne factor facilitating growth and development in mice when they are communally rather than singly housed is another recent experimental demonstration of the possibility of the universal character of this level of organization (Herreid & Schlenker, 1980).

However, with increasing neural and endocrine complexity, the number of systems involved in social facilitation increases, and there is a qualitative change in the mechanisms through which social facilitation works. Thus, in the monkey, although the chemical stimulation afforded by conspecifics may be significant for growth and development (particularly during nursing), the effects of conspecifics can be mimicked by providing moving objects and increased heterogeneity in the environment. This did much to promote growth and development in an animal reared alone. However, this was not as salutory as the social experience of being reared with conspecifics (Anderson, Kenney, & Mason, 1977). Whereas some processes, such as biochemical influences, may operate on all levels of social organization, others are particular to only some levels. Similarities *and* differences must be taken into account in seeking to formulate general principles about the role of social facilitation in growth and development.

To understand the process that led to the formation of a particular individual in *particular circumstances*, it is necessary to understand the historical circumstances of the level of organization characteristic of that species. These circumstances are a function of the evolutionary history of the species, that is, the ecological circumstances that made it possible for the species to evolve and survive. As the circumstances (or environment) changed, the *relationship* between an individual member of the species and its contemporary environment also changed. The unresolved question is: What is the process relating the adjustments and changes of the individual to the morphologic and physiological variations that are seen in the next generation of that species? For example, when an individual is modified in its interaction with the environment, or through its action on the environment, do those modifications affect the genetic material, the only system thus far known to be necessary for the production of the succeeding generation? For most evolutionary biologists, the answer to this question lies in a better understanding of the genetic process. Evolutionary change is seen as operating only through the genes. The individual organism plays a role through its dereliction, only by not reproducing; it plays a role by subtraction, not by contribution to the process. The genes themselves may also play a role by disappearance, and by their frequency increase or their change in spatial relationship to each other. But there is little evidence of the effects of the organism's activities or developmental history on the genetic material, or the genetic process. The individual plays a role only by the failure to reproduce sexually or asexually, either because it has been eliminated from the population before it had the opportunity to reproduce, or because of some malfunction or inefficient structure.

The reason for the lack of evidence regarding possible effects of the developmental history of the individual on genetic processes is not that experiments have been tried and have failed. Rather, the question seems trivial in the context of the scientific philosophy that informs most evolutionary biologists (Tobach, in press). The dominant ideology is of Popper (1972), which, as a hypothetic–deductive philosophy, encourages experiments that start from an untested assumption: In this case the assumption is that the genetic process is the ultimate causal mechanism of all change in evolution and development. This ideology may be the explanation for the general ignorance of Waddington's (1952, 1953a) experiment with "veinless-wing" fruit flies. This experiment requires replication and further analysis in the light of new knowledge about genetic processes in general and in the fruit fly in particular (Ehrman & Parsons, 1976), but the complexity of the experiment makes it difficult to repeat. In this experiment, through use of temperatures within the range of changes that might take place in the environment in which wild flies lay their eggs, Waddington was able to increase the number of veinless-wing flies in succeeding generations, without subjecting every generation to the temperature shock. In other words, the genetic processes seemed to have been affected. It is rather significant that although Waddington's concept of the chreod (Waddington, 1971) is fairly well accepted in one form or another, the experiment, which probably did much to develop his theoretical formulation, is not cited in any of the discussions about genetic processes and evolutionary change.

Relationships of the individual with external forces (or environment) are expressed on many levels within the organism: For example, on the biochemical level, the temperature effects may have been on enzyme systems responsible for embryological development, or on proteins that were differentially involved in the elaboration of cells. The effects of such biochemical changes on structures may then have been amplified to affect the physiology of the other structures of the wing (effects on muscles?) so that wing beat was affected. This in turn may have affected social and reproductive behavior (Bastock, 1956), thus affecting the frequency of the veinless characteristic in succeeding generations. It is the interconnectedness of all these levels of organization that is at the base of understanding the evolution of species and how genetic processes are expressed in it.

The functional and structural integrations of these internal and external relationships bring about the unique growth, development, and maturation of the individual. Understanding the evolutionary history of the species provides a basis for understanding the special circumstances of the ways in which the individual establishes its integrity through its relationship to the environment (i.e., both the social [biotic] and the physical [abiotic] aspects of that environment).

Continuity and Discontinuity

Another reason for analyzing development in an evolutionary context is the elucidation of the continuity and discontinuity of processes underlying developmental phenomena. A process may be considered continuous, or may be seen on a continuum when it is present *in some form* in all phyletic levels. The variations in mechanisms, involved structures, and other characteristics provide the basis for defining the discontinuities in that continuum. Delineation of the continuities and discontinuities provides clues to the relationshp among different species and how changes might have come about.

An example of such a continuous process is "irritability." All living matter, like all matter, is continuously changing. But living matter changes differently than nonliving matter: It incorporates the energy that acts on it; it can grow; and it in turn changes the environment by releasing that part of the transmuted energy that it does not incorporate. Furthermore, it not only changes internally but it "responds" to internal and external changes by changing its spatial relationship to the surround. The response to the changing relationship between internal and external changes is coordinated (see Lerner & Busch-Rossnagel, Chapter 1, this volume; Liben, Chapter 5, and Meacham, Chapter 15, this volume).

The parts of the individual are interconnected, and each is affected by internal and external change, directly or indirectly because each in turn affects another. The property of transmission of response to change to other parts of the system has been termed *irritability*, that is, the ability of protoplasm to respond to such changes by involvement of parts not directly affected by the change. For example, changes in ciliary beating in an acellular animal when the focus of change has been in an area without cilia (chemical change at the mouth area) is one form of irritability. Irritability is present in all cells in plants and animals and in all acellular organisms such as bacteria and amoebae. In this respect, irritability may be seen as a continuous process in all groups of living animals.

In contrast to the irritability response described in a protist, the response of a cell in a mimosa leaf to changes in external pressure is a mechano-physical change in structure that affects its fluid dynamics. This change is transmitted to other cells in the leaf so that it changes its position. These changes are accompanied by an electrical charge resembling a nerve action potential (Roblin, 1979). On this level of organization, the process of irritability shows qualitative changes that are discontinuous with characteristics shared with organisms on a simpler and lower level of organization and integration. Although the electrical charges on the surfaces of the protist change in relation to electrical charges on the internal surfaces of intracellular structures, the form of such changes is not an action potential.

Although irritability of living matter is present in all species, its organization and interconnection with other structures and functions is varied, bringing about qualitative differences that are discontinuous. The specialized irritability of a neuron, and its participation in a system of neurons, as receptors (specialized to change in regard to certain types of energy in the environment), as effectors (specialized to change motor systems of the individual), or as parts of the system connecting receptors and effectors, can be seen as different levels on the continuum of irritability. From the simpler irritability of the protist to the most complex integrated organization of specialized neurons known as the human brain, the continuum has evolved through a series of discontinuities in types of organization, such as nerve nets (in the medusa), or ganglia (in worms), and the increased, qualitatively more complex organization of networks and ganglia in mollusks and in arthropods.

THE CONCEPT OF LEVELS OF ORGANIZATION AND INTEGRATION

The concept of continuity and discontinuity of phenomena and processes on the level of species evolution and the concept of continuity and discontinuity on the level of the individual development or the intraorganismic levels are related through the more general concept of levels of organization and integration. In brief, this concept orders all matter in a hierarchical increase of complexity of structure and function. The broadest hierarchical order of levels is that of inanimate (abiotic) and animate (biotic) matter. There are also mesolevels; for example, the virus represents a mesolevel, a level representing both the lower (abiotic) and higher (biotic) level. The virus is both living and nonliving, depending on its relation to a living organism. Within the animate, or living level of organization of matter, one can define plants on a lower level, and animals on a higher one. Again, there are entities belonging to both levels, as for example, euglena. Although this organism has no cell wall, a characteristic of animals, it does have chloroplasts containing chlorophyl so that it produces its own food (autotroph), a characteristic of most plants. However, with heat or chemical treatment, these organisms can lose their chlorophyl, at which time they become heterotrophs (depending on other sources of food than on their own production), which is a characteristic of animals. Thus euglena is both plant and animal, and represents a mesolevel.

Many categories of phenomena may be analyzed in terms of hierarchical levels. Species may be hierarchically arranged in increasing orders of complexity, and integration of specialized and interdependent subunits or parts. Behavioral plasticity may be so ordered and correlated with a concomitant grading of neural organization, beginning with the irritability of the protista and higher plants in which coordination of response is comparatively simple (but with qualitative differences between the two), depending for the most part on fewer elements and relatively less integration among elements, to increasingly complex specialization and differentiation of neural organization.

The organism, too, can be seen to be an integration of many levels. Intraorganismic organization, beginning with the molecular level, on which biophysical and biochemical functional phenomena are evident, is further characterized on the next level, the cellular level; that, in turn, becomes integrated as tissue, as an organ, as a system, and, finally, as an integration of many systems identifiable as an individual.

The concept has several corollaries that are useful in the analysis and synthesis of phenomena. For example, each succeeding level is subsumed in the next higher level and continues to function, but in the context of the higher level. One cannot, therefore, predict on the next higher level what the specific characteristics of function of the lower level will be without further knowledge of the new level. Each level has its own laws and properties requiring its own methods, and instrumentation for study. On any one level, causal explanations are necessarily limited; fuller causality can only be understood by integrating the preceding lower levels and succeeding higher levels in their interrelationships. Thus, knowledge about hormonal function is necessary to understand response to stress. However, without knowledge about how hormonal function is in turn affected by neural function (on the systems level) and knowledge about the interrelationships of the two systems on their molecular, cellular, tissue, and organ levels (e.g., neurotransmitter effects in relation to hormone metabolism) and on the behavioral level, one cannot predict how an individual will respond to stress under extreme ideational motivation. For example, the neural system can be superordinate to the hormonal system (extraordinary control of respiration and circulation) under conditions of societal pressure, as in combat, or emergency social situations. To understand the response of the individual in such situations, the history of the individual needs to be known in addition to the foregoing knowledge. This is another application of the concept of levels of organization and integration, the developmental or historical concept. For the individual, developmental phenomena are seen in a hierarchy of stages in which all the levels of intraorganismic organization are differently integrated at each stage of development as the individual grows, develops, and matures.

There is a continuity and discontinuity between levels that applies to all categories to which the concept may be applied. In discussing the relationship between the molecular level and the cellular level, continuity is the inclusion of the molecular level within the cellular level. The molecular level now functions differently because of its interconnections with other structural and functional characteristics of the cell; but the molecular level *in its function* is continuous in regard to its "essence" (its structure and function; its history; the laws by which it comes into existence and by which it changes into something else).[2] Although it is incorporated, it is analyzable on its own level.

The discontinuity between levels exists in the qualitative change in molecular function because of its interconnection and its "contradictory" function in the cell. On the molecular level, it is "necessary" that it have certain energy-changing relationships with the surround—to obtain those energy sources that will maintain the integrity of the molecular structure and function. However, because of its interconnection with other molecules and structures in the cell, it "gives" of itself in the process that maintains the cell. This contradiction is the inner contradiction in the cell that keeps the cell integrated and functioning—the integrity of the cell qua cell may be destroyed if the molecules require too much to maintain their integrity. At the same time, the special characteristics arising out of the inner contradictions of the cell are discontinuous with the molecular level. The cell requires new methods of study, new laws, and so on.

Continuity and discontinuity on the intraorganismic level, are well recognized in developmental psychology, although there is no universally accepted formulation of the concept (Werner, 1957). As much as the individual changes in development, the constancy of the integrity of the

[2] Spencer in his *First Principles* proposed the contradictory of evolution (or development) as "dissolution," a conceptualization having much in common with Hegel's philosophy, as well as those of Marx and Engels (Lawler, in press). The following quotes come from his chapter entitled "Evolution and Dissolution" (Chapter XII, Spencer, 1880): "The formula [ET: for integrating all knowledge] must be one comprehending the two opposite processes of concentration and diffusion [p. 243]." "All things are growing or decaying, accumulating matter or wearing away, integrating or disintegrating [p. 244]."

individual is self-evident. This might be said to be the primary contradiction in development. Given certain processes of development (internal contradictions) in interconnections with specific circumstances, the integrity of the individual is or is not maintained; the individual is or is not the same. The experience of seeing a person who is not "himself" or "herself" is sufficiently widely shared to make it evident that there are indeed times when constancy seems not to be maintained. Of course, the most dramatic change is the one in which the individual becomes significantly disturbed in behavior and relatedness to society to be described as psychotic or neurotic—when the "persona," the individual's integrity, seems to have become its opposite. And the final point on the continuum is death, or dissolution of integrity.

The evolutionary continua and discontinua can be significant in understanding the relationship between the individual and changing circumstances leading to continuity and discontinuity in development. But, to analyze and synthesize the phenomena of the evolutionary process and the individual's development, one must identify the level of the phenomenon to be studied and determine qualitative, as well as quantitative, change. Identifying the level emphasizes the appropriate lower levels to be considered for understanding causal relationships. The evolutionary continua and discontinua that are pertinent can help to identify the appropriate level of investigation.

A study of the effects of stimulation[3] (external energy change), whether it is in the abiotic or biotic aspects of the environment, reveals the significance of phyletic or evolutionary discontinuities. Abiotic and biotic stimulation are both important to the growth, development, and maturation of many species. One could compare three vertebrate species on the continuum of "effects of stimulation," to discover the continuity and discontinuity of the process, as well as to provide the context for studying the continuity and discontinuity of the process in individual development. The comparison of these three species is appropriate because they are being discussed within the context of a behavioral process on a continuum, and because no conclusion is being drawn about their phyletic relationship, nor are any assumptions being made about such a relationship (Aronson, 1980). If one wanted to discuss how differences in the effects of stimulation might relate to the evolutionary history of the three species,

---

[3] The term *stimulation* implies effective energy change, in the sense of Schneirla's concept of approach–withdrawal systems (Schneirla, 1972, pp. 344–412). In the parsimonious terms formulated in this chapter, I prefer to use the term *energy change* as an indication of the need to be aware of the subliminal quantitative changes that may act on the organism before the threshold of effectiveness is reached. Furthermore, the ability of the organism to store and integrate past experience plays an important role in the determination of an energy change as a *stimulus*. For these reasons, one would be advised to consider the desirability of using a less assumptive term such as energy change in place of stimulus.

the degree of phyletic relationship among the three would be appropriately involved. Issues of time and ecological location of origin as well as contemporary features of species adaptation would be pertinent. In the broadest sense, the three species have much in common; but they have much not in common. The comparison of the three species on the continuum is restricted because the data were derived from experiments that asked different questions. Nonetheless, within the boundaries of their data, a similar conclusion was reached by all: Stimulation during development is important.

The effects of social deprivation on mice and rats have been studied primarily at the biochemical and physiological level (Brain, 1975). However, in two behavioral studies, the effects of social isolation in young, male, laboratory rats were found to increase response to other rats (Latane, Schneider, Waring, & Zweigenhaft, 1971) but there was no discriminatory response to familiar rats as contrasted with strange rats. In the case of virgin female rats (approximately 50% of which retrieved 5- to 10-day-old rat pups) kept in conditions of social deprivation, a significant decrease in responsiveness to rat pups (Herrenkohl & Lisk, 1973) was found. Although profound hormonal changes take place in socially deprived rats (e.g., increased gonadal activity in both females and males; Brain, 1975), reproductive function is not significantly affected, as evidenced by routine laboratory management.

In the case of the monkey, effects of decreased social stimulation lead to profound changes in reproductive function (Harlow & Harlow, 1965). Some of these effects were mitigated by creating a more heterogeneous and complex developmental environment in which objects were manipulable. Although these monkeys were not as damaged in respect to social behavior as were monkeys reared without such stimulation, they were still different from monkeys reared with other monkeys (Anderson *et al.*, 1977). Mimicking some of the physical aspects of social stimulation was not sufficient; whether the deficiency was due to a lack of other forms of energy considered irrelevant, such as chemical stimuli, remains to be elucidated.

In the case of the human (Bowlby, 1961; Orlansky, 1949; & Spitz, 1965), effects of lack of social stimulation are more profound, and such deficiency affects the physiology of children so that they are more susceptible to disease.

The implications of these discontinuities for the study of the effects of stimulation on the development of an individual are far-reaching. Regardless of the phyletic level of organization of the individual involved, effects of stimulation on growth and development can be expected. Within intraorganismic levels of organization, effects on the molecular level would be found in all organisms, but with significant differences among different phyletic levels. In the case of acellular organisms, the biochemical reaction

would be studied rather directly in terms of change in molecular configuration within the animal. In the case of vertebrates, such as the rat, the
biochemical response would be measured in terms of the products of
physiological systems involving many different subunits such as circulating hormones, changes in water metabolism, and so on. But in both
cases, the continuity of a biochemical response would be a relevant factor.
The relevance of social stimulation would vary, not only in terms of types
of stimulation possible and types of systems affected, but also of stages
at which stimulation would be differentially significant (Schneirla & Rosenblatt, 1972, pp. 340–343).

LEVELS AND DEVELOPMENT: AN INTEGRATIONIST
APPROACH TO CONTEMPORARY THINKING

Those who view individual development as an unfolding of a program
that evolved and is species-specific would ask very different questions
about continuity and discontinuity in development. The integrationist
approach (Tobach, in press) first seeks to understand the phenomenon
in terms of the levels involved, within the context of the history of the
organism, and then within the history of the species. An evolutionary
approach without a levels approach leads to the kind of confusion cited
by Baltes, Reese, and Lipsitt (1980). In all the orientations listed by them
under the headings of "Development as expression of ontogenetic and
evolutionary principles" and "Pluralistic conceptions of development,"
the evolutionary aspect of development is viewed as related to species
survival; in individual development, "biological" factors are related to
reproductive maturity and disease. There is little evidence that the individual's relationship to society focuses on the survival of the species.
There is rather a consciousness about the continuity of the self as a societal
entity, that is, to perpetuate the self as a member of a nationality to
counter genocidal actions by another group, or nationality; or an identity
with family name, property, reputation, or other idealized reflections of
societal processes. The most self-conscious behavior in regard to the survival of the species is evidenced by groups who are concerned about
overpopulation, and are willing to forego having their own children. These
are a small proportion of contemporary society.

In the multicausal factors approaches listed by Baltes *et al.*, the various
factors are seen as equivalent. Interaction of the factors is seen as dominated early in development by "biological," or genetic "influences" with
a weakening of such influences later in life because "evolutionary selection
appl(ies) [ET change] primarily to the preproductive stages of the life
course [p. 77]." As Baltes *et al.* state "much of the work has been conceptual . . . rather than empirical [p. 101]." Yet, these approaches will
determine the kinds of questions asked; and the implications for research
and societal policy are profound (Hirsch, 1970; Tobach, in press).

Whereas it is true that, at different stages of development in different processes relating to different situations, different levels are preeminent, all levels continue to function, and all preceding stages are determinative of later stages. Thus, during embryonic development, the biochemical and biophysical factors in the milieu (referring in this discussion particularly to human beings, in the context of the discussion by Baltes *et al.*) are significant in determining growth and development of the embryo. The biochemical levels include the genetic processes as well as the circulating hormones and other substances that are derived from the incubating mother. However, as indicated in the preceding discussion, the levels on which the mother is operating are also relevant to the developing embryo. In this respect, the societal processes of which she is a part are preeminent in determining what shall be the biochemical and biophysical factors in the developing embryo. Indeed, the very determination of which sperm and which egg shall form the zygote are a function of societal processes— whether the mother shall be a victim of rape, of slavery, of bride barter, of "assortive mating" by class and race in an advanced technological society or of union arranged by a sperm bank for Nobel Prize winners.

The lower levels of organization and earlier stages of development continue to function throughout life, their effects integrated not only with subsequent events but with the particular situation in which the individual is acting. These factors are not "mediated" through the developing organism; they *are* the developing organism.

It is not only desire for species survival that operates through the genes. Gene function is expressed in enzymes and proteins that are fundamental and ubiquitous to all aspects of molecular function and derivatively in physiological integration. However, the preeminence of societal factors in human development in determining the significance of these biochemical processes is also never lost. If the child is discovered to have an enzyme deficiency that is corrected through dietary supplementation, the outcome will depend on whether the child is in a society in which such knowledge is not available, or if the knowledge is available, whether the treatment is available to the individual child. Extremes in chromosomal structures and function such as trisomy-21, despite their demonstrated molecular base, are also variably vulnerable to societal processes.

The current interest in developmental processes throughout life raises questions about the effects of war and economic disruption on development. Some of the authors cited by Baltes *et al.* (1980) attempt to see these as interactions between "biological" and "environmental" determinants. Such an approach leads to questions and research formulations that ignore the societal laws of these phenomena. For example, let us analyze the proposal to have 18- to 20-year-old men register for possible service in the military forces in the United States in terms of evolutionary processes leading to species survival or the perpetuation of one's own genes. (See

Baltes *et al.*, p. 71 and p. 77.) This approach might lead to the conclusion that those who propose to send off these young men to possible death and loss of their contributions to the human gene pool were doing so to increase the possibility that the proposers' genes would be perpetuated instead (Wilson, 1978). This conclusion is based on the assumption that the proposers are not sending their own sons off to battle. A demographic analysis of the lawmakers and personnel in the armed forces leadership and of the racial, ethnic, and class composition of the armed forces would probably seem to support that conclusion. Such an analysis ignores alternative explanations. The concept of levels of organization would view these phenomena as societal processes and relate them to various levels of societal organization. Unemployment, need for greater consumption of certain products, inability of society to provide training in nonmilitary pursuits, and so on, would be considered. The analysis and understanding of developmental processes in an evolutionary context based on preformationistic, genetic determinist approaches such as those cited by Baltes *et al.* (1980) tend to obfuscate the questions to be asked and the experimental approaches needed to answer them (Schneirla, 1972; pp. 192–196).

How Does the "Integrationist" Approach Differ from Other Approaches to Development?

SOME APPROACHES TO DEVELOPMENT

Although the following definitions of development have some elements of a levels approach, they do not make clear the interrelationship of the organism and the environment. They emphasize the intraorganismic aspect of the developmental process, which is close to the "unfolding" view of development. For instance, Werner (1957) says[4]

> one regulative principle of development . . . is an orthogenetic principle which states that whereever development occurs it proceeds from a stage of relative globality and lack of differentiation, articulation, and hierarchic integration [p. 126]. . . . The orthogenetic law, by its very nature, is an expression of unilinearity of development [p. 137].

> When one considers the development of behavior, there remain many paradoxes. A greater differentation of the organism is accompanied by greater integration and organization of the parts. The more the organism reduces random activities to skill or habits, the freer it becomes to formulate new patterns of behavior. In the development of the individual case we are confronted with continuous change and also with undeniable continuities or rigidities. These are but some of the seeming paradoxes which beset developmental

[4] I have rearranged the sentences for purposes of clarity. I believe I have not altered the meaning.

studies. If a paradox means that we have failed to make a necessary distinction, then we must work out these distinctions for future research to be fruitful [Harris, 1972, p. 481]. . . . There is its characteristic *complexity* and *organization*, its apparent *directionality*, its *process* nature, the problem of *stages*, the question of *hierarchical relationships*, and finally the concept of potentials [Harris, 1972, p. 487].

These definitions are reminiscent of the one offered by Spencer. One must remember that his "formula," as Spencer called it, pertained to all phenomena, including individual development, societal development, and evolution. Whereas he achieved notoriety for his contribution to the infamous ideology of social Darwinism, he also contributed significantly to our concepts of evolution and survival of the fittest in the modern sense.

Evolution is an integration of matter and concomitant dissipation of motion; during which the matter passes from an indefinite incoherent homogeneity to a definite coherent heterogeneity; and during which the retained motion undergoes a parallel transformation [Spencer, 1880, p. 343].

A definition by Bronfenbrenner (1979) stresses the environment and activity of the individual as important parts of the developmental process:

Development is defined as the person's evolving conception of the *ecological environment*, and his relation to it, . . . as the person's growing capacity to discover, sustain, or alter its properties [p. 9]. . . . The ecological environment is conceived topologically as a nested arrangement of concentric structures, each contained within the next . . . the *micro-*, *meso-*, *exo-*, and *macrosystems* [p. 22].

Schneirla's (1972) definition integrates the significant aspects of development within the context of his approach–withdrawal theory, which is formulated within the concept of levels of organization and integration:

behavioral development . . . progressive, changing relationships between organism and environment in which the contributions of growth are always inseparably interrelated with those of the effects of energy changes in the environs. . . . "maturation" and "experience" . . . are not simply interrelated but constitute a fused system in each stage. . . . the concept of "maturation," redefined as the contributions of tissue growth and differentiation and their functional trace effects at all stages, and "experience," defined as the contributions of stimulation from the developmental medium and of related trace effects. . . . These terms are not to be taken as representing a mutually exclusive separation, but as convenient abstractions [p. 352].

There is fairly good agreement about the concept of growth, although differences in the definition of development are evident. The definition of the maturation process is also problematical. As defined by Schneirla, it is open-ended, and does not define a developmental stage that may be considered maturity. *Maturity* is viewed by many as an end point, as the full development or growth of the organism. For some biologists, the concept of maturity is defined in the context of reproductive process, that is, maturity is related to the production of the egg and sperm, ready for the formation of the zygote. Despite the fact that there are species, such as axolotl, in which the subadult form is capable of reproduction, in general, maturity may be seen as that stage of development when reproduction of the total individual, that is, the production of a new individual, is possible.

An analysis of the concept of maturity explicates the concept of levels of organization and integration, and of the concepts of continuity and of discontinuity. As Schneirla defines growth, development, and maturation, these processes apply to all organisms, to all animals, and maturation and maturity are consonant. However, on the human level, the meanings of maturation and maturity become dissonant. The determination of when an individual is mature, that is, ready to reproduce, varies with the society in which the individual lives, not with a defined physiological stage of development. Usually, the society's criteria of maturity have some reference to the physiological stage of reproduction. Individuals who have reached a certain age are considered mature, however, whether or not they have reproduced or are capable of reproducing.

HOW CONCEPTUALIZATIONS OF DEVELOPMENT REFLECT HISTORICAL REALITY

The concept of development has gone through several stages: development as unfolding, passive (both in genetic determinist definitions), reactive (e.g., Harris, 1972), and interactive (e.g., Bronfenbrenner, 1979; Schneirla, 1972). In a sense, all development may be said to encompass these characteristics, and these earlier definitions did reflect reality in a limited way. In one sense, development is a kind of unfolding. Those processes that are intraorganismic (molecular through systematic levels, biochemical through physiological levels), in the course of their changing, do "push" the organism out, or cause the organism to "unfold" into the environment, through the products that are excreted, changes in shape, size, number of parts, and so on. All organisms share this expression of inner process.

As changes in the external milieu penetrate the individual, the effects of such energy changes may be at quantitatively low or subliminal levels. During these quantitative changes, the developmental process of the organism may be "passive," that is, the changes take effect on an internal level of organization only. As the external forces continue to operate, or as they change sufficiently in intensity, amplitude, or in other parameters, the internal changes undergo a qualitative change, and the organism as an integrated whole changes its spatial relationship to the surround: It becomes reactive. Finally, as the organism reacts to the changing relations between external and internal forces, its reactions are modified by the changes resulting from the reaction, in an *interactive* process between the two, that is, between the reactions and the changes in the external situation and in the inner process.

The viewing of these processes as unfolding, passive, reactive, and interactive events in which the changes in the organism lead to growth and development, however, all are based on the individual as not acting through any kind of self-generating, self-organizing process. Schneirla (1972) and Bronfenbrenner (1979) both included related notions of the role of the individual in their discussions of the stimulating effects of the organism's own activity. Bronfenbrenner discusses the concept of self-organized activity only in regard to human activity. Leontyev (1977) also proposes that activity, as a self-originating, goal-directed process is crucial for development, and he also applies the concept to humans primarily. In Schneirla's (1972) discussion of self-stimulation, the process is discussed within an evolutionary context. Describing a series of developmental phenomena in insects, amphibia, birds, and mammals, he elaborates the significance of the actions of the developing organism as integral to its growth and development (pp. 270–273). These effects are seen in an interactive, spiraling process in which previous events form the basis for later events in development. His formulation makes clear the need to understand the organism as integrally self-organizing, and its development is a reflection, not only of its internal changes, but of the changes it has made in the environment (see also Lerner & Busch-Rossnagel, Chapter 1, this volume).

How Does the Levels Concept Apply to the Analysis of the Integration of Organism and Environment?

In discussing the category of organism–environment integration, one is struck by the similarity between the levels of processes in which the integration comes about and the levels of developmental processes just described. With the exception of the unfolding characteristic of development, which is the expression of internal processes (never really independent of external processes), the internal and external processes can only be separated as convenient abstractions for discussion, analysis, and synthesis. The individual is thus integrated with the environment through a series of processes that may be hierarchically arranged as passive, reactive, interactive, and active. To understand how these processes are carried out, the general concept of environment needs to be discussed.

ENVIRONMENT

Generally speaking, the environment may be seen to consist of abiotic (nonliving) and biotic (living) aspects. The abiotic aspects are physical, chemical aspects of the environment, processes related to climate, geography, cosmic structures, and so on; or they may be the result of the activity of living organisms releasing chemicals and other products into the environment.

The biotic aspects of the environment may be disspecific,[5] or conspecific, that is, organisms that are in different groups (e.g., plants and other animals) or in the same group. The relationship of the organism to the abiota and biota is expressed in the activity of the organism on and in that environment; the environment is contradictory in the unity of opposites defined by organism and environment. The organism is the other contradictory. The contradiction between the living organism and the environment is a special form of a more general contradiction, because it deals with living matter rather than inanimate matter. The primary contradiction for all matter, and in a special form for living matter, is the contradiction between those apsects of the environment that promote the integrity of the organism and those that bring about disintegration. The living organism may become the opposite of what it is, that is, nonliving. "Death," whether in a one-celled organism, in a complex plant, or in a human being is the result of the contradiction between those two processes.

Within the organism, a similar contradiction exists between processes that promote integrity and those that bring about disintegration (cf. Schneirla, 1972, pp. 344–412; Tobach, 1970). This inner contradiction is sharpened or stabilized by the contradiction between the organism and the environment. In regard to the changes in both the abiotic and biotic aspects of the environment, the animal may be passive, reactive, interactive or active. However, in the case of the abiotic aspects of the environment, the earliest and most frequent types of change in the animal are passive (see previous discussion). The reactive activities are tropisms and taxes. For the most part the organism can adjust to the abiotic aspects of the environment through passivity or reactivity. There are instances in which the organism interacts with the abiotic aspect of the environment

---

[5] In an earlier publication I used the words *homospecific* and *heterospecific* to denote animals which belonged to the same group, and animals which belonged to different groups, respectively. These words were criticized because they "mixed" Latin and Greek roots. As the term conspecific is well-known and understood, I am proposing that the opposite of conspecific be the word *disspecific*, in which the Latin root *species* meaning form, or shape, is combined with the prefix *dis* meaning separation from, parting from, reversal, or negation. In other words, *conspecific*, meaning together with the species, is contrasted with *disspecific*, meaning separated from the species [Tobach, 1963].

(i.e., as the animal reacts to the nonliving aspect of the environment, the environment is changed and acts back on the organism). An example of this is a sea hare's burrowing under the sandy substrate and being covered by it. Interactions may come about directly through tangoception; or the animal's changing a current of air by moving into it.

Actions by the organism, that is, directed, integrated operations that change the abiotic environment are most frequently seen in the modification of the substrate through digging, creation of tunnels (as in the case of desert-dwelling rodents and in the case of fish which spawn on sandy bottoms of bodies of water). The next largest category of action on the environment is seen in the manipulation of plant materials for nests by insects, fish, birds, and other animals.

In the category of organismic–environmental integration with the biotic aspects of the environment, the response to disspecifics can also be categorized in the way that the response to the abiotic environment was described. Passive, reactive, interactive, and active integrations with disspecifics also take place. For purposes of this discussion, parasitism and inquilism will be omitted; these are passive integrations primarily. The most common disspecific integration is predation. The category of conspecific integration is generally conceptualized as social activity or social behavior. This, and predation, are the most significant integrations of the organism with the environment, varying with the stage of development.

DISSPECIFIC ASPECTS OF THE ENVIRONMENT: PREDATION; CONSPECIFIC ASPECTS: SOCIALIZATION

The continuous adjustment (e.g., passive, reactive, interactive and active processes) of the organism to changes in the abiotic aspects of the environment are significant for the growth, development, and maturation of the organism. Actions as directed, integrated modifications of the environment by the organism are critical in two types of adjustment to the biota: feeding and socialization. Animals must act on the environment to incorporate energy; almost all animals are heterotrophs (i.e., depending on other organisms for energy).

The feeding activity of animals can also be seen on a continuum. The two major categories of action on the environment in feeding are those in which the organism does not change its location in time and place to obtain food, and those in which it does. Animals which live in a medium containing the nutriments may be filter feeders, that is, the energy source is simply circulated through the animal either by specialized structures that require an orientation on the part of the animal or a simple closing or opening of sphincters (oral, through the skin or membranes of the body, etc.).

These categories are usually thought of in regard to adult organisms. However, it should be noted that this category includes immature stages of many species (e.g., larval forms of both invertebrates and vertebrates, marsupial young, insects which hatch in a medium of food as in the case of some moths and flies, egg-laying species and many of the neonates among vertebrates). In the mature stage, these same species may belong to the other category of feeding activity.

The other major category is one in which the organism moves in time and space to where the food is, and some further changes in time and space occur during which the energy source is taken internally. The elaboration of patterns of action in this regard is an important part of evolutionary history and the specialization of structures and the complexity of the sensory–action systems are as varied as are the species to be enumerated. In these activities, the developing organism modifies its relation to the environment at different stages of development to feed; the mode of feeding is differentially dependent on the organism's own activity.

In the invertebrate groups, many of the animals will show both types of feeding, at different stages of development. For example, sponges become filter feeders after having been active larval predators. In the case of social insects (e.g., ants and bees), feeding by the growing organism is dependent on the organism's own activities in reaction and interaction with the conspecific aspects of the environment, as in the army ant. The activity of the larva, an expression of both internal change and external forces, by changing its spatial relationship to the environment affects the conspecifics in the colony, that is, the workers which are actively moving in and out of the colony. The workers are feeding but also carrying materials back to the colony. The activity of the larva affect the workers; the workers palpate the larva with antennae and legs. The larva, during activity brought about by internal change, releases chemicals and other moieties that affect the actions of the workers. They drop the materials near the larva, which then feeds on the materials. This interaction (reciprocal stimulation, Schneirla, 1972, pp. 458–461) affects the workers, which then leave the colony to feed and return with materials.

However, the activity of the workers in leaving and returning is not only a function of the colony situation, but also a function of the characteristics of the environment around the colony. The novelty of the area, along with the other characteristics not yet elucidated, brings about an increase in the activity of the workers both to leave and to return to the colony (Topoff, 1975; Topoff & Mirenda, 1980; Topoff, Mirenda, Droual, & Herrick, 1980). This interrelationship between the changes *within* individuals in the colony and the changes in the environment brings about quantitative–qualitative change, which is the next step of development, pupation. The physiological activities of the larvae change, producing a material that encloses the larva. During the pupal stage, the larva metamorphoses into the next stage of development, the callow worker (Schneirla, 1971).

The socialization of organisms so that they may feed and thus grow, develop, and mature represents a significant discontinuity in the continuum of the relationship between the organism and different aspects of its environment. One cannot hierarchically arrange groups of animals according to their usual taxonomic categories and correlate position on the continuum of "dependence on conspecifics" with the taxonomic classification. For example, dependence on conspecifics for survival is highly significant in the social insects; interdependence of individuals to survive is equally significant in the case of medusa, coral, and other colonial organisms. However, in these cases, the individuals, by becoming connected to conspecifics, lose some of the physiological and structural characteristics that made it possible for them to survive as individual entities. In these cases, the contradictions between the individual and the group bring about a sharpening of the inner contradictions of the individual, so that the individual becomes the opposite of what it was as a free-swimming organism before it "colonized." It is no longer an individual; rather, it is a structural level of organization in a new entity—a colonial animal. In these instances, growth, development, and maturation are reversed in the sense that there is no development beyond a certain stage; maturation in the sense of reproduction does not occur; reproduction is part of the developmental process of the colonial organism of which it is now a part, not of the individual cell.

The individual social insect also loses identity as an individual but in a significantly different way from that of the colonial individual. The social insect moves about in the environs as a separate entity; it shows a variety of behavior patterns related to obtaining food, carrying members of the colony, and many more. However, it has also undergone structural and functional modification in the course of development so that it is not able to reach maturity in the sense of being able to reproduce. The differences between these two levels of organization are concomitant with levels of neural and hormonal organization, the social insect being more complex than the colonial organism.

In the vertebrates also, there are many instances in which the species may be categorized for the most part as to whether the offspring are predominantly independent of, or dependent on adults for survival, growth, and development. In general, the traditional taxonomic ordering of vertebrates agrees with an ordering of the continuum from least dependence on adults to most dependence on adults: The offspring of fish, amphibia, and reptiles generally show less dependence on adults than do those of birds and mammals. Nonetheless, there are in each taxon examples of both types of relationships. In all three groups, there are species in which the egg donor or the sperm donor incubates the offspring until they are individuated and become active in the environment as individuals.

Young may be born precocial or altricial, so that the young may be more or less dependent on adults for survival. In the case of many invertebrates, the lower vertebrates, and precocial birds and mammals, it is the activity of the young organism in relation to the nonconspecific environment that makes survival, growth, and development possible. When the young organism is dependent on the adult, the contradictions between the young and the adult make the action of the young organism on the adult or conspecific of significant value in the growth and development process of the young organism (Carr, 1960; Rosenblatt, 1970, 1971). The reciprocal stimulation of the two organisms in these situations is not only important for development but is the basis for the formation of the social organization which is the context in which the organism develops and matures (Alexander & Williams, 1964; Butler, Suskind, & Schanberg, 1978; Galef & Clark, 1976; Schneirla, 1972; pp. 358–361).

Levels of Activity in Organism–Environment Integration as Developmental Processes

In all the activities of the individual, the fundamental contradiction is to maintain integrity and to survive. The fundamental activity is the adjustment of the organism to internal and external change: passive (quantitative), reactive (tropism and taxis), and interactive (organism acts on environment, which acts back on it). The highest level is one in which the organism carries out an integrated and directed action that changes the surround: All levels of organization within the organism are coordinated in carrying out the activity with a maximum of effect and efficiency; that is, the activity is an integration of all levels. The activity is directed in the sense that the organism is integrating the activity with the consequence of such activity. For example, the organism engages in learned behavior to obtain food (e.g., returning to a previously visited source); it engages in detour behavior to arrive at a particular place in which it then rests (takes a route that avoids a predator rather than a shorter one); the individual plants seeds in a predetermined program. All of these are directed activities, but they may be hierarchically ordered as to level of directedness. Some of the characteristics that are the basis for such ordering are: the degree to which the individual integrates past experience related to the consequence of the activity; and the degree to which the behavior involves planning without the direct physical presence of the result of such planning. These other aspects of the activity provide the framework for arranging such directedness in order of increasing complexity. The labor carried out by humans with tools that may or may not have been fashioned by the individual but are obtained through abstract symbolic communication (language) is different from the use of a rock by a monkey to open a clam shell.

POSITIVE FEEDBACK AND AUTOCATALYSIS

The organism–environment integration, that is, the action aspect of development, has characteristics of positive feedback, and autocatalysis.[6] The continuous interpenetration of the results of the action by the organism, that is, the changes within the organism and the changes in the environment is in effect a growing quantitative relationship in which the "explosion" results in the qualitative change that brings the organism into a new stage of development, a qualitatively new integration with the environment. The end point of the positive feedback brings about a cessation of the particular activity. This type of activity characterizes such quantitative–qualitative types of change, as in copulatory activity or, nest building by fish, birds, and mammals.

The autocatalytic type of action is more qualitative and more related to inner processes. Autocatalysis is the potentiation of a reaction brought about by a product of that reaction. Thus, as the bird builds the nest, the product produced accelerates the action because the part produced (presence of twigs) further stimulates the bird to deposit more twigs. The significance of the results of activity is qualitatively such as to cause the activity to be continued. The relationship of the lower levels of activity (passive, reactive, interactive) to directed actions such as positive feedback, and to autocatalysis varies with the phyletic level of the organism and the individual's history and stage of development.

ACTION AND DEVELOPMENT

Three processes (contradictions) intercept in time to bring about qualitative changes in the individual (development, which includes growth and maturation): (a) the inner contradiction of the organism; (b) the inner contradiction of the environment; and (c) the outer contradiction between the organism and the environment. Some of the inner contradictions would be the metabolic cycle, and neurohormonal cycles; these have characteristics of negative and positive feedback that bring about continuous change with more or less stability in the organism. The environment expresses its own contradictions in diurnal and seasonal variations, faunal and floral interrelations, and so on. Given different lighting conditions (environmental contradictions), the effects on the hormonal function (in-

---

[6] It is to be noted that this concept of autocatalysis is also used by Wilson (1975). However, he does not indicate the qualitative differences in this process on different phyletic levels. In the concept of levels of organization and integration, the autocatalytic process is seen as a lower level of activity than self-organization, self-directed activity, which is an integration of many processes, including the auto-catalytic, as a lower level. Wilson sees much of human social activity as only autocatalytic.

traorganismic contradictions) bring about changes in the organism's activity that bring it into changing relationships with the abiota and biota, and particularly with conspecifics (contradiction between organism and environment). The intersect of these three processes (contradictions) brings about developmental change in the organism. The organism may act on the environment (the social aspect), resulting in copulation, bringing about a new developmental stage.

What is the value of analyzing this well-known neurohormonal relationship within this context? In this formulation, the changing nature of the relationship still needs the elucidation and careful study that would be required by any other theoretical basis. This analysis yields different questions, however. The intergrationist approach stresses the historical or developmental approach; it asks questions as to which intraorganismic and interorganismic levels were involved; it asks what were the relations between the levels or systems. Within the levels context, one would predict that, at the biochemical level, circulating hormones would change the functional characteristic of cells. For the most part, the investigation of such changes has dealt with changes in so-called "target" organs—reproductive glands, sexually dimorphic structures, and so on. But the integrationist approach (contradictions) in the context of levels would suggest that higher levels affect lower levels, just as lower levels change in higher levels. One would also seek ways in which the biochemical changes at the cellular level, in either direct or indirect connections, operate on many systems, such as the visual system. The interconnectedness of these changes would affect the integration of the organism with the environment, and thus affect its action on the environment.

For example, it is well known that changing colors in conspecifics affect other conspecifics in a particular manner at certain stages of development but not at others. It has been proposed by ethologists and sociobiologists that these changes in reaction to the environment are encoded genetically as a result of the evolutionary process. To state that the action is coded or programmed describes the general historical framework within which one might place such phenomena; it is not a statement of causality; it is a descriptive statement. The integrationist approach requires the elaboration of the function of the biochemical level (genetic; hormonal; neurotransmitter) in the history of the organism on all intraorganismic levels to bring about such a change in reaction–action–reaction–integration as seen in the changing effect of conspecific color. This approach asks: Were there changes in the visual system?

Another example of the different types of questions that are formulated on the basis of this approach is to be found in the analysis of social deprivation and the "enriched environment" studies. For the most part, the actions of the organism on the environment are not taken into account. Behavioral and physiological changes are sought in the systems that seem immediately of interest to the investigators—the social bond formation between infant and adult; or between peers; or reproductive behavior. In the case of the enriched environment, the effects on biochemical and anatomic changes were looked at in the hormonal and neurosensory systems (Bennett & Rosenzweig, 1971; Bennett, Rosenzweig, & Diamond, 1970; Cummins & Livesey, 1979; Krech, Rosenzweig, & Bennett, 1960; Rosenzweig, Krech & Bennett, 1960). How did the organisms act with the objects in the enriched environment and how was this reflected in the physiology of the organisms? How did these changes then express themselves at different levels of organization? In some studies, the activity of the organisms was discussed but this was in regard to species characteristics of gerbils, rats, and mice (Rosenzweig, 1971; Rosenzweig & Bennett, 1970).

Levels of Action

Self-organizing and self-organized action, the integration of many levels and processes, is the highest level of activity possible. Such activity and its role in development also represents a continuum on many levels of phyletic organization and integration, and may be ordered hierarchically. Self-organizing activity that results from the inner contradictions of the individual may be short-term, dependent on the immediate contemporary situation with positive feedback characteristics. Such activity ends with changing internal and external conditions and is "forgotten"; or the trace effects are weak and transient and likely not to be involved in any future activity. Such self-organizing activity (described in earlier sections) is typical of invertebrates.

Self-organizing activity at the highest level of organization is characterized by symbolized reflection of experience, including the experience of other individuals. These symbolic representations have been incorporated in the consciousness and knowledge of the individual. Such activity may have no relevance to the biotic or abiotic characteristics of the immediate situation. Positive feedback and autocatalysis are evident in such activity, but they are internalized at a higher level, as criteria for determining the significance of the outcome of the activity, rather than expressed in immediate feedback phenomena. Human activity, such as tilling the soil, making a design for a building, or writing a chapter in a book are examples of such activity.

Between these two extremes, on the continuum of activity, there are other levels. In the case of the bird building a nest, some aspect of the completedness of it probably has some effect on the starting and stopping point of its being built. The ability of apes to perform complex tasks in communication through self-organizing action is another point on the continuum.

Action as Environmental Control

The outstanding difference between humans and other animals is that humans use activity to control the environment better than any other species. This evolved ability to control the environment through self-organizing, self-directed symbolized activity has a necessary corollary in the developmental process. As the adult or mature organism achieves greater control of the environment, the necessity of the young organism to act on the developmental environment to bring about survival, growth, development, and maturation, becomes greater.

As organisms achieve more control of the environment (rather than metabolic processes producing substances that create a specific environment for the organism, e.g., a coral reef, a worm tube), the more they become dependent on conspecifics for survival. In the case of the social insects, control of the environment is through production of materials from the body as in the case of bees; or the actual use of the body to create the nest as in the case of the army ants; or through the actual manipulation of other species thus providing food and other life necessities as in the case of the "slave-making" or gardening ants. And in these species, the dependence on conspecifics for survival is critical, as exemplified by the activity of the larvae to bring about growth and development.

It is in the vertebrates that the elaboration of environmental modification to bring about survival become most clearly evident. This is more evident in fish than in amphibia and reptiles. A new level of organization and integration is reached in birds, with building of nests and colonization of nest sites. The survival of the altricial individual is possible only through its relationships with its group. There are many advances and retreats in the evolution of increasingly complex relationships between the environment and individual and the group in regard to mammalian survival.

One must be cautious in synthesizing such observations. In general, such generalizations are valid, but the exceptions are the nodal point of evolutionary processes where the contradictions between the two types of processes are seen. The species can go on to higher levels of organization and integration, or stay at the same level, somewhat reduced in complexity and not progressing to increased independence of the environment.

New types of control of the environment came about through the use of tools and fire, and the storage and integration of knowledge about the flora and fauna of the environment. Activities could, then, be projected into the future, thus affecting the tense characteristics of communication. Such a qualitative change in the type of activity may well have affected the process or abstraction and symbolization. Hunting activity may have been overemphasized as a critical activity in the evolution of humans. Hunting is another way of feeding; the elaboration of tools for hunting and gathering, as well as for the use and control of fire, may all have led to a change in the kinds of activity possible. Through storage of information about the environment—where to find game based on their life cycle, or where to find edible vegetation—a change came about in the self-organizing, self-directed, goal-oriented activity. Consequent or integrated change in communication, language, and thought made increased control of the environment possible, and required increased directed activity (e.g., training) of young individuals to be integrated in the group without which they could not survive as individuals. As to who hunted and gathered, given the human capacity for work and control of the environment shared by both sexes, and the need for young individuals to be trained, there is as little basis for thinking that one or another activity was restricted to one sex, as there is for asserting otherwise. It is a question that can only be answered by increased study of early hominid evolution.

Special Characteristics of Action

Certain characteristics of self-directed, self-organizing activity should be examined and reviewed.

In analyzing development, one has to deal with reproductive function. That is where the development of the newly individuated organism begins. It is not surprising, therefore, that much of the activity seen on all phyletic levels is activity that changes as a result of the reproductive stage. This tends to obscure the fact that it is engaged in for a relatively short period of time in the organism's life. Again, the relative amount of time spent in such activity by different species varies. In the invertebrates, the end point of life frequently is reproductive activity, and reproduction seems to take very little time.

In the case of mammals, which survive long after reproduction, selection pressures are such that, frequently, old animals become so ill or sufficiently wounded to die earlier than they would have if they were in protected human-organized situations. The amount of time in which the modification of the environment takes place during reproductive activity is very small contrasted with the amount of time the individual engages in activity to survive through feeding, resting, and avoidance of predators. This is also true on the human level; most of the life history of the individual is engaged in modification of the environment and controlling of the environment to survive. The amount of time spent in reproductive activity, however, changes with the culture.

Recapitulation

Throughout this chapter I have stressed that activity of the organism in bringing about growth, development, and maturation is variously related to the phyletic and individual history of the organism. These lawful relations make it possible to understand and appreciate that the analysis of developmental processes has to take place on the appropriate level of organization and integration. In this way, generalizations about the similarities among species do not lead to underestimating the significance of certain types of experience for the growing individual, or to overemphasizing limitations of growth and development because species are seen as more similar than dissimilar. The value of looking at the problem in an evolutionary context lies in the formulation of questions based on concepts of change rather than on concepts of fixity and predeterminism. Living organisms are seen as active forces in these processes of change, and phyletic comparisons point to the increasing significance of action for individual development as species become more complex.

Acknowledgments

I wish to thank Professor Susi Koref-Santibanez, Professor Rosamond Gianutsos, and Dr. John Gianutsos for their critical reading of the manuscript. They are, of course, not responsible for the contents thereof.

References

Alexander, G., & Williams, D. Maternal facilitation of sucking drive in newborn lambs. *Science*, 1964, *146*, 665–666.

Anderson, C. O., Kenney, A., & Mason, W. A. Effects of maternal mobility, partner, and endocrine state on social responsiveness of adolescent Rhesus monkeys. *Developmental Psychobiology*, 1977, *10*, 421–434.

Aronson, L. R. Evolution of telencephalic function in lower vertebrates. In P. Laming (Ed.), *Brain mechanisms of behaviour in lower vertebrates.* Cambridge, Eng.: Cambridge University Press, 1980, in press.

Baltes, R. B., Reese, H. W., & Lipsitt, L. P. Life-span developmental psychology. *Annual Review of Psychology*, 1980, *31*, 65–110.

Bastock, M. A gene mutation which changes a behavior pattern. *Evolution*, 1956, *10*, 421–439.

Bennett, E. L., & Rosenzweig, M. R. Chemical alteration produced in brain environment and training. In A. Lajtha (Ed.), *Handbook of neurochemistry* (Vol. 6). New York: Plenum, 1971. Pp. 173–201.

Bennett, E. L., Rosenzweig, M. R., & Diamond, M. C. Time courses of effects of differential experience on brain measures and behavior of rats. In W. L. Byrne (Ed.), *Molecular approaches to learning and memory.* New York: Academic Press, 1970. Pp. 55–89.

Bowlby, J. B. F. Separation anxiety: A critical review of the literature. *Journal of Child Psychology and Psychiatry*, 1961, *1*, 251–269.

Brain, P. What does individual housing mean to a mouse? *Life Sciences*, 1975, *16*, 187–200.

Bronfenbrenner, U. *The ecology of human development.* Cambridge, Mass.: Harvard University Press, 1979.

Butler, S. R., Suskind, M. R., & Schanberg, S. M. Maternal behavior as a regulator of polamine biosynthesis in brain and heart of the developing rat pup. *Science*, 1978, *199*, 445–447.

Caplan, A. L. (Ed.). *The sociobiology debate*. New York: Harper & Row, 1978.

Carniero, R. L. The devolution of evolution. *Social Biology*, 1972, *19*, 248–258.

Carr, A., & Hirth, H. Social facilitation in green turtle siblings. *Animal Behaviour*, 1960, *9*, 68–70.

Cummins, R. A., & Livesey, P. J. Enrichment–isolation, cortex length and the rank order effect. *Brain Research*, 1979, *178*, 89–98.

Dobzhansky, Th. *Evolution, genetics, and man*. New York: Wiley, 1955.

Ehrman, L., & Parsons, P. *The genetics of behavior*. Sunderland, Mass.: Sinauer, 1976.

Eigen, M. Self-organization of matter and the evolution of biological macromolecules. *Die Naturwissenschaften*, 1971, *10*, 465–523.

Fisher, R. A. *The genetical theory of natural selection*. Oxford: Clarendon, 1930.

Freese, E. B., & Freese, E. The influence of the developing bacterial spore on the mother cell. *Developmental Biology*, 1977, *60*, 453–462.

Galef, B. G., Jr., & Clark, M. M. Non-nutrient functions of mother–young interactions in the Agouti (*Dasyprocta punctata*) *Biology*, 1976, *17*, 255–262.

Gould, S. J. *Ontogeny and phylogeny of behavior*. Cambridge, Mass.: Harvard University Press, 1977.

Haldane, J. B. S. *The causes of evolution*. London: Longmans, Green, 1932.

Harlow, H. F., & Harlow, M. K. The affectational systems. In A. M. Schrier, H. F. Harlow, & F. Stolnitz (Eds.), *Behavior of nonhuman primates* (Vol. 2). New York: Academic Press, 1965. Pp. 287–334.

Harris, D. B. The development of human theoretical coincidents for future research. In L. R. Aronson, E. Tobach, & E. Shaw, (Eds.), *The biopsychology of development*. New York: Academic Press, 1971. Pp. 473–502.

Herreid, C. F., II, & Schlenker, E. H. Energetics of mice in stable and unstable social conditions: Evidence of an air-borne factor affecting metabolism. *Animal Behaviour*, 1980, *28*, 20–28.

Herrenkohl, L. R., & Lisk, R. D. The effects of sensitization and social isolation on maternal behavior in the virgin rat. *Physiology and Behaviour*, 1973, *11*, 619–624.

Hirsch, J. Behavior genetic analysis and its biosocial consequences. *Seminars in Psychiatry*, 1970, *2*, 89–105.

Huxley, Julian: Evolution: The Modern Synthesis. London: George Allen and Unwin Ltd.

Krech, D., Rosenzweig, M. R., & Bennett, E. L. Effects of environmental complexity and training on brain chemistry. *Journal of Comparative and Physiological Psychology*, 1960, *53*(6), 509–519.

Latané, B., Schneider, E., Wanng, P., & Zweigenhaft, R. The specificity of social attraction in rats. *Psychonomic Science*, 1971, *23*, 28–30.

Lawler, J. R. Hegel in formal and dialectical contradictions, and misrepresentations from Bertrand Russell to Lucio Colletti, in press.

Leontyev, A. N. Activity and consciousness. In *Philosophy in the USSR: problems of dialectical materialism*. Moscow: Progress, 1977. Pp. 180–202.

Lwoff, A. Interaction among virus, cell, and organism. *Science*, 1966, *152*, 1216–1220.

Orlansky, H. Infant care and personality. *Psychological Bulletin*, 1949, *46*, 1–52.

Popper, K. R. *Objective knowledge: An evolutionary approach*. Oxford: Clarendon, 1972.

Roblin, G. *Mimosa pudica*: A model for the study of the study of the excitability in plants. *Biological Review*, 1979, *54*, 135–153.

Rosenblatt, J. S. Views on the onset and maintenance of maternal behavior in the laboratory rat. In L. R. Aronson, E. Shaw, & E. Tobach (Eds.), *Development and evolution of behavior: Essays in memory of T. C. Schneirla*. San Francisco: W. H. Freeman, 1970. Pp. 489–515.

Rosenblatt, J. S. Suckling and home orientation in the kitten: A comparative developmental study. In E. Tobach, L. R. Aronson, & E. Shaw (Eds.), *The biopsychology of development*. New York: Academic Press, 1971. Pp. 345–410.

Rosenzweig, M. R. Effects of environment on development of brain and behavior. In E. Tobach, L. R. Aronson, & E. Shaw (Eds.), *The biopsychology of development*. New York: Academic Press, 1971. Pp. 303–342.

Rosenzweig, M. R., & Bennett, E. L. Effects of differential environments on brain weights and enzyme activities in gerbils, rats, and mice. *Developmental Psychobiology*, 1970, 2(2), 87–95.

Rosenzweig, M. R., Krech, D., & Bennett, E. L. A search for relations between brain chemistry and behavior. *Psychological Bulletin*, 1960, 57(6), 476–492.

Sahlins, M. D. *The use and abuse of biology: An anthropological critique of sociobiology*. Ann Arbor, Mich.: University of Michigan Press, 1976.

Schneirla, T. C. *Army ants: A study in social organization* (H. R. Topoff, posthumous ed.). San Francisco, Cal.: W. H. Freeman, 1971.

Schneirla, T. C. *Selected writings of T. C. Schneirla*. L. R. Aronson, E. Tobach, D. S. Lehrman, & J. S. Rosenblatt (Eds.). San Francisco, Cal.: W. H. Freeman, 1972.

Schneirla, T. C., & Rosenblatt, J. S. "Critical periods" in the development of behavior. In L. R. Aronson, E. Tobach, D. S. Lehrman, & J. S. Rosenblatt (Eds.), *Selected writings of T. C. Schneirla*. San Francisco, Cal.: W. H. Freeman, 1972. Pp. 340–343.

Spencer, H. *The principles of biology*, New York: D. Appleton, 1866.

Spencer, H. *First principles*. New York: A. L. Burt, 1880 (Reprinted from the Fifth London Edition, unaltered and unabridged).

Spitz, R. A. Total emotional deprivation (hospitalism). In *The first year of life*. New York: International Universities Press, 1965. Pp. 277–284.

Tolbach, E. The synthetic theory of evolution and psychology as a science. In G. Tembrock and H. D. Schmidt (Eds.), *Evolution and psychology*. New York: Springer-Verlag, in press.

Tobach, E. The potential for telemetry in the study of the social behavior of laboratory animals. In L. E. Salter (Ed.), *Bio-Telemetry*. New York: Pergamon, 1963. Pp. 33–42.

Tobach, E. Some guidelines to the study of the evolution and development of emotion. In L. R. Aronson, E. Tobach, D. S. Lehrman, & J. S. Rosenblatt (Eds.), *Development and evolution of behavior: Essays in memory of T. C. Schneirla*. San Francisco, Cal.: W. H. Freeman, 1970. Pp. 238–253.

Tobach, E. The meaning of the cryptanthroparion. In L. Ehrman, G. Omenn, & E. Caspari (Eds.), *Genetics, environment, and behavior*. New York: Academic Press, 1972. Pp. 219–239.

Tobach, E. Evolution of behavior and the comparative method. *International Journal of Psychology*, 1976, 11(3), 185–201.

Tobach, E. Developmental considerations of chemoception. *Annals of the New York Academy of Sciences*, 1977, 290, 226–269.

Tobach, E. The synthetic theory of evolution and psychology as a science. In H. R. Schmidt & G. Tembrock (Eds.), *Evolution and determination of animal and human behavior*, in press.

Tobach, E., & Schneirla, T. C. The biopsychology of social behavior in animals. In R. E. Cooke (Ed.), *The biologic basis of pediatric practice*. New York: McGraw-Hill, 1968. Pp. 68–82.

Topoff, H. R. Behavioral changes of army ants during the nomadic and statary phases. *Journal of the New York Entomological Society*, 1975, 83, 38–48.

Topoff, H., & Mirenda, J. Army ants on the move: Relation between food supply and emigration frequency. *Science*, 1980, 207, 1099–1100.

Topoff, H., Mirenda, J., Droual, R., & Herricks, S. Onset of the nomadic phase in the army ant, *Neivamyrmex nigrescens*: Distinguishing between larval and callow excitation by brood substitution. *Insectes Sociaux*, 1980, 27, 175–179.

Waddington, C. H. Selection of the genetic basis for an acquired character. *Nature*, 1952, 169, 278.

Waddington, C. H. Genetic assimilation of an acquired character. *Evolution*, 1953, 7, 118–126. (a)

Waddington, C. H. The "Baldwin effect," "genetic assimilation," and "homeostasis." *Evolution*, 1953, *7*, 386–387. (b)

Waddington, C. H. Concepts of development. In L. R. Aronson, E. Tobach, & E. Shaw (Eds.), *The biopsychology of development.* New York: Academic Press, 1971. Pp. 17–23.

Werner, H. The concept of development from a comparative and organismic point of view. In D. B. Harris (Ed.), *The concept of development: An issue in the study of human behavior.* Minneapolis, Minn.: University of Minnesota Press, 1957. Pp. 125–148.

Webster's unabridged dictionary (3rd ed.). Springfield, Mass.: G. & C. Merriam, 1965.

Wilson, E. O. *Sociobiology.* Cambridge, Mass.: Harvard University Press, 1975.

Wilson, E. O. *On human nature.* Cambridge, Mass.: Harvard University Press, 1978.

CHARLES M. SUPER
SARA HARKNESS

3

Figure, Ground, and Gestalt: The Cultural Context of the Active Individual[1]

The history of the behavioral sciences plays out, in one sense, like a good Freudian dream. So many diverse forces combine to yield the final symbolic forms that alteration of any one need not alter the outcome. The history, like the dream content, seems overdetermined. In the emergence of sociology, anthropology, and psychology as separate disciplines, each has elaborated a distinctive combination of substantive topic, research techniques, and style of deliberation. Each has formal and informal networks of communication and self-regulation. Each has its own origin myth, complete with founding parent(s), to teach the young the singular features that bind its members as a community and that distinguish it from its neighbors. These and other aspects of the disciplines' paradigms reinforce each other in a synergistic way, resisting as a whole the weakening of any single element. Behavior by the institutions and individuals that constitute social science is directed by a variety of motives and structural forces only partly related to the objective demands of scientific knowledge. The development of the disciplines, again like a dream, has a "logic" of its own—in this case, the human endeavor of science reflects in part a fantastic abstraction of the behavioral realities it is trying to understand.

[1] The preparation of this chapter was facilitated by support from the National Institute of Mental Health (grant no. 1-ROI-MH33281), the Spencer Foundation, and the William T. Grant Foundation. All statements made and views expressed are the sole responsibility of the authors.

69

The underlying theme of the present chapter is that the historical divergence of professional disciplines concerning human behavior has abetted an artificial dismemberment of the scientific issues. Although this divergence has served some important purposes and has yielded many significant findings, it has frustrated the emergence of more comprehensive theory. Psychology has claimed the individual as the fundamental unit of its analysis, anthropology and sociology the larger social organism (these latter two differing historically on the kinds and features of society of interest). Within each discipline there is a small, deviant tradition that has strained to incorporate the other perspective: psychological anthropology, social psychology, and sociology based on symbolic interaction theory. Both the intra- and interdisciplinary tensions involve thesis and antithesis concerning the proper locus of attention: Is it the individual or the community?

The more direct theme of this chapter centers on the importance of cultural context for understanding how individuals influence their own development. The theoretical tension outlined previously can be resolved, at least in metaphor, by considering the individual and the context as figure and ground in a mutually adapting, dynamic gestalt. A static parallel is presented in Figure 3.1. Is there a white vase shaped by the black background, or are there two dark faces set across a light field? We cannot see the individual psyche without acknowledging its larger context,

FIGURE 3.1   *A static parallel to the concept of the individual and the context as figure and ground. Is a white vase shaped by the black ground, or are two dark faces set across a light field?*

and we cannot understand the context without knowledge of individuals (see Lerner & Busch-Rossnagel, Chapter 1, this volume). There is a gestalt, a multiplicity of perspectives that together yield a new picture and a new insight.

Figure

Psychology, in archetype, has chosen the experiment as its method and the individual as its turf. There is a symmetry here, for with the individual as the focus, the surrounding stimuli can be varied systematically for an understanding of psychological functioning. It is fitting, in this regard, that the word "individual" is, in effect, a Latin version of the Greek derivative "atom"—not divisible, not capable of being cut, the irreducible unit of analysis and synthesis. Individuals in psychology are the elements to understand and the building blocks of the social universe. Through the experimental method, American psychologists have sought to uncover the underlying rules of behavior by detaching it from its usual context. This approach has met with spectacular success in many areas, but it is limited in the face of some larger issues of human development (cf. Belsky & Tolan, this volume).

The limits are partly technical, in that one cannot easily or ethically experiment with individuals' lives. A more profound problem, however, intimated in our opening paragraph, grows from the mutually reinforcing properties of a discipline's professed topic, unit of analysis, research style, and mode of discourse. The ethos formed by these features becomes a professional culture. It defines an identity and operates as a partially closed and self-regulating system of beliefs and values. Change the method and the topic is changed; change the unit of analysis and the methods must change; change the paradigm and one has altered the traditional discipline.

A significant feature of the ethos of psychology as a professional field is blindness to the organization of the environment. Individual features of the environment, ranging from social reinforcement by peers to parental education, are familiar elements in psychology's tables of ANOVA and correlations. However, the synergistic relationship of such features with each other and with less visible influences such as parental values is rarely a topic of inquiry. Of even greater importance, the developmental structure of the environment is invisible, so that its regularities are more easily attributed to an inherent structure of development (see Meacham, Chapter 15, this volume). Without an appreciation of culture as a phenomenon, there has grown in psychology an unwarranted confidence that the human psyche is everywhere the same in all interesting aspects. If the psyche is not altered in any critical way by culture, then studies within a single society are adequate as a method for investigating human functioning. Hence experiments concerning visual perception in middle-class American babies report conclusions about the human infant; studies of their older siblings yield principles of human development; and examination of their parents teaches about human information processing. The overwhelming problem of systematically sampling the species is not considered.

One unintended consequence of this disciplinary constellation of analytic unit and research tradition is a nativist bias to psychological theory. Observed variations in behavior are readily attributed to constitutional disposition (e.g., genes), to differing stages of allegedly universal sequences of development, or to other causes that lie within the individual (see Meacham, Chapter 15, this volume). The generality of this bias in academic psychology can be illustrated by three diverse examples, from the domains of motor, cognitive, and moral development.

NATIVISM IN MOTOR DEVELOPMENT

Early work in the study of motor development drew explicitly from biological models for species-specific behavior: "[J]ust as the science of embryology is clarifying the phenomena of physical growth through countless sectional studies, so may genetic psychology attain an insight into the obscure developmental mechanics of the growth of behavior" wrote Gesell in 1925 (p. 26), using "genetic" in the now less common sense of "developmental." Gesell, Shirley, Bayley, and other pioneers in infant research devoted great energy to the detailed observation and description of behavioral growth as a species-specific process. They documented a reliable order of appearance of motor "milestones" such as sitting and crawling, and this order was seen as unfolding under direction of the biological potential. There is a continuing minority interest in experimental approaches to understandiing the role of environment in the emergence of motor skills (e.g., McGraw, 1935; Zelazo, Zelazo, & Kolb, 1972), but the major focus has remained strongly individualistic. The dominant view as it stabilized in postwar academic psychology seemed to classify the emergence of motor skills more with internally determined biological traits such as hair color than with environmentally shaped psychological variables.

Recently, research inspired by developmental genetics tends to confirm the importance of internal regulation. The Louisville Twin Study found greater similarity between identical twins than fraternal twins in the timing of normal "spurts and lags" in the growth of motor skills (Wilson & Harpring, 1972). It is important to note that subjects in this large scale study included the full range of socioeconomic and ethnic variation within the Louisville area; from the perspective of mainstream psychology, therefore, environmental influences were not artificially restricted by sampling.

It has been professionally documented and widely known for decades, among anthropologists, that American techniques of infant care are deviant in world perspective (e.g., Barry & Paxon, 1971; Whiting & Child, 1953). The approach to early motor development is no exception. As reviewed elsewhere (Super, 1980a), the child-rearing variation critical to early motor skills is in (a) deliberate practice organized by caretakers in accord with culturally defined traditions and values regarding the acquisition of walking, crawling, and so on; and (b) incidental opportunity for practice resulting from customary techniques of holding, carrying, and laying down of infants. Cultural variation in the relative timing of different skills is associated with these factors, so that rural Kenyan infants, who are encouraged to sit, generally learn to do so earlier than American infants. With little chance or encouragement to crawl, however, they lag in attainment of this milestone. Whereas there may also be a general physiological effect of certain kinds of physical activity, it has been demonstrated that the two discrete factors can account for the different timing of some motor skills among several distinct culture groups (Super, 1976). The pattern of emergence of motor skills reflects in each case the pattern of infant care.

The Louisville sample, broad as it was, did not include the relevant kind of environmental variation (or, possibly, did not measure it). In the absence of relevant environmental variation, variations in development are controlled almost entirely by genetic factors; if individual genetic variation is pooled within culture groups, as it was in the African research, experience dictates the variations in average timing. The lesson is a familiar one in genetic studies: Comparison of the variation controlled by genetic versus environmental factors addresses only the kind and extent of variation assessed, not the possible results under different circumstances. Both the Louisville and Kenyan studies are correct, and each tells only half the story. Without the cultural perspective, monocultural research would yield only a nativist interpretation.

NATIVISM IN COGNITIVE DEVELOPMENT

Monocultural studies of cognitive development have focused theory on the individual locus of variation for related, though more complex, reasons. Because the broad sweep of developmental change in thinking appears so regularly in American and European children, we are tempted to see the growth as maturationally engineered. Classic works on the emergence of intellectual ability as measured by IQ are clearly in this tradition. An "interactionist" or "constructionist" position does not entirely avoid the temptation, for it usually concentrates on the individually directed construction of a universal physical reality. In its most persuasive form, regarding infancy (Piaget, 1952), the assumption of universality of the environment is reasonable (e.g., object permanence operates similarly in all cultures and contexts). In childhood and beyond, however, the reality of classical physics may be less important than the reality of socially regulated habits of thought. Nevertheless, the elegance of the constructionist approach to the sequential stages of understanding in Euro-American culture has focused theoretical energies on the internal logic of the progression, to the neglect of the cultural supports for that progression.

Inhelder and Piaget's (1958) *The Growth of Logical Thought*, one of the most influential works in the area, illustrates the limitations of the individualist perspective (only partly recognized in Piaget, 1972). Their diagnostic tests of formal operations, derived from classical physics, chemistry, and geometry, provide a rich description of the progression of children's thought in mastering the relevant intellectual tools. There is no mention, however, of the extent of subjects' classroom training in mathematics and laboratory science. The propositional logic and other features of formal thought do not emerge independently of such tutoring, nor are they unrelated to other aspects of Western culture. Traditional dance forms, the spatial arrangement of physical objects in everyday life, classical music, and many other facets of our culture embody aspects of formal thought (Super, 1980b). It seems likely that long-term exposure to these cultural features predisposes European and American children to learning, or constructing, their formal statement in the adolescent years. Psychological studies of individual development that ignore the pervasive invariants of the individual's culture find it difficult to describe the role of culture in structuring cognitive behavior. Nativist theory necessarily follows more easily.

NATIVISM IN SOCIAL DEVELOPMENT

Our final example concerns an important aspect of social development: How do people regulate conflicting rights and responsibilities? How do they think about the resolution of disputes and how do they see the issues involved? The socialization of behavior and thought in this domain lies squarely at the interface of individual and community; it is a central part of a child's enculturation to adult functioning, and it is the nuts and bolts of a society's daily operation and continuity. In recent times, research in this area has been dominated by the psychological approach. The leading work of Kohlberg (1969, 1971) has drawn heavily on Piagetian stage theory and has helped define the "cognitive developmental" view. Again, the focus is on the individual's progression along a hypothetically universal track, and those who pause too long at one station are considered less adequate, or even less moral, than those who reach the terminus (Kohlberg, 1973).

Examination of the social context in which this progression typically develops, however, combined with empirical research in other settings, suggest that the six-stage sequence belongs as much to the culture as it does to the psyche. Gibbs (1977, 1979) has characterized Stages 5 and 6, the upper two, "principled" modes of reasoning, as reflective or metaethical extensions of earlier stages, not true stages themselves. They may be ways of thinking about morality that are particular to some subcultures within highly differentiated societies. Stage 4, in turn, has been identified by Edwards (1975, 1980) as an abstraction relevant only to Western legal–judicial systems, which emphasize individual rights, and the separation of principles of authority from the persons who exercise it. In rural, face-to-face communities in non-Western societies, Stages 2 and 3 may be more common because they are more appropriate to the nature of the social reality being regulated. We have demonstrated this with a sample from rural Kenya, where, in addition to the societal pattern, we found a coordination of social reasoning with social role (Harkness, Edwards, & Super, in press). Men who were customarily involved in mediating community disputes were more likely to use Stage 3, which gives particular importance to interpersonal concordance and community solidarity, whereas men not active in a mediating role were more sensitive to the particular authority relations involved (Stage 2). Again, the point is that the monocultural research tradition places the locus of variation in the individual, whereas a cultural perspective is better able to see the relations among individual growth, social roles, and social structure.

SUMMARY: THE BIAS OF PSYCHOLOGY

In summary, research focusing exclusively on the individual ignores the relationship between individual functioning and the larger culture. This tends to be true in both observational and experimental approaches, although the limited treatment of "stimuli" is an additional burden of the completely decontextualized method (cf. Lerner & Busch-Rossnagel, Chapter 1, this volume). The monocultural research traditions that have developed in psychology are mutually reinforcing to a nativist orientation. The bias of this approach lies not in the imposition of arbitrary cultural values (although this is occasionally a problem), but rather in the exclusive use of a paradigm that does not recognize the central role that culture plays in human functioning. The widespread use of monoculturally derived theory is not just careless ethnocentricity—it follows logically from the individually oriented, nativist focus of psychology as a discipline.

Ground

The roots of anthropology are embedded in concern with the history of human societies, the origin and evolution of cultures (Harris, 1968). In the early decades of this century, however, Franz Boas and his students looked beyond "cultural laws" to explain the regularities of cultural phenomena and began to seek instead the role of the human mind. If culture resides in the individual mind, as it must in some sense, then a theory of culture should encompass how it gets there (enculturation), how it functions there (personality), and how it is passed on to the next generation (child rearing). The well-known work of Margaret Mead on adolescence in Samoa (Mead, 1928) can serve to mark the emergence of the "culture and personality" approach to these issues in psychological anthropology.

In searching for the connections between culture and personality, anthropologists naturally looked to psychological theories of individual learning and functioning. One of the central topics in psychology during these decades was, usefully enough, the relationship between early experience and adult personality, inspired to large degree by the work of Freud. Until some point in the 1950s, therefore, there was a vital symbiosis among cultural anthropology, psychoanalytic theory, and child development studies. The work of Benedict (1934), Mead (1951), Whiting (Whiting & Child, 1953), and others share in aspects of this symbiosis. The collaboration was fruitful and had considerable impact on the development of both psychology (e.g., Yarrow & Yarrow, 1955) and anthropology (Harris, 1968).

In retrospect, however, a recurring impediment to the success of this interdisciplinary endeavor was its asymmetry. By and large, psychological anthropology borrowed existing psychological theory, developed in the West, for testing in foreign lands and for explaining foreign behavior. Built into these theories were a variety of assumptions that seemed as reasonable to the Western anthropologist as to the Western psychologist. Often the underlying assumptions were not given adequate examination, and a confirmation of expectations was too easily interpreted as validation of the original theory. The psychological continuity from infancy and early childhood to adult personality, fundamental to Freudian theory, was one such assumption. In the classic work of Du Bois (1944) among the Alorese, as in other studies of the time, the relationship that was found between experience in early childhood and adult personality was readily assimilated by psychoanalytic theory. The descriptive material presented by Du Bois provides raw material for other analyses, such as one concerning continuity in environmental regulation of behavior, but few anthropologists looked beyond the confirmation of psychologically based expectations.

Ironically, observations incompatible with psychologically based theory also failed to generate a more widely accepted approach, even within anthropology. The work of Malinowski (1927) on the Oedipal complex stands as a good example. As conceptualized by Freud, the Oedipal complex involves hostility on the part of young boys toward their fathers resulting from an assumed sexual rivalry for the mother. This antagonism was postulated as a universal characteristic of the human psyche. Among the Trobriand Islanders, however, Malinowski found a different picture. Trobriand fathers did not act as a disciplinary authority. Rather, the maternal uncle was more likely to fill this role, as well as to have economic responsibilities for the mother (his sister) and children. Malinowski analyzed dreams, folktales, gossip, and other cultural materials, and failed to find evidence of hostility for the father or themes of sexual rivalry for the mother. Whereas this work and the generalizations drawn from it are of obvious importance for theories of individual development, they have not been incorporated into a full exposition for anthropological purposes, nor, indeed, have they been assimilated by much of psychology and psychiatry.

Thus anthropologists have often been willing, if unwitting, collaborators in rendering their discipline without import for the central tenets of Western-based psychological theories, useful only in some cases to "bear on the outer limits of their generality [LeVine, 1980, p. 75]." This is the assessment common among psychologists today (see Harkness & Super, 1980). With rare but important exceptions (e.g., Whiting & Whiting, 1974), the anthropological focus continues to be on the context of development, only peripherally on its content. Without pursuing an appropriately general theory of individual development, traditional anthropology has indeed merely tested the limits of psychologically (and monoculturally) based theory. When such theory fails, anthropology is left with the mensa rasa of complete cultural relativism and determinism.

Gestalt

Individuals as producers of their development play out their propensities and creativity, and they do so in their own particular environment; the enviornment contributes, in turn, to their propensities and creativity, and it is influenced by them as well. The challenge to a comprehensive theory of human development is to see the structure of the figure, of the ground, and of their interplay. There are presumably a number of levels at which the interplay operates, but it is not possible at this point to spell out a general description. Instead, we present here some considerations that have emerged from our continuing work on behavior problems in early infancy and that have stimulated the gestalt metaphor used in this chapter. Following that metaphor, we group our comments according to the individual infant, the cultural environment, and the gestalt of their mutual adaptation. In this last section, we expand the time frame of discussion beyond infancy and beyond the life span.

DISPOSITIONS AND ADAPTABILITY IN THE INFANT

A major portion of the current work on individual differences in the first years of life is derived directly or indirectly from the seminal studies of Thomas, Chess, and their associates (e.g., 1977; Chapter 9, this volume). Through a variety of methods, particularly parental interviews, they derived nine dimensions of individual variation among the children of mid-dle-class families in New York. These dimensions, which seemed theo-retically separable, include rhythmicity of feeding and sleeping behaviors, distractibility, intensity of reaction, quality of general mood, activity level, approach–withdrawal to new situations, adaptability, attention span, and threshold of responsiveness. Three clusters of the dimensions appeared of particular importance. One characterized an infant who was difficult and demanding: The baby was not regular in schedule, tended to with-draw from new situations or persons, was slow in adapting, and had intense, negative reactions. In contrast, other babies were easy to care for, as they were regular, highly adaptable, and had positive, approaching responses. A third group of babies was termed "slow to warm up," for they initially withdrew from new situations and were sometimes negative in mood, but they were less intense and less irregular than the more difficult infants. Roughly half of the New York sample fit one of the three characterizations. A large body of research has related the clusters of behavioral differences in infancy to problems, or their absence, in later phases of childhood (see Thomas & Chess, 1977; Chapter 9, this volume).

It was pointed out in the earlier discussion of monocultural studies that, however valuable may be the conclusions, such studies are intrinsically unable to distinguish the structure of the environment (as it affects de-velopment) from the inherent structure of development itself. In the pres-ent discussion, this distinction yields the question: Can one find in all human settings the same dimensions of individual differences and the same clusters of dimensions, or do these patterns of development only reflect the pattern of environmental forces as they occur in middle-class America?

Working with infants in a rural farming community in Kenya, called Kokwet, and in suburban families in metropolitan Boston, we have found evidence that the dimensions of individual difference are not, by and large, artifacts of the American setting. One can recognize from maternal interviews in both samples dimensions of mood, adaptability, intensity of reaction, and rhythmicity. Naturalistic observations of daily behavior provides evidence that these similarities are not simply conceptual artifacts of common biases of judgment. Babies who were reported by their mothers to be generally happy, for example, compared to those described as less cheerful, were observed to engage in more happy, face-to-face interaction and to require less quieting by the caretakers (e.g., rocking, nursing).

One might be tempted on the basis of this cross-cultural similarity to apply further the American theories—irregular, negative, unadaptable traits will cluster into a "difficult" pattern of dispositions, and children who fit this description will be at risk for particular developmental prob-lems at home and as they enter the wider social environment. Such predictions of the longitudinal structure of development, however, are no more sound, a priori, than assumptions about the cross-cultural universality of individual differences. To understand the meaning and import of individual differences, we must shift our gaze from the figure to the ground.

DISPOSITIONS AND ADAPTABILITY IN THE ENVIRONMENT

The infant's environment is structured by three kinds of influences: the physical and social setting, culturally regulated customs involved in care and rearing, and the psychology of the caretakers. Each of these contributes to the initial shape, or "disposition," of the family "niche" entered by the new baby, as well as its points of flexibility and rigidity in adapting to the infant's particular traits.

In many homes in our American sample, the physical space was altered in anticipation of the arrival of the baby. A separate room was set aside as "the baby's room," redecorated and furnished with a crib, bassinet, and other items uniquely for infants. In succeeding months, all parents had to move fragile and dangerous objects out of reach, and family rules were set about whether the infant should be permitted on the white couch, the yellow rug, or other easily damaged furnishings. The social environment of the home was also adjusted. The mother made plans to be home all day or, in later months, for the father or outside help to cover certain times. In none of the families in our sample, however, was there more than one person generally at home during most of the day, so moment-to-moment flexibility in the social setting was limited.

These arrangements are in accord with the American customs and parental psychology that usually accompany them. The baby customarily sleeps in his or her own room, and is customarily cared for by a single caretaker, the mother. It is usually believed that close, consistent care primarily by the mother is essential to healthy development. The importance of healthy early development is emphasized in this system by a belief in the lasting consequences of disturbance in the opening period of life. Because one task for the parents is to lead the child to independence and self-reliance, the emerging individuality must not go astray. Parents are quick to notice indications of future personality, and they are quick to share and discuss the baby's temperament with each other, with neighbors, acquaintances, and relevant professionals such as the pediatrician.

Although this description of the setting for infancy in our American sample is necessarily brief, it emphasizes the coherence of elements in the physical and social setting, the traditional customs, and the relevant beliefs and values of the parents. The culture, in other words, is a synergistic integration of psychology, custom, and ecology. There may be inconsistent elements as well, especially in rapidly changing societies, but culture plays an important integrative role there too, as the whole changes with its parts.

Consider, now, the infant's niche in Kokwet. The people of Kokwet are Kipsigis, members of the Kalenjin grouping that comprise about 20% of the population of Kenya. Kokwet is in the Western Highlands, where good land makes it possible for families to feed and support themselves through their small herds of dairy cattle and plots of maize (corn) and other crops for home consumption and sale on the national market. (A more detailed description of Kokwet is available in Super & Harkness, 1981.) Daily life for infants and young children takes place in and around the straw-roofed, mud houses, as they observe or participate in the flow of everyday activity—cooking and cleaning, resting, weeding, watering the cows, playing tag, weaving a basket, and fetching firewood in the brush.

For the first few months, a new baby is in the exclusive care of the mother, rarely separated, in fact, from physical contact with her. The baby rides on her back or hip, sits in her lap, or sleeps under the same blanket for most of the time. The mother and infant are not alone, however. One finds during the day an average of five additional people at home: other siblings or half-siblings, the father, a neighbor, a co-wife, or a visitor who has come to greet the new baby. At around 3 or 4 months, moment-to-moment care of the baby becomes increasingly shared with, typically, a 6- or 7-year-old sister who will carry, hold, and entertain the infant while the mother resumes more of her chores and responsibilities. The mother is usually near by, in the yard or the adjacent fields. The mother takes on more of what has been called an executive role, directing and supervising infant care, and taking over when the baby is too fussy or hungry. Nursing is frequent during both the day and night, and weaning is not completed until well into the second year. In sum, while the Kokwet setting is different from the American one, the culture still presents a coherence of psychology, custom, and ecology.

THE DEVELOPING GESTALT

The disposition and adaptability of the context form the structure in which individual infants act as agents of their own development through their own dispositions and adaptabilities. There is a mutual adjustment, over time, of the individual and the environment, and that process is the developmental gestalt introduced earlier.

The organization of behavior within time is a major dimension of contrast between our samples in Kokwet and Boston. Activities for the baby in Boston are often scheduled by the clock. The schedule itself may be set to meet the infant's, as well as the mother's, needs, but there is usually a nap time and a feeding time that are carefully integrated into the mother's day. Because balancing the checkbook, grocery shopping, working at the office, and attending a committee meeting are more difficult with a baby in the lap; because bottle feeding is a customary alternative and easy for a babysitter; because the baby has a quiet room set aside; for these reasons it is often easier for the mother to divide her activities into baby care and, separately, other activities. An important aspect of infant adaptation in the first year is to the temporal and spatial arrangements designed for regulating interaction.

In Kokwet, the daily chores and pleasures of the Kipsigis mother are more compatible with infant care than is the case in Boston. The resources, such as a child caretaker, that she can use are different too. The overall effect of these differences is a particular embeddedness, for the Kipsigis baby, in the continuing social and economic functioning of the family. The Kipsigis infant adapts to the particular caretakers and their changing activities to a greater extent than does the American baby. The baby in Kokwet spends much of the waking day being held or sitting in the lap, while the mother pursues her chores or rest; when the mother needs a break, or faces a chore that is less suitable to carrying the baby (such as some kinds of weeding), the infant is passed to the sibling caretaker. This secondary caretaker, in turn, holds or carries the child, cajoles and entertains, until the mother returns. Within this pattern, the baby is free to sleep and eat. Sleeping can be on someone's lap or back, or on a blanket set in the shade or in the house. Eating is usually nursing at the breast, for the mother is almost always at hand or a few minutes' walk for the caretaker.

There are several developmental consequences of this divergence of setting in the niches for early infancy. Many activities for the American infant become concentrated into fewer but longer blocks of time. For example, although measures of sleep–wake activity are initially quite similar in the two samples, they rapidly diverge (Super & Harkness, in press). The American infants begin to concentrate their sleep into specified periods. By 4 months of age, the average American baby sleeps for a solid 8 hours at night. The parents are then freed from the midnight chore of waking up, getting a bottle, going to the baby's room, feeding the baby, and changing the diapers. The Kipsigis infant, who sleeps next to the mother, develops approximately the same day–night ratio of sleep–wake as does the American baby, but continues to wake briefly and nurse. Thus the long episodes of uninterrupted sleep do not develop until many months later. Feeding undergoes a parallel divergence in time patterning in the samples. Even in circadian patterns of social interaction, one can identify accumulating "chunks" in the American sample, with a less pronounced grouping for the Kipsigis. There, shorter periods of playful socializing remain more frequent.

It is evident from these brief examples that a temperamental disposition toward regularity and "chunking" has different significance in Kokwet

and Boston, as does disposition toward adaptability to the styles of multiple caretakers. A mismatch in either case provides a nucleus around
which behavior problems develop. Night waking by a 1-year-old can severely stress American parents whose own daytime lives are rigidly scheduled; in Kokwet, night waking is normal and not particularly stressful.
However, the Kipsigis baby who will not be comforted by anyone but
the mother, who will refuse to quiet on the back of a sister, drives the
Kipsigis mother to despair. Most mothers in our American sample did
not use supplementary caretakers to a significant degree in the first year
and did not confront this aspect of adaptability as a serious problem.

The definition of an emerging behavior problem does not depend exclusively on the physical and social surround; customs and parental psychology play critical roles as well. In the realm of custom, back-carrying
could be a standard part of American parents' routines of care, as the
current trend to use soft carrying pouches indicates. But for a full generation of parents in midcentury America, carrying the baby around on
the back would have seemed odd. The availability of this custom might
have added a dimension to both the definition and the potential resolution
of some infant care problems, but for a variety of reasons it was not an
option.

Similarly, parents' beliefs and values affect their interpretation of
whether or not there is a problem. Of particular importance is their evaluation of the long-term significance of behavioral dispositions during infancy. Part of the widespread attention to night waking in America (e.g.,
Spock, 1968) derives from an assumption that the problem is intimately
related to the infant's emerging personality, and to the parents' wisdom
in rearing their child. Correctly or not, night waking is seen not only as
a problem itself, but also as a symptom of a larger, long-term concern.
Parents in Kokwet do not share the American belief in persistence of
dispositions from infancy to maturity. Their typical belief is better summarized by the common statement that one cannot know about personality
until the child is old enough, about 6 or 7 years to take responsibility in
household economic chores. Thus, while a Kipsigis mother may be an-
noyed at the baby who fusses for her to stay when she needs to go to
the garden, she may be more comfortable, in one sense, with simply
leaving because of her belief that the problem is of little long-term significance for her child's sound development.

NICHES IN THE LIFE SPAN

The concept of niche developed for early infancy applies as well to the
later stages of development and maturity. At each period there is an
agenda, a set (or sets) of structured demands and points of negotiation.
At each period the niche reflects the physical and social setting, the rel-

evant cultural customs, and the ethnopsychology of other people about one's presumed motivations, one's reasonable needs and responsibilities, and the value and significance of particular behaviors.

Thematic parallels in the niches at various life stages are often easy to identify. To pick up our examples from infancy, it is evident that the American baby who is scheduled to bottle and bed is later scheduled to the school bell and, in turn, to the time card or deadline. In Kokwet, the baby who has to adapt to the personal styles of several caretakers will, as an adult, need to accept the community insistence on maintaining social cohesion in the settlement of disputes.

The sequence of niches that are available to form the developmental gestalt varies from culture to culture. The nature and number of thematic parallels is fashioned in part by the developmental pattern of niches in the life span, through two possible mechanisms. First, there may be structural similarities from niche to niche in the physical and social ecology, the customs, and the psychology of beliefs and values. Second, the niches have a cumulative psychological meaning. The meaning of infancy, in effect, is different depending on what follows, and the meaning of childhood depends in part on what preceded. Longitudinal studies of development in the West provide insight into one pattern of cumulative meaning, but it is difficult to separate the structural–cultural elements of that pattern from the more fundamentally psychological threads.

Niches at maturity increase, in many societies, in their diversity. In coordination with changing patterns of growth and behavior (see Scarr-Salapatek, 1976), perhaps, the adult niches are less canalized. The larger social structure does regulate, however, the influence a person may have in choosing and shaping later niches. In American society, with its individualist ideology, and with social status as an adult being based largely on achievement rather than ascribed on the basis of social origin, the individual may have (and especially may appear to have) considerable influence on future development. The choice to attend college, for example, is available to a large percentage of young Americans and substantially influences their future lives. For people born in a more rigid caste or class society, or in a structurally simpler group that has less differentiation of role and status, the ways individual talents can be used in self-direction must be different.

BEYOND THE LIFE SPAN

The spectre of Social Darwinism swoops to embrace our thesis. Each society provides a certain set of niches that interact with individual dispositions to create, in some instances, a problem of mismatch; if the contours of the figure do not match the ground, healthy development is threatened. Over generations, the misfits will be "selected out" through the familiar processes of survival of the fittest, and the distribution of temperament types in the genetic pool of each culture will gradually shift toward the ideal type for that culture.

There are several reasons why this syllogism is false, and they are best tied together with the notion put forward by Clarke (1975) that species survival is assured, in the long run, by an emphasis, not on narrowing individuals to an ideal type as functional clones, but rather by maintaining enough variety to assure survival of at least some members under unknown future conditions. The evidence for this hypothesis is diverse. At the species level, a genetically diverse population can often better exploit its environment. At the individual level, unusual characteristics (which by definition increase group diversity) may provide a relative advantage. The individual may be more successful in utilizing a neglected resource, or may be less vulnerable to a predator who is most effective in identifying and capturing the "typical" member of the prey species. For humans, who stake their success on creative adaptation, the case is obvious. In the long run, it is likely to be advantageous to a human group to have individuals with a variety of talents and dispositions, as long as they are open to positive use, because of the variety of circumstances for success that humans encounter and create (see Lerner & Busch-Rossnagel, Chapter 1, this volume).

The evolutionary mechanisms for diversity are themselves diverse. Slobodkin and Rapaport (1974) have emphasized the advantage of behavioral solutions, rather than genetic solutions, to environmental threats. Because selection actually operates on the phenotype (surface characteristics or behaviors) rather than at the level of the gene, adaptation at the behavioral level is more direct as well as less "costly" in terms of loss of future adaptive capability. The ability to adapt behaviorally, to learn, is of course a salient characteristic of our species.

When Slobodkin and Rapaport's analysis is applied to particular issues in development, as Chisholm (1980) has done, it is evident that behavior changes by the infant and caretakers, as well as features of the interactive system provide a number of effective escape routes from mismatches between environment and individual. Given the complexity of developmental niches, their sequencing, their possible interactions with temperament, and the frequent diversity of routes to reproductive success in human populations, it is difficult to generalize from a single arena of difficulty to genetic selection.

A final caution about simplistic evolutionary extension of our thesis speaks to the assumption of cultural stability over many generations. The short-lived individual mind probably overestimates such stability. All cultures, including our own, are in the process of disappearing, as LeVine (1980) points out, and it has probably always been so. The ever-unfolding sequence of generations, the diffusion of cultural ideas and artifacts, climatic, economic, and geographic change, all contribute another level of variety to the niches in which individuals adapt and create.

Conclusion

The division of the study of human development into separate disciplines, each with its own ethos of research, has frustrated the growth of comprehensive theory. The figure for one discipline is ground for another, and this perceptual trick makes it difficult to focus on the whole picture. We have presented in some detail the kinds of analysis of both the developing individual and the context of development, which we think might contribute to progressing beyond the illusion. The active individual works within a structured and active context, and it is their interplay over the stages of life that makes the gestalt of human development.

References

Barry, H., III, & Paxon, L. M. Infancy and early childhood: Cross-cultural codes 2. *Ethnology*, 1971, *10*, 466–508.

Benedict, R. *Patterns of culture*. New York: Houghton Mifflin, 1934.

Chisholm, J. S. Development and adaptation in infancy. In C. M. Super & S. Harkness (Eds.), Anthropological perspectives on child development, *New Directions for Child Development*, 1980, *8*, 15–30.

Clarke, B. The causes of biological diversity. *Scientific American*, 1975, *233*, 50–60.

Du Bois, C. *The people of Alor*. Minneapolis: University of Minnesota Press, 1944.

Edwards, C. P. Societal complexity and moral development: A Kenyan study. *Ethos*, 1975, *3*, 505–527.

Edwards, C. P. The development of moral reasoning in cross-cultural perspective. In R. H. Munroe, R. L. Munroe, & B. B. Whiting (Eds.), *Handbook of cross-cultural development*. New York: Garland, 1980.

Gesell, A. *The mental growth of the preschool child*. New York: Macmillan, 1925.

Gibbs, J. C. Kohlberg's stages of moral judgment: A constructive critique. *Harvard Educational Review*, 1977, *47*, 43–61.

Gibbs, J. C. Kohlberg's moral stage theory: A Piagetian revision. *Human Development*, 1979, *22*, 89–112.

Harkness, S., Edwards, C. P. & Super, C. M. Social roles and moral reasoning: A case study in a rural African community. *Developmental Psychology*, in press.

Harkness, S., & Super, C. M. Child development theory in anthropological perspective. In C. M. Super & S. Harkness (Eds.), Anthropological perspectives on child development, *New Directions for Child Development*, 1980, *8*, 1–6.

Harris, M. *The rise of anthropological theory*. New York: Crowell, 1968.

Inhelder, B., & Piaget, J. *The growth of logical thinking from childhood to adolescence*. New York: Basic Books, 1958.

Kohlberg, L. Stage and sequence: The cognitive–developmental approach to socialization. In D. Goslin (Ed.), *Handbook of socialization theory and research*. Chicago: Rand McNally, 1969.

Kohlberg, L. From is to ought. In T. Mischel (Ed.), *Cognitive development and epistemology.* New York: Academic Press, 1971. Pp. 151–235.

Kohlberg, L. The claim to moral adequacy of a highest stage of moral judgment. *Journal of Philosophy,* 1973, *70,* 630–646.

LeVine, R. A. Anthropology and child development. In C. M. Super & S. Harkness (Eds.), Anthropological perspectives on child development, *New Directions for Child Development,* 1980, *8,* 71–86.

Malinowski, B. *Sex and repression in savage society.* London: Routledge & Kegan Paul, 1927.

McGraw, M. B. *Growth: A study of Johnny and Jimmy.* New York: Appleton Century, 1935.

Mead, M. *Coming of age in Samoa.* New York: Morrow, 1928.

Mead, M. The study of national character. In D. Lerner & H. D. Haswell (Eds.), *The policy sciences.* Stanford: Stanford University Press, 1951.

Piaget, J. *The origins of intelligence in children.* New York: International Universities Press, 1952.

Piaget, J. Intellectual evolution from adolescence to adulthood. *Human development,* 1972, *15,* 1–12.

Scarr-Salapatek, S. An evolutionary perspective on infant intelligence: Species patterns and individual variations. In M. Lewis (Ed.), *Origins of intelligence.* New York: Plenum, 1976.

Slobodkin, L., & Rapaport, A. An optimal strategy of evolution. *Quarterly Review of Biology,* 1974, *49,* 181–200.

Spock, B. *Baby and child care (revised edition).* New York: Pocket Books, 1968.

Super, C. M. Environmental effects on motor development: The case of "African infant precocity." *Developmental Medicine and Child Neurology,* 1976, *18,* 561–567.

Super, C. M. Behavioral development in infancy. In R. H. Munroe, R. L. Munroe, & B. B. Whiting (Eds.), *Handbook of cross-cultural human development.* New York: Garland, 1980. (a)

Super, C. M. Cognitive development: Looking across at growing up. In C. M. Super & S. Harkness (Eds.), Anthropological perspectives on child development, *New Directions for Child Development,* 1980, *8,* 59–69. (b)

Super, C. M., & Harkness, S. The development of affect in infancy and early childhood. In H. W. Stevenson & D. A. Wagner (Eds.), *Cultural perspectives on child development.* San Francisco: Freeman, 1981.

Super, C. M., & Harkness, S. The infant's niche in rural Kenya and metropolitan America. In L. L. Adler (Ed.), *Cross-cultural research at issue.* New York: Academic Press, in press.

Thomas, A., & Chess, S. *Temperament and development.* New York: Brunner/Mazel, 1977.

Whiting, B. B., & Whiting, J. W. M. *Children of six cultures: A psychocultural analysis.* Cambridge, Mass.: Harvard University Press, 1974.

Whiting, J. W. M., & Child, I. *Child training and personality: A cross-cultural study.* New Haven: Yale University Press, 1953.

Wilson, R. S., & Harpring, E. B. Mental and motor development in infant twins. *Developmental Psychology,* 1972, *7*(3), 277.

Yarrow, M. R., & Yarrow, L. Child psychology. *Annual Review of Psychology,* 1955, *6,* 1–28.

Zelazo, P. R., Zelazo, N., & Kolb, S. "Walking" in the newborn. *Science,* 1972, *176,* 314–315.

JAY BELSKY
WILLIAM J. TOLAN

4

Infants as Producers of Their Own Development: An Ecological Analysis

Introduction

The dual focus of this volume, the child as producer of his or her own development and the life-span perspective, reveals strengths as well as weaknesses of research on infant behavior and development. Although students of infancy have been very much responsible for promulgating the notion of the individual child as an active agent contributing to his or her own development, they have generally failed to appreciate, at least until recently, the implications of a life-span view of human development. To introduce this chapter, we briefly consider each of these issues.

THE LIFE-SPAN PERSPECTIVE

The initial research on infant development that grew out of Freud's (1940) theory of the origins and consequences of the infant–mother relationships represented an effort to establish predictive links between patterns of infant care (e.g., breast versus bottle feeding) and later personality development (see Caldwell, 1964; Orlansky, 1949, for reviews of this work). The basic metatheoretical assumption underlying this work and much subsequent infancy research was that early experience was a direct cause of later development. Whereas the initial inability of investigators to demonstrate strong (or even consistent) relationships revealed the inherent weakness of available theory, it was not until many years later that basic questions were raised regarding the implicit assumptions that guided this work and the infancy–early experience research that followed it.

Some, like Kagan (Kagan, Kearsley, & Zelazo, 1978; Kagan & Klein, 1973) and the Clarkes (Clarke & Clarke, 1976) eventually came to question the very notion that infancy–early experience is of consequence to later development. Others, like Sameroff (1975), raised issues regarding the presumed manner by which organism–environment interactions influence development. In our minds, these latter process-oriented questions (e.g., How does early experience influence later development?) are far more appropriate at this stage of scientific inquiry than simplistic outcome-oriented questions (e.g., Is infancy–early experience of consequence to later development?). In fact, given the research done to date, we do not believe that these outcome-oriented questions can yet be answered. This is because investigations attempting to relate measures of infant functioning and early experience to later development, but skipping intervening developmental epochs, implicitly ignore the basic tenets of a lifespan view of human development: that complex organism–environment transactions characterize development throughout the life span and make possible the continual modification of developmental trajectories established in infancy, childhood, adolescence, or even in adulthood (Baltes, Reese, & Lipsitt, 1980; Lerner, 1978; Riegel, 1975).

In our minds, the appropriate strategy for investigating continuities–discontinuities in development, and thus the significance of early experience, entails making developmentally sequenced, longitudinal assessments of individual development and interrelating only those measurements made during contiguous developmental periods. Unless an explicit, theory-derived "sleeper effect" is presumed to exist, we see little justification for calculating (and interpreting) measures of association between widely spaced assessments. This latter analytic strategy, which characterizes most early experience research, completely ignores the probabilistic epigenetic quality of human development that most assuredly characterizes growth and change throughout the life span (Lerner, 1978). In the case of infancy, then, psychological functioning and experience during the first 2 years will be of consequence to subsequent development only to the extent that it influences the experience the preschooler has and the manner in which he or she filters this experience.

THE CHILD AS PRODUCER OF HIS OR HER OWN DEVELOPMENT

Students of infancy have long recognized the active role the child plays in contributing to its own development. Piagets's (1952) detailed observational studies of his own three children during their infancies clearly documents the child's role in "constructing" his own reality (see Liben, Chapter 5, this volume), and Thomas, Chess, and Birch's (1970) early work on temperamental variation among infants highlights the role that characteristics of individuality play in determining one's experience.

In the field of developmental psychology, this notion of the child as an active contributor to his or her own development has exerted its greatest impact upon the study of socialization, most probably as a consequence of R. Q. Bell's (1968) now classic review reinterpreting the direction of effects in studies of the parent–child relationship. We see clear evidence of this impact in research documenting the effect of the newborn's responsivity and alertness on maternal feeding behavior (e.g., Osofsky & Danzger, 1974), in work highlighting the contribution of the infant to his own poor development when malnourished (Pollitt, 1973), and, as a final illustration, in microanalytic analyses illuminating the reciprocal interchanges that characterize parent–infant relations (e.g., Brazelton, Koslowski, & Main, 1974).

Given the primary focus of Bell's critique, it is not surprising that most of the work stimulated by his seminal paper focused upon how infants influence parenting behavior (e.g., Lewis & Rosenblum, 1974). Only recently has systematic attention been given to the wider influence of the infant (Belsky, 1981; Lamb, 1978), specifically, to the effect of the infant on the marital relationship. Because Belsky's and Lamb's reports only begin to elucidate the far-reaching impact of the infant, one major goal of the present chapter will be to push beyond infants' influences upon their primary care givers—as both parents and spouses—and consider their impact upon the wider ecological context in which the family itself is embedded. In this chapter we shall endeavor to show how infants influence their own development by systematically considering the ecology of human development and the multifaceted and complex reciprocities that transpire in the infant's social world.

We have chosen to employ Bronfenbrenner's (1977a, 1979) model of the ecology of human development to guide our analysis because we find it to be particularly useful when considering the familial, social, cultural and historical contexts in which development takes place. Its ability to reveal neglected areas of inquiry has been documented in several applications of the model to public policy concerns for which developmentalists have shown a special interest: child abuse (Belsky, 1980a; Garbarino, 1977), day care (Belsky, 1980c), adolescent labor (Steinberg & Greenberger, 1979), and developmental disabilities (Young & Kopp, 1979). As in these endeavors, we shall see in our analysis of the infant as producer of his or her own development that the ecological model raises issues to which available theory has not drawn attention. This characteristic consequence of an ecological analysis results from the primary strength of Bronfenbrenner's conceptual framework. In contrast to more broad-based pleas for contextual analyses of developmental processes (e.g., Lerner, 1978; Riegel, 1975), Bronfenbrenner's model of the ecology of human development provides a detailed map for considering "development in context." In the present chapter, it is our intent to demonstrate the applicability of this scheme to basic process concerns of developmentalists and, in so doing, highlight its capacity for bridging the chasm that supposedly separates basic and applied developmental psychology. Such a demonstration, we believe, should show it to be an extremely useful analytic paradigm for a science of human development—a science that purports concern for understanding the developmental process of the developing organism in its constantly changing familial–social–cultural–historical milieu (cf. Bronfenbrenner, 1979; Lerner, 1978; Riegel, 1975).

We shall begin our ecological analysis of the infant as producer of his or her own development by considering *the microsystem* of infancy. Following Bronfenbrenner (1977a, 1979) we employ this term to denote "the complex of relations between the developing person and environment in an immediate setting containing that person [1977a, p. 515]." For us, the immediate setting of concern will be the family system, and the "complex of relations," the *reciprocal pathways* of social influence that exist within the three-person family; that is, those bidirectional pathways of influence that link mother–wife, father–husband, and infant in the family system.

After discussing the microsystem of the family during infancy, we extend our analysis beyond the immediate setting in which development takes place and consider the community, cultural, historical, and evolutionary contexts in which the individual and the microsystem of the family are embedded. Such an ecological inquiry will reveal two things. First, that the infant's influence can extend beyond the family and feedback and affect his or her development. Second, that the wider ecology in which the family is embedded sets significant constraints upon how the infant's behavior will be interpreted and, thereby, upon the infant's ability to affect his or her care givers and, consequently, his or her own development.

Before proceeding to a consideration of the microsystem, one caveat is in order. When we say, as we already have, that infants "produce" their own development we do not mean that infants are the sole producers of their growth and functioning. Rather we mean that they actively contribute to the developmental process. The infant's influence on patterns of parenting and the marital relationship will receive special attention, then, as such infant effects are likely to feed back and affect the child's development.

The Microsystem of Infancy: The Family System

As already noted, a microsystem is any immediate setting containing the developing person. For older children, home, school, and playground are microsystems of significance. Given the relative immaturity of infants and their extreme dependence upon their care givers, particularly in the first year of life, access to multiple microsystems, at least for extended periods of time, is limited. For this reason, we direct our attention in this section to the major and single most important microsystem for American infants—the family. We recognize that other microsystems are of significance to infant development, most notably the hospital where the first days of postnatal life are usually spent, and the day care center or day care home where increasing numbers of young children spend rather extended periods of each day. To keep our analysis within manageable limits, we reserve consideration of these two latter contexts to a subsequent section of this chapter, one that focuses upon the wider ecology of human development and, more specifically, what Bronfenbrenner (1977a, 1979) refers to as the mesosystem, or the intersection of two or more microsystems.

As far as the microsystem of infancy is concerned, consideration of the infant's role in producing his or her own development has been restricted primarily to the frequent discussion of the reciprocal pathway of influence that links parent and child (e.g., Lewis & Rosenblum, 1974). More specifically, data have been offered that indicate that the infant influences the care it receives, and it has been assumed, though rarely documented, that this care feeds back and affects the child. We see four major limitations of this work. The first is that it lacks a developmental perspective. That is, no efforts have been made to determine whether the characteristics of individuality that are of most significance in influencing parenting behavior at one point in time are the same as those that are most responsible for influencing parenting behavior at a later point. The second limitation is that research on infant effects has focused primarily on patterns of mothering. Hence, the possibility that the infant's influence varies as a function of the particular person with whom it is engaged has not been explored. We do not know, as a result, whether mothers and fathers are differentially sensitive to certain characteristics of individuality. The third limitation is analogous to the second, and stems from the disciplinary narrowness that characterizes most infancy research. As all efforts to understand the infant's role in producing his or her own development have focused upon parenting, the possibility has not been entertained that the characteristics of individuality affecting patterns of mothering and fathering may differ from those that affect the marital relationship or the nonmarital and nonparental roles of parents. Finally, the available research is limited by its failure to consider the context in which the infant develops. Here we are specifically concerned with the mediating influence that parents' individual developmental, and joint marital, histories may play in determining the nature of the effect which the infant exerts.

In response to these limitations, we offer Figure 4.1 as a model of the development of the microsystem of infancy. As can be seen from this figure, the family is considered to have a developmental history that not only predates the conception of the infant but also parents' acquaintance with one another; to consist of mothering (M) and fathering (F) roles, a marital relationship (P_1/P_2) and individual adults who function in non-parental and nonmarital roles (P_1, P_2); and to be affected by changes that characterize infant growth and development ($I_{T1}...I_{Tn}...I_{Tn+}$). Additionally, each developmental period (i.e., I, II...IX) is presumed to exert an influence upon subsequent periods (see arrowed brackets in Figure 4.1).

In this model of the microsystem of infancy, we include the period labeled "Individual Development," because we believe parents' developmental histories set constraints upon the influence that infants can exert on their care givers and thus upon their own development. Evidence that substantiates this contention can be found in the research literature on child abuse. Repeatedly, an association has been discerned between the experience of mistreatment in one's own childhood and the subsequent mistreatment of one's offspring (Belsky, 1980a; Parke & Collmer, 1975; Spinetta & Rigler, 1972). In this regard, Frodi, Lamb, Leavitt, Donovan, Neff, and Sherry (1978) have demonstrated experimentally that child-abusing parents, in comparison to nonabusive controls, respond less sympathetically and more aversively to the cries and smiles of young babies; when considered in light of experiences that might differentiate the developmental histories of these two groups of parents, these findings suggest that the effects that infants have upon their care givers (e.g., distress evoking sympathy or anger) may be partially determined by factors that predate not only the baby's birth, but parents' acquaintance with one another as well. To the extent that this is so, the first section of Figure 4.1 is underscored as a necessary component of any analysis of the infant's role in producing–contributing to its own development.

The significance of the period labeled "Spousal Relation" is similarly underscored by research from family sociology and developmental psychology. In studying the transition to parenthood, several sociologists have suggested that the degree to which "crisis" is experienced by couples having their first baby is dependent upon the quality of the marital re-

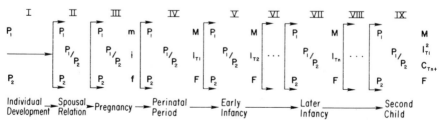

FIGURE 4.1.   *The development of the microsystem of infancy.* P_1 = adult male: present experience and developmental history; P_2 = adult female: present experience and developmental history; P_1/P_2 = "spousal relation": present experiences and shared developmental history; m = implicit role of mother; f = implicit role of father; i = implicit infant; M = role of mother; F = role of father; I = infant; T = time; C = infant as child; I^2 = second baby.

lationship *before* the baby is conceived (Dyer, 1963; Feldman & Rogoff, 1968; Russell, 1974). Furthermore, several developmentalists have observed that the quality of the marital relationship is directly related to patterns of mother–infant interaction. Specifically, a husband's supportiveness of his wife as a mother and his positive feeling for her as a spouse have been found to predict competent and sensitive mothering styles (Feiring & Taylor, 1977; Pedersen, 1975; Price, 1977; see Belsky, 1981, for a review). There can be little doubt as to the necessity of including the second section of Figure 4.1 in this analysis of the infant as contributor to its own development if, as these observations suggest, the infant's impact upon the marital relationship is mediated by the quality of the spousal relationship prior to the child's conception, and maternal care giving is affected by marital adjustment.

As we proceed to consider the prenatal and infancy period in this microsystem analysis of the infant as producer of its own development, a serious limitation of Figure 4.1 becomes evident. Although this model sketches the elements of the microsystem of infancy, and suggests the role of its developmental history, it communicates little about the processes by which the infant actually affects his or her own development. Thus, we offer Figure 4.2 as a model of the reciprocal pathways of influence within the three-person family system. It will serve to guide our efforts to illuminate the infant's influence on its own development during the pregnancy and infancy periods. We reserve a discussion of the perinatal period to a later section in which we concern ourselves with the hospital setting as a second microsystem in the ecology of infancy.

THE PRENATAL PERIOD

After conception, but prior to birth, infants can influence the course of their own development. That this is so is suggested by a recent study of unwed parents. Upon interviewing 14,000 expectant mothers, Altemeir,

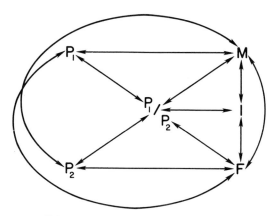

FIGURE 4.2. *Microsystem reciprocities.*

Vietze, Sherrod, Sandler, Falsey, & O'Connor (1979) found that impending parenthood terminated the relationship that many unwed couples had established prior to the baby's conception. As the available evidence on the developmental consequences of father absence indicates that boys without fathers display low levels of social control and achievement motivation as they grow up (for review, see Hetherington, Cox, & Cox, 1978), we can see that the unborn child may inadvertently undermine his or her subsequent development. Unfortunately, the same appears to be true of infants who, through their conception, encourage their parents to wed. As Furstenburg (1976) has shown, such marriages run a high risk of eventual dissolution; such a direct influence of the infant on the marital relationship does not bode well for the child either.

The infant's influence on its development may work in more subtle ways, for example, through mothers' and husbands' evaluation of the pregnant women's changing physique. Such a physical transformation could make the mother resentful of the child, and even lead her to restrict her diet to maintain her figure. Alternatively, this physical evidence of the baby's presence could assist the mother in investing herself psychologically in the unborn child. In many families, it is likely that a mother's attitude to her new body configuration will vary as a function of her spouse's attitudes. In this regard, Masters and Johnson (1966) have observed that many husbands have their first extramarital affair during the pregnancy period. As Brenner and Greenberg (1977) note that many husbands find the pregnant body especially attractive, it would be mistaken to regard the infant's influence upon his or her own development, as mediated by responses to the pregnancy physique, as invariably negative.

We suspect also that pregnancy and impending parenthood will have a maturing effect upon individuals. For example, the infant may influence a father by altering his perception of himself and of his responsibilities; this might influence his performance at work and his commitment to his spouse. That this process of growth might feed back upon the husband's own parenting as well as his spouse's, and thereby influence the yet unborn infant, is certainly conceivable. Unfortunately, we are aware of no studies that directly test this speculation. Heath (1978) has found, however, in a longitudinal study of young men, that competent fathering and psychological maturity are positively correlated. Additionally, Belenky and Gilligan (1979) have observed that pregnancy can stimulate moral development by raising ethical concerns regarding abortion.

THE INFANCY PERIOD

Following birth, the infant will continue contributing to its own development. The exact nature of this influence is likely to vary as a function of the child's characteristics of individuality (e.g., Goldberg, 1977; Thomas, Chess, & Birch, 1970). This is most certainly true not only with respect to the infant's direct influence upon care-giving behavior but also with regard to his or her indirect influence upon the care parents provide as mediated by the spousal relationship and mother's and father's nonparental and nonspousal roles (see Figure 4.2). The characteristics of individuality we see as most important to the infant's role in producing its own development include gender, activity level, cuddliness, responsivity, physical attractiveness, alertness, affective expressiveness, susceptibility to illness, and what Goldberg (1977, 1979) describes as readability (i.e., clarity of signaling) and predictability (i.e., regularity of behavior). These latter two characteristics, Goldberg notes, may be particularly important to the feelings of efficacy that care givers derive from their interactions with the baby. Because so much has been written about how individual differences between infants can determine the care they receive (e.g., Lewis & Rosenblum, 1974; Thomas, 1975; Thomas & Chess, 1977), we have chosen, in this chapter, neither to reiterate these comments nor to illustrate how these characteristics may affect the child's experiences and thus his or her development. Instead, we shall consider, through illustrations, various ways in which the complex of relations depicted in Figure 4.2 applies to the infant's role in producing its own development during the infancy period.

Lamb (1979) has suggested that parenthood serves to traditionalize family roles, and Cowen, Cowen, Coie, and Coie (1978) report clinical evidence supportive of this thesis. Because the division of labor within the family system will most assuredly influence children's eventual sex-role development, this traditionalizing impact of parenting highlights one way in which children influence their own development.

The literature in family sociology repeatedly suggests that the birth of the infant can create a crisis for married couples (see Russell, 1974, for review). In attempts to account for this crisis, several have argued that it is mother's physical exhaustion, and her resulting lack of interest in sexual relations, that is partially responsible for the stress experienced by couples (Dyer, 1963; Hobbs & Wimbish, 1977; LeMasters, 1957). As we have already noted that the quality of the marital relationship influences the sensitivity of maternal care giving, which is known to foster cognitive–motivational and social–emotional development (e.g., Clarke-Stewart, 1973), we see again evidence of a complex and indirect process through which infants can influence their own functioning postnatally by affecting the relationship that their parents have with each other.

We would be making a grave mistake if we were only to consider the negative ways in which infants affect their own development. On the positive side, Belsky (1979a) reports correlational data linking shared pleasure between spouses while parenting with high levels of marital harmony. Although these data do not document cause–effect relations, they do suggest that the infant may serve to bring spouses together to partake of enjoyable experiences. As Belsky (1979b) also reported high levels of spousal harmony to be associated with father involvement in parenting, which was itself correlated with competent infant functioning, there is again suggestive evidence that infants can contribute to their own development by influencing the spousal relation (Belsky, 1981).

Reciprocal pathways of influence within the family system are also highlighted by a consideration of the infant's impact upon his or her parents as individuals. In most households, the birth of the infant will force the mother to discontinue her work or schooling, at least temporarily. When the loss of the wife's salary presents serious financial burdens for the family, the husband may be compelled to seek a second job. This, of course, may not only place stress upon the marital relationship and thereby affect the care mother provides her infant, but may also restrict the quality and quantity of the time father is available to the infant. As evidence continues to accumulate documenting the positive influence that paternal involvement has in promoting infant social and cognitive–motivational development (e.g., Belsky, 1980b; Pedersen, Rubenstein, & Yarrow, 1979; Spelke, Zelazo, Kagan, & Kotelchuck, 1973), there is again reason to believe that infants can inadvertently influence their own development through rather complex processes within the three-person family system.

The only pathway of influence depicted in Figure 4.2 that has yet to be implicitly or explicitly addressed involves the reciprocal influence of patterns of mothering and fathering on each other. A recent study provides evidence of just such a pathway as well as of the role of the infant in contributing to its own development. Upon analyzing data gathered at 15, 20, and 30 months on an intensively studied sample of 14 families, Clarke-Stewart (1978a) concluded that fathers do not so much affect their toddler's social and cognitive development as they are influenced by it. Specifically, the more competent infants were at 15 months, the more involved fathers were at 20 months. The fact that father involvement at 20 months predicted maternal involvement at 30 months, which had been found at 15 months to predict infant functioning at 20 months, led Clarke-Stewart to propose a complex process of family influence whereby mother influences infant, who affects father who, coming full circle, influences mother.

In this section, we have put forth a model of reciprocal pathways of influence within the microsystem of the family and have illustrated the potentially complex processes through which infants, both pre- and postnatally, may contribute to their own development. By drawing upon research evidence and speculation, we have in Figure 4.2 suggested (a) that infants can influence their care givers' behavior, which in return can influence their own development; (b) that infants can influence the marital relationship by affecting parenting behavior, and that this influence on the marital dyad can feed back and affect parenting and, thereby, the infant; and (c) that infants can affect parents as individuals in their non-parental and nonspousal roles which can, in turn, affect mothering and fathering behavior and the relationship that exists between them and, ultimately, the child's own development.

The only influence process we have yet to consider (and one not in-cluded in our Figure 4.2) is that involving the infant's *direct* effect upon his or her development. In this regard, some recent data gathered by the second author deserve mention, as do several recent reports concerning sudden infant death. In studying the play and temperaments of 9-month-olds, Tolan (1979) found that highly active infants engaged in less com-petent play than did their less active counterparts. As Smith and Dutton (1979) have recently demonstrated experimentally that exploration and play enhance the child's problem-solving skills, these results are sugges-tive of one way in which infants serve as direct producers of their own development. Piaget's (1952) analysis of the active role the infant plays in repeating and experimenting with organism–environment contingen-cies initially discovered by chance (i.e., secondary and tertiary circular reactions) also documents the contribution that infant exploration plays in promoting development, as does the recent work of Rovee-Collier and Gekoski (1979) concerning the effect of conjugate reinforcement on the infant's ability to control the motion of mobiles suspended over his or her crib.

Recently, Lipsitt (1979) has suggested that, in the sudden infant death syndrome (SIDS), certain behavioral characteristics of the infant may be responsible, in part, for his or her own demise. Whereas we generally take this kind of reasoning for granted in connection with many aspects of adult health, welfare, and safety (witness how inadequate sensory responsivity or motor reflexes may result in vehicular accidents, poor judgment about distances and one's capabilities may result in drowning, smoking and drinking behavior may produce cancer and hepatitis, etc.), the infant's behavioral contribution to its own mortality is not often rec-ognized. Lipsitt notes that the normal newborn is equipped with a rep-ertoire of protective reflexes that help to guard against respiratory occlu-sion or threat of it. Sudden infant death may result, he speculates, in part, because infants without strong reflexes may, as a consequence, fail to learn appropriate voluntary behaviors that must supplant the con-genital reflexes as they wane over the first few months of life. Thus, by 2–4 months of age, when infants are most likely to succumb to SIDS, the unprotected infant lacks the skills required to act on threats to normal air flow (pressure against the face, mucus clogging, or reduction of oxygen content in the lungs).

In the course of studying another possible cause of sudden death in infancy, apnea, Black, Steinschneider, and Steele (1979) have found that even when infants do not succumb to periods of breathlessness, these episodes may still impair future functioning. Infants who frequently stopped breathing during the first week of life, in comparison to more healthy controls, were found to have lower developmental quotients (though none were retarded) in the last quarter of the first year of life even when potentially influential antecedent and background variables (e.g., sex, race, birth weight, parental education) were statistically controlled. The infant's role in directly producing its own development is suggested by one explanation offered by the investigators to account for their findings: Cerebral anoxia, secondary to prolonged apneic episodes during sleep, disrupts brain development, and thereby impairs mental functioning.

We would be in error, however, if we failed to recognize that the very process of influence detailed here may itself be the product of early experience of which the infant has little control. For example, it may well have been the mother's poor health habits prenatally (e.g., smoking) that resulted in a premature birth, which is responsible for the episodes of apnea under discussion. And, moreover, whether or not such early experience causes extended periods of breathlessness may be a function of the quality of care provided to the child postnatally. Thus, we see that the extent to which the child can produce its own development is a function of the context in which he or she is reared.

In summary, consideration of the work reviewed on exploration–play and on sudden infant death suggest both positive and negative ways in which infants directly produce their own development.

The Wider Ecology of Human Development

To this point in our analysis of the infant as producer of his or her own development, we have restricted our discussion to the immediate setting of the family, the microsystem of infancy. Basic to an understanding of the ecology of human development, however, is an appreciation of the multiple and nested contexts in which development takes place. There are two reasons why it is imperative that we consider this wider ecology, given the focus of the present chapter. The first is that the infant exerts an impact that extends beyond the immediate family system and this impact feeds back and affects what transpires in the family, thereby influencing the infant's development. The second reason for considering the wider ecology of human development is that what transpires beyond the family system sets constraints upon the very processes of influence outlined in the preceding section. Thus, to understand the manner in which infants produce their own development, one needs to understand the context in which they develop.

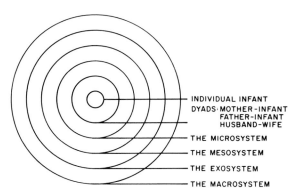

FIGURE 4.2. *The ecology of infancy.*

In the latter half of this chapter, we shall examine the outer rings of Bronfenbrenner's (1977a, 1979) concentric circle model of the ecology of human development. Beyond the microsystem, the innermost ring, lies the mesosystem, and beyond that the exo- and macrosystem. We shall consider each of these levels of the ecology of human development in turn. Finally, before making some concluding remarks, we shall briefly discuss evolutionary considerations that bear upon the focus of this chapter. Although Bronfenbrenner fails to consider the role of evolution in his ecological scheme, there can be little doubt of its significance in human development (see Lerner & Busch-Rossnagel, Chapter 1, this volume), particularly in the case of infancy (see Figure 4.2).

THE MESOSYSTEM

In Bronfenbrenner's (1977a) words, "a mesosystem comprises the interrelations among major settings containing the developing person at a particular point in his or her life [p. 515]." As our concern is infancy, we shall restrict ourselves to the interface of the home with two additional settings that have developmental significance for the infant, the hospital, and the day-care environment.

The Hospital

What transpires in the hospital during the perinatal period has direct bearing upon how infants contribute to their own development in the family. The most certain evidence of this comes from the rather extensive study of the premature infant. Observational studies not only indicate that these children are less alert, less responsive, and more fussy than their full-term counterparts, but also that their parents must work harder to maintain interaction with them (see Goldberg, 1977, for review). That such consequences are, in turn, of importance to infant development is suggested by repeated observations linking prematurity and child abuse

(Belsky, 1978; Friederich & Boriskin, 1976; Lamb, 1978; Parke & Collmer, 1975), and evidence that abused toddlers are less inclined to make direct and friendly approaches to peers and adults in a group setting (George & Main, 1979).

Work by Leifer, Leiderman, and Barnett (1972) also indicates that stress placed upon families bearing premature infants .nay increase the likelihood of divorce if special efforts are not made in the hospital to minimize the "interactive deficit" experienced by parents and their premature infants. This finding suggests that the negative effects of placing at-risk newborns in intensive-care nurseries may extend beyond the disruption of parent–child bonds to which Klaus and Kennell (1976) have drawn attention.

Recent studies of infants at-risk for SIDS also highlight the significance of the hospital–family interface for understanding infants' contributions to their own development. When hospital-supplied apnea monitors were attached to a group of experimental infants, two-thirds of their mothers reported that the machines had "drastic effects" on family life (Black, Hersher, & Steinschneider, 1978). Not only were these infants more closely watched and more frequently held than were a group of controls, but these machines, which emitted a loud alerting signal when respiration ceased, were frequently the cause of marital quarrels. Evidence gathered on the monitored infants themselves did not indicate that these hospital-supplied machines actually affected the child. But given our earlier comments regarding the importance of marital support for sensitive care giving, and the results of Belsky's (1979b) correlational study linking high levels of maternal holding and low levels of infant exploratory competence among 15-month-olds, we believe that there is good reason to reserve judgment on the ultimate effects that apnea monitors have on the infant's role in producing his or her own development.

Recent work by Parke, Hymel, Power, and Tinsley (1979) manipulating the experiences of the father during the perinatal period highlights the importance of the hospital–family interface for normal infants. These investigators reported that showing fathers videotaped demonstrations of newborn perceptual and motor competencies, and styles of paternal play and care giving, significantly enhanced father involvement during the first months of life and husbands' appreciation of their wives' roles as mothers. To the extent that this hospital intervention positively influenced paternal sensitivity to infant cues and signals, and maternal sensitivity (by increasing husband's supportiveness of his wife), infant capacity to affect the care received is most assuredly enhanced.

Day Care

In a recent review of relevant research, Belsky and Steinberg (1978) noted that the effects of day care are likely to be mediated by children's experiences at home. To date, however, very little research has examined the interface of day care and the family. Two notable exceptions to this generalization are an interview study documenting limited communication between these two rearing environments (Powell, 1978), and an observational study detailing relationships between care giving experienced in day care at 12 months of age and at home 2½ years later (Rubenstein, Howes, & Boyle, 1979). Although Powell's descriptive study provides an in-depth understanding of care giver–parent communication, it sheds no light upon an issue of special importance to an ecological analysis of day care (Belsky, 1980c), that is, how does the quality and quantity of such interaction influence the child's experience at home and in day care? We suspect that the more friendly and informative parent–care giver contacts are, the more the infant's behavior in each context will be understood and, consequently, the more sensitively he or she will be cared for. If this could be demonstrated, there would be clear evidence that the home–day-care interface affects the manner in which infants influence their care givers and is thus of importance to understanding the manner in which infants produce their own development.

A study by Rubenstein *et al.* (1979) sheds more light on this issue. Correlational analysis revealed that infants frequently played with in day care experienced more positive interactions at home with their mothers and evidenced advanced performance on infant tests. The role played by the infant in producing its own development and in determining the influence of day care on home care are suggested by Rubenstein *et al.*'s speculation that the infants' day-care experiences were a function of their own characteristics of individuality. Some infants, it seems, displayed more positive social behavior, which appeared to account for their more frequent positive interactions with day-care staff. As noted, it was these day-care experiences that correlated significantly with subsequent development and maternal care. It would appear, then, that infants in day care create certain experiences for themselves and these experiences influence later experience and, ultimately, their future developmental status.

In summary, we believe that the interaction of the family and day care, as well as that of the family and the hospital, influence the manner in which the infant's behavior is interpreted and responded to. An appreciation of these mesosystems, or "systems of microsystems" as Bronfenbrenner (1977a, p. 515) describes them, assists us in systematically analyzing these contextual determinants of the infant's role in producing his or her own development.

THE EXOSYSTEM

Beyond the mesosystem in Bronfenbrenner's (1977a) topographical model of ecology of human development is the exosystem, representing "an extension of the mesosystem embracing other specific social structures, both formal and informal, that do not themselves contain the developing person but impinge upon or encompass the immediate settings in which that person is found, and thereby delimit, influence, or even determine what goes on there [p. 515]." Given the focus of this chapter, the exosystem factors we shall consider are the social networks of parents, their places of work, and the media. Although Bronfenbrenner primarily emphasizes the indirect impact of these formal and informal social structures on the developing person, it is important to recognize that these pathways of influence, however indirect, are at times reciprocal. Thus, we intend to show not only that infants are affected by parents' social networks and their places of work, but that infants also affect them and, in so doing, contribute to their own development.

It should be noted that in this discussion of the exosystem we shall rely heavily on speculation. This is because we have been unable to find much research data regarding ways in which infants influence or are influenced by parents' social network, the world of work, and the media. One reason for this, we believe, is that available developmental theory has not drawn attention to the existence and importance of these domains of the ecology of human development. As noted in our introduction, the major strength of Bronfenbrenner's contextual model is the attention it draws to potentially rich and important, but neglected, areas of inquiry. It is our hope that the following exosystem analysis will stimulate research on these neglected topics.

Social Networks

The discovery of pregnancy, the preparation for childbirth, and the rearing of the baby most certainly influence parents' social relationships. Particularly in the case of the first child, it is likely that the infant affects the quality of parents' ties with their own families. In some households, parents' renewed relations with their own families of origin are likely to be positive, as when the parents' parents (or other relatives) provide emotional and material (including financial) assistance. In such cases, infants probably positively affect their own development by drawing support to their parents so that they can more effectively fulfill their parental obligations. In contrast, when the baby serves as the impetus for in-laws' meddling in family affairs, it is likely that the infant inadvertently increases the stress his or her parents experience and, thereby, undermines their ability to respond sensitively to his or her cues. Moreover, this stress may well create conflict between spouses, which we have already suggested may alter the way in which parents might otherwise have responded to their infant's behavior.

Preparation for childbirth and the birth of the baby are likely to influence nonfamilial members of the family's social network too (Lee, 1977). The widespread utilization of childbirth education and parenting classes has a most certain, but to our knowledge unstudied, impact upon the support system of parents. As persons with shared interests (e.g., pregnancy and parenthood) are brought together, it must frequently be the case that friendships, some of which may prove long-lasting, are established. The importance of such networks for infant development is implicated by the repeated observation that social isolation and child maltreatment are closely, and probably causally, related (Belsky, 1980a; Garbarino, 1977). Thus, by being conceived, some children may stimulate the formation of social relationships within the community that support parents in their child-rearing function and, thereby, affect their development.

Such friendships are also likely to influence parents' appraisal of their infants, as the tendency to compare the developmental achievements of young children is so widespread among American parents. In some cases, this may be helpful—as when a developmental delay might have otherwise gone unnoticed—but, in most cases, we suspect it simply generates unnecessary parental anxiety, and possibly encourages parents to push their children inappropriately.

In addition to expanding parents' social networks, the infant may also serve to reduce them. We have observed, for example, the expression of resentment by childless couples regarding the intrusion of a demanding baby into what previously had been mature adult relationships. In fact, the high levels of attention parents pay to their children and their continual interest in domestic matters are viewed with distaste by some nonparents. In certain cases, this must cause friends to grow apart. If this is so, and parents resent the child's influence upon their friendships, the infant may inadvertently harm its own relationship with the parents.

Employment

In addition to social networks, the infant may also affect parents' occupational performance and career plans (Kanter, 1978). In a recent review of major influences upon employee attendance, Steers and Rhodes (1978) cite numerous studies linking family responsibilities with occupational absenteeism, but provide no evidence suggestive of the positive influence that family responsibilities may have on missed work days. Nevertheless, we hypothesize that in families in which the addition of a child creates financial burdens, the working parent(s) may be less inclined to skip a day of work. Indirect support for this hypothesis comes from an intensive study of 25 dual-working-parent families with preschoolers. Lein (1979) found that the birth of the first child stabilized men's employment. Parents indicated that it was the family's need for a stable income and additional benefits (e.g., health insurance, pension) that kept fathers from changing jobs.

In addition to the effect of the child on absenteeism and employment stability, we suspect that family responsibilities may also increase parents' desire for job promotion and thereby enhance job performance. Of course, this may not bode well for the child; as we noted earlier in discussing reciprocities within the family system, such occupational concerns can create stress on marital relations and limit parents' availability to their children, thereby influencing their development.

Steers and Rhodes (1978) also cite evidence documenting declines in absenteeism rates for women throughout their work careers (in contrast to increases for men) and suggest these result from the traditional family responsibilities assigned to women that keep them home to care for their sick young children during their early stages of career development. In the case of a sickly infant, it seems possible that many missed work days could threaten a woman's employment security. The same holds true of course for difficulties encountered in trying to manage substitute child-care arrangements, particularly when frequent changes must be made with regard to who is taking care of the child. As Steinberg and Green (1979) recently discovered, responsibility for dealing with these periodic crises invariably falls on the shoulders of mothers. Under such conditions, it is certainly conceivable that the child, if construed as the cause of mother's occupational problems, might negatively affect mothering behavior and thus his or her own development.

On-the-job pressures that are not caused by the infant may also mediate the infant's influence in producing its own development. Required overtime and dangerous work conditions, for example, may sufficiently stress the parent and limit the capacity to care for and respond sensitively to the infant's demanding and dependent behavior. Such sensitive, responsive, and appropriate care giving is of significance to the infant, a fact that has been demonstrated repeatedly, as in Ainsworth's (1973) and Yarrow, Rubertein, and Pedersen's (1975) studies linking such mothering styles with secure (as opposed to anxious) emotional development and advanced test performance.

The Media

As our final illustration of the role that exosystem influences can play in determining the infant's contribution to his or her own development, we consider the media, especially television and popular literature on child care.

During the past 15 years, research on television has primarily focused upon the *direct* effect of TV content on child development (e.g., Liebert, Neale, & Davidson, 1973; Stein & Freidrich, 1975). An alternative view of TV points to the possibility of its *indirect* influence on the child (Parke, 1978). Unfortunately, little evidence has been gathered on the way in which television may alter family interaction and, thereby, child development. Maccoby (1951) did document, though, in an early study, the depressive influence of television ownership upon non-TV-related joint family activity. In a similar vein, Steiner's (1963) national survey revealed that TV is often employed by parents as a babysitter. These findings suggest to us that TV may limit the infant's access to parents and, thereby, his or her ability to influence their behavior. To the extent that parents are less responsive and sensitive to the infant, one route by which the child contributes to its own development becomes circumscribed.

Like television's effect on family interaction, the influence that popular child-rearing literature has had on parental behavior has received little attention from child developmentalists. Bronfenbrenner's (1958) early analysis of social class differences in parenting strategies represents a single exception to this statement. He noted that changes in middle-class patterns of child rearing tended to mirror the changes Wolfenstein (1951) described in her historical analysis of the government publication *Infant Care*. In fact, he concluded "that mothers not only read such books but take them seriously, and that their treatment of the child is affected accordingly [Bronfenbrenner, 1958, p. 15]."

If this was true in 1958, we suspect it is even more true today, as publication data "show a clear monotonic increase over the past 17 years in both absolute number and proportion of new child-care books published each year—a trend that apparently is continuing [Clarke-Stewart, 1978b, p. 360]." In a series of recent studies, Clarke-Stewart (1978b) found that parents who most frequently turn to books written by child-care "experts," and who report being most influenced by them, are those for whom more traditional family supports are unavailable, that is, those without relatives living nearby. This suggests that the social context of the family influences parents' susceptibility to advice provided by child developmentalists. Because such advice affects parents' strategies of care giving (e.g., whether or not to respond to infant crying), popular literature on child development and parenting represents a dimension of the ecology of human development, like social networks and work, that is of importance for understanding contextual constraints upon the infant's ability to produce its own development.

THE MACROSYSTEM

What goes on in the exosystem, as well as at the levels of the meso- and microsystems, is influenced by cultural values and beliefs and historical events. To fully understand how children influence their own development, these macrosystem forces must be appreciated.

Certain evidence of the macrosystem's influence on the microsystem of the family, and particularly upon parent–infant relations, is found in historical evidence concerning the role of gender. In ancient Sparta, being born a girl placed one at risk of infanticide (Sameroff, 1979). It is certainly hard to imagine a more dramatic manner in which infants (inadvertently) produced their own development (in this case, their own demise), except perhaps in the laws of primogeniture, which assured the first-born male property rights to his father's estate.

Interestingly, although infanticide is no longer legally practiced in Western societies and primogeniture is no longer the law of the land in many countries, there are still strong preferences for sons and benefits to being born male. In this country, Hoffman's (1977) recent examination of reproductive patterns revealed that if couples have only daughters, they will bear more children than originally planned. This cultural (and perhaps universal) desire for sons most certainly affects the influence children have on their own development. For example, Jacobs and Moss (1976) report, on the basis of their systematic observational work, that, although later borns receive less attention than do first-born infants, if the later-born child is a first son, he elicits the same amount of care giving from his mother as do his first-born counterparts (for a replication study, see Lewis & Krietzberg, 1979). A more striking example of the cultural valuing of sons, and of its relevance to understanding the infant as producer of its own development, comes from a report appearing in the *China Medical Journal* in 1975 (cited in Hetherington & Parke, 1979, p. 49). Of approximately 100 pregnant women screened to determine the gender of their unborn child, over 60% carrying girls wished to abort, whereas only one of 53 carrying males did so!

An examination of cross-cultural belief systems serves to identify additional macrosystem determinants of children's contributions to their own development. Of particular significance would seem to be ideologies concerning the infant's nature and the importance of infancy. With respect to the latter, Kagan *et al.* (1978) argue that the beliefs that the child is father to the man, and that early experience is of consequence to subsequent development, may be particularly western and rooted in the early writings of Plato and Aristotle. The implication of such a world view for understanding the infant as producer of its own development is apparent when the American mother and her Rajput counterpart of Northern India are compared. Because American care givers tend to believe in the connectedness of early and later development, they respond to their infants' cues in hopes of promoting the child's future functioning. The Rajput mother, in contrast, adopts a relatively inactive role in her care giving, because she considers her infant's destiny to be under supernatural control. Cultural beliefs regarding the significance of early experience determine at least in part, then, the infant's ability to influence his or her care giver, and thereby set constraints upon one process through which the child can affect its subsequent functioning.

The significance of cultural perceptions of the infant, rather than of the stage of infancy, for understanding the process through which children produce their own development is underscored by Caudill and Weinstein's

(1969) classic study comparing Japanese and American mothers. Because Japanese mothers view their infants as untamed and autonomous, needing to be brought into dependent personal relationships, they are inclined to respond with short delay when their infants cry. American mothers, however, project dependence and helplessness onto their infants and are likely to let them cry for a few minutes. To the extent that Bell and Ainsworth (1972) are correct in their analysis linking responsiveness to crying with lower levels of subsequent crying, these cross-cultural comparisons provide suggestive evidence that the effect of the infant on its care giver, and thus upon its future development, is itself determined by the culture's view of the nature of the infant.

In a study by deVries and Super (1979) of differences in the way parents in several African tribes respond to the evaluation of their babies on the Brazelton Neonatal Exam, additional evidence is provided about the significance of cultural conceptions of the infant. Whereas the Mosai, Kikuyu, and Kipsigs perceive their infants "as fragile creatures, easily threatened by rough handling or overstimulation, . . . the Digo appear to think of their babies as relatively hardy and not in need of special protection from physical distress [p. 95]." These differing ideologies undoubtedly affect the way in which the infant is responded to and, thereby, highlight the role of the macrosystem in determining the infant's contribution to its own development.

Although the macrosystem puts constraints upon the individual infant's ability to influence its own development, it is unlikely that any individual infant can affect the macrosystem. This does not mean that infants as a group cannot exert such far-reaching impact. Indeed, evidence of just such an influence is provided by the thalidomide tragedy. As a result of the large number of physical deformities that resulted from the administration of this drug to pregnant women, Great Britain instituted an expensive and comprehensive health-care system to serve these individuals and their families. From the perspective of this analysis, then, these thalidomide babies exerted an influence at the level of the macrosystem by affecting the social policy of Great Britain.

Such a far-reaching impact of children, which must certainly feed back and influence their development, may become apparent over the next several decades in this country. As the distribution of age cohorts in the United States becomes increasingly "top heavy," we believe that the generations of older Americans will recognize that they have a "generational stake" (Bengtson & Kuypers, 1974) in assuring the optimal development of the young. Specifically, as more and more citizens become dependent upon the productivity of fewer and fewer citizens, this country will be less able to afford to waste valuable human resources. In a sense, then, by being a scarce commodity, future birth cohorts should draw resources to them that will insure their optimal development.

EVOLUTIONARY CONSIDERATIONS

This analysis of the infant as producer of his or her own development, and especially of the role of context in determining the nature of this influence process, would be incomplete without a discussion of evolution. As the human infant is, above all else, a carefully selected product of a lengthy evolutionary history, all that has been said is predicated upon what has been designed into, or left out of, this organism. Consideration of several of these characteristics not only highlights the active contribution that infants make to their own development, but also the organism–environment reciprocities that embody life.

Evidence to support this contention can be found even before the infant is born. The fact that sperm are equipped with mobile flagella, which propel them on their 7-inch journey through the birth canal and womb to the waiting egg, documents the active role of the organism-to-be in producing its own development. Progress in the journey is not entirely dependent upon the sperm, however. As Rossi (1978) has recently noted, transport through the female is much too rapid to be accounted for by purely the locomotive ability of the male germ cell. Uterine contractions, which are stimulated by the release of the hormone oxytocin from the posterior pituitary, are instrumental in the transport of sperm. Here, then, is evidence of the organism–environment reciprocity that characterizes not only conception and prenatal development, but development throughout the life span.

Such reciprocity is evident in other ways during the time of conception. Once the egg is fertilized, the zygote must maneuver itself down the fallopian tube and attach itself to the intrauterine wall. Just as not every sperm succeeds in reaching or in penetrating the ovum, not every zygote successfully implants itself. Approximately 25% succumb to spontaneous abortions in the earliest stage of life (Hetherington & Parke, 1979), as not every zygote can establish satisfactory reciprocal relations with its host.

By the time of birth, evolution has so programmed the human infant, the modern view of the competent newborn teaches us (cf. Stone, Smith, & Murphy, 1973), that the infant is "preadapted to be selectively attentive to the methods of stimulation provided by people and . . . is equipped with a repertoire of behaviors which effectively *capture* adult attention and facilitate effective adult–infant interactions [Goldberg, 1977, p. 163, emphasis added]." Not only does the human newborn see and hear, but it evidences preferences for facelike visual stimuli (Hoaf & Bell, 1967); is selectively attentive to the band-width frequencies that include human voices (Eisenberg, 1965); is able to discriminate voices (Boyd, 1975); and is capable of synchronizing movement with the articulated structures of adult speech (Condon & Sander, 1974).

Complementing the infant's selective attention to human features is the normal behavior of adults toward infants, which also appears to be preadapted to capitalize on the skills and preferences of the infant (Goldberg, 1977): Crying is perceived as aversive (Wolf, 1969); the tendency to lift the infant to the shoulder is especially effective in quieting distress (Korner & Thoman, 1972); the configuration of the infant's face is judged to be especially cute (Hildebrandt & Fitzgerald, 1979); and as a final example, the inclination to exaggerate tonal changes, articulate speech, and increase the pitch of the voice (Stern, 1974) systematically enhance the attention-getting features of speech for the baby.

Thus, the active contribution of the infant appears "built-in" by the dovetailing of the young infant's skills and the care giver's proclivities. This does not imply, of course, that development is assured, only that the healthy newborn has been provided by evolution with the tools and a context that affords reciprocal interchange between organism and environment, one that fuels growth and enables infants to contribute to their own development.

Evolution's influence on the infant's ability to actively engage the environment and to foster his or her future functioning is not restricted to the basic competencies provided the newborn. Recent formulations of attachment theory clearly highlight the importance of evolutionary considerations and the increasingly active role of the infant (Ainsworth, 1973). According to Bowlby (1969) the neonate is "programmed" with a set of skills that promote proximity to adults. And as it develops, the infant becomes increasingly capable of integrating these and other skills in a selective and discriminating fashion to help maintain its own security. Finally, with the onset of locomotion, the infant develops the capability of moving away from the attachment figure in the service of exploration and learning.

The balance that the infant achieves between the behavioral systems of attachment, exploration, and fear by the end of the first year of life may well determine much later development. A secure attachment, Arend, Gove, and Sroufe (1979) note, in their report relating the quality of infant–mother attachment with preschool functioning, "'supports the toddler's early attempts at exploration and object-mastery and promotes a developing sense of effectance (White, 1973).' The early confidence resulting from mastery promotes further affectively positive engagement in the world, in turn leading to subsequent competence [p. 956]." In other words, the balance achieved *within the infant* between competing behavioral systems, which itself derives from the infant's early care-giving experience (Ainsworth, 1979), fuels subsequent growth so that, on the basis of this early foundation, infants produce their own development.

Again, we feel compelled to point out that early development does not, by itself, determine the entire course of later development (see chapter Introduction). Thus, a secure attachment does not guarantee optimal functioning during future developmental periods, though it does provide a foundation upon which future experience will build. If the ecology of human development fails to support future functioning, there is no guarantee, and indeed no reason to expect, that a positive developmental trajectory forecast at 1 or 2 years of age will maintain its course. Moreover, there is reason to believe that a negative developmental trajectory can be redirected with subsequent therapeutic experiences (Rutter, 1979). We do not mean to imply, however, that development is totally open-ended, as the human organism is not an infinitely changing system. Under certain conditions (e.g., severe anoxia in the postpartum period) it is likely that some developmental possibilities (e.g., normal intellectual functioning) will be foreclosed. Later behavior is not totally devoid, then, of earlier experience, as this extreme example illustrates (also see Introduction).

Under less extreme circumstances, we suscribe to the principle that development is the product of the complex and continuous interaction between a much changing organism and a much changing environment. Evidence to support this contention comes from a recent study of the cross-age stability of infant–mother attachment. Although Waters (1978) observed marked stability in the attachment ratings (i.e., secure, avoidant, ambivalent) of 50 middle-class infants between 12 and 18 months, Vaughn, Waters, Egeland, and Sroufe (1979) discerned just the opposite pattern in an even larger sample of lower-class infants. Internal analyses revealed that the infants who showed unstable attachment classifications across the 6-month period were likely to have undergone several major environmental disruptions, as indicated by frequent changes of residence. Thus, continuity–discontinuity in development is, at least in part, dependent upon the continuity–discontinuity of the environment (Wohlwill, 1979).

Conclusion

In the field of developmental psychology, it is widely recognized that development takes place in context and is characterized by the complex interplay of organism and environment. Students of infancy have displayed appreciation of this perspective through their studies of parent–infant interaction, which document the infant's influence on parenting behavior as well as on the influence of parenting on the infant.

In our minds, such work represents only the beginning of an empirical evaluation of the implications of the concepts of "contextualism" and "organism–environment reciprocity." As we have endeavored to show in this chapter, infants influence the marital relationship and parents' nonmarital and nonparental responsibilities. And these infant effects feed back and influence the infant. The implication of these observations should be clear. Researchers of infant development must move beyond a consideration of bidirectional influence processes within the parent–child dyad; they must recognize that the infant and the parent–infant relationship are embedded within a family system. To understand how infants produce their own development, then, the components of the family system (e.g., mothering, fathering, the marital relationship) must be examined.

Bronfenbrenner's (1977a, 1979) model of the ecology of human development demands that we move beyond the family system in our efforts to understand the significance of context. Most importantly, it provides an analytic scheme for carrying out systematic contextual analyses. In this chapter, we have applied Bronfenbrenner's conceptual framework to the problem focus of this volume and found it useful for guiding inquiry into the infant's role in producing its own development. We argued, for example, that infants may effect their parents' social networks and performance at work and that such infant effects can feed back and influence parental behavior, thereby influencing the infant's development. Additionally, we observed that contextual forces set constraints upon the infant's ability to contribute to the developmental process by influencing parents' responsiveness and sensitivity to the young child. In this regard, we discussed, for example, parents' developmental and marital histories, their interactions with day-care staff, and cultural beliefs regarding the significance of infancy for later development.

In summary, we have endeavored to outline an "ecology of infancy" and conduct an ecological analysis of the infant's role in producing its own development. It is our hope that our efforts will stimulate others to move beyond the parent–infant relationship, and even the family system, in their attempts to understand the nature and determinants of infant behavior and development.

Acknowledgments

We would like to thank Dr. Lewis P. Lipsitt for the critical feedback he provided on an early draft of this manuscript.

References

Ainsworth, M. *Attachment: Retrospect and prospect*. Presidential address to the biennial meetings of the Society for Research in Child Development, San Francisco, March, 1979.

Ainsworth, M. D. S. The development of infant–mother attachment. In B. Caldwell & H. Ricciuti (Eds.), *Review of child development research* (Vol. 3). Chicago: University of Chicago Press, 1973.

Altemeir, W., Vietze, P., Sherrod, K., Sandler, H., Falsey, S., & O'Connor, S. Prediction of child maltreatment during pregnancy. *Journal of the American Academy of Child Psychiatry,* 1979, 205–218.

Arend, R., Gove, F., & Sroufe, L. Continuity in early adaptation: From attachment theory in infancy to resiliency and curiosity at age 5. *Child Development,* 1979, *50,* 950–959.

Baltes, P., Reese, H., & Lipsitt, L. Life-span developmental psychology. *Annual Review of Psychology,* 1980, *31,* 65–110.

Belenky, M., & Gilligan, C. *Predicting clinical outcomes: A longitudinal study of the impact of abortion crisis on moral development and life circumstance.* Unpublished manuscript, Harvard University, 1979.

Bell, R. A reinterpretation of the direction of effects in studies of socialization. *Psychological Review,* 1968, *75,* 81–95.

Bell, S., & Ainsworth, M. D. S. Infant crying and maternal responsiveness. *Child Development,* 1972, *43,* 1171–1190.

Belsky, J. Three theoretical models of child abuse: A critical review. *International Journal of Child Abuse and Neglect,* 1978, *2,* 37–49.

Belsky, J. Child maltreatment: An ecological integration. *American Psychologist,* 1980, *35,* 320–335. (a)

Belsky, J. The interrelation of parental and spousal behavior during infancy in traditional nuclear families: An exploratory analysis. *Journal of Marriage and the Family,* 1979, *41,* 62–68. (a)

Belsky, J. *The interrelation of parenting, spousal interaction, and infant competence: A suggestive analysis.* Paper presented at the biennial meeting of the Society for Research in Child Development, San Francisco, March, 1979. (b)

Belsky, J. A family analysis of parental influence on infant exploratory competence. In F. Pedersen (Ed.), *The father–infant relationships: Observational studies in a family context.* New York: Praeger Special Studies, 1980. (b)

Belsky, J. Future research in day care: An ecological analysis. *Child care Quarterly,* 1980, *9,* 82–99. (c)

Belsky, J. Early human experience: A family perspective. *Developmental Psychology,* 1981, *17,* 3–23.

Belsky, J., & Steinberg, L. The effects of day care: A critical review. *Child Development,* 1978, *49,*929–949.

Bengtson, V., & Kuypers, J. Generational differences and the developmental state. *Aging and Human Development,* 1974, *2,* 249–260.

Black, L., Hersher, L., & Steinschneider, A. Impact of the apnea monitor on family life. *Pediatrics,* 1978, *62,* 681–685.

Black, L., Steinschneider, A., & Sheehe, P. Neonatal respiratory instability and infant development. *Child Development,* 1979, *50,* 561–564.

Bowlby, J. *Attachment.* New York: Basic Books, 1969.

Boyd, E. Visual fixation and voice discrimination in 2-month-olds. In F. Horowitz (Ed.), Visual fixation, auditory stimulation, and language discrimination in young infants. *Monographs of the Society for Research in Child Development,* 1975, *39,* No. 158.

Brazelton, T. B., Koslowski, B., & Main, M. The origins of reciprocity: In early mother–infant interaction. In M. Lewis & L. Rosenblum (Eds.), *The effect of the infant on its caregiver.* New York: Wiley, 1974.

Brenner, P., & Greenberg, M. The impact of pregnancy on marriage. *Medical Aspects of Human Sexuality,* 1977, *11,* 15–21.

Bronfenbrenner, U. Socialization and social class through time and space. In E. Maccoby, T. Newcomb, & E. Hartley (Eds.), *Readings in social psychology.* New York: Holt, 1958.

Bronfenbrenner, U. Toward an experimental ecology of human development. *American Psychologist,* 1977, *32,* 513–531. (a)

Bronfenbrenner, U. *The ecology of human development.* Cambridge, Mass.: Harvard University Press, 1979.

Caldwell, B. The effects of infant care. In M. Hoffman & L. Hoffman (Eds.), *Review of child development research* (Vol. 1). New York: Russell Sage Foundation, 1964.

Caudill, W., & Weinstein, H. Maternal care and infant behavior in Japan and America. *Psychiatry,* 1969, *12,* 32–43.

Clarke, A. M., & Clarke, A. D. *Early experience; Myth and evidence.* New York: Free Press, 1976.

Clarke-Stewart, K. Interactions between mothers and their young children: Characteristics and consequences. *Monographs of the Society for Research in Child Development,* 1973, *38* (6–7, Serial No. 153).

Clarke-Stewart, K. And daddy makes three: The father's impact on mother and young child. *Child Development,* 1978, *44,* 466–478. (a)

Clarke-Stewart, K. Popular primers for parents. *American Psychologist,* 1978, *33,* 359–369. (b)

Condon, W., & Sander, L. Synchrony demonstrated between movements of the neonate and adult speech. *Child Development,* 1974, *45,* 456–462.

Cowan, C., Cowan, P., Coie, L., & Coie, J. Becoming a family: The impact of a first child's birth on the couple's relationship. In L. Newman & W. Miller (Eds.), *The first child and family formation.* Chapel Hill: Carolina Population Center, 1978.

deVries, M., & Super, C. Contextual influences on the neonatal behavior assessment scale and its implications for its cross cultural use. In A. Sameroff (Ed.), Organization and stability of newborn behavior: A commentary on the Brazelton Neonatal Behavior Assessment Scale. *Monographs of the Society for Research in Child Development,* 1979, *43,* (Serial Nos. 5–6).

Dyer, E. Parenthood as crisis: A restudy. *Marriage and Family Living,* 1963, *25,* 488–496.

Eisenberg, R. Auditory behavior in the neonate. *Journal of Auditory Research,* 1965, *5,* 159–177.

Erikson, E. *Childhood and society.* New York: Norton, 1950.

Feiring, C., & Taylor, J. *The influence of the infant and secondary parent on maternal behavior: Toward a social systems view of infant attachment.* Unpublished manuscript, University of Pittsburgh, 1977.

Feldman, H., & Rogoff, M. *Correlates of changes in marital satisfaction with the birth of the first child.* Paper presented at the American Psychological Association Meeting, San Francisco, 1968.

Freud, S. An outline of psychoanalysis. *The Complete Works of Sigmund Freud* (Vol. 23). London: Hogarth Press, 1940.

Friederich, W., & Boriskin, J. The role of the child in abuse: A review of the literature. *American Journal of Orthopsychiatry,* 1976, *40,* 580–590.

Frodi, A., Lamb, M., Leavitt, C., Donovan, W., Neff, C., & Sherry, D. Fathers' and mothers' responses to the faces and cries of normal and premature infants. *Developmental Psychology,* 1978, *14,* 490–498.

Furstenburg, F. Premarital pregnancy and marital instability. *Journal of Social Issues,* 1976, *32,* 67–86.

Garbarino, J. The human ecology of child maltreatment: A conceptual model for research. *Journal of Marriage and the Family,* 1977, *39,* 721–736.

George, C., & Main, M. Social interactions of young abused children: Approach, avoidance, and aggression. *Child Development,* 1979, *50,* 306–318.

Goldberg, S. Social competence in infancy: A model of parent–infant interaction. *Merrill-Palmer Quarterly,* 1977, *23,* 163–177.

Goldberg, S. Premature birth: Consequences for the parent–infant relationship. *American Scientist,* 1979, *67,* 214–270.

Heath, D. What meaning and effects does fatherhood have on the maturing of professional men? *Merrill-Palmer Quarterly,* 1978, *24,* 265–278.

Hetherington, E., Cox, M., & Cox, R. The development of children in mother-headed families. In H. Hoffman & D. Reiss (Eds.), *The American family: Dying or developing.* New York: Plenum, 1978.

Hetherington, E., & Parke, R. *Child Psychology.* New York: McGraw-Hill, 1979.

Hildebrandt, K., & Fitzgerald, H. Facial feature determinants of perceived infant attractiveness. *Infant Behavior and Development,* 1979, *2,* 329–340.

Hobbs, D., & Wimbish, J. Transition to parenthood by black couples. *Journal of Marriage and the Family,* 1977, 677–689.

Hoffman, L. Changes in family roles, socialization, and sex differences. *American Psychologist,* 1977, *32,* 644–658.

Jacobs, B., & Moss, H. Birth order and sex of sibling as determinants of mother–infant interaction. *Child Development,* 1976, *47,* 315–322.

Kagan, J., Kearsley, R., & Zelazo, P. *Infancy: Its place in human development.* Cambridge, Mass.: Harvard University Press, 1978.

Kagan, J., & Klein, R. Cross-cultural perspectives on early development. *American Psychologist,* 1973, *28,* 947–962.

Kanter, R. Families, family processes, and economic life: Toward systematic analysis of social historical research. In J. Demos & S. Boocock (Eds.), *Turning points.* Chicago: University of Chicago Press, 1978.

Klaus, M., & Kennell, J. *Mother–infant bonding.* St. Louis: C. V. Moss, 1976.

Korner, A., & Thoman, E. The relative efficacy of contact and vestibular proprioceptive stimulation in soothing neonates. *Child Development,* 1972, *43,* 443–454.

Lamb, M. F. Influence of the child on marital quality and family interaction during the prenatal, perinatal, and infancy periods. In R. M. Lerner & G. B. Spanier (Eds.), *Child influences on marital and family interaction: A life-span perspective.* New York: Academic Press, 1978.

Lee, G. Effects of social networks on families. In W. Burr, R. Hill, F. Nye, & I. Reiss (Eds.), *Contemporary theories about the family (Vol. 1).* New York: The Free Press, 1977.

Leifer, A., Leiderman, R., Barnett, C., William, J. Effects of mother–infant separation on maternal attachment behavior. *Child Development,* 1972, *43,* 1203–1218.

Lein, L. Male participation in home life: Impact of social supports and breadwinner responsibility on the allocation of tasks. *Family Coordinator,* 1979, *28,* 489–495.

LeMasters, E. Parenthood as crisis. *Marriage and Family Living,* 1957, *19,* 352–355.

Lerner, R. M. Nature, nurture, and dynamic interactionism. *Human Development,* 1978, *21,* 1–20.

Lerner, R. M., & Spanier, G. B. (Eds.). *Child influences on marital and family interaction: A life span perspective.* New York: Academic Press, 1978.

Lewis, M., & Feiring, C. The child's social world. In R. Lerner & G. Spanier (Eds.), *Contributions of the child to marital quality and family interaction through the life-span.* New York: Academic Press, 1979.

Lewis, M. & Krietzberg, V. Effects of birth order and spacing on mother–infant interactions. *Developmental Psychology,* 1979, *15,* 617–625.

Lewis, M. & Rosenblum, L. (Eds.), *The effect of the infant on its care giver.* New York: Wiley, 1974.

Liebert, R., Neale, J., & Davidson, E. *The early window: Effects of television on children and growth.* New York: Pergamon, 1973.

Lipsitt, L. Critical conditions of infancy: A psychological perspective. *American Psychologist,* 1979, *34,* 973–980.

Maccoby, E. Television: Its impact on school children. *Public Opinion Quarterly,* 1951, *15,* 423–444.

Masters, W., & Johnson, V. *Human sexual response.* Boston: Little, Brown, 1966.

Orlansky, H. Infant care and personality. *Psychological Bulletin,* 1949, *46,* 1–48.

Ofsofsky, J. D., & Danger, B. Relationships between neonatal characteristics and mother–infant interaction. *Developmental Psychology,* 1974, *10,* 124.

Parke, R. Children's home environments: Social and cognitive effects. In I. Altman & J. Wohlwill (Eds.), *Children and the environment* (Vol. 3), New York: Plenum, 1978.

Parke, R., & Collmer, C. Child abuse: An interdisciplinary review. In E. M. Hetherington (Ed.), *Review of child development research* (Vol. 5). Chicago: University of Chicago Press, 1975.

Parke, R., Hymel, S., Power, T., & Tinsley, B. Fathers and risk: A hospital-based model of intervention. In D. Sawn, R. Harkins, L. Walker, & J. Penticuff (Eds.), *Psychosocial risks in infant–environment transactions,* 1979.

Pedersen, F. Mother, father, and infant as an interactive system. Paper presented at the annual convention of the American Psychological Association, Chicago, 1975.

Pedersen, F., Rubenstein, J., & Yarrow, L. Infant development in father-absent families. *Journal of Genetic Psychology,* 1979, *35,* 51–61.

Piaget, J. *The construction of reality in the child.* New York: Basic Books, 1954.

Piaget, J. *The origins of intelligence in children.* New York: International Universities Press, 1952.

Pollitt, E. Behavior of infant in causation of nutritional marasmus. *The American Journal of Clinical Nutrition,* 1973, *26,* 264–270.

Powell, D. The interpersonal relationship between parents and care givers in day-care settings. *American Journal of Orthopsychiatry,* 1978, *48,* 680–689.

Price, G. *Factors influencing reciprocity in early mother–infant interaction.* Paper presented at the biennial meeting of the Society for Research in Child Development, New Orleans, March, 1977.

Riegel, K. Toward a dialectical theory of development. *Human Development,* 1975, *18,* 50–64.

Rossi, A. A biosocial perspective on parenting. In A. Rossi, J. Kagan & T. Harevan (Eds.), *The family.* New York: Norton, 1978.

Rovee-Collier, C., & Gekoski, M. The economics of infancy: A review of conjugate reinforcement. In H. Reese & L. Lipsitt (Eds.), *Advances in child development and behavior* (Vol. 13), New York: Academic Press, 1979.

Rubenstein, J., Howes, C., & Boyle, P. *A two year follow-up of infants in community based day care.* Paper presented at the biennial meeting of the Society for Research in Child Development, San Francisco, March, 1979.

Russell, C. Transition to parenthood: Problems and gratifications. *Journal of Marriage and the Family,* 1974, *36,* 294–301.

Rutter, M. Maternal deprivation, 1972–1978: New findings, new concepts, and new approaches. *Child Development,* 1979, *50,* 283–305.

Sameroff, A. *Theoretical and empirical issues in the operationalization of transactional research.* Paper presented at the biennial meeting of the Society for Research in Child Development, San Francisco, March, 1979.

Sameroff, A. Transactional models of early social relations. *Human Development,* 1975, *18,* 65–79.

Smith, P., & Dutton, S. Play and training in direct and innovative problem solving. *Child Development,* 1979, *50,* 830–836.

Spelke, E., Zelazo, P., Kagan, J., & Kotelchuck, M. Father interaction and separation protest. *Developmental Psychology,* 1973, *9,* 83–90.

Spinetta, J., & Rigler, D. The child-abusing parent. A psychological review. *Psychological Bulletin,* 1972, *77,* 296.

Sroufe, L. The coherence of individual development. *American Psychologist,* 1979, *34,* 834–841.

Steers, R., & Rhodes, S. Major influences on employer attendance: A process model. *Journal of Applied Psychology,* 1978, *63,* 391–407.

Stein, A., & Freidrich, L. Impact of television on children and youth. In E. Hetherington

(Ed.), *Review of child development research* (Vol. 5). Chicago: University of Chicago Press, 1975.

Steinberg, L., & Greenberger, E. *The part-time employment of high school students: An ecological perspective on research and policy.* Manuscript submitted for publication, November, 1979. (Available from authors, Program in Social Ecology, University of Irvine, Irvine, Cal. 92717.)

Steinberg, L., & Green, C. *How parents may mediate the effects of day care.* Paper presented at the biennial meeting of the Society for Research in Child Development, San Francisco, March, 1979.

Steiner, G. *The people look at television.* New York: Knopf, 1963.

Stern, D. N. Mother and infant at play: The dyadic interaction involving facial, vocal, and gaze behavior. In M. Lewis & L. Rosenblum (Eds.), *The effect of the infant on its care giver.* New York: Wiley, 1974.

Stone, L., Smith, H., & Murphy, B. (Eds.), *The competent infant: Research and commentary.* New York: Basic Books, 1973.

Thomas, E. How a rejecting baby affects mother–infant synchrony. In Ciba Foundation (Ed.), *Parent–infant interaction.* New York: Associated Scientific Publishers, 1975.

Thomas, A., & Chess, S. *Temperament and development.* New York: Brunner/Mazel, 1977.

Thomas, A., Chess, S., & Birch, H. The origins of personality. *Scientific American,* 1970, *223,* 102–109.

Tolan, W. *Infant temperament and exploration.* Unpublished doctoral dissertation, Cornell University, 1979.

Vaughn, B., Waters, E., Egeland, B., & Sroufe, L. *Individual differences in infant–mother attachment at 12 and 18 months: Stability and change in families under stress.* Unpublished manuscript, University of Minnesota, 1979.

Waters, F. The reliability and stability of individual differences in infant–mother attachment. *Child Development,* 1978, *49,* 489–494.

White, B. Motivation reconsidered: The concept of competence. *Psychological Review,* 1959, *66,* 297–333.

Wohlwill, J. Stability and change in cognitive development. In O. Brim & J. Kagan (Eds.), *Constancy and change in human development.* Cambridge, Mass.: Harvard University Press, 1979.

Wolf, P. H. The natural history of crying and other vocalizations in early infancy. In B. M. Foss (Ed.), *Determinants of infant behavior II.* London: Methuen, 1969.

Wolfenstein, M. Fun morality: An analysis of recent American child-rearing literature. *Journal of Social Issues,* 1951, *7,* 15–25.

Yarrow, L. Maternal deprivation: Toward an empirical and conceptual reevaluation. *Psychological Bulletin,* 1961, *58,* 459–490.

Yarrow, L. Rubenstein, J., & Pedersen, F. *Infant and environment.* New York: Wiley, 1975.

Young, M., & Kopp, C. *Handicapped children and their families: Research directions.* Unpublished manuscript, University of California at Los Angeles, 1979.

LYNN S. LIBEN   **5**

Individuals' Contributions to Their Own Development during Childhood: A Piagetian Perspective

The substantive problem of how individuals contribute to their own development during childhood is approached here from the perspective of Piagetian theory. The utility of this perspective is discussed in the first section of the chapter, with emphasis on how the constructivistic nature of Piagetian theory makes it particularly appropriate for the substantive topic of the volume. The next section of this chapter contains a review of the major state and process components of development proposed by Piaget, with a focus on how individuals contribute to and influence each of these components. Particular attention is given to the ways in which Piaget's views of maturational and experiential influences on development differ radically from traditional nativist and empiricist views. To illustrate individuals' contributions to their own development, the next section contains a review of selected empirical data drawn from the literature on childhood. The concluding section of this chapter contains a brief discussion of the fundamental compatibility of proposing that individuals contribute to their own development and simultaneously holding that individuals are affected by, and themselves are affecting, the cultural context in which they develop.

117

Individuals as Producers of Their Development

Why Piaget?

Two qualities of Piagetian theory make it particularly appropriate for examining individuals' contributions to their own development during childhood. First, Piagetian theory posits qualitative, structural change in individuals as they develop from infancy, to childhood, to adulthood, and is therefore well-suited for the age-segmented organization of this section of the volume. Second, Piagetian theory is highly constructivistic. As a consequence, there is a match between the substantive focus of this volume—how individuals contribute to their own development—and constructivism, which holds that development can be understood only as the outcome of individuals' own active constructions.

The constructive nature of Piagetian theory is most easily presented by first describing the two epistemological positions that contrast most sharply to it. Although there have been many variations in how these alternative positions have been formulated, their essence can be characterized fairly simply. One view is that there is a reality that exists external to the individual, and that the individual's developmental task is to come to know that external reality by producing some sort of internal copy of it. Befitting the mechanistic world view within which this positivist position is found (see Overton & Reese, 1973), this conceptualization posits an essentially passive individual. That is, although the individual is physically active in the acquisition of knowledge (for example, to learn about the visually observable qualities of an object, an individual would need to turn his or her head toward the object, the lens of the eye must be accommodated and so on), the individual plays no part in determining the *structure* or *form* of what is known. There might be differences in the completeness of one's internal representation, but the content and form of that internal representation are determined by the content and form of the external reality.

At the other extreme is the position that the structure and development of knowledge are determined by the biological makeup of the individual. The individual comes equipped with knowledge or with the predisposition to structure knowledge in certain ways (as in the a priori categories of Kant) and the individual's developmental task is to play out a biologically provided script. Insofar as the plan of development is contained in the individual, the individual might seem to play an active role in development. But this activity is trivial, because, in essence, the individual is now simply the servant of biology rather than the servant of the environment. Again, the individual does not determine the structure of his or her knowledge.

In neither of the two cases just described is the individual seen as having a fundamental impact on the structure of knowledge. In contrast, the constructivistic theory offered by Piaget does assert that individuals are responsible for the form of their knowledge. This is not to deny biological and experiential influences on development (see the following section), but it is to assert that knowledge arises neither directly from objects nor directly from the individual, but rather from interactions between them. Knowledge is not simply a functional copy of the external world, but instead, is *"richer* than what the objects can provide for themselves [Piaget, 1970, p. 714]." The thrust of Piaget's work has been to describe how individuals progress in constructing, or, more precisely, in "inventing" knowledge through these interactions.

> objective knowledge is not acquired by a mere recording of external information but has its origin in interactions between the subject and objects . . . It follows that objective knowledge is always subordinate to certain structures of action. But those structures are the result of a *construction* and are not given in the objects, since they are dependent on action, nor in the subject, since the subject must learn how to coordinate his actions [Piaget, 1970, p. 704].

As illustrated in this quotation, Piaget holds that interactions between subject and object are at the core of the development of knowledge. Nevertheless, Piagetian theory has been criticized for failing to give the environment its due. Riegel (1973), for example, states that "For Piaget, the individual, through his own activities, creates his conceptual world. But the activities of and within the environment are disregarded [p. 367]." Riegel prefers to substitute a dialectic approach that is concerned with developmental changes in individuals, with historical changes in society, and with their necessary interdependence. From this perspective, there is need to consider simultaneous movements along inner–biological, individual–psychological, cultural–sociological, and outer–physical dimensions (Riegel, 1976; Riegel & Meacham, 1976). Similarly, Lerner (1979) has suggested that, at most, Piaget is a "moderate" interactionist, arguing that although Piaget emphasizes that development "arises from an interaction between organismic and environmental processes, it is only the organism that is seen as going through changes [p. 145]." However, one would be hard pressed to find a more dialectic, interactive statement than the following:

> The subject S and the objects O are therefore indissociable, and it is from this indissociable interaction $S \leftrightarrows O$ that action, the source of knowledge, originates. The point of departure of this knowledge, therefore, is neither S nor O but the interaction proper to the action itself. It is from this dialectic interaction $\leftrightarrows$ that the object is bit by bit discovered in its objective properties by a "decentration" which frees knowledge of its subjective illusions. It is from this same interaction that the subject, by discovering and conquering the object, organizes his actions into a coherent system that constitutes the operations of his intelligence and his thought [Piaget, 1977b, p. 31].

The apparent discrepancies between these interpretations may be reconciled by recognizing that they emphasize two somewhat different concerns. In each, there is an interest in the individual (a "personological" focus, see Baltes, Cornelius, & Nesselroade, 1977; Lerner & Ryff, 1978). But beyond this, Riegel and Lerner are interested in the *environment as environment*. This focus is evidenced in their preference for interdisciplinary study of development, including sociological, biological, and historical perspectives, in addition to psychological analyses (see Baltes & Brim, 1979; Lerner & Spanier, 1978).

In contrast, when examining ontogenetic development, Piaget is interested in the *environment as known*, or *as used*. For Piaget, the way the environment functions for a particular individual (or even *if* it functions at all) is dependent upon what schemes or structures the individual has or uses to assimilate that environment. Thus, a particular "veridical" stimulus (if, indeed, we could ever determine what that stimulus is, see Piaget, 1977b; von Glasersfeld, 1979) may be understood (assimilated) in many different ways. A rattle, for example, might be understood (assimilated) simply as something to be sucked. In this case, neither the rattle's shakability nor its noisiness would constitute a part of the child's environment. Or, a crowd of people might be understood only as an undifferentiated collection of individuals, or instead be understood as subgroups of men, women, boys, and girls. These subgroups, in turn, might be understood as isolated classes, or conceptually cross-classified with respect to age and sex. This latter example is particularly useful for illustrating the difference between an interest in how individuals affect the environment as environment, versus how they affect the environment as known: An individual's application of multiple classification schemes to a group of people does little to alter the group of people themselves (environment as environment), but it significantly affects (transforms) the environment as known.

To suggest that Piaget focuses on the environment as known is *not* to attribute a solipsistic position to Piaget. Piaget would not deny that rattles can be shaken or can make sound. Nor would he suggest that these properties are unimportant for the individual. But, it is only when the individual uses this environmental aliment that these qualities have an impact upon the individual. For example, accidentally knocking the rattle against the side of the crib might lead an infant to attempt to reproduce the interesting sound, thereby leading to the expansion of banging schemes, a better understanding of causality, and so on.

Furthermore, to assert that Piaget focuses on the environment as known in his theory of ontogenetic development does *not* imply that Piaget ignores the importance of environmental variation. Piaget's interest in the environment is readily apparent in the fact that the concept of adaptation is such a central one for the theory. Different environments make possible different adaptations, at both biological and intellectual levels. That there is a reciprocal influence of individuals and environments is also apparent in Piaget's work. This is particularly evident in his writings on evolution, in which he argues that, collectively, individuals' behaviors ultimately alter their environment and even their own biological makeup (also see Brent, 1978; in particular, see Piaget, 1971b, 1978).

In general, however, Piagetians assert that human environments— across cultures if not across millennia—do provide the appropriate aliment for individuals to construct certain intellectual structures. There are undoubtedly differences among environments with respect to their facilitation of structural development and the determination of content areas for specialization (Dasen, 1972, 1977; Fein, Chapter 10, this volume; Feldman, 1980; Forman & Kuschner, 1978; Gallagher & Easley, 1978; Kamii & DeVries, 1978; Murray, 1979; Piaget, 1972; Sigel, 1979). More controversial, however, is whether profound differences in social environments—as in the contrast between industrialized and nonindustrialized societies—might affect even the most fundamental characteristics of cognition—as in the development of abstract formalism (see Buck-Morss, 1975; Mangan, 1978). Regardless of the role one ultimately attributes to environmental influences, however, it is clear that Piagetian theory is focused on the processes individuals use in the construction of their own knowledge, and in the cognitive structures that result from the functioning of these processes. The next section of this chapter is focused on these processes and structures in more detail.

Piagetian Theory:
Structure and Developmental Process

In the preceding discussion, two qualities of Piagetian theory—its emphasis on qualitative change across portions of the life span and its constructivistic nature—were linked, respectively, to the age-graded organization and the substantive focus of this book. These two aspects of Piagetian theory may also be linked to a distinction drawn in developmental psychology more generally, between (a) describing the individual at any given point in the life span; and (b) explaining how the individual arrived at (and progresses beyond) that particular point. This distinction has been referred to as the distinction between the "states" and "rules of transition" of development (Kessen, 1962).

There are, of course, fundamental disagreements across world views with respect to both "state" and "process." For example, with respect to the former, there are major differences concerning whether or not one infers underlying, unobservable, holistic structures at different points in development; with respect to the latter, there are major differences concerning the types of cause of development (material, efficient, formal, final) that are sought (see Overton & Reese, 1973, for a thorough discussion of distinctions between organismic and mechanistic world views with respect to these issues). But, despite these controversies, virtually every developmentalist recognizes the importance of both components.

This section of the chapter contains, first, brief comments about the state components of Piagetian theory, and second, detailed discussions of the process components of Piagetian theory. Some of the process factors identified by Piaget have also been invoked by other theorists in their explanations of development, and thus, particular attention is given to ways in which Piaget's interpretations of these factors are fundamentally different from the interpretations of theorists rooted in different world views.

STATE

For Piaget, the "state" task consists of describing the structures of the various stages of development, represented through formal logic. An extensive, meaningful description of these structures cannot be accomplished within a single chapter, and, furthermore, would be redundant with the many excellent reviews that already exist. Thus, other than pointing out that the portion of the life span commonly referred to as "childhood" includes the preoperational and concrete operational periods (approximately the years 2–7 and 7–12, respectively), and discussing particular aspects of these stages in the discussions of illustrative empirical data of the next section, no attempt will be made to discuss characteristics of these periods in general. The reader who is not already familiar with the structures of these stages is referred to existing reviews (e.g., see Brainerd, 1978a; Flavell, 1963; Furth, 1969; Ginsburg & Opper, 1979; Piaget, 1970; Piaget & Inhelder, 1969; Tuddenham, 1966).

PROCESS

The "process" aspect of Piagetian theory is the central focus of this section of the chapter, again, with particular attention to the ways in which individuals affect these processes.

Piaget (1964, 1970; Piaget & Inhelder, 1969) has identified four factors that are responsible for developmental progress; (a) maturation; (b) experience with objects; (c) social experience; and (d) equilibration. On first reading, the first three of these factors seem to correspond to those found in other developmental theories. The first factor is reminiscent of physical growth and development emphasized in maturational theories such as Gesell's. The next two factors suggest experiential influences like those linked with associationistic explanations of development. Only the fourth of the factors—equilibration—is clearly distinguished from traditional maturational and associationist explanations of development, and is thus easily recognized as a new contribution.[1]

Despite the seemingly obvious equation of maturation with biological explanations of development, and of experience (physical and social) with environmental explanations of development, the correspondence is not that simple. In part, this is because Piaget uses these terms in special ways, and, in part, it is because the fourth factor, equilibration, is not simply tacked onto the others as yet another cause, but rather, serves to regulate the other factors, that is, "to coordinate them in a consistent, noncontradictory totality [Piaget, 1970, p. 722]." Thus, the ways in which biological and experiential factors operate to yield developmental progress are profoundly modified or transformed through the equilibration process. Again, this reflects the underlying constructivistic nature of Piagetian theory: Nothing of importance simply "happens" to the individual, either through biological or through environmental forces. A major purpose of this section of the chapter is to show how these maturational and experiential factors cannot be equated with classic nativistic and empiricistic views.

Piaget typically discusses the four factors in the order listed earlier, but this order does not reflect the hypothesized order of importance. Instead, Piaget (1977a) sees equilibration as the most central of the processes: "No one of the three [factors] is sufficient in itself. Each one of them implies a fundamental factor of equilibration, upon which I shall place special emphasis [p. 3]." In view of the priority of equilibration, it is the first of the four factors to be discussed. Without an understanding of the equilibration process, it is not possible to appreciate the constructivistic nature of the other seemingly more traditional biological and experiential factors (and hence, of course, of the individual's contribution to each).

Equilibration

The concept of equilibration has sometimes led to considerable confusion because Piaget uses the term "equilibrium" in reference to state as well as in reference to process. As Piaget (1977b) has stated, "For me, it [equilibration] refers above all to a process. But, in some cases, there can be states that are in equilibrium [p. 19]." The structures that evolve as products of the equilibration process may be equilibrated states, but it is

---

[1] It should be noted that Piaget (1967) recognizes that he has not created the concept of equilibrium for psychological theories, explicitly noting the use of the concept by Janet, Freud, Claparède, and Lewin. Meacham (personal communication) has suggested, however, that Piaget's concept of equilibrium may be substantially different from that of other theorists with respect to the role of activity. For Piaget, activity not only brings about higher levels of equilibrium but, in addition, is essential for *maintaining* equilibrated states. For other theorists (e.g., Freud), equilibrium suggests a state of rest, achieved when activity (or tension or conflict) *ceases.*

the process of "a further search for better equilibria [p. 19]" which is the fundamental *developmental* process.[2] Although it has sometimes been suggested that it is the structural component of Piagetian stage theory that is offered as an explanation of development in Piagetian theory (Brainerd, 1978a, 1979), it is actually the *process* of equilibration that serves this function. More complete discussions of the relationship between the process and state aspects of equilibrium are found in Furth (1977), Gallagher (1977), Piaget (1967, esp. Chapters 4 and 6; 1970; 1977c), and Mischel (1971).

In view of the centrality of the equilibration process, it is not surprising that virtually every one of Piaget's works contains at least some description of this process. One of the most complete and concise definitions is found in the summary work written by Piaget and Inhelder (1969), *The Psychology of the Child:*

> An internal mechanism . . . is observable at the time of each partial construction and each transition from one stage to the next. It is a process of equilibrium . . . in the sense . . . of self regulation; that is, a series of active compensations on the part of the subject in response to external disturbances and an adjustment that is both retroactive (loop systems or feedbacks) and anticipatory, constituting a permanent system of compensations [p. 157].

There are several important components and implications of this description of the equilibration process. First, the equilibration process is an internal, self-regulating one. The impetus for this process is ultimately attributable to the invariant function of adaptation, a goal of all living organisms, which implies a strong biological component. Indeed, as Piaget (1977c) has noted, biology plays a more straightforward role in the equilibration process than in maturation, which, ironically, is the one of the four factors typically cited by those who argue that Piaget's position is essentially a nativistic one (e.g., Beilin, 1971a; Brainerd, 1978c; Stevenson, 1962). "It seems to me that this notion of self-regulation, which consequently is one of equilibration, is much more fundamental and much more general than the more narrow notion of variable hereditary programming. It is, then, self-regulation that is the important idea for us to take from biology [Piaget, 1977c, p. 9]." Although the general motivation to achieve balance may be biological in origin, the source of imbalance and the actual activities used to compensate for that imbalance are, again, attributable to the constructions of the individual rather than to biological inheritance. Furthermore, this biological inheritance is itself, in part, the product of individuals' behaviors (see Piaget, *Behavior and Evolution*, 1978, for a full discussion of these issues).

___

[2] Thus, equilibrium as a state is closer to other theorists' concepts of equilibrium (see Footnote 1), whereas equilibration as a process implies its prior converse, disequilibrium and is, therefore, closer to the concept of dialectic conflict offered by Riegel (1973).

A second critical aspect of the definition, implied by the reference to "active compensations," is the role of the assimilative and accommodative processes. The point of assimilation (one that will become even more critical in the later discussion of the role of experience in development) is that any behavior "is always grafted onto previous schemes and therefore amounts to assimilating new elements to already constructed structures (innate, as reflexes are, or previously acquired) [Piaget, 1970, p. 707]." Whereas assimilation allows new elements to be integrated into existing schemes, it is accommodation that simultaneously modifies the structures or schemes used in assimilation, thereby resulting in developmental progression.

Third, the processes just described (the motivational drive to regulate or balance the system as accomplished through the assimilation and accommodation processes) function in both microgenetic and ontogenetic development. The former is implied by the reference to "each partial construction" and the latter by the reference to "each transition from one stage to the next."

Fourth, there is a structure that is both developed by and, in turn, used by the regulatory assimilative and accommodative processes. It is apparent, then, that equilibration as a process is linked directly to the equilibrated structures referred to earlier.

Finally, the reference to both "retroactive" and "anticipatory" compensations in the definition given is important in implying that intrusions may be presented in two different ways:

> In the case of the lower, unstable (sensorimotor and perceptual) forms of equilibrium, the intrusion consists of real and actual modifications of the environment, to which the compensatory activities of the subject respond as best they can without a permanent operational system.

> In the case of the higher or operational structures, on the other hand, the intrusion to which the subject responds may consist of virtual modifications; i.e., in optimum cases they can be imagined and anticipated by the subject in the form of the direct operations of a system (operations expressing transformations in some initial sense). In this case, the compensatory activities will also consist of imagining and anticipating the transformations but in an inverse sense (reciprocal or inverse operations of a system of reversible operations) [Piaget, 1967, p. 113].

In a specific illustration of this point, Mischel (1979) notes that the acquisition of conservation concepts takes place via " 'internal factors of coherence . . . the deductive activity of the subject himself (Piaget, 1959: 32).' Equilibration here is a response to *internal* conflict between the subject's conceptual schem[e]s, rather than a response to any disturbance from outside [Mischel, 1979, p. 95]." Thus, individuals themselves, as well as their responses to their external environments, are ultimately responsible for perturbations, and thus, for development.

To return more directly to the focus of this book, it should be readily apparent that the individual plays a critical role in the various aspects of the equilibration process just discussed. First, as noted, the individual is the source of internal disturbances. Second, it is the individual who is using assimilative and accommodative processes to respond to these as well as to external disturbances. Furthermore, because the structure at any given point is an outcome of prior adjustments, the existing schemes to which stimuli are assimilated in the first place are consequences of the individual's activity. Indeed, virtually everything but the external events themselves may be understood as individually motivated. And, even the "external" events are functionally determined by the individual, because, as noted earlier, nothing acts as a stimulus in the first place unless the appropriate schemes exist for its assimilation. Thus, it is readily apparent that individuals contribute to their own development through the process of equilibration.

Maturation

Piaget's view of maturation as a factor in development can be understood only in contrast to traditional maturational theories of development. In their purest forms, maturational theories of development hold that the biological material of the individual contains "a developmental program (blueprint) [that] consists of a set of instructions (preformed guidelines) determining the developmental process [Kitchener, 1978, p. 152]." That is, the *form* of developmental outcome is predetermined in the genetic material of the individual. This is not, of course, to assert that the environment is totally irrelevant. The environment must provide the supportive conditions for the expression of the genetically given program. The individual's final height, for example, is determined not only by the boundaries established by inheritance, but also by a variety of environmental influences such as nutrition, exposure to disease, and so on.

Strong forms of maturational theories—theories in which it is proposed that ultimate forms of developmental outcomes are biologically determined—have been proposed not only for physical development (e.g., Hamburger, 1957), but for psychological and behavioral development as well. The classic proponent of this position is Gesell (1943): "How does the mind grow? It grows *like* the nervous system; it grows *with* the nervous system. Growth is a patterning process. It produces patterned changes in the nerve cells; it produces corresponding changes in patterns of behavior [p. 18]." As in maturational theories of physical development, maturational theories of behavioral development do not ignore the importance of the environment, but again, the role of the environment is to provide the conditions (e.g., social interaction, exposure to a particular language) that are necessary to permit the expression of the biologically given program. (This discussion is necessarily abbreviated. The reader is referred to Kitchener, 1978 and Lerner, 1979, 1980, for more extended discussions of these issues).

Although Piaget, too, lists maturation as one of the factors responsible for development, there are important distinctions between the view of maturation presented earlier and the view of maturation held by Piaget. For Gesell, maturation per se is responsible for important psychological development; for Piaget, maturation affects psychological development indirectly by opening up new possibilities for an individual to interact with the environment, and thus, in turn, to extend assimilatory schemes: "Maturation simply indicates whether or not the construction of a specific structure is possible at a specific stage. It does not itself contain a pre-formed structure, but simply opens up possibilities [Piaget, 1971a, p. 193]." In a sense, then, there is a parallel in the way that environmental and biological factors operate. Each provides the material for the construction of knowledge. As noted in the earlier discussion of the constructive nature of Piagetian theory, the environment provides the aliment for the exercise and expansion of schemes. Thus, for example, there are things in the environment that can be sucked, looked at, pulled, dropped, and so on, thereby giving the individual the opportunity to apply (and modify) existing schemes to these materials of the environment. Similarly, the biological equipment (which itself changes as a consequence of maturational processes) provides the aliment for the development of schemes. The development and refinement of schemes for sucking, looking, dropping, and so on can take place only because physical prerequisites such as sucking reflexes, lens accommodation, and muscle development, are met.

It should be clear, then, that Piaget's position, which *does* assert that physical structures and their development serve an important role in the development of psychological structures, does *not* assert that the psychological structures *themselves* develop through maturational processes.

Piaget's claims notwithstanding, Piagetian theory has often been taken as a maturational theory (e.g., Beilin, 1971a; Brainerd, 1978c; Stevenson, 1962). The evidence typically cited in support of this interpretation is that the developmental stages postulated in Piagetian theory occur in an invariant order of succession. Only species-specific preprogramming, it is argued, could explain why all individuals would follow the same path to the same conclusion (barring premature termination of the sequence). One of the clearest expositions of this position may be found in a statement by Beilin (1971a):

> Piaget's primary criterion for the theory of stages, the invariant order of structural achievements, to which Piaget accepts no qualification, suggests, in fact almost requires, an explanation defined in terms of genetic control. When the effects of experience are accepted only in the rate of structure acquisition, it is difficult to see why Piaget would explain structural achievement other than by genetically controlled mechanisms [p. 178].

There are, however, at least two other viable interpretations of these invariances. First, it is possible that *environments* are fundamentally identical across the human experience. Although our awareness of differences across cultures and historical periods may immediately lead us to dismiss this interpretation, it is quite reasonable to suggest that the seemingly large differences across cultures and historical periods are actually rather trivial. It is only in radically different environments (e.g., one without permanent objects, see Wartofsky, in press) that one might expect different outcomes. With this interpretation, however, one runs the risk of taking Piaget out of the pan of the maturationists and into the fire of the empiricists. That is, the reasoning given here might lead one to conclude that the developmental similarity across individuals is attributable to similarity across environments, and thus to return to a copy theory of knowledge. Indeed, as Piaget has noted in an amused—if frustrated—manner, he has been subjected to both misclassifications: "My friend, Daniel Berlyne, wrote an article maintaining that I was a neobehaviorist, and today Beilin has read a paper showing that I am a maturationist. In fact, I am neither one nor the other. I refuse to admit the necessity of a choice between these alternatives [Piaget, 1971a, p. 192]."

The second nonmaturational interpretation of the invariant sequence is Piaget's. Again, it is an interpretation that is constructive in nature: "Let us simply recall that while the coordinations of the nervous system determine the framework of possibilities and impossibilities within which the logical structures will be constructed, these logical structures do not exist within the nervous system as embryonic instruments of thought. An entire construction is necessary in order to lead from the nervous system to logic, so logic cannot be considered innate [Piaget, 1967, p. 127]."

Given that individual members of the species come equipped with certain reflexes and the self-regulatory equilibration mechanism, and given that they have available the aliment provided in the normal human environment, early sensorimotor structures will be constructed. These sensorimotor structures are, however, inadequate so that, by their very functioning, they are led to higher-level structures. In essence, the exercise of a given structure, in view of its imperfectly equilibrated state (until the level of formal operations), contains within it the seeds of its own development. The succession of structures, and the tasks used to tap them, are not, then, arbitrary measurement sequences (as suggested by Brainerd, 1978c) but, instead, are what could be called "logically necessary sequences [Flavell, 1971]."

Thus, from Piaget's perspective, the invariance of structural development arises neither as a direct consequence of a genetic blueprint, nor as a direct consequence of exposure to particular sequences in the environment, but rather as the consequence of individuals' constructions, which make use of biological and environmental aliments.

Experience with Physical Objects

Piaget identifies two types of knowledge gained through the child's interactions with objects in the world that act as an impetus for developmental progress. The first focuses on knowledge derived from the objects themselves, while the second focuses on knowledge derived from actions *on* objects. The first type of knowledge is referred to as "physical knowledge." It is derived through the process of simple or *empirical abstraction*, in which children learn about the properties of objects by manipulating them. For example, by handling balls and cubes, the child learns that balls roll and cubes stack; by handling bricks and feathers, the child learns that bricks are heavy and feathers are light. In this case, the child constructs knowledge about objects in the physical world through interacting with these objects.

The second type of knowledge is referred to as "logicomathematical knowledge," and is derived through the process of *reflective abstraction*. This process permits the formulation of new realities through "reflections," in both the physical and mental senses of the word.

> First, in the physical sense, the results of abstractions carried out on an inferior level are reflected (like a ray reflected by a mirror) onto a superior one. Consequently, it is necessary to reconstruct on this superior plane that which existed on the inferior one. And here lies the importance of the second sense (mental) of "reflexion": in order to reconstruct this structure on the superior level, richer and new constructions have to be made, since it is not just a question of translating the inferior into the superior, but of simultaneously adding the operations which make possible the passage from the inferior to the superior level [Piaget, 1971a, p. 193].[3]

The classic example used by Piaget to illustrate logicomathematical knowledge is that of a mathematician friend who reports that, as a child, he discovered that regardless of the arrangement of and order in which he counted a group of pebbles, the sum remained constant. Unlike knowledge of the pebbles' weight or hardness (derived from empirical abstraction), neither sum nor order is a property of the pebbles but rather, each

---

[3] There has been considerable confusion in the terminology related to reflective abstraction. The broadest term is "reflective abstraction" which concerns knowledge derived from the subject's own actions, thus contrasting with empirical abstraction. There are three types of reflective abstraction. "Reflecting abstraction" (*abstraction réfléchissement*) is a mirror-like projection. "Reflection," also called "reflexion" (*réflexion*), concerns reorganization on the new plane, rather than an isomorphic projection. "Reflected abstraction" (*abstraction réfléchie*) concerns yet higher-order combinations, and is also known as "reflected thought" and "retrospective thematization" (see Piaget, 1980, pp. 26–27). Thus, reflecting abstraction refers to shifting elements to a higher plane, reflexion refers to reorganizing elements on that higher plane; and reflected abstractions refers to thought about those reorganizations. It should be evident that the word "reflected" found in the quotation from Piaget (1971a) cited in the text is used as a verb, and concerns reflecting rather than reflected abstraction.

is derived through reflective abstraction. Admittedly, certain characteristics of pebbles are particularly conducive to the activity of counting
(grains of sand, for example, would not serve this counting activity as
readily), but the knowledge gained is not about pebbles, but about the
operations themselves, such as associativity.

It should be immediately apparent that the second of these types of
knowledge—logicomathematical—is highly constructive in its origin, as
it would not exist in any sense without the individual's own activities and
reflections on these activities. Less apparent, perhaps, but equally true,
is that physical knowledge is also inseparable from the individual's own
constructions. As noted earlier in this chapter, whether or not objects in
the environment function as stimuli in the first place depends upon the
individual's cognitive structure. Furthermore, the ability to recognize specific qualities of objects rests upon the appropriate schemes. For example,
without classification schemes, a child would be unable to classify some
objects as heavy and others as light, and thus would not be in a position
to recognize the heaviness of bricks and the lightness of feathers. Or,
without seriation schemes, the child could not appreciate the increments
in size associated with a growing plant. Thus, even the seemingly straightforward empirical knowledge about objects *qua* objects is dependent upon
the individual's capacity to construct that knowledge. (An excellent discussion of the inseparability of physical and logicomathematical knowledge is found in Piaget, 1977b, Section 2). Again, the Piagetian position
is distinguished from a classic empiricistic position. The individual's
knowledge is always mediated by the individual's cognitive structures.
Empirical examples of this mediation are discussed at length in a later
section of the present chapter.

Social Experience

The fourth factor identified by Piaget as a cause of developmental progression is much like the third factor just discussed, except that the focus
is on what the child constructs from interactions with the social, rather
than with the physical world. Included within the realm of social experience are exposure to a particular language, the opportunity to play and
work with others, socialization to a particular set of mores and values,
and so on.

Most of what has been said about the role of experience with the physical
environment is also applicable to the role of social experience. Indeed,
one could divide the social experience factor into two components that
parallel the physical and logicomathematical knowledge just discussed.

Analogous to physical knowledge is knowledge gained directly from
the social environment. Included, for example, would be the acquisition
of vocabulary; learning the dress appropriate for males and females; learning social rites such as shaking hands, and so on. Direct social knowledge

of this kind is acquired both through observation and through direct instruction (as, for example, the formal educational setting of the school). The qualities are found in people and social institutions rather than in inanimate objects, but there is still an exogenous source of data as there was in physical knowledge.

The second type of socially derived knowledge is derived from the individual's reflected constructions, and is therefore like the logicomathematical knowledge derived from interaction with physical objects. (In fact, this might instead be classifed as logicomathematical knowledge, except with social rather than with physical content.) For example, by interacting with others and discovering that not everyone shares identical viewpoints, the young child may be helped to decenter and overcome the egocentric perspective of the preoperational period. Similarly, social interaction is important for recognizing that rules—be they for a game of marbles or for a business transaction—are arbitrary, changeable agreements, rather than immutable laws handed down by a deity (see Piaget, 1965). Thus, although knowledge of particular rules of marbles is achieved through social empirical abstraction, knowledge of abstract concepts of rules such as their origins, arbitrariness, and reciprocity is constructed through reflective abstraction.

The individual's cognitive structure affects what can be observed or assimilated of the social world, just as it affects what can be taken from the physical world. One cannot, for example, learn what dress or behavior is appropriate for boys versus girls if one lacks the ability to classify individuals as male or female. Even when the transmission of knowledge appears to be direct as in traditional classroom instruction, the child must possess the necessary structures to assimilate the information. The recognition that children cannot absorb information without the appropriate schemes is, of course, one of the classic tenets of Piagetian approaches to education referenced earlier. "There can be no effect of social or linguistic experience unless the child is ready to assimilate and integrate this experience into his own structures [Piaget, 1977a, p. 9]."

Furthermore, the child's cognitive level has a major impact on the types of social interactions that are possible, and thus, in turn, on the knowledge that can be extracted from social exchanges. In observing children's language, for example, Piaget notes that very young children do not actually communicate with one another, but rather talk aloud in "collective monologues [Piaget, 1926]." Only later in development can children take their listeners' perspectives into account and modify their communications appropriately. Similar observations have been made about the changes from solitary play, to parallel play, to cooperative play (Parten, 1932). Thus, the way in which individuals are able to interact with others in social contexts is highly dependent upon cognitive structures, and this in turn affects what can be gained from the social encounter. There is, then, a strong interdependence between the development of logical structures and social interactions. It must be recognized, of course, that having cognitive structures that enable individuals to act and interact in particular ways does not imply that behaviors will uniformly reflect these structures. Similarly, two seemingly identical behaviors may be motivated by qualitatively different structures (see Turiel, 1969). What is important here is simply the recognition that individuals are responsible for how the social environment is actually used, and thus that the individual contributes to this fourth factor of development just as to the previous three.

CONCLUSIONS

It should be evident from the previous discussions that individuals play a critical role in their own development. Not one of the four factors discussed may be understood as influencing development in isolation from the individual. Constructivism pervades every aspect of Piagetian theory, even affecting the way that classic developmental factors such as physical maturation and environmental experience are understood. Furthermore, because the structure of the individual at any given point in time must be understood as the product of these developmental processes, both state and process are ultimately attributable to the individual. In the next section of the chapter, empirical data are presented to illustrate the impact of the individual in the acquisition, storage, and utilization of knowledge and in the further development of structure.

Empirical Illustrations

The preceding section of this chapter concerned the processes that Piaget has identified as leading to developmental progress, and of the ways in which individuals contribute to each of these processes. In this section, selected empirical research is reviewed to illustrate these contributions more concretely.

To organize the discussion of relevant empirical data, empirical work is grouped into two major categories. The first is concerned with how an individual's cognitive structure affects the knowledge constructed by that individual at any given time. Empirical research demonstrates that the knowledge the individual takes (or, more properly, constructs) from any stimulus depends upon what schemes are available to that individual. For example, as discussed in more detail later in this section, a child who has not yet constructed Euclidean spatial concepts has difficulty in perceiving that liquid remains horizontal in a tipped bottle.

The second type of research reviewed is focused on the ways in which the individual's current cognitive structure influences further structural development. Empirical research in this category is concerned with demonstrating that the "same" experiences effect further development differently as a function of the individual's initial cognitive structure. The prototype of this type of research (again, discussed more extensively later in this chapter) is training research in which the effects of various experiences are found to differ as a function of the child's initial operative level.

Although the empirical data included have been organized into these two separate sections, it should be apparent from the earlier sections of this chapter that state and process issues can never be divorced from one another, just as Piaget (1964) asserts the fundamental connection between learning and development. Knowledge is influenced by the individual's level of development, and this knowledge, in turn, serves as an aliment for the individual's further structural development.

STRUCTURE AND THE ACQUISITION
AND RETENTION OF KNOWLEDGE

Overview

There are several opportunities for the individual's cognitive schemes to affect the knowledge acquired from interactions with the environment. First, as already discussed, the individual's cognitive schemes influence what aspects of the environment are attended to in the first place. However, even given that one's attention is focused on a particular aspect of the environment, schemes also influence the way in which the particular stimulus is perceived. Once particular information from the environment has been perceived, schemes operate to affect the retention and use of that knowledge. Thus, over time, knowledge may be differentially forgotten, distorted, or used, depending upon the knower's operative structure. A range of work is sampled to illustrate the ways in which these influences occur.

Perception

There are several types of empirical research that may be cited to support the generalization that operative schemes affect the way that stimuli are perceived. One of the most obviously relevant of these is the program of research on perception carried out over the last several decades by Piaget and his colleagues (Piaget, 1969). Space limitations permit only a sample of the Genevan theory and research on perception, a sample that cannot help but oversimplify and therefore distort a very complex area. Nevertheless, a brief discussion can at least illustrate the ways in which operative schemes may influence perception. (For more comprehensive reviews of the Piagetian work on perception, see Elkind, 1969a; Flavell, 1963; Piaget, 1969; and Wohlwill, 1960).

In Piaget's view, basic perceptual acts consist of "encounters" between some aspect of the perceptual system (in actuality, of the visual system, since vision is focused on to the exclusion of other sensory systems) and some aspect of the stimulus. An encounter may be thought of as something like an eye fixation on a line. It is the conglomeration of encounters that determines how the stimulus is perceived. In the case of a line, for example, perceived length is dependent upon the number of encounters, itself determined by (a) time—more encounters occur with more time; and (b) fixation—more encounters occur when the line is centered or fixated than when it is in peripheral vision.

In addition, there are "couplings," which refer to the joining of encounters. For example, encounters with one line are linked to encounters with another line, as might occur, for example, when one is asked to compare the length of two lines. To the extent that every point is coupled with every other point, the viewer will be able to determine the relative length of the two lines accurately; to the extent that the couplings are incomplete, one line will tend to be overestimated. Encounters and couplings may be understood as centration and decentration processes, as described by Flavell (1963). "An encounter is an agent of *centration;* the building up of encounters in the course of centering on a stimulus leads to a perceptual overestimation (distortion) of that stimulus, relative to neighboring, noncentered stimuli. A coupling, on the other hand, is seen as an agent of decentration—a coordination between centrations leading to objectivity [pp. 230–231]."

These two different processes are tied to the more general distinction between (a) "primary perceptions" (also called "field effects") which are perceptions based on single centrations in a fixed field of vision; and (b) "perceptual activity," which refers to the active processes used by the individual to overcome distortions resulting from the more passive primary perception. In general, the importance of perceptual activity relative to primary perception increases with development, as part of the child's generally increasing ability to approach stimuli systematically.

Piaget has studied the development of these perceptual processes by investigating a variety of visual illusions. According to Piaget (1969), illusions may be divided into two categories. Primary illusions result from field effects, and consistent with decreasing importance of primary perception, Piaget reports that these illusions diminish with age. (Pollack, 1969, however, argues that the decreasing power of these illusions is more appropriately attributed to age-related changes in the receptor system, rather than to structural changes in intellectual functioning.)

In contrast, secondary illusions are thought to result from perceptual activity; these show an increase with development. The Müller-Lyer illusion, for example, is a primary illusion, stronger in younger than in older children (see Figure 5.1a). In contrast, the illusory overestimate of the vertical line when viewing horizontal and vertical lines (see Figure 5.1b), is greater in 9–10-year-olds than in 5–6-year-olds. This is hypothesized to occur because older, but not younger children link the two lines together by using a coordinate system that leads to distortions. Further decentration in still later childhood causes the illusion to diminish again, although never to the low level found in the youngest children. Thus, from this perspective, the perception of even simple stimuli such as lines is hypothesized to be tied to individuals' operative levels. Unfortunately, the empirical evidence that links the two is usually indirect insofar as operative level is typically inferred from age rather than being assessed directly.

Perhaps even more interesting from the point of view of demonstrating the effect of general intellectual level on perception are data reported by Piaget (1969, pp. 191–196) concerning the ways in which general intellectual structures can be used to overcome illusory effects. Although the Müller-Lyer illusion decreases with age, it is still rather strong even in older children. When the Müller-Lyer lines are embedded in a square (see Figure 5.1c) however, older subjects are able to overcome the illusion almost completely. Presumably, the square encourages perceptual activities (such as evaluating the four angles as right angles and recognizing that the sides are parallel), activities made possible by the ability to use Cartesian coordinate axes, knowledge of qualities of a square, and so on. Younger children are not able to make use of these activities, and thus continue to show the Müller-Lyer illusion even with the support of the square.

A similar effect is found when the task is to determine the relative length of two straight lines, continuous either horizontally, or at a 135° angle. These judgments were required either with, or without, a circle, as shown in Figure 5.2. To benefit from the circle as an index, it is necessary to appreciate that all radii of a circle are equal. Consistent with expectations derived from Piagetian theory, the circle functioned fully only for the children about 8 years or older. (Detailed results from these studies are reported by Piaget, 1969, pp. 343–345.)

Piaget (1969) reports a large body of empirical data on the consequences of field effects and perceptual activity on a variety of other illusions as well, although the use of illusions to investigate perception has been criticized as ecologically invalid (e.g., see Gibson, 1969). Fortunately, Piagetian studies of perception have not used illusions exclusively. Other

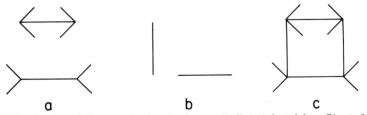

FIGURE 5.1.   *Visual illusions showing developmental effects (adapted from Piaget, 1969).*

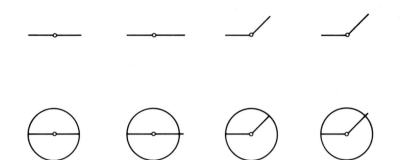

FIGURE 5.2. *Stimuli used for comparing line segments with and without circular index (adapted from Piaget, 1969).*

researchers have used entirely different kinds of stimuli to study the effects of operativity on perception. Elkind (1969a,b), for example, has been interested in the isomorphisms between conceptual and perceptual abilities, in particular, perceptual reorganization, schematization, and exploration in relation to logical structures.

Perceptual reorganization concerns the ability to rearrange a stimulus mentally, and, according to Elkind, is isomorphic with (although not identical to) logical abilities involved in classifying the same objects in different ways. To assess children's abilities in perceptual reorganization, Elkind (1964; Elkind & Scott, 1962) devised a series of ambiguous pictures that could be interpreted in two different ways, such as the duck in the tree illustrated in Figure 5.3a. The ability to detect the hidden figures was found to increase developmentally, consistent with the position that children's increasing abilities to decenter and reclassify affect perception.

The second process studied, perceptual schematization, refers to the ability to recognize the parts and whole of a configuration simultaneously, an ability isomorphic to the logical abilities involved in class inclusion. To assess schematization, Elkind, Koegler, & Go (1964) used drawings in which the whole was composed of identifiable, independent parts, such as a man made out of fruit, as illustrated in Figure 5.3b. Elkind and his colleagues (e.g., Elkind et al., 1964; Whiteside, Elkind, & Golbeck, 1976) have found that there are developmental changes in the way that children describe these drawings, with preschoolers mentioning either the parts or the whole, but not both ("a man" or "apple, banana, grapes"); kindergartners and first graders naming both the whole and the parts, but in a sequential rather than an integrated manner ("man, apple, grapes"), and older children giving integrated responses ("man made of fruit").

The last of the abilities studied by Elkind, perceptual exploration, refers to the systematicity with which children scan visual displays. When asked to name items in an array, young children name them more or less randomly, and hence often miss certain items. In contrast, older children are

a   b

FIGURE 5.3. *Examples from the Picture Ambiguity Test (a) and the Picture Integration Test (b) for measuring perceptual reorganization and perceptual schematization, respectively (from Elkind, 1969a).*

able to use conceptual abilities such as seriation schemes to approach the task, and thus name items systematically, for example, in clockwise order when items are displayed in a circle. This program of research adds to Piaget's own work on illusions in suggesting the importance of underlying operative schemes for the individual's perceptions. With immature perceptual exploration, the child may overlook particular aspects of the stimulus entirely; with immature perceptual schematization, the child may ignore the pieces of an array, its overall structure, or the part–whole relationship; and, with immature perceptual reorganization, the child may see only one aspect of a pictorial display.

A third line of research that may be cited as evidence for the effects of operativity on perception is actually an outgrowth of the Piagetian memory research. The hypothesis underlying the Piagetian memory research is that the viewer's operative level affects the way that pictures or events are recalled. As part of their memory studies, several investigators have also examined the way individuals process stimuli while the stimuli remain in view, thus providing data on perception that are of interest here. Furth, Ross, and Youniss (1974) showed kindergarten, first-, second-, and fourth-grade children a picture of a tipped, half-filled glass and asked them to copy it. The liquid was copied in its correct, horizontal position by 8, 29, 37, and 60% of children in each grade, respectively. Liben (1975) asked children in kindergarten, first, second, and third grade to copy a seriated array of 10 sticks. Perfectly seriated drawings were produced by 38, 69, 79, and 92% of the children in each grade, respectively. Finally, as part of a recent memory study in which children's operative levels were assessed directly rather than being inferred from age, Liben (1978) found that the accuracy with which children were able to copy a stimulus was related to operative level. Of children who had previously demonstrated mature concepts of verticality, 92% were able to copy a picture of a tree on a hill correctly. In contrast, only 63% of children with transitional verticality concepts, and 45% of children with immature verticality concepts were able to copy the vertical position of the tree. The findings from these studies all demonstrate that children have difficulty even in copying—and, by implication, in perceiving—stimuli that are more advanced than their own conceptual levels.

In summary, evidence from a wide range of work suggests that the way in which an individual perceives information from the environment is profoundly influenced by the individual's own cognitive structure. This generalization is based on findings from a diverse range of tasks, including those that assess the perception of the length of lines (as in visual illusions); the ability to attend to stimuli systematically (as in perceptual exploration tasks); the ability to interpret stimuli flexibly (as in perceptual schematization and reorganization tasks); and the ability to perceive pictures accurately (as in copying stimuli related to seriation, horizontality, and verticality concepts).

Memory

The data just reviewed suggest that individuals extract (construct) different information from their interactions with the environment as a function of their own conceptual levels. Intellectual structure continues to influence knowledge beyond intitial encoding, as shown most directly by the research on memory that has been conducted from a Piagetian perspective. Highlights of the Piagetian memory literature are therefore reviewed here. Following this review, illustrations from the more traditional (i.e., non-Piagetian) research on memory development are included to demonstrate that operative levels have a more general influence on memory than might be surmised if one focused exclusively on the highly specialized paradigms and stimuli of "Piagetian" memory research.

As mentioned earlier, the hypothesis underlying the Piagetian research on memory is that individuals' intellectual structures influence their memories for particular stimuli and events. To demonstrate this relationship, Piaget and Inhelder (1973) asked children to recall pictures or events after varying time intervals. Cross-sectional data showed that children of different ages—and, by implication, of different operative levels—reproduce stimuli differently, apparently reflecting differences in their operative levels. Longitudinal data showed that individual children's memories changed in conjunction with operative development.

The example most frequently cited concerns children's memories for an array of seriated sticks. Children ranging in age from 3 to 8 years were shown an array of 10 sticks, arranged in size order from smallest to largest. After a retention interval of about one week, children were asked to reproduce the array from memory. The overall pattern of results was consistent with the operative thesis just outlined. That is, children whose relevant schemes were not yet developed were unable to reproduce the stimulus as shown, whereas children with mature operations were able to reproduce the stimulus accurately. Thus, the 3- and 4-year-old children typically drew sticks of equal size, or reproduced the sticks in random order, 4- and 5-year-olds were able to show only limited patterning such as alternating large and small sticks, whereas 6–8-year-old children were able to reproduce the stimulus accurately.

Without having seen the stimulus array again, children were asked to reproduce the stimulus again after about 8 months. The findings from this retest were surprising: Of the children available for retesting, most (74%) produced drawings that were *more* like the original stimulus after the 8-month interval than were the drawings produced only 1 week after viewing the stimulus. These "long-term memory improvements" were explained in relation to operativity: memory is tied to the individual's operative schemes, operative schemes develop naturally over the 8-month retention interval, and thus memories improve as well. Similar results were reported with a variety of other stimuli related to logical and infralogical concepts, although the magnitude of the effects was smaller.

Subsequent investigators have been concerned with determining whether the memory phenomena observed by Piaget and Inhelder are reliable, and whether the Genevan interpretation of the empirical data is justified. With respect to the first issue, a variety of studies using the Genevan paradigm and stimuli related to concepts of horizontality, verticality, conservation, and seriation suggest that the cross-sectional differences are robust. There is less consensus with respect to the longitudinal improvements: Recent investigators have found a far smaller incidence of improvements, and in addition, evaluate the statistical significance of these improvements more conservatively than did Piaget and Inhelder (see Liben, 1977a, 1977b; Maurer, Siegel, Lewis, Kristofferson, Barnes, & Levy, 1979). Nevertheless, most investigators would probably accept the overall generalization that reproductions of stimuli are significantly influenced by individuals' conceptual levels, that these influences can be distinguished from developmental improvements in memory more generally (see Trepanier & Liben, 1979), and are therefore primarily interested in understanding how and where operative influences occur.

One of the central concerns of this work is whether or not operative schemes actually affect memories of stimuli during the time they are stored internally. Instead, operative schemes might have a temporally prior effect, that is at time of encoding. (Indeed, such influence is demonstrated by the data on perception just reported.) Alternatively, or in addition, schemes might affect reproductions at time of retrieval. Although the resolution of this issue may well determine whether or not this research literature is properly construed as "memory" research, it is of relatively little importance for the present argument. That is, even if a substantial portion of operative control occurs at the time of encoding or retrieval rather than during storage (Liben, 1975; 1980), the general point remains the same: The knowledge available to an individual is significantly affected by his or her general intellectual structure.

In summary, the Piagetian memory literature shows striking influences of individuals' conceptual levels on the way in which stimuli are remembered after varying intervals. Although these effects are attenuated to some extent by using recognition and reconstruction tasks rather than reproduction tasks, the overall pattern of results remains unchanged. Similarly, artifacts such as practice effects or increasing abilities to draw appear to account for some, but not all of the observed effects (see Liben, 1977a, 1977b). However, just as one may criticize the original Piagetian work on perception for its reliance on visual illusions, one might similarly criticize the initial Piagetian work on memory for its reliance on stimuli that are derived directly from Piaget's general theory of intellectual development. It is, therefore, useful to consider whether the more traditional, non-Piagetian work on memory development also demonstrates a relation between individuals' conceptual levels and memories.

The research literature on memory development in children (see Kail & Hagen, 1977; Ornstein, 1978) is replete with paradigms that may be used to demonstrate influence of conceptual levels on memory. One of the most direct links is derived from the paradigm developed by Bransford and Franks (1971) to study constructive memory in adults, and which was subsequently extended to children by Paris (see Paris, 1978; Paris & Lindauer, 1977). Bransford and Franks (1971) presented a series of separate, but related sentences, and later asked subjects to discriminate old from new items in a recognition task. Subjects falsely—but confidently—"recognized" test sentences that were actually new, but which expressed information that could be inferred from the original acquisition sentences. In later research with children, Paris and Carter (1973) found evidence of similar processes. For example, children were given the following sentences: "The bird is inside the cage. The cage is under the table. The bird is yellow." Second- and fifth-grade children falsely recognized a test sentence "The bird is under the table," which is a true inference derived from the original premises.

Of particular interest for the present discussion are several subsequent investigations in which the tendency to recognize true, but new inference sentences was examined in relation to children's operational levels. Prawat and Cancelli (1976) argued that active, inferential constructions would depend on concrete operations. Consistent with this hypothesis, they found that children who were able to conserve gave more false recognitions to true inferences than did nonconservers.

In an attempt to identify the operations underlying these inferences in memory more precisely, Liben and Posnansky (1977) assessed kindergartners' and first-graders' abilities to make transitive inferences rather than to conserve, as the former appeared to be more closely related to the inferential processes tapped by the prose memory task. The predicted relationship was not demonstrated in this study, apparently because young children were accepting new sentences as old because inferences contained specific words that had been found in the original premises, rather than because they represented semantically true information.

A relationship between operations and sentence memory was, however, found in a study by Johnson and Scholnick (1979). The link between logic and memory was examined in two areas, specifically, class inclusion and seriation. Children were given standard Piagetian tasks to determine whether they were able to solve class inclusion problems and/or seriate. In addition, memory materials tapped each of these concepts independently. As predicted, seriaters recognized more true seriation inferences than did nonseriaters. Contrary to predictions, however, children who were able to solve class inclusion problems did not show a greater tendency to give false recognitions to the inclusion inferences in memory than did children unable to solve class inclusion problems.

Thus, the evidence to date with respect to the relationship between logical abilities and prose memory suggests that children's logical abilities do influence the inferences made in memory, although the correspondence is far from perfect or fully understood.

Many other types of research on memory development may be cited in support of the assertion that cognitive skills and knowledge affect memory, including studies of the development of classification schemes in relation to the use of semantic categorization in free recall tasks (e.g., see Lange, 1978; Moely, 1977; Tenney, 1975); the effects of operational schemes on the child's ability to process and remember information from organized pictorial scenes (e.g., Hock, Romanski, Galie, & Williams, 1978), and the ways in which the growth of general knowledge affects memory for prose, pictures, and events (e.g., Chi, 1978; Myers & Perlmutter, 1978; Paris, Lindauer, & Cox, 1977). Although space constraints preclude more than alluding to these various types of data, the illustrations given serve to suggest that individuals' operative schemes and knowledge influence memory not only for stimuli derived directly from Piagetian tasks, but also for a wide range of verbal and pictorial material.

Conclusions

The data reviewed provide a diverse group of examples to demonstrate that the way in which knowledge is acquired, stored, and used varies in relation to individuals' operative levels. Although this review concentrated on highly cognitive topics, the arguments presented could also be illustrated with data drawn from the social realm. For example, children's cognitive structures have been shown to influence the interpretation of defense mechanisms (e.g., Chandler, Paget, & Koch, 1978), understanding of social institutions (e.g., Damon, in press; Furth, 1980), and person perception (e.g., Chandler, 1977). Indeed, virtually any topic under the burgeoning area of "social cognition" is concerned with the ways in which cognitive processes affect children's interpretations of, and transactions with, the social world (Shantz, 1975; Overton, in press).

STRUCTURE AND THE DEVELOPMENT OF NEW STRUCTURES

Overview

As mentioned briefly in the introductory comments to this section of the chapter, individuals' structures affect not only the way stimuli are perceived, remembered, and used (as just discussed), but also affect the extent to which they permit or support further structural progress. Thus, the "same" experiences have different effects on individuals' developmental progression, depending upon the individual's developmental level at the time these experiences are encountered. To study the effects of the "same" experiences on different individuals, it is, of course, necessary to have control over these experiences, and thus, they are typically (although not always) provided in the laboratory setting. Reviewed here, then, are illustrative research findings concerning how laboratory interventions affect further development in interaction with individuals' initial operative levels.

Most investigators concerned with the effects of laboratory intervention on children's operative concepts have used a variety of direct instructional methods. Typically, some kind of direct feedback is given to children regarding the accuracy of their responses to particular problems, usually dealing with some aspect of conservation. Dependent measures concern the child's ability to give correct conservation responses on the particular type of problem trained, and often, the ability to generalize to related problems. For example, a child might be trained on conservation of number, and tested on conservation of number and conservation of length. The emphasis on direct feedback in most of this research reflects the fact that much of this work is rooted in the tradition of learning theory, rather than within the perspective of Piagetian theory itself. In contrast, intervention research inspired within the Genevan approach has typically been designed to engage normal developmental mechanisms, most notably, equilibration. Thus, the Genevan intervention research has generally tried to induce cognitive conflict and, as a consequence, progressive equilibration.

The purposes of the two kinds of work have typically differed as well. The direct instructional methods have usually been aimed at accelerating development in an attempt to disprove the position (falsely attributed to Piaget) that development can occur only over extended periods of time in the everyday environment, or in an attempt to accelerate development under the apparent assumption that "sooner is better." The conflict induction research, in contrast, has generally been motivated by an interest in determining what mechanisms operate to yield cognitive growth.

Studies on the effect of individuals' operative levels with respect to "direct instruction" and "conflict induction" are illustrated in what follows. As before, the studies reviewed are chosen to be illustrative; no attempt is made to provide an exhaustive review. Alternative organizational systems of the training research, and more inclusive reviews of the relevant theoretical issues and empirical findings may be found in Beilin (1971b), Brainerd (1973b; 1978b), Brainerd and Allen (1971), Kuhn (1974), Overton (1976), and Strauss (1972; 1974).

Direct Instruction

By far the large majority of Piagetian training studies fall into the category of direct instruction. Although several extensive reviews of this empirical literature already exist, there is little consensus among those writing the reviews with respect to what we can conclude from this literature. Brainerd (1978b; Brainerd & Allen, 1971), for example, concludes that even short-term experimental training procedures are successful in inducing conservation, a conclusion supported by Glaser and Resnick (1972). Strauss (1972), in contrast, concludes that training is successful only insofar as it engages appropriate structures, so that, for example, interventions aimed at developing isolated operations such as addition–subtraction have met with extremely limited success, whereas interventions aimed at developing several related operations in a coordinated fashion have been successful. In an excellent review of the controversies surrounding the interpretation of the Piagetian training literature, Kuhn (1974) delineates some of the reasons for these discrepant interpretations, including disagreements with respect to what criteria should be used for inferring conservation (e.g., the necessity of explanations, see Brainerd, 1973a; the necessity of showing resistence to extinction through disconfirmation, see Brainerd, 1973b; Miller, 1971, 1976; Strauss, 1972); and even more fundamentally, disagreements with respect to what conservation consists of in the first place.

A review of the issues and empirical literature concerning training is neither possible nor necessary here. Of concern instead is the more limited question of whether the impact of direct instruction does, in fact, vary with the individual's initial operative level. Unfortunately, only a relatively small portion of the training studies have included an assessment of individuals' operative levels. On the basis of the data that are available, however, most reviewers (e.g., see Beilin, 1971b; Overton, 1976) agree that training is more effective when rudiments of the concept are already present prior to intervention. (The reader is referred directly to Brainerd, 1978b, for an extended discussion of the opposite interpretation, that is, that no such relationship has been demonstrated in more than a trivial fashion.)

Consistent with the hypothesized importance of individuals' initial operative levels, for example, are the results of an early training study by Beilin (1965), which showed that didactic instruction on conservation of number and length was maximally effective for children who had some, but not complete, conservation ability at the beginning of training. Using operant conditioning techniques, Cooley (1973) found that, although he was able to train a very young child (3;11) to criterion on conservation of continuous quantity, this child—unlike the 5- and 6-year-olds given the same training—gradually lost all understanding of conservation in later tests. Parker, Sperr, and Rieff (1972) found that training on multiple classification differed in effectiveness depending upon subjects' ages. Similar results from a variety of studies are reviewed by Beilin (1971b), Overton (1976), and Strauss (1972).

It appears, then, that the effectiveness of direct instruction does vary as a function of the individual's initial developmental level. (Again, however, see Brainerd, 1978b, for the opposite conclusion.) Research bearing on the relationship between the effectiveness of inducing cognitive conflict and individuals' operative levels is reviewed next.[4]

Conflict Induction

Given the importance of the equilibration process within Piagetian theory, it is understandable that investigators working within a Piagetian perspective and interested in effecting developmental progress should try to do so by inducing cognitive conflict. Although the concepts of cognitive conflict, equilibration, and the relationship between them are complex (see especially Mischel, 1971), the general point is clear: A conflict between what the individual expects and what the individual observes should lead to disequilibrium, and thus be likely to induce developmental progression as a way to achieve a better-equilibrated state. Importantly, for conflict to occur at all, the individual must already have the structures necessary to recognize the inconsistencies. Herein lies the relationship between conflict and the individual's structural level which is of concern here: "the 'surprise' element has no effect if the child does not yet possess the cognitive equipment which enables him to fit the unforeseen phenomena into a deductive or inferential framework [Inhelder, Sinclair, & Bovet, 1974, p. 267[.''

---

[4] The distinction between training research motivated by learning theory and training research motivated by constructivism may be fuzzier in practice than in theory. In a review of a wide range of studies of conservation training, Cooley (1978) concluded that disequilibrium may have been induced in all successful cases (e.g., Gelman, 1969). Indeed, when Cooley avoided disequilbrium by using errorless discrimination training, conservation was not successfully maintained at posttests.

The most direct translation of this theoretical position into the design of intervention experiences has been to ask children to make specific predictions, to demonstrate an outcome which is discrepant with those predictions, and then assess the child's appreciation of the disparity and any resulting cognitive growth.

This paradigm has been used in an extensive program of research by Inhelder, Sinclair, and Bovet (1974) (summarized briefly by Inhelder & Sinclair, 1969). In studying conservation of continuous quantity, for example, Inhelder et al. (1974) first directed children to attend to the initial equality of the liquid in identical beakers, and then to make various predictions, such as where the level of the liquid would be when the liquid is allowed to flow out into two different-sized jars. After making and explaining predictions, children were shown the outcome. In addition, all children were given pretests and posttests on conservation. Of particular importance here is the finding that the growth produced as a function of these laboratory experiences was directly linked to the individual's initial operative level. Virtually all children who were truly preoperational at the beginning made no progress at all on the elementary notions of the conservation of physical qualities. The two preoperational children who did show progress reached only intermediate levels, characterized by oscillations between conserving and nonconserving responses. For children who began at intermediate levels, however, the picture was different: Three-fourths of these children made substantial progress. Similar results are reported by Inhelder et al. (1974) with a variety of other concepts and laboratory experiences.

In the cases described, conflict is created through a discrepancy between the child's initial prediction and the physical world. Another means of engendering cognitive disequilibrium is by social conflict. Specifically, children are exposed to social models who reason at levels more advanced than their own. In the first study using this approach, Turiel (1966; 1969) gave subjects Kohlberg's moral judgment interview as a pretest. Two weeks after the pretest, children were asked to make additional moral judgments about new dilemmas, but in this case, the child was asked to seek advice from two "friends." The friends, played by the experimenter, gave advice that was either one stage above ($+1$), two stages above ($+2$), or one stage below (-1) the child's own level of development. One week later, children were given another test of moral development. Of particular interest is the finding that children in the $+1$ condition showed the maximum change from pretest to posttest.

Kuhn (1972) used the same paradigm, but applied it to classification skills rather than to moral judgments. Children were exposed to a model who used a classification system that was either more or less advanced than the system that had been used by the child on a pretest (again, $+1$, $+2$, and -1). Results paralleled those just described: Maximum cognitive growth was found in children exposed to reasoning that was one stage more advanced than their own. These data again suggest that the subject's own level of development is important in determining what is learned from experiences.

It should be noted, however, that not all empirical data are consistent with the thesis that individuals' initial levels influence the profit derived from exposure to more advanced thinking. Murray (1972) for example, asked conservers and nonconservers to reach a joint decision about a conservation problem. The nonconservers showed improvement in their conservation concepts following this interaction, but surprisingly, gains were equivalent in children who had exhibited no conservation on the pretest and in those who had exhibited some rudimentary conservation concepts. Unfortunately, subsequent studies using this social persuasion paradigm have not compared posttest performance as a function of subjects' initial operative level. Instead, subjects who are transitional on pretests have been systematically excluded from further testing (e.g., Miller & Brownell, 1975; Silverman & Geiringer, 1973). Thus, the generalization offered earlier with respect to the apparent importance of children's initial level must be regarded with caution until more empirical evidence is available.

Conclusions

The evidence cited from various kinds of intervention studies does suggest a relation between the individual's initial operative level and the progress made as an outcome of participation in the intervention. This conclusion must be taken as tentative, however, for several reasons. First, very few studies provide data bearing directly on this issue, as many of the best-designed training studies have failed to include children at varying initial operative levels. Most commonly, pretests are used only for the purpose of selecting subjects who do not yet "have" the concept of interest. Although such studies can provide data to show that training leads to better performance than that found in subjects in an untrained control group, these studies cannot provide data bearing upon the relative impact of training among children of differing initial levels. Second, of those studies that do differentiate among children's initial states, not all provide data that are consistent with the hypothesized relationship (e.g., the study by Murray, 1972). Third, as mentioned earlier, there is considerable controversy with respect to what constitutes evidence for "having" a particular concept. Although this controversy may well be unresolvable because the positions are rooted in different world views (see Overton, 1973; Overton & Reese, 1973; Pepper, 1942; Reese & Overton, 1970), the controversy nevertheless precludes a definitive interpretation of the empirical findings.

Finally, as in virtually every other area of developmental research, this area is plagued by a competence–performance problem: It may be that training is effective for transitional children not because it permits *acquisition* of the concept, but simply because it promotes *activation* of the concept (Overton, 1976).

SUMMARY

Although there are obviously many controversies surrounding the interpretation of the empirical work reviewed in this chapter, the data do illustrate the ways in which individuals' own cognitive structures mediate the impact of the environment. Knowledge derived from pictures, events, social interactions, and other stimuli appears to vary significantly in relation to the individual's operative level. Furthermore, the extent to which the individual can use the aliment of the environment in enhancing further structural development appears to vary with existing structure. In summary, empirical data support the theoretical arguments made earlier that individuals contribute to their own development in fundamental ways.

Conclusions

Piagetian theory provides a useful perspective from which to view individuals' contributions to their own development. Each of the developmental processes identified by Piaget—maturation, experience with objects, social experience, and equilibration—is profoundly influenced by the individual in nontrivial ways. The responses one has to environmental material, the structures into which these experiences are fit, and the resulting disequilibria and adjustments are all determined by the individual. The empirical data cited earlier illustrate the futility of trying to understand development without careful attention to the individual's own influence.

Before closing, it should be reiterated that, although the emphasis throughout these discussions has been upon the individual's role in development, this emphasis should not be taken to imply that contextual influences on structure and content are unimportant (see, for example, Buck-Morss, 1975; Feldman, 1980; Riegel & Meacham, 1976). The imbalance in the present chapter reflects the theme of the book, rather than a belief that development is insulated from environmental effects. It is important to recognize that Piaget is not primarily concerned with showing that all people in all cultures at all times follow a predestined path. Instead, Piaget is concerned with novelty:

> the main problem here is . . . to establish the method of construction of true novelties. During development, we witness a whole series of original and new

constructions. [There are] species-specific novelties. There are also, however, the novelties which are *invented* by the individual. The whole of human history is a history of *inventions* and *creations* which do not stem simply from the potentialities of the human race as a whole—we cannot yet even imagine to what heights human inventions will lead us—but which are also empowered by initiatives, by individual activities (and, of course, interindividual activities, since one cannot dissociate the individual from his social environment) [Piaget, in Inhelder & Piaget, 1971, p. 212].

Furthermore, Piaget (1978) argues that organisms' behaviors ultimately affect the evolution that occurs over millennia. In short, from the perspective of Piagetian theory, individuals contribute profoundly to their own development, and, simultaneously, to the development of the society in which they live.

Acknowledgements

I would like to express my deep appreciation to Richard Lerner for his intellectual and personal support in my preparation of this chapter, and to Jay Belsky, Susan Golbeck, John Meacham, Nora Newcombe, Willis Overton, Avron Spiro, and Ernst von Glasersfeld for providing valuable comments on an earlier draft of the manuscript.

References

Baltes, P. B., & Brim, O. G., Jr. (Eds.), *Life-span development and behavior* (Vol. 2). New York: Academic Press, 1979.

Baltes, P. B., Cornelius, S. W., & Nesselroade, J. R. Cohort effects in behavioral development: Theoretical and methodological perspectives. In W. A. Collins (Ed.), *Minnesota symposium on child psychology* (Vol. 11). Hillsdale, N.J.: Erlbaum, 1977.

Beilin, H. Learning and operational convergence in logical thought development. *Journal of Experimental Child Psychology*, 1965, *2*, 317–339.

Beilin, H. Developmental stages and developmental processes. In D. Green, M. Ford, & G. Flamer (Eds.), *Measurement and Piaget*. New York: McGraw-Hill, 1971. (a)

Beilin, H. The training and acquisition of logical operations. In M. Rosskopf, L. Steffe, & S. Taback (Eds.), *Piagetian cognitive–development research and mathematical education*. Washington, D. C.: National Council of Teachers of Mathematics, 1971. (b)

Brainerd, C. J. Judgments and explanations as criteria for the presence of cognitive structures. *Psychological Bulletin*, 1973, *79*, 192–179. (a)

Brainerd, C. J. Neo-Piagetian training experiments revisited: Is there any support for the cognitive–developmental stage hypothesis? *Cognition*, 1973, *2*, 349–370. (b)

Brainerd, C. J. *Piaget's theory of intelligence*. Englewood Cliffs, N.J.: Prentice-Hall, 1978. (a)

Brainerd, C. J. Learning research and Piagetian theory. In L. S. Siegel & C. J. Brainerd (Eds.), *Alternatives to Piaget*. New York: Academic Press, 1978. (b)

Brainerd, C. J. The stage question in cognitive–developmental theory. *The Behavioral and Brain Sciences*, 1978, *2*, 173–213. (c)

Brainerd, C. J. Continuing commentary. *The Behavioral and Brain Sciences*, 1979, *2*, 137–154.

Brainerd, C. J., & Allen, T. W. Experimental inductions of the conservation of "first-order" quantitative invariants. *Psychological Bulletin*, 1971, *75*, 128–144.

Bransford, J. D., & Franks, J. J. The abstraction of linguistic ideas. *Cognitive Psychology*, 1971, 2, 331–350.

Brent, S. B. Individual specialization, collective adaptation, and rate of environmental change. *Human Development*, 1978, *21*, 21–33.

Buck-Morss, S. Socioeconomic bias in Piaget's theory and its implications for cross-culture studies. *Human Development*, 1975 *18*, 35–49.

Chandler, M. J. Social cognition. In W. F. Overton & J. M. Gallagher (Eds.), *Knowledge and development* (Vol. 1). New York: Plenum, 1977.

Chandler, M. J., Paget, K. F., & Koch, D. A. The child's demystification of psychological defense mechanisms: A structural and developmental analysis. *Developmental Psychology*, 1978, *14*, 197–205.

Chi, M. Knowledge structures and memory development. In R. Siegler (Ed.), *Children's thinking: What develops?* Hillsdale, N.J.: Erlbaum, 1978.

Cooley, L. W. *An empirical test of Piaget's operational theory of knowledge.* Unpublished master of science thesis, University of Manitoba, 1973.

Cooley, L. W. *An experimental analysis of the role of equilibration in the development of conservation of continuous quantity.* Unpublished doctoral dissertation, University of Manitoba, 1978.

Damon, W. The nature of social–cognitive change in the developing child. In W. F. Overton (Ed.), *The relationship between social and cognitive development.* Hillsdale, N.J.: Erlbaum, in press.

Dasen, P. R. Cross-cultural Piagetian research: A summary. *Journal of Cross-Cultural Psychology*, 1972, *3*, 23–29.

Dasen, P. R. (Ed.), *Piagetian psychology: Cross cultural contributions.* New York: Gardner, 1977.

Elkind, D. Ambiguous pictures for the study of perceptual development and learning. *Child Development*, 1964, *35*, 1391–1396.

Elkind, D. Developmental studies of figurative perception. In H. W. Reese & L. P. Lipsitt (Eds.), *Advances in child development and behavior.* (Vol. 4). New York: Academic Press, 1969. (a)

Elkind, D. Reading, logic, and perception. *Educational Therapy*, 1969, *2*, 195–207. (b) (Reprinted in D. Elkind, *Children and adolescents*, New York: Oxford, 1970).

Elkind, D., Koegler, R. R., & Go, E. Studies in perceptual development II: Part–whole perception. *Child Development*, 1964, *35*, 81–90.

Elkind, D., & Scott, L. Studies in perceptual development I: Decentering of perception. *Child Development*, 1962, *33*, 619–630.

Feldman, D. H. *Beyond universals in cognitive development.* Norwood, N.J.: Ablex, 1980.

Flavell, J. *The developmental psychology of Jean Piaget.* New York: Van Nostrand, 1963.

Flavell, J. H. Comments on Beilin's "The development of physical concepts." In T. Mischel (Ed.), *Cognitive development and epistemology.* New York: Academic Press, 1971.

Forman, G. E., & Kuschner, D. *The child's construction of knowledge.* Monterey, Cal.: Brooks/Cole, 1978.

Furth, H. G. *Piaget and knowledge.* Englewood Cliffs, N.J.: Prentice-Hall, 1969.

Furth, H. G. Comments on the problems of equilibration. In M. H. Appel & L. S. Goldberg (Eds.), *Topics in cognitive development* (Vol. 1). New York: Plenum, 1977.

Furth, H. G. *The world of grownups: Children's conceptions of society.* New York: Elsevier-North Holland, 1980.

Furth, H. G., Ross, B., & Youniss, J. Operative understanding in children's immediate and long-term reproductions of drawings. *Child Development*, 1974, *45*, 63–70.

Gallagher, J. M. Piaget's concept of equilibration: Biological, logical, and cybernetic roots. In M. H. Appel & L. S. Goldberg (Eds.), *Topics in cognitive development* (Vol. 1). New York: Plenum, 1977.

Gallagher, J. M., & Easley, J. (Eds.). *Knowledge and development* (Vol. 2). New York: Plenum, 1978.

Gelman, R. Conservation acquisition: A problem of learning to attend to relevant attributes. *Journal of Experimental Child Psychology*, 1969, *7*, 167–187.

Gesell, A. *Infant and child today.* New York: Harper, 1943.

Gibson, E. *Principles of perceptual learning and development.* New York: Appleton-Century-Crofts, 1969.

Ginsburg, H., & Opper, S. *Piaget's theory of intellectual development.* Englewood Cliffs, N.J.: Prentice-Hall, 1979.

Glaser, R., & Resnick, L. B. Instructional psychology, *Annual Review of Psychology*, 1972, *23*, 207–276.

Hamburger, V. The concept of "development" in biology. In D. B. Harris (Ed.), *The concept of development.* Minneapolis, Minn.: University of Minnesota Press, 1957.

Hock, H. S., Romanski, L., Galie, A., & Williams, C. Real-world schemata and scene recognition in adults and children. *Memory and Cognition*, 1978, *6*, 423–431.

Inhelder, B., & Piaget, J. Closing remarks. In D. Green, M. Ford, & G. Flamer (Eds.), *Measurement and Piaget.* New York: McGraw-Hill, 1971.

Inhelder, B., & Sinclair, H. Learning cognitive structures. In P. H. Mussen, J. Langer, & M. Covington (Eds.), *Trends and issues in developmental psychology.* New York: Holt, 1969.

Inhelder, B., Sinclair, H., & Bovet, M. *Learning and the development of cognition.* Cambridge, Mass.: Harvard University Press, 1974.

Johnson, J. W., & Scholnick, E. K. Does cognitive development predict semantic integration? *Child Development*, 1979, *50*, 73–78.

Kail, R. V., Jr., & Hagen, J. W. *Perspectives on the development of memory and cognition.* Hillsdale, N.J.: Erlbaum, 1977.

Kamii, C., & DeVries, R. *Physical knowledge in preschool education.* Englewood Cliffs, N.J.: Prentice-Hall, 1978.

Kessen, W. "Stage" and "structure" in the study of children. In W. Kessen & C. Kuhlman (Eds.), Thought in the young child. *Monographs of the Society for Research in Child Development*, 1962 (Whole No. 83, 65–82).

Kitchener, R. F. Epigenesis: The role of biological models in developmental psychology. *Human Development*, 1978, *21*, 141–160.

Kuhn, D. Mechanisms of change in the development of cognitive structures. *Child Development*, 1972, *43*, 833–844.

Kuhn, D. Inducing development experimentally: Comments on a research paradigm. *Developmental Psychology*, 1974, *10*, 590–600.

Lange, G. Organization-related processes in children's recall. In P. A. Ornstein (Ed.), *Memory development in children.* Hillsdale, N.J.: Erlbaum, 1978.

Lerner, R. M. The stage concept in developmental theory: A dialectic alternative. *Brain and Behavioral Sciences*, 1979, *2*, 144–145.

Lerner, R. M. Concepts of epigenesis: Descriptive and explanatory issues. *Human Development*, 1980, *23*, 63–72.

Lerner, R. M., & Ryff, C. D. Implementation of the life-span view of human development: The sample case of attachment. In P. B. Baltes (Ed.), *Life-span development and behavior* (Vol. 1). New York: Academic Press, 1978.

Lerner, R. M., & Spanier, G. B. (Eds.), *Child influences on marital and family interaction.* New York: Academic Press, 1978.

Liben, L. S. Evidence for developmental differences in spontaneous seriation and its implications for past research on long-term memory improvement. *Developmental Psychology*, 1975, *11*, 121–125.

Liben, L. S. Memory in the context of cognitive development: The Piagetian approach. In R. V. Kail, Jr. & J. W. Hagen (Eds.), *Perspectives on the development of memory and cognition.* Hillsdale, N.J.: Erlbaum, 1977. (a)

Liben, L. S. Memory from a cognitive–developmental perspective: A theoretical and empirical review. In W. F. Overton & J. M. Gallagher (Eds.), *Knowledge and development (Vol. 1): Advances in research and theory.* New York: Plenum, 1977. (b)

Liben, L. S. *Children's reproductions of operative stimuli: Perceptual or mnemonic distortion?* Paper presented at the 86th Annual Convention of the American Psychological Association, Toronto, 1978.

Liben, L. S. The effect of operativity on memory. In H. Beilin (Chair), *The Operative basis of reading, memory, information processing, and self instructions.* Symposium presented at the Southeastern Conference on Human Development, Alexandria, Virginia, 1980.

Liben, L. S., & Posnansky, C. J. Inferences on inference: The effects of age, transitive ability, memory load, and lexical factors. *Child Development,* 1977, *48,* 1490–1497.

Mangan, J. Piaget's theory and cultural differences: The case for value-based modes of cognition. *Human Development,* 1978, *21,* 170–189.

Maurer, D., Siegel, L. S., Lewis, T. L., Kristofferson, M. W., Barnes, R. A., & Levy, B. A. Long-term memory improvement? *Child Development,* 1979, *50,* 106–118.

Miller, S. A. Extinction of conservation: A methodological and theoretical analysis. *Merrill-Palmer Quarterly,* 1971, *17,* 319–334.

Miller, S. A. Extinction of Piagetian concepts: An updating. *Merrill-Palmer Quarterly,* 1976, *22,* 257–281.

Miller, S. A., & Brownell, C. A. Peers, persuasion, and Piaget: Dyadic interaction between conservers and nonconservers. *Child Development,* 1975, *46,* 992–997.

Mischel, T. Piaget: Cognitive development and the motivation of thought. In T. Mischel (Ed.), *Cognitive development and epistemology.* New York: Academic Press, 1971.

Mischel, T. Piaget and the nature of psychological explanations. In F. B. Murray (Ed.), *The impact of Piagetian theory.* Baltimore: University Park Press, 1979.

Moely, B. Organizational factors in the development of memory. In R. V. Kail, Jr. & J. W. Hagen (Eds.), *Perspectives on the development of memory and cognition.* Hillsdale, N.J.: Erlbaum, 1977.

Murray, F. B. Acquisition of conservation through social interaction. *Developmental Psychology,* 1972, *6,* 1–6.

Murray, F. B. (Ed.), *The impact of Piagetian theory.* Baltimore: University Park Press, 1979.

Myers, N., & Perlmutter, M. Memory in the years from two to five. In P. A. Ornstein (Ed.), *Memory development in children.* Hillsdale, N.J.: Erlbaum, 1978.

Ornstein, P. A. *Memory development in children.* Hillsdale, N.J.: Erlbaum, 1978.

Overton, W. F. On the assumptive base of the nature–nurture controversy: Additive versus interactive conceptions. *Human Development,* 1973, *16,* 74–89.

Overton, W. F. Environmental ontogeny: A cognitive view. In K. F. Riegel & J. A. Meacham (Eds.), *The developing individual in a changing world.* Chicago: Aldine, 1976.

Overton, W. F. (Ed.). *The relationship between social and cognitive development.* Hillsdale, N.J.: Erlbaum, in press.

Overton, W. F., & Reese, H. W. Models of development: Methodological implications. In J. Nesselroade & H. Reese (Eds.), *Life-span developmental psychology: Methodological issues.* New York: Academic Press, 1973.

Paris, S. G. The development of inference and transformation as memory operations. In P. A. Ornstein (Ed.), *Memory development in children.* Hillsdale, N.J.: Erlbaum, 1978.

Paris, S., & Carter, A. Semantic and constructive aspects of sentence memory in children. *Developmental Psychology,* 1973, *9,* 109–113.

Paris, S. G., & Lindauer, B. K. Constructive aspects of children's comprehension and memory. In R. V. Kail, Jr. & J. W. Hagen (Eds.), *Perspectives on the development of memory and cognition.* Hillsdale, N.J.: Erlbaum, 1977.

Paris, S. G., Lindauer, B. K., & Cox, G. The development of inferential comprehension. *Child Development,* 1977, *48,* 1728–1733.

Parker, R., Sperr, S., & Rieff, M. Multiple classification: A training approach. *Developmental Psychology,* 1972, *7,* 188–194.

Parten, M. B. Social participation among preschool children. *Journal of Abnormal and Social Psychology*, 1932, *27*, 243–269.

Pepper, S. *World hypotheses.* Berkeley: University of California Press, 1942.

Piaget, J. *The language and thought of the child.* New York: Harcourt Brace, 1926.

Piaget, J. Apprentissage et conaissance. In P. Greco & J. Piaget (Eds.), *Apprentissage et conaissance.* Etudes d'epistimologie genotique, 7. Paris: Presses Universitaires de France, 1959.

Piaget J. Development and learning. In R. Ripple & V. Rockcastle (Eds.), *Piaget rediscovered.* Ithaca: Cornell University Press, 1964.

Piaget, J. *The moral judgment of the child.* New York: The Free Press, 1965.

Piaget, J. *Six psychological studies.* New York: Random House, 1967. (Translated from the French by A. Tenzer, trans. Edited by D. Elkind).

Piaget, J. *The mechanisms of perception.* New York: Basic Books, 1969.

Piaget, J. Piaget's theory. In P. Mussen (Ed.), *Carmichael's manual of child psychology.* New York: Wiley, 1970.

Piaget, J. Comments on developmental stages and developmental processes. In D. Green, M. Ford, & G. Flamer (Eds.), *Measurement and Piaget.* New York: McGraw-Hill, 1971. (a)

Piaget, J. *Biology and knowledge.* Chicago: University of Chicago Press, 1971. (b)

Piaget, J. Intellectual evolution from adolescence to adulthood. *Human Development*, 1972, *15*, 1–12.

Piaget, J. Chance and dialectic in biological epistemology: A critical analysis of Jacques Monod's theses. In W. F. Overton & J. M. Gallagher (Eds.), *Knowledge and development (Vol. 1).* New York: Plenum, 1977. (a)

Piaget, J. The role of action in the development of thinking. In W. F. Overton & J. M. Gallagher (Eds.), *Knowledge and development (Vol. 1).* New York: Plenum, 1977. (b)

Piaget, J. Problems of equilibration. In M. H. Appel & L. S. Goldberg (Eds.), *Topics in cognitive development* (Vol. 1). New York: Plenum, 1977. (c)

Piaget, J. *Behavior and evolution.* New York: Pantheon Books, 1978.

Piaget, J. The psychogenesis of knowledge and its epistemological significance. In M. Piattelli-Palmarini (Ed.), *Language and learning: The debate between Jean Piaget and Noam Chomsky.* Cambridge, Mass.: Harvard University Press, 1980.

Piaget, J., & Inhelder, B. *The psychology of the child.* New York: Basic Books, 1969.

Piaget, J., & Inhelder, B. *Memory and intelligence.* New York: Basic Books, 1973.

Pollack, R. H. Some implications of ontogenetic changes in perception. In D. Elkind & J. Flavell (Eds.), *Studies in cognitive development.* New York: Oxford, 1969.

Prawat, R., & Cancelli, A. Constructive memory in conserving and nonconserving first graders. *Developmental Psychology*, 1976, *12*, 47–50.

Reese, H., & Overton, W. Models of development and theories of development. In L. Goulet & P. Baltes (Eds.), *Life-span developmental psychology: Research and theory.* New York: Academic Press, 1970.

Riegel, K. Dialectic operations. The final period of cognitive development. *Human Development*, 1973, *16*, 346–370.

Riegel, K. F. The dialectics of human development. *American Psychologist*, 1976, *31*, 689–700.

Riegel, K. F., & Meacham, J. A. (Eds.). *The developing individual in a changing world.* Chicago: Aldine, 1976.

Shantz, C. The development of social cognition. In E. M. Hetherington (Ed.), *Review of child development research* (Vol. 5). Chicago: University of Chicago Press, 1975.

Sigel, I. E. Piaget and education: A dialectic. In F. B. Murray (Ed.), *The impact of Piagetian theory.* Baltimore: University Park Press, 1979.

Silverman, I. W., & Geiringer, E. Dyadic interaction and conservation induction: A test of Piaget's equilibration model. *Child Development*, 1973, *44*, 815–820.

Stevenson, H. W. Piaget, Behavior theory, and intelligence. In W. Kessen & C. Kuhlman (Eds.), Thought in the young child. *Monographs of the Society for Research in Child Development*, 1962 (Whole No. 83).

Strauss, S. Inducing cognitive development and learning: A review of short-term training experiments. *Cognition*, 1972, *1*, 329–357.

Strauss, S. A reply to Brainerd. *Cognition*, 1974, *3*, 155–185.

Tenney, Y. J. The child's conception of organization and recall. *Journal of Experimental Child Psychology*, 1975, *19*, 100–114.

Trepanier, M. L., & Liben, L. S. The operative basis of performance on Piagetian memory tasks: Evidence from normal and learning disabled children. *Developmental Psychology*, 1979, *15*, 668–669.

Tuddenham, R. Jean Piaget and the world of the child. *American Psychologist*, 1966, *21*, 207–217.

Turiel, E. An experimental test of the sequentiality of developmental stages in the child's moral judgments. *Journal of Personality and Social Psychology*, 1966, *3*, 611–618.

Turiel, E. Developmental processes in the child's moral thinking. In P. Mussen, J. Langer, & M. Covington (Eds.), *Trends and issues in developmental psychology*. New York: Holt, 1969.

von Glasersfeld, E. Radical constructivism and Piaget's concept of knowledge. In F. B. Murray (Ed.), *The impact of Piagetian theory*. Baltimore: University Park Press, 1979.

Wartofsky, M. From genetic epistemology to historical epistemology: Kant, Marx, and Piaget. In L. S. Liben (Ed.), *Piaget and the foundations of knowledge*. Hillsdale, N.J.: Erlbaum, in press.

Whiteside, J. A., Elkind, D., & Golbeck, S. L. Effects of exposure duration on part–whole perception. *Child Development*, 1976, *47*, 498–501.

Wohlwill, J. Developmental studies of perception. *Psychological Bulletin*, 1960, *67*, 249–288.

NORMA HAAN   **6**

Adolescents and Young Adults as Producers of Their Development

The task undertaken in this chapter is the analysis of the dialectical transactions that typify the person's activity during two adjacent and not clearly separable segments of the life span—adolescence and young adulthood. Before this discussion begins, its limits and the propositions underlying its perspective are stated.

Limits and Clarifications

Adolescents and young adults have probably been the subjects of more empirical investigations than have any other age group. Because they can read, follow directions, and are often readily available and even captives of investigators, youths are subjects of convenience. The special age characteristics of adolescents have interested many theorists, but college sophomores as young adults have more often served as the model of the "generalized human being" in psychological theories. If young adults are age distinctive in important ways, this circumstance can only mean that much general theory is erroneously based.

Small wonder that the adolescent period has not lacked for theorists. Adolescents are often surprising, multifaceted, interesting creatures com-

Individuals as Producers of Their Development

Copyright © 1981 by Academic Press, Inc.
All rights of reproduction in any form reserved.
ISBN 0-12-444550-0

pared to young adults, who often seem single minded, driven, proper, and predictable. Moreover, extensive sociological and historical analyses of adolesence (e.g., Bengston & Kuypers, 1971; Gillis, 1974; Mannheim, 1952) suggests the motivations of the older generation, including the theorists'. Adolescence is the last time that the old can expect to have potent influence on the young. Developmentalists' past suppositions that adulthood was a seamless period, probably suggested to most theorists that there was little special to know about young adults once they passed adolescence.

In view of the many sensitive, penetrating analyses of adolescence provided by theorists like Erik Erikson, Anna Freud, Margaret Mead, Barbel Inhelder, Jean Piaget, Fritz Redl, Peter Blos, James Tanner, Elizabeth Douvan, Daniel Offer, Joseph Adelson, James Coleman, Kenneth Keniston, and others, it is not clear whether further important contributions can be made unless an organization of these disparate but relevant views can be proposed. Clearly, there is no gain in each generation of social scientists discovering anew insights of previous generations; moreover, because social scientists lack consensus about the nature of the knowledge they are trying to accrue, discovery via renaming is not infrequent (Sarason, 1978).

Because these many excellent analyses are available, this discussion is based on a rearrangement of our understandings about adolescence; however, a partially new view of the young adult period is suggested. The task is to suggest, always from the standpoint of the self, several basic dialectical reciprocities that are especially salient during adolescence and young adulthood. The literature is not reviewed, instead the rich but disparate array of existing accounts are used to build a consecutive view of movement from adolescence through young adulthood.

The calendar years and the particular life events that set childhood off from adolescence, adolescence from young adulthood, or young adulthood from middle adulthood vary with persons and societies. Calendar years are subject to experiential and biological qualifications and surely no one marker event includes all the concatenated meanings that define most life transitions, no matter how vigorously a society ritualizes an age transition. Keniston (1968), among others, believes a period of "youth" between adolescence and young adulthood is now discernible and he celebrates it as a highly desirable opportunity for the "talented and privileged," to deepen their self-understandings. Alternatively, youth can be viewed as a prolonged period of noncommitment that is experienced—whether enjoyed or suffered—by young people in societies that have surplus workers and thus a need to keep their young citizens off the job market (Freeman, 1976; O'Connor, 1973). Whatever the case, youth is not an invariant period of life. It is instead an example of sociohistorical conditions interacting with young "privileged" people to reinforce their understandable human reluctance to narrow their life prospects and select one vocation and one spouse.

We commonly think of adolescence as the time from puberty on and young adulthood, as appearing in our society, at about age 20 and terminating at about age 35. Little would be gained for this discussion by my being more precise with regard to chronological age.

Conceptual Perspectives

The perspective taken here will be better understood if account is taken of its constructivist–structuralist frame and its roots in those parts of psychoanalytic theory that define ego as processes. My initial derivation (Haan, 1977) revised psychoanalytic theory to make its view of ego as processes logically congruent with a cognitive–structuralist position. At the same time, structural theory needed to be made into a more open system. The approach is literally dialectic, that is, not dialectical in the sense of a metaphor (Baltes & Cornelius, 1977). Instead, people's functioning is seen as ceaseless and successively organized by activities that follow the sequence of thesis–antithesis–synthesis. Here, I draw more differentiated implications from this earlier work in an account of adolescent and adult development and in so doing avail myself of the language of dialectical change.

The strong version of psychological interaction, now frequently identified as dialectical, is always evident in the therapeutic context, being explicitly conceptualized as the operation of the defensive mechanisms, resistance, transference, working through, and the like. I argue that it is better to work with variables like ego processes, instead of inventing new names for processes, for several reasons:

1. We keep faith with the past, stand on accrued stored knowledge, and access old insights.
2. Psychoanalytic insights in regard to defensive functioning (poor functioning) enrich our formulations.
3. Understandings in regard to poor functioning lead to definitions of optimal functioning and optimal ways of development. This last point is fully developed later.

A number of basic strategies and propositions underlie the perspective outlined in the following pages:

1. The psychologist's interest in dialectical processes—both diachronic and synchronic—must logically take the self as the starting and central point. Clearly, sociologists, historians, and economists will prefer other foci (e.g., social organizations, historical forces, business cycles, etc.).

However, for the psychologist, dialectical reciprocities will include—moving from the proximal to the distal—the self's metacognitive and affective transactions with other aspects of the self, with the soma, biological capabilities including the sexual, with requirements and expectancies of family, friends, and colleagues, and with the opportunities and pressures of society, culture, and history. Thus, the psychologist's interest is in one kind of reality, that of the individual person involved in varied and unceasing transactions.

2. These transactions are often conflictual, although "conflict" is often much too strong a word to describe the phenomenon, but the English language seems not to have another with the proper connotations. Perturbance comes close to describing the impingements that impose on stases that then encourage the person to work for resolutions. The temporality of this activity means that the prime descriptive variables must literally be processes and that greater clarity is achieved if they are not inferred processes (e.g., change inferred between two points in time). Piaget's words, assimilation and accommodation, drawn from biology and seen by him as the functional invariants of adaptation, identify two broad functions performed by ego processes. Clinical experience provides finer distinctions in the forms of the classical defense mechanisms, although these are not always adaptive. I argue that common sense also identifies a series of coping processes that have the same form as the defense processes, but different properties. More is said about these coping processes in following sections. In the present view then, the prime descriptive variables are processes of coping and defending; both kinds can be either assimilatory or accommodatory. The person uses these processes in varying patterns to carry on his or her daily transactions and negotiations with life conflicts or perturbances.

3. The conceptualization of the active organism in the active world requires that the whole person, as the organizer of multiinteractions, be kept in view. This tack counteracts the positivists' historic reductionism, but is close in intent to many previous efforts in the study of personality, a field distinguished, on the one hand, by the humanists' vagueness and ambitious polemic and, on the other hand, by the pretentious rigor and scientism of the psychometricians (Bernstein, 1976; Habermas, 1973).

Forewarned by our own history, we need, in taking a unitary view of the person, to keep the limits of social science in mind so we know what we can say in a precise way. As Einstein is reported to have observed, "Describing the taste of chicken soup is clearly not the same as tasting chicken soup." Naivete characterized the earlier positivist ambitions that a science of behavior would so completely and accurately predict human activity that full control would eventually be possible. We have been under the sway of what Rudner (1966) called the "reproductive fallacy" that is the hope that a mature social science would come to explain all of life.

The contrary conceptual view is taken here: Social science's general and abstract descriptions and explanations will necessarily be limited to the person's processes and structures. The contents of people's lives infinitely vary across time, place. The person is only comprehensively known by lovers, next of kin, psychotherapists, and biographers. The goals of social science must be more modestly drawn to include more probabilistic conclusions than earlier generations of psychologists thought would be necessary.

4. In view of the risks involved, people's "motivations" for changing or developing need to be made explicit. The traditional answer, given by both psychoanalysts and behaviorists, was that aroused tensions cause people to learn to act in ways to quiet their tensions. The goal was peace and calm. The psychoanalytic account also relies heavily on biological maturation as an independent propellant of psychological development. In the present perspective, premises of both carrot and stick and biological maturation are viable partial explanations. Broader, however, is the conception that development follows on dialectical conflict and, critical to the present view, is the idea that development follows on curiosity and attempts to enhance life. To roughly paraphrase Piaget, once life is in motion, it continues to move. At any rate, development is not always driven by noxious tensions or biology. People also have interest in enhancement.

5. Important to this perspective are three characteristics of human adaptation; ordinary people assume all three as part of their everyday epistemology: (a) In their accommodations, people normatively develop a stake in being rational because it works better for them; (b) they develop expectancies that other people generally make this same accommodation; and (c) all additionally assume that their rational working consensus represents reality and that they may intersubjectively revise it from time to time. Thereby, we develop reality by our social accommodations to one another.

Nonetheless, as rational person and practical reality dialectically interact, the individual will insist that his or her resolutions must be his or her own. Thus, particular resolutions may fit intrasubjective logic but not intersubjective logic. Observers think that actions based on intrasubjective logic are irrational or idiosyncratic. This dialectic—the tension between self and society—is the root interaction that psychologists try to understand.

Seligman (1975) has shown the pervasive and deleterious effects of forcing helplessness on a variety of organisms. Lefcourt (1973) reviewed the extensive experimental literature concerning "freedom" and the control of one's destiny and cautiously concluded that whether people actually have freedom and control over their lives can never be decided, but the results from many investigations make it clear that subjects are better off for thinking they do. De Pres (1975) has documented the "secret" coping—

the freedom—of concentration camp survivors in the most dire and oppressive of social circumstances.

Because people's "reality" is developed in a dialectical interchange between their intrasubjective points of view and the social consensus of their milieu, their ego processes come to form a utilitarian hierarchy: (a) normatively, people sustain their usual allegiance to social reality, abandoning it only when they will do no harm to themselves or others. They cope when they can; (b) however, they demand that they be their own persons and that solutions be theirs. Thus they readily sacrifice their usual commitments to a consensual, social reality when they are stressed. Then, they will distort or negate their situation and intents by using defensive strategies or even by fragmenting and breaking with reality to preserve their private intrasubjective sensibilities. In other words, they choose compartmentalization to avoid disintegration. These shifts from coping to defending to fragmenting involve sharp discontinuities in social implications wherein slight changes in the meaning of the stimulus yield "catastrophic" changes in the modes of functioning, much as Freedle (1977) recently discussed for Thomian topological models.

6. Behind all formulations of adaptation is the idea of equilibration. This view has been most extensively used in describing cognitive development. However, we can more broadly and simply say that people intend sustaining some kind of reasonable relations with the world. The further supposition is usually made that the child or the adult's equilibrated adaption represents a "success," being based on the most accurate and complete use of his or her cognitive capacity; in this event performance equals capacity. Of course, this result does not always occur; habitually, we blame the methods or instruments of data collection. To the contrary, an essential principle of adaptivity is involved.

I argue (Haan, 1977) that the person's equilibration not only involves many more structures than the cognitive and moral, but also that "false" equilibrations are often achieved by dint of defensive negation, distortion, and narrowing. Equilibrations can occur even when proportionately greater weight is given to nonlogical, socially intuitive, or affective factors because the situation itself may not call for realistic, logical, or instrumental actions. Being a "subject" may be a time when defensive narrowing in an unrealistic situation may serve intrasubjective logic, whether or not it serves intersubjective adaptivity. Evidence that this is the case for older people and black children, whose intelligence has been the subject of many investigations, is accruing. Various "extraneous" factors, such as the elderly's anxiety in reaction to the widespread supposition that they deteriorate intellectually, influence performance (see Labouvie-Vief & Chandler, 1978). Such findings suggest the operation of processes, like the self-fulfilling prophecy, found in the testing and education of black children (Rosenthal & Jackson, 1968). Both the old and the black children "intelligently" preserve their intrasubjective logic, as they see it, in the situation of testing.

Thus, the equilibrations of everyday life are frequently "false" and achieved at the cost of the person negating unbearable aspects of internal or external reality. In other words, the person forfeits allegiance to intersubjective reality to preserve intrasubjective logic and sensibility. Thus, defensiveness and fragmentation also serve adaptation, but of a different kind, and in these cases performance and capacity do not match because the situation is not one that permits "good" functioning.

7. Rational minds in interaction with practical social reality are evaluative, whether these reactions are explicitly articulated or not. Because social–psychological reality is constructed and scientists are people, they select, emphasize, and protect some values over others; life is never a matter of disinterest. The early positivists forbade investigators to take evaluative stances but these prohibitions served to impoverish conceptualization. Moreover, from the standpoint of a constructivist epistemology, fact and value cannot logically be separated (Bernstein, 1976), so the important question is no longer whether or not values enter social–psychological accounts, but concerns which values social science *should* adopt and use in investigations. Bernstein (1976) has developed a detailed and persuasive argument that social scientists' impoverished findings are not due to their disciplines' infancy but result from their failure to deal with the epistemological issues of value choice. However, not just any value will do for social science. Its choice cannot be capricious or parochial. Avoiding value issues often produces contorted and nonsensical accounts of humans and their affairs.

In the present context, this evaluative or "critical" position is required for two reasons: It clarifies the direction of optimal development, and makes it possible to distinguish synchronic resolutions based on defensiveness from those based on coping or those that are "emancipatory," to use Habermas' (1973) words.

Unrestricted, undistorted communication with the self, others, and the world is the unacknowledged core value of psychoanalysis (Habermas, 1973), Hartmann's (1960) attempt to declare psychoanalysis value-free to the contrary notwithstanding. Likewise, Piaget (1969a) takes a value position based on the idea of intersubjective integrity or accuracy as he notes the child can only become truthful in the presence of others; Swanson (1968) comments in an analysis of intersubjectivity that people require of one another that they actually be what they publicly allow themselves to seem to be.

A related value is fundamental to my formulation of coping. Negation or distortion of truth has always been the hallmark of defensiveness and fragmenting. I argue (Haan, 1977) that the core value of coping, as we commonly use the word, is being accurate about one's self to one's self

(self-insight in psychoanalytic theory) and about others to one's self (Habermas', Piaget's and Swanson's intersubjective integrity). More could be said, but here I can only say that the value of interpersonal and intrapersonal accuracy is neither metaphysically nor ideologically biased; instead it is very simply derived from the scientific ethic, which also rests on the notion of intersubjective accuracy. Both kinds of accuracy are everyday, pragmatic requirements we make of ourselves and of others. If the implicit consensus they represent were explicitly used, social science might gain the same vigor and direction that psychoanalytic theory did when the conceptualization of the ego's reality testing was introduced.

Specifying the synchronic and diachronic forms of optimal life resolutions would make it possible to know when psychological life and development are either environmentally or situationally facilitated or deterred. Thus, the confused, convoluted, and infinitely regressive interpretation of results from relativistic points of view could be avoided along with the impoverishments of psychology searching for explanations of actions at deeper levels, in new complex methodologies and statistical procedures, or in other "hard" disciplines, such as genetics, demography, or brain physiology. Debate might take up the substantive issues of psychology. As Piaget (1969b) has said, we can have no better preparation for convergence with biology than an adequate psychology.

Implications for Conceptualizing Adolescence and Young Adulthood

All times in the life span, adolescence and young adulthood included, have a history and a future, and the life-span view requires that both be taken into account; at the same time period-centrism is avoided. Several postulates about the self, its development and functioning follow on the perspective outlined in the previous section:

1. For the individual, the core developmental dialectic is changes in the self versus conservation of the self (Haan & Day, 1974; Haan, 1974). To stay the "same," the self develops by adaptational transformations, rather than by ruptures. On the one hand, if persons defend themselves against changing, little development will occur. On the other hand, precipitous, unexpected self-changes that are out of the person's control do not result in development. Instead, the first outcome is stress and the second may be symptom formation. Examples of the results of unbidden self-changes are provided by clients in crisis intervention clinics, the disruptive effects of insight therapy with some borderline patients, and the panic experiences of some sensitive adolescents. Other examples of traumatic reactions

to radical self-changes include being an obedient immoral subject in an experiment like Milgram's (1974), finding that one's face has radically changed as a result of cosmetic surgery, one has an incurable genetic disease, or one is adopted. Thus, people need to conserve a modicum of self to sustain their self-sensibility, which partly depends on their maintaining some ties with the past.

Researchers know very little about this self-dialectic of change and sameness, because systematic study of the self has not been done. Its measurement by the psychometricians has usually focused on its multiple contents. However, recent interesting work concerning the structural properties of the self may give us a purchase on this problem (see Markus, 1977; Rogers, Kuiper, & Kirker, 1977).

This position assumes that selfhood, as a sense of self, is an important concern throughout the life span; however at some ages when rapid physiological changes and rapid social redefinitions of the self occur, selfhood becomes problematic; then we recognize and accentuate the self and speak of identity crises. Clearly this phenomenon of self reorganization especially occurs at adolescence so the dialectic of change and sameness is importantly involved in the adolescent's development.

2. The internal dialectic of self-change versus self-conservation has a temporal macroversion. Some periods in life seem disproportionately devoted to assimilation, that is, taking in and absorbing new information in regard to self. Adolescence and old age seem such times. Other periods of life seem disproportionately devoted to accommodation, that is, inventing and working out ways to incorporate potentially desirable possibilities or change what seems undesirable in the self. Childhood and the early to middle adult years seem to be such times. From this perspective, life-span development is composed of periods of exploration (assimilating) alternating with ones of consolidation (accommodating); perhaps there are also some periods of equilibration, such as late infancy, late childhood, and late middle adulthood.

To regard adolesence as a time of assimilation—as I think many theorists have implicitly done—has important implications. As adolescents cognize and reconstruct their experience in their own lights, they are not yet exposed, nor does society require them to be entirely exposed, to corrective social feedback; thus their assimilations are sometimes slightly off base, abstract, imaginative, or overly formal in nature. More pejorative words have been used to suggest adolescents are egocentric and narcissistic or, more recently, unable to understand the Protestant Ethic. At some places and times in history, societies prolong and accentuate adolescents' assimilatory experience by not permitting them to begin accommodating, like our own society now does with large numbers of minority group youth.

Assimilatory activity is a private pursuit. As such, it was investigated in a recent study conducted by Larson and Csikszentimihalyi (1978). They installed electronic pagers on a number of adolescents and buzzed them at random times. The adolescents responded by writing about their immediate thoughts and circumstances. Although time spent alone was generally evaluated as a negative experience, those who spent a moderate amount of time alone (about 30%) were less alienated and better adjusted than those who spent very little or a great deal of time alone. The authors conclude that time alone may be needed for the adolescents to reflect in order to integrate.

Whereas adolescents are distinctively assimilatory, young adults seem to be distinctively accommodatory. Much of high symbolic and real value must be concretely accomplished by the young adult: a career advanced, a spouse selected, money made, personal property acquired, housing secured, a mortgage signed, a family started. If these activities are to be successful, they must jibe with the self's desires and capabilities and the milieu's social possibilities and others' expectancies. In general, other people do not cooperate if the young person does not make social sense. Thus, of necessity, the assimilating adolescent becomes an adult, recommitted to a definition of self and to social reality. Possibly, the birth of offspring is the clearest turning point. As someone has said, when we have children we gave hostages to fortunes; Peter DeVries (1963) has a character say in *The Blood of the Lamb*, that children make grown-ups out of their parents.

Analyses of the personality descriptions of the longitudinal subjects at the Institute of Human Development (Haan, in press) suggest that when the participants were young adults they were more self-confident than they were as adolescents. However, at early adulthood compared to themselves at middle age, they were less cognitively invested, less open to their own thoughts and feelings, and less expressive of themselves, both sexually and socially. Their score changes on the scales of the California Psychological Inventory were consistent with this comparative picture. As young adults, they had greater investment in being socially effective and appropriate; at middle age, they had greater investment in being self-expressive and self-aware.

Another kind of evidence for the young adult's disproportionate accommodation comes from Inglehart's (1977) study of materialism and postmaterialism in six countries of the European community. Inglehart analyzed his survey data by six age groups and found greater materialism in the older age groups; he attributed the findings to historical–social trends. However, close examination of his data suggests that life-cycle effects are superimposed on historical trends. The drops in the percentage of "postmaterialists" between the adjacent age groups was clearly the greatest between adolescent and young adult periods for all six countries. Gains in the portions of materialists for the same interval were the highest in Belgium, Italy, and France and second highest in West Germany, Netherlands, and Britain. We should not conclude from these findings that becoming a young adult necessarily means abandoning one's social values, as we will see in later sections concerned with adolescents' and young adults' moral and political commitments; however, these results suggest that the young adults' value priorities necessarily become more complicated as they acquire spouses and children.

3. Adolescents are especially vulnerable to their own confusions because they are undergoing many personal and unbidden changes and are neither entirely committed to nor accepted by society. In contrast, young adults undergo few personal changes and are usually cognizant of and committed to society's necessities. In fact, they are so committed to society that they usually hope to bend it to their own purposes, so society marks this respect and reciprocates by recognizing and respecting them. Comparisons of the kinds of transactions that engage adolescents and young adults are shown in Table 6.1.

TABLE 6.

Developmental Transactions Typical of Adolescents and Young Adults (from the Standpoint of the Person)

Adolescents	Young Adults
Proximal	
Self with self	Self with self
(Who am I?)	(How much can I make of me and what will society let me make of what I am?)
Self with soma	Self with soma
(Dramatic shifts in size, proportions, appearance, and sex characteristics)	(Little change beyond filling out)
Self with qualitative cognitive gains (new view of reality and ideality)	Self with refinements of cognitive gains
Self with proximal social experience (others' evaluations of the new physical, cognitive, and social self)	Self with proximal social experience (others' approval and disapproval of progress)
Distal	
Self with distal social experience (self as an observer of historical trends; only a participant in times like the 1960s)	Self with distal social experience (Self as affected and affecting social trends.)

4. From the critical, evaluative position, we directly ask how these two periods are best traversed. All theorists have implicit answers to this question; Erikson (1959) suggests that the best way to traverse and conclude adolescence is to form an authentic identity. In adopting this position, he, knowingly or unknowingly, endorses a variant of the root value of psychoanalysis: Human affairs work better if they are based on "unrestricted, pathologically undistorted communication [Habermas, 1973, p. 43]." In other words, Erikson expects that the adolescent experience is optimally concluded—an authentic identity is formed—when the adolescent deals in free and undistorted ways with his or her changing self and with his or her shifting world. In this light, the task for adolescents is to assimilate their new possibilities, others' evaluations of them, and the prospects that society offers. Then as young adults their task is to construct accommodations that accurately respond to self, others, and situation. Erikson (1959) observes that some adolescents use nonoptimal ways of traversing the period: foreclosing or diffusing the experiential opportunity or assuming a negative identity. In my view, these processes are subsumed by the classical defensive processes of repression, isolation, and reaction formation, whereas an authentic identity is formed by the use of coping processes.

No one—as far as I know—has suggested an optimal way to traverse the young adult period. Inasmuch as young adults recognize society and join it and in turn are recognized (Erikson, 1959), there is no ambiguity: They are best off if they relate accurately to their new community and are attentive to its rules, regulations, rewards, and punishments. Perhaps the predominance of achievement and adjustment themes in many psychological theories arises from the frequency with which young adults are subjects. If the young adult's course is complicated by society—the Viet Nam War, high unemployment—decisions in regard to optimal accommodations to society become more complicated.

5. If an adolescent copes with the opportunity, there is still no guarantee that his or her course will be smooth or that the outcome will be an authentic identity. Actual "success" will be determined by self–situation interaction. Perhaps the most accurate, undistorted, unrestricted path that some adolescents can follow, given their situation or their time in history, is to rebel, to withdraw, or to bide their time. Clearly many activists and hippie youth of the 1960s felt rebellion or withdrawal was their only moral choice, when they faced the necessity of accommodating to society's demand that they or their male compatriots become soldiers and die and kill in Viet Nam.

Analysis of the longitudinal data at the Institute of Human Development suggests that the female study members (who were adolescents during the 1930s) fitted the picture of classical adolescent rebellion more closely than did males of the same cohorts. Parents' rearing practices are generally more protective and restrictive of girls and these may create situations that girls can resolve only by rebelling to achieve an accurate identity. In a small study (Haan, 1974), I divided 37-year-old adults into groups on the basis of their predominant usage of coping or defensive processes and then prospectively studied the archival record to learn about their adolescent experiences. Coping at adulthood was preceded by progressive reorganization in adolescence, that is, copers changed as a period of transition basically requires, whereas the eventual defenders changed very little. These differences at adolescence were more marked for females than for males. Later work (Haan, in press) suggests that the interval between adolescence and young adulthood was the time of greater change for the males. This difference between the sexes in the timing of the periods of their greatest developmental changes undoubtedly follows on (a) the earlier sexual maturing of females and the greater difficulty girls have in separating from their parents; and (b) the males' later physiological changes and the strong interest this generation of men (born 1921) had in vocational achievement.

The mothers of the predominantly coping or defensive subjects presented complimentary pictures: The mothers of the eventually coping adults were objectively but openly concerned with their struggling offspring, whereas the mothers of the eventually defensive adults described the smoothness of their offsprings' development and were concerned only with conventional matters of whether their offspring ate appropriate food and more proper clothing.

With a different longitudinal sample at the Institute of Human Development, Weinstock (1967) found that family conflict during the subjects' infancy was associated with adult defensiveness at age 30, but family conflict during adolescence was associated with coping at age 30. These results are consistent with mine for the other longitudinal sample in suggesting that family readjustment at adolescence is a prelude to offspring's adult coping.

Universality of the Adolescent Rebellion

When the life-span approach is taken, adolescence is seen as the time of transition between childhood and adulthood, whatever calendar ages are assigned in different cultures. From this view, adolescents are liable to all the emotional reactions that humans experience when they are in personal and social transition: worrying about future risks, erratic interim solutions, and panic about losing the self and longstanding interpersonal relations. Thus, whether individual adolescents are rebellious or whether the period always involves Sturm und Drang experiences, depends on the nature of the social supports adolescents are offered and the obstacles put in their way. In some families, life situations, and societies, the adolescent's transit may be so fully facilitated that the redefinitions that he or she necessarily makes go almost unnoticed. However, western societies have placed various obstacles in the path of adolescents for some time; for example, difficulties in regard to vocational commitment exist at present, resulting from various strains and contradictions in our economy (Freeman, 1976) that increasingly make occupational entry difficult for the young.

Developmental Reciprocities during Adolescence and Young Adulthood

This discourse has so far concerned developing persons' transactions between their old and newly emerging selves and their eventual adaptations. In this section, other self-transactions are considered: the self's transactions (a) with the proximal changes of soma, cognitive qualities, moral concerns, and social expectancies and requirements, like those of the family's; and (b) with distal changes in social expectancies and requirements like those of the government's and more general sociohistorical trends and pressures. As indicated by the entries in Table 6.1, the breadth and depth of changes in the self, and thus the dialectical activity of adolescents in regard to these transactions, is undoubtedly greater than that of young adults.

SELF WITH SOMA

Tanner (1971), considering the sequence, tempo, and individual variation of adolescents' physical growth, writes "the years from twelve to sixteen are the most eventful ones of their lives [p. 907]." Although he admits that physical growth during the first 2 years of life is faster, he notes that the difference lies in the fact that "the subject himself was not a fascinated, charmed, or horrified spectator (of his own developments at age two) [p. 907]." The facts of adolescents' physical growth are well known. Probably in all cultures, teenagers are understandably concerned with their bodies, which are growing larger, changing shape, and acquiring new features and functions (more muscle and less fat; disproportionate growth—head, hands, and feet first grow large; breasts, axillary and pubic hair and beards appear; menstruation, ejaculations occur, and sex and reproduction become more possible). Girls are approximately 2 years ahead of boys in all these respects, but great individual variations in growth velocity occur within each sex. Complicating our understandings of the self–soma transaction is the evidence that a secular trend is underway, although Tanner (1971) thinks it may have reached an outer genetic limitation in some affluent countries with optimal nutrition. The young are maturing physically approximately 2 years earlier than they did 40 years ago and their terminal height continues to increase.

Kimmel (1974) described the paradoxical biohistorical–social situation by noting that "young people appear to be growing up faster and taking a longer time to do it [p. 77]." Clearly Kimmel had adolescents in western societies in mind as he pointed to the contradictions between precocious biological maturation and the social and economic prohibitions and deprivations that prevent these personal possibilities from being enacted. A later section concerned with sociohistoric trends includes a discussion of society's reasons for prolonging adolescence.

Pointing to the more proximal transactions between self and soma, Tanner (1971) writes that the superficially different aspects of physical development—accruing power, skill, and endurance—are all of a piece, biologically, so adolescents' uneven achievements in these respects can only be due to emotional reactions that they have to their bodies. Following the same reasoning, he notes that the timing of boys' first ejaculation is partially culturally determined. Likewise, the value placed on thinness for girls in Western culture seems to have resulted, for not entirely understood reasons, in a recent epidemic of anorexia nervosa (Thompson, 1979). More young women than those who are hospitalized treat food and eating in bizarre ways. These varying self–soma transactions serve to illustrate an interacting network: The adolescent's somatic changes have meaning to the self and the self's and society's reaction have implications for the soma, particularly when striking somatic changes must be assimilated and accommodated, as regularly occurs during adolescence, infancy, and old age. By young adulthood, somatic growth has decelerated so less active and extensive adaptation is required.

Considering the self's dialectical reciprocities as central suggests ways to reorganize conceptualizations in psychosomatic medicine that would change the present emphasis from identifying "types of people," who are at risk of acquiring certain diseases to observing the ways people process expected and fortuitous life stresses during their development (Haan, 1979).

The adult social–emotional sequalae of different rates of physical maturing during adolescence illustrates the long-term implications of the self's transactions with somatic changes. Jones and Bayley (1950) first reported that early maturing adolescent boys were accepted and treated by both adults and peers as being socially more mature. These boys did not need to strive for status for it was simply given to them; as an example, many were student leaders. In contrast, the late maturing boys seemed to counter their physical disadvantage by frenetic activity and striving for attention, or in some cases, by withdrawal.

However, it was the late not the early maturing girls who enjoyed the more favored social position, an expected finding in view of the culturally different evaluations made of the sexes' physiques. Harold Jones (1949) suggested two reasons for the difference:

1. slow maturing girls and their parents have more time to get used to (assimilate and accommodate) the girls' changes, an important consideration, as girls' sexuality is always a greater source of anxiety for parents than is boys'.
2. late maturing girls' physical status is more nearly congruent with the status of boys of the same age, so these girls can readily find opposite sex companions.

So far no study has been made of the adult characteristics of the early and later maturing females; however, Mary Jones (1965) finds that males made radical and interesting personality shifts by young adulthood despite their similarity in adult intelligence and socioeconomic status. The anxious and frenetic late maturing boys had become the more flexible, according to personality inventory scores, and tolerant of ambiguity, playful, and initiating of humor, according to observers; altogether, Jones concluded, they appeared to have greater insight and ability to cope. In contrast, the early maturers as adults were sociable, socialized, self-controlled, and interested in making a good impression, according to personality inventory scores; they were more objective, conventional, power oriented, condescending, and satisfied with their own appearance, according to observers' ratings.

These outcomes suggest complex dialectics occur between social attributions and the self's evaluations of physical status and the self's adaptational needs that resulted in different equilibrations at different points in time. The late maturing boys seem to have "suffered" as adolescents, but perhaps at the same time they discovered how to cope in self-reflective, expressive, sensitive ways that then provided them with particular social rewards and personal satisfactions at adulthood. The early maturing boys seemed to have found their adolescence, with all its easy rewards, a most satisfying time so they may have later experienced difficulty in accommodating to the role of junior worker. Only top slots would be consistent with their adolescent preparation.

SELF AND COGNITIVE GAINS

That young adolescents acquire a qualitatively new way of thinking by means of hypothetical–deductive logical operation is now well-documented by the extensive Piagetian research. The concomitant qualitative shifts in the ways they view themselves and the world are not as widely considered. Inhelder and Piaget's (1958) classical account described the cognitive changes. Adolescents become capable of superimposing propositional logic on the logic of classes and relations and thus come to structure formal mechanisms based on the mathematical vehicles of lattice structures and the inversion, negation, reciprocity, and correlativity group (INRC). From these cognitively based transformations in the way thought proceeds, changes in the self-views follow (or perhaps proceed!).

Adolescents become interested in the future and in the ideal person, life, and society; they acquire certain hypothetical, and thus invariably impractical attitudes toward life and people at the same time their impracticability permits a mad, gay humor. They criticize the way things are and speak confidently and favorably of how they will improve matters in their own lifetimes. Piaget (1971) has related his own adolescent attraction to the formalism of a career in philosophy, a fate he seems to feel he narrowly escaped. As all humans do with newly acquired competencies, adolescents' overexercise their new cognitive virtuosity and some become quite literally drunk with thought. Adolescents' imminent departures from home and family and their justifiable wishes for better future lives for themselves, their generation, and the families they expect to create also instigate strong interests in the morality of exchanges, on both the personal and societal levels. The next section concerns their moral development.

Some theorists disagree with a conclusion frequently drawn from Piagetian theory that cognitive development stops at early adolescence following the acquisition of formal operations (Arlin, 1975; Murphy & Gilligan, 1980; Labouvie-Vief & Chandler, 1978). In an important analysis of structural changes in the life span, Labouvie-Vief (1979) asks, "What, if any, are the failures of limits of this logic (formal operations) from the perspectives of adult development? [p. 6]." She answers that only an open logic that is reactive to pragmatics can be truly adaptive and she goes on to show that this position is consistent with sentiments Piaget has expressed in passing. Critical to the argument here are two statements of Piaget's (which Labouvie-Vief cites as well), "Just as experience reconciles formal thought with the reality of things, so does effective and enduring work, undertaken in concrete and well-defined situations, cure dreams . . . once the last crises of adaptation have been surmounted, professional work definitely restores equilibrium and thus definitely marks the advent of adulthood [Piaget, 1967, pp. 68–69]."

In essence, Piaget and Labouvie-Vief suggest that adolescents' cognitive development is not equilibrated because they still do not accommodate to reality in a practical sense but, when they do, adulthood begins. In one sense, this suggestion agrees with the present proposal that young adulthood is a time of accommodation. For Piaget, "undertaking professional work" is the turning point; for Labouvie-Vief, the pragmatic accommodation of formal logic to reality marks the event. However, this argument only results in structural development being terminated a few years later in the life span and we are brought to see that programmatically, the Piagetian system is an open one. More conceptualization and investigation about adult development are needed for us to understand in what ways this open system continues to develop.

Alternatively, I argue that understanding young adults' cognitive development is to be understood in the light of the following considerations:

1. Real-life adaptation (equilibration) is never final and more than cognitive structures are always involved.
2. Whatever cognitive structures develop between adolescence and middle adulthood, people make increasingly greater investments in cognitive means of problem-solving and increasingly consider their own thought and feelings relevant (as assessed in lengthy clinical interviews, Haan, in press), probably because such strategies work better.
3. Given our present political economy, many young adults probably "successfully" adapt, not by accommodating, but by overaccommodating, a trend that can only be relieved at middle age when a person is either a clear success or reconciled to what achievements are possible (Clausen, in press; Stroud, in press).
4. When we seriously consider those ineffable entities inside the person that we blithely label "structures," it is obvious that there must be more kinds of structures than those of formal logic (structures being defined as holistic, organized, and logically consistent understandings). Other structures such as morality, understandings of human embeddedness and attachments, and affective–attitudinal organizations likely exist.
5. The primarily accommodatory cognitive changes of young adults cannot be understood apart from social contexts and fortuitous life events that both facilitate and deter development. Young adults discover the implications for themselves of definitive choice and use the results of their investigations to further their accommodations because neither they nor society can allow further delay.

SELF AND MORALITY

I found in my moral research with lower- and middle-class, black and white adolescents that they were eager, even yearned to discuss moral issues (Haan, 1978). Adolescents have every reason to have deep interest in morality: They are moving into uncharted contexts that expose them to moral strains that can be neither fully articulated nor understood; they want to decide for themselves and cannot usually bear to seek guidance from the old, being well aware that the latter cannot resist opportunities to instruct.

Fundamentally, morality is the dialectic between the self's and other's interests and the terms of these transactions clearly shift for the person at adolescence and again at young adulthood. Because young adults have usually acquired moral capabilities equal to or better than their parents, as well as reasonable social–economic resources, readjustments in existing moral imbalances within the family become necessary. Typically, parents in all times and places have greater moral concern for their offspring than is reciprocated, an historic injustice, Rawls (1971) says. But if moral equity between now-adult offspring and parents is not achieved, their relationship cannot continue to survive as an emotionally honest one.

When the young take the critical step that repeals their moral advantage in relation to their parents, they have terminated their adolescence. The move is not usually an easy one for either party. Parents must forfeit their sense of moral superiority and realize their aging; the offspring must forego personal advantage and cast themselves out to take their chances as a nonspecial person among other people.

Following a process–dialectical view of development, arising from the formulation of coping and defending, I constructed an interactional formulation of morality (see Haan, 1977; 1978), based on the supposition that people perpetually engage in important and trivial moral dialogues within dyads, groups, and society for the sake of preserving their social relations and conserving their sense of themselves as moral beings. Given the lengths to which people will go to defend themselves against recognizing their wrongdoings, we can conclude that belief in one's moral righteousness is a deep and abiding human motivation that must arise from the social context—the assimilations and accommodations—of our living and rearing. These moral dialogues are often preconscious but they have structure and rules that are widely accepted and understood, although not often articulated. For a dialogue and its conclusion to be considered moral, three criteria need to be met: All concerned must be allowed to speak, none can dominate, and all can veto. This formulation of morality is similar to other procedural theories of justice advanced by Habermas (1973) and Rawls (1971).

Several years ago, we engaged six different friendship groups of approximately 10 adolescents each to take part in a research project—three groups were black and three white, three were middle-class, and three, lower-class and in all groups half were girls and half were boys (Haan, 1977; 1978). First, they were individually interviewed in regard to several hypothetical moral dilemmas; then, as friendship groups, they confronted moral dilemmas presented in the form of five different games and simulations lasting for 3 hours each; and finally, they were interviewed twice again, immediately after the completion of the group sessions and again 3 months later.

Independent measures were made of each adolescent's forms of coping and defending and levels of moral resolution in reaction to the moral strain posed by the group dilemmas. Most instances of moral default probably occur as the result of self-protective, defensive distortion and negation, whereas coping gives some assurance that the "truth" will be discovered in moral dialogues and that the participants will act on it. Under moral strain, several upper-middle-class white adolescents of brilliant academic achievements proved to be morally less differentiated and sensitive than some lower-class black adolescents of meager academic achievements. In general, the black groups became more cohesive under moral strain, perhaps because they were sensitive to the fact that they were dealing with a white institution (although one-half the staff was black), but more likely because most oppressed groups, like blacks and women, develop interpersonal, integrative skills for protection. The group most debilitated by moral strain was composed of the lower-class white youngsters. Individually, they lacked interpersonal skills to help themselves and their group. Their moral argumentation—no matter what the game suggested in the way of content—drifted toward the moral relationship between men and women. Manifestly they argued about men and women sharing housework, child care, and financial support, but their real problem was basic equity between the sexes. Current social pressures toward changing sex roles were not lost on the girls who seized the opportunity to discuss the moral balance between sexes with their male peers. The girls wanted to avoid the fate of their own mothers, who were raising their children without husbands' or relatives' help, mostly on waitresses' salaries.

The quantitative results for this study showed the expected; correlations between the adolescents' levels of moral reasoning about hypothetical dilemmas and their levels of moral actions in the games were not high. The contexts of game or interview and hypothetical or real moral dilemmas sharply contrast; if people are rational, it can be expected that they will respond with differentiation. However, the adolescents' moral action levels were more fully explained when the stress of the games and the individuals' kinds and levels of ego processing were taken into account. Moral levels were high for those adolescents who coped empathically with others' points of view, who tolerated ambiguities, and who objectively assessed the situational circumstances and group conflict. Moral levels fell for those who became actively defensive by rationalizing and intellectualizing or who failed to cope. The adolescents generally raised their initial levels of skill in moral dialogues by the end of the five sessions and retained these gains when they were interviewed again 3–4 months later.

Other results occurred, but I conclude by emphasizing the dialectical, life-span aspects of this study. Several reciprocities are involved:

1. The self's interests versus the group's interests is the root dialectic of morality. Being self-interested in this group context resulted from stress and turned out to be stressful.

2. The self's old ways of moral resolution versus new ways possibly incited by the games, other's needs, and the adolescent's own need to regard him or herself as moral; the basic developmental dialectic of self-conservation versus self-transformation is involved.
3. The sociohistorical context as it penetrated these situations, resulted in the black groups' cohesiveness and fomented argument concerning equity between the sexes with the lower-class white group.

SELF AND PROXIMAL SOCIAL EXPECTANCIES

In their assimilatory binges, adolescents are alert and diffusely vulnerable to the mirror of others' criticisms, blandishments, and offers of love; at the same time they do not readily accommodate to these rewards and punishments. In their accommodatory bent, young adults are reactive and adaptive but particularly liable to frustrations and angers because they now forgo so much self-interest to accommodate. Margaret Singer (1979) contends after her extensive work with former cult members that all young people are liable to cult recruitment and its promises of interpersonal peace if they are in limbo (e.g., between love affairs or jobs) and meet a skilled proselytizer. However, according to Singer, upper-middle-class white youngsters are considerably more likely to be recruited because of the nature of their social expectancies than blacks or chicanos who recognize a street hustle when they see one and who realistically know when people give, they expect some kind of return. Clearly, young adults have not yet achieved virtuosity in handling human affairs, if any age group does.

Early adolescence marks the expansion of the person's actual social network, and for the first time, serious relations with nonfamily persons occur. However, at young adulthood, the self is engaged in multiple and serious transactions with a larger variety of people than is the case at adolescence (i.e., at adolescence: mothers, fathers, sibs, close friends; additions at young adulthood, lovers, spouses, co-workers, bosses). Each of these transactions is potentially infused with concerns of attachment, dependency, morality, love, power, and so forth. All the permutations of the array of objects and contents available to young people cannot be considered here so this exposition focuses on the self's relations with family as a transacting, organic unit.

The adolescent's ontogeny requires that familial roles be redefined. Reference was made earlier to the necessities of families' transforming their moral balances; however, this is not the only family reorganization because the family's love and dependency relations and its governance also change in concert with the young person's moral and cognitive developments. As the family undergoes change, all members are involved in a complex dialectic, which most families appear willing to undertake, presumably because the unit has value to its members (and the unit values individual members). There is ample evidence that families generally wish to preserve themselves as social–emotional entities (Bengston & Kuypers, 1971; Bengston & Troll, 1978; Haan, 1971, 1977; Troll & Smith, 1976), so the family has reason to want to change.

Just as the fundamental dialectic for the individual's development involves changing while staying the same, so it is with the family. It must maintain tradition but faciliate its members' changes and development. If it does not achieve this synthesis, it may be necessary for the developing offspring to resign their membership. Bengston and Kuypers (1971) report that parents consistently overestimate the degree of closeness, understanding, and communication in the family compared to young adult offspring. This antithesis reflects the life situation of young people. They have the primary and stronger developmental interest in changing the status quo by redefinition and separation: They hope for emotional gain, whereas the parents have only the consolation prize of a job well done. Bengston and Kuypers conclude from their studies that although patterns of solidarity and warmth are consistently found between generations, each interprets their mutual interaction from different developmental perspectives. For the parents, family disagreements are trivial ones of personal habits and traits, whereas, for the offspring, fundamental matters of value, morality, politics, and life goals are at issue. These investigators suggest older generations have "developmental stakes" in the younger ones; equally important are the young's stakes in the older people that arise from their love and their needs for the family's continued validation of their self-changes and their enduring identities. Bengston and Troll (1978) conclude from their literature review that parent–child bonds persist through the years. However, the family's bond is the more embracing and it usually persists despite geographic separation, economic and social differences, and disagreements about values.

SELF AND DISTAL SOCIAL EXPECTANCIES: INSTITUTIONS AND SOCIOHISTORIC TRENDS

When the life span is the focus, the possibilities that sociohistorical trends have differential effects on the development of successive generations becomes more evident. This "cohort effect" has long interested sociologists in their studies of society. However, psychologists have recently developed interest in the effect for different reasons and answers to several questions help to determine whether such trends are relevant for their enterprise:

1. What is the sociohistoric trend? (Many studies do not say.)
2. What is the evidence that the particular sociohistoric trend *actually* impinged on the subjects' life in important ways (e.g., not all persons

living during the time of some calamity or some historical shift are personally affected)?

3. Are the psychological characteristics of focus the sort that can be reasonably expected to be affected by a distal sociohistorical trend?
4. What precisely are the critical features of the identified sociohistorical trend that seem to have affected personal development?
5. What are the effective mechanisms of transactions and transmission between self and the environment trend?
6. How important and/or permanent are the cohort effects (i.e., as scientists, we are presumably more interested in durable influences than in passing fashions)? For example, Elder (1974) found strong concurrent effects of the Depression on adolescent subjects from economically deprived families but neither these nor other discontinuous effects could be discerned by age 37.

If statistical analyses suggest cohort effects may have occurred but suitable answers to these questions are not provided, the conclusion that a sociohistorical trend affected results cannot be drawn. Results could very well be due to conditions of testing and observation or the peculiar nature of the samples drawn. The contents of people's lives readily change with passing trends, but their basic structures and processes may not easily fluctuate; I argue that the latter variables are of greater interest to psychologists.

Turning to consider historic effects on adolescents and young adults, we have no more complete account than Gillis' (1974) history of youth and society since 1770. He defines youth as the period between childhood and adulthood, and uses adolescence as a special designation for a period of prolonged dependency invented by the middle classes in the late 1880s to control their offspring following the revolutions of the mid-nineteenth century. According to Gillis' careful work, a period of "youth" has always existed (Aries, 1965, to the contrary), and he focuses on the "interface where the expectations of the young and those of the elders' interact in a dynamic manner (Gillis, 1974, p. x)." Thus, on the macrolevel, Gillis is suggesting that the dialectic between generations reflects the inevitable differences in the ontogenesis of the two age groups' self-interests. The age grading of society and the personal characteristics of young people— their vigor, need to seek their fortune, and their oppression by elders— cause youth to make its own history at the same time that they draw on youth's traditions. Their expectancies and demands are never entirely congruent with the life possibilities offered by society that most likely reflect society's current economic and social needs. In the eighteenth century and in some countries now, families and societies need large numbers of children because few survive, parents need protection in their old age, and the economy or the military need young workers or soldiers.

Patently, none of these purposes represents the self-interests of the young. According to Gillis, when generational tensions grow, authority tightens and the youth become more group conscious and strengthen their resistance by horizontal bonding. A recent example is young Americans' effective organization against the Viet Nam War.

The nature of human interchange means that parents and statesmen always need to morally legitimize themselves to the young in some fashion whether or not they do so adequately or accurately. Not to do so threatens society; if the young do not cooperate in society, the elderly's future may be in jeopardy. Moreover, the older generation has emotional stakes (Bengston & Kuypers, 1971) in their offspring because they love them, the offspring are the fruition of their long-term intent to "rear a child" and they represent the continuity and the continuation of the parent's own lives. For their part, the young must make a place in society for themselves often at the elders' expense. Optimistically, the young hope for "room at the top." Thus the two generation's needs constitute a dialectic in themselves. The psychologist's question, at the microlevel of the self's transaction with distal social factors, is whether and how individual persons' development, as processes and structure, is affected by their generation's prospects and how young persons' point of entry into history affects their immediate transactions as well as their long-term prospects.

Understandably, history and the larger society are usually matters of indifference to the young, given reasonable intergenerational equity. However, history (Gillis, 1974) suggests that when equity is clearly violated, youth are easily and understandably swept up with ambition to preserve their future living space and avoid society's plans for them. For instance, contemporary young seem to be concluding that their future living space may be seriously violated by further development of nuclear energy. Tice (1976) predicts a new era of student activism which will be different from the 1960s because American youth's traditions now include considerably more sophisticated knowledge about how social change can be brought about beyond the simple pressures of sit-ins, rallies, and marches (Inglehart, 1977; Tice, 1976). Of course, neither youth nor elders are always clear or fully informed about the contingencies.

For youth these times become ones of moral issue—their future is on the line; the shoes are on their feet and their future orientation inspires them to avoid repeating the fate of their hapless elders. For society, these are times of confusion, but also potentially of structural renewal and enhancement as the old accommodate to the young and the young to the old. Bengston and Troll (1978) have recently provided cogent evidence for "reverse socialization" wherein the young are agents of the old's changes.

From a developmental point of view, adolescents' opportunities to engage in real transactions with society make it possible for them to quit their assimilatory binges as they examine their contexts and prospects and clarify their options. A prospective study of Peace Corp Volunteers (Haan, 1974) found that, after overseas tours of duty, they had not only morally gained in Kohlberg (1969) scores but they had also become more liberal politically, more introspective and autonomous personally, and further differentiated from their parents. Experiences that inform citizens about the force of political participation and assure them of their efficacy in influencing governmental processes are widely assumed to be to their own and society's good.

Using the key concepts of the forerunner effect (a nucleus of attitudes evolved and practiced by persons isolated in their own generation; Mannheim, 1952) and the keynote effect (the particular area of life a generation might want to change (e.g., sexual behavior), Bengston and Troll (1978) evolve a striking and detailed analysis of individual's contributions to the process of social change in which each new generation is mediator, both to their parents and their children and recipient of their own generation's keynote interests. Thus, as Reese (1977) observes, "there is a dialectical relation between the individual's activities and the activities of the society, and the result is the individual's knowledge, which, however, changes society's knowledge [p. 208]."

Summary Ideas

The unifying themes of this chapter are not particularly new, except for the contention that it is important and clarifying to distinguish normatively expected behavior from self-protective, socially voiding behavior.

A process perspective suggested that normatively (a) the young person is active in an active world that is reactive to him or her; (b) the young person has his or her own directions but obstacles are met in the form of oppositional inclinations of other people or in contradictive aspects of situations, or metacognitively, in the countering multiple intentions of the self; so (c) the young person negotiates varying settlements that compromise or synthesize his or her intents with what is possible. The temporality of cognizant persons' lives is evident in this unceasing, dialectical cycling of intent–conflict–resolution and it can be seen with especial clarity in adolescents and young adults. In their naiveté, orientation to the future, and need to make a place for themselves, young people are "naturally" and frequently at odds with the status quo whether their primary adaptive mode is assimilatory, as it seems during adolescence, or accommodatory, as it seems during young adulthood.

The different, if not new ideas presented in this chapter follow on the critical position that the rules governing social scientific inquiry—objective, public, and repeatable procedures—are the same ones people informally use to discover practical consensual validations and thus social psychological truth and that truth-finding and freedom to find truth are inseparable (Habermas, 1971). These procedures do not define the contents of the good life span or the best adolescence or determine which kind of "mature" behavior is the best (Labouvie-Vief & Chandler, 1978; Reese, 1977). Instead, values are represented in the kind of processes people use to secure pragmatic, everyday forms of truth, to traverse developmental transitions, and to resolve fortuitous stress.

Psychoanalysis' and Habermas' values of undistorted, unrestricted communication and my suggestion that the integrity of coping processes rests on their accuracy are related. However, Erikson likewise takes a value position when he suggests that adolescents normatively form authentic identities by accurately appraising who they are and what they can become, whereas other adolescents' nonnormative processes negate or distort their opportunities so they do not form authentic identities.

The psychologist's proper focus is the self's reciprocities with all else; here it was with the self's developmental opportunities during adolescence and adulthood within the context of Frenkel-Brunswik's (1954) earlier remonstration, "there are richer and poorer, more efficient and less efficient orientations or ways of dealing with reality and as scientists we are not entitled to obscure or circumvent this fact [p. 486]."

References

Aries, P. *Centuries of childhood: A social history of family life.* New York: Vintage, 1965.

Arlin, P. K. Cognitive development in adulthood. A fifth stage? *Developmental Psychology,* 1975, *11*, 602–606.

Baltes, P., & Cornelius, S. The status of dialectic in development psychology: Theoretical orientation versus scientific method. In N. Datan & H. Reese (Eds.), *Life-span developmental psychology: Dialectical perspective on experimental research.* New York: Academic Press, 1977.

Bengston, V., & Kuypers, J. Correlational difference and the developmental stake. *Aging and Human Development,* 1971, *2*, 249–259.

Bengston, V., & Troll, L. Youth and their parents: Feedback and intergenerational influence in socialization. In R. Lerner, P. Baltes, & G. Spanier (Eds.), *Child Influences on marital and family interaction.* New York: Academic Press, 1978, 215–240.

Bernstein, R. *Restructuring of social and political theory.* New York: Harcourt Brace Jovanovich, 1976.

Clausen, J. Men's occupational careers in the middle years. In D. Eichorn, P. Mussen, J. Clausen, N. Haan, & M. Honzik (Eds.), *Present and past in middle life.* New York: Academic Press, in press.

Des Pres, T. *The survivors.* New York: Oxford University Press, 1975.

De Vries, P. *The Blood of the lamb.* New York: Little, Brown, 1963.

Elder, G. *Children of the Great Depression.* Chicago: University of Chicago Press, 1974.

Erikson, E. H. Identity and the life cycle. *Psychological Issues*, 1959, *1*(1), 171 pp. (whole issue).

Freedle, R. Psychology, Thomian topologies, deviant logics, and human development. In N. Datan & H. Reese (Eds.), *Life-span developmental psychology: Dialectical perspectives on experimental research.* New York: Academic Press, 1977, pp. 317–340.

Freeman, R. *The overeducated American.* New York: Academic Press, 1976.

Frenkel-Brunswik, E. Social research and the problem of values. *Journal of Abnormal and Social Psychology*, 1954, *49*, 466–471.

Gillis, J. R. *Youth and history: Tradition and change in European age relations, 1770–present.* New York: Academic Press, 1974.

Haan, N. Moral redefinition in families as a critical aspect of the generational gap. *Youth and Society*, 1971, *2*, 259–283.

Haan, N. Changes in young adults after Peace Corps experience. *Journal of Youth and Adolescence*, 1974, *3*, 177–194.

Haan, N. "Change and sameness" reconsidered. *International Journal of Aging and Human Development*, 1976, *7*, 59–65.

Haan, N. *Coping and defending: Processes of self-environment organization.* New York: Academic Press, 1977.

Haan, N. Two moralities in action contexts. *Journal of Personality and Social Psychology.* 1978, *36*, 286–305.

Haan, N. Psychological meanings of unfavorable medical forecasts. In G. Stone, F. Cohen, & N. Adler (Eds.), *Health psychology.* San Francisco: Jossey-Bass, 1979.

Haan, N. Common dimensions of personality development: Early adolescence to middle life. In D. Eichorn, P. Mussen, J. Clausen, N. Haan, & M. Honzik (Eds.), *Present and past in middle life.* Academic Press, in press.

Haan, N., & Day, D. Change and sameness in personality development: adolescence to adulthood. *International Journal of Aging and Human Development*, 1974, *5*, 11–39.

Habermas, J. *Knowledge and human interests.* (Trans. J. J. Shapiro). Boston: Beacon Press, 1971.

Habermas, J. *Legitimation crisis.* (Trans. Thomas McCarthy). Boston: Beacon Press, 1973.

Habermas, J. Moral development and ego identity. *Telos*, 1975, *24*, 41–55.

Hartmann, H. *Psychoanalysis and moral values.* New York: International Universities Press, 1960.

Inglehart, R. *The silent revolution.* Princeton, N.J.: Princeton University Press, 1977.

Inhelder, B., & Piaget, J. *The growth of logical thinking from childhood and adolescence.* New York: Basic Books, 1958.

Jones, H. Adolescence in our society. In Community Service Society of New York (Eds.), *The family in a democratic society.* New York: Columbia University Press, 1949, 70–84.

Jones, M. Psychological correlates of somatic development. *Child Development*, 1965, *36*, 899–911.

Jones, M., & Bayley, N. Physical maturing among boys as related to behavior. *Journal of Educational Psychology*, 1950, *41*, 129–148.

Keniston, K. *Young radicals.* New York: Harcourt, Brace, & World, 1968.

Kimmel, D. *Adulthood and aging.* New York: Wiley, 1974.

Kohlberg, L. Stage and sequence: The cognitive-developmental approach to socialization. In D. A. Goslin (Ed.), *Handbook of socialization.* Chicago: Rand McNally, 1969. Pp. 347–380.

Labouvie-Vief, G. *Uses of logic in life-span development: Piaget revisited.* Paper presented at the annual meeting of society of Research on Child Development, San Francisco, March 15, 1979.

Labouvie-Vief, G., & Chandler, M. Cognitive development and life-span developmental theory: Idealistic versus contextual perspectives. In P. Baltes (Ed.), *Life-span development* (Vol. 1). New York: Academic Press, 1978.

Larson, R., & Csikszentimihalyi, M. Experimental correlates of time alone in adolescence. *Journal of Personality*, 1978, *46*, 677–693.

Lefcourt, H. The function of illusions of control and freedom. *American Psychologist*, 1973, *28*(3), 417–425.

Mannheim, K. The problem of generations. In K. Mannheim (Ed.), *Essays on the sociology of knowledge*. London: Routledge & Keagan, 1952. (Originally published 1923.)

Markus, H. Self-schemata and processing of information about the self. *Journal of Personality and Social Psychology*, 1977, *35*, 63–78.

Milgram, S. *Obedience to authority*. N.Y.: Harper, 1974.

Murphy, J. M., Gilligan, C. Moral development in late adolescence and adulthood: A critique and reconstruction of Kohlberg's theory. *Human Development*, 1980, *23*, 77–104.

O'Connor, J. *The fiscal crisis of the State*. New York: St. Martin's Press, 1973.

Piaget, J. *Six psychological studies*. New York: Random House, 1967.

Piaget, J. *The child's conception of the world*. Patterson, N.J.: Littlefield Adams, 1969. (a)

Piaget, J. *The mechanisms of perception*. New York: Norton, 1969. (b)

Piaget, J. *Insight and illusion in psychology*. New York: World, 1971.

Rawls, J. *The theory of justice*. Cambridge, Mass.: Harvard University Press, 1971.

Reese, H. Discriminative learning and transfer: Dialectical perspectives. In N. Datan & H. Reese (Eds.), *Life-span developmental psychology: Dialectical perspectives on experimental research*. New York: Academic Press, 1977.

Rogers, T. B., Kuiper, N. A., & Kirker, W. S. Self-reference and the encoding of personal information. *Journal of Personality and Social Psychology*, 1977, *35*, 677–688.

Rosenthal, R., & Jackson, L. *Pygmalion in the classroom: Teacher expectation and pupils' intellectual development*. New York: Holt, Rinehart, & Winston, 1968.

Rudner, R. S. *Philosophy of social science*. Englewood Cliffs, N.J., 1966.

Sarason, S. The nature of problem solving in social action. *American Psychologist*, 1978, *33*, 370–380.

Seligman, M. E. P. *Helplessness*. San Francisco: Freeman, 1975.

Singer, M. Cults as an exercise in political psychology. Invited address International Society of Political Psychology, annual meeting, Washington, D. C., May 24, 1979.

Stroud, J. Women's careers: Work, family, & personality. In D. Eichorn, P. Mussen, J. Clausen, N. Haan, & M. Honzik (Eds.), *Present and past in middle life*. Academic Press, in press.

Swanson, G. E. *Self processes and social organization: An interpretation of the mechanisms of coping and defense*. Unpublished manuscript, 1968.

Tanner, J. Sequence, tempo, and individual variation in the growth and development of boys and girls aged twelve to sixteen. *Daedalus*, 1971, *100*(4), 907–930.

Thompson, M. *Anorexic-like behavior among normal college women*. Paper presented at the conference on the psychology of adolescence, Michael Reese Hospital, Chicago, June 15, 1979.

Tice, T. *Student rights, decision making, and the law*. Washington, D. C.: American Association for Higher Education, 1976.

Troll, L., & Smith, J. Attachment through the life span: some questions abut dyadic bonds among adults. *Human Development*, 1976, *19*, 156–170.

Weinstock, A. Family environment and the development of defense and coping mechanisms. *Journal of Personality and Social Psychology*, 1967, *5*, 67–75.

DEAN RODEHEAVER
NANCY DATAN

7

Making It: The Dialectics of Middle Age

Introduction: Middle Age and the Dialectics of Control

The developmental dynamics of middle age have only recently become a fashionable focus for empirical inquiry. The second half of the life span is being increasingly studied by developmental psychologists who find that transitions do not end in adolescence, by clinicians who discover that each age in the life cycle has its own unique problems, and by sociologists who explore the position of the middle-aged and older adult in the social structure (Datan & Lohmann, 1980).

Social and historical changes have been at least partly responsible for attracting the attention of social scientists to the entire life span. Fewer children, spaced closer together, have created an extended postparental period, adults who have increasing numbers of years to call their own. This trend has been accompanied by a greater status and influence in middle age. The result has been the creation of a period of life charac-terized by the ability and time to make choices in one's life. With these choices have come difficulties; the contributions to one recent volume (Norman & Scaramella, 1980) on the midlife crisis repeatedly contend that researchers have paid little attention to middle adulthood except to claim losses and to count casualties. The transitions of middle age provide a challenge for those interested in understanding development across the life span.

183

Individuals as Producers of Their Development

FREEDOM WITH QUALIFICATIONS:
MIDDLE AGE AND CONTROL

Middle age encompasses both remembrance and anticipation. The individual leaves adolescence with a claim to an independent life and strengthens that claim throughout adulthood. Increasingly, though, the autonomy of middle adulthood is tempered by the anticipation of a final ending; the deaths of friends and relatives become reminders of one's own death. The pressures of time require some readjustment of earlier goals as one begins to "fear that it may be too late to accomplish some of the things one had hoped to accomplish in one's life time [Mann, 1980, p. 132]." It becomes clear in middle age that the final authority over life rests in the hands of the individual (Gould, 1978). Competence in and control over one's life become important developmental issues in middle age.

Neugarten (1968) has portrayed for us the executive capacities of middle age. As she notes, "Middle-aged men and women, while they by no means regard themselves as being in command of all they survey, nevertheless recognize that they constitute the powerful age-group vis-a-vis other age groups [p. 93]." Their sensitivity extends beyond their social position to their sense of control over their own lives. "Middle adulthood is the period of maximum capacity and ability to handle a highly complex environment and a highly differentiated self [p. 97]." Their handling of the environment and the self is expressed through feelings of maturity, a good grasp of reality, and the experience of a sense of expertise, and is maintained through a constant reassessment of the self. A similar picture is painted by Lowenthal, Thurnher, Chiriboga, Beeson, Gigy, Lurie, Pierce, Spence, and Weiss (1976): They note that middle-aged men consider themselves "more masculine and frank . . . (and) rated themselves as less lazy, less self-pitying, less disorderly, more cautious, and less sarcastic [p. 71]" than men of other ages. Although this sense of self control emerged later in women, by preretirement age they too felt that they were less dependent and more competent and assertive; they generally assumed a position of greater effectiveness (Lowenthal, *et al.*, 1976).

Yet life in middle age comes to be measured by time left to live rather than time since birth (Neugarten, 1968), perhaps bringing the realization that not all of one's goals can be achieved. Paradoxically, at the height of personal control over one's personal and social self, the personalization of death, as Neugarten puts it, creates what we might call a dialectical tension between autonomy and vulnerability. We shall explore this developmental dialectic in the following section.

THE DEVELOPMENTAL DIALECTIC OF CONTROL

From a dialectical perspective, the major goal of life-cycle development is synchronization—a balance both within the individual and between the individual and the world (Riegel, 1979). Synchronization is very rarely spontaneous: Where it does occur, it is the result of action performed by the developing individual. This activity is a response to the crises, contradictions, and doubts indicating that inner or outer relations are not in synchrony. Such an imbalance leads the individual to act toward synchrony within the temporal constraints of the life cycle.

It is consistent with the dialectical view that developmental goals can never actually be reached. Development is characterized by continuous activity because the act of achieving synchrony creates the conditions that lead to further imbalance: In acting on the world, the individual changes that world, creating a need for further action.

This general dialectical view suggests that control over development is an issue across the life span. The activity emerging from conflict is the individual's assertion of control over the course of the life cycle. At any point in development, inner and outer relations will determine the nature of the conflict and the form taken by the controlling resolution.

In middle age, the salience of the themes of competence and effectiveness in directing a dwindling life span would suggest that control may be the very issue over which the conflict arises. One's accomplishments and failures are attributable to past resolutions. One's hopes depend on the ability to gain control over conflicts yet to come. At a time when one has accomplished a large measure of control over the personal and social self, a recognition of inefficiency in control over any facet of development, resulting from earlier conflict resolutions, will present an imbalance and a new conflict.

We will consider two developmental interfaces where conflicts over control may arise. First, we shall explore the relationship between the developing individual and the changing family world, which includes other individuals on independent developmental trajectories. We will illustrate this interface with a discussion of intergenerational relations. Second, we shall explore the relationship between the developing individual and those earlier resolutions of developmental conflicts—the dynamics of control between the developing self and the reflective self. The interaction of these development interfaces will be illustrated by the phenomenon of the empty nest. Throughout, we will suggest that these crises are expressions of ongoing conflicts between the individual's need to control the remaining life cycle and inner (personal) and outer (interpersonal) relations opposing that control.

Intergenerational Relations:
The Developing Self and Developing Others

In middle age, the individual is typically at the center of three generations of adults: both the parent of adult children and the adult child of one's own parents. The control of the personal self, a major developmental issue for the middle aged, requires coordination of personal development with that of two other adult generations. Successful control of adult life cannot be achieved at the expense of relations to adult children or parents, and requires an orchestration of multiple developmental trajectories.

Troll, Miller, and Atchley (1979) have given careful attention to the relationship between the generations. They see middle age as a liaison period; whereas few young couples visit their grandparents, middle-aged couples unite both ends of the generation span with frequent visits to both children and parents. In one study, Troll et al. (1979) report that 40% of the middle-aged respondents saw their parents weekly and 70% saw their children weekly. Generations remain in close contact not only physically but emotionally: "Most parents and children report positive feelings for each other at all ages [p. 94]." Parents seem to remain important to their children throughout the life cycle of the child: When asked to describe any person, adults of all ages spontaneously described their parents more than anyone else.

What is the role of this generational closeness in the development of middle-aged individuals? How does maintaining close physical and emotional contact with parents and children affect the control of one's own development in middle age? How do three generations of adults balance close contact with the coordination of independent lives?

Erikson's (1963) stage of generativity versus stagnation recognizes the importance of the younger generation in the psychosocial development of the older generation. The ability of adults to expand their ego interests to the establishment and guidance of the next generation is a necessary step in the development of the individual. The alternative, stagnation, results in investment only in the self—as if one were one's only creation— rather than in the next generation. Erikson (1959) has also discussed the importance in middle age of a changed perspective toward one's parents; at this stage their importance is better appreciated.

Troll et al. (1979) speculated that children's maturity may come when they begin to make decisions and to assume responsibilities for some aspect of their parents' lives. Through the development of "filial maturity" (Blenkner, 1965), parents and children come to know each other better and to appreciate the importance each has for the development of the other:

> For the child to achieve filial maturity, the parent must participate in the process, first in a modeling capacity, and second in a rewarding capacity. There is reason to believe that the inverse is also true. For the parent to continue to develop, the child must participate in the process in both a modeling and a rewarding capacity. In other words, the significance of the parent/child relationship does not end with launching but continues throughout life. Parents and children who continue to develop throughout their lives—to accept their

own development as meaningful and satisfying—are helping their children and parents to develop in turn [p. 105].

In short, the importance in middle adulthood of intergenerational relations, conceptualized as generativity or filial maturity, is gaining recognition. Theorists agree that the development of each generation is contingent on the development of preceding and succeeding generations.

Conflicts between the generations are due to the "stake" (Bengtson and Kuypers, 1971) each generation has in its own development and in the development of other generations. The youngest generation, faced with the task of achieving independence, will maximize the differences between it and the older generations. The middle generation, facing its own developmental tasks—generativity and filial maturity—will perceive greater continuity across the generations (Bengtson & Troll, 1978; Lerner, 1975; Lerner & Knapp, 1975).

The "generational stake" is a recognition that the development of each generation is partially controlled by at least one other generation. For the middle generation, this issue of control arises at a time when control is increasingly salient in the individual domain as well.

As an example of the demands intergenerational relations place on adult development, consider the process of intergenerational transmission. Traditionally, this process has been interpreted as the unidirectional influence of the old upon the young. Bengtson and Troll (1978), however, asserted that transmission implies feedback—an exchange of information—that may be assumed to include the influence of the young upon the old. Parents are not simply the keepers of information who relentlessly try to convince the child of its value; there is also evidence of the influence of children upon political and sex-role orientations of parents. Furthermore, there is a lifelong bond between parents and children and a developmental trend toward greater affective solidarity that reflects an intergeneration exchange and the dialectically linked development of parent and child.

This is not to suggest that there is no conflict of opinion between parents and children, but that parenthood is not defined by rigid adherence to adult values in opposition to those held by children. As both parents and children move into maturity and young adulthood, respectively, a capacity for change develops out of the intergenerational dialogue. The development of generativity or filial maturity is not merely a recognition of change in others but is also the realization of one's own capacity and need for change. Parents recognize that, if they are to continue to be generative, to nurture their children, the kind of nurturance they give must change as the child grows older. If there is no parental change, the child is unable to sustain the filial tie, nor can the parents learn to accept the child as an adult whose developing needs demand parental change.

Intergenerational relations exemplify the conflicts in control between

the developing middle-aged and developing others. In the preceding discussion, the development of middle-aged parents was seen in the context
of their relationships with their young adult children. Maintaining these
relationships introduces tension over control by middle-aged parents,
whose own development is partially dependent on the development of
their children through their rejection of parental control. The autonomy
of each generation is closely related to the autonomy of other generations,
and the progression of intergenerational relationships can lead to change
in both generations as ideas, attitudes, and beliefs are exchanged and a
capacity for change is realized.

Troll *et al.* (1979) suggest that, for most adults, such intergenerational
conflicts are resolved through a mutuality of expectations: "The evidence
indicates that most parents understand and comply with the norms for
older-parent/adult–child relationships [p. 99]." Thus parents recognize the
independence of their children, whereas children "leave behind the
emancipation-oriented behavior of early adulthood to turn again to their
parents [p. 99]," not as children, but as adults recognizing the individuality
of the people with whom they have grown up.

The intergenerational conflict over control reflects the interdependence
of developmental tasks and their timing between the generations. The
issues of tasks and timing in intergenerational relations deserve further
research. First, normative research on the nature of these developmental
tasks and their timing across generations should be considered and combinations of these tasks explored, addressing such questions as: What
tasks do parents and children typically face at the same time? What tasks
are timed in ways that induce conflict? Second, this research should consider the extent to which a cooperative effort between the generations
results in the resolution of these tasks. Third, variations in task resolutions
should be studied as a function of intergenerational timing: Do some
combinations of tasks make the coordination of intergenerational development more difficult than others?

The research of Gilligan and Notman (1978) reflects this intergenerational orientation. They investigated differences in the ways adolescents
and adults face problems: Adolescents, with their view of infinite time,
externalized conflicts, and sought idealistic solutions that would enable
them to escape further conflict; adults, with a more finite view of time,
sought to understand the conflict rather than to escape it. This difference
in coping style may cause one or both to face developmental transitions
in different ways, a difference that might be reflected in intergenerational
relations.

To sum up, the family sociology approach, as we have seen, emphasizes
the interdependence of the development of family generations. The reciprocity of developmental tasks means that individual control of any stage
of the life cycle involves coordinating one's own development with the

development of others. In middle age, the salience of personal control makes this a particularly important task. In the following section, we shall suggest that this dialectical process may be intrapsychic as well as intergenerational.

Growing Up in Middle Age: The Reflective Self and the Developing Individual

Individual models of development (Gould, 1978; Levinson, 1978) suggest an intrapsychic equivalent to intergenerational conflict: the individual's confrontation with the self. This is a confrontation between the developing self and the assumptions and perspectives of the past, which constitute the reflective self. The conflict over control is between past and present facets of the individual's development.

On the basis of clinical observations, Gould (1978) described development in middle age in terms of the relationship between adult consciousness and early development. In the course of growing up, a child encounters painful experiences in coping with the world. The child's fragile control is frequently overwhelmed by these painful emotional and physical experiences. Only the child's parents can remove the pain; their failure to do so can produce intense anger in the child. This anger is not destroyed as one grows and develops one's own control; instead, "it reappears in a subtle but very real new form, in which we overestimate our own hostile powers and the hostile powers of others to control us [p. 18]." Gould calls this "demonic" anger, the key ingredient of the childhood consciousness that persists into adulthood.

The anger of the child is rooted in physical separations; similar "separation situations [p. 24]" reactivate childhood anger even in adulthood, and the individual faces two conflicting views of reality: a current reality of adulthood and a demonic reality through which self-definitions created in the separation situations of childhood enter the experiences of adult life. Gould argues that leaving childhood and the demonic reality is not easy, even in adulthood. Development requires ongoing separations from earlier self-definitions and elicits the demonic anger of childhood separations. Aware that development can be dangerous, the developing individual may retreat under pressure of the childhood consciousness to the safety of the world of the parents. Through a set of rules that limit individual identity, the omnipotence of one's parents can be assured and a separation from past self-definitions avoided. One task of adult development, then, is the recognition that the safety of the parental world is inadequate protection against childhood demons precisely because they reside in one's past; growth away from that past is the only protection.

The task of adulthood is the wresting of control from the childhood consciousness and the assumption of control of one's own development.

Because the middle-aged have three generations of adults to contend with, family power struggles typically mark the middle of the life span. Each generation faces its own version of the childhood consciousness. Young adult children are still reluctant to give up their illusion of safety; they delay their independence. Meanwhile, aging parents fortify their own illusion of safety by maintaining their control over their middle-aged children. For the middle-aged, power may be maintained over children and simultaneously surrendered to parents for the sake of the illusion of safety.

Even when parents' control of their children is relatively complete, any failure of control may produce doubts about their effectiveness as parents. As the children begin to challenge their own false assumptions of safety and to desire independence from the parents who created that sense of safety, parents may feel threatened by a complete loss of control. This loss of control can lead to tremendous fear for their own as well as their childrens' safety; neither will survive the independence of the children.

If an attempt is made to keep that sense of safety intact, the growth of both generations may be jeopardized. By keeping the children in the family and prolonging their dependence, feelings of safety may be maintained. However, this form of control avoids a confrontation with the true source of conflict over life control—the reflective self. By challenging the fear of the loss of safety, by bestowing their own development with significance, parents confront the false assumptions of safety that guard the reflective self and also help their children prepare to face their own versions of this reflective self. By valuing the childrens' position in the life cycle and acknowledging that they too have childhood consciousnesses, parents can help their children confront their weaknesses and accentuate their strengths so that they are better prepared for adulthood. At the same time, middle age becomes a significant time of change in the parents' own life cycle.

Gould's hypotheses, based on his clinical experiences, gain some support from extensive interviews with middle-aged men conducted by Levinson (1978) and his colleagues, who have studied the conflict between the developing self and the reflective, childhood reality. This period is a time of reappraisal, a time when the desires that inspired the young man are found wanting in light of the reality of middle age.

Just as it seems that so much has been accomplished, the middle-aged man asks, "How much of the past really has any meaning for me now?" This reappraisal can lead to the discovery that much of his life has been based on illusions; many of his assumptions and beliefs reflect the awareness of a growing youth, not a middle-aged adult. As a young man moves toward valued goals, he combines discipline with an exaggerated belief in himself and his abilities, shaping even his relationships with others in the service of achieving his goals. This early period is one in which illusions thrive. One task of the middle-aged man is to relinquish those illusions when they become inappropriate for the realities of middle age.

With the discovery that much of what he believes is based on illusions comes the discovery that his life is actually controlled by a "dream" (Levinson, 1978, p. 245). This dream is the core of the life structure created in young adulthood, when the young man felt that if he single-mindedly pursued his dream, his life would be legitimized by that pursuit and all facets of his life would fall into place. Others—wives and mentors—have been coopted into his life as supporting players in the quest for the dream, which becomes so important that he may minimize those aspects of himself that are inconsistent with the image of himself presented in his dream; thus the dream masters his life. Middle age becomes a period in which future development depends on the recognition of the dream as the tyrannical ruler of his life—the recognition of the conflict between the developing self and the reflective self.

To create a life structure with a better sense of his place in the world, the middle-aged man must integrate his past with his future, reassessing his dreams in terms of the course of his life. By accepting his mortality, his creative and destructive potentials, his feelings of intimacy and dependency, and his sense of separateness from the world, the middle-aged man can restructure his life toward greater involvement with others and awareness of his place in the world. Recognition of the illusion of the dream controlling his life is a recognition that his control of the world may have little effect on his own growth and development. The external world can be dominated and controlled, but this external control does not guarantee control over his life. Developmental control necessitates a reworking of the dream—a recognition of the control of the reflective self.

Levinson (1978) and his colleagues illustrate how the changing nature of middle life—the intrapsychic dialectic of control—can lead to activity directed toward regaining control. By reworking the dream so that its demands are less absolute, "success less essential and failure less disastrous [p. 248]," a man's goals become tempered, realistic, and their pursuit enjoyable. By recognizing his own aging, he can enjoy the rejuvenation that comes with nurturing the development of a new generation. By overcoming illusions about his marriage and the role it plays in the pursuit of the dream, he can develop mature relationships with women. In summary, by recognizing the intrapsychic dialectic that generates conflicts in the control of his life, a man can begin to work toward regaining that control and toward integrating his reflective self, the changing world, and his own development so that he controls his own life course within the boundaries of adult life.

The psychodynamic approach of Gould (1978) and Levinson (1978) explores individual growth through a series of confrontations with outdated versions of the self. The conflict over control between the developing self and the reflective self persists throughout adulthood. This conflict may be resolved through the creation and maintenance of protective false assumptions about the source of conflict. It can also be resolved through a confrontation with the demonic realities (Gould, 1978) and dreams (Levinson, 1978) formed by the reflective self. In middle age, one must face this reflective self to continue to grow and to help one's children to grow. The alternative form of control allows the individual a sense of safety and preservation of the past only at the cost of further development. Development in middle adulthood conjures up childhood demons and dreams; it requires, finally, separation from the self one wished one could be and the self one always thought one would be in middle age.

The notion that middle age is marked by a tension between current developmental realities and past conceptions of the self is supported by the work of Sarason (1977) and Gutmann (1964, 1980). Sarason's exploration of the life cycle of work revealed a dialectic between the self of middle age and a previous self-conceptualization. Although they face a need for great changes in their lives and careers, middle-aged men must confront the "one life–one career imperative"—a confrontation with the meaning of work in the lives they have created. Gutmann's cross-cultural research on psychological changes in middle and late life has shown a dismantling of earlier established psychological structures and a "return to the repressed [1980, p. 44]"—the increased saliency in middle age of psychological aspects of the self that were repressed in the service of parenthood. Thus, the middle-aged female demonstrates a long-abandoned aggressiveness and the male a sense of community and nurturance. Once again we see a dialectical conflict between a self created in the past and new developmental tasks.

Synchrony of Control: The Empty Nest

The two previous examples of midlife control reflect the interpersonal— a conflict between the developing individual and developing others—and the intrapsychic—a conflict between the developing self and the reflective self. Development requires the synchronization of both these conflicts and the activity that results from them; throughout the life cycle there is a tension between the individual and the world outside and between the individual and the world within. We believe that these tensions are interwoven so closely that any attempt to resolve one must affect the other. Our last example—the empty nest—will illustrate the relationship of the interpersonal to the intrapsychic.

Middle age in the family life cycle is characterized by the departure of children from the home. This period of the "empty nest" has been seen as a time of stress as well as renewal for middle-aged parents (Deutscher, 1968). Whether stressful or renewing, this event is an important developmental step because it usually marks the first stage in the redefinition of the parents by children; leaving home can bring about the child's first sense of what adulthood and parenthood mean. For the parent, a long investment of time, energy, and love is perhaps best repaid by their children's acceptance of adulthood, including an acceptance of their investment, the promise of future love from the adult offspring, and the promise of continued change and development throughout the middle years of adulthood.

Datan (1980) has suggested a complement to the empty nest: the "crowded nest," the period when the children are grown up but not yet out of the parental house. Folklore, she says, does not dwell on the theme of the empty nest but rather on the children who are turned out of the home. These children, "too hungry, too beautiful, too dangerous [p. 17]," pose a threat to resources and are forced out to make their own living. For the parents, the message of these folk tales is that parenthood ends when children are grown; if they do not leave willingly, folklore suggests, they are likely to be cast out of the nest.

Both the empty nest and the crowded nest are examples of the dialectical tension over control in the life of the middle-aged parent. If the children depart from the home, the maintenance and growth of their relationship with their parents depends on their emotional return. This may require the parents to redefine their relationship with their children as one of mutuality between adults. The children, however, also play a role in this relationship; they are part of whatever new relationship the parents come to define. The parents' development, then, depends not only on the redefinition of their relationship with their children, but on the children's response to this new relationship. We believe that the data on the empty nest show it to be an important period of transition not because of the structural change that departure of the children from home represents but because of the dialectical issues of this period: It is a time when parents come to realize the fragility of their control over their lives, and both interpersonal and intrapsychic struggles with control characterize this transition.

The research of Lowenthal et al. (1976) supports our view of the empty nest. The responses of women who have been through this transition are indicative of conflicts with developmental questions of control. Most felt that the departure of children from the home was not frustrating, nor was it seen as a turning point in their lives: Satisfaction with parenting continued in spite of the change (Lowenthal & Chiriboga, 1972). However, women whose children had left home did not feel in control of the transition; they attributed control over this transition to their children. The degree of control they felt was related to the extent to which their children were doing what the women wanted them to be doing (Lowenthal *et al.*, 1976). Those who felt in control of this change made generally negative comments about it, suggesting that their feelings of control over the empty nest transition were tempered by the realization that their own control depended on their children's.

Why did this conflict of control not lead to feelings of frustration? This appears to be due partly to evolving relationships outside the family. During this period, these women seemed to be particularly interested in social problems and community activities. Thus, diminishing intensity of relationships within the family was compensated by expanding relationships outside the family.

Relationships outside the family are a clue to development on another level—the tension between the developing self and the reflective self. Social activity and concern may represent significant steps in a mother's redefinition of the parent–child relationship. Perhaps as part of the loss of control over relationships with children, women in the empty nest period move from expressive to instrumental modes of response. They evaluate themselves in relation to a wider range of personality characteristics and no longer believe that only a "feminine" role is acceptable. They are "looking forward to establishing a somewhat less complex life style [Lowenthal & Chiriboga, 1972, p. 14]." If the empty nest transition is not frustrating, it is perhaps because these women are redefining their relationships with their children through personal control: They are resolving the tension with their reflective selves.

Although there is little research on the period Datan calls "the crowded nest," some speculation is possible on the basis of available data (e.g., see Lowenthal & Chiriboga, 1972). Women whose children have not yet left home show signs of having less control over both interpersonal and intrapsychic dimensions of their development; they are generally dissatisfied with their interpersonal relations, more selfish, and more self-pitying. Unlike the mother in the empty nest, whose children's departure precipitates personal change, the mother in the crowded nest feels the need for change before the children do. Their presence prevents the mother in the crowded nest from assuming complete control over the remainder of her life course.

The empty nest transition is an illustration of the developmental dialectic of control in middle age. Women facing this transition must integrate two conflicting sources of control over their lives. On the one hand, they recognize that their own development depends on the development of their children: Their personal sense of control has not become independent of the management of their children's lives. On the other hand, they also experience tension from the reflective self. Changes in children and within the self demand new relationships between the empty nest mother and her offspring. Relationships developed in the course of the children's early development must give way to new relationships reflecting new directions in the development of both mother and child.

Conclusion: The Dialectics of Middle Age

In this chapter, we have noted some of the special tasks and potentialities of middle age, a period with unique features created as the achievements of youth encounter the anticipation of a diminishing life span.

The existential discovery that the life span will end makes middle age a time of reflection with a sense of urgency. The goals set earlier in the life cycle may require reappraisal and change; yet, paradoxically, these changes require control over one's own development at a time when the self is seen as newly vulnerable.

In middle age, one's own development is also bound up with the development of others. The middle-aged confront not only their own developmental tasks, but also those facing their adult children and their aging parents. Thus, personal control in middle age involves the coordination of one's own development with that of developing others. In relations with adult children, the individual must realize a personal potential for change as well as that of the children's potential; the alternative is to deny development by forcing an unchanging relationship on independent adult children.

Middle age may highlight differences between early ideals and present realities; moreover, the goals and ideals set early in adulthood may lose their importance with the growing realization of finite time left to live. Dreams, childhood illusions of safety, career, and life imperatives are reevaluated in light of new life challenges.

To date, many theories of midlife crisis grow out of clinical observations and a focus on stressful life events. Unfortunately, such a focus evokes images of the social scientist gingerly stepping over battlefield casualties, whereas too little is known of the survivors. If, as Bakan (1979) suggests, psychology is literary criticism, the developmental psychology of middle age cannot ignore plot, character conflicts, and transitions, and read only final chapters. It is our hope that we have provoked some such study for the future.

References

Bakan, D. Humanistic psychology and the idea of the person. In H. Alker (Chair), *The great humanistic debate*. Symposium presented at the 87th Meeting of the American Psychological Association, New York, September 3, 1979.
Bengtson, V. L., & Kuypers, J. A. Generational differences and the developmental stake. *Aging and Human Development*, 1971, 2, 249–260.

Bengtson, V. L., & Troll, L. E. Youth and their parents: Feedback and intergenerational influence in socialization. In R. M. Lerner & G. B. Spanier (Eds.), *Child influences on marital and family interaction: A life-span perspective*. New York: Academic Press, 1978.

Blenkner, M. Social work and family relations in later life with some thoughts on filial maturity. In E. Shanas & G. F. Streib (Eds.), *Social structure and the family*. Englewood-Cliffs, N.J.: Prentice-Hall, 1965.

Datan, N. Midas and other midlife crises. In W. H. Norman & T. J. Scaramella (Eds.), *Midlife: Developmental and clinical issues*. New York: Brunner/Mazel, 1980.

Datan, N., & Lohmann, N. (Eds.). *Transitions of aging*. New York: Academic Press, 1980.

Deutscher, I. The quality of postparental life. In B. L. Neugarten (Ed.), *Middle age and aging*. Chicago: University of Chicago Press, 1968.

Erikson, E. H. Identity and the life cycle: Selected papers. *Psychological Issues*, 1959 (Monograph No. 1).

Erikson, E. H. *Childhood and society* (2nd Ed.). New York: Norton, 1963.

Gilligan, C., & Notman, M. *The recurrent theme in women's lives: The integration of autonomy and care*. Paper presented to the Eastern Sociological Meetings, Philadelphia, Penn., March, 1978.

Gould, R. L. *Transformations: Growth and change in adult life*. New York: Simon and Schuster, 1978.

Gutmann, D. L. An exploration of ego configurations in middle and later life. In B. L. Neugarten (Ed.), *Personality in middle and later life*. New York: Atherton, 1964.

Gutmann, D. L. The postparental years: Clinical problems and developmental possibilities. In W. H. Norman and T. J. Scaramella (Eds.), *Midlife: Developmental and clinical issues*. New York: Brunner/Mazel, 1980.

Lerner, R. M. Showdown at generation gap: Attitudes of adolescents and their parents toward contemporary issues. In H. D. Thornburg (Ed.), *Contemporary adolescence* (2nd ed.). Belmont, Cal.: Brooks/Cole, 1975.

Lerner, R. M., & Knapp, J. R. Actual and perceived intrafamilial attitudes of late adolescents and their parents. *Journal of Youth and Adolescence*, 1975, 4, 17–36.

Levinson, D. J. *The seasons of a man's life*. New York: Alfred A. Knopf, 1978.

Lowenthal, M. F., & Chiriboga, D. Transition to the empty nest: Crisis, challenge, or relief? *Archives of General Psychiatry*, 1972, 26, 8–14.

Lowenthal, M. F., Thurnher, M., Chiriboga, D., Beeson, D., Gigy, L., Lurie, E., Pierce, R., Spence, D., & Weiss, L. *Four stages of life*. San Francisco: Jossey-Bass, 1976.

Mann, C. H. Midlife and the family: Strains, challenges, and options of the middle years. In W. H. Norman and T. J. Scaramella (Eds.), *Midlife: Developmental and clinical issues*. New York: Brunner/Mazel, 1980.

Neugarten, B. L. The awareness of middle age. In B. L. Neugarten (Ed.), *Middle age and aging*. Chicago: University of Chicago Press, 1968.

Norman, W. H., & Scaramella, T. J. (Eds.). *Midlife: Developmental and clinical issues*. New York: Brunner/Mazel, 1980.

Riegel, K. F. *Foundations of dialectical psychology*. New York: Academic Press, 1979.

Sarason, S. B. *Work, aging, and social change: Professionals and the one life–one career imperative*. New York: The Free Press, 1977.

Troll, L. E., Miller, S. J., & Atchley, R. C. *Families in later life*. Belmont, Cal.: Wadsworth, 1979.

Proactive and Reactive Aspects of Constructivism: Growth and Aging in Life-Span Perspective[1]

"All men have the stars," he answered, "but they are not the same things for different people. For some, who are travelers, the stars are guides. For others they are no more than little lights in the sky. For others, who are scholars, they are problems. For my businessman they were wealth. But all these stars are silent. You—you alone—will have the stars as no one else has them [Saint Exupéry, THE LITTLE PRINCE]."

The purpose of the present chapter is not to convince the reader of the value of the tenets of constructivism in the analysis of aging processes— or even of life-span development. At the very outset, the author una-bashedly confesses the belief that individual development, for better or worse, is the result of an active response to the challenge posed by the environment. Constructivism, however, comes in many shapes. The point of view developed here has been most profoundly influenced by Piaget's writings. With his arguments for a genetic (i.e., developmental) structuralism, Piaget has offered an integration between nativism (which is, in effect, an agenetic structuralism) and astructuralist environmental positions. Briefly put, his position implies that, at any developmental level or choice point, the next integration results from the action of the organism on the environment, thereby creating a continuous line of syntheses of increasing spatiotemporal stability.

This position immediately exposes a contrapuntal theme central to the thesis of this chapter. If structural organization results from a juncture of the constraints of *both* organism and environment, developmental structuralism actually incorporates two seemingly paradoxical propositions.

[1] Preparation of this chapter was supported by NIA Research Career Development Award 5 K04–AG00018–02, and by funds provided by the Institute of Gerontology at Wayne State University.

197

Individuals as Producers of Their Development

The first is the one most usually allied with interpretations of developmental–structural models and states that individuals construct themselves, as it were, from the inside out. But the second one is just as important: As each new synthesis presupposes the discovery of a conflict or constraint to be surmounted, it is also inevitably true that individuals construct themselves from the outside in. Thus, to elucidate the meaning of developmental structuralism in its fullest sense, we must attend to this recurrent dualism: Development is a process both *pro*active and *re*active.

It is in an exposition of this duality that lies the resolution of several conceptual puzzles that have become most cumbersome for researchers interested in the whole of the human life span. For, whereas it has proven heuristically useful to view development from birth to adolescence as a unilinear succession of stages, researchers in adulthood and aging have been overwhelmed by variability rather than uniformity. In the absence, however, of theories that were tailored specifically to problems of *adult* adaptation, aging research has been profoundly influenced by available child development models. This influence has slowly given rise to a feeling that, having thus put the cart before the horse, the field of adult development and aging had conceptualized itself into a blind alley in which several key issues could only be resolved by retreating backwards into the arena of child development.

The first problem, already mentioned, is that of variability. Here, most models of the unilinear kind have us believe that variability can be accounted for either by notions of fixation or regression. The concept of fixation provides a cumbersome interpretation because it forces us to view adult differences due to cultural (e.g., Greenfield, 1976), professional (e.g., Sabatini & Labouvie-Vief, 1979) or historical (e.g., Baltes & Schaie, 1976) specialization as being a result of different levels of achievement or adaptation. It does not allow for the possibility of different specialized achievements that, in their own contexts, are of equal adaptive value— or, in any case, that are profoundly different from the behavior of the child (Bowlby, 1973; Werner, 1948). Interpretations relying on notions of regression are no less problematic, as most theoreticians of development have remained vague on the meaning of regression.

When confronted with apparent deficits in adulthood, many researchers therefore have tended to opt for a distinction between competence and performance (see Baltes, Reese, & Lipsitt, 1980; Labouvie-Vief & Chandler, 1978) with a concomitant emphasis on modifiability and plasticity of adult cognitive structure. This framework has provided a useful heuristic stance, as indeed purported deficits are often quite readily alleviated and thus should not be called a normal component of aging. Still, it has failed to answer the question: "Are there normative structural changes unique to adulthood?" In the absence of an answer to this question, the standards held up for adult performance were those specified by youth-centered

theories. Thus adulthood, at best, could display stability rather than continued growth.

This dilemma leads us immediately to the second problem. To the
researcher rooted in child developmental theory, the variability of adulthood appears so chaotic, so mechanistic (Flavell, 1970; Reese, 1973), that
it seems obvious that one cannot talk of growth in the sense of new
structural change. Yet, we must ask at once, is this not a foregone conclusion as long as we examine adulthood through the eyes of the child
developmentalist? For each mode of viewing—each level of structural
organization—primes us to *re*act to a specific segment of reality as if it
were ordered and meaningful. But it also delimits our ability to impart
similar order on other parts of reality.

This constraining, reactive property of structures may work in two
directions. One of these is a "bottom-up" direction and corresponds to
the familiar dictum of the child developmentalist that we are unable to
perceive the coherence of a higher stage from the vantage point of a lower
stage. Thus, is it not more appropriate to say that the view of adulthood
as erratic reflects the absence of a proper model (i.e., a model of wide
enough generality)?

A second reactive property is, however, of equally vital importance.
This is the fact that new forms of organization act back, in "top-down"
fashion, on older ones, weeding out ways of acting, knowing, and perceiving typical of older levels. Adults, for example, when presented with
a deck of red spades, will typically "see" a deck of hearts (Bruner, 1962),
giving up a perhaps more accurate sensory impression in favor of a cognitive judgment. Thus, whereas cognitive growth models have almost
exclusively emphasized movements toward greater perfection, they have
failed to point out that regression—far from being a defining element of
aging—is part and parcel of the process of development. Indeed, we will
argue that many of the changes of adulthood are readily seen to be
developmental once the juxtaposition of growth and regression is given
up to make way for a view in which the two are seen as being interwoven
at all points of the life span.

Indeed, the third and most pervasive problem is the fact that regression
has been treated as an anomaly in development, whereas growth has
been treated as granted. Yet, in a very real sense, regression is a process
just as "natural" as growth: Systems or structures will naturally tend to
regress—lose in orderliness—*unless* they feed on information provided by
systems of higher structural order (see Brent, 1978b, c). Thus development
by its very nature is a reactive process. And rather than taking development for granted and asking about the conditions that will result in
regression, we may ask just as logically, "What are the conditions that
will *prevent* regression and lead to further structural growth?"

The present chapter will argue that, once these various issues are given full consideration, adulthood and aging can be interpreted within a model of progressive development. This argument will be presented in two steps. The first of these is to discuss a number of theoretical concepts that may help to point out continuities between earlier and late parts of the life span. Here, we shall of necessity occasionally trespass on the territory of other authors of this volume, although we will keep such transgressions at a minimum. The second step will be more empirically oriented, pointing to a reinterpretation of selected areas of research in aging within a growth-oriented model of life-span change.

Theoretical Issues

It is particularly unfortunate for research into adaptive processes in adulthood and later life that cognitive–developmental structuralism often tends to be identified with a particular research method rather than with a more abstract point of view. Thus adult and aging individuals have been examined with tasks developed for children and adolescents with little concern for how these tasks fit into the adaptive context of the age groups concerned. This is, of course, a violation of *the* very basic tenet of developmental–structural models: No special meaning attaches to the isolated act: Rather, individual adaptation is a system of coordinations and regulations of behaviors.

It is the basic thesis of this chapter that the preoccupation with regression in adulthood derives from a misunderstanding of this basic premise. Instead of being indicative of generalized regression, many forms of adult behavior can be seen to fit into a sequence of logical developmental progression. It is necessary, therefore, to put questions of research methods aside for the present and instead to pose the question: "What, at a more abstract level, defines a logically progressive sequence of development?" Only after this question is clarified is it possible to examine if aging does, or does not, constitute a basic deviation from this sequence.

LEVELS OF ANALYSIS: THE CORRELATIVITY OF FORM AND CONTENT

In Piaget's terminology, a structure, or system of regulations is defined both by its formal features and by the contents coordinated by those features (Piaget, 1970). It is easy, however, to commit the logical error of attempting to infer formal features from isolated contents alone. The child-like language of an adult, for example, may indicate either a regressive breakdown or an adaptive flexibility in which the complexity of the communicative act is tailored to the needs of the receiver. Thus notions of form and content are never absolute, but statements about formal complexity depend, in large part, on the wisdom with which the boundaries are drawn around a content field of behavioral repertoires.

Piaget (1970) refers to this interdependency between form and content as the correlativity of form and content. For the purposes of our discussion, this interdependency has two important implications. The first of these is best exemplified by Bartlett's (1932) view of memory, in which each act of remembering is an assimilation of past cognitive constructions. Thus formal features of mnemonic acts will vary widely across behavioral contents, depending on the historicity of the individual's cognitive structure. Each individual, when confronted with material that is alien, may evidence fragmented, unstructured remembering; conversely, advanced forms of mnemonic organization are likely only if they tap familiar concept fields. The crux, therefore, is to carefully tailor one's concept field to the individual's cognitive structure as it has evolved in his or her unique adaptive context.

The second implication derives from the fact that what one calls "form" and "content" will vary with one's level of analysis. The forms of concrete thought (classes, relations, quantities), for example, become the contents of formal thought. What is merely content, therefore, in one context, is a series of highly differentiated structures in another. And vice versa, each highly differentiated structure, in another context, takes on the property of mere content to a superordinate structure. Thus, for the purposes of life-span analysis, if we are concerned with a particular structural level, we must always look for the next higher-order structure within which the level under examination can be said to be regulated.

The form–content correlativity has such important theoretical and methodological repercussions that a biological analogy may be useful here. As in individual psychological development, so in embryological development systems—namely, cells—undergo a transformation from a state of undifferentiated *potency* (i.e., ability to, under different conditions, differentiate into a variety of different tissues) to different states of *determination* in which each differentiated cell system takes on a characteristic structure and function (Jacobson, 1978; Lund, 1978). They thereby necessitate, however, a new system that interregulates all these structures by means of stabilizing feedback loops. Both of these processes incorporate proactive and reactive components. Proactively, the cell has self-constructive "abilities" to divide and reproduce; but reactively, its competence (ability to respond) is restricted at any moment to specific inducers that must be provided to insure normal development. Thus developing embryological systems require that they be embedded in systems that in turn provide these regulating influences. If the embedding system itself contains errors, such errors may be the cause of embryological damage or death (Moore, 1977).

It is obvious, therefore, that developing systems can be studied at many levels of analysis. At the most general level, we may talk about the move from potency to determination, stating the role of different inducers at each state of competency. At a more specific level, however, we must be careful to realize that the exact meaning of the terms varies from cell system to cell system. Each of those systems is eventually characterized by different metabolic components, for example, and it would be meaningless to conclude from this difference that any one system takes on a "more developed" role. Rather, statements about more or less developed states of development take on meaning only within the next higher system: That of the interregulation of component processes. And at this level of analysis, such comparative statements are valid only insofar as they may bear on the effective regulation of the *total* system. Ideally, therefore, to avoid the logical fallacy of mixing levels of analysis, we want to specify the most general level of analysis *before* we can talk about normative deviations.

Developmental psychologists have been highly individualistic in defining such normative deviations. In general, deviations have been gauged by youth centered standards of the mode of "abstract thinking" typical of highly educated males (Riegel, 1977; Sampson, 1977). Questions of adaptation are, however, not resolved by referring to the specialized adaptations of only a single group of individuals. Instead, we must ask how the accomplishments or competencies of individuals specialized for different functions become intercoordinated to regulate the survival of a population.

Many biological adaptations, in fact, can be understood only in this supraindividual context. The courtship dance of the stickleback fish described by Tinbergen (1951) is a specific example of the fact that many adaptively vital behavioral displays result from the coordinated movements of different individuals of a species (e.g., males and females). Thus, even in species of relatively low complexity, we find a kind of social interregulation which Piaget (1971) refers to as "trans-individual cycles." And, in this framework, it becomes unjustified to polarize individual–biological and social levels of description. Instead, social levels of explanation become part and parcel of biological explanation.[2] As Piaget says:

> the social group plays the same role that the population does in genetics and consequently in instinct. In this sense, society is the supreme unit, and the individual can only achieve his inventions and intellectual constructions insofar as he is the seat of collective interactions that are naturally dependent, in level and value, on society as a whole [p. 368].

[2] It is important here to point out that this view does not endorse a biological reductionism as, for example, in Wilson's (1975) *Sociobiology*. Rather, social phenomena are seen to be an emergent property, as discussed in the sequel.

STRUCTURE AND CONTEXT

The constructivist aspect of cognitive–structural theories has emphasized that, at whatever level of analysis one studies the organism, one needs to consider the organism's capacity for self-regulation. This important property derives from the view of structures as neither temporally nor spatially punctate, but as displaying a degree of continuity or stability.

Such continuity presupposes several activities of which a structure is capable. First, it needs to be able to *transform* information to a form appropriate to its structural level. Thus, in cognition, we typically "perceive" the environment in characteristic modes (e.g., sensorimotor, concrete, etc.) which are themselves the transformed product of the information provided by the environment.

Second, transformations are typically achieved through some mechanism of *conservation* or "memory" by which information is retained in a particular form. This is merely to say that from spatially and temporally disconnected and apparently random events (e.g., the pulling of a tablecloth and the movement of an object on the cloth) the organism is able to conserve their spatial and temporal relationships or feedback. In this way, a certain degree of "abstraction" is achieved through which relationships are represented as single units such that the occurrence of either event allows an inference about the other: Thus, a new form of information is produced.

Finally, this new mode of information will be transferred to new situations, as it is the formal feature (e.g., causal relationship) rather than merely the specific contents that are conserved. Thus structures are able to proliferate by providing a matrix within which new contents can be organized: They are means of *anticipation.*

All of these activities are important, of course, because they serve to delineate merely reactive physical systems from the proactions characteristic of living systems. In this way, they provide a *potential* for autoregulation and growth.

While providing a *necessary* condition, however, for adaptive regulations, they do not entail a *sufficient* criterion. Whether applied at biological, psychological, or social levels, the proactive extensions are merely tentative and "hypothetical": Some lead to "useful" feedback, others do not. Thus, a second criterion is necessitated according to which "useful" and "useless" anticipations become selected.

The dialectical interplay between proaction and reaction, or variation and selection, is of course a standard ingredient of theories of evolution (e.g., Mayr, 1978). But it applies to other levels of analysis as well. One telling example is offered by recent theories of neuronal development. Here, one appears to discern two substages at any stage of development. The first of these is characterized by a period of rapid proliferation of young neurons, followed by a second substage in which only those neurons that have established appropriate target connections are retained (Jacobson, 1978; Lund, 1978). Thus, there is a cycle beginning with an oversupply of young neurons and ending with a trimming down, via selective depletion and programmed cell death, of a portion of those neurons.

This variation–selection cycle can be similarly discerned at the level of psychological functioning. The young child, for example, actively puts forward anticipatory explorations of the environment. Yet not all of those explorations prove functional, as the environment provides specific constraints that will select some and eliminate others. The resulting dialectical interplay between proactive, explorative activity and the restraining action of the environment has been addressed, in particular, by Soviet psychologists (e.g., Leontiev, 1977; Vygotsky, 1962). Leontiev (1977), for example, points out that cognitive structures are built up in interaction with *specific* objects or concepts that afford specific modes of action and reaction. Hence, to the extent that cultures differ in terms of these material contexts, there is no need to polarize organismic and social–structural theories.

Piaget occasionally (e.g., Piaget, 1971, 1977) appears to endorse such a perspective, although he has no doubt put almost exclusive emphasis on the proactive side of the organism–environment equation. Even so, he has argued in his book *Insights and Illusions of Philosophy* (Piaget, 1965) that even at the level of formal logic one needs to distinguish between necessary and sufficient conditions of adaptability. The adaptive *potential* (i.e, necessary condition) of formal logic consists in the fact that it offers a mechanism by which all possibilities can be generated by permutations and recombinations. But only some of those will stand pragmatic tests, whereas others will need to be discarded. Thus again, logical growth provides a necessary but not sufficient condition for continued development. Unless it is integrated with pragmatic constraints, for example, no logical limits could be drawn between a brilliant delusional system and a heuristic scientific system. Or, as Piaget (1971) states

> with hypothetico–deductive operations, by a system of all combinations of propositions, a formal logic can emerge in the form of an organizing structure applicable to any content whatever. This is what makes possible the constitution of "pure" mathematics as a construction of forms of organization, ready to organize everything, *but from time to time organizing nothing, insofar as it becomes dissociated from its application* [p. 358; emphasis added].

Then again, the same cycle can be seen on a time scale yet broader, as when discussing the evolution of scientific theories. Kuhn (1970), Popper (1963; Popper & Eccles, 1978), and Campbell (1974) all have described similar cycles of variation–selection in scientific discourse and argued that the proliferation of data and hypotheses, generated by paradigmatic permutation at one point in time, is eventually trimmed down considerably once a new paradigm supersedes the old.

In summary, then, we conclude that structural change is typically the result of a two-tiered process. A particular level of structural development permits a proliferation of anticipatory extensions. But it does so typically in the form of an oversupply. This oversupply will eventually be trimmed down by a context that provides a framework of both regulation and deselection.

For the purpose of our analysis, it is significant here to note two features that are implied in this model. First, it is assumed that the substages are temporally ordered such that a proliferative phase precedes a "trimming down" phase (see Campbell, 1974; Mayr, 1978; Piaget, 1965). It is for this reason that the adaptive value of each proaction (hypothesis, etc.) *cannot* be defined at the time it occurs, but only at a later time. A particular structural level cannot, therefore, judge its own adaptive value, as it were—hence the dictum that a stage of development appears coherent only in the aftermath. Or, to put it more directly, as long as one examines the life span from the perspective of formal operations only, one has no way of judging which of the apparent losses following that stage are part of adaptive deselection and which indicate maladaptive or regressive losses.

Second, we see that two views of development are equally correct. One is the process view here discussed in which development will display periods of exploration, fumbling, and searching in blind alleys. The second is a product view arrived at by retrospectively examining the finished system from which all these temporary deviations have already been weeded out. If looked at from the latter perspective, development appears to be of a unilinear goal directedness which belies, however, its process perspective. Put differently, adult researchers examining childhood are easily led to neglect the losses implied in growth, because, from the retrospective perspective of the adult viewpoint, such losses are indeed interpreted as net gains (Toulmin, 1971). The adult examining later parts of the life span, in contrast, is faced with a more ambiguous situation, as criteria of "loss" and "gain" are inherently indeterminate as long as they are examined from the perspective of an earlier stage.

STRUCTURES AS TRADE-OFFS

To the child developmentalist, development often displays a picture of conjunctive, cumulative continuity. This view is expressed, for example, in the use of Guttman scales in developmental research (see Achenbach, 1978; Wohlwill, 1973) reflecting the assumption that each new stage integrates and *adds on to* a former one. This linear view, Piaget argues, ultimately rests upon an elementaristic deterministic model by which "simple" stages are logically prior, and complex stages are derived from them by an abstraction of common elements. Elsewhere, we have shown that this deterministic view of necessity posits a model in which aging is equated with regression (Labouvie-Vief, 1980a).

Piaget (e.g., 1972), however, rejects such a view as one of impoverishment rather than gain, and we will argue in this section that, from his view as well as from those of others (e.g., Brent, 1978 b, c; Popper & Eccles, 1978), follows an ordering relationship altogether different from that of a Guttman (see Wohlwill, 1973) scale. Specifically, whereas the notion underlying a Guttman scale is one of a linear order of difficulty levels, structuralism predicts, on the contrary, a nonlinear ordering of what is to be called "simple" and what "complex." This nonlinear view follows from several properties of structures.

Transformation

As Piaget (1972) has argued, linear views see the organism's perceptions and cognitions as becoming more and more removed from a physical or phenomenal context. This is a mistaken view, however, because at each structural level the contact with the phenomenal context is direct rather than derived. The formal operational child, for example, perceives a volume not as a derived quality (i.e., derived from the relations of length, width, and height), but rather as an immediate totality. The object of perception simply has become a higher-order variable that permits a new mode of knowledge and action. It is in this sense that Piaget (1972) talks about the causal relationships between sensation and perception at the level of the mature individual:

> There is immediate perception as totality and sensations are now merely structur*ed* elements and no longer structur*ing*. . . . When I perceive a house, I do not see at first the color of the tile, the height of the chimney, and the rest, and finally the house! . . . The neurologist Weizsaecker said . . . "When I perceive a house, I do not see an image which enters through the eye; on the contrary, I see a solid into which I can enter!" [pp. 65–66; emphasis added].

This mode of transformed sensation depends, of course, on the individual's experience with (past actions on) objects. Once restructured, however, sensations no longer serve a deterministic function. They merely serve a signaling function for a percept or cognition that supplies elements not contained in sensations themselves. Thus what we perceive of a phenomenal context is no longer "determined" in a bottom-up causality (as assumed, for example, by many current models of information processing), but rather in a top-down direction. Our cognitions determine what we see. It is in this sense that Gibson (1959), too, maintains: "Sensations are the occasional symptoms of perception, not the cause of it [p. 460]."

Again, this view shows that the functioning of structures is profoundly different depending on whether one examines them from a process or a product perspective. From a process perspective (i.e., the process of their formation), we must refer to an earlier stage in which the elements themselves are structuring—that is, more readily available or activated than the eventual superordinating structure. From a product perspective, however, the superordinating structure has become dominant such that even only a component process activates the macrostructure (see Labouvie-Vief & Schell, in press, for a discussion of this superordination process in terms of an information-processing model). Thus from a process perspective, the higher-order structure directs a unidirectional, recursive or irreversible mode of information intake.

Nonlinear Ordering

It is important, now, to realize that from the view of structures as a mode of dominant, recursive, and transformative information assimilation follows on ordering property that is nonlinear: Once the child has attained, for example, a concept of an object as a series of invariant temporal and spatial transformations, it becomes almost unthinkable to revert to perceiving merely a series of isolated images.

The implication of this process is perhaps best demonstrated by referring to the domain of mnemonic transformations. Here, most research has examined memory changes with tasks that were fashioned after a view of memory as a passive event recorder. Thus, in examining the retention of verbal material, "accuracy" was scored as the ability to retain the verbatim content of such verbal messages as lists of words and, less frequently, sentences or paragraphs. The nonlinear view rejects, however, any single criterion of accuracy. Rather, it starts with the assumption that individuals may perform different kinds of transformation on the messages given. In sentence memory, for example, coding may be primarily in terms of verbatim content (e.g., "A rolling stone gathers no moss"), or it may be in terms of a meaning preserving transformation such as a paraphrase (e.g., "Only a resting stone gathers moss"), or it may even be in terms of a meaning-expanding transformation (e.g., "A restless soul remains rootless")—and the important point is that different criteria for accuracy may be partially *exclusive*.

The state of affairs to which this example alludes is often captured by the notion that structuralism is inherently nondeterministic. A more appropriate way, however, to conceptualize causal relationships is to say that whether or not structures function in a deterministic way depends on one's level of analysis (e.g., Prigogine, 1976). To exemplify, let us call the first two modes of the example just given Modes A and B and let us assume that a particular individual functions at Mode B. We may then say that the causal relationship of A to B or B to A is stochastic, as a variety of verbatim surface forms can express the same meaning. However, if we apply a criterion appropriate to B, we face a deterministic relationship: the meaning-preserving constraints of level B permit us, with relative facility, to distinguish between transformations that preserve meaning and those that do not. It is when we mix levels of analysis, however, that a degree of stochastic slippage is inevitably introduced.

It is because of this property of structures that acquisitions of a higher level of functioning may imply a loss of ability to reproduce the surface detail that is assimilated into the structure. Information is encoded (conserved) in conformity with the constraints of the formal or deep structural properties, and so it will be decoded in conformance with the same rules of transformation.

This important feature is only occasionally pointed out by child developmentalists. Still, Piaget (e.g., 1972) has shown that the superordination of cognition often brings with it a loss of accuracy at a perceptual level. Other examples have been discussed by Labouvie-Vief (1980 a, c) and Labouvie-Vief and Schell (in press). Suffice it, at this juncture, to elucidate briefly two implications of such a nonlinear view. The first of these contrasts with the usual view of development as a move toward perfection. Instead, it conceptualizes development as a series of trade-offs: Adaptation is not some constantly improving quality, but each mode of adaptation is a specialized capacity to deal with a certain mode of transformation. By virtue of this specialization, however, it gives up adaptive features of earlier levels. It is preferable, therefore, to talk of each structural level as being *locally* adapted, thereby forcing us at once to realize that local adaptation to one mode of thought implies a failure to be equally adapted to another mode.

Second, it is also apparent that the meaning of context varies from level to level. Each mode of adaptation, due to the conservation properties of structures, implies a correlated context to which it is adapted. In the mnemonic example given, for example, one individual may define the context at a concrete, verbatim level in conformity with his structural capacities; for a second individual, the context may be defined by all possible meaning-preserving transformations; for a third, the context may be broader still and include all metaphoric permutations of the verbatim surface form. The sentence per se, in other words, may convey all kinds of different meanings.

The view expressed in this example is one that is profoundly different from views usually held about development. Elsewhere (Labouvie-Vief, 1980a) we have called it the "nonlinear" view to capture the fact that, as we develop, we not only achieve integrations of higher spatiotemporal order, but we also tend to give up those of lower order unless they can be integrated into higher-order concepts. Thus the linear view of development is profoundly misleading in suggesting that, throughout development, we become better and better information processors. In contrast, it proposes a view of life-course development in which different periods are characterized by dominant modes that supersede and replace earlier ones. The whole course of the life span thus can be conceptualized as a succession of single peaked functions of different modes each of which undergoes a period of growth, achievement of a functionally mature form, and then decline as it is superseded by a new mode.

Flexibility

Assuming that the organism at a particular level functions in accordance with a particular mode of information intake does not, however, imply that this mode is inflexibly "wired in"; it is merely to say that this mode takes preference or dominance over earlier modes. Thus earlier modes are less accessible, but they may be reactivated under special circumstances.

Age-related differences on a Stroop task offer a good example. To the young child whose behavior is not strongly superordinated by linguistic meanings, the reading off of the color of words written in discrepant linguistic messages provides no particular difficulty. To the older child, conversely, it becomes a more difficult task (e.g., Comalli, Wapner, & Werner, 1966), and this difficulty increases systematically until old age. It is quite impossible, indeed, for adults to (re-) acquire great facility in disregarding the linguistic label (e.g., Jensen & Rohwer, 1966)—unless they adopt such strategies as squinting the eyes or focusing on a single segment of the label.

In general, we may assume that a good deal of flexibility is lost as development progresses. In comparisons between children and college students, for example, many examples may be found (see Labouvie-Vief & Schell, in press) that demonstrate that a developmentally earlier strategy is not readily adopted unless the experimental (or, for that matter, ecological) context provides strong pressures to do so. Such pressures may take the form of increased practice or specific information that cues in the individual to the fact that a different (nondominant) response mode is asked for.

CONTEXTUAL STRUCTURE AND INDIVIDUAL SPECIALIZATION

We have emphasized so far the trade-off nature of structural development from stage to stage. Hand in hand with this trade-off, however, another trade-off occurs by which the individual gives up unrealized potential for realized, specialized structure. We have already pointed out, by way of a biological analogy, that the resulting trade-off of potential for functioning structures is not to be seen as a generalized adaptive loss, but part and parcel of an adaptive process by which the individual eventually takes on specialized capabilities.

This view is modeled after Waddington's (1975) epigenetic landscape where development is pictured as the progressive channeling of systems into distinct though interdependent routes. Bowlby (1973) has captured particularly well the fact that out of such a model arise interpretations distinctly different from the emphasis on regression and fixation of unilinear models:

> One alternative that . . . fits presently available evidence far closer than does the traditional one conceives of personality as a structure that develops unceasingly along one or another of an array of possible and discrete developmental pathways. All pathways are thought to start close together so that, initially, an individual has access to a large range of pathways along any one of which he might travel. The one chosen, it is held, turns at each and every stage of the journey on an interaction between the organism as it has developed up to that moment and the environment in which it then finds itself [p. 364].

The result of such a process is both an intraindividual move toward stability, on the one hand, and specialization and an increasing interindividual variability, on the other. Specifically, this movement follows from several interrelated features.

The Epigenetic Environment

Waddington (1972) has referred to the regulatory systems upon which the organism "turns" at different choice points as the "epigenetic environment." At the most general level of analysis, this environment consists of the material objects and symbolic systems of a culture Leontiev, 1977). These systems themselves encode ways of doing and modes of knowing. Developing organisms are, of course, exposed to these systems in a gradual manner. Thus the epigenetic context itself is represented via many specialized structures through which socially encoded transformation is transmitted—families, institutions, and so forth.

Note, now, that a differentiation must be made between levels of analysis of this epigenetic context. At the most general and most stable level, we are facing the total storehouse of knowledge that represents, in effect, the structure resulting from the collaborative efforts of all individuals. At the other extreme, this information is filtered down to small groups. By this process, these groups become more and more specialized; thus from level to level, a degree of slippage is introduced. From this perspective, one must be careful to specify one's level of analysis when judging individual competence: Clearly, for example, individual slippage or specialization must not be confused with formal logic as a complex scientific system.

Each social group exerts, of course, specific regulatory pressures: It serves as an adaptive context. These pressures are codified along dimensions of sex and age (see Neugarten & Hagestad, 1976), among many others. Much as cell systems are created through the interaction of similar cells in spatial proximity, so individuals will tend to conserve, and act on, information in accordance with parameters of social proximity. The net result of this move along different "social channels" is a trade-off process by which flexibility in *all* contexts is given up for specialized efficiency in *some*.

It is not possible, therefore, to talk about development and adaptation without talking, at the same time, about the context within which they propagate. As Maccoby and Modiano (1966) conclude, for example, from their comparative study of North American and Mexican children:

> A city child coming from an industrial society starts by dealing with objects in terms of their perceptible, concrete characteristics. He soon comes to consider them in the light of what he can do with them. In time, he is led to more abstract formulations as to how things are, how they are alike and different. Some go so far that they lose the sense of the concreteness of things and become buried in a dry nominalism. . . . Peasant children do not change that much. They are much more similar to their older brothers; they both look. The older one looks at things more closely and considers more concrete ways to use them. While the older peasant child can say how things are alike, he feels more at home with their differences, for that is where reality lies for him. He does not think in generalities. . . . Essentially, such cognitive styles reflect the demands of a culture. The modern industrialized world demands abstractions. . . . What is demanded of the peasant, on the other hand, is that he pay attention to his crops, the weather, and the particular people around him [p. 268].

At the other extreme, the infant is first exposed to the social environment in a much smaller group—the family. This, as Bowlby (1973) argues, creates a first working model of social reality; and future modes of cognition and action are, in turn, built upon this working model.[3]

Stability

Once started on a certain pathway, the very process of development tends to keep the developing structure on this course. On the one hand:

Structural features of personality, once developed, have their own means of self-regulation that tend also to maintain the current direction of development. For example, present cognitive and behavioural structures determine what is perceived and what ignored, how a new situation is construed, and what plan

---

[3] Piaget (e.g., 1970) occasionally is not too fond of such contextual views, as they have often claimed causal priority over the proactive activities of the organism. However, no such a priorism is implied here. As Waddington (1972) points out, on the contrary, social information itself will coevolve with biological and psychological development; it is, however, much more stable than individual–psychological development and thereby functions as a regulatory context—that is, one that feeds back on individual growth.

of action is likely to be constructed to deal with it. Current structures, moreover, determine what sorts of person and situation are sought after and what sorts are shunned. In this way an individual comes to influence the selection of his own environment; and so the wheel comes full circle [Bowlby, 1973, pp. 368–369].

On the other hand, the context structures which have initiated a particular pathway themselves tend to reinforce this process stability (e.g., Bloom, 1964). As a result, the whole process of development becomes more and more buffered, that is, less and less likely to deviate from the pathway it is already on. Waddington (1975) has referred to this stabilizing feature as homeorhesis.

Note that the hemeorhetic feature of development implies a successive restriction of potential or *plasticity*. This does not mean, however, that readjustments become impossible. It is merely to say that, as development advances, it is more and more supported by a matrix of wider and wider structures (e.g., family, friends, work, etc.). As a result, major readjustments can result only from a readjustment in the total social matrix as well as of the individual. Bloom's (1964) classic study has demonstrated particularly well the effect of such readjustments on instability and plasticity in intelligence.

DEVELOPMENTAL PROGRESSIONS: SYNOPSIS

We are ready, now, to return to the question posed at the outset: Is aging, in principle, a process that differs from development? Before attempting an answer proper, it may be useful to provide a summary of the main points developed thus far.

First, we have argued that decline at one level may go along with growth at another. It is crucial, therefore, to carefully delimit one's statements to a particular level of analysis. A decline in age–performance functions per se does not constitute a meaningful criterion of adaptive loss; it may, in fact, indicate the opposite.

Second, whereas development is characterized by a move toward higher spatiotemporal stability, it also implies that previous modes of behavior of lower stability are superordinated and even weeded out. The result may be a loss of intraindividual flexibility over time.

Third, the move toward higher stability implies increasing specialization and a loss of plasticity. This is not to say that plasticity is, of necessity, lost altogether, but that it is bought at a higher price: Developmentally more advanced systems will require a greater input of information to counteract homeorhetic pressures than systems less advanced.

Finally, the role of the context is an overriding one at all stages of development. Its function is, however, a correlate of a particular level. At each level, the individual puts forward proactive attempts to adapt—cope with—a level of context appropriate to the current structural level.

However, at each level, too, we must look for a superodinate context that reactively trims down these proactions to guarantee regulated growth.

Aging and Growth: Empirical Issues

It remains, then, to be demonstrated to what extent many known phenomena of aging can be interpreted within a general model of development. The author has touched upon selected areas of research elsewhere (Labouvie-Vief, 1980a, 1980b, 1980c; Labouvie-Vief & Schell, 1980). Here, for reasons of brevity, we will merely offer a synopsis of a number of domains.

DEFINITION OF AGING AND LEVELS OF ANALYSIS

On both biological and psychological levels, aging has been defined as an irreversible deteriorative process. If we adopt this definition, however, we discern that many processes subsumed under the term of aging are not a unique part of later life. Rather, we see a view of the life span in which processes of growth and aging are interwoven at any temporal segment. Some phenomena of aging, by this interweaving, represent an active suppression of elements that have failed to establish successful connections with a regulatory context. Others, in turn, may be the result of a failure to establish such a regulatory context in the first place, thus creating unregulated proliferation. Theories of cancerous growth, for example, may be mentioned in this second category (e.g., Makinodan, 1977).

Theories of neuronal cell death may offer, once again, a useful starting point. Often (see Wisniewski & Terry, 1976) neuronal deterioration or death has been implicated in cognitive deterioration. Yet a number of recent studies have claimed either stability of neuronal loss over the adult life span of verious species (e.g., Dayan, 1971; Diamond, 1978) including humans (e.g., Brody, 1955), or else that losses affect specific areas of the brain rather than being diffuse, and thus may have an impact on specific modes of information processing only. In contrast, neuronal loss is thought to be an integral part of brain *growth* (Brody, 1955; Diamond, 1978; Jacobson, 1978; Lund, 1978) where indeed it provides an adaptive regulatory mechanism. This, indeed, is a common problem encountered in theories of biological aging (Kohn, 1971): Extrapolations made from growing organisms may severely distort our view of what are "normal" aging processes.

However, the very stability of neuronal structures can be seen to be an exemplar of the kind of move toward stability and resistance to change characteristic of developmental processes as outlined here. And, some authors believe, such resistance to change may be reinforced by brain structures (e.g., the hippocampus) which are relatively specialized for the synthesis of *novel* information (e.g., McGough, Jensen, Martinez, Messing, & Vasquez, 1979; Wisniewski & Terry, 1976). Even so, however, it is important to note that plasticity is not foreclosed. First of all, the brain is able to tolerate enormous tissue loss with little apparent effect on normal functioning (Timiras, 1972), as information is stored with great redundancy. Second, there appears to be considerable dendritic growth in the *normal* aging human brain (in at least the parahippocampal gyrus), whereas regression and cell death may be limited to senile pathology (Buell & Coleman, 1979). Third, even in the adult brain, lost functioning may be replaced by new systems (Lund, 1978). But finally, even stable neuronal populations are able to reorganize their interconnections through processes of reactive synaptic regrowth (Scheff, Bernardo, & Cotman, 1978).

Of course, such adaptive potential for plasticity does not *guarantee* further adaptive growth. The extent to which such growth may occur or fail to happen should to a great extent depend on the informational context in which the older individual is embedded. The point is merely that mechanisms for plasticity certainly are available.

This is not to say, however, that questions of the adaptive value of aging hinge on the issue of plasticity per se. Rather, there are circumstances under which the very stability of the information accumulated by the older organism may serve adaptive advantages. However, much as the advantageous or deleterious contribution of the life cycle of a cell must be evaluated within the system in which it functions, so the adaptive advantage of individual aging cannot be judged by an individual-level analysis, but rather hinges on whether or not the aging individual serves to contribute to the system of which it is a part—the social group. At this level, high stability and long-term conservation may well serve an important role in positively contributing to the continuity of the social system. Ethologists have pointed out, for example, that in many primate species older individuals may function to identify food sources, control potential danger situations, and effectively cope with events that have a low probability of occurrence and thus are more likely to be stored by older individuals (e.g., Hinde, 1974; Jolly, 1972; Kummer, 1971). Even though this function is bought, at times, at the expense of misidentifying novel adaptive behaviors as dangerous, it may provide an important counterforce to the unchanneled exploratory curiosity of the young. As Kummer (1971) notes:

> There is little doubt that conservatism, too, is adaptive. The inflexible adults of the . . . troop form a safety reservoir of the previous behavioral variant, which will survive the invention for at least ten years. If the new behavior should turn out to be harmful, say because of parasitic infection, they would survive. In spreading new behaviors, adult rigidity has the same function as low mutation rates in evolution [p. 129].

Whether or not aging is adaptive, therefore, cannot be judged at a level of simple biological reductionism. Even though aging does bring a reduction in biological resilience, aging organisms may have evolved new structures that increase the coping efficiency of the population as a whole.

It would be absurd to claim, however, that because of this potentiality aging universally leads to greater adaptation of any system (e.g., the individual person). Nevertheless, we would claim that it is the outcome of a logical developmental progression. Indeed, it would seem that most developmental models have confounded these two logically distinct criteria and thus imposed youthful standards of "maturity" on the older organism. Thus, we are really facing two issues. First, much as Piaget has argued that our understanding of children is little aided by viewing them as quantitatively diminished adults, so our understanding of aging should be guided by a view of normal, stage-appropriate capacities from which normative deviations can be gauged. We are merely arguing, therefore, that aging can be encompassed by a general developmental program. But second, although such a general progression may at times bring adaptive advantages, it may eventuate in a deleterious outcome to the individual and the population if this program is no longer subordinated by new contexts of regulation (Kohn, 1971). Thus sooner or later, individual death may be the price paid for population flexibility.

GROWTH VERSUS REGRESSION

Although aging has been equated with the deteriorative regression of certain systems, we maintain that such deterioration of subsystems within a larger system may constitute an inherent component of developmental growth of the larger system. In the face of certain declining functions, therefore, we can never logically conclude that these constitute a more general deterioration; rather, we must see whether such subsystem decline is compensated, at a more general level of analysis, by a more stable trade-off. From this perspective, we will argue here, many demonstrated changes in the aging organism indeed can hardly be called maladaptive at all, but often constitute a logical progression from adaptations characteristic of earlier parts of the life span. In this section, we will first be concerned with change dimensions that are often claimed to display a fair degree of robustness. This is not to neglect the problem of interindividual variability, which will be taken up in the next section.

Cognition and Social Development

A first domain, more fully elaborated elsewhere (Labouvie-Vief, 1980a; 1980b, 1980c), is that of cognitive development. In this area, demonstrations of all sorts of deficit have been so numerous (see Botwinick, 1978; Horn, 1978) that it may appear a logical tour de force to argue them away as growth. Nevertheless, as argued earlier, demonstrations of decline are *not* logically inconsistent with claims of growth. In fact, they may logically derive from the fact that virtually all demonstrations of cognitive deficit have adhered to a youth centered model.

The standard par excellence of such models is that of formal operations—here understood in the widest sense to encompass the kind of purely symbolic thinking reflected in tasks of fluid intelligence and formal problem solving. This kind of thinking does, of course, represent an adaptive potential of enormous proportions, as it frees the youth to operate on pure symbols and thereby achieves a degree of extension in space and time never reached before.

Nevertheless, Piaget (e.g., 1967) argues, this kind of thinking entails its dangers as well.

> With the advent of formal intelligence, thinking takes wings and it is not surprising that at first this unexpected power is both used and abused . . . each new mental ability starts off by incorporating the world in a process of egocentric assimilation. Adolescent egocentricity is manifested by a belief in the omnipotence of reflection, as though the world should submit itself to idealistic schemes rather then to systems of reality [pp. 63–64

Formal thinking thus ensnares the youth in a kind of idealistic grandeur of the omnipotence of "pure logic," and only once this intellectual egocentricity is adapted to the pragmatic constraints of reality can we talk of mature adaptation: "True adaptation to society comes automatically when the adolescent reformer attempts to put his ideas to work. Just as experience reconciles formal thought with the reality of things, so does effective and enduring work, undertaken in concrete and well-defined situations, cure dreams" [pp. 68–69].

Several lines of research bear, in effect, on the progression thus alluded to. Perry (1970), for example, has analyzed the conflicts, and their eventual resolution, experienced by college students. Here conflicts resulted from exactly that feature of logic which Piaget calls the egocentricity of youth—a belief in the omnipotence of reflection. And this feature creates, according to Perry, specific social and cognitive vulnerabilities: a search for absolute values, for authoritative statements, for ideological certainty. College life, however, may induce a slow erosion of this absolutism of adolescent logic:

> Reason reveals relations within any given context; it can also compare one context with another on the basis of metacontexts established for this purpose. But there is a limit. In the end, reason itself remains reflexively relativistic, a property which turns reason back upon reason's own findings. In even its farthest reaches then reason will leave the thinker with several legitimate contexts and no way of choosing among them—no way at least that he can justify through reason alone. If he is still to honor reason he must now also transcend it; he must affirm his own position from within himself in full awareness that reason can never completely justify him or assure him [pp. 135–136].

The eventual resolution of this conflict, in Perry's study, is the realization of the inherent logical relativity of multiple perspectives. At the same time, however, this cognitive realization signals a new integration: One needs to discontinue one's search for logical certainty and accept the pragmatic constraints of adulthood. One needs to give up absolutism and idealism for commitment and specialization.

A somewhat similar analysis has been offered by Gilligan and Murphy (1980) in a reanalysis, based upon Kohlberg's model, of moral development. Here, a move from college age to adulthood demonstrated an increased awareness of social concentions and pragmatic constraints. This movement originally had been thought to constitute regressive change. Yet, Gilligan and Murphy argue, a closer look at the individual's thinking reveals new and progressive qualities. Reflecting after 7 years on their earlier responses to Kohlberg's moral dilemma, these young adults realize that their earlier thinking reflected an overidealization that was, however, divorced from their own affect and actions. As one subject reflects upon his earlier response to the dilemma of whether Heinz should steal a drug that might save his dying wife:

> This is a very crisp little dilemma and you can latch onto that principle pretty fast, and in that situation you can say that life is more important than money. But then, when you reflect back on how you really act in your own life, you don't use that principle, or I haven't yet used that principle to operate on. And none of the people who answer the dilemma that way use that principle to operate on because they were blowing $7,000 a year for their education at Harvard instead of giving it to the Children's Fund to give porridge to the kids in Botswana, and to that extent, answering the dilemma with that principle is not hypocritical, it's just that you don't *recognize it*. I hadn't recognized it at the time, and I am sure they didn't recognize it either [p. 24].

As Birren (1969) has shown, this eventual giving up of individualistic, grandiose egocentricity may bring a new mode of thinking in which decision making is integrated with affective needs and pragmatic constraints. Older adults, according to Birren, may have developed a sharp awareness of their own limitations in dealing with information overload. Yet in so doing they have also come to view decisions as embedded in a complex social matrix, and they have learned to utilize that matrix to optimize decisions.

We are maintaining, therefore, that different criteria of cognitive maturity must be applied in middle and later adulthood than in youth. Issues of commitment, specialization, and channeling one's energies in the service of social system stability become mature concerns and they invalidate, therefore, youth's fascination with the exercise of logic *qua* logic (also see Ahammer, 1979; Erikson, 1978; Schaie, 1977).

The point here, it must be noted, is not to deprecate this fascination. For youth, it will permit a circulatory exercise of skills that are to be put to use later on. Nevertheless, from the perspective of adult maturity it constitutes but a temporary, local adaptation: The tools perfected in youth must be subordinated to a higher-order goal. In Schaie's (1977) words, if the theme of youth is acquisitive flexibility, that of mature adulthood is responsibility.

To the researcher who overidentifies with the buoyant optimism inherent in logical overassimilation, adulthood may, as a consequence, be marked by an overly concrete, pragmatic orientation. However, it would certainly misrepresent the context of adulthood to call the resulting demand for meaning and pragmatic payoff a regressive change. From the perspective of adulthood it can instead be argued that an integration of these demands reflects a realistic fit into the constraints of adult life—far from indicative of a return to a childlike concrete stage as is often intimated in life-span research (see Labouvie-Vief, 1980a, c).

However, even the theme of generativity reflects only a local transcendence of egocentrism as each stage brings its unique form of egocentricity (Elkind, 1974). Those of the generative adult are the preoccupations with executive power and generative competence, and eventually, many adults may come to view even those preoccupations from the perspective of the chains of their past. To Jung (1933), for example, midlife becomes the truly pivotal period of life-span development, as the middle-aged adult may face the dilemma that even the integration of generativity was the result of a specific social fabric with its pressures toward restraining the process of individuation. Later life, for Jung, therefore brings the most crucial turning point—a chance for freedom from, and transcendence of, those constraints.

Cumming and Henry (1961) have referred to this process as disengagement and, like other authors (e.g., Ahammer, 1979; Erikson, 1978; Kohlberg, 1973; Neugarten, 1964; Sheehy, 1976), have stressed the resulting potential for growth: A concern, on a yet higher level of analysis, with wide-reaching metaphysical issues, with the ultimate meaning of life.[4]

Few empirical analyses are available, as yet, of this process. Ahammer (1979) has, however, offered examples from philosophical and literary sources. Even more pertinent is Feuer's (1974) analysis of the life spans of twentieth century physicists, as it helps not only to clarify the point that each life stage brings unique and locally adapted skills, but also to show how these are progressively integrated into the contexts of different life stages. Thus it is the belief in youthful omnipotence that impels many

[4] The interpretation of disengagement here differs from the argument over whether or not high degrees of social involvement are important in late life. It stresses, instead, a cognitive integration by which the individual may transcend earlier socially enforced specializations and thereby achieve a new level of individuation (Jung, 1933).

eminent physicists to reject prevailing paradigmatic orientations. The resulting discovery, in turn, reinforces a stage of commitment in which issues are equally important: the working out in detail of one's discovery, the building up of a social group to propagate the resulting theoretical framework, and then the exeuction of power and social control as the framework becomes a new paradigm itself. Upon having thus established social control, however, one often discerns a wholistic concern with the ultimate principles pervading the universe. It is this very move that compelled the young Einstein, for example, to vehemently reject idealized laws of time, space, and cause and effect, only to end up, in his later life, searching for a unifying harmony that led him to criticize the young Heisenberg's indeterminacy principle with the quip "God does not play dice!"

It might be argued, of course, that Feuer's (1974) analysis pertains to highly exceptional individuals only. Nevertheless, Gutmann (1977) has argued that very similar movements are discerned in more mundane life spans. In a careful analysis of cross-cultural similarities, he finds that the aging individual is considered more integrative and meditative, and often will control religious, moral, and magical resources. Indeed, this theme may be so generally related to aging that it even characterizes the content of psychopathological thought disorders in aging (Gutmann & Grunes, 1980).

Information Processing

If our discussion of social–cognitive changes is perhaps overly general and speculative, no area shows the postulated movement on a more fine-grained level than that of information processing. In this area (see, e.g., Craik, 1977) aging deficits have been said to affect primarily more complex abstract, or "deeper," modes of processing. Most of the pertinent research has been based, however, on stimulus materials of a low order of structural complexity (e.g., isolated words). To that extent, deficits may be specific to the structural complexity of the tasks utilized; they may fail to show up, however, on other materials.

Such trade-off processes in which more complex modes come to superordinate developmentally prior ones are well demonstrated in the childhood literature. As language and conceptual functioning come to supersede information intake, for example, one typically finds a decrease in the analysis of fine perceptual detail (see White, 1965) and reduced attention to the spatial and temporal distribution of detail (Stevenson, 1972)—indeed, the list is far too exhaustive to replicate here (see, however, Labouvie-Vief & Schell, in press). It is not appropriate therefore (as shown in the earlier quoted study by Maccoby & Modiano, 1966) to view development as a move toward perfection. Rather, each level implies a trade-off—a view expressed particularly well in Borges's (1962) short story

"Funes the Memorious." Funes, the story tells, once took a fall from a horse and thereafter forgot how to forget.

> On the falling from the horse, he lost consciousness; when he recovered it, the present was almost intolerable, it was so rich and bright . . . He remembered the shapes of the clouds in the south at dawn on the 30th of April, 1882, and he could compare them in his recollection with the marbled grain in the design of a leather-bound book which he had seen only once . . . He told me . . . 'My memory, Sir, is like a garbage disposal' [p. 112].

Yet this perfection imprisoned him in a mindless, "stammering greatness":

> He was . . . almost incapable of general platonic ideas. It was not only difficult for him to understand that the generic term 'dog' embraced so many unlike specimens of different sizes and forms; he was disturbed by the fact that a dog at three-fourteen (seen in profile) should have the same name as the dog at three-fifteen (seen from the front) . . . Without effort, he had learned English, French, Portuguese, Latin. I suspect, nevertheless, that he was not very capable of thought. To think is to forget a difference, to generalize, to abstract [pp. 114–115].

In fact, we have proposed elsewhere (Labouvie-Vief, 1980a; Labouvie-Vief & Schell, 1980) that older adults' difficulty with many current mnemonic tasks is exactly due to their ability to forget a difference. For example, whereas older adults have poor memory for verbatim surface detail, there is no forceful at evidence that such deficits extend to more deep structural retention—the preservation of sentence meaning (Labouvie-Vief, 1980a; Hurlbut, 1976; Walsh & Baldwin, 1977), or the abstraction of abstract kernel propositions from text (see Labouvie-Vief & Schell, 1980; Zelinski, Gilewski, & Thompson, 1980).

It does not appear too far fetched, indeed, to conclude that this trade-off between surface detail and deep structural meaning represents an altogether adaptively useful strategy. Birren (1969) has referred to it as the "race between the bit and the chunk": The mature and older adult has experienced the limitations of his or her memory, and has learned to attend to those codes that are less likely to be transitory, thus more permanent and stable.

This adaptive interpretation of the adult's attention to higher-order units of meaning receives support from several further empirical sources. First, it is known that, if recall is followed for a prolonged period of time, lower-order information tends to decay rather rapidly, whereas the recall of meaning-preserving kernel transformations displays more temporal stability (e.g. Bartlett, 1932; Dooling & Christiansen, 1977). Second, a few studies also have demonstrated that the elderly may have acquired more accurate knowledge of the functioning of their mnemonic system (Lachman & Lachman, 1979; Zelinski et al., 1980). Thus it is possible that they have learned to attend selectively to more informative and temporally stable units of meaning.

INDIVIDUAL DIFFERENCES:
FLEXIBILITY AND SPECIALIZATION

The general outline of stages of cognitive and mnemonic development in adulthood has served to elucidate the point that what is to be called "intelligence" or "cognitive structure" in adulthood and old age are dimensions that are qualitatively different from the youth centered ones usually used to assess these dimensions. To the extent that such stages represent relatively broad, dominant levels of information analysis, or modal levels, they then serve as an ordering principle by which such concepts as "task difficulty" change their meaning from mode to mode.

Note now that apparent deficits may enter into this model in at least two ways. One is by requiring a subject to perform a task that corresponds to a developmentally prior mode. In that case, we are not really concerned with questions of developmental deficit, but rather of *flexibility*. The second source of apparent deficit may arise from the fact that, although modal levels may be relatively broad, they nevertheless are realized in different contexts and contents: To talk about a move to the metaphysical in Einstein's theory or in Shakespeare's literature or even in Gutmann and Grunes' (1980) cases of late adult psychoses requires that we recognize that, despite commonalities, there also exist differences. In this case, we are facing the issues of *specialization* and—if remedial efforts are deemed important—of *plasticity*.

In reality, a differentiation between flexibility and plasticity may not always be a very sharp one. It is possible, however, for two reasons. First, it is a logically different issue to ask if a mode once present in an individual's repertoire, although subordinated, can in principle be reactivated, or whether an individual can be brought to acquire specialized contents not previously in his or her repertoire. But second, we would also expect time functions of the acquisition process that are quite divergent. As Shiffrin and Schneider (1977) have shown, the acquisition of new material is an exceedingly slow process if it is to be brought to automated efficiency, often taking many thousands of trials. The reacquisition of material already in the repertoire, however, can be exceedingly fast.

A good example of this differentiation is a longitudinal study performed in the Wisconsin Primate Laboratory (Suomi, personal communication). Old rhesus monkeys who in their youth had learned to master an oddity learning task were compared to old monkeys who never had done so. The acquisition curves for the two groups were dramatically different. That of the latter group showed a slow rise over a long time interval. That of the former group showed a very brief period of high error rates, but then almost immediate recovery of high accuracy.

The issue is worth detailing at some length because it shows that the older organism, when presented with certain stimulus materials, may tend to relate them to a current modal level, and thus be fairly inefficient in information analysis and retention. However, once the experimenter provides a context for what is to be required in the task (e.g., by verbal instructions or practice), an altogether different picture may emerge.

Numerous cognitive and mnemonic experiments do, of course, fit this general pattern. When presented with lists of words and instructions to recall them, for example, most elderly individuals show low efficiency. But when a context is provided (e.g., by asking the subjects to utilize organizational strategies of a specific nature), one typically finds a dramatic rise, often to the level of college students (see Botwinick, 1978; Craik, 1977; Labouvie-Vief & Schell, in press).

Usually, this phenomenon is interpreted as a failure on the part of older subjects to "deep process" information. We would argue, however, that this is an inherently relative interpretation as, without instructions to process material in a specific way, the experimental context leaves inherently ambiguous both what the subjects are *actually doing* and what they *are to do*. A persuasive example is provided by Riegel and Birren (1969) who tested young and old subjects on their latency to produce a word given a discrete first syllable (i.e., CAN → CANDY), and in addition asked the subjects to write as many words as they could, given the same constraints (i.e., CAN → CANDY, CANCER, CANDID, etc.). In the initial trials of the experiments the researchers found that the older subjects were slower in responding and that their responses were more "random" than those of the younger subjects. As the test continued the older subjects eventually achieved the same response latency as the younger subjects. Concomitantly, though, there was also a decrease in the "randomness" of the older subjects responses. This process may, however, reflect a stylistic tendency to search for unique, creative answers, and an eventual realization that this is not what is being asked for. As Riegel and Birren (1966) state: "By restricting their responses to the most common ones and by avoiding unique and original answers, they (the older subjects) increase their speed during continual performance [p. 169]."

Elsewhere (Labouvie-Vief & Schell, in press) we have argued that it may be a misrepresentation to interpret such data as evidence of deficits in processing, abstraction, and so forth. And indeed, one can only be surprised, from this perspective, at the facility with which older subjects, with a minimum of instructions and practice, raise performance levels all of a sudden, generalize them to other tasks, and even maintain this level for a period of weeks (for review, see Baltes & Baltes, 1977; Labouvie-Vief, 1977; Labouvie-Vief & Chandler, 1978).

We do not want to argue, at this point, about the exact degree of flexibility maintained by the older individual. To do so would require a more careful analysis of (*a*) the adaptive pressures acting against flexibility; and (*b*) the degrees of relative information input that will result in maximum flexibility in different age groups. We do, however, maintain, that the contextual fluctuation of behavior resulting from research aimed at this issue is not at all a failure of the adult organism to adhere to organismic–structural laws (e.g., Reese, 1973). On the contrary, to a research subject who has developed organization of information at a particular level, most experimental contexts are inherently ambiguous and must be disambiguated.

A somewhat different case is encountered if one deals with individual differences resulting from specialization. These, we have argued, are also valid from a structural–developmental viewpoint; that is, they may not indicate generalized regressive changes. Sabatini and Labouvie-Vief (1979) have shown, for example, that differences in formal reasoning were altogether accounted for by professional specialization rather than by age. Similarly, Schaie and his collaborators (e.g., Baltes & Schaie, 1976; Nesselroade, Schaie, & Baltes, 1972; Schaie & Labouvie-Vief, 1974) have shown that apparent decrements on many dimensions of intellectual functioning may represent history-related changes in educational exposure. On a more general level, others have argued that culture-related differences in modes of thinking may reflect specialized adaptations to the contexts of a culture (e.g., Cole & Scribner, 1974; Scribner, 1979; see Labouvie-Vief, 1980c, for review).

Similar effects of specialization also occur in the area of social development. Typically, for example, we find that no one social life style can be called optimally adapted (e.g., Mass & Kuypers, 1974; Neugarten, Crotty, & Tobin, 1964) as long as individuals see themselves as embedded in a matrix of meaningful activities. And on a still longer time scale, different individuals may move through different life lines, sequencing their contexts (e.g., childbearing, career start) in different orders (see Labouvie-Vief & Zaks, 1980).

At this level of specialization, one may expect a high degree of stability that results from the homeorhetic tendencies of development discussed earlier. Nevertheless, evidence indicates that, even so, adults may achieve major cognitive and cognitive–social restructuring, although at this level one may be dealing with a time scale of years. Luria (1976), for example, has shown that relatively short periods (several months) of formal education raise the level of formal thinking in an Uzbekistan peasant culture, although the level achieved in Western college students may demand many years (Scribner, 1979). In general, however, a formal mode of thinking appears to be primarily related to length of education rather than age (Scribner, 1979).

Similarly, in the development of personality structure, high stability over long time intervals appears to be the rule. Such stability, however, appearś to go hand in hand with the individual's tendency to maintain a stable context; to the degree that adaptive styles change, they usually co-occur with changes in context (e.g., Mass & Kuypers, 1974). Many adults, for example, are socialized into particular roles, and whether or not they move out of them may depend entirely on whether they experience a change in context initiating a role shift. For some, this may be divorce (Sedney, 1977); for others, the "empty nest"; for some, widowhood (Lopata, 1975); for others still, their particular course of early socialization which has created a sense of being trapped in traditional but ill-fitting roles (Livson, 1975). It also appears that such a role shift may be more likely in women, possibly because current sex-role prescriptions permit greater flexibility for women (Lynn, 1969; Mass & Kuypers, 1974). A good example is offered by Maas and Kuypers' (1974) 40-year follow-up of young couples. Here, high stability both of behavior and context was observed in men. This was not true of women, however. One group of women, in particular, early in their adulthood were highly dissatisfied with their marriages, unhappy in their parenting roles, socially withdrawn and in general poorly adapted. As older and no-longer-married women, however, they were highly satisfied, dividing their time between rewarding involvements with friends, children, and occupations.

CONTEXTUAL REGULATION AND REGRESSION

The reader may well have wondered, by now, how the present framework leaves room for the type of regression observed in senility and loss of orientation. Is any purpose served by arguing these away?

The answer is an unqualified no. For the process that we have outlined may, or may not, be adaptive in a particular context—only in some cultures have these qualities gained prestige for the older individual and have helped to reinforce a degree of gerontocracy:

> Thus, extremes of climate appear to reduce gerontocracy, as does impermanency of residence. Conversely, male gerontocracy increases as society becomes more stable and more complex. In organized folk settings, the usefulness and prestige of the age depends on their wisdom, their experience, their acquired property rights, and their ritual powers [Gutmann, 1977, p. 312].

Consistent with this, the loss of traditional culture associated with modernization has often brought a loss of status and enforced disengagement with all the detrimental consequences these conditions imply for the elderly person. As Mead (1970) has stated, in such cultures the young must define their own adaptive context, and the skills and long-term experience of the old may easily be considered obsolete. This general view is perhaps best exemplified in Bengtson and Kuypers' "social breakdown model" (cf. Bengtson, 1973). In this conceptualization, the relationship between aging and intellectual and social competence is to be viewed as a feedback loop through which social groups in marginal positions are actively inducted into a role of social and intellectual incompetence. Once begun, this induction initiates a cycle of self-fulfilling prophecies buttressed by mythologies and stereotypes surrounding socially held views of "normal" aging. As a result, a two-fold socialization process is reinforced. First, many social institutions will actively discourage competent behaviors. But second, the target individuals themselves are subjected to a life-long socialization process that leads them to internalize negative expectations. Rosenmayr (cf. Rosenmayr & Rosenmayr, 1978) has coined the phrase of a "societally induced individual responsibility" to capture the implication that many elderly surrender to negative social stereotypes and thereby contribute toward their own decline.

Demonstrations for this cycle are to be found particularly in marginal groups of the elderly, such as those who are institutionalized. Often, the social expectation in such groups is one of irreversible decrement, and it is one in which interactions with patients is actively translated into a discouragement of competence-related behaviors by the staff (Baltes & Baltes, 1977; Macdonald & Butler, 1974). Yet often relatively minor interventions into this breakdown cycle have resulted in dramatic effects. Schulz (1976) and Langer and Rodin (1976) for example, have shown that the patients' subjective control of events affects their cognitive, emotional, and even physical well-being. Such control may be heightened by simply involving the patient in decisions about everyday happenings such as taking care of plants or knowing visitation schedules. Langer (Langer & Rodin, 1976), in the same vein, has argued that memory deficits may result from institutional failures to make events memorable. Even more dramatically, the increased mortality often reported following intstitutional relocation was significantly alleviated when administrators implemented programs to familiarize and involve patients with the events and circumstances of the move (Schulz & Brenner, 1977). Decrements, in other words, certainly continue to be a part of aging. As often as not, however, they may result from a removal of the individual from an informative social matrix, a regulatory context.

Concluding Note

Development and aging have typically been treated as processes which are antithetical and polarized. In contrast, the view of aging here elaborated is one asserting that growth and regression are part of any reorganization at any segment of the life span. In this way, many phenomena currently subsumed under the notion of "aging" are structurally part of a general developmental progression, and vice versa.

This view may offer several advantages. First, it circumvents the cumbersome problem of postulating different evolutionary programs, one aimed at increasing structural development, the other at its destruction (e.g., Sacher, 1978). Second, it asserts that, much as child developmentalists have insisted on stage-appropriate definitions of adaptability, so normative deviations in aging are to be gauged by a stage-appropriate concept of the normalcy of aging, as opposed to the superiority of youth.

Nevertheless, it is necessary to reiterate several cautionary remarks. We are not claiming that aging constitutes some ultimate apogee of adaptability. Rather, by virtue of the very processes that lead to it, aging may imply a loss of flexibility and resilience. This loss, on the background of a social context, which itself evolves, may eventually lead to destructive outcomes at the individual level. Neither are we claiming that earlier phases of the life span are mere preparatory stages to aging. Rather, each life stage may bring unique adaptations, but also unique failures to be adapted. Ultimately, the adaptive value of each life stage can be judged only in the context of how different stage-specific adaptations are corregulated in a population. As Brent (1978a) has put it:

> The younger cohorts in any collective at any given time—i.e., those which most recently came into existence—seem to be specialized for providing the flexibility necessary for adpating to changes in existing environmental conditions and for expansion into new environmental niches, while the older cohorts appear to be specialized for maintaining the existing organismic collective within the environmental niches to which they have already adapted—thus providing a secure base of operations from which the younger cohorts can venture out [p. 25].

Acknowledgments

The conceptualization in the current chapter has significantly been influenced by numerous discussions with Sandor B. Brent. James E. Birren, Jurgis Karuza, Carolyn U. Shantz, and Glenn E. Weisfeld, and many graduate students—especially Karen Olsen, David Schell, Mark Speece, and Shelly Weaver—have also provided useful conceptual and corrective feedback. To all of them my sincere thanks are due.

References

Achenbach, T. M. *Research in developmental psychology: Concepts, strategies, methods.* New York: Free Press, 1978.

Ahammer, I. M. *A positive growth model for adult development and aging: The model of experience.* Unpublished manuscript, University of Frankfort, W. Germany, 1979.

Baltes, M. M., & Baltes, P. B. The ecopsychological relativity and plasticity of psychological aging: Convergent perspectives of cohort effects and operant psychology. *Zeitschrift fuer experimentelle und angewandte Psychologie.* 1977, 24, 179–197.

Baltes, P. B., Reese, H. W., & Lipsitt, L. P. Life-span developmental psychology. *Annual Review of Psychology*, 1980, *31*, in press.

Baltes, P. B., & Schaie, K. W. On the plasticity of adult and gerontological intelligence: Where Horn and Donaldson fail. *American Psychologist*, 1976, *31*, 720–725.

Bartlett, F. C. *Remembering*. Cambridge, Eng.: University Press, 1932.

Bengtson, V. L. *The social psychology of aging*. New York: Bobbs-Merrill, 1973.

Birren, J. E. Age and decision strategies. In A. T. Welford & J. E. Birren (Eds.), *Interdisciplinary topics in gerontology* (Vol. 4). Basel: S. Karger, 1969.

Bloom, B. S. *Stability and change in human characteristics*. New York: Wiley, 1964.

Borges, J. L. *Ficciones*. New York: Grove Press, 1962.

Botwinick, J. *Aging and behavior*, (2nd ed.) New York: Springer, 1978.

Bowlby, J. *Attachment and loss. II: Separation*. New York: Basic Books, 1973.

Brent, S. B. Individual specialization, collective adaptation, and rate of environmental change. *Human Development*, 1978, *2*, 21–33. (a)

Brent, S. B. Motivation, steady-state, and structural development: A general model of psychological homeostasis. *Motivation and Emotion*, 1978, *2*, 229–332. (b)

Brent, S. B. Prigogine's model for self-organization in nonequilibrium systems: Its relevance for developmental psychology. *Human Development*, 1978, *21*, 374–387. (c)

Brody, H. Organization of the cerebral cortex. III: A study of aging in the human cerebral cortex. *Journal of Comparative Neurology*, 1955, *102*, 551–556.

Bruner, J. *On knowing: Essays for the left hand*. Harvard University Press, 1962.

Buell, S. J., & Coleman, P. D. Dendrite growth in the aged human brain and failure of growth in senile dementia. *Science*, 1979, *206*, 854–856.

Campbell, D. T. Evolutionary epistemology. In P. A. Schilpp (Ed.), *The philosophy of Karl Popper* (Vol. 1). La Salle, Ill.: Open Court, 1974.

Cole, M., & Scribner, S. *Culture and thought: A psychological introduction*. New York: Wiley, 1974.

Comalli, P. E., Jr., Wapner, S., & Werner, H. Interference effects of Stroop color-word test in childhood, adulthood, and aging, *Journal of Genetic Psychology*, 1966, *100*, 47–53.

Craik, F. I. M. Age differences in human memory. In J. E. Birren & K. W. Schaie (Eds.), *Handbook of the psychology of aging*. New York: Van Nostrand Reinhold, 1977.

Cumming, E., & Henry, W. H. *The process of disengagement*. New York: Basic Books, 1961.

Dayan, A. D. Comparative neuropathology of aging: Studies of the brains of 47 species of vertebrates. *Brain*, 1971, *94*, 31–42.

Diamond, M. C. The aging brain: Some enlightening and optimistic results. *American Scientist*, 1978, *66*, 66–71.

Dooling, J. D., & Christiaansen, R. E. Levels of encoding and retention of prose. In G. H. Bower (Ed.), *The psychology of learning and memory* (Vol. 11). New York: Academic Press, 1977.

Elkind, D. Egocentrism in children and adolescents. In D. Elking (Ed.), Children and Adolescents: Interpretive essays on Jean Piaget (2nd ed.). New York: Oxford University Press, 1974.

Erikson, E. H. *Adulthood*. New York: Norton, 1978.

Feuer, L. *Einstein and the generations of science*. New York: Basic Books, 1974.

Flavell, J. H. Cognitive changes in adulthood. In P. B. Baltes & L. R. Goulet (Eds.), *Life-span developmental psychology*. New York: Academic Press, 1970.

Gibson, J. J. Perception as a function of stimulation. In S. Koch (Ed.), *Psychology: A study of a science*. New York: McGraw-Hill, 1959.

Gilligan, C., & Murphy, J. M. Development from adolescence to adulthood: The philosopher and the dilemma of the fact. In D. Kuhn (Ed.), *Intellectual development beyond childhood*. New York: Jossey-Bass, 1980.

Greenfield, P. M. Cross-cultural research and Piagetian theory: Paradox and progress. In

K. F. Riegel & J. A. Meacham (Eds.), *The developing individual in a changing world* (Vol. 1). *Historical and cultural issues.* Chicago: Aldine, 1976.

Gutmann, D. The cross-cultural perspective: Notes toward a comparative psychology of aging. In K. W. Schaie & J. E. Birren (Eds.), *Handbook of the psychology of aging.* New York: Van Nostrand Reinhold, 1977.

Gutmann, D., & Grunes, J. The clinical psychology of later life: Developmental paradigms. In N. Datan & N. Lohmann (Eds.), *Transitions of aging.* New York: Academic Press, 1980.

Hinde, R. A. *Biological bases of human social behavior.* New York: McGraw-Hill, 1974.

Horn, J. L. Human ability systems. In P. B. Baltes (Ed.). *Life-span development and behavior* (Vol. 1). New York: Academic Press, 1978.

Hurlbut, N. L. *Adult age differences in sentence memory.* Unpublished doctoral dissertation, University of Wisconsin, 1976.

Jacobson, M. *Developmental neurobiology* (2nd ed.). New York: Plenum, 1978.

Jensen, A. R., & Rohwer, W. D., Jr. The Stroop color–word test: A review. *Acta Psychologica,* 1966, *25,* 36–93.

Jolly, A. *The evolution of primate behavior.* New York: Macmillan, 1972.

Jung, C. G. *Modern man in search of a soul.* New York: Harcourt, Brace & World, 1933.

Kohlberg, L. Continuities in childhood and adult moral development revisited. In P. B. Baltes & K. W. Schaie (Eds.), *Life-span developmental psychology: Personality and socialization.* New York: Academic Press, 1973.

Kohn, R. R. *Principles of mammalian aging.* Englewood Cliffs, N.J.: Prentice-Hall, 1971.

Kuhn, T. S. *The structure of scientific revolutions.* 2nd ed. Chicago: University of Chicago Press, 1970.

Kummer, H. *Primate societies: Group techniques of ecological adaptation,* 1971.

Labouvie-Vief, G. Adult cognitive development: In search of alternative interpretations. *Merrill-Palmer Quarterly,* 1977, *23,* 227–263.

Labouvie-Vief, G. Adaptive dimensions of cognitive aging. In N. Datan & N. Lohmann (Eds.), *Transitions of aging.* New York: Academic Press, 1980. (a)

Labouvie-Vief, G. Beyond formal operations: Uses and limits of pure logic in life-span development. *Human Development,* 1980. (b)

Labouvie-Vief, G. Individual time, social time, and intellectual aging. In T. K. Hareven (Ed.), *The life-course and aging in interdisciplinary and cross-cultural perspective.* New York: Guilford, 1980. (c)

Labouvie-Vief, G., & Chandler, M. J. Cognitive development and life-span developmental theory: Idealistic versus contextual perspectives. In P. B. Baltes (Ed.), *Life-span development and behavior.* New York: Academic Press, 1978.

Labouvie-Vief, G., & Schell, D. Learning and memory in later life: A developmental view. In B. Wolman & G. Stricker (Eds.), *Handbook of developmental psychology.* Englewood Cliffs, N.J.: Prentice-Hall, 1980.

Labouvie-Vief, G., & Zaks, P. M. Adulthood and aging. In A. Kazdin, A. Bellack, & M. Hersen (Eds.), *New perspectives on abnormal psychology.* New York: Oxford University Press, 1980.

Lachman, J. L., & Lachman, R. Age and the actualization of world knowledge. In L. W. Poon, J. L. Fozard, L. Cermak, D. Arenberg, & L. Thompson (Eds.), *New directions in memory and aging: Proceedings of the George Talland Memorial Conference.* Englewood Cliffs, N.J.: Earlbaum, 1979.

Langer, E., & Rodin, J. The effects of choice and enhanced personal responsibility: A field experiment in an institutional setting. *Journal of Personality and Social Psychology,* 1976, *34,* 191–198.

Leontiev, A. N. *Probleme der entwicklung des psychischen* (2nd ed.). West Germany: Fischer, 1977.

Livson, F. *Sex differences in personality development in middle adult years: A longitudinal study.* Paper presented at the 28th annual meeting of the Gerontological Society, Louisville, Kentucky, October, 1975.

Lopata, H. Z. Widowhood: Societal factors in life-span disruptions and alternatives. In N. Datan & L. H. Ginsberg (Eds.), *Life-span developmental psychology: Normative life crises.* New York: Academic Press, 1975.

Lund, R. D. Development and plasticity of the brain. New York: Oxford University Press, 1978.

Luria, A. R. *Cognitive development: Its cultural and social foundations.* Cambridge, Mass.: Harvard University Press, 1976.

Lynn, D. B. *Parental and sex-role identification: A theoretical formulation.* Berkeley: McCutchan, 1969.

Maas, H. S., & Kuypers, J. A. *From 30 to 70.* San Francisco: Jossey-Bass, 1974.

Maccoby, M., & Modiano, N. On culture and equivalence. In J. S. Bruner, R. R. Olver, P. M. Greenfield, (Eds.), *Studies in cognitive growth.* New York: Wiley, 1966.

Macdonald, M. L., & Butler, A. K. Reversal of helplessness: Producing walking behavior in nursing home wheelchair residents using behavior modification procedures. *Journal of Gerontology,* 1974, *29,* 97–101.

Makinodan, T. Immunity and aging. In C. E. Finch & L. Hayflick (Eds.), *Handbook of the biology of aging.* New York: Van Nostrand Reinhold, 1977.

Mayr, E. Evolution. *Scientific American.* 1978, *239,* 46–55.

McGough, J. L., Jensen, R., Martinez, J., Messing, R., & Vasquez, B. Age-related changes in drug modulation of learning and memory. Paper presented at the 1979 Annual Meeting of the American Psychological Association, New York, September, 1979.

Mead, M. *Culture and commitment: A study of the generation gap.* New York: Doubleday, 1970.

Moore, K. L. *The developing human: Clinically oriented embryology* (2nd ed.). Philadelphia: W. B. Saunders, 1977.

Nesselroade, J. R., Schaie, K. W., & Baltes, P. B. Ontogenetic and generational components of structural and quantitative change in adult cognitive behavior. *Journal of Gerontology,* 1972, *27,* 222–228.

Neugarten, B. L., Crotty, W. J., & Tobin, S. S. Personality types in an aged population. In B. L. Neugarten (Ed.), *Personality in middle and late life.* New York: Atherton, 1964.

Neugarten, B. L., & Hagestad, G. O. Age and the life course. In R. H. Binstock & E. Shanas (Eds.), *Handbook of aging and the social sciences.* New York: Van Nostrand Reinhold, 1976.

Perry, W. I. *Forms of intellectual and ethical development in the college years.* New York: Holt, Rinehart & Winston, 1970.

Piaget, J. *Insights and illusions of psychology.* New York: New American Library, 1965.

Piaget, J. *Six psychological studies.* New York: Random House, 1967.

Piaget, J. *Structuralism.* New York: Basic Books, 1970.

Piaget, J. *Biology and knowledge.* Chicago: University of Chicago Press, 1971.

Piaget, J. Intellectual evolution from adolescence to adulthood. *Human Development,* 1972, *16,* 1–12.

Piaget, J. Chance and dialectic in biological epistemology: A critical analysis of Jaques Monod's Theses. In W. F. Overton & J. M. Gallagher (Eds.), *Knowledge and development* (Vol. 1). New York: Plenum, 1977.

Popper, K. R. *Conjectures and regulations: The growth of scientific knowledge.* New York: Harper & Row, 1963.

Popper, K. R., & Eccles, J. *The self and its brain.* New York: Springer, 1978.

Prigogine, I. Order through fluctuation: Self-organization and social system. In E. Jantsch & C. H. Waddington (Eds.), *Evolution and consciousness.* Reading, Mass.: Addison-Wesley, 1976.

Reese, H. W. Life-span models of memory. *Gerontologist,* 1973, *13,* 472–478.

Riegel, K. F. History of psychological gerontology. In J. E. Birren & K. W. Schaie (Eds.), *Handbook of the psychology of aging.* New York: Van Nostrand Reinhold, 1977.

Riegel, K. F., & Birren, J. E. Age differences in verbal associations. *The Journal of Genetic Psychology,* 1966, *108,* 153–170.

Rosenmayr, L., & Rosenmayr, H. *Der alte Mensch in der Gesellschaft.* Reinbek, Ger.: Rowohlt, 1978.

Sabatini, P., & Labouvie-Vief, G. *Age and professional specialization in formal reasoning.* Paper presented at the 1979 Annual Meeting of the American Gerontological Society, Washington, D. C., November, 1979.

Sacher, G. A. Longevity, aging, and death: An evolutionary perspective. *Gerontologist,* 1978, *18,* 112–120.

Sampson, G. Psychology and the American ideal. *Journal of Personality and Social Psychology,* 1977, *8,* 129–138.

Schaie, K. W. Toward a stage theory of adult development. *International Journal of Aging and Human Development,* 1977, *8,* 129–138.

Schaie, K. W., & Labouvie-Vief, G. Generational versus ontogenetic components of change in adult cognitive behavior. A 14-year cross-sequential study. *Developmental Psychology,* 1974, *10,* 305–320.

Scheff, S. W., Bernardo, L. S., & Cotman, C. W. Decrease in adrenergic axon sprouting in the senescent rat. *Science,* 1978, *202,* 775–778.

Schulz, R. Aging and control. In J. S. Carroll & J. W. Payne (Eds.), *Cognition and social behavior.* New York: Wiley, 1976.

Schulz, R., & Brenner, G. Relocation of the aged: A review and theoretical analysis. *Journal of Gerontology,* 1977, *32,* 323–333.

Scribner, S. Modes of thinking and ways of speaking: Culture and logic reconsidered. In R. O. Freedle (Ed.), *New directions in discourse processing* (Vol. 2). Norwood, N.J.: Ablex, 1979.

Sedney, M. A. *Process of sex-role development during life crises in middle-aged women.* Paper presented at the 1977 annual meeting of the American Psychological Association, San Francisco, August, 1977.

Sheehy, G. Passages: *Predictable crises of adult life.* New York: E. P. Dutton, 1976.

Shiffrin, R. M., & Schneider, W. Controlled and automatic human information processing: II. Perceptual learning, automatic attending, and a general theory. *Psychological Review,* 1977, *84,* 127–190.

Stevenson, H. W. *Children's learning.* New York: Appleton-Century-Crofts, 1972.

Timiras, P. S. (Ed.). *Developmental physiology and aging.* New York: Macmillan, 1972.

Tinbergen, N. *The study of instincts.* New York: Oxford University Press, 1951.

Toulmin, S. The concept of "stages" in psychological development. In T. Mischel (Ed.), *Cognitive development and epistemology.* New York: Academic Press, 1971.

Vygotsky, L. S. *Thought and language.* Cambridge, Mass.: The M.I.T. Press, 1962.

Waddington, C. H. *The evolution of an evolutionist.* Ithaca, N. Y.: Cornell University Press, 1975.

Walsh, D. A., & Baldwin, M. Age differences in integrated semantic memory. *Developmental Psychology,* 1977, *13,* 509–514.

Werner, H. *The comparative psychology of mental development.* New York: International Universities Press, 1948.

White, S. Evidence for a hierarchical arrangement of learning processes. In L. P. Lipsitt & C. C. Spiker (Eds.), *Advances in child development and behavior* (Vol. 2). New York: Academic Press, 1965.

Wilson, E. O. *Sociobiology.* Cambridge, Mass.: Harvard University Press, 1975.

Wisniewski, H. M., & Terry, R. D. Neuropathology of the aging brain. In R. D. Terry & S. Gershon (Eds.), *Neurobiology of aging.* New York: Raven Press, 1976.

Wohlwill, J. F. *The study of behavioral development.* New York: Academic Press, 1973.

Zelinski, E. H., Gilewski, M. J., & Thompson, L. W. Do laboratory tests relate to self-assessment of memory ability in the young and the old? In L. W. Poon, J. L. Fozard, L. Cermak, D. Arenberg, & L. Thompson (Eds.), *New directions in memory and aging: Proceedings of the George Talland Memorial Conference.* Hillsdale, N. J.: Earlbaum, 1980.

ALEXANDER THOMAS
STELLA CHESS

9

The Role of Temperament in the Contributions of Individuals to Their Development

Introduction

The dictionary (Webster, 1977) defines temperament as "one's customary frame of mind or natural disposition." In the study and conceptualization of psychological functions, we (Thomas, Chess, & Birch, 1968) have viewed temperament "as a general term referring to the *how* of behavior. It differs from ability, which is concerned with the *what* and *how well* of behaving, and from motivation, which seeks to account for *why* a person does what he is doing [p. 4]." This formulation of temperament corresponds to the formal analysis of behavior made by other workers (Cattell, 1950; Guilford, 1959), and to current usage in psychological and psychiatric theory and practice (Thomas & Chess, 1977).

Temperament can thus be characterized as comprising those behavioral attributes that show some overall degree of consistency at any one time over various, although not necessarily all, life situations, and that do not reflect motivation or ability. Two young children may feed themselves with equal dexterity and play ball with similar ability, and have the same goal in mind. Two older children or adolescents may function in school with the same intellectual competence and interests. Two adults may work at similar jobs with the same expertise and objectives. Yet these children,

231

adolescents, or adults may show significant differences in the liveliness of their movements, the ease with which they adapt to an environmental change, the manner and quality of their emotional expressiveness, and the degree of persistence in the face of difficulty.

Temperament, as thus conceptualized, refers to the behavioral style of the individual, and contains no inferences as to genetic, endocrine, somatologic, or environmental etiologies. There is, furthermore, no implication as to immutability. On the contrary, like any other characteristic of the organism—whether it be height, weight, cognitive characteristics or perceptual patterns—temperament must be influenced by environmental factors in its expression and even in its nature as development proceeds. In recent years, several authors have attempted to narrow the definition of temperament to make it a hereditary–constitutional behavioral characteristic. Thus, Buss and Plomin (1975) take the position that the crucial criterion for temperament is inheritance, and that "this is what distinguishes temperament from other personality attributes [p. 9]." And Betz and C. B. Thomas (1979) define temperament as "a dispositional tendency, a given at birth, with variance among individuals, but constant over time for a single individual [p. 81]." There is evidence, as will be indicated in what follows, for a genetic factor for temperament, and that individual differences in behavioral style can be identified in the newborn. However, other personality attributes may also conceivably be genetically influenced, and the presence of a characteristic at birth should in no way imply constancy over time. To dichotomize and separate biology and culture, heredity and environment in this way represents a reversion to outmoded one-sided views of development. The modern view, by contrast, emphasizes the dialectical unity and continuous interaction between the biological and the social. "Human evolution is now the resultant of the interaction between biological and sociocultural forces, and it involves a constant feedback between them. In this respect also man differs qualitatively from the rest of the animal creation [Dubos, 1965, p. 13]."

Temperament and the Active Role of the Individual

The theme of this volume is that people are active participants in their own development. This activity occurs within the context of a reciprocal dynamic and continuously evolving organism–environment interaction; changes in one are embedded in changes in the other. It was exactly this view of the individual that influenced our own first formulations in the early and mid-1950s of the nature of temperament and its significance for individual psychological development. At that time, in the United States, personality theory, child-care advice and psychiatric practice were dominated by a one-sided environmentalist approach. The two most influential schools of psychological theory, psychoanalysis and behaviorism, differed fundamentally in the concepts of the biological substrate in the child upon which the environment acted. But both agreed that individual differences in development were the exclusive result of specific life experiences in the early years of life. Organismic differences in developmental level were recognized, but were considered to influence time sequences in which universals in personality organization were achieved, but not the emergence and elaboration of individuality in behavioral functioning.

It is true that Freud (1964) had asserted that "Each ego is endowed from the first with individual dispositions and trends [p. 240]" and that Pavlov (1927) had attempted to explain features of normal and pathological behavior on the basis of differences in the balance between excitation and inhibition in the central nervous system. However, these speculations and their possible implications for human psychological development were never explored systematically by either the psychoanalytic or behaviorist schools.

There was no doubt that the focus on environmental influences, both intra- and extrafamilial, had led to a host of productive studies of both normal and pathological psychological development. As evidence accumulated of the crucial importance of life experience and learning in shaping the individual's behavioral functioning, one after another of the static, mechanistic constitutionalist concepts so popular in the past were discredited and rejected. But crucial is not the same as exclusive. However, the environmental emphasis went on from its challenge to a one-sided heredity–constitution view to the assertion of a similar exclusive determinism of its own. The newborn child became a tabula rasa on which the environment, first and foremost the mother, wrote its psychological future. As we (Thomas & Chess, 1957) wrote in our first paper on this issue,

> Perhaps the most important concept currently influencing the direction of studies and formulations in the field of child development is that concerning the decisive role of the mother or mother substitute. The theoretical approaches vary but the specific emphasis is on the fundamental importance not only of maternal behavior, but also of unexpressed maternal attitudes in determining the cause of the child's psychological development. This focus has stimulated a host of psychological studies in which child development in its various phases, and disturbances ranging from simple physiological upsets in the young infant, through the various psychosomatic and behavior disorders as well as delinquency and schizophrenia, are examined with the only variable considered being that of the behavior and attitude of mother [p. 348].

Some writers also emphasized the role of other intrafamiial influences and the larger social environment (Rose, 1955; Soddy, 1956), but the child still remained as a passive participant in his own development.

We ourselves became increasingly critical of this exclusively environmentalist approach for several reasons. Like innumerable other parents, we were impressed by the striking individual differences in our children's behavior, even in the first month of life. We were also struck by the same phenomenon in the infant children of our relatives and friends. And we could see no clear correlation between these differences in the children and the attitudes and child-care practices of the parents. As clinicians, we noted repeatedly a lack of any direct one-to-one correlation between environmental influences and the course of a child's behavioral development. Even when disturbed parental functioning appeared to be the cause of a child's behavior problem, we could not identify any consistent relationship between the nature of the parents' attitudes and practices and the specific symptoms of the child. As mental health professionals, we were appalled at the unjustified and destructive guilt and anxiety created in so many mothers who were held responsible for any and all behavioral deviations in their children, from minor transient symptoms to malignant mental illnesses. A few voices were raised in that period challenging the validity of the dominant environmentalist ideology (Bruch, 1954; Levy, 1957; Orlansky, 1949), but these were indeed unheard even if they came from respected professionals.

Our own observations led us to the hypothesis that the newborn infant was no tabula rasa, no purely passive respondent to the influence of the family into which he or she was born. Rather, all the evidence suggested to us that the infant came into the world with a behavioral repertoire that actively shaped his or her reactions to stimuli from the environment, and that, at the same time, influenced the responses of his or her caretakers. The parent–child relationship, in other words, was not a unidirectional influence of parent on child, but a mutually interactive process from the beginning. This behavioral repertoire, furthermore, varied significantly from one infant to another, so that the course of development was determined not only by differences in the family and extrafamilial environment, but also by individual differences in the child himself, by the child's temperamental characteristics.

The New York Longitudinal Study

By the mid-1950s, the time we were formulating our own views and approach to the study of temperament, a number of observations had been reported on individual differences in children and adults that appeared to have an organismic base. These included data on behavior, perceptual, biochemical, and neurophysiological characteristics (see Thomas & Chess, 1977, p. 2) for a list of references to these reports). Some of these reports suggested that these individual patterns might influence the behavior and attitudes of the mother or other significant persons toward the child. However, this possibility had remained speculative, as none of the studies had carried through any comprehensive investigation of the influence of the young child's behavioral individuality on his psychological development.

To test our own view that individual differences in temperament could be identified systematically from the first weeks of life onward, and that these temperamental characteristics played an active role in the continuously evolving organism–environment interactional process, a long-term longitudinal study was required. With these objectives in mind, we began our first and most comprehensive longitudinal study in 1956, the New York Longitudinal Study (NYLS).

METHODS AND CATEGORIES

Our methods of data collection and analysis have been reported extensively in a number of papers and three volumes (Thomas & Chess, 1977; Thomas, Chess, & Birch, 1968; Thomas, Chess, Birch, Hertzig, & Korn, 1963), and will be summarized briefly at this point.

The NYLS comprises 133 subjects from middle- and upper-middle-class professional and business families. With only a few exceptions, all the pregnancies were uneventful, carried to term, and there were no perinatal complications. To obtain contrasting populations for comparison purposes, several other samples were gathered and also followed longitudinally: (a) 95 children of working-class Puerto Rican parents living in New York City; (b) 68 children born prematurely; (c) 52 children with mild mental retardation; and (d) 243 children whose mothers were infected with rubella during pregnancy.

Data collection was initiated at 2–3 months of age. A pilot study had indicated that the neonate's behavior varied significantly from hour to hour, and that the inclusion of data from this period would be both very demanding and inconclusive. Information of the objective details of the child's behavior in a wide range of daily activities was obtained through periodic semistructured interviews with the parents. These were supplemented as the child grew older by direct observations in nursery school, kindergarten, and elementary school, by teacher interviews, and by direct observation of behavior during standard psychometric testing. Parental attitudes and practices were assessed through simultaneous but separate interviews with both parents when the child was 3 years of age. At 3 and 6 years, IQ scores and academic achievement scores were obtained from the elementary school records. Standard, detailed clinical evaluation and follow-up was carried through in all cases where behavior disorder was suspected. Each subject has been interviewed directly at 16 years of age and, currently, again in the early adult age period; these have been supplemented by concurrent but separate interviews with the parents.

Inductive data analysis of the behavioral protocols resulted in the delineation of nine categories of temperament, as follows.

1. *Activity Level:* the motor component present in a given child's functioning and diurnal proportion of active and inactive periods. Pro-
   tocol data on motility during bathing, eating, playing, dressing, and
   handling, as well as information concerning the sleep–wake cycle,
   reaching, crawling, and walking, are used in scoring this category.
2. *Rhythmicity (regularity):* the predictability and/or unpredictability in
   time of any function. It can be analyzed in relation to the sleep–wake
   cycle, hunger, feeding pattern, and elimination schedule.
3. *Approach or Withdrawal:* the nature of the initial response to a new
   stimulus, be it a new food, new toy, or new person. Approach
   responses are positive, whether displayed by mood expression (smil-
   ing, verbalizations, etc.) or motor activity (swallowing a new food,
   reaching for a new toy, active play, etc.). Withdrawal reactions are
   negative, whether displayed by mood expression (crying, fussing,
   grimacing, verbalization, etc.) or motor activity (moving away, spit-
   ting out new food, pushing away new toy, etc.).
4. *Adaptability:* response to new or altered situations. One is not concerned with the nature of the initial responses, but with the ease
   with which they are modified in desired directions.
5. *Threshold of Responsiveness:* the intensity level of stimulation that is
   necessary to evoke a discernible response, irrespective of the specific
   form that the response may take, or the sensory modality affected.
   The behaviors utilized are those concerning reactions to sensory stimuli, environmental objects, and social contacts.
6. *Intensity of Reaction:* the energy level of response irrespective of its
   quality or direction.
7. *Quality of Mood:* the amount of pleasant, joyful, and friendly behavior
   as contrasted with unpleasant, crying, and unfriendly behavior.
8. *Distractibility:* the effectiveness of extraneous environmental stimuli
   in interfering with or in altering the direction of the ongoing behavior.
9. *Attention Span and Persistence:* two categories that are related. Attention span concerns the length of time a particular activity is pursued
   by the child. Persistence refers to the continuation of an activity in
   the face of obstacles to the maintenance of the activity direction.

A 3-point scale was established for each category. Item scoring was
used, and the item scores transformed into a weighted score for each
category on each record.

Two opposite temperamental constellations were determined by qualitative analysis and separate factor analysis of the quantitative scores for
the first 5 years of life. The *Easy Child* is characterized by biological regularity, approach responses to new stimuli, quick adaptability to change,
and predominantly positive mood of mild or moderate intensity. The
Difficult Child, by contrast, is characterized by biological irregularity, fre-

quent withdrawal responses to new stimuli, slow adaptability to change, and relatively frequent negative mood expressions, with high intensity of both positive and negative mood. A third constellation, the *Slow-To-Warm-Up Child*, was also identified qualitatively, but not in the factor analysis. This type of child, like the difficult child, is characterized by frequent withdrawal responses to new stimuli and slow adaptability, but, by contrast, has mild intensity of mood expression and less tendency to biological irregularity and negative mood.

In the NYLS, about 40% of the sample have been easy, about 10% difficult, and about 15% slow-to-warm-up children. Similar percentages have been present in our other longitudinal samples. Some children cannot be classified into one of these three temperamental categories. Also, for those who fit one of these three patterns, there is a wide variation in degree of manifestation from child to child and from situation to situation. It is also important to emphasize that the different rating on the nine temperamental categories and the three constellations all represent variations within normal limits, and indicate the wide range of behavioral styles that normal children can display.

The traits and constellations we have defined in no way exhaust the possibilities for identifying functionally significant temperamental categories. As other workers have taken up the investigation of temperament, other categories have been suggested (Keogh, 1979, personal communication; Plomin & Rowe, 1977; Thomas & Chess, 1977, pp. 9–10). As these studies develop, a consensus for a comprehensive categorization of temperament should be attainable.

Origins and Continuity Over Time

As indicated earlier, the operational definition of temperament carries no implications as to origins or etiology. A review of our own data and those from other studies

> Suggests an appreciable, but by no means exclusive, genetic role in the determination of temperamental individuality in the young infant. Prenatal or perinatal brain damage does not appear to influence temperament in any striking fashion. The data also indicate that parental attitudes and functioning, as shaped by the sex of the child or special concerns for a premature infant, at the very most have a modest etiological influence on temperament. Sociocultural factors appear to have some influence. Special idiosyncratic parental characteristics such as chronic anxiety preceding or at least starting in pregnancy may also be significant. [Thomas & Chess, 1977, p. 152].

Whatever the combination of genetic, prenatal, perinatal, and early postnatal influences that shapes the emergence of individual patterns of temperament in the young infant, environmental influence may very well accentuate, modify, or even change temperamental traits over time. No psychological characteristic, whether cognitive capacity, perceptual patterns, coping and adaptive mechanisms, or value systems, remains immutable and impervious to environmental influences as development proceeds. The same must be true for temperament.

The evaluation of consistency and change in temperament over time is a complex issue. A number of special methodological problems exist, above and beyond those involved in the measurement of any behavioral attribute at sequential developmental periods (Kagan, 1971; Rutter, 1970). As Rutter (1970) points out, for temperament there are measurement problems resulting from the reliance on the adjectives used by parents in describing their children's behavior, the possibility of bias in the selection of items reported by the parent or other observer, the difficulty at times in separating behavioral style content, and the effect that the changing context of the child's behavior might have on the ratings.

Beyond these methodological issues, the dynamics of the developmental process makes for complexity in the study of the vicissitudes of temperamental individuality over time. A child or adult's typical expression of temperament may be attenuated or absent at any specific age period. If few or no new situations and demands arise, the determination of approach–withdrawal, adaptability, or quality of mood may be difficult or distorted. Lack of motivation or commitment to definite goals and activities may influence the expression of persistence and distractibility. Presence or absence of opportunity for physical activity may affect the level and type of motor activity.

In addition, continuity or change may be different for specific temperamental traits or constellations. One or several traits may be strikingly consistent over time in one individual and others not, and the reverse correlation may be true for another person. A temperamental attribute or constellation may show significant continuity from one specific age period to the next, and then change its expressive character in the following age period.

In reviewing the available data from various studies reported thus far, a number of tentative statements can be made. Temperament is unstable in the neonatal period and does not reach stability until after the second month of life (Torgersen & Kringlen, 1978). This most probably reflects the influences of various biological factors in the birth process and the adaptation to extrauterine life. Quantitative ratings of temperament in the first 7 years of life show varying degrees of stability of different traits and constellations from year to year, with diminishing number of significant correlations as the time span for the comparison is increased (Carey & McDevitt, 1978; Thomas & Chess, 1977, Ch. 12). Qualitative longitudinal studies of the subjects in the NYLS from infancy through adolescence have indicated that, in general, five patterns of consistency can be identified: (a) overall significant consistency of most or all attributes; (b) consistency in some aspects of temperament at one time period and in other aspects at other times; (c) modification of temperament by motivational or other factors; (d) consistency in temperament but modification of its expression because of significant change in temperament–environment interaction; and (e) actual change in one or more temperamental traits.

Currently we are making new quantitative assessments of temperament in the NYLS subject at the early adult life period. When these ratings are completed, they will be compared with the temperament scores for the first 5 years of life.

It is a temptation to look for linear continuity of temperament over time, as others have done for other psychological attributes. Such linear continuity would give us the predictive power that appears to be so desirable. However, the research evidence indicates strongly that such predictability is not possible (Clarke, 1978; Kagan, Kearsley, & Zelazo, 1978; Sameroff, 1975; Thomas & Chess, 1977, Ch. 15). Indeed, an interactionist view of psychological development as proceeding through a constantly evolving process of organism–environment interaction is entirely at variance with any formulation of simple linear continuity. As Sameroff (1975) puts it, "Linear sequences are non-existent and . . . development proceeds through a sequence of regular restructurings of relations within and between the organism and his environment [p. 295]." The identification of a variety of patterns of continuity–discontinuity over time, whether for temperament or any other psychological attribute, should be seen as a research opportunity and not as a limitation. The analysis of such patterns, just as the analysis of intersituational consistency or inconsistency in behavior at the same time period, will undoubtedly prove fruitful in the identification of different types of interactional patterns in specific individuals, groups, or cultures.

Measurement of Temperament

Our own original work in developing methods for the identification and rating of temperament necessarily involved relatively elaborate and time-consuming data collection and data analysis procedures. These methods have resulted in the establishment of specific objective criteria for each of the nine categories. The studies from our own research unit, as well as from many other centers in this country and abroad, have demonstrated that these nine categories can be identified and rated in all children of different ages and sociocultural and national backgrounds, and in those suffering from various cognitive and physical handicaps, as well as in normal children. Beginning studies of adolescent and adult samples indicate that similar evaluations of temperament are possible for these age periods (see Thomas & Chess, 1977, for a review of some of these studies).

These findings have stimulated the development of a number of questionnaire forms to make the determination of temperament economically feasible for research workers, health care professionals, and educators. For infants, Carey (1970, 1973) developed a brief, simple parent questionnaire for the 4–8-month age period, which has been used productively in a large number of studies. Carey and McDevitt (1978) have revised this questionnaire to improve its psychometric characteristics (e.g., the number of items have been increased and rating options increased). Carey is currently completing parent questionnaires for the 1–2- and 7–10-year age periods. A separate parent questionnaire for the rating of the nine temperament categories for 6-month-old infants has been developed in Sweden by Persson-Blennow and McNeil (1979).

We have worked out separate parent and teacher questionnaires for the 3–7-year age periods (Thomas & Chess, 1977, Appendix B). McDevitt and Carey (1978) have separately elaborated a similar parent questionnaire for this same childhood period. The two 3–7-year parent questionnaires are currently in use in a number of ongoing studies.

For the adolescent period, no short rating forms have as yet been developed. For the early adult age period we are currently completing a questionnaire with a 7-point scale for each of the nine categories. This form has already been extensively pretested and the final testing is in progress. Scholom and co-workers (Scholom, Zucker, & Stollak, in press) have used the Thorndike Dimensions of Temperament questionnaire and a brief global rating scale for the nine temperamental categories to assess temperament in the adult. Further reliability and validation studies of this approach to adult temperament is required before its usefulness can be evaluated. In addition to these questionnaires, several short parental interview protocols have been devised for the school-age child (Garside, Birch, Scott, Chambers, Kolvin, Tweedle, & Barber, 1975; Graham, Rutter, & George, 1973), and for clinical practice with children of all ages (Thomas & Chess, 1977, Appendix D).

These various questionnaires and short interview protocols have been and are being utilized extensively in many centers in the United States and abroad. As the data from these studies are analyzed and compared, it can be expected that a consensus among the various rating schemes can be developed. Experience with Carey's 7–10-year measure and our young adult questionnaire should make the necessary modifications possible for the elaboration of questionnaires for adolescents and for older adults.

Functional Significance of Temperament

Our studies of the functional significance of temperament for normal and deviant psychological development have involved from the beginning a commitment to an interactionist viewpoint (Thomas & Chess, 1957). As we have put it (Thomas & Chess, 1977)

> temperament is never considered by itself, but always in its relationship to, or interaction with, the individual's abilities and motives and external environmental stresses and opportunities. This interactive process produces certain consequences in behavior, which then interact with new and recurrent features of the environment to reinforce certain previous patterns, or attenuate some, or produce new behavioral consequences, or all three. To analyze this constantly evolving process of development requires the view that new behaviors or personality attributes that appear at new age-stage developmental periods may represent older patterns in new form, as is commonly assumed, but also may constitute the emergence of qualitatively new psychological characteristics [p. 10].

Within this interactionist framework, we have found the concept of *goodness of fit* versus *poorness of fit* to be very useful. At any age period, if environmental demands and expectations are *consonant* with the individual's capacities, abilities, motivations, and temperament, a goodness of fit will exist, and favorable psychological functioning and development will be possible. If, to the contrary, environmental demands and expectations are *dissonant* with the individual's capacities, abilities, motivations, and temperament, a poorness of fit will exist, and unfavorable psychological functioning and development will occur.

This concept of fit requires a simultaneous consideration of the characteristics of the environment and the organism and their mutual interaction in any analysis of the dynamics of normal or deviant behavior development. Both the environment and the individual are seen to enter as active agents at all times in this continuously evolving interactional process. The specific factors that are most influential in determining goodness or poorness of fit may vary significantly from one person to another, and from one age period to another in the same individual. No a priori assumptions of a fixed hierarchy of importance of different environmental or organismic variables applicable in all cases are possible.

Goodness of fit does not in any way imply absence of stress or conflict. Healthy development progresses through the sequential mastery of new environmental demands that may occasion temporary mild to even severe stress and/or conflict. The elimination of the specific stresses and conflicts that inevitably accompany increasing competence and scope of functioning occurs through success in coping, and not through avoidance of new demands. It is *excessive* stress and conflict, the result of demands and expectations that the individual cannot master, that has unfavorable consequences for psychological functioning and development.

Our studies of the functional significance of temperament have involved both quantitative and qualitative analyses. Our objective has been to utilize quantitative methods to their maximum. When dealing with a complex body of longitudinal data within an interactionist framework, however, the traditional simple analytic models are of limited value (McCall, 1977). As Spanier, Lerner, and Acquilino (1978) put it, "current statistical techniques, based on linear mathematical models and buttressed by Aristotelian logic, are not fully appropriate to analyze continual reciprocities. Circular statistical models, based on dialectical logic. . . . will have to be devised [pp. 329–330]."

Furthermore, quantitative methods require routine methods involving a minimum of judgment and evaluation. Judgment is involved in the development of categories and in the formulation of scoring criteria and methods. Once established, however, quantitative methods must of necessity be routine. The demand for reliability in scoring also limits the possibility of the full utilization of the available data. The rigors of quantitative methods of data treatment often preclude the identification of meaningful subtleties in the developmental course of specific individuals.

As an example, our item scoring of the temperamental traits for one child showed a high weighted score for persistence. Although high, this quantitative score did not indicate that this youngster differed remarkably from a number of other children with high persistence ratings. However, inspection of the records showed that for selective activities in which he was highly motivated, this boy's persistence level was extraordinary. Also, when such focused attention and activity was disturbed by parent or teacher, an intense tantrum frustration response occurred. Thus, at 18 months, he determined to learn to tie his shoelaces. For several days he spent most of his waking hours tying and retying his brother's and father's shoelaces, as well as his own, until he mastered this task. One evening, during this period of persistent effort, his mother forcibly interrupted him to put him to bed. He responded with a prolonged violent tantrum. Single episodes of this character occurred at various times in elementary school. He would become highly motivated for some activity (reading a specific book, making a poster, etc.), and devote all his attention to the task. The teacher would forcibly interrupt him without explanation, because of the class schedule and assignments, and he would respond with a violent outburst. This led to a number of serious problems with various teachers and schools, with a significant effect on overall psychological development. The quantitative scores by themselves would not have illuminated the dynamics of these child–school interactional sequences.

As an additional example, another youngster in the NYLS had the characteristics of the temperamentally difficult child to a marked degree.

His initial reaction to most new situations was an intensely negative one, with slow adaptation and eventual positive responses, which were also intense. His parents handled these situations appropriately and the boy did not become a behavior problem. In the middle childhood and high school years, there were very few new situations that arose and quantitative scoring would never have identified this difficult temperamental pattern. However, in the few new situations that did arise, such as his starting piano lessons on his own initative, the same sequence of strong initial negative reactions, slow adaptation, and final enthusiastic pleasurable involvement was evident. And when he went away to college, which presented him with a whole set of new demands and situations simultaneously for the first time since the infancy and preschool periods, the difficult temperamental pattern again reappeared.

For these reasons, it therefore becomes desirable to supplement the routine techniques of scoring and analysis by qualitative judgmental methods employed by professional persons with psychological and psychiatric skill and competence. The richest treatment of a body of behavioral data necessitates both quantitative and qualitative methods. Different issues require different proportions of these methods and the relative emphasis is best determined in the course of the study of specific issues. In our own studies of the functional significance of temperament, we have paid special attention to the analysis of the relationship of the etiology and dynamics of behavioral disorders to temperament. This is in line with a long tradition in medicine, in which, repeatedly, the study of pathological deviations led to the elucidation of normal physiological functioning. We were also concerned with extending the ability to advise parents, child-care professionals and educators in child management more effectively— in other words, adding a new dimension to prevention in the mental health field.

In addition, our data have permitted various other analyses, such as the significance of temperament for school functioning, and cross-cultural comparisons between the middle-class native born NYLS families and our Puerto Rican working-class sample. We will first summarize the findings of the significance of temperament for behavior disorder development, from our quantitative analyses, as well as from the work of other investigators. Following this, we will outline the different ways in which temperament actively contributes to the phenomenon of individuals as producers of their development.

Temperament and Behavior Disorders

The findings from the NYLS are detailed in two of our volumes (Thomas & Chess, 1977; Thomas, Chess, & Birch, 1968), and in several publications (Cameron, 1978; Terestman, in press), and will be summarized here.

Our overall quantitative analysis included 108 children who had reached 5 years of age at the time the analysis was done. Of this group, 42 children had been diagnosed as having a behavior disorder, of mild severity in all but 6. This number was cumulative; at any one time the actual prevalence of children with behavior disorders was lower than this total figure. For the purposes of analysis, the 42 clinical cases were divided into those with "active" versus "passive" symptoms. The active symptoms included overt manifestations of anxiety, tension symptoms, and problems with sleep, speech, tantrums, aggressive behavior, and so on. The passive children showed nonparticipation or active avoidance of group activities. The active cases were also divided into those identified before and after 5 years of age. The control comparison group comprised 66 children all over 5 years of age.

The mean temperamental scores for each of the nine categories and Factor A (corresponding to the Difficult Child constellation in the first 5 years of life) were compared for the overall clinical group and its subgroups and the nonclinical control sample. Both before and after symptom development, the total active clinical group showed a significantly higher frequency of high activity, irregularity, low threshold, nonadaptability, intensity, persistence, and distractibility, as compared to the nonclinical group. The passive clinical sample showed only a few significant differences from the nonclinical groups—in mood in the fourth and fifth years, and in activity level, approach–withdrawal, and persistence only in the fifth year. The comparisons of Factor A values of the total active clinical group with the control sample were significant at 3, 4, and 5 years, and for the passive clinical group at 4 and 5 years. In both clinical groups, the differences were in the direction of the Difficult Child pattern, and became larger as the group grew older. The findings for the active clinical subgroup with onset of behavior disorder before 5 years of age closely resembled the total active group, but were expressed more sharply.

Cameron (1978) further analyzed the NYLS data for the first 5 years to obtain correlations between parental attitudes, the child's temperament, and the incidence and form of behavioral problems in the child. Seventy items from the separate parental interviews done when the child was 3-years-old were subjected to cluster analysis by means of the Tyron system. Only the mother's responses were used, because, in the overwhelming majority of cases, both parents provided identical responses. Eight parental dimensions were derived from this cluster analysis: (a) parental disapproval, intolerance, and rejection; (b) parental conflict regarding child rearing; (c) parental strictness versus permissiveness; (d) maternal concern and protectiveness; (e) depressed living standards; (f) limitations of the child's material supports; (g) inconsistent parental discipline; and (h) large family orientation. From his analysis, Cameron (1978) concluded that, with regard to behavior disorder development:

First-year temperament scores were found to be predictive of mild cases of either sex. Prediction of moderate-to-severe cases, however, could not be achieved on the basis of temperament data alone, but could be achieved for girls' cases by resorting to a global parental pathology score. While moderate-to-severe male clinical cases were harder to predict, there was evidence that escalations in temperament accompanied their progress into behavior problems. In addition, in a retrospective analysis of first-year temperament profiles of those children who subsequently became clinical cases, the trends suggested a correspondence between the *form* of the children's symptoms and their temperament during their first twelve months [p. 146].

Terestman (in press) analyzed the temperament scores obtained from nursery school teacher interviews in 58 of the oldest children in the NYLS. The teacher interview protocols were structured to obtain similar behavioral data on the children to that obtained from the parent interviews. Of the 58 children, those placed in the highest quartile for negative mood or mood intensity showed a significantly higher incidence of behavior disorder, either concurrently or before 9 years of age. Most significantly, all the 10 children in the highest negative mood–high intensity quartile were, or became, behavior problems.

Carey (1972, 1974) has utilized his infant temperament parental questionnaire to study the relationship of temperament to certain behavioral symptoms in infancy. In 13 babies with colic, he found significant correlations with low sensory threshold and the Difficult Child constellation (1972). In an unselected sample of 60 infants 6 months of age, he found a significant correlation between night awakening and low sensory threshold (1974).

Graham *et al.* (1973) have reported a study of 60 British children, 3–7 years of age, each of whom had at least one mentally ill parent. Quantitative ratings of nine temperamental traits, plus an additional category they identified as "fastidiousness," were correlated with the presence or absence of behavior disorder in the child. They found that irregularity and low fastidiousness, and, to a lesser degree, negative mood, low adaptability, and high intensity were predictive of the development of later psychiatric disorder.

In another study by Lambert and Windmiller (1977), 35 elementary school children were classified as hyperactive, 126 as poorly adjusted, and 55 as low achievers. An additional 111 children who had no discernible school problems served as a control group. Data on the nine temperament traits for the early childhood and school-age years were obtained retrospectively from the parents. From their analysis of the data, the authors concluded that on six of the temperament categories that emerged from factor analysis:

The hyperactive group showed the most extreme scores; however, they differed significantly from the others only on distractibility. Findings suggest that hyperactive children appear to have a biological system that overreacts in both home and school environments, which makes it difficult for parents and teachers to accommodate to their behavior, producing a circular, persistent pattern of overactive and overresponsive behavior in the child [p. 37].

No quantitative studies of the significance of temperament for psychiatric disorders in the adolescent or adult have as yet been reported. An extensive discussion of the issue and its application in psychotherapy, based on qualitative clinical data has just been published by Burks and Rubenstein (1978). We are now beginning a quantitative analysis of the relationship of temperament and the level of behavioral functioning in the early adult period, as we complete the current follow-up of the NYLS.

THE DIFFICULT CHILD AND BEHAVIOR DISORDER

As the summarized studies indicate, a number of temperamental traits may show significant correlations with one or another type of behavioral disturbance in children. The most striking correlation is with some or all of the Difficult Child characteristics—irregularity, withdrawal, slow adaptability, frequent negative mood, and high intensity of mood response. Thus, in the NYLS, only 14 children, or approximately 10% of the sample, were rated as difficult children temperamentally. Yet they made up 23% (10 cases) of the behavior problem group, and only 4% (four children) of the nonclinical sample.

When children with physical or cognitive handicaps are considered, the correlation of the Difficult Child constellation with behavior disorder incidence is even more striking. We have explored this relationship in our samples of 52 mildly retarded children and 243 children with congenital rubella (Thomas & Chess, 1977, Ch. 5). For these comparisons each child was designated as having zero to five signs of the Difficult Child, depending on whether he was above or below the median of the group in the five temperamental categories making up this constellation.

Of the 52 retarded children, 31 were identified as having a behavior disorder. In these 31 cases, 19, or 61%, had three or more signs of the Difficult Child, whereas, of the other 21 children without behavior disorder, only 3, or 14%, had these three or more signs. Furthermore, all 5 of the children in the total sample of 52 who had all five signs of the Difficult Child had a behavior disorder, as did 8 of the 10 with four signs, and 6 of the 7 with three signs. By contrast, of the 30 children with two or less signs, only 12 had behavior disorders.

The congenital rubella group showed similar findings. Almost half (40.9%) of this sample who had behavior disorders had four or five signs of the Difficult Child, as contrasted to only 14.5% of the group who had no behavior disorders.

Children with special handicaps, as seen in our mentally retarded and

congenital rubella samples, have a higher incidence of behavior disturbances than do nonhandicapped children. The presence of the temperamental characteristics of the Difficult Child in effect adds another vulnerability, and significantly increases the incidence of behavioral disturbance
in such handicapped children.

It is, of course, also true that no temperamental trait or constellation,
such as the Easy Child pattern, can render a child invulnerable to behavior
disorder development. Poorness of fit in the organism–environment interactional process can occur with any and all temperamental traits, cognitive levels, parental attitudes and practices, and so on.

Temperament as a Contributor to Individuals' Production of Their Development

The quantitative and qualitative analyses of our longitudinal data, as
well as the reports from other centers, suggest several broad generalizations with regard to the active contribution of temperament to the developmental process. First and foremost, no generalization can be made
that can be applied in the same way to all individuals of the same age
and socioeconomic status, let alone persons of different ages, cultures,
and class position. So many interacting variables influence the course of
development, that no single factor, whether it be temperament or any
other variable, operates in isolation or in exactly the same way in all
individuals. To generalize further, different temperamental traits may be
more significant at different age periods, in different cultures, in different
social classes, and in males versus females.

To spell out these generalizations, specific formulations will now be
presented schematically by age groups. Unless otherwise indicated, the
statements derive primarily from the middle-class native-born families of
the NYLS.

INFANCY: BIRTH TO 2 YEARS

This is the period in which the critical demands for socialization within
the family are mastered. For the establishing of regular sleep and feeding
patterns, and the beginning of self-feeding, self-dressing, and the acceptance of family rules and prohibitions, the temperamental constellation
of the easy versus difficult child is most significant. The easy child typically
masters these demands quickly and easily, and adapts quickly to other
changes, such as the birth of a younger sibling or a family move to new
living quarters. The parents react with pleasure to such a child and often
attribute the ease of child care to their own competence as parents. This
facilitates the development of a mutually reinforcing positive parent–child
relationship.

By contrast, the temperamentally difficult child's mastery of these early socialization demands are typically stormy and protracted. Nurturing such a child places special burdens on parents. Depending on their own psychological characteristics and their attitudes toward child rearing, the irregular, negative, intense, and slowly adaptive responses of the difficult child can stimulate a variety of disturbed reactions in the parents. These can include self-doubt, guilt, anxiety, and helplessness. The anger and exasperation engendered toward the child who appears to be creating such problems for them may compound such guilt and anxiety. The sense of helplessness may lead to intimidation and appeasement, the anger and sense of loss of control to punitive attitudes and behavior toward the child.

Given these sequences of interaction, it is not surprising that the majority of the difficult children in the NYLS developed behavior problems of varying degrees of severity in the first decade of life. Beyond this, it is a reasonable hypothesis that these temperamental traits may contribute to child abuse by the parent (Gregg, 1973). Although the causes of child abuse must be evaluated within a broad socioeconomic framework, there is evidence that deviant or difficult behavior on the child's part may be a contributing cause (Alvy, 1975).

Some parents are able to respond to the difficult child's pattern of behavior constructively and to avoid negative judgments on themselves or on the child. One parent in the NYLS even took pride in his young son's "lustiness." In these cases, parent–child interaction can proceed positively. Thus, as has been pointed out, it is the goodness of fit with the context, and not the temperamental style, per se, that may be most important in promoting adaption. Also, child-care attitudes and practices of different cultures may make for more benign responses to the difficult child than is true most typically in the present-day middle-class American parent. Thus, Super and Harkness (1978), in a comparison of infant temperament and maternal responses in an upper-middle-class Boston community and a farming and herding community in Kenya, found strikingly different responses to infant night awakening. The American families made a major effort to get the baby to sleep through the night, and night wakening or irregular sleep became a distinct annoyance. The Kenyan families made no such effort, inasmuch as the baby slept in direct skin contact with the mother, and night awakening resulted in immediate breast feeding. The sleep irregularity of the difficult child (or the child with a low sensory threshold), one source of the negative parent–infant interaction in American middle-class families, does not have this impact in Kenyan families.

Similarly, in our Puerto Rican working-class sample, parents also did not make the same demand on their young children for regular sleep schedules as did the middle-class NYLS parents. As a result, the former group of children showed very few sleep problems in the preschool years. A significant number of such problems did develop, however, when the children started school, and the parents had to enforce regular bedtime and awakening schedules (Thomas *et al.*, 1974).

THE PRESCHOOL CHILD: 2–6 YEARS

In these years, certain major demands for socialization of the infant continue to be significant, such as sleep schedules, acceptance of family rules and prohibitions, and, quite typically, the birth of a younger sibling. Other substantial new expectations also arise, such as adaptation to peer group activities and to nursery school and kindergarten. For these continued and new demands, the temperamental constellation of the easy versus difficult child influences the parent–child interaction, as in the infancy period. In addition, the intense negative and slowly adaptive responses of the difficult child may affect negatively the attitudes of peers, older children, teachers, and other adults, as the child's range of activities begins to extend beyond the immediate home environment.

In contrast to the infancy period, the easy child's temperament does not always make for a benign parent–child interaction at older ages. An occasional parent may consider the child a "pushover" because of the lack of loud protests when upset and the easy adaptability to the expectations of others. Some parents may give insufficient attention to the needs and interests of an easy child who adapts quickly and fusses very little. In most cases, however, the temperamental characteristics of the easy child tend to stimulate positive parental responses and favorable outcome, as during infancy.

The slow-to-warm-up temperamental constellation may occasionally produce negative reactions in parents or other caretakers during the infancy period. This is most likely with a fast-moving quickly adaptable parent who becomes impatient at the child's slow adaptation to the bath, to new foods, or to strangers. However, the low intensity of such an infant's negative responses, and the absence of marked irregularity of biological functions, usually minimizes negative parental reactions, in contrast to the responses to a difficult child.

As the slow-to-warm-up child reaches the toddler stage, however, the situation may change. Parents who can easily tolerate a slow adjustment to the bath and new foods in infancy may show quite a different reaction to the toddler's slow pattern of adaptation with peer groups and nursery school. The contemporary middle-class American parent typically has little concern over idiosyncrasies of a child's feeding habits, but gives high importance to the youngster's level of social functioning. Once the slow-to-warm-up child begins to show apparent lags in making friends, entering into play groups quickly, and adapting quickly to new school settings, parents may become impatient, threatened, or anxious, as with the difficult child in infancy. Pressure on the child to adapt at a rapid pace may then only increase the child's discomfort in the new situation and retard, if not actually prevent, the achievement of a positive social integration into a group.

Nursery school teachers who tend to interpret a child's behavior psychodynamically may easily misjudge the meaning of a slow-to-warm-up child's initial responses to the school setting. For such a teacher, a child who stays quietly at the periphery of the group, and does not respond immediately to invitations to enter actively into the school's activities, must be anxious and insecure. Such an incorrect diagnosis may well lead parent and teacher into an approach that results in a self-fulfilling prophecy, so that the child actually does become anxious.

THE SCHOOL-AGE CHILD: 6–12 YEARS

Positive or negative patterns of child–environment interaction initiated in early childhood frequently have consequences that ensure their continuation and even intensification as the child grows older. Parental approval of an easy child's responses may enhance the youngster's positive mood and easy adaptability, which gains further approval and encouragement. Parental pressure on a difficult or slow-to-warm-up child may enhance the temperamental traits that stimulated the parental reaction, resulting in greater parental disapproval or pressure. However, a new attribute of the child or an environmental change, or a combination of both may change the developmental course significantly. Thus, one difficult child in the NYLS stimulated highly critical attitudes in both parents and punitive behavior in the father. The girl developed a neurotic behavior disorder, with explosive anger outbursts, fear of the dark, hair-pulling and poor peer relationships. Psychotherapy was instituted with some improvement. But a truly dramatic positive change when the girl was 9- to 10-years-old and showed evidence of musical and dramatic talent. This brought approval and respect from teachers and classmates. Fortunately for the girl, these talents also ranked high in her parents' value system. Her intense negative reactions and slow adaptability were now accepted as "artistic temperament" instead of condemned as previously. Positive interaction with parents, teachers, and peers crystallized, her symptoms diminished, and this further reinforced positive responses from others. Within a few years, she was symptom free.

By contrast, another girl in the NYLS with an easy child pattern adapted well and developed smoothly in the preschool years, with a strongly positive child–parent interaction and relationship. However, her peer relationships and school functioning showed a different sequence, so that, by age 7 years, she was socially isolated and falling behind in reading, in spite of superior intelligence. Her parents had valued uniqueness of expression and creative individuality, and the youngster had adapted enthusiastically. In the process, however, she developed a disregard for rules and schedules in play with peer groups and in learning situations in school, with unfavorable social and academic consequences. Once the problem was clarified and her parents modified their approach, the girl's highly adaptive capacities did allow her to make a quick resolution of her maladaptive behavior.

The new demands and expectations of the family, school, and community on the school-age children can make for a poorness of fit with specific temperamental traits, when contrasted to these relations in younger age-periods. The extremely high persistence of the boy cited earlier was easily consonant with the expectations of the home environment in the preschool years but became dissonant with the demands of teachers for rapid shift in attention and activity. In the middle-class families of the NYLS, the combination of high distractibility and low persistence typically became dissonant with parental value judgments for their school-age sons. These parents attached great importance to the qualities of persistence and "stick-to-it-iveness," especially for boys, as necessary for educational and career goal achievement. A son's tendency to drop a difficult task or to be easily distracted from it were all too frequently considered as lack of self-discipline and laziness. As a result, the therapeutic procedure of parent guidance for the behavior problem cases in the NYLS, which showed positive outcome in the majority of cases, was a dismal failure for the children who were distractible and nonpersistent (Thomas, et al., 1968, Ch. 16). A key requirement for the success of parent guidance is the acceptance of the temperamental individuality of the child as normal. These parents as a group could do so for all the temperamental patterns except the combination of distractibility and nonpersistence.

By contrast, and for different reasons, in our Puerto Rican working-class sample the temperamental trait of high activity became dissonant with environmental demands (Thomas et al., 1974). These families lived in small apartments with no safe play areas in the neighborhood. If anything, the high activity youngsters were more likely than their less active sibs to be cooped up at home because of parental fears of dangerous accidents if they let these restless children roam the dangerous streets. These restrictions on physical outlets often became excessively stressful for the high activity children, with consequent behavior disorder development. The middle-class youngsters of the NYLS, however, had ample living space at home, play areas in the immediate neighborhood, and safe streets. This contrast between the two groups was sharply demonstrated in the clinical samples. In the NYLS, no child was brought to psychiatric notice with the specific complaint of excessive motor activity except for one brain-damaged youngster. In the Puerto Rican working-class sample, 53% of the clinical cases under 9 years of age had this symptom. The difference was highly significant ($p < .001$).

In the school setting itself, teacher misinterpretation of temperamental characteristics can lead to harmful misjudgments. In the NYLS sample, we have seen teachers label slow-to-warm-up or low activity children as "sluggish" and dull intellectually when they were in fact bright youngsters. The slow-to-warm-up pattern to a new peer group in school has also been interpreted as anxiety. For impatient teachers the "restlessness" of the distractible or high activity child may be labeled as inattentiveness or deliberate disobedience.

This issue of teacher misjudgments of temperament is highlighted in a study of 93 children in a suburban middle-class kindergarten (Gordon and Thomas, 1967). Two experienced teachers were asked to rate each child on a 4-point behavioral scale that differentiated the quick from the slow-to-warm-up child. The four ratings, in terms of the quickness of a child's involvement in new activities and situations, were labeled as plungers, go-alongers, sideliners, and nonparticipants. The teachers also estimated each child's general intellectual level on a 7-point scale ranging from very inferior to very superior. When the children entered first grade 6 months later, their actual IQ levels were determined by group testing. Discrepancies between the kindergarten teachers' estimates of intellectual level and these IQ scores were compared with the behavioral ratings. The teachers overestimated the intelligence of 6 children. Of these, 5 had been rated as plungers. The intelligence levels of 50 children were underestimated. Of these, 11 had been rated as plungers, 28 as go-alongers, and 11 as sideliners. In addition, the underestimation was greater for the sideliners than for the plungers. (One child had been rated as a nonparticipator, but had moved out of the school district before the IQ test was administered.)

This study confirms the finding in the NYLS sample that teachers may underestimate the intelligence of a slow-to-warm-up child. Such incorrect estimates could affect teacher expectations and the child's actual academic performance (Rosenthal & Jacobsen, 1969).

ADOLESCENCE AND ADULT LIFE

As has been indicated, systematic quantitative studies of the functional significance of temperament in adolescence and adult life have not yet been reported. Our own analyses of the data for the adolescent and early adult age periods are currently in progress and should be completed within 2 years. Our preliminary impressions are that temperament continues to enter significantly into the organism–environment interactional process at these age periods. However, when compared to the earlier childhood age periods, the delineation of the role of temperament—as well as of other influential variables—becomes increasingly complex as the individual grows into adolescence and adult life. Increasingly elaborate repertoires of abilities and talent mature, motivational patterns crystallize and become conceptualized, and environmental demands and expectations become differentiated and diversified for specific individuals and groups. As a consequence of these changes, the determination of the temperamental element is any individual item or pattern of behavior becomes more demanding. Experience with the use of the early adult life temperament questionnaire that we have just developed should expedite the development of appropriate methodologies for the identification of adult temperament.

Burks and Rubenstein (1979) have reported a systematic qualitative clinical study of temperament and its functional significance in the adult. They have suggested six temperament clusters in the adult, derived from different combinations of our nine categories. They describe various patterns of adult interactions utilizing these six clusters, and the active influence of an adult's temperament on others and on the life course of the individual is emphasized. The authors also postulate that temperament in the adult can have certain dynamic consequences having a motivational aspect. Thus, for example, they suggest that the individual with withdrawal and slow adaptability responses may tend to control situations or people around him to minimize unexpected or rapid change. Or the person with high persistence may develop perfectionist tendencies. As the authors emphasize, their formulations are inductively derived from their extensive case material and counseling experience and require systematic testing and verification.

Conclusions

Temperamental characteristics are an important, active factor for individuals in the production of their development. The data for this generalization are most abundant and detailed for the infancy and childhood periods. In addition, the available evidence suggests that the active influence of temperament extends through the adolescent and adult years.

Temperament influences the course of both normal and deviant psychological development. The role of temperament at any age period can never be considered in isolation from other organismic characteristics and from environmental demands and expectations. It is but one factor in the constantly evolving interactional process among all these variables. One or several temperamental attributes may be significant influences in one individual at one age period, and other attributes at later periods. The temperamental characteristics that are important at any age may also vary from one individual to another, depending on sociocultural factors, special intra- or extrafamilial expectations and demands, other attributes of the individual, and his past life experiences. Generalizations can be made that may be useful guides to child rearing, education, and counseling, but their application must be shaped and modified as necessary for idiosyncratic features of any individual's characteristics and life situation.

References

Alvy, K. T. Preventing child abuse. *American Psychologist*, 1975, *30*, 921–928.

Betz, B. J., & Thomas, C. B. Individual temperament as a predictor of health or premature disease. *Johns Hopkins Medical Journal*, 1979, *144*, 81–89.

Bruch, H. Parent education, or the illusion of omnipotence. *American Journal of Orthopsychiatry*, 1954, *24*, 723–732.

Burks, J., & Rubenstein, M. *Temperamental styles in adult interaction.* New York: Brunner/Mazel, 1978.

Buss, A. H., & Plomin, R. *A temperament theory of personality development.* New York: Wiley, 1975.

Cameron, J. R. Parental treatment, children's temperament, and the risk of childhood behavioral problems: 2. Initial temperament, parental attitudes, and the incidence and form of behavior problems. *American Journal of Orthopsychiatry*, 1978, *48*, 140–147.

Carey, W. B. A simplified method of measuring infant temperament. *Journal of Pediatrics*, 1970, *77*, 188–194.

Carey, W. B. Clinical applications of infant temperament measurements. *Journal of Pediatrics*, 1972, *81*, 823–828.

Carey, W. B. Measurement of infant temperament in pediatrics. In J. Westman (Ed.), *Individual differences in children.* New York: Wiley, 1973. Pp. 293–306.

Carey, W. B. Night awakening and temperament in infancy. *Journal of Pediatrics*, 1974, *84*, 756–758.

Carey, W. B., & McDevitt, S. C. Stability and change in individual temperament: diagnosis from infancy to early childhood. *Journal of Academic Child Psychiatry*, 1978, *17*, 331–337.

Cattell, R. B. *Personality: A systematic and factual study.* New York: McGraw-Hill, 1950.

Clark, A. D. B. Predicting human development: Problems, evidence, implications. *Bulletin of British Psychology and Sociology*, 1978, *31*, 947–961.

Dubos, R. *Man adapting.* New Haven: Yale University Press, 1965.

Freud, S. Analysis, terminable and interminable. In J. Strachey (Ed.). *The complete psychological works of Sigmund Freud.* London: Hogarth Press, 1964 (originally published 1937).

Garside, R. F., Birch, H. G., Scott, D. M., Chambers, Kolvin, I., Tweedle, E. G., & Barber, L. M. Dimensions of temperament in infant school children. *Journal of Child Psychology and Psychiatry*, 1975, *20*, 1–13.

Gordon, E. M., & Thomas, A. Children's behavioral style and the teacher's appraisal of their intelligence. *Journal of School Psychology*, 1967, *5*, 292–300.

Graham, P., Rutter, M., & George, S. Temperamental characteristics as predictors of behavior disorders of children. *American Journal of Orthopsychiatry*, 1973, *43*, 328–339.

Gregg, G. Clinical experience with efforts to define individual differences in temperament. In J. Westman (Ed.), *Individual differences in children.* New York: Wiley, 1973. Pp. 306–322.

Guilford, J. P. *Personality.* New York: McGraw-Hill, 1959.

Kagan, J. *Change and continuity in infancy.* New York: Wiley, 1971.

Kagan, J., Kearsley, R. B., & Zelazo, P. R. *Infancy, its place in human development.* Cambridge: Harvard University Press, 1978.

Lambert, N. M., & Windmiller, M. An exploratory study of temperament traits in a population of children at risk. *Journal of Special Education*, 1977, *11*, 37–47.

Levy, D. M. Capacity and motivation. *American Journal of Orthopsychiatry*, 1957, *27*, 1–8.

McCall, R. B. Challenges to a science of developmental psychology. *Child Development*, 1977, *48*, 333–344.

McDevitt, S. C., & Carey, W. B. The measurement of temperament in 3–7-year-old children. *Journal of Child Psychology and Psychiatry*, 1978, *19*, 245–253.

Orlansky, H. Infant care and personality. *Psychological Bulletin*, 1949, *46*, 1–48.

Pavlov, I. P. *Conditioned reflexes: An investigation of the physiological activity of the cerebral cortex*, (G. V. Anrep, trans. and Ed.). London: Oxford University Press, 1927.

Persson-Blenow, I., & McNeil, T. F. A questionnaire for measurement of temperament in 6-month-old infants: Development and standardization. *Journal of Child Psychology and Psychiatry*, 1979, *20*, 1–13.

Plomin, R., & Rowe, D. C. A twin study of temperament in young children. *Journal of Psychology*, 1977, *97*, 107–113.

Rose, A. M. (Ed.). *Mental health and mental disorder*. New York: Norton, 1955.

Rosenthal, R., & Jacobsen, L. *Pgymalion in the classroom*. New York: Holt, Rinehart & Winston, 1969.

Rutter, M. Psychological development: Predictions from infancy. *Journal of Child Psychology and Psychiatry*, 1970, *11*, 49–62.

Sameroff, A. J. Early influences on development: Fact or fancy? *Merrill-Palmer Quarterly*, 1975, *20*, 275–301.

Scholom, A., Zucker, R. A., & Stollak, G. E. Relating early child adjustment to infant care and parent temperament. *Journal of Abnormal Child Psychology*, in press.

Soddy, K. (Ed.). Internal seminar. *Mental health and infant development* (Vol. 1). New York: Basic Books, 1956.

Spanier, G. B., Lerner, R. M., & Aquilino, W. The study of child–family interactions—a perspective for the future. In R. M. Lerner & G. B. Spanier (Eds.), *Child influences on marital and family interactions*. New York: Academic Press, 1978.

Super, C. M., & Harkness, S. The infant's niche in rural Kenya and metropolitan Boston. In *Anthropological studies of infancy: Some recent directions*, symposium at the annual meeting of American Anthropological Association, Los Angeles, 1978.

Terestman, N. Mood quality and intensity in nursery school children as predictors of behavior disorder. *American Journal of Orthopsychiatry*, in press.

Thomas, A., & Chess, S. An approach to the study of sources in individual differences in child behavior. *Journal of Clinical and Experimental Psychopathology and Quarterly Review of Psychiatry and Neurology*, 1957, *18*, 347–357.

Thomas, A., & Chess, S. *Temperament and development*. New York: Brunner/Mazel, 1977.

Thomas, A., Chess, S., & Birch, H. G. *Temperament and behavior disorders in children*. New York: New York University Press, 1968.

Thomas, A., Chess, S., Birch, H. G., Hertzig, M. E., & Korn, S. *Behavioral individuality in early childhood*. New York: New York University Press, 1963.

Thomas, A., Chess, S., Sillen, J., & Mendex, O. Cross-cultural study of behavior in children with special vulnerabilities to stress. In D. Ricks, A. Thomas, & M. Roff (Eds.), *Life history research in psychopathology* (Vol. 3). University of Minnesota Press, 1974, pp. 53–67.

Torgersen, A. M., & Kringlen, E. Genetic aspects of temperamental differences in infants. *Journal of American Academic Child Psychiatry*, 1978, *17*, 433–444.

Webster's New World Dictionary (2nd concise ed.) Cleveland: Collins World, 1977.

GRETA G. FEIN **10**

The Physical Environment: Stimulation or Evocation

Introduction: Sensation, Arousal, and Knowledge

Lightning flashes across the sky followed a few seconds later by a roll of thunder. A young child sees the lightning and hears the thunder. How is the child's experience of these events to be described? The possibilities are numerous, but three stand out as especially respected traditions in child psychology. In one tradition, the experience is described as a stimulus of a given wavelength, luminance and duration followed by another of a given frequency and amplitude. In another, the experience is described according to the unexpectedness or novelty of the events. In the third, the experience is identified with the child's concept of lightning and thunder. In the first view, the environment is a source of sensory stimulation. In the second, it is a source of uncertainty or fear. In the third, it is a source of knowledge. To establish the facts of seeing or hearing, the occurrence of arousal, or the properties of the child's concepts, each view calls upon a carefully chosen system of responses and a particular set of investigative procedures. These ingredients, the definition of environment, the specification of responses and the processes presumed to mediate the two, yield fundamentally different visions of the developing individual's relation to the physical environment.

The purpose of this chapter is to examine the implication of these visions for a view of individuals as contributors to their own development. When the individual is viewed as either a sensory surface or a neural network,

257

interest is drawn to behavior in the immediate presence of activating stimulation. The individual is dominated by environmental exigencies and development is viewed as changes in the correspondence of exigency and activation. But suppose the child imagines lightning and thunder; suppose the child renders these things on paper or drum, or talks and thinks about them. In a sense, the environment is inside the child, and once inside, the child can control its evocation. Environment as evocation in the sense of events represented and understood provides for reciprocity between the individual and an environment of objects rather than of stimuli.

The evocation of environment, as expressed in children's pretend play, is the major concern of the present chapter. In the first section, the role of organism-dominated behavior is discussed with respect to Berlyne's (1960, 1966, 1969) theory of exploratory behavior. In the second, the development of the ability to create imaginary situations and objects in pretend play is presented as a mark of the transition from stimulation-dominated to organism-dominated behavior. In the third section, evidence concerning the environment that supports pretense is reviewed. Finally, several implications for future research and practice are examined.

Environment as Stimulation

At one time, environment as stimulation dominated the study of environment–behavior relations. Countless studies were designed to examine whether children discriminated physical dimensions of stimulation such as hue, brightness, or area and whether stimuli selected from positions along these dimensions exercised control over subsequent behavior under a variety of presentational, training, and transfer conditions. These investigations required rigorous experimental arrangements free of unwanted, confounding, and distracting sources of stimulation. They also required a single, invariant, and unambiguously observable response, the proverbial look, point, and bar press.

This view of environment–behavior relations led to what Fiske and Maddi (1961) characterized as the study of restricted behavior in monotonous environments. Critics of the established view argued that everyday behavior consists of a splendid variety of responses directed to multiple aspects of the environment, and that organisms produce, choose, and vary stimulation. Animals and children "play" (Beach, 1945), "explore" (Barnett 1958; Welker, 1961), and encounter the environment as active, stimulation-organizing agents (White, 1959). The challenge was epistemological as well as methodological. The view of environment as stimulation drew its assumptions from Locke, its categories from physics, its methodology from sensory psychology, and its metaphors from engineering. But, if psychology was to abandon a vision of restricted behavior in a monotonous environment, what vision might it embrace?

The impending crisis was forestalled temporarily by a compromise promoted most brilliantly by Berlyne (1960, 1966, 1969). Of course people respond to hue, brightness, size, and form; but, more importantly, they respond to the temporal patterning, organization, and sensibleness of the physical environment. Berlyne argued persuasively in behalf of the motivating properties of novelty, complexity, incongruity, and other variables derived from the meaningful arrangement of physical energy. Berlyne also offered a conceptualization of behavior as a general mode of responding, defined functionally rather than topographically. Exploratory behavior, for example, includes any activity that maintains the individual's exposure to one or more elements of the environment (looking, pointing, bar pressing as well as smelling, fondling, pushing, or shaking). Berlyne described two types of exploratory behavior, specific and diversive. Specific exploration is a positive response to particular dimensions of stimulation such as novelty, complexity, or incongruity. Diversive exploration, by contrast, is a stimulation-seeking response that occurs when there is too little novelty, complexity, incongruity, or other form of arousing stimulation in the environment. A third type of behavior, avoidance or withdrawal, includes behaviors that reduce an individual's contact with excessive environmental stimulation. The glue binding these forms of behavior comes from the construct of arousal, a motivating state that can be too low, too high, or just right. When the organism's level of arousal departs from a comfortable optimum, it engages in exploration or avoidance until the optimum is restored.

When compared with previous views, Berlyne's motivational theory of stimulation has much to recommend it. First, the theory offers psychological, organism-based definitions of stimulation to replace definitions borrowed from physics and sensory psychology. Second, the organism is presented as a stimulation seeker as well as a responder. Third, the psychological status of stimulation changes as a function of the organism's behavior. When a novel stimulus is explored, its novelty decreases as a function of this exploration. The bored organism explores until it finds novelty, complexity, or some other stimulation that ameliorates the boredom. A psychological view of stimulation, a mobile organism, and, especially, an organism that changes itself (and, in a sense, its environment) as a function of activity, constitute theoretical achievements of considerable importance.

However, the theory produced as many problems as it solved. First, different forms of exploratory behavior are distinguished by stimulus conditions rather than by patterns of behavior. Although several investigators have attempted to identify the behavioral features of exploration (e.g., Fein & Apfel, 1979b; Weisler & McCall, 1976), these attempts seem arbitrary and post hoc. Second, and more serious, the theory does not provide a way of determining when a given level of novelty or complexity will be optimal, too much, or too little. If studies repeatedly find that individuals seem to have an insatiable appetite for novelty (Mendel, 1965), complexity (Switsky, Haywood, & Isett, 1974) or some other collative variable (McCall, 1974; Nunnally & Lemond, 1973), does this mean that insufficient variation was sampled, that these dimensions are confounded, or that the theory is incomplete, if not wrong (Hutt, 1970, in press; Weisler & McCall, 1976)? In effect, the theory recognizes the need for a subjective definition of stimulation based on the individual's encounters with the environment. But the theory fails to recognize the need for an objective definition of the behavioral or mental capacities of the stimulated individual. In the absence of a clear vision of the experiencing individual, the environment disappears "in" the person. Paradoxically, a subjective description of stimulation requires an objective account of the stimulated subject. To be complete, this account may need to recognize that environmental objects are cultural products before they become personal constructions.

Finally, key aspects of the concept of an optimum level of arousal are underdeveloped. According to Berlyne (1966), the arousal state accompanying specific exploration (curiosity or uncertainty) is mildly aversive; the organism is disturbed by a "lack of information and thus left prey to uncertainty and conflict [p. 26]." Diversive exploration is also precipitated by a negative state (understimulation or boredom). Specific and diversive exploration function similarly to reduce discomfort produced by environmental conditions beyond the organism's control. In Berlyne's discomfort reduction theory, the optimum emerges as a momentary state that a labile organism sweeps through as it cycles from boredom to uncertainty. Missing in Berlyne's theory is a positive conception of comfort and comfort-maintaining behavior. Essentially, arousal theory is about relatively short-term motivational states rather than enduring dispositions (e.g., children's fondness for familiar toys and games or sustained and deepening interests). In the present chapter, the credentials of a candidate for the latter are examined. The particular candidate is "play," a behavior presumably associated with pleasure, engagement, and the organism's control over the environment (Garvey, 1977; Sutton-Smith, 1972). But the concept of play poses innumerable problems that have made it an elusive, contentious construct.

Play: A Generic Category in Need of an Exemplar

If behavior can be treated as a general mode of reacting to the environment that includes a great variety of particular responses (e.g., exploration), then why not admit play as one such mode? The possibility has been considered by several investigators. After reviewing definitions of play drawn from the literature, Berlyne (1969) recommended that the concept be abandoned in favor of "both wider and narrower categories [p. 843]." Other investigators, attempting to distinguish play from exploration, have concluded pessimistically that the effort is not likely to be fruitful (Weisler & McCall, 1976). Still others have suggested that play might be identified with diversive exploration (Ellis, 1973), or, more provocatively, with the positive affect occurring when arousal reaches optimum levels (Hutt, in press). Nunnally and Lemond (1973) offered a temporal definition of play within the framework of arousal theory. According to these investigators, a stimulus with collative properties produces heightened attention followed by specific exploration. The stimulus is explored or manipulated until the uncertainty concerning its physical properties is reduced. Uncertainty reduction is followed by a form of play identified with autistic thinking. Finally, boredom sets in, the organism sets off in search of boredom-alleviating stimulation, and the sequence repeats itself. In the Nunnally and Lemond (1973) scheme, play is no longer a generic category of behavior, but rather a particular play behavior known as pretense. In placing pretend play between uncertainty and boredom, Nunnally and Lemond introduced a "both wider and narrower" behavioral category that directly confronts the issue of an optimum level of arousal maintained by stimulation generated and dominated by the individual.

The position developed in the following sections contains several parts. With respect to the general theme of the present volume, pretend play is viewed as a provocative example of reciprocity between person and environment. With respect to human development, pretend play marks the transition from stimulation-dominated to organism-dominated behavior. Because components of this transition have been documented to some degree, it is possible to examine how pretense functions to produce, modify, and control stimulation by way of dominating its meaning. Finally, although pretend play is often viewed as a behavior in which the physical environment is dominated by the child's ideas and interests, there is growing evidence that the child's domination is only partial during the preschool years. There are features of the environment that exercise an influence on children's pretense, and, not surprisingly, those features are related to a view of the physical environment as meaningful objects (see Fein, in press for a comprehensive review of the empirical literature).

In the following sections, the discussion will focus primarily on pretend play as a spontaneous overt behavior. But, as overt behavior, it exhibits an inverted-U-shaped developmental function. The behavior first appears during the second year of life, it increases in frequency and complexity over the preschool years, and then declines in middle childhood (Eifermann, 1971). Most certainly, older children and adults are able to pretend. The fate of pretend play has attracted speculation but little evidence. Some theorists argue that the symbolizing functions of pretend play are retained in games, rituals, and religious ceremonies, but the symbols are social and conventional rather than personal and idiosyncratic, and their functions are to transmit and preserve rather than to innovate and change (Huizinga, 1955; Sutton-Smith & Roberts, 1970). According to Piaget, pretend play is supplanted by activities that reflect the individual's recognition of reality and mastery of logical forms of thinking. From this perspective, pretend play is an aberrant phenomenon, precipitated by dysynchronies peculiar to preoperational thinking (Piaget, 1962). According to others, pretend play reflects imaginal or divergent processes that become covert in later childhood while continuing to serve creative functions (Klinger, 1971). Or, perhaps, the play of childhood becomes differentiated into public forms on the one hand, and private forms on the other; and, perhaps, these differentiated forms come to serve differentiated functions. Because these possibilities have yet to receive the attention they merit, the following discussion will deal primarily with the overt pretend behavior of young children.

Pretend Play: Environment as Evocation

Some years ago, Wolff (1959) urged those studying the environment of the young child to respect the distinction between stimulation and reality. As *stimulation,* the physical environment is viewed as energy impinging on the organism and evoking or eliciting a reaction. As *reality,* the environment is viewed as objects or events that the organism may see, touch, use, imagine, or produce. Pretend play is of special interest because it illustrates the latter view.

In pretend play, children behave toward a situation as though it were something other than it actually is. Children evoke objects, persons, and events from the past, but the evocations themselves are often crude, loose, fanciful, distorted depictions of the past. Real and not real are juxtaposed. When children say "Let's play house," they are, among other things, declaring an intention to produce, in a setting that is not what it will be held to be, the familiar everyday reality of household objects, occasions, and persons. "Pretend this is . . ." and "You be the . . ." are conventional play expressions that communicate unambiguously to adult and child the conversion of a thing or person from what it is into something else. In fully developed pretense, reality travels on multilayered tracks, parallel yet firmly tied. The reality of the immediate stimulus field travels on one, and the reality of previous experience on another. There may even be a third track for a reality that is pure invention, a combination that is conceivable, although never experienced. The tracks are tied by conversion rules that permit one reality to be treated "as if" it were another. In pretend play, stimulation comes from several sources: immediate objects, motor actions, and thoughts as separate elements and as elements combined in interesting and appealing ways.

The Development of Pretense

Between the age of 1 and 3 years, a profound change occurs in the play of human children (Fenson, Kagan, Kearsley, & Zelazo, 1976; Inhelder, Lezine, Sinclair, & Stambak, 1972). Prior to this period, the baby sleeps when tired and eats when hungry; objects are banged, waved, pushed; a spoon might be put into a cup, a top on a jar, but even these gestures of relatedness are brief and tentative. Then, quite suddenly, a new element appears. Piaget's classical observation vividly illustrates the nature of this new element:

> Obs. 64 . . . In the case of J., . . . the true ludic symbol with every appearance of "make-believe" first appeared at 1;3 (12) in the following circumstances. She saw a cloth whose fringed edges vaguely recalled those of her pillow; she seized it, held a fold of it in her right hand, sucked the thumb of the same hand, and lay down on her side laughing hard. She kept her eyes open, but blinked from time to time as if she were alluding to closed eyes. Finally, laughing more and more, she cried "nene" (nono) [Piaget, 1945, from the 1962 edition, pp. 96–97].

Then, over the next year and a half, these fleeting gestures become elaborated and enriched. At first a doll is simply an object to be touched, moved, or banged. Somewhat later, the doll (rather than the child) is used as the recipient of pretend food and eventually the recipient of a complex array of care-giving activities; the doll is put to bed, dressed, patted, and spanked (Fein & Apfel, 1979a,b; Nicolich, 1977; Piaget, 1962; Watson & Fischer, 1977). The child's voice quality might change to sound like a parent; gestures, clothing, and other elements might be added as elaborations of the adult identity (Garvey & Berndt, 1977; Sachs & Devin, 1976).

At first, the objects used in pretense tend to be similar to the things used in the real life situations that pretend activities mimic (babylike dolls, cuplike cups). Gradually, the need for verisimilitude weakens and assorted objects (sticks and shells) can be used as substitutes in pretend enactments (Fein, 1975; Piaget, 1962; Vygotsky, 1967). Eventually, the child can create the semblance of an object (cupped hand; molded clay) or use pantomime gestures in the absence of a physical entity (hand holding absent cup or arms rocking absent doll). In adulthood, ideas can be concretized in physical models of abstract concepts.

Initially, pretend play is a solo activity. Adults may participate and organize it, but children under 3 years of age rarely share pretend sequences with one another except, perhaps, in brief, imitative, parallel exchanges (Parten, 1932). By 2½ years of age, the beginnings of sociodramatic play appear and, by the age of 5 years, what began as a few simple gestures begins to encompass intricate systems of reciprocal roles, ingenious improvisations of materials, and increasingly coherent themes and plot weaving.

Components of Pretense

The development of pretend play reveals the phasing and coordination of several discrete components that seem to reflect the child's ability to represent the environment (Fein, 1979a). Some components have attracted more attention than others, but each constitutes an element of the child's juxtaposition of real and unreal. More importantly, these components illustrate the sense in which children in play are able to control the immediate stimulus environment. Two components are of special interest in a discussion of the physical environment: situations as frames, and substitute objects.

SITUATIONS AS FRAMES

According to Bateson (1955; 1956) and Goffman (1974) people bracket ordinary life situations (family mealtime, a doctor's waiting room, a cocktail party) into clearly marked units. The units are constructed and defined "in accordance with principles of organization which govern events and our subjective involvement in them [Goffman, 1974, p. 10]." Framed situations have rules that govern entry and define appropriate behavior once inside. In several respects, pretend play satisfies the requirements of a framed situation.

One requirement of bracketed situations is that a special set of signals indicates that the situation is being constituted. Metacommunicative signals that say, "This is play" are used by infrahuman primates as well as by children. Although these signals may be gestural as well as verbal, verbal forms such as "Let's play house" and "You be the . . ." illustrate the situational framing of pretend most clearly. Such signals or metacommunications are used by two 3½-year-olds in the following example (metacommunications are italicized):

H: Knock, knock (fist pounding air).
S: Who is this?
H: It's baby.
S: (Talks baby talk.)
H: *You want to play house?*
S: Yes.
H: *O.K. you be the mommy.* Mommy . . .
S: What, baby?
H: Is this the morning, mom? (baby voice)
S: Yes.
H: Can I play in the morning?
S: Yes.

As the play unfolds, the children give the baby (a doll) a bath, go for a drive, and then to a wedding. The baby's bath is represented by vigorously rubbing the doll's unclothed body, the drive by walking hand in hand around the room. The wedding is in a corner opposite from the house, and one of the children dresses for the occasion by wrapping a scarf around her shoulders. Because the wedding posed problems, the play comes to a temporary halt as the children step out of the play frame to discuss what happens at a wedding and what they need to do to "play" wedding.

S: You get married, three times—you go to the wedding with me and the baby, too.
H: Then what do we do at the wedding?
S: And then we'll . . .
H: And then we'll kiss.

The evidence is clear that by 3 years of age children deliberately manipulate pretense as a situation about situations (Garvey, 1974). By 5 years of age they can talk about it as a distinctive situational form. In a Merrill-Palmer pilot study, 5-year-olds were asked to discuss the difference between work and play, what they play, and how they play. Our informants noted without exception that work is what people "have to" do, and play is what people do when they can choose to do whatever they want to do. Pretend play is the form of play most frequently mentioned by these children and they have little difficulty describing how they play house, doctor, fireman, or monster. These descriptions are often accompanied by animated accounts of especially memorable play sessions punctuated by laughter, vocal imitations, and gestures.

Moreover, the situations rendered in play have to some extent been conceptualized by the children as specific, distinctive, life activities. Evidence that by 4 years of age pretend situations originate in the child as well as in the immediate environment comes from a recent study of pretend initiations. Matthews (1977) noted that pretend frames may be initiated in two ways. One is ideational: The initiation depends on ideas of things not actually present in the immediate environment (the wedding or the house in the above example). The other is material: The initiation depends on an actually present object (the doll that eventually became the baby). When these modes of initiation were compared in 4-year-old children, the results indicate that approximately half the initiations are ideational. The immediate environment, then, serves a limited role in the initiation and content of pretend situations. Whether or not that role can be dispensed with entirely will be considered in a later section.

The idea that children view pretense as a situation about situations raises the question of when in development an awareness of pretending appears. In the earliest form of pretend play, the child's behavior (pretending to eat or sleep) seems detached from the real-life situation in which it ordinarily occurs (mealtime, bedtime) and the motivational underpinnings ordinarily associated with it (hunger, fatigue). In a sense, a familiar, well-practiced behavior is reproduced in a novel context, free of social and tissue demands. Piaget claims that early in the development of pretend behaviors, the child is consciously aware of having decontextualized the behavior, a claim difficult to confirm, as the "knowing smile" observed by Piaget (1962) does not always occur.

> As for symbols, they appear towards the end of the first year . . . For the habit of repeating a given gesture ritually gradually leads to the consciousness of "pretending." The ritual of going to bed . . . is sooner or later utilized "in the void," and the smile of the child as it shuts its eyes in carrying out this rite is enough to show that it is perfectly conscious of "pretending" to go to sleep [p. 32].

Exactly when the child becomes aware of pretending and exactly when pretense becomes a deliberate, planned act are surely unresolved issues. But as Piaget (1962) and Nicolich (1977) note, the verbalizations that appear in solitary play by about 2 years of age indicate that awareness and intention are present. At least it is possible to say that sometime between 12 and 24 months of age, pretend play is treated by the child as a framed situation.

The results of a study by Fein and Apfel (1979a) suggest that some form of intentionality is present at 12 months of age. In the study, children between the ages of 12 and 30 months were presented a set of realistic play materials that were either actual eating utensils (cup, spoon, bottle, pot), or toys (doll, doll bottle, toy tea cup). The question was how pretend feeding changed with respect to who was fed (child or doll) and with what utensils. One of the major findings was that the 12-month-olds, all of whom had been bottle fed, rarely used the bottle to feed themselves but preferred the spoon and the cup. If the behavior reflects merely a generalized tendency to use objects in a functional manner, why was the bottle ignored? The doll was ignored until 18 months when it was fed with the bottle rather than with other utensils.

The results help to make two points. First, even at 12 months, the child's choices do not seem to be haphazard. Pretense in its earliest form seems to be a selective and deliberate activity. Second, the results bear upon the function of pretend play. At 12 months, the children avoided a familiar object, the bottle. However, they also ignored the doll, as if the symbolic equation "doll stands for baby" had not yet been formed. Instead, they initiated a familiar activity (eating or drinking) with familiar objects (cups and spoons) that they were just beginning to use in real life, and which posed a real challenge when filled with real liquid or food.

If pretense is motivated by uncertainty, the uncertainty is not emanating from the novelty of the object per se, but rather from the novelty of its use. The notion that pretense might provide special opportunities for the partially understood and the dimly grasped to become firmly mastered is not new. Vygotsky (1967) stated the case quite clearly "play creates the zone of proximal development . . . In play a child is always above his average age, above his daily behavior [p. 16]." The children in the earlier example recognized a wedding as a special occasion involving something called "marriage," a male and a female, kissing, dressing up, and traveling to the place where it happens. The details are hazy and confused, nonetheless, the situation merited inclusion in the play. One might argue that the content of pretend play characteristically contains some degree of uncertainty, but the uncertainty is generated and controlled by the child (Fein, 1979a; Fein & Apfel, 1979a). If the child chooses to reproduce uncertain events, one might suppose that the net affect is positive rather than negative. If so, pretend play might provide a mechanism by which the organism generates pleasurable feelings of control over such events, a position in keeping with psychoanalytic theory (Waelder, 1933).

In summary, pretend play can be viewed from the perspective of both observing adult and participating child as a rule-governed situation. The first rule is that activity is drawn from real-life situations that have been experienced either directly or indirectly. The second rule is that these situations must be rendered convincingly, but not literally. As a framed situation, pretense has an immense appeal to young children. In the preceding discussion, it was suggested that the appeal might be derived from the children's control over the arousal level generated in the play.

OBJECT SUBSTITUTIONS

During the early stages of pretend play, an object must be present in its familiar form if it is to be used as an object in pretense. Initially, the spoon must be spoonlike, but eventually an object which does not appear to have any apparent spoonlike features (a leaf) can be used as if it were a spoon provided it can be held, lifted, and brought in some fashion to the child's mouth.[1] Piaget's (1962) observations of a child pretending to sleep nicely illustrate these changes:

> The same cloth started the same game on the following days. At 1;3 (13) she treated the collar of her mother's coat in the same way. At 1;3 (30) it was the tail of her rubber donkey which represented the pillow! And from 1;5 onwards she made her animals, a bear and a plush dog also do "nono" [pp. 96–97].

The child's use of a substitute object is viewed by Vygotsky (1967) as the first step in the detachment of meaning from the actual object. The substitute object serves as a "pivot" and, in a sense, precipitates the detachment. Symbolic play is the behavioral mechanism that precipitates the transition from "things as objects of action" to "things as objects of thought." According to Vygotsky (1967),

[1] Most likely the system is not symmetrically reversible. The child can treat a tiny pebble as if it were a gigantic boulder, but cannot treat the boulder as if it were a tiny pebble. The world can be miniaturized in action; it can only be giganticized in thought.

> Play is a transitional stage . . . At that critical moment when a stick—i.e. an object—becomes a pivot for severing the meaning of horse from a real horse, one of the basic psychological structures determining the child's relationship to reality is altered . . . To a certain extent, meaning is emancipated from the object with which it had been directly fused before [pp. 12–13].

In the most advanced forms of pretense, the child's liberation from the immediate situation is complete:

> Some objects can readily denote others, replacing them and becoming signs for them, and the degree of similarity between a plaything and the object it denotes is unimportant. What is most important is the . . . possibility of executing a representational gesture with it . . . The child's self-motion, his own gestures, are what assign the function of sign to the object and give it meaning [Vygotsky, 1978, p. 108].

According to theorists such as Vygotsky and Piaget, object substitutions are a striking example of child-dominated behavior liberated from the control of external stimulation. But is the child's domination of the environment as complete as these theorists imply? In the next section, evidence concerning the environmental conditions that support pretense is examined.

The Environment for Play

A deeply held conviction among preschool educators is that playthings with highly realistic details limit the imaginativeness of children's play. Certainly, one aspect of the development of play is the ability to create imaginary situations and objects. If children are able to create such things, they will presumably do so most richly if the environment is neutral and unintrusive. The evidence suggests that the relationship between objects in the immediate environment may not be so simple.

Consider first the pretend behavior of 2-year-olds. The issue of object substitutions was examined in a study by Fein (1975) and in another by Fein and Robertson (1975). In the former study, it was argued that by 2 years of age, the child who feeds a horselike toy horse with a cuplike cup knows that real animals eat and that a cup is for drinking. Pretense is operating insofar as the child behaves as if attributing living functions to an inanimate object, adding liquid to an empty cup and, importantly, establishing the relation between horse and cup. In a sense, neither the horselike horse (a toy) nor the cup (empty) are "real" but when realistic, prototypical objects are used the child pretends to "feed the horse" with little difficulty.

What happens when less realistic objects are substituted for a horselike horse or a cuplike cup? Substitutions can be presented singly (either horse or cup) or in pairs (horse and cup). When 2-year-olds were asked to "feed the horse" under double, single, or no substitution conditions, the results were in accord with predictions derived from a transformational analysis. Over 90% of the children were able to enact the pretense when no substitutions were involved, 70% could do so when single substitutions were involved, and only 33% could do so when double substitutions were involved. The children required a more or less realistic anchor to support substitution behavior. The symbolic function is operating, but symbols and symbol making is not completely emancipated from perceivable objects.

Additional evidence comes from the Fein and Robertson (1975) study. In a free play situation, children who were 20- and 26-months-old were presented two toy sets—a highly prototypical set with realistic dolls, trucks, and other toys and a less prototypical set with less realistic toys. Toys in the latter set were scaled according to their degree of realism as judged by adults. Results indicated that, within the less prototypical set, the pretend use of objects increased as the objects became more realistic. In addition, the use of less realistic materials increased between 20 and 26 months.

Between the ages of 3 and 5 years, children's ability to pretend with less realistic objects increases (Elder & Pederson, 1978; Golomb, 1977). As development progresses, the dependency of pretending upon a perceivable object of any form is reduced and eventually, by school age, the child is able to produce an imaginary object with a simple gesture (Overton & Jackson, 1973).

For young children, the best environment for pretense may be one containing an ample supply of realistic objects. For older children, such an environment may limit rather than enhance play. Pulaski (1973) compared the influence of highly structured and moderately structured materials on the play of middle-class children in kindergarten, first, and second grade. The highly structured set contained costumes designating specific roles, toys, realistic play buildings, and realistic male and female dolls. The moderately structured set contained bolts of fabric, blocks and cartons, and nondescript rag dolls. The amount of play with the two play sets did not differ. Differences appeared, rather, in the inventiveness and imaginativeness of the themes generated by the children. Play with the highly structured toy set tended to adhere to the content suggested by the materials, whereas play with the moderately structured set was more varied and inventive. Moreover, the activity level of the children was higher with the less realistic materials.

In an attempt to extend this issue to architectural aspects of the play environment, Fields (1979) presented 4- and 5-year-old disadvantaged children with two, large enterable play boxes (see Figures 10.1 and 10.2).

FIGURE 10.1.   *Playbox decorated in a simple abstract pattern (from Fields, 1979, reprinted with permission).*

The boxes were identical in size, shape, openings, and coloring. They differed in that one box was painted to look like an automotive vehicle, whereas the other was decorated in a simple abstract pattern. Play was observed over 15 consecutive days for approximately 1 hr. each day.

Contrary to Pulaski's findings, children spent more time playing in the realistic box ($F = 5.07$, $df / 28$, $p < .05$) and more pretend elements were generated in the realistic box ($t = 2.56$, $p < .05$). Finally, the play elements generated in the realistic box were more diverse. The particular themes

FIGURE 10.2.   *Playbox painted to look like an automotive vehicle (from Fields, 1979, reprinted with permission).*

and variations generated by the children indicate how the boxes were used (Table 10.1). Clearly, the automotive motif provoked the play theme of transportation, a theme that never occurred when the motif was absent. Motif-specific play elements account for 58% of the play elements generated in the realistic box. Although the children imagined several types of vehicles (plane, train, bus, car, and camper), the stereotyped activity of driving accounts for 61% of the transportation play. If motif-specific elements are excluded from the calculation, more play elements appear when children play in the less realistic box. Note, also, the high occurrence of house play in both boxes. When the children "drove" the camper, the scene shifted rapidly to basic house play activities, as if the camper idea was too limited to stand on its own. Basic house play activities, eating and sleeping, occurred in 8 of the 24 house episodes in the realistic box, and in 15 of the 31 house episodes in the other box. The fire theme occurred only in the unrealistic box, possibly as an extension of the house play. At any rate, the theme was never developed. In brief, Fields' findings suggest that realistic structures might have a facilitating effect on the pretend play of disadvantaged 4- and 5-year-old children, especially when the structure suggests a theme that is not likely to occur spontaneously.

But why do Fields and Pulaski find such different effects? One possibility is that Pulaski's children came from middle-class families and Fields' children came from poor families; generally, children from middle-class backgrounds pretend more imaginatively than children from disadvantaged backgrounds (Fein & Stork, in press; Smilansky, 1968). There is also a considerable age difference between the samples. Social class and age are individual characteristics likely to produce person–context interactions.

Indirect evidence from a study by Enslein (1979), suggests that the pretense of middle-class preschool children is limited in an environment lacking realistic props. Enslein observed children's play in the housekeeping area over a 7-week period. The area contained wooden play furniture (a stove, refrigerator, cupboard, bed, table, and chairs), a couple of worn rag dolls, some bedding, and little else. Pretend play occurred occasionally during the first 2 weeks, but decreased steadily thereafter, until by the sixth week it was down to zero. Enslein then added a set of

TABLE 10.1
Number of Different Play Elements in Enterable Realistic and Nonrealistic Play Boxes

Theme	Realistic box (automotive motif)	Nonrealistic box (abstract motif)
House	17	29
Transportation	39	0
Fire	0	3
Miscellaneous	11	13

realistic pots, pans, and dishes, dress-up clothes, and empty food containers. During the first day after the new materials were added, the children engaged largely in exploratory activity rummaging through the boxes of new materials, trying on the new clothes, and so forth. The novelty effect was brief, but seemed to preclude pretend play. Pretend play emerged on the second day as exploratory behavior receded. The dominant themes initially were material-specific: cooking, serving and eating food, dressing up to represent family roles. Cooking activities continued into the third day, but the food changed from a general substance to specific kinds (soup, spaghetti, hot dogs). Pretend play showed little sign of diminishing over the next few days.

As proposed by Nunnally and Lemond (1973), exploratory behavior seemed to be the first response to novel objects and pretend play appeared when the effect of novelty was attenuated. Although the children were observed for a week, there was no sign of the boredom that Nunnally and Lemond (1973) predicted would follow pretend play. Of course, these observations cover days and weeks, rather than the minutes of typical laboratory studies. They also consider children in groups, rather than in solitary play situations.

OTHER FACTORS

In the presence of a novel object, children explore; but when the novelty wears off, they play (Hutt, 1970; Nunnally & Lemond, 1973). Limited evidence suggests that novelty may have a positive influence on exploratory behavior and a negative or inhibitory influence on pretense. This possibility merits further investigation for two reasons. First, the inverse relation suggests that exploration and pretend play are different behavioral systems. Second, it suggests that a familiar environment and familiar objects provide a supportive condition for play. In keeping with the view presented earlier, the element of uncertainty produced in play does not come from the need to gather information about the physical properties of immediate environmental events. Uncertainty comes from previously experienced events being introduced into the stream of play. The pretending child knows what the immediate object is or what it will be held to be in the play. Characteristics of stimuli in the immediate environment that challenge the child's confidence in this knowledge disrupt the generation of open associations that seem so crucial to pretense.

What about complexity? Again, the evidence is limited, but when exploration and play are examined under varying levels of complexity, the two behaviors function differently. Switsky, Haywood, & Isett (1974) presented children with 2-dimensional, vinyl shapes varying in complexity according to the number of turns on the edges. These investigators distinguished between exploratory behaviors (visual and tactual investigation) and play behaviors (sensorimotor behaviors such as bouncing or bending an object and symbolic activities such as using an object as if it were a gun). In children between 4 and 7 years of age, exploratory behavior increased with the complexity of the vinyl shapes, but play behavior peaked at moderate levels of complexity. In 2-year-olds, however, both play and exploratory behavior peaked at moderate levels of complexity and then declined. These results provide additional support for the notion that exploration and play are functionally different behaviors at least in older children. Moreover, moderately complex figures of the kind used by Switsky, *et al.* tend to look like real objects, and people tend to attribute meaning to them (Munsinger & Kessen, 1966). As discussed in an earlier section, meaningfulness tends to favor play.

Several other studies offer provocative possibilities for future research. For example, Gramza (1970, 1973) examined children's preference for enterable play boxes. Children in a group situation were found to prefer boxes that were more opaque and with fewer entry ports. Unfortunately, Gramza did not observe what children actually did in these boxes and, therefore, the case cannot be made that "encapsulating" objects attract children because they support pretend play.

From Stimulation to Evocation

In the present chapter, two views of environment have been contrasted. In one, the environment is conceptualized as stimulation, an activating and directing force for behavior. In the other, environment is conceptualized as evocation, and the activation and direction of behavior is attributed to the organism. Berlyne's theory of exploratory behavior was taken as a departure point for considering sources of mental arousal other than those stemming from excess, uncertainty, or boredom.

The particular source chosen for discussion was pretense, a kind of play in which the child treats one thing as though it were something else. In pretense, the child evokes situations and objects that are actually not present in the immediate environment. The evocation is deliberate and recognized by the child as an evocation; or, in the language of Bateson (1956) and Goffman (1974), pretense is a well-framed behavior about the well-framed behaviors of ordinary life. Within the frame, one object, by its treatment, is transformed into another; the real and immediate properties of things are ignored, and the physical correspondence between the immediate object and the object represented is relatively casual. And, as Vygotsky (1967, 1978) so astutely noted, the situations and objects of ordinary life that are evoked by the child are largely cultural inventions.

Although theorists often assume that in pretense anything can be substituted for anything else (Piaget, 1962; Vygotsky, 1978), recent evidence suggests that the loosening of physical constraints is gradual and, possibly, never complete. Children's ability to pretend that one thing is something else reveals how children represent the environment and how rules of representation change with age (Fein, 1979b).

Early in the development of pretense, children require the presence of a realistic object. But consider what is meant by the term *realistic*. If the term is used to refer to things that look like they are supposed to look, the young child by 12 months of age must be credited with a special kind of representational capacity such that, among the diverse physical appearances of things known as cups and horses, some appearances are better exemplars of the general category than are others (see Fein, 1975, 1979b, for more discussion of this issue). In young children, pretense is enhanced by the presence of a highly prototypical object. Stimulation as object is the basis of evocation. As pretense unfolds developmentally, less prototypical objects can be used, which means that a greater variety of objects can serve as substitutes. Pretense, thereby, becomes less restricted by immediate environmental circumstance; evocation dominates stimulation. But, the domination is relative rather than absolute. In one study, when children between the ages of 3 and 6 were offered a number of substitution alternatives for food to feed the "hungry baby," they tended to reject incongruous alternatives such as a realistic toy animal or a hair brush (Golomb, 1977). Highly prototypical objects, good exemplars of one class, may be especially difficult to treat as if they were members of another class. Complete liberation from the immediate appearance of things may require a capacity to suspend belief not found until the school-age years. And yet, incongruity of this type is the basis of humor in even preschool children (Schultz & Horibe, 1974). But, of course, pretense is not exactly joke making. If pretense is about framed situations, the rules of pretense may be violated by the introduction of incongruous frames.

Although much more is known about pretense today than was known a decade ago, major features of the behavior have not been examined. For example, what on earth suddenly possesses the child at 12 months of age to do such a thing? Why not earlier, later, or never? Some investigators have suggested that pretense is directly taught (El'Konin, 1966), and others have suggested that its general principles are modeled in the course of parent–child play (Garvey, 1977; Sutton-Smith, 1979). But these explanations cannot account for the developmental data, nor are they consistent with the observation that, whereas most parents play relatively infrequently with their children (Dunn & Wooding, 1977), pretense as a play form is a widespread, if not universal phenomenon (Kagan, Kearsley, & Zelazo, 1978).

If pretense is not to be explained as an outgrowth of childhood socialization, what else might it be attributed to? Suppose that the repetition of partially mastered activities maintains a pleasant level of arousal. For the 12-month-old just learning to drink from a cup, the absence of liquid eliminates the messy consequences of clumsiness. Suppose, too, that the child becomes able to monitor its activity and recognize that a familiar but uncertain activity is being repeated in a new, penalty-free context. From that recognition, the child might draw the conclusion that life's activities are not necessarily context bound. This conclusion might become the basis of a new form of behavior that presents possibilities for countless recyclings, innovations, variations, and an immense new potential for self-stimulation. Of course, this hypothetical child possesses attributes of self-awareness, conclusion drawing, voluntary control, and a desire for pleasant experiences.

Pretense is a childhood behavior as natural and ubiquitous as talking, crawling, or crying. As such, it poses fascinating problems of structure, content, function, and consequence. Pretense occurs in a physical environment and is influenced by environmental factors. But, pretense is also behavior about the environment. As such, it reveals the process whereby the environment gets inside the person, thereby providing an opportunity to understand the relation between in and out. In pretense, the child deals with the reality of things, people, and events, with objects rather than with physical stimulation.

Underlying the child's discovery of pretense as a situation about situations is the child's capacity to distinguish real from nonreal, literal from nonliteral and, more basically, to distinguish stimulation from evocation. The distinction is an active process through which the individual gains possession of immensely expanded opportunities for exchanges within and between the environment as felt and as evoked. Among other things, pretense illustrates the notion that even the physical environment, as palpable, independent, and enduring as it may seem, can be recast and usurped in the imaginings of a young child.

But the capacity to recast is a slowly emerging function between the years of 1 and 6. Early in life, the idea of an object is tied to its immediate and prototypical appearance and pretense reflects these ties. Over time, the ties are loosened, and pretend play becomes increasingly ideational. Finally, pretend play may be supplemented by newer functions such as the capacity to fantasize and daydream in the absence of both activity and object.

Pretend play as a spontaneous overt behavior appears over a relatively brief period of life. As such, it illustrates an unusual inverted-U-shaped developmental function. Before vanishing, pretense changes from an activity in which children themselves enact central roles to an activity in which children direct and orchestrate the actions of Ken, Barbie, or R2D2. Although these older children are capable of abstract representations, they are perversely enchanted by the most literal and realistic representations of stereotyped cultural forms. At the very age when the capacity for internal, personal fantasy is fully formed, when romantic or adventurous figures can be invented at will, children submerge themselves in the commercial, prepackaged fantasies of adult artists and writers. But the perversity may be more apparent than real. According to Piaget, pretend play, even in the absence of commercial toys, becomes more realistic before vanishing. Piaget uses this observation to support the position that pretense, initially an expression of the child's ignorance and confusion, vanishes when ignorance is replaced by knowledge and confusion by logical thinking. The controversial question is whether pretense truly vanishes.

Suppose fantasy making is an enduring disposition of the mature individual. Suppose, as others have suggested (e.g., Klinger, 1971), that fantasy making becomes transformed from an overt behavior in childhood to a covert imaginal process in adulthood. What mechanism might precipitate this transformation? One possibility is that fantasy-made-literal exposes the inherent fixedness of physical stimulation in relation to the fluidity of mental evocation. Barbie is simply too pathetically stiff and explicit to express fully the personal, romantic, ethereal, and sensuous fantasies of adolescence. A doll is just a doll. But the attempt to make the nonliteral literal confronts the inherent opposition between real and not real and the orthogonality of stimulation and evocation. The confrontation finally frees fantasy from its last, lingering dependence on immediate stimulation. Now stimulation can be entirely subordinated to evocation and new forms of fantasy expression become possible (e.g., overt, public forms such as theater and covert, private forms such as daydreams).

In view of these observations, it might be instructive to reconsider the implications of pretense in childhood. In the solitary pretense of infants, pretense is primarily representational. In the sociodramatic play of older children, presentation appears but presentation and representation are fused. In adulthood, presentation and representation are differentiated, and a new form of reciprocity between stimulation and evocation emerges. Now stimulation can be selected and produced to serve evocational purposes. The literal can be made nonliteral; reality can become hypothetical. In placing stimulation at the service of evocation, great theater vividly illustrates the human capacity to present as hypothetical the real dilemmas of human existence. In actual time, the transition from childhood pretense to adult fantasy requires less than a decade; but in psychic time, the transition from Barbie to Desdemona is millennial.

Stated in a general way, reciprocity between the individual and the physical environment occurs at several levels. At the level of immediacy, there is stimulation as a sensory or motivational experience and reality as a cognitive experience. At a distant level, there is stimulation and reality as they are organized, remembered, and transformed in mind. At the level of the interface, immediacy and distance act upon one another to produce new immediacies for distant transport. The pretend play of young children provides a special opportunity to understand basic aspects of a developing process. If, in childhood, pretense entails the ability to abstract from the concrete, in adulthood, pretense involves the ability to concretize the abstract (Piaget & Inhelder, 1971; Sutton-Smith, Botvin, & Mahoney, 1975). One aspect of individuals' contributions to their own development involves the exercise of both abilities.

References

Barnett, S. A. Exploratory behavior. *British Journal of Psychology*, 1958, *49*, 289–310.

Bateson, G. A theory of play and fantasy. *Psychiatric Research Reports*, 1955, *2*, 39–51.

Bateson, G. The message "This is play." In B. Schaffner (Ed.), *Group processes: Transactions of the Second Conference*. New York: Josiah Macy Foundation, 1956, pp. 145–246.

Beach, F. A. Current concepts of play in animals. *American Naturalist*, 1945, *79* (785), 523–541.

Berlyne, D. E. *Conflict, arousal, and curiosity*. New York: McGraw-Hill, 1960.

Berlyne, D. E. Curiosity and exploration. *Science*, 1966, *153*, 25–33.

Berlyne, D. E. Laughter, humor, and play. In I. Lindzey & E. Aronson (Eds.), *The handbook of social psychology* (Vol. 3). Reading, Mass: Addison-Wesley, 1969.

Dunn, J., & Wooding, C. Play in the home and its implications for learning. *Biology of play*. London: William Heineman, 1977.

Eifermann, R. R. Social play in childhood. In R. E. Herron & B. Sutton-Smith (Eds.), *Child's play*. New York: Wiley, 1971.

Elder, J. L., & Pederson, D. R. Preschool children's use of objects in symbolic play. *Child Development*, 1978, *49*, 500–504.

El'Konin, D. B. Symbolics and its function in the play of children. *Soviet Education*, 1966, *8*, 35–41.

Ellis, M. J. *Why people play*. Englewood Cliffs, N.J.: Prentice-Hall, 1973.

Enslein, J. *An analysis of toy preference, social participation, and play activity in preschool aged children*. Unpublished Master's Thesis, The Merrill-Palmer Institute, 1979.

Fein, G. G. A transformational analysis of pretending. *Developmental Psychology*, 1975, *11*, 291–296.

Fein, G. G. Play and the acquisition of symbols. In L. Katz (Ed.), *Current topics in early childhood education*. New Jersey: Ablex, 1979a.

Fein, G. G. Echoes from the nursery: Piaget, Vygotsky and the relation between language and play. *New Directions in Child Development*, 1979, *6*, 1–14b.

Fein, G. G. Pretend play: An integrative review, *Child Development*, in press.

Fein, G. G. & Robertson, A. R. *Cognitive and social dimensions of pretending in 2 year olds*. ERIC #ED 119 806, 1975.

Fein, G. G. & Stork, L. Sociodramatic play in an integrated setting. *Journal of Applied Developmental Psychology*, in press.

Fein, G. G. & Apfel, N. Some preliminary observations on knowing and pretending. In M. Smith & M. B. Franklin (Eds.), *Symbolic functioning in childhood*. Hillsdale, N.J.: Erlbaum, 1979a.

Fein, G. G. & Apfel, N. The development of play: Style, structure, and situation. *Genetic Psychology Monograph*, 1979, *99*, 231–250b.

Fenson, L., Kagan, J., Kearsley, R. B. & Zelazo, P. The developmental progression of manipulative play in the first two years. *Child Development*, 1976, *47*, 232–235.

Fields, W. *Imaginative play of four year old children as a function of toy realism*. Unpublished Master's Thesis. The Merrill-Palmer Institute.

Garvey, C. Some properties of social play. *Merrill-Palmer Quarterly*, 1974, 20, 163–180.

Garvey, C. *Play*. Cambridge, Mass. Harvard University Press, 1977.

Garvey, C., & Berndt, R. Organization of pretend play. *Catalogue of Selected Documents in Psychology*, 1977, 7 (No. 1589), American Psychological Association.

Goffman, E. *Frame analysis: An essay of the organization of experience*. Cambridge, Mass.: Harvard University Press, 1974.

Golomb, C. Symbolic play: The role of substitutions in pretense and puzzle games. *British Journal of Educational Psychology*, 1977, 47, 175–186.

Gramza, A. F. Preferences of preschool children for enterable play boxes. *Perceptual and Motor Skills*, 1970, 31, 177–178.

Gramza, A. F. An analysis of stimulus dimensions which define children's encapsulating play objects. *Perceptual and Motor Skills*, 1973, 37, 495–501.

Huizinga, J. Homoludens: A study of the play element in culture. Boston: Beacon Press, 1949.

Hutt, C. Specific and diverse exploration. In H. W. Reese & L. P. Lipsitt (Eds.), *Advances in child development and behavior* (Vol. 5). New York: Academic Press, 1970, pp. 120–172.

Hutt, C. Towards a taxonomy and conceptual model of play. In S. J. Hutt, D. A. Rogers, & C. Hutt (Eds.), *Developmental Processes in Early Childhood*, London: Routledge & Kegan Paul, in press.

Inhelder, B., Lezine, I., Sinclair, H., & Stambak, M. Les Debut de la function symbolique. *Archives de Psychologie*, 1972, 41, 187–243.

Kagan, J., Kearsley, R. B., & Zelazo, P. R. *Infancy: Its place in human development*. Cambridge, Mass.: Harvard University Press, 1978.

Klinger, E. *Structure and functions of fantasy*. New York: Wiley, 1971.

Matthews, W. S. Modes of transformation in the initiation of fantasy play. *Developmental Psychology*, 1977, 13, 212–216.

McCall, R. B. Exploratory manipulation and play in the human infant. *Monographs of the Society for Research in Child Development*. 1974, 39 (No. 155).

Mendel, G. Children's preferences for differing degrees of novelty. *Child Development*, 1965, 36, 453–465.

Munsinger, H., & Kessen, W. Stimulus variability and cognitive change. *Psychological Review*, 1966, 73, 164–178.

Nicolich, L. Beyond sensorimotor intelligence: Assessment of symbolic maturity through analysis of pretend play. *Merrill-Palmer Quarterly*, 1977, 23, 89–99.

Nunnally, J. C., & Lemond, L. C. Exploratory behavior and human development. In H. Reese (Ed.), *Advances in child development and behavior* (Vol. 8). New York: Academic Press, 1973, pp. 60–106.

Overton, W. F., & Jackson, J. P. The representation of imagined objects in action sequences: A developmental study. *Child Development*, 1973, 44, 309–314.

Parten, M. B. Social participation among preschool children. *Journal of Abnormal Social Psychology*, 1932, 27, 243–269.

Piaget, J. *Play, dreams, and imitation in childhood*. New York: Norton, 1962.

Piaget, J., & Inhelder, B. *Mental imagery in the child*. New York: Basic Books, 1971.

Pulaski, M. A. Toys and imaginative play. In J. L. Singer (Ed.), *The child's world of make-believe*. New York: Academic Press, 1973.

Sachs, J., & Devin, J. Young children's use of age appropriate speech styles in social interaction and role playing. *Journal of Child Language*, 1976, 3, 81–98.

Schultz, T. R., & Horibe, F. Development of the appreciation of verbal jokes. *Developmental Psychology*, 1974, 10, 13–20.

Smilansky, S. *The effects of sociodramatic play on disadvantaged preschool children*. New York: Wiley, 1968.

Sutton-Smith, B., Botvin, G., & Mahoney, D. *Developmental structures in fantasy: Narratives.* Paper presented at the meeting of the American Psychological Association, Chicago, September, 1975.

Sutton-Smith, B., & Roberts, J. M. The cross-cultural and psychological study of games. In G. Luschen (Ed.), *The cross-cultural analysis of games.* Champaign, Ill.: Stipes, 1970.

Sutton-Smith, B. Play as a transformational set. *Journal of Health, Physical Education, and Recreation,* 1972, *43,* 32–33.

Sutton-Smith, B. A sociolinguistic approach to ludic action. In H. Lenk (Ed.), *Handlugen theorieu interdisziplinar.* West Germany: Karlsbad University, 1979.

Switzky, H. N., Haywood, C. H., & Isett, R. Exploration, curiosity, and play in young children: Effects of stimulus complexity. *Developmental Psychology,* 1974, *10,* 321–329.

Vygotsky, L. S. Play and its role in the mental development of the child. *Soviet Psychology,* 1967, *5* (3), 6–18.

Vygotsky, L. S. *Mind in society: The development of higher mental processes* Cambridge, Mass: Harvard University Press, 1978.

Waelder, R. The psychoanalytic theory of play. *Psychoanalytical Quarterly,* 1933, *2,* 208–224.

Watson, M. W., & Fischer, K. W. A developmental sequence of agent use in late infancy. *Child Development,* 1977, *48,* 828–836.

Weisler, A., & McCall, R. B. Exploration and play: Resume and redirection. *American Psychologist,* 1976, *31* (7), 492–508.

Welker, W. I. An analysis of exploratory and play behavior in animals. In Fiske, D. W., & Maddi, S. R. (Eds.), *Functions of varied experience.* Homewood, Ill.: Dorsey Press, 1961.

White, R. W. Motivation reconsidered: The concept of competence. *Psychological Review,* 1959, *66,* 297–333.

Wolff, P. H. Observations on newborn infants. *Psychosomatic Medicine,* 1959, *21,* 110–118.

NANCY A. BUSCH-ROSSNAGEL **11**

Where Is the Handicap in Disability?: The Contextual Impact of Physical Disability

*Deviant behavior and skill deficits lead to
exclusion from society. . . .When individuals
are consistently excluded from the
environments where socially appropriate
behavior and skills are learned, their
development will become increasingly retarded
[Pomerantz & Marholin, 1977, p. 130].*

From the moment of birth or the occurrence of a disability, the physically handicapped experience a pattern of socialization that is definitely atypical. Their parents have different expectations for them; childhood peers may exclude them; colleagues in adulthood may overcompensate for the disability. To understand the development of the physically disabled, various models and theories have been utilized. These include the behaviorist approach (Bijou, 1966) and social role theory (Gordon, 1966) within the mechanistic world view, and psychoanalytic theory, the individual psychology of Adler, and body-image theory (English, 1971; McDaniel, 1976) within the organicist paradigm. An alternative world view, that of dialectics (Riegel, 1975; 1976a, 1976b) or contextualism (Pepper, 1942) stresses the interdependency of biological, psychological, sociocultural, and historical variables and that these variables are constantly changing. This pardigm has not yet been systematically applied to the study of physical handicaps. One test of the contextual model is to examine its ability to account for atypical as well as for normal development. The purpose of this chapter is to indicate that the contextual model increases our understanding of the development of the individual with a physical disability.

Individuals as Producers of Their Development

Definition of Physical Disability

Before the contextual model is applied to the development of the physically disabled, we must first understand what is encompassed under the rubric of "physical disability." Diller (1972) outlines six handicapping conditions, five of which are physical. Mental retardation–emotional disturbance, by itself, is not considered a physical handicap, but it often occurs with such a physical condition. The largest group of physical handicaps is that of the orthopedically impaired, which includes conditions such as cerebral palsy, spina bifida, amputation and limb deformation, paraplegia, and muscular dystrophy. All of these conditions are visible and involve limitations of movement. The other four types of handicapping conditions are: (*a*) blind and partially blind; (*b*) deaf and partially deaf; (*c*) cardiac problems; and (*d*) tuberculosis and respiratory problems. Using the categories of the United States Office of Education, Bureau of Education for the Handicapped, crippled and other health impaired, deaf, hard of hearing, visually handicapped, and multiply handicapped children represent 1.3% of all school age children (USOE–BEH cited in Sontag, 1977). Physical disabilities may also be found in the categories of speech-impaired, mentally retarded, learning disabled, and emotionally disturbed, which would increase the incidents to approximately 4.9% or 348,000 children (Gellman, 1974).

A clarification must also be made as to the components of the handicap. Using Susser and Watson's (1971) terminology, three components of a handicap can be differentiated. The organic component is static and is referred to as an *impairment;* the analogue from medicine would be disease. The functional component involves the limitation of function and is called a *disability;* it is the analogue of illness. The social component, the *handicap,* limits the performance of social roles and relations; handicap is the analogue of the sick role. Throughout this chapter, the use of impairment, disability, and handicap will be in accordance with these distinctions of Susser and Watson.

An Application of the Contextual Model

A contextual model is applied to the development of individuals with a physical disability in Figure 11.1. The physically disabled have an organic deviance that makes their functioning at the biological level atypical; this is their impairment. Examples of such impairments are limb deformities or deterioration of the retina. Their impairments have both response characteristics and stimulus characteristics.

Response characteristics are functional limitations resulting from the impairment. These disabilities include the inability to walk or the inability

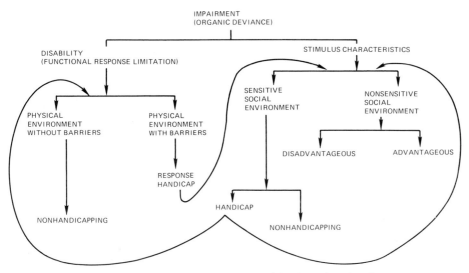

FIGURE 11.1.   *A contextual model of the development of handicaps from impairments.*

to see (blindness). A disability will constitute a handicap only within certain physical environments and at certain developmental stages. For example, there is a sizable segment of the population who are unable to walk, but for whom this functional limitation is not a handicap. These individuals are, of course, infants. The older child who is unable to walk will be handicapped in an environment where mobility is required. However, if that environment is modified so that mobility may be achieved with wheelchairs, the child has a disability but need not experience a handicap. An alternative method of ameliorating the handicap is through the use of prostheses. If the child is fitted with an artificial limb and learns to walk, the functional limitation has been modifed to reduce both the disability itself and the associated handicap.

However, the impairment still acts as a stimulus to others (i.e., it has stimulus characteristics). The social environment may or may not be sensitive to these characteristics. If the other individuals in the environment are not aware of the impairment, the stimulus characteristics may not result in a handicap. In addition, when the disability has been modified and the response limitation reduced, the stimulus characteristics may also be reduced. For example, the use of an artificial limb covered with clothing may mean that the individuals in the environment are not aware of the impairment. Thus, the result may be a nonsensitive social environment. However, this nonsensitive social environment may not always be advantageous. For example, a partially deaf person who has learned to lip read can carry on a conversation so that other individuals may not know that the person is partially deaf. However, if the other persons turn away, the hearing-impaired person will lose the conversation. Far more serious consequences may result when the parent of an impaired child is not aware of the impairment or denies its existence. The parent may then not provide desirable experiences (e.g., medical treatment or educational intervention) to keep the impairment from progressively deteriorating.

When the individuals in the social environment are sensitive to the stimulus characteristics of the impairment, they may respond in an advantageous or disadvantageous way. Advantageous ways of responding include providing appropriate developmental stimulation for the child or employment opportunities for the adult. The result of this sensitive environment is nonhandicapping because there is no limitation of social roles. However, the sensitive social environment usually responds in a disadvantageous way (at least at one level; see Figure 11.2 and following discussion). The result is a handicap. At the first level of analysis this is a socially induced handicap. This handicap may occur without a real impairment; the simple perception of an impairment and the social reaction to it are enough to create this type of handicap.

A circular function between handicaps and the environment exists. The response handicap of not being able to walk in an environment that requires walking acts as a stimulus. When orthopedically impaired children cannot play ball with their peers, the result of not walking may be a lessened opportunity to participate in other activities. The exclusion may in turn feedback on the child, leading to a negative self-image and/or less

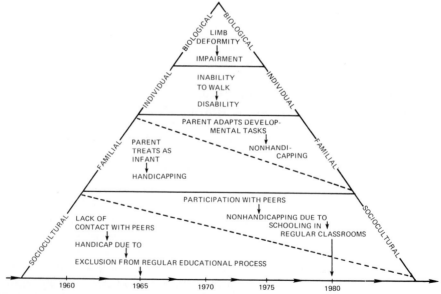

FIGURE 11.2. *Levels of functioning for the physically disabled individual.*

accurate perception of social cues over time as a function of lessened learning opportunities.

These circular functions occur at different levels: the biological, the individual, the familial, the sociocultural, and the historical; these levels are shown in Figure 11.2, which shows that impairment occurs on the biological level, whereas disability occurs on the individual level (although it may be the result of a sociocultural event such as war). Whereas handicaps may result from a conflict between the individual level (disability) and the physical environment, the focus of this chapter will be on the social environment. At the familial level, the child who is unable to walk may be treated as an infant. In this circumstance, the parents may not recognize the child's striving for independence and mastery because one aspect of development, mobility, is still in the stage of infancy. This is a handicapping social environment. A handicapping condition at the sociocultural level is the child's lack of contact with peers. This is the result of the child's exclusion from the regular educational process as shown on the time line. Nonhandicapping social environments may also be described for these levels. For example, at the familial level, parents may adapt developmental tasks to the child's lack of mobility, by seeing that objects are close enough to recover. At the sociocultural level, the child may use a wheelchair to participate in a "special Olympics."

Handicapping and nonhandicapping social environments occur on a variety of levels, and a variety of them occur within the same level. For example, the mandates of Public Law 94–142 insure that every child has a right to education, which has resulted in sociocultural changes. However, on the sociocultural level, there is still a prevalent societal attitude of "handicapism" (Blatt, Bogdan, Biklen, & Taylor, 1977), suggesting that the handicapped are innately incapable and naturally inferior. Thus, while one part of one level of a social environment may be nonhandicapping, there are always some handicapping conditions present for the physically disabled. Thus, Figure 11.2 shows that some handicapping conditions were alleviated with the historical occurrence in 1975 of the passage of The Education for All Handicapped Children Act, Public Law 94–142, but that handicapping conditions still exist. The diagonal dotted lines show the hope that the incidence of handicapping social environments will continue to decrease.

When applied to the development of the physically disabled, the contextual model suggests two ideas for research in the area of physical disability. First, stimulus characteristics and the social environment should be investigated as well as functional limitations. However, to date these functional limitations have been the primary focus of inquiry in the area of rehabilitation and exceptional children (cf., Trapp & Himelstein, 1972), partly as a result of the predominance of medical personnel and approaches in these fields (Richardson, 1970). Second, to understand the development of the physically disabled, we must examine their functioning at a variety of levels and examine the interdependence of these levels.

This chapter reviews research in the area of physical disability using the proposed model of person–context relations. Studies pertaining to the development of the physically disabled from infancy through adolescence are emphasized.[1] Literature that deals with the functional limitations of specific disabilities or with mental retardation or emotional disturbance without an associated physical problem is not included. Because of the nature of the problems in the fields concerned with physical disability, the criterion of utility for application must be one important aspect of any model attempting to integrate knowledge in the field. Therefore, intervention studies are used as examples of the possible applications of the model proposed in this chapter.

Physical Disability at Birth and during Infancy

To understand the impact of the birth of a physically disabled child, one must first realize that the expectations concerning the child precede birth and even precede pregnancy. Veevers (1973), Flapen (1969), and Ryckman and Henderson (1965) have analyzed child-bearing motivations and the meanings of parenthood. According to their ideas, having an impaired child reflects negatively on the parents' emotional adjustment and requires the development of coping mechanisms. These speculations about the meaning of parenthood suggest that parents do not expect a child who is impaired. However, the implications of parenting an impaired child and the expectations for a healthy baby go beyond the level of the family to both the sociocultural and the individual and biological level. At the sociocultural level, the family network and the network of friends are preparing for a healthy baby. At the individual level, the pregnant woman is preparing herself psychologically for the birth of her baby (Davids, 1968; Davids & Holden, 1970). At the biological level, there is a wealth of information showing the effect of various toxins during pregnancy (e.g., ingestion of the drug thalidomide or maternal infection with rubella during early pregnancy).

In summary, the expectations preceding and during pregnancy from the total social environment are for a healthy, intact baby. However, the

---

[1] This emphasis reflects the different emphases of the literature through adolescence and the literature in adulthood. Research on physical disability during infancy, childhood, and adolescence is often concerned with psychological development and with the effects of disabilities on interactions. The adulthood literature may be characterized by a greater emphasis on the effect of functional limitations on such tasks as job performance and home management. Rather than examining socially induced handicaps in their own right and as a potential source of development, the researchers see handicaps as by-products of functional limitations. Concern with the social environment is not completely lacking in the adulthood literature as can be seen in the trend toward normalization.

mother's biological and psychological functioning during pregnancy may put the child at risk. If the child is subsequently impaired, the mother is then at great risk for self-blame and guilt. Thus, an examination of the social environment of the disabled child and an understanding of the circular functioning between the child's disability and the social environment must begin prenatally and even prior to the pregnancy.

NEONATAL EXPERIENCE

Because the social environment expects a healthy infant, the birth of an impaired child requires the adjustment of the individuals involved. This process has been most carefully studied in parents of disabled children.

Based on their clinical experience, Solnit and Stark (1961) characterized the reaction of parents to the birth of a defective child as consisting of several key elements. The first is that the infants do not match the expectations of the parents, so the parents must mourn the loss of the perfect infant before relating to the real infant. The parents will experience guilt and anger, some of which is directed toward the professionals with whom the parents have contact. The mother's mourning can be interrupted by caring for the handicapped infant, and this can be emotionally and physically exhausting.

Klaus and Kennell (1976) enlarged the ideas of Solnik and Stark (1961) and suggested a sequence of five stages through which parents of children with congenital malformations may pass. These are: (*a*) shock; (*b*) denial or disbelief; (*c*) sadness, anger, or anxiety; (*d*) equilibrium; and (*e*) reorganization. Individual differences may alter the process or the timing, but the ultimate result can be a new sense of confidence (Daniels & Berg, 1968) and a positive self-image (Voysey, 1972). Research on mothers' personalities and motivations by this author (Busch-Rossnagel & Peters, 1980) supports these ideas. In a longitudinal study, first-time mothers were tested three times in the early months of motherhood. There were no differences in anxiety between mothers of disabled and normal children, but mothers of disabled children had higher career sentiment themselves and lower aspirations for their children. These findings suggest that mothers respond to the birth of a disabled child with a reorganization of their expectations for the future. However, the differences in maternal personality found by other researchers (e.g., higher anxiety, lower self-esteem; cf. Cummings, Bayley, & Rie, 1966 and discussion that follows) are not a part of the familial social environment during the early months of a disabled child's life. Later differences in maternal personality may be the result of interaction with the disabled child, a position consistent with the idea that these children are producers of their own development.

On the sociocultural level, the environment of the physically disabled newborn is different as well. For example, the rituals surrounding the birth are upset (Battle, 1974). Religious services may be canceled. The network of family and friends may stay away or not phone because of uncertainty or embarrassment. As Richardson (1969) points out, there are no well-known guidelines of behavior for the family or friends of the newborn disabled child. Thus the infant has a handicap as well as a disability because the roles ascribed to the newborn are disrupted.

The research has thus described the social environment of the disabled child during the neonatal period. The individuals involved are certainly sensitive to the stimulus characteristics, although there may also be some denial. The explanation for the differing social environment is that the expectations surrounding the birth process are upset. However, the intervention implications have not been well-applied as yet. Certainly no one would suggest preparing all mothers to expect a disabled child. Still, medical professionals could be better trained to deal with the parents instead of reacting to what they may perceive as their failure to deliver a healthy, intact baby. Klaus and Kennell (1976) have shown that concern for the attachment process may be applied to mothers of infants with congenital malformations. By presenting the normal attributes of the child to the parents and by allowing the mother more opportunity for prolonged contact with her baby, the parents' expectations can be revised, and the mother's attachment to her infant may be fostered.

THE IMPACT OF DISABILITY DURING INFANCY

The physical disabilities of infants may not be noticed or diagnosed at birth. The parents themselves are often the ones who perceive that something is wrong with the child because the baby is not meeting the parents' expectations. For these children, the possible handicapping conditions are similar to those of the neonatal period. When the diagnosis is finally made, the parent will experience emotions similar to the impact at birth. However, the intensity will probably be lessened, in part because the parents probably already suspected something was wrong, and in part because they have already attached to the child. The physician's worry about maternal attachment is thus of less importance than during the neonatal period, although it is of continuing concern. However, the parents are faced with the problem of revising their expectations.

Regardless of whether the infant's disability was diagnosed at birth or occurred later, the differences in the social environment are often explained by the lack of agreement between the infant's behavior and the social expectations. This may cause the individuals in the environment to revise their expectations, thus creating a different social environment for the infant with a disability.

What are the characteristics of this social environment? Consider two studies on the lingustic development of Down's syndrome infants. Buium, Rynders, and Turnure (1974) examined the linguistic environments of normal and Down's syndrome infants who were learning language. When they compared the linguistic characteristics of the mother's speech to these children, they found the following differences. The speech directed to the Down's syndrome infants had a higher number of utterances, but a lower mean length of utterance. The linguistic environment of the Down's syndrome infants had a higher frequency of less-complex grammatical forms and a lower use of more complex grammatical forms when compared with the linguistic environment of the normal children.

Buckhault, Rutherford, and Goldberg (1978) studied the maternal language of Down's Syndrome and normal infants approximately 1 year younger than the subjects of Buium *et al.* They found no differences in the mean length of utterance to the Down's syndrome and normal infants. The two studies together show that the mothers of normal infants provided a higher mean length of utterance for the 24-month-olds than for the 12-month-olds, but the mother's mean length of utterance remained constant across this age span for the Down's syndrome children. Since studies of maternal language have shown that maternal language complexity increases only after the child shows more complex language, Buckhault *et al.* suggest that the mothers in both groups in both studies were showing appropriate language. Thus, the different linguistic environment of Down's syndrome toddlers may be due to their differing linguistic behaviors which create differing expectations in the mothers.

A different example may more clearly demonstrate the circular function effect of the differing social environments and thus show how physically impaired infants produce their own development. A number of children with physical disabilities exhibit an extreme level of muscle tension (e.g., cerebral palsied children,Smith & Neisworth, 1975). A low level of muscle tension may be associated with a low level of arousal, which Johnson and Olley (1971) suggest may be psychological as well as medical. The model outlined by Goldberg (1977) suggests such a psychological effect. The model that she proposes focuses upon the contingencies that *each* member of the parent–infant dyad provides for the other. That is, the contingency of experiencing an infant's response is critical in developing an "expectation of effectiveness" in the mother. Although parental histories determine their initial expectation of being effective, this expectation will be influenced by the parent's experiences with the infant. Thus the infant with an impairment may not respond to the parent and contributes to the parental feeling of ineffectiveness or "helplessness." This may in turn lead to unresponsive care giving leading to further deterioration of muscle tone and lower levels of arousal. However, the negative circular function is not automatic. "A newborn with distinct limitations or handicaps may be extremely effective (in eliciting attention and appropriate care) when complemented by an unusually sensitive and responsive caregiver [p. 167]."

Support for Goldberg's model comes from the work of Prechtl (1963).

He found that mothers of hyperkinetic or hypokinetic babies were anxious about whether or not they treated the baby correctly because they assumed that the source of the problem was not the baby, but themselves. There appeared to be a relationship between the baby's not meeting the mothers expectations and the mothers' overprotective or rejecting attitude and behavior. Studies such as these need to look at maternal personality and health before birth and the delivery circumstances as well as the baby's abnormal behavior to explain more fully the interactions involved.

IMPLICATIONS FOR INTERVENTION

Historically, disabled infants produced their own development because they were placed in an institution simply as a result of being impaired. As a result of many studies (cf. Skeels & Dye, 1939; Tizard, 1962) that have documented detrimental effects of traditional institutional practices, we are experiencing two intervention trends to modify this differing social environment. The first trend is to modify the traditional practices of the institution. The reasons for improper stimulation are many, such as low staffing levels and low salaries for the staff that is there. To modify these practices, we need to use the knowledge of child development to provide appropriate care and stimulation for the residents of institutions. For Kugel (1970), this implied providing experiences similar to those of a middle-class home, such as socialization with adults and peers and an emphasis on motor skills. In a pilot study, Kugel (1970) found that seven children who were given such experiences were developing better than the earlier prognosis would have predicted.

The second trend stresses the desirability of home care over institutional care and is modifying the percentage of disabled children who are institutionalized. Because professional advice is often the basis for placing children in institutions, there are intervention programs in which professionals encourage home care and upgrade parental teaching practices. Townsend and Flanagan (1976) suggested that the parental decision whether or not to institutionalize the child was based on four factors: (a) maternal attitudes toward homemaking and child rearing; (b) use of local social service agencies; (c) the presence or absence of objectionable child behaviors; and (d) maternal perception of the hope of the child returning home or the required intensity of care. In an experimental preadmission program, Townsend and Flanagan tried to modify these factors. Their results showed that the experimental program, which included child training, did help to keep the child at home by decreasing objectionable child behaviors. The traditional intervention, counseling alone, also helped to keep the child at home, but with the cost of increased maternal conflict over homemaking and child rearing. This conflict certainly has implications for future decisions about the care of the child.

This idea of parent training has been enlarged upon by several researchers (cf., Hanson, 1977; Hayden & Dmitriev, 1975; Nielsen, Collins, Meisel, Lowry, Engl, & Johnson, 1975). These interventions are consistent with the model of this chapter and with Goldberg's (1977) model in that they seek to modify a very significant aspect of the social environment of the young disabled child by changing parental expectations and effectiveness. As one parent in Hanson's program stated, "Each time the teacher came into my home my thoughts were that my child cannot achieve this task, but through the parent training and desire to teach, I see results achieved every time [Hanson, 1977, p. 190]." Evaluations show that, indeed, these parents are effective. The infants in Hanson's program exhibited developmental milestones at earlier ages than did comparison groups of disabled infants, and these ages were close to the normal age range (Hanson, 1976).

Such interventions help to evaluate the notion of circular functioning because they are often applied to prevent the occurrence of handicaps. These preventive interventions are also important in explicating the contextual model, because research has shown that the development (even of risk children) "cannot be predicted independently of subsequent caretaking experiences. [Beckwith, 1976, p. 120; also see Sameroff & Chandler, 1975]."

The Influence of Disability during Childhood

As the young child grows out of infancy, increasing pressures are exerted to socialize the child in activities such as feeding, toileting, language, and cooperation. However, the young disabled child may not experience such socialization pressures. Battle (1974) suggested that this is due to the similarities between the infant and the older, severely handicapped child. These infants and children are totally dependent on others and "must be fed, cleaned, moved, stimulated not to fret, protected from danger [p. 132]." Just as society does not expect infants to acquire any social skills, neither does it expect social skills of the handicapped child. This may be due to the delay in achieving locomotion which is associated with many physical disabilities during childhood. The acquisition of walking skill is the usual demarcation of infancy, and toddlerhood is a period of increasing independence and socialization. When a child cannot walk, societal expectations are for immature socialization, and the disability thus becomes a handicap. However, there is great variability among handicapped children. Even a child who is immobile may be responsive and initiate social interaction.

The dependency associated with physical disability can often create a crisis in child rearing. The normal pattern of development allows the care giver to provide a decreasing intensity of care as the child grows. However, the intensity of the care of the physically disabled child often increases. Moving a 10- to 20-lb. infant is of little difficulty for most care givers. Although carrying a 30-lb. 3-year-old is more difficult, it is not beyond the physical ability of most adults. However, moving or even restraining an older child or adolescent becomes impractical for many care givers. The type of crisis thus created is what Farber (1960) termed a "role organization crisis." It stems from an inability to cope with the child over a long period of time and is associated with poor maternal health.

Obviously, the intensity of care giving and subsequent child-rearing crises are influenced by the nature and severity of the child's impairment. Kogan and Tyler (1973) observed interaction in mother–child pairs with a physically handicapped (mostly cerebral palsied) child, a mentally retarded child, and a normal child. Mothers of physically handicapped children used more assertive control and warm responses when compared to mothers of normal children. Stinson (1978a) suggested that "the hearing-impaired child may not respond readily to the mother's effort to teach social conduct, even if these efforts are extensive [p. 80]." Immature social skills and the lack of response probably lead to frustration in the mother, thereby making it even more difficult for her to try to teach her child in the future.

Cummings (1976; Cummings, Bayley & Rie, 1966) studied the personality of parents of disabled children. In their study of maternal personality variables, Cummings et al. (1966) found support for the clinical observation that having a child with a deficit is a psychologically stressful experience. Personality variables of 240 mothers of mentally retarded, chronically ill, neurotic, and control (no diagnosed deficiencies) children were assessed using the Edwards Personal Preference Schedule. The variables of concern were self-esteem, dysphoric affect (depression), interpersonal satisfaction, and child-rearing attitudes. In general, the mothers of handicapped children showed greater dysphoric affect, less self-esteem, and less interpersonal satisfaction than control mothers (there were no significant differences in child-rearing attitudes). The mothers of the neurotic children were the most deviant in comparison to the controls, and the mothers of chronically ill children were the least deviant. In the study of paternal personality using the same methodology, Cummings (1976) found that the mentally retarded child had a greater negative impact on the father than did the chronically ill child. These fathers showed greater depressive feeling, a preoccupation with the child, but less enjoyment of the child, lower self-acceptance, higher order and lower dominance. Cummings (1976) described this as a pattern of neurotic-like constriction in these fathers of mentally retarded children.

These differences in parental personality may be the partial cause of what some researchers have termed the "vulnerable child syndrome." Green and Solnit (1964) hypothesized that children whose parents expect (or expected) them to die (e.g., because they had a serious illness from which they were not expected to recover) would often react with a psychosocial disturbance. In examining the clinical records of 25 such children ages 17 months to 14 years, they discovered a pattern of parent behavior including pathological separation difficulties, inability to set disciplinary limits, overprotection, and overconcern with child's bodily functions; they label this a "vulnerable child syndrome." Because not all parents of children who recover from critical illnesses develop this syndrome, Green and Solnit suggest that there are variables in the family history that might predict this. Thus a contextual model that includes the familial level is helpful in understanding this syndrome.

Rose (1961; Rose, Boggs, Adlerstein, Trigos, Rigg, & Crowther, 1960) also studied the mothers of such vulnerable children. When 90 mothers of children with Rh incompatibility were studied, Rose et al. (1960) found that these mothers saw their children as less viable both at birth and as the child grew. Reassurances from physicians about the health of the children did not affect this attitude. While these mothers had reared other children successfully, their inaccurate perception of the meaning of state changes in these infants was an impediment to the fostering of healthy development. In a follow-up study, Rose (1961) suggested that the original anxiety about the viability of the child with physical abnormalities is again produced at each new maturational period. This new period brings rapid change and thus insecurity about the earlier assurances regarding the child's good health. These mothers are unable to respond appropriately to changes or to develop close ties with the infant–child. However, if substitute caretakers were available, these children did not develop physical disorganization.

These studies show that even when an impairment does not still exist, the threat of one in the past is capable of producing a handicap. The parents of vulnerable children showed a preoccupation with the physical well-being of their children. Similarly, Richardson (1969) concluded that parents of the physically disabled child focus on physical and motor functioning with a resultant loss of concern for cognitive or social development.

However, this overprotection by mothers of physically disabled children is not always negative. In a study of deaf children, Stinson (1978b) suggested that professionals need to understand how deafness is related to child rearing, especially maternal overprotectiveness. He found that maternal help, one aspect of overprotection, was related to achievement motivation if the mother was flexible. A high level of achievement in the child was associated with maternal help and reward that matched the child's capabilities. Thus professionals should concentrate on helping mothers evaluate their children's abilities, rather than on seeking to eliminate overprotectiveness.

In addition to mothering disability, the disabled child may be a "vulnerable child" because of the potential for child abuse. In a review paper, Friedrich and Boriskin (1976) suggested that the child plays more than a passive role in child abuse because "particular children produce parental stress reactions [p. 581]" that may lead to abuse. Prematurity, mental retardation, and physical handicaps have all been associated with greater incidences of abuse. Therefore, Friedrich and Boriskin (1976) conclude that "the special child is at greater risk for abuse [p. 589]."

THE IMPACT ON THE FAMILY

Beginning with the classic reports of Farber (1959), Tizard and Grad (1961), and Ross (1964), researchers have looked at the effect of a child's physical disability on family functioning. In a study of physically hand-icapped children and their families, McMichael (1972) found that psychological stress was imposed on the rest of the family by the presence of the disabled child. The parents experienced anxiety about their child and about themselves. The anxiety over their children was related to the severity of the disability, the prognosis, the child's future, and the ultimate care of the child (i.e., whether or not to institutionalize the child). Their personal anxieties concerned future pregnancies, marital disharmonies, and their health (both physical and mental). When there was an element of rejection in the parent–child relationship, the adjustment of the child was poor. McMichael also found that the psychological stress in siblings was related to the severity of the disability, the extent of maternal anxiety, and the handicapped child's own emotional difficulties. She concluded that realistic acceptance of the handicap by both parents was the key to the successful adjustment of the family.

Carver and Carver (1972) and McAllister, Butler, and Lei (1973) studied the social interaction of families with a disabled child. McAllister *et al.* compared the social interaction of 281 families with a retarded child to 784 families without a retarded child. They found systematic differences in interaction among the families that were related to the degree of retardation and subsequent visibility of the handicaps. More severe retardation was associated with less extrafamilial interaction and distortions in intrafamilial interactions. Carver and Carver (1972) also found patterns of decreased interaction in social relationships.

Howard (1978) summarized most families' adjustment to having a handicapped child. The first reactions are depression and denial, interspersed with anger. There is great anxiety about the future, the child's disability and role, and the family's social adjustment. The healing process, when it begins, must include a partial acceptance of the problem. However, "it seems unrealistic to expect parents to fully accept their situation and to have the same confidence in parenting their handicapped child as they do in parenting their normal children [p. 279]."

SOCIOCULTURAL INFLUENCES

The impact of the physically disabled child on the family and on the child's subsequent development is not mediated solely by parental personality, the severity of the disability or any other individual or familial variable. The social climate also mediates the effect of a handicapped child. When economic resources and community support are scarce, greater stress is placed on the family (Farber, 1959; Gorham, des Jardins, Page, Pettis, & Schieber, 1975; McMichael, 1972; Tizard & Grad, 1961). In part, this is because the needs of these families are greater. Thus, the parents of disabled children need to be released periodically from the unusually heavy demands of parenting (Gordon, 1977). Parents of normal children get such relief as the children grow; for parents of disabled children it must come from outside. A second reason for this greater stress is the inability to obtain generic services. These are the "typical services which families with nonhandicapped children either receive outright or purchase for a standard price [Kenowitz, Gallaher, & Edgar, 1977, p. 31]." These include medical and dental care, insurance, child care, public transportation, social activities, ability to eat in a restaurant, cosmetic services (such as haircuts), and access to religion. An analysis of these services indicated that "few services are equally available to the handicapped and nonhandicapped [Kenowitz, *et al.*, 1977, p. 38]."

IMPLICATIONS FOR INTERVENTION

In describing and explaining the development of the physically disabled child, the research just presented is relevant to the contextual model in a number of ways. First, the work of Green and Solnit (1964) and Rose (1961; Rose *et al.*, 1960) strongly suggests that a sensitive social environment is sufficient to create a handicap. Even when there is no biological impairment, according to physicians, the parents' perception of a health threat can result in physical and/or psychosocial disturbance. Rose's (1961) suggestion for primary prevention also makes use of the life-span perspective in assessing the effect of the period of crisis on later period. Because the maternal perception of the viability of the child can be manipulated more effectively during the crisis, Rose suggested that physicians consider the long-term effect of how they tell the parents that the child might die.

The work of Battle (1964), Gordon (1977), and others also emphasizes the importance of examining the constant changes that are a part of every level of functioning. As physically disabled children grow, their care requires adaptation on the part of their families, communities, and even society. Thus, it is not enough to document the adjustment of the family at birth or at the time of diagnosis of the impairment. The long-term changes of the child and every level of the social environment must be studied to see the transactions between them.

Two intervention programs may serve as examples. Shere and Kastenbaum (1966) studied 13 mother–child pairs in which the child was severely afflicted by cerebral palsy. The children who were between the ages of 2½ years and 4 years, 8 months could neither walk nor speak. The mothers of these children focused their attention on their child's physical functioning. They defined the child's happiness as a lack of crying, and the child's passivity was equated with being a good child. Thus, the mothers did not negatively evaluate the lack of activity and responsiveness in the children. The medical personnel concerned with the children also focused on their physical functioning. In Shere and Kastenbaum's opinion, these children were in double jeopardy, once due to their organic impairments and again due to the mother–child interaction pattern. The intervention program focused on the importance of play and toy-related activities to cognitive development. For example, they stressed the importance of having toys within reach and helping the child recover those toys to develop object permanence. Shere and Kastenbaum (1966) suggest that success in the intervention was due to greater previous involvement with the child and a favorable shift in maternal attitude. They concluded that the design of intervention efforts must "take into consideration the total life situation of the mother and child [p. 326]." Thus, the pattern of interaction already established and maternal attitudes should be evaluated before intervention.

In a later intervention, Bromwich (1976) used a developmental sequence of interaction to deal with the constant change. Rather than teaching the mother to teach skills to the child, Bromwich suggested that positive mother–child interaction could be taught and that this would carry over to later developmental periods. She suggested six steps for the sequence of positive mother–child interaction starting with the mother enjoying being with the child and ending with the mother independently generating activities appropriate to the child's stage. This sequence was derived from the assumptions that mother–child interaction is a reciprocal process with each changing the other, that the affective aspect of the interaction is important, and that the ultimate goal of the intervention should be the mother's independence.

In criticizing programs that focused solely on the functional limitations of the child, these programs instead sought to modify the child's social environment to foster the development of the disabled children. However, they have not analyzed the sociocultural level of functioning that influences the development of the physically disabled child. Consistent with our contextual model, research strongly emphasizes the importance of sociocultural influences and the reciprocal nature of the influence. McMichael (1972) showed that social conditions affect the families' adjustment to the presence of a physically disabled child. In her estimation, the study also demonstrated that a relatively small number of disabilities complicated the lives of a considerably larger group.

In addition to sociocultural influences there are also historical effects to consider. Dunlap and Hollingsworth (1977) studied how disabled children affected their families. They concluded that the families in their study were not significantly affected. This is in contrast to earlier studies, which found that disabled children seriously disrupt their families' pattern of life. The discrepancy may be due to two factors. First, the disabilities in the earlier research may have been more severe. However, the discrepancy may also reflect a "cohort effect." As historical changes have brought more community services and better acceptance of disabled children, the negative impact of these children on their families may have indeed been lessened. In the last decades, a number of sociocultural changes have resulted from the historical events of federal legislation and litigation, especially in the area of education.

The School Experience of Physically Disabled Children

The educational process is a major socializing force in modern western culture. During middle childhood and adolescence, teachers and peers become major influences in the social environments of children. However, the school experience of physically disabled children may be very different from that of their peers.

Before the 1970s, many physically disabled children were excluded from the regular educational process. For the school year 1972–1973, 386,000 physically disabled children were unserved by the educational system. This represents 48% of all such children aged 0–19 years (USOE–BEH cited in Sontag, 1977). Even when these children were receiving schooling, a majority of them were receiving it in segregated settings such as special schools or residential institutions. The social environment of these schools isolated the physically disabled from their nondisabled peers, and such isolation often resulted in a handicap.

Legislation and litigation in recent years have changed the patterns of both exclusion and institutionalization for the physically disabled child. Court decisions since 1971 have given the right to appropriate education to all children who had previously been excluded, including the physically disabled (Abeson, 1972; 1974). Following this litigation, the Education for All Handicapped Children Act, Public Law 94–142, was passed and signed in November 1975. This law reaffirms the right of every child to a free appropriate public education. Among its provisions are guarantees for appropriate evaluation, the right to an individualized educational program, the right to education in the least restrictive environment, and procedural safeguards, including due process guarantees. As the provisions of Public Law 94–142 were gradually phased in between 1978 and 1980, the status of schooling for the physically disabled also changed. Thus, research on the school experience of these children may be dated, and its findings need to be reexamined using our knowledge of historical and sociocultural changes.

One way in which the school experience changed is through the provision of education in the "least restrictive environment." The law man-

dated that handicapped and nonhandicapped children be educated together to the greatest extent possible. This means that the handicapped
children will be moved from segregated settings to settings where they
can interact in more normal ways with peers. In studies of the effects of
such integration, researchers have found that integration does not automatically create interaction. Esner (1977) found that, whereas parent involvement increased in integrated Head Start classrooms, those children
with serious handicaps experienced the greatest social distance from their
peers. Guralnick (1976) concluded that the simple presence of nonhandicapped children was not beneficial to handicapped children. Instead,
interactions, such as using nonhandicapped peers as resources, must be
planned and guided. Keeping in mind that sociocultural events have
probably changed the school experience of disabled children, previous
research provides some indication of this social environment.

RELATIONSHIPS WITH TEACHERS

When children enter school, the significant adults in their lives include
not only their parents, but also their teachers. In most cases, the influence
of the teacher is different from that of the parent. For example, Newman
and Doby (1973) found that social competence in brain-damaged and
Down's syndrome children was related to teacher expectations, but not
to parental expectations. This is not to imply that teacher expectations
caused social competence, but to suggest that with more realistic expectations teachers may exert a different influence from that of the parents.

One influence on teachers' relationships with their pupils is the physical
attractiveness of the child. (See Sorell and Nowak, Chapter 13, this volume, for a review pertaining to nonhandicapped children.) Ross and Salvia
(1975) studied teachers' reactions to unattractive, but not deformed, children. They found that the teachers suggested placement in an educable
mentally retarded (EMR) class and that further psychological evaluation
would reveal lower functioning than that presented in the case history.
The teachers also predicted future difficulties in peer relationships and
future academic difficulties. Richman (1978) studied teachers' perceptions
of children with cleft lips and/or palates; the teachers knew the children
they were ranking. Although there were no differences in the behavior
ratings or in academic performance, there were differences in the ratings
of intellectual ability. Children with noticeable facial disfiguration were
rated less accurately by their teachers than children with relatively normal
appearances. The intelligence of children with facial disfigurement and
above average intelligence was underestimated, a finding consistent with
the work of Ross and Salvia (1975) and other previous research. However,
the teachers overestimated the intellectual ability of those children with
lower than average intelligence and facial disfigurement. Richman (1978)
suggested that this may be a sympathetic response to children who are

below average in both intelligence and physical attractiveness. Such an hypothesis has many implications when considered within the contextual model, but it needs further investigation.

Physical attractiveness and the variability of the visibility of physical impairments (i.e., the degree of disfigurement), are also critical for the understanding of peers' responses to children with physical disabilities.

PEER RELATIONSHIPS

In a review article, Levitt and Cohen (1976) have shown that peer attitudes toward handicapped children are age-related. Children are aware of physical disabilities at about 4 years of age, and they hold negative attitudes about children with disabilities by 5 years of age. Younger children hold less negative attitudes. Consistent with the research on integrated settings, Levitt and Cohen suggested that contact with handicapped peers alone does not lessen negative attitudes, and indeed, may intensify them. However, Rapier, Adelson, Carey, and Croke (1972) found that a year after classes for orthopedically impaired children were established in a school, the normal children in third, fourth, and fifth grades did show some attitude changes. Most of the children had positive attitudes before the integration, but after the contact, the older children were also more realistic. In general, when assessing the attitudes of children using the Attitude Toward Disabled Scale, girls express more favorable attitudes and there are no differences in attitudes between normal and gifted children (Lazar, Orpet, & Revie, 1972).

A series of studies has examined children's attitudes toward specific disabilities. Richardson, Goodman, Hastorf, and Dornbusch (1961) found a uniformity of rankings for pictures of children with physical disabilities. The ranking (from most to least preferred) was (a) child with no handicap; (b) child with crutches and leg brace; (c) child in a wheelchair with a blanket covering the legs; (d) child with the left hand missing; (e) child with facial disfigurement; and (f) an obese child. This ranking was uniform across sex, presence of a physical handicap, race, socioeconomic status, and urban–rural settings. Almost a decade later, Alessi and Anthony (1969) replicated the findings of Richardson *et al.*, in a study of 42 physically handicapped children. Using an expanded set of 21 pictures, Richardson (1971a) found that amputations were the least liked of the disabilities, although the use of artificial limbs (especially for legs) increased the ranking. Because artificial limbs may be more easily made to look "normal" (e.g., by clothing that covers it) than an amputation, the visibility of the handicap may be one critical variable in children's attitudes toward disabled peers. However, this study used pictures of the disabilities, which probably enhanced the "visibility" variable because clues about movement or functional limitations were not available. Richardson (1971a) concluded that not only do disabled children need to be taught better social skills, but peers and adults need to be helped in developing more favorable attitudes toward these children.

Richardson (1971a) thus seems to adopt a model of circular functioning to prevent further handicaps in social skills. In his review chapter (Richardson, 1969), he suggested that the voluntary social relations of physically disabled children are negatively affected in both direct and indirect ways. Directly, there are functional limitations in mobility and both verbal and nonverbal communication that may limit disabled children's interaction with their peers. Indirectly, the children's physical appearance may subtly influence the interaction. For example, before integration, Rapier *et al.* (1972) found that physically disabled children were perceived as weak and in need of attention. Richardson (1969) suggested that the nonhandicapped child who is likely to initiate contact with a disabled peer is isolated, has had less social experience, and has learned peer values less accurately than the child who does not initiate contact.

The stereotypes that Richardson (1969) suggested affected social interaction were investigated by Willey and McCandless (1973). In comparing stereotypes for orthopedically handicapped and educable mentally retarded children, the orthopedically disabled were perceived by normal children to be "ideal" children and given favorable characteristics. The unfavorable characteristics ascribed to the disabled children were probably realistic: not healthy, not strong, sick, weak, nervous, and gets teased. In contrast, the retarded children were only given one favorable characteristic, happy, and many unfavorable ones. The stereotype of the orthopedically handicapped child was thus positive, but that is no guarantee of social interaction with peers (Willey & McCandless, 1973).

How do attitudes and stereotypes translate into social status for physically disabled children? Kennedy and Bruininks (1974) investigated the social status of hearing-impaired children in integrated first- and second-grade classrooms. After evaluating group status, peer acceptance, and self-status, they found no significant differences between the status of normal and disabled children. Indeed, those children with a profound hearing loss enjoyed the highest group status and were better accepted than were children with a less severe loss. In addition, at this age, the disabled children were as perceptive in evaluating their own status in the group as the normal children. Thus these disabled children are not handicapped with regard to social status.

Richardson (1971b) enlarged upon this idea by suggesting that preferences are made on more than just the presence of a disability. Factors such as the behavior skills and emotions of the child come into play. Thus, disabilities should be more salient in the initial meeting than over time. To study this, Richardson looked at the friendship choices of children who were not handicapped, who had visible disabilities, or who had disabilities that were not visible. At first, the nonhandicapped child with normative peer values picked a nonhandicapped child for a friend, whereas the nonhandicapped child with atypical peer values picked a child with a visible disability. After 13 days of mutual experience at summer camp, no association was found between values and friendship choices for the nonhandicapped children. The pattern was reversed for handicapped children with a visible disability; the children with normative values picked a child with a visible disability, and the child with atypical peer values picked a nonhandicapped child.

IMPLICATIONS FOR INTERVENTION

In attitudes and initial meetings, the visibility of the disability is a critical variable in determining whether or not the social environment is handicapping. Over time, the behaviors of the children become more important, and a less visible disability can even be glorified into an advantage. This might be one way of explaining the high social status of hearing-impaired children found by Kennedy and Bruininks (1974). Disabilities that are visible to peers also serve as explanations for atypical behaviors, whereas dysfunctions having no visible source (e.g., retardation) are harder to understand. The favorable behavior of physically disabled found by Willey and McCandless (1973) is an example of this type of social environment.

As the research shows no differences or greater social status for physically disabled children, are these children handicapped? Possibly not, if we only analyze one level of functioning (i.e., peer relationships, at one point in time). However, the contextual model suggests that such a static approach does not yield a complete understanding. To better examine the socialization of these children, we need to look at different levels of functioning across time. Richman and Harper (1978; Richman, 1976) suggest that the disabled have learned to avoid situations that may lead to negative responses. This avoidance may be adaptive at some levels, but the disabled children were less competitive and confident in the classroom situation where independence and competitiveness are important.

Lynch and Arndt (1973) looked not only at different levels, but also at different ages when examining response to frustration. They found that physically disabled children were not significantly different from their nonhandicapped peers in their external expression of aggressive reactions to frustration. Thus, their behaviors on this level did not set them apart from their peers. However, on an individual–psychological level, there were differences in secondary coping strategies and developmental changes in these strategies. At 6 years of age, the physically disabled children minimized or denied the frustration. At age 10, the children took a greater intropunitive approach and blamed themselves as the cause of the frustration more than their nonhandicapped peers. These findings underline the importance of a developmental, life-span approach. Whereas there may be no differences on one level, at one point in time, the differences on another level at that time may later result in differences on the first level. For example, the differences in self-blame on the psychological level may result in differing social status during adolescence.

As another illustration, consider research on a group of atypical children: those with growth deficiency. Extremely short stature is the result of a deficiency in growth hormones in some humans. The syndrome of hypopituitary dwarfism is characterized by normal intellectual capacity and normal height at birth. Half of these dwarfs are below the third percentile of height norms by 2 years. In a study of the personality development of children with growth hormone deficiency, Rotnem, Genel, Hintz, and Cohen (1977) found that these children had normal IQs, but were socially immature. Their disturbances included social isolation, powerlessness, a sense of incompetence, low self-esteem, and the inhibition of aggression. Although some central nervous system maturation may be related to the endocrine disorder, Rotnem *et al.*, suggested that their development may be better understood in relation to parenting. They suggested that personality normally develops with the size of the child, but these children are seen as too young to take on family roles. Because the responses of parents and physicians are those suitable to younger children, the children retreated to the passivity and infantilism ascribed to them. The overprotection of the parents also limits the child's self-reliance.

Thus, the social environment is sensitive to the children's impairment of short stature, but not to their normal intellectual development. The expectations of the social environment are for behaviors appropriate to a younger child, and age-appropriate behaviors may be overlooked. The children are thus handicapped. This explanation is supported by another finding of Rotnem *et al.* Children whose families foster a sense of competence by having age-appropriate expectations see themselves as socially integrated and useful and do not develop problems.

Therapy for hypopituitary dwarfism is available, but restricted because of the scarcity of human growth hormone. What happens to the personality development of these children after treatment? Kusalic and Forten (1975) found that the treatment affected their height, but not necessarily their adjustment. The children remained depressed and apathetic, but were able to verbally express aggression. However, those who were younger (starting at age 5 years, 10 months) showed better adjustment. Our model would lead to this expectation and suggest that follow-ups should show a continuation of better adjustment for the younger children. The model would also suggest that the reactions of teachers and peers would be critical to the personality development of these children. Thus, children who began treatment before extended contact with teachers and peers (e.g., before school entrance) should also show better adjustment.

This discussion of research in the area of growth deficiency allows two conclusions. First, the contextual model usefully integrates research findings. Second, the contextual model has utility in that it delineates avenues for further research. In this example, the model would include the socio-cultural influence of schooling by examining teacher and peer relations. These influences become even more important during adolescence.

Physical Disability during Adolescence

During the adolescent period, the influences on the lives of children change. As ties with parents loosen, the peer group assumes greater importance. For example, the onset of dating emphasizes the need for social skills and physical attractiveness. Adolescents are also pressured to make educational and vocational role decisions that will shape the rest of their lives. Whereas the striving for identity occurs in both the non-disabled and disabled, the physically disabled adolescent continues to exist in a different social environment.

PEER RELATIONSHIPS

In his review, Richardson (1969) noted that nondisabled adolescents perceive that relationships with disabled peers require more commitment and are more difficult to disengage than relationships with nondisabled peers. As a result, the disabled peer may have reduced opportunities for social interaction. After continued contact with disabled peers, the non-disabled distort their opinions, show less variability of opinions and give shorter responses in social interaction with the disabled. Therefore, disabled adolescents are handicapped because they do not receive accurate or spontaneous feedback and they are thus hampered in developing appropriate social skills.

Schiff (1973) found that deaf and hearing adolescents were different in one particular social skill, perceptions of social cues. Although hearing and deaf adolescents paid equal attention to nonverbal cues from mouth, deaf adolescents paid more attention to gross motor activity in judging hostility. Hearing adolescents gave more attention to the eyes.

When disabled adolescents receive care outside the home, the demands for new social skills in adolescence are often overlooked. Hawke and Auerbach (1975) suggest that opportunities for independence are difficult to find in centers designed to carry through on doctors' orders. In addition, the increasing sexuality of the adolescent is ignored or restricted.

According to Bansavage (1968), individuals with congenital defects have lower social status than do those with later acquired disabilities because of limited social interactions as well as the more severe natures of their physical disabilities. Greater degrees of deviance and disability are related to lower social acceptance during adolescence, but this relationship is modified by personality and intelligence.

With limitations on their social interactions, are the self-perceptions of disabled adolescents negatively influenced? Weinberg-Asher (1976) says that physically disabled college students do not incorporate negative stereotypes in their self-images. Using the 29 dimensions of the Self-Description Questionnaire, she found only three differences between disabled and able-bodied college students. The disabled saw themselves as more religious, more opposed to abortion and more dependent on others for help. The lack of differences may not be surprising as disabled adolescents who go to college are probably a select sample. Other researchers have found lowered self-esteem in physically disabled adolescents. As McDaniel (1976) concluded, "the increasing emphasis on physique and appearance during adolescence serves as a critical variable in the process of personality development for the physically disabled adolescent [p. 21]."

PSYCHOLOGICAL ADJUSTMENT

Just as physical appearance influences self-esteem, it also influences other areas of adjustment such as vocational aspirations. Using questions derived from the Scale for Vocational Development, Goldberg (1974) compared children with an invisible handicap, congenital heart disease, to children with a visible handicap, facial burns. Vocational aspirations, post high-school career plans, work values, and self-image were all higher for those with congenital heart disease. Goldberg concluded that a visible disability without physical limitations had a more deleterious effect than an invisible disability with severe limitations. He also suggested that children with heart problems have had a long time to adjust to their limitations, whereas those with burns had experienced a sudden trauma.

From other studies that compared various handicaps, we can conclude that self-disclosure is an issue for the juvenile epileptic, but not for the juvenile diabetic, apparently because greater stigma is attached to epilepsy than to diabetes, although both are serious, chronic diseases (Davis, Shipp, & Pattishall, 1965; Goldin, Perry, Morgolin, Stotsky, & Foster, 1971). There are sex differences as well. Boys adapt better to amputation and the "use of a prosthesis than girls because they are better able to accept the cosmetic limitations of an artificial limb [McDaniel, 1976, p. 23]."

Psychological adjustment is affected by other critical variables such as locus of control and locus of evaluation. Deaf, blind, and other disabled youth perceive themselves to be under the external control of such factors as luck, opportunity, and the pressures of the significant adults in their lives (Blanton & Nunnally, 1964; Vigliano & Shontz, 1964). Deaf adolescents also exhibit an externalized locus of evaluation, which means they depend upon an external frame of reference to judge actions. Because the disabled adolescent "views much of the control of his life as being imposed upon him rather than self-determined [McDaniel, 1976, p. 21]," his vocational role decisions and emotional maturity are impaired.

IMPLICATIONS FOR INTERVENTION

Because of the importance of the peer group and the emphasis on physical appearance, physically disabled adolescents appear likely to be handicapped. They have lower social status, self-esteem and vocational aspirations than their nondisabled peers. However, to truly understand the consequences of physical disability we must examine the adjustment of the disabled before their impairment (when this is possible). In a rare example of prospective data in this area, Barton and Cattell (1972) tested New Zealand high school students. Upon retesting 5 years later, 25% (148) of these adolescents had experienced a major chronic illness in the interim. On the pretest using the 16 Personality Factor Questionnaire, those adolescents who were later to have serious illnesses were lower on ego strength (C), higher in sensitivity and dependency (I), and more unconventional (M), radical (QI), and anxious (QII). These differences raise the question as to whether certain personality factors affect the probability of chronic illness. Certainly, studies of adult patients have shown that survivors of chronic diseases significantly differ from non-survivors (McDaniel, 1976).

Barton and Cattell (1972) also found an interaction of groups and occasions. Those adolescents without chronic illness followed the usual pattern of personality development, showing an increase in ego strength (C) and a decrease in guilt proneness (O), ergic tension (Q4), and anxiety (QII). The chronically ill adolescents decreased in ego strength (C) and were stable in guilt proneness (O), ergic tension (Q4) and anxiety (QII). This study offers credible evidence that physical disability does alter personality functioning. During the adolescent period, such disability interferes with the normal growth of emotional maturity and independence.

What are the intervention implications of such findings? Some researchers have tried to modify the attitudes of the nondisabled toward the disabled. Wilson and Alcorn (1969) used a simulation in which 80 college students "experienced" blindness, deafness, or the loss of the dominant hand. The Attitude Toward Disabled Persons scale was given before and after the simulation; there were no significant changes. However, the students reported feelings of frustration and insights into the behavior of the disabled. For example, they noted their embarrassment, their dependence on others, and the tendency to become isolated.

Unfortunately, greater insight by the disabled adolescent's peers does not provide a comprehensive intervention program. Our model suggests that intervention needs to occur on other levels in addition to that of the social network. In addition, the life-span perspective emphasizes both prevention and modification. The data of Barton and Cattell (1972) pose some challenging questions in this regard. Do the personality differences between disabled and nondisabled adolescents represent effective coping skills by the disabled? Can modification in the form of opportunities for emotional maturity and independence be achieved without sabotaging the disabled adolescent's truce with the disability?

The finding of pretest differences by Barton and Cattell raises the possibility of prevention. Another study documenting the need for prevention also demonstrates the circular aspect of disability and psychological functioning. Littlemore, Metcalfe, and Johnson (1974) found a lag in the skeletal maturity of psychiatrically disturbed adolescents after age 14. As Littlemore *et al.* were able to eliminate environmental deficiencies as a cause, they suggest that the skeletal immaturity may be the result of long-standing severe emotional distress. Barton and Cattell suggest that disability may cause changes in psychological functioning. Littlemore *et al.* suggest that atypical psychological functioning may cause disability. Both are possible and, from the perspective of our model, psychological functioning and disability are best understood in relation to each other and to familial sociocultural, and historical influences as well.

Conclusions

There are two ways to evaluate the use of the contextual model in understanding physical disability. The first approach is to analyze whether or not the research has been usefully integrated by this model and whether meaningful suggestions for further research can be made. The second way is to evaluate the feasibility of interventions suggested by the model. Both approaches were used in this chapter.

The research reviewed in this chapter has been integrated by our model, but the usefulness is limited by the unitemporal nature of the research. There are also variables that have been neglected in the research and that should be included in these research strategies. The age of onset of the disability is often mentioned as a mediating influence on the effect of physical disability, but little research has examined this variable (McDaniel, 1976). Examinations of age differences and sex differences in the effect of disabilities are likewise often lacking (Richardson, 1969). The hypothesized influence of sociocultural variables also needs further examination with cross-cultural research. Important sociocultural variables to be considered are attitudes of "handicapism," levels of technology, and exposure of the disabled in the media.

Many interventions during the past decade have resulted from the trend of "normalization." The severely disabled who were confined to institutions a generation ago are now the focus of public attention as a result of increasing participation in the mainstream of life. What is normalization? It is the participation in the normal events of the time, and unfortunately, that includes trouble and strife. As Park (1975) points out, normalization includes the right of the disabled to leave the "sanitized life" and be exposed to risk. The possibility of failure must exist along with the possibility of success.

Interventions that stress normality are analogous to contextual approaches because they emphasize the effect of all levels of functioning. For example, behavioral disturbances that are correlated with physical disability may not be the direct result of the disability but of the sensory isolation of hospitalization and home confinement or special education placement. However, evaluations of these normalizing interventions have not used the contextual approach. For example, because deinstitutionalization has been mandated on the sociocultural level (i.e., through legal processes), many individuals have been moved to institutions of smaller size. However, the risks as well as the benefits of such moves have not been examined.

In spite of the trend toward normalization, the majority of the interventions still influence only one level of functioning at one point in time. Reeducation of the helping professions may be necessary to achieve comprehensive rehabilitation services, but our model suggests that such approaches will be more efficient. In total, the ideas of the model proposed in this chapter are often seen as ideals by rehabilitation professionals; they embrace the usefulness of the contextual model for interventions. The research is also usefully integrated by the contextual approach. However, additional research and application are necessary to test the utility of the contextual model because all of its implications have not been explored. Consistent with the assumptions of the contextual approach, further study must always examine the developmental nature of the influence of physical disability and the interdependence of different levels of functioning.

Acknowledgments

The author thanks Mary Katherine Hawryluk, Richard Lerner, Donald Peters, Stephen Richardson, and Annette Vance for their comments on an earlier version of this manuscript and Anne Goldman for her assistance with the library research.

References

Abeson, A. Movement and momentum: Government and the education of handicapped children. *Exceptional Children*, 1972, *39*, 63–66.

Abeson, A. Movement and momentum: Government and the education of handicapped children II. *Exceptional Children*, 1974, *41*, 109–116.

Alessi, D. F., & Anthony, W. A. The uniformity of children's attitudes toward disabilities. *Exceptional Children*, 1969, *35*, 543–545.

Bansavage, J. Social acceptance in a group of orthopedically impaired adolescents. *Proceedings of the 76th Annual Convention of the American Psychological Association*, 1968, 647–648.

Barton, K., & Cattell, R. Personality before and after a chronic illness. *Journal of Clinical Psychology*, 1972, *28*, 464–467.

Battle, C. U. Disruptions in the socialization of a young, severely handicapped child. *Rehabilitation Literature*, 1974, *35*, 130–140.

Beckwith, L. Care giver–infant interaction and the development of the risk infant. In T. Tjossem (Ed.), *Intervention strategies for high-risk infants and young children*. Baltimore: University Park Press, 1976.

Bell, R. Q., & Harper, L. V. *Child effects on adults*. Hillsdale, N.J.: Erlbaum, 1977.

Bijou, S. W. A functional analysis of retarded development. In N. R. Ellis (Ed.), *International review of research in mental retardation* (Vol. 1). New York: Academic Press, 1966.

Blanton, R., & Nunnally, J. Evaluative language processes in the deaf. *Psychological Reports*, 1964, *15*, 891–894.

Blatt, B., Bogdan, R., Biklen, D., & Taylor, S. From institution to community: A conversion model. In E. Sontag (Ed.), *Educational programming for the severely and profoundly handicapped*. Reston, Va.: The Council for Exceptional Children, 1977.

Bloom, J. L. Sex education for the physically handicapped. *Sexology*, 1970, *36*, 62–65.

Bray, G. P. Reactive patterns in families of the severely disabled. *Rehabilitation Counseling Bulletin*, 1977, *20*, 236–239.

Bromwich, R. M. Focus on maternal behavior in infant intervention. *American Journal of Orthopsychiatry*, 1976, *43*, 439–446.

Buckhault, J. A., Rutherford, R. B., & Goldberg, K. E. Verbal and nonverbal interaction of mothers with their Down's Syndrome and nonretarded infants. *American Journal of Mental Deficiency*, 1978, *82*, 337–343.

Buium, N., Rynders, J., & Turnure, J. Early maternal linguistic environment of normal and Down's syndrome language-learning children. *American Journal of Mental Deficiency*, 1974, *79*, 52–58.

Busch-Rossnagel, N. A., & Peters, D. L. Parental development in first-time mothers of handicapped, at-risk, and normal children. *International Journal of Rehabilitation Research*, 1980, 32, 229–231.

Carver, J. N., & Carver, N. E. *The family of the retarded child*. Syracuse: Syracuse University Press, 1972.

Cummings, S. T. The impact of the child's deficiency on the father: A study of fathers of mentally retarded and chronically ill children. *American Journal of Orthopsychiatry*, 1976, *46*, 246–255.

Cummings, S. T., Bayley, H. C., & Rie, H. E. Effects of the child's deficiency on the mother: A study of mothers of mentally retarded, chronically ill, and neurotic children. *American Journal of Orthopsychiatry*, 1966, *36*, 595–608.

Daniels, L. L., & Berg, C. M. The crisis of birth and adaptive patterns of parents of amputee children. *Clinical Proceedings, Children's Hospital, Washington, D.C.*, 1968, *24*, 108–117.

Davids, A. A research design for studying maternal emotionality before childbirth and after social interaction with the child. *Merrill-Palmer Quarterly*, 1968, *14*, 345–354.

Davids, A., & Holden, R. H. Consistency of maternal attitude and personality from pregnancy to 8 months following childbirth. *Developmental Psychology*, 1970, *2*, 364–366.

Davis, D., Shipp, J., & Pattishall, E. Attitudes of diabetic boys and girls toward diabetes *Diabetes*, 1965, *14*, 106–109.

Diller, L. Psychological aspects of physically handicapped children. In B. B. Wolman (Ed.), *Manual of child psychopathology*. New York: McGraw-Hill, 1972.

Dunlap, W. R., & Hollingsworth, J. S. How does a handicapped child affect the family? Implications for practitioners. *Family Coordinator*, 1977, *26*, 286–293.

English, R. W. The application of personality theory to explain psychological reactions to physical disability. *Rehabilitation Research and Practice Review*, 1971, *3*, 35–47.

Esner, G. L., Blatt, B., & Winschel, J. F. Head Start for the handicapped: Congressional mandate audit, *Exceptional Children*, 1977, *43* (4), 202–210.

Farber, B. Effects of a severely mentally retarded child on family integration. *Monographs of Society for Research in Child Development*, 1959, *24* (2, Serial no. 71).

Farber, B. Perceptions of crisis and related variables in the impact of a retarded child on the mother. *Journal of Health and Human Behavior*, 1960, *1*, 108–118.

Flapan, M. A paradigm for the analysis of child-bearing motivations prior to the birth of the first child. *American Journal of Orthopsychiatry*, 1969, *39*, 402–417.

Friedrich, W. N., & Boriskin, J. A. The role of the child in abuse: A review of the literature. *American Journal of Orthopsychiatry*, 1976, *39*, 402–417.

Gellman, W. Projections in the field of physical disability. *Rehabilitation Literature*, 1974, *35*, 2–9.

Goldberg, Richard T. Adjustment of children with invisible and visible handicaps: Congenital heart disease and facial burns. *Journal of Counseling Psychology*, 1974, *21*, 428–432.

Goldberg, S. Social competence in infancy: A model of parent–infant interaction. *Merrill-Palmer Quarterly*, 1977, *23*, 162–177.

Goldin, G., Perry, S., Morgolin, R., Stotsky, B., & Foster, J. *The rehabilitation of the young epileptic*, Lexington: D. C. Heath, 1971.

Gordon, G. *Role theory and illness.* New Haven, Conn.: College and University Press Services, 1966.

Gordon, R. Special needs of multihandicapped children under 6 and their families: One opinion. In E. Sontag (Ed.), *Educational programming for the severely and profoundly handicapped.* Reston, Va.: The Council for Exceptional Children, 1977.

Gorham, K. A., des Jardins, C., Page, R., Pettis, E., & Scheiber, B. Effect on parents. In N. Hobbs (Ed.), *Issues in the classification of children.* San Francisco: Jossey-Bass, 1975.

Green, M., & Solnit, A. J. Reactions to the threatened loss of a child: A vulnerable child syndrome. *Pediatrics*, 1964, *34*, 58–66.

Guralnick, M. J. The value of integrating handicapped and nonhandicapped preschool children. *American Journal of Orthopsychiatry*, 1976, *46*, 236–245.

Hanson, M. J. Evaluation of training procedures used in a parent implemented intervention program for Down's syndrome infants. *American Association for the Education of the Severely–Profoundly Handicapped*, 1976, *1*, 36–52.

Hanson, M. J. *Teaching your Down's syndrome infant: A guide for parents.* Baltimore: University Park Press, 1977.

Hawke, W. A., & Auerbach, A. Multidiscipline experience: A fresh approach to aid the multihandicapped child. *Journal of Rehabilitation*, 1975, *41*, 22–24.

Hayden, A. H., & Dmitrier, V. The multidisciplinary preschool program for Down's syndrome children at the University of Washington Model Preschool Center. In B. Z. Friedlander, G. M. Sterritt, & G. E. Kirk (Eds.), *Exceptional infant* (Vol. 3): *Assessment and intervention.* New York: Brunner/Mazel, 1975.

Howard, J. The influence of children's developmental dysfunctions on marital quality and family interaction. In R. M. Lerner & G. B. Spanier (Eds.), *Child influences on marital and family interaction: A life-span perspective.* New York: Academic Press, 1978.

Johnson, J. T., Jr., & Olley, J. J. Behavioral comparisons of mongoloid and nonmongoloid retarded persons: A review. *American Journal of Mental Deficiency*, 1971, *75* (5), 546–559.

Kennedy, P., & Bruininks, R. H. Social status of hearing-impaired children in regular classrooms. *Exceptional Children*, 1974, *40*, 336–342.

Kenowitz, L. A., Gallaher, J., & Edgar, E. Generic services for the severely handicapped and their families: What's available? In E. Sontag (Ed.), *Educational programming for the severely and profoundly handicapped.* Reston, Va.: The Council for Exceptional Children, 1977.

Klaus, M. H., & Kennell, J. H. *Mother–infant bonding.* St. Louis: C. V. Mosby, 1976.

Kogan, K. L., & Tyler, N. Mother–child interaction in young physically handicapped children. *American Journal of Mental Deficiency*, 1973, *77*, 492–497.

Kugel, R. B. Combating retardation in infants with Down's syndrome. *Children*, 1970, *17*, 188–192.

Kusalic, M., & Fortin, C. Growth hormone treatment in hypopituitary dwarfs: Longitudinal psychological effects. *Canadian Psychiatric Association Journal*, 1975, *20*, 325–331.

Lazar, A. L., Orpet, R. E., & Revie, V. A. Attitudes of young gifted boys and girls toward handicapped individuals. *Exceptional Children*, 1972, *38*, 489–490.

Levitt, E., & Cohen, S. Attitudes of children toward their handicapped peers. *Childhood Education*, 1976, *52*, 171–174.

Littlemore, D., Metcalfe, M., & Johnson, A. L. Skeletal immaturity in psychiatrically disturbed adolescents. *Journal of Child Psychology and Psychiatry*, 1974, *15*, 133–138.

Lynch, D. J., & Arndt, C. Developmental changes in response to frustration among physically handicapped children. *Journal of Personality Assessment*, 1973, *37*, 130–135.

McAllister, R. J., Butler, E. W., & Lei, T. J. Patterns of social interaction among families of behaviorally retarded children. *Journal of Marriage and the Family*, 1973, *35*, 93–100.

McDaniel, J. W. *Physical disability and human behavior*. New York: Pergamon Press, 1976.

McMichael, J. K. *Handicap: A study of physically handicapped children and their families*. Pittsburgh: University of Pittsburgh Press, 1972.

Newman, H. G., & Doby, J. T. Correlates of social competence among trainable mentally retarded children. *American Journal of Mental Deficiency*, 1973, *77*, 722–732.

Nielson, G., Collins, S., Meisel, J., Lowry, M., Engl, H., & Johnson, D. An intervention program for atypical infants. In B. Z. Friedlander, G. M. Sterritt, & G. E. Kirk (Eds.), *Exceptional infant* (Vol. 3): *Assessment and intervention*. New York: Brunner/Mazel, 1975.

Park, L. D. Barriers to normality for the handicapped adult in the United States. *Rehabilitation Literature*, 1975, *36*, 108–111.

Pepper, S. C. *World hypotheses*. Berkeley: University of California Press, 1942.

Pomerantz, D. J., & Marholin, D. Vocational habilitation: A time for a change. In E. Sontag (Ed.), *Educational programming for the severely and profoundly handicapped*. Reston, Va.: The Council for Exceptional Children, 1977.

Prechtl, H.F.R. The mother–child interaction in babies with minimal brain dysfunction (a follow-up study). In B. M. Foss (Ed.), *Determinants of infant behavior II*. New York: Wiley, 1963.

Rapier, J., Adelson, R., Carey, R., & Croke, K. Changes in children's attitudes toward the physically handicapped. *Exceptional Children*, 1972, *39*, 219–223.

Richardson, S. A. The effect of physical disability on the socialization of a child. In David A. Goslin (Ed.), *Handbook of socialization theory and research*. Chicago: Rand McNally, 1969.

Richardson, S. A. Patterns of medical and social research in pediatrics. *Acta Paediatrica Scandinavia*, 1970, *59*, 265–272.

Richardson, S. A. Handicap, appearance, and stigma. *Social Science and Medicine*, 1971, *5*, 621–628. (a)

Richardson, S. A. Children's values and friendships: A study of physical disability. *Journal of Health and Social Behavior*, 1971, *12*, 253–258. (b)

Richardson, S. A., Goodman, N., Hastorf, A. H., & Dornbusch, S. M. Cultural uniformity in reaction to physical disabilities. *American Sociological Review*, 1961, *26*, 241–247.

Richman, L. C. Behavior and achievement of cleft palate children. *Cleft Palate Journal*, 1976, *13*, 4–10.

Richman, L. C. The effects of facial disfigurement on teachers' perception of ability in cleft palate children. *The Cleft Palate Journal*, 1978, *15*, 155–160.

Richman, L., & Harper, D. School adjustment of children with observable disabilities. *Journal of Abnormal Child Psychology*, 1978, *6*, 11–18.

Riegel, K. F. Toward a dialectical theory of development. *Human Development,* 1975, *18,* 50–64.

Riegel, K. F. From traits and equilibrium to developmental dialectics. In W. Arnold (Ed.), *Nebraska Symposium on Motivation.* Lincoln: University of Nebraska Press, 1976. (a)

Riegel, K. F. The dialectics of human development. *American Psychologist,* 1976, *31,* 689–700. (b)

Rose, J. A. The prevention of mothering breakdown associated with physical abnormalities in the infant. In G. Caplan (Ed.), *Prevention of mental disorders in children.* New York: Basic Books, 1961.

Rose, J., Boggs, T. R., Adlerstein, A., Trigos, W., Rigg, I., & Crowther, P. The evidence for a syndrome of "mothering disability" consequent to threats to survival of neonates: A design for hypothesis testing including prevention in a prospective study. *American Journal of Diseases of Children,* 1960, *100,* 776.

Ross, A. O. *The exceptional child in the family.* New York: Grune & Stratton, 1964.

Ross, M. B., & Salvia, J. Attractiveness as a biasing factor in teacher judgments. *American Journal of Mental Deficiency,* 1975, *80,* 96–98.

Rotnem, D., Genel, M., Hintz, R., & Cohen, D. J. Personality development in children with growth hormone deficiency. *Journal of the American Academy of Child Psychiatry,* 1977, *16,* 412–416.

Ryckman, D. B., & Henderson, R. A. The meaning of a retarded child for his parents: A focus for counselors. *Mental Retardation,* 1965, *3* (4), 4–7.

Sameroff, A. J., & Chandler, M. J. Reproductive risk and the continuum of caretaking casualty. In F. D. Horowitz (Ed.), *Review of Child Development Research* (Vol. 4). Chicago: University of Chicago Press, 1975.

Schiff, W. Social perception in deaf and hearing adolescents. *Exceptional Children,* 1973, *39,* 289–297.

Schwartz, C. Normalization and idealism. *Mental Retardation,* 1977, *15* (6), 38–39.

Shere, E. S., & Kastenbaum, R. Mother–child interaction in cerebral palsy. Environmental and psychosocial obstacles to cognitive development. *Genetic Psychology Monographs,* 1966, *73,* 255–335.

Skeels, H. M., & Dye, H. B. A study of the effects of differential stimulation on mentally retarded children. *Proceedings of the American Association of Mental Deficiency,* 1939, *44,* 114–136.

Smith, R. M., & Neisworth, J. T. *The exceptional child: A functional approach.* New York: McGraw-Hill, 1975.

Solnit, A. J., & Stark, M. Mourning and the birth of the defective child. *Psychoanalytic Study of the Child,* 1961, *16,* 523–537.

Sontag, E. (Ed.), *Educational programming for the severely and profoundly handicapped.* Reston, Va.: The Council for Exceptional Children, 1977.

Stinson, M. Effects of deafness on maternal expectations about child development. *Journal of Special Education,* 1978, *12,* 75–81. (a)

Stinson, M. Deafness and motivation for achievement: Research with implications for parent counseling. *Volta Review,* 1978, *80,* 140–148. (b)

Susser, M. W., & Watson, W. *Sociology in medicine.* London: Oxford University Press, 1971.

Tizard, J. The residential care of mentally handicapped children. *Proceedings of the London Conference on the Scientific Study of Mental Deficiency,* 1962, *2,* 659–666.

Tizard, J., & Grad, J. C. *The mentally handicapped and their families.* London: Oxford University Press, 1961.

Townsend, P. M., & Flanagan, J. J. Experimental preadmission program to encourage home care for severely and profoundly retarded children. *American Journal of Mental Deficiency,* 1976, *80* (5), 562–569.

Trapp, E. P., & Himelstein, P. *Readings on the exceptional child: Research and theory.* New York: Appleton-Century-Crofts, 1972.

Veevers, J. E. The social meanings of parenthood. *Psychiatry,* 1973, *36* (3), 291–310.

Vigliano, E., & Shontz, F. Physical disability and perceived adult control in preadolescent boys. *Rehabilitation Counseling Bulletin,* 1964, *8,* 8–12.

Voysey, M. Impression management by parents with disabled children. *Journal of Health and Social Behavior,* 1972, *13,* 80–89.

Weinberg-Asher, N. The effect of physical disability on self-perception. *Rehabilitation Counseling Bulletin,* 1976, *20,* 15–20.

Willey, N. R., & McCandless, B. R. Social stereotypes for normal, educable mentally retarded, and orthopedically handicapped children. *Journal of Special Education,* 1973, *7,* 283–288.

Wilson, E. D., & Alcorn, D. Disability simulation and development of attitudes toward the exceptional. *Journal of Special Education,* 1969, *3,* 303–307.

Life-Span Sex Roles: Development, Continuity, and Change

Introduction

In every culture, the impact of gender assignment on life-span development is profound. The label of male or female provides a structure around which behavioral expectancies, role prescriptions, and life opportunities are organized. There appear to be few variables in the developmental literature as potent as gender in predicting categorically diverging life activities. From the dissimilar toy provisions for the 2-year-old, the segregated play and work groups of the elementary child, the separate athletic and social preoccupations of the adolescent, and the career and family pathways of both young and mature adults—the distinctive patterns of gender orientation predominate.

In contrast to these divergencies in life pursuits, there is now considerable evidence to support the conclusion that in most cognitive, behavioral, and affective spheres, males and females are more alike than they are different (Gullahorn, 1979; Maccoby & Jacklin, 1974; Sherman, 1978; Unger, 1979; Waber, 1979; Weitz, 1977; Williams, 1977; Wittig & Peterson, 1979). This apparent contradiction between the contrasting life experiences of males and females and the paucity of evidence for many tangible and categorical differences between them provides the foundation for the study of psychological sex roles. It seems that the differences that do exist

313

between males and females contribute less to the course of our lives than the nature of the sociocultural sex roles assigned, the characteristics attributed to them, and the constraints engendered by these sex roles on the opportunities that are made available.

Rather than examine sex differences as an independent variable, then, the appropriate focus of individual development will be on the changing course of sex-role behaviors as persons move forward in space and time. In the context of pervasive sex-role socialization practices in every society (Barry, Bacon, & Child, 1957; Block, 1973, Whiting & Edwards, 1973), this chapter will consider some of the ways that individuals contribute to the development, continuity, and potential for change in their own sex-role behaviors over the life span. The introductory section defines key terms and discusses three major problems in designing a psychology of life-span sex-role development: interactions between gender and sex-role conceptions; research problems inherent in the study of male and female development; and the limitations of current theorizing to account adequately for the changing organization of sex-role behaviors over time. In response to these limitations, a set of guidelines for an adequate theory of life-span sex-role development is suggested, and some recent theoretical models are offered. The section on development reviews selected examples of theory and research on how individuals become traditionally sex typed, how these sex-typed orientations persist over time and across situations, and what may be the possibilities for individual change. With the view that human development and change involve a reciprocal interaction between the behaving individual and a complex social-learning environment (Bandura, 1977; Mischel, 1973, 1977), it is proposed that individuals alone are relatively powerless to implement far-reaching changes in traditional sex-role prescriptions.

Defining Sex, Gender, Sex Roles, and Sex Typing

SEX AND GENDER

The most obvious contribution of each person to his or her own development is, for the most part, out of the individual's control. From the day of birth, and even before, parents and others react to the developing individual in terms of attributed gender (Rubin, Provenzano, & Luria, 1974; Seavy, Katz, & Zalk, 1975; Will, Self, & Datan, 1976). Here, the term *gender* is used to denote the social determination that the person is either male or female (Katz, 1979a). Although at birth, gender is assigned automatically on the basis of the presence or absence of male genitalia, chromosomally there may be at least four sexes (Grady, 1979). Money and Ehrhardt (1972) suggest that, in addition to external genitalia and chromosomes, hormonal and gonadal criteria may be used to determine sex assignment. Therefore, the term *sex*, although often used interchangeably with gender, carries a different connotation for many by including re- productive capabilities and sexuality (*Webster's New World Dictionary*, 1979). As the male or female designation is a dichotomous one for practical purposes, and usually disregards criteria other than visible anatomical ones, gender can be seen as a social, as well as a biological, construct.

SEX ROLES AND STEREOTYPING

Social responses to the real or perceived attributes of assigned male and female gender will continue to provide an environment in which the developing individual appears to have limited control over external events. The expectancies of others for the emergence of broad personality traits such as assertiveness or passivity, the social and physical environments provided, the tasks to which individuals are assigned or steered, and the rewards and punishments for specific behaviors all converge to shape sex- role socialization (Emmerich, 1973; Laws, 1979; Mischel, 1970). The concept of *sex roles*, then, in contrast to sex or gender, includes a set of organized expectancies for behaviors and activities that are considered to be appro- priate and desirable for either males or females in a particular culture (Bem, 1974; Katz, 1979a). These sex roles have been referred to as mas- culine or feminine, denoting the expected sets of behaviors for each gender.

When judgments are made about the characteristics or behavior of a particular individual on the basis of membership in a gender group, *sex- role stereotyping* is said to occur. The stereotype serves as a kind of "cog- nitive economy" (Unger, 1979) that reduces perceived intragroup varia- bility and exaggerates the differences that are assumed to exist between the groups.

SEX TYPING

Prior to 1970, it was generally assumed by developmentalists that gender and stereotyped sex roles should coordinate in the developing individual to produce the appropriate masculine and feminine *sex typing*. A boy or girl was judged to be sex typed if he or she preferred behaviors and activities that were culturally gender-related, such as playing with trucks for boys and with dolls for girls (Kagan, 1964; Mussen, 1969; Rabban, 1950). Additionally, it was thought that crossed sex-typed behavior was an indication of abnormal and maladaptive development, such as a boy or girl preferring the activities or demonstrating the traits culturally as- signed to the other gender (Lynn, 1969). Such "failure" to adopt one's "proper" masculine or feminine sex typing was viewed as deviant and changeworthy.

SEX TYPING AND ANDROGYNY

More recently, newer conceptions of sex roles and sex typing have been introduced (Bem, 1975; Constantinople, 1973; Spence, Helmreich, & Stapp, 1975). Rather than viewing masculinity and femininity as opposite, bipolar attributes, these investigators proposed that masculinity and femininity are separate, orthogonal dimensions of personality, and can be measured in varying amounts in the same individual. Persons are considered to be sex typed on certain personality dimensions to the extent that they endorse relatively more of one set of sex-typed characteristics than the other. The more revolutionary outcome of this approach to sex typing was the suggestion that *androgyny,* or an equally high endorsement of both masculine and feminine interpersonal characteristics, was the more desirable state of affairs (Bem, 1975, 1976; Kaplan, 1976). Indeed, if psychological well-being is correlated with an absence of significant sex typing, then the entire body of psychological literature on sex differences, which is based on gender rather than on sex roles, needs some serious reconsideration.

The introduction of androgyny as an alternative to sex typing has opened up the research arena without clarifying the conceptualization of sex roles. A current dialogue among androgyny researchers concerns the extent to which androgyny should be restricted to a circumscribed set of personality traits, defined as psychological masculinity and femininity, or whether it can be usefully extended to broader areas of interpersonal functioning (Bem, 1979; Locksley & Colten, 1979; Helmreich, Spence, & Holahan, 1979; Spence, 1979; Spence & Helmreich, 1979). Some researchers (cf. Lott, 1980) suggest that all sex-typing terminology that refers to teachable behavior—masculinity, femininity, and androgyny—should be replaced by "human" descriptors that refer only to individual differences. These issues will be sidestepped here by emphasizing that current measures of androgyny assess only a limited set of interpersonal traits. In the context of individual life-span development, it appears that a broadened view is required that incorporates concepts of gender, sociocultural role prescriptions, interpersonal skills or traits, and ideographic, internalized, person variables. One way to approach this task is by viewing the concept of sex roles as a job description within a particular culture.

SEX ROLE AS A JOB DESCRIPTION

From the viewpoint of each individual, the multiple nature of sex roles can be conceived in terms of a sociocultural job description (Worell, 1979). Within this framework, sex roles can be classified into four broad components: job assignment or selection; job analysis of tasks to be accomplished; job performance, or skills, knowledge and behaviors needed to complete the tasks; and job satisfaction, or personal, self-engaged reactions to each of the three previous components. The first two are generally related to job assignment or choice, whereas the third and fourth determine job functioning and satisfaction. Each of these four components can be described further:

1. *Job selection:* Here, there are only two choices for most individuals, male or female. Job assignment (gender) begins at birth and usually remains constant throughout life.

2. *Job analysis:* Cultural expectations for tasks to be performed on the job are both age graded and gender correlated. Males and females are socialized to participate in certain tasks, but the opportunities for individual choice on most are hypothetically available. These tasks include leisure-time activities, athletic participation, household chores, financial management, dating and mating games, parenting activities, political engagement, and career–vocational commitments.

3. *Job performance:* Completion of and competence in sex-role tasks involves mastery of functionally related behavior patterns to be used in completing the job. These response patterns encompass knowledge and information about task requirements, and interpersonal, achievement, and task-related skills that contribute to effective task completion. Important skills include some personal "traits" such as dominance, assertiveness, competitiveness, nurturance, and persistence.

4. *Job satisfaction:* Each individual develops internalized and personal reactions that determine task effectiveness and satisfaction. Self-generated responses (e.g., a good mother stays home), values (e.g., women are more sensitive), preferences (e.g., I wish I were a man/woman), expectancies (e.g., if I am too smart, the boys won't like me), attributions (e.g., it was just a lucky break), and various other types of cognitive and evaluative reactions can become engaged with any of the previous three components of sex roles.

This last category encompasses the phenomenology of the individual, and is frequently the only portion of sex role that is assessed. It has been pointed out by others that self-engaged responses, such as preferences and evaluations, frequently conflict with job, task, and behavioral prescriptions (Angrist, 1969; Horrocks & Jackson, 1972; Lynn, 1969). Thus, individuals may adhere to stereotyped tasks and behaviors but would prefer to behave in other ways. In the summary discussion of sex-role change, it will be seen that any of the four components of the job description can be altered for or by a particular individual. The ease with which this can be accomplished by the individual, however, is related to the number and strength of both internal and external barriers to change.

The foregoing framework for sex roles as a job description is constructed to point out the multivariate nature of the sex-role concept. In view of the range of activities involved in both the male and female cultural definitions of sex roles, it seems important to expand our measurement beyond the range of a single set of stereotyped responses. At this point, we can begin to consider the problems appearing in the research on gender, sex typing, and sex roles.

Problems in Gender and Sex-Role Research

Some of the differences that are found between the behaviors and experiences of males and females will be reviewed here to describe and account for the influence of sex-role dichotomization on development. It is clearly beyond the scope of this chapter to examine and critique the range of studies that discuss and report these differences. However, it is important to document some of the problems and pitfalls appearing in the research related to male–female differences. The following section considers three major concerns about sex-role research. Each area of concern is one that threatens to confound our knowledge about how gender and sex roles enter into the person–environment formula for individual development. Many of these research outcomes are intertwined with one or more methodological problems that render their interpretations inconclusive for arriving at firm statements about the distinctive developmental paths of men and women.

GENDER AND SEX-ROLE INTERACTION

The concepts of gender and sex role appear in varying contexts in the research literature. Two major approaches to gender-related research will be explored here: (a) gender as an independent variable; and (b) gender as a stimulus or sex-role variable. The position is taken that these two conceptualizations interact in human development research; this interaction should be considered in designing experiments and in interpreting the data. We can control for, but can seldom remove, the variance due to gender and sex-role contributions.

Gender as an Independent Variable

A traditional approach to sex differences in research treats gender or sex as a simple predictor variable. Accordingly, subjects are divided into two groups, male and female, and are observed on a task or subjected to an experimental manipulation. The outcome measures or dependent variables are regarded as the result of the sexual dimorphism and as legitimate properties of each group. Frequently, biological implications are drawn that relate the response differences, when found, to genetic, hormonal, or structural differences between the groups.

A number of writers have pointed to the limitations of this biological position for clarifying the useful predictive properties of gender (Gullahorn, 1979; Mednick, 1979; Unger, 1979). The question is raised about how gender contributes directly to these observed differences. In the area of cognitive development, for example, the bulk of research suggests that males outperform females on spatial visualization tasks. One set of explanatory models relates these sex differences to some form of brain lateralization, or differential specialization by the left and right hemispheres of the cerebral cortex (Gullahorn, 1979; Maccoby & Jacklin, 1974; Sherman, 1978). Although the apparent superiority of males on various visual–spatial tasks is not an issue here, the relevant antecedents and correlates of this performance difference are being questioned. In particular, researchers have looked at such factors as differential maturation rates (Waber, 1977, 1979), experience and practice with spatial toys and activities (Coates, Lord, & Jacabovics, 1975; Connor, Serbin, & Schackman, 1977; Fennema & Sherman, 1977), and the effects of sex typing and sex preferences (Nash, 1975).

A few examples will suggest the complexity in gender correlates of spatial performance. Waber (1977) examined maturation rates and gender as predictors of auditory lateralization, and of verbal and spatial skills. Late maturing in fifth- through eighth-grade girls and eighth-through tenth-grade boys was associated with spatial, as compared to verbal, skills and to increasing right-ear lateralization. Waber (1979) points out that the within-gender differences between early and late maturers are considerably greater than the between-gender differences on these same measures. Mossip and Unger (1977; cited in Unger, 1979) found that activity with spatial toys (wheeled vehicles, etc.) showed an increasing correlation with spatial lateralization performance in 3- to 11-year-old boys, but not in girls. Coates, et al. (1975) reported that field articulation performance was related for girls, but not for boys, to the amount of time they spent playing with blocks in preschool. Finally, Nash (1975) found that visual–spatial skills in both sixth- and ninth-grade boys and girls were correlated with masculine sex-role preference. Moreover, gender differences in spatial skills disappeared entirely among ninth-grade girls who stated that they preferred to be boys.

The implications of studies such as these on lateralization do not dismiss the findings on overlap (rather than dichotomies) in particular characteristics such as spatial or verbal skills. Rather, they emphasize the interaction of these measures with a variety of social and developmental variables. The important task for the developmental researcher would seem to focus on those person and situational variables that interact with categorical gender assignment rather than pursuing direct cause–effect relationships.

Gender as a Stimulus Variable

A second way to view gender-related behavior is to treat the male–female dichotomy as a stimulus variable. Here, the stimulus can be the applied label, appearance, or any other attribute that denotes gender assignment.

These gender discriminators serve as cues to elicit from self or others previously held expectancies, attributions, and stereotypes that shape and direct the form and expression of the obtained responses. Recent literature contains abundant evidence that these self- or other- expectancies can produce gender-related response differences (Deaux, 1976; Frieze, Fisher, Hanusa, McHugh, & Valle, 1978; Frodi, Macaulay, & Thome, 1977; Lenney, 1977). Moreover, the biasing effects of gender information on evaluative responses such as judgments of product quality or personal characteristics have been found when nothing varied between the two sets of stimuli but the male or female designation (such as the name Jane or John embedded in a standard paragraph stimulus). People tend to use gender as a descriptive or evaluative variable even when it is irrelevant for the task (Grady, 1979).

The stereotyped stimulus value of gender assignment was nicely demonstrated by Rubin, *et al.* (1974). These investigators asked the parents of first-born infants, 15 boys and 15 girls, to rate their babies on a set of bipolar adjectives within 24 hr after birth. According to the hospital records, these male and female infants did not differ on length, weight, or activity scores at birth. Infant girls were more likely to be described by both parents as softer, finer-featured, little, and more inattentive. Interactions were found between gender of child and parent. Fathers, more than mothers, rated their sons as firmer, larger, better coordinated, more alert, stronger, and hardier than did fathers of girls; fathers rated girls as weaker and more delicate. The authors point out that, as information about these characteristics was minimal at birth, the gender-related labels ascribed to the newborns might affect subsequent parent expectations and socialization practices as well as the behavior of the developing child in response to these expectations.

The implications for individual development throughout the life span of gender-related expectancies and attributions are multiple. In response to sex-role expectations, the developing child, as well as the mature adult, may react by playing out selected components of the stereotype with selected persons in particular situations. The "self-fulfilling prophecy" becomes realized. Additionally, individuals tend to ascribe some of these stereotypes to themselves (Bem, 1974; Spence & Helmreich, 1978), and may behave in some situations as though the gender-related attributions were valid. The procedural problems for researchers emerge in separating the complex stimulus and response components of the male–female dichotomy and in determining the conditions under which differential outcomes are elicited (Worell, 1978).

From a life-span perspective, it is also necessary to examine the differential occurrence and effects of these expectancies for males and females in relation to age–stage categories. It has been observed that age-graded norms interact with sex-role norms (Neugarten & Datan, 1973; Sales, 1978).

This interaction suggests that some components of sex-role expectations will affect men and women differently at certain age–stage levels. Here it is particularly important to unravel the separate effects of age, gender, and life situations as well as personal and sex-role expectations for behavior. For example, both men and women have been shown to fluctuate periodically in mood. For many postpubertal women, however, some of these periods of irritability have been associated with the menstrual cycle, and are attributed to its recurrence. The monthly female cycle itself, however, has negative social connotations (Ernster, 1975) that may then serve to trigger the attribution to mood swings. To what extent have women and men been trained to express dissatisfaction in the presence of different discriminative stimuli? The causal attributions that individuals themselves provide may confound gender, age, and sex-role expectations. The challenge of examining the complex interactions between societal and personal expectations may be twofold: to explain the apparent continuity of sex-role behaviors across major life periods, and to suggest opportunities for personal change.

DESIGN AND MEASUREMENT CONSIDERATIONS

For almost any gender-related characteristic that is reported in the psychological literature, a disconfirming study can be found. Maccoby and Jacklin (1974) solved this problem, in part, by cataloging the research outcomes into "pro" and "con," (that girls are more dependent than boys, for example) and reporting the resulting balance as a gender difference–no difference. Although these authors were careful to break down some areas further into categories such as use of rating scales versus direct observational studies, the catalog procedure has some serious limitations. By lumping together studies with dissimilar methodologies and construct assessment, the catalog approach may mask important data or "reveal" group differences that in individual studies contributed to only minor portions of the total variance (Block, 1976). Understandably, it is desirable to draw some broad conclusions about the lives of men and women if we are to derive a psychology of life-span sex-role development. Nevertheless, measurement problems should not be overlooked. The following is a sample of continuing problems in the sex-role literature; many others have been discussed (e.g., Frieze *et al.*, 1978; Lenney, 1979; Locksley & Colton, 1979; Mednick, 1979; Sherman, 1979; Unger, 1979; Worell, 1978, 1979).

Correlations among Measures of Sex-Role Behavior Are Low

Whether the measures of sex-role behavior are directed at concepts of "identity," "flexibility," "preference," or "androgyny," low to moderate intercorrelations among measures suggest that they may be assessing constructs which overlap only partially or not at all (Katz, 1979a; Kelly & Worell, 1977; Mischel, 1970; Spence, 1979; Spence & Helmreich, 1978;

Worell, 1978). In view of the multifaceted nature of the sex-role concept, no one set of measures can be expected to encompass all aspects into a single measure. In addition to the diversity of constructs being measured, the content domain and testing format of current measuring instruments vary widely: self-descriptive adjectives (active or passive); true–false self-descriptions (I like to help my friends); toy choices (trucks or dolls); activities (needlework or hammering a nail); jobs around the house (cooking or taking out the trash); career choices (teacher or doctor); traditional or liberated attitudes toward roles (women should stay home or be free to choose a career).

These variations in measurement strategies result in low correspondence from one set of measures to another. Some traditional measures, such as the widely used children's "It" test (Brown, 1957; Sher & Lansky, 1968) may fail to predict a simple behavioral criterion such as observed toy activities or peer playmates (Smith, Goldman, & Keller, 1979). In comparing four measures designed to assess a similar construct (androgyny), Kelly, Furman, and Young (1979) found that a majority (61%) of people were classified discrepantly into one of the four sex-typed categories by any pair of scales. It is clear that multiple problems are being described here: overly broad definitions of sex roles and sex-typing concepts, lack of correspondence among measuring instruments, and poor predictability from scale measurement to observed behavior. Several inclusive research programs are currently attempting to obviate these difficulties by means of careful definitions, multimeasurement of sex-role components, and extensive field testing of predictive measures (Katz, 1979b; Spence & Helmreich, 1978).

Gender and Sex-Roles Are Confounded

The inconsistency in use of gender and sex-role constructs as independent or stimulus variables is matched with a similar trend in measurement procedures. This inconsistency appears in two major contexts: construction and scoring of sex-role measures, and selection of experimental tasks. In both kinds of activities, researchers have apparently not decided whether they wish to demonstrate that response differences exist between categorically defined males and females or whether social judgments are made that these characteristics or tasks are culturally typical–appropriate–desirable for either males or females. In the first instance, a task or measure is constructed or validated according to gender differences in response (more boys choose trucks than do girls). The assumption here is a bipolar one: that categories of responses are divided according to categories of gender. In the second instance, social judgments are obtained about what tasks are desirable or typical for males or females. The assumption in this procedure is that categories of activities can be ordered from least to most desirable or typical for males and females and that, therefore, response frequencies between them will overlap. The second assumption is reflected in the construction of recent androgyny scales and in careful preassessment for male or female typing and valuing of tasks (Stein & Bailey, 1973). The result is a more precise assessment of gender-related or unrelated responses. For particular purposes, both categorical and dimensional procedures are legitimate. The confounding occurs when purpose and procedure fail to match, as when researchers measure *sex-role* behavior in terms of *gender* differences in response.

An interesting offshoot of this measurement problem is the reexamination of the extensive literature on parent–child relations for evidence of new relationships between parent behavior, parent sex typing, and child sex typing. Some recent studies have included sex-role characteristics, as well as gender, of both parent and child. Many of the reported failures to obtain strong evidence for parental socialization effects on child sex typing (Maccoby & Jacklin, 1974) may relate to the gender-typed measurement of both parent predictor and child outcome variables. Although the recent research is only correlative, it is nevertheless suggestive and appealing, in that it leads us one step beyond the simple effects of gender. A salient finding is immediately apparent: within-sex differences in perceived or observed parent or child sex-typed behavior may be as great as that between males and females. Several recent studies suggest that clear differences in perceived parent behavior are obtained for male and female subjects who have been classified as masculine, feminine, androgynous, or "undifferentiated" on separate measures of self-reported sex-role characteristics (Kelly & Worell, 1976; Orlofsky, 1979; Spence & Helmreich, 1978).

Kelly and Worell (1976) hypothesized that perceived parental behavior patterns of acceptance, cognitive encouragement, and control, would be related to college students' classification as masculine, feminine, androgynous, or undifferentiated. Using the Parent Behavior Form (PBF) (Worell & Worell, 1976) as a measure of perceived parent behavior, and the Personality Research Form Androgyny Scale (PRF ANDRO) (Berzins, Welling, & Wetter, 1978) as a measure of self-reported sex-role orientation, these authors found that the presence of parents who model and reinforce cross-sex behavior is related to nontraditional (androgynous or cross-sex) orientations in children. In particular, it was principally the presence of warmth in the reported behavior of mothers *and* fathers of males that differentiated the sex-role categories, and the presence of cognitive–intellectual achievement encouragement as well as lax discipline from *both* parents that predicted nontraditional orientations in females. Orlofsky (1979) also reports high paternal warmth in androgynous males and high encouragement for cognitive and intellectual achievement in androgynous females. As with gender differences in sex-role orientation, these parental behavior findings reflect more similarities than differences between parents for sex-role groups.

Spence and Helmreich (1978) looked at both the reported parental behaviors as well as the perceived and reported sex-role traits (as measured by the Perceived Attributes Questionnaire (PAQ) in relation to high school and college students' sex-typed categories. Looking at the combined father–mother category for sex-role traits, these authors found the androgynous–androgynous parent pattern produced the highest level of child self-esteem and the highest probability for androgyny in male children (for females, high androgyny was predicted best for a parent pattern of androgyny–femininity). In addition, Spence and Helmreich report that parent behavior patterns and parental sex-role category each contributed separately to children's sex-role orientation and self-esteem.

From these complex findings, summarized briefly here, it seems clear that the inclusion of both gender and sex-role considerations provides increased information about parent–child relations, sex typing, and self-esteem. With measurement by orthogonal sex-role categories as a relatively recent introduction, we may see some interesting changes in established "facts" in the developmental literature as more researchers include these kinds of measures in their designs.

Gender-Related Variables are Uncontrolled

Finally, we can catalog a number of design procedures that may confound the gender-related effects with uncontrolled variables; some of these will be listed briefly. Gender of experimenter has been demonstrated time and again to bias some responses in some situations, but is frequently unreported or uncontrolled (Harris, 1971; Rumenik, Capasso, & Hendrick, 1977). For females especially, gender of experimenter may be facilitative or inhibitive, depending on the task or situation. With a female experimenter, females have shown increased quantitative performance on the Wechsler Intelligence Scale for Children (Pederson, Shinedling, & Johnson, 1968) and increased aggression (Larwood, O'Neal, & Brennan, 1977). These experimenter effects are not assumed to account for all gender-related differences, but may contribute, in some situations, to their absence or exaggeration.

Cohort or generational effects may appear in either longitudinal or cross-sectional data attempting to compare changes over time or with age (Neugarten & Datan, 1973). Although the effects of differing social and historical measurement times probably contribute to the variance in most research involving cross-age comparisons, it seems particularly salient for men and women today. Probably, the changes in role prescriptions, attitudes, and legal support systems in the United States have at no time in recent history been so dramatic as those that have occurred in this area. In particular jeopardy are studies attributing to age or stage of life those changes that are occurring at many age levels at a particular time in history (attitudes toward the women's movement, for example). Again, the solution is not to dismiss such data, but to question it carefully. Generation effects may also contribute to differences in measuring instruments across age groups. We are still discovering that the content domain of sex-role measurements varies across age groups. We cannot always ask the same questions to the 2- and 20-year-olds. For children, adolescents, and adults, we are still discovering the complex and multifaceted components of sex-role conceptions. Are constructs that are measured by instruments with differing content similar in terms of their predictive power to other behaviors? This is a question that has been frequently assumed but seldom tested empirically.

Finally, the failure to control for prior experiences with stimuli, tasks, and situations, may encourage task-specific differences that appear to be gender-related. Examples of this problem were brought up earlier in the chapter in relation to visual–spatial abilities. Similar problems exist in the assessment of mathematical skills (Sherman, 1978), leadership skills in male-dominated groups (Cytrynbaum & Brandt, 1979), and conformity to group pressure (Sistrunk & McDavid, 1972).

The discussion of methodology problems in gender-related developmental research covered gender and sex-role considerations, measuring instruments, and considerations about gender of experimenter, age of cohorts, and task experience. Doubtless, other problems becloud the sex-role scene; the challenge is to detect, control, or circumvent them.

THEORETICAL PERSPECTIVES

At the present time, no single theory adequately accounts for the acquisition, continuity, and change of sex-role behaviors across the life span. It may be that a unified theory of sex-role development is not possible because the conceptual and behavioral domains are too broadly defined. Indeed, each theory has tended to limit its focus to certain restricted domains of knowledge or behavior. The traditional psychological theories fall into three rather distinct categories: identification theories, cognitive theories, and social learning. There are many recent reviews of these major theories and of their strengths and limitations and a comprehensive review will not be repeated here (Emmerich, 1973; Frieze *et al.*, 1978; Maccoby & Jacklin, 1974; Mussen, 1969; Weitz, 1977). The following discussion will present a capsule view of each of the three types of theories and will summarize some of the major objections that are thought to limit their utility. A useful theory of sex-role development should provide for a progression in sex-role orientation over the life span, should include equal treatment of male and female development, and should accommodate individual differences in sex-role behaviors.

Identification theories propose that introjection, or adoption of the behaviors, attitudes, and values of the same-sex parent by the age of 5 or 6 years leads to a stable and enduring personality organization that is consistent across time and situations. Deviations from the stereotyped model of appropriate sex-typed behaviors are viewed as failures in the strength and timing of identification (Erikson, 1963, 1968; Freud, 1965; Kagan, 1964). Critics of identification theories point to the early consolidation, and therefore the inflexibility of sex typing; the requirement of same-sex parent as the major role model; the assumption that moral and ethical structures are tied into successful sex typing; the treatment of sex-role adoption as a trait that resists situational influences; the explanation of female development in terms that are analogous, but different from the male; the devaluing and stereotyping of female development and characteristics; and the assumption that nontraditional sex-role adoptions are deviant.

Cognitive theories of sex typing emphasize the acquisition of knowledge about one's own and others' gender and the active efforts of the individual to acquire and retain relevant sex-typed information. The development and utilization of this knowledge appears in a structured sequence and is motivated by the positive value attached to one's own gender assignment (Kohlberg, 1966, 1969; Lewis & Weinraub, 1979). Here, critics point to problems such as androcentrism, in that for Kohlberg the male is the prototype of development; females are assumed to value their sex-roles as strongly as do males; individual differences within each gender are either ignored or are treated as deviations from the normal; sex-role stereotypes are assumed to reflect some universal "givens" in human nature; sex-role identity is isomorphic to cognitive structures; and that the most cognitively mature position is a sex-typed one.

Social learning theory emphasizes principles of observational learning, and direct, symbolic, and vicarious reinforcement and punishment as the major mediators of sex-role development. The theory provides for multiple sources of modeling and reinforcement, from which the individual gradually selects same-sex behaviors and develops standards for same-sex role behavior that become increasingly self-monitored. In addition, a distinction is made between learning and performance, so that individuals have knowledge of many behaviors that they choose not to display. Flexibility is possible through variations in models, reinforcers, and novel situations (Mischel, 1966, 1970). Critics of social learning theory contend that the theory fails to account for active cognitive monitoring by the individual; it emphasizes discrete behaviors rather than cohesive "internalized" orientations; it assigns too much weight to the reinforcing power of parents; and it underestimates the cognitive and motivational functions of self-labeling on the subsequent modeling behavior of the child.

Recent reformulations of social learning theory have attempted to integrate certain cognitive and social learning variables into a "cognitive social learning" theory (Bandura, 1977, 1978; Mischel, 1973, 1977; Rosenthal & Zimmerman, 1978; Worell, 1981; Worell & Stilwell, 1981). The emphasis is on "reciprocal determinism," which posits a continuous interaction between environmental variables, observed behavior, and covert person variables. A cognitive social learning approach is useful, in this author's view, for encompassing both external control variables (objective antecedents and consequences of behavior) and covert internal variables (selecting, storing, evaluating, and utilizing gender-related information). Furthermore, a cognitive social learning model incorporates individual covert responses, such as self-generated expectancies, standards, attributions, and evaluations, that have been shown to discriminate male and female performance in many situations. Some of these internal, self-generated responses will be used later in the chapter to account for both continuity and change in individual sex-role orientations. The reciprocal influence position is particularly applicable to sex-role behavior in assuming that individuals create their own environments partly by means of their stimulus value to others, in this case, assigned gender as well as by their gender-differentiated behavior. Finally, the assumption of reciprocal influence suggests that substantial change in an individual's sex-role behaviors requires modifications in both self and others.

Conclusions

Aside from specific empirical validation, on which all theories ultimately depend, an overview of these theories suggests the need to specify a set of prescriptions for a useful sex-role theory that will be applicable to life-span development. It seems clear that the press of environmental and historical events and their demonstrated power to change the course of sex-role behaviors, denies the exclusive applicability of theories that rely primarily on internal variables, such as cognitive structure or personality organization. Theories that propose useful procedures to facilitate developmental continuity and change (such as social learning) need to be integrated with approaches that are applicable to varying age-related contents (such as puberty, parenthood, retirement). It appears to this author that neither identification–trait models, internal cognitive models, nor procedural-change models are sufficient to cover and explain the range of stability and change that are encompassed by the multiple conceptions of sex-role and gender-related behaviors.

Alternative Models of Life-Span Sex-Role Development

Given the list of sins and omissions in previous theories, it seems that only the intrepid would dare to devise a new theory of sex-role development. However, a number of models with a life-span approach have appeared in the recent literature. These recent theories contain both the attraction of a new approach and the liability of being unsubstantiated

by large bodies of research. In the following section, some broad prescriptions are presented that appear to this author to form the minimal
requirements for an acceptable theory of life-span sex-role development.
These prescriptions do not constitute a theory, but suggest some guidelines for the evaluation of alternative models. A flexibility model is then
presented that conforms in several, but not all, ways to these prescriptions.

PRESCRIPTIONS FOR A
LIFE-SPAN SEX-ROLE APPROACH

Integration of Life-Span Considerations

The major theories of sex-role development have tended to focus on
early influences in sex-role orientation at the expense of later modification.
In a recent review of life-span developmental psychology, Baltes, Reese,
and Lipsett (1980) discussed the assumptions underlying this approach
to development. The following four ideas appear particularly relevant to
the present topic. A life-span view assumes that development (a) is a lifelong process, in which behavior change can occur at any point in time
in the individual's life; therefore maturity is not an end state, nor can an
ideal end state be determined; (b) is influenced by the historical time in
which it is occurring, so that cohort (generational) effects must be considered; (c) is multidetermined and complex for any one area of behavior,
so that an individual exhibits considerable heterogeneity over time and
across situations and age is not the primary determinant of change; and
(d) is best described, not in terms of traits or orderly sequences of change,
but by a flexibility model in which multiple determinants may induce
continual change.

Applied to life-span sex roles, these assumptions suggest that sex-role
behaviors are not fixed in people, time, or situations, but are potentially
in flux. The traits and role prescriptions we observe as inflexible may be
as much a function of the historical prescriptions as they are of the individuals that play out the roles. The more desirable theory, then, is one
that includes the contributions of situations, tasks and life stages, as well
as the historical milieu in which these events are taking place. From the
perspective of this chapter, it should also include an active and interactive
individual who assumes a reciprocal and self-monitoring response system
for integrating the events that take place in the external environment.

Acceptance of Cultural Relativism

Most traditional theories of sex-role acquisition have focused on the
universal "givens" in the natures of women and men and have treated
nontraditional sex-role behavior as deviant. A life-span theory to satisfy
a flexibility model will be able to account for within-, as well as between-
gender differences in development. The search for antecedents and cor-

relates of traditional sex-typed behaviors will target differences among males or females who distribute themselves along relevant dimensions. The recent work on androgyny and the behavioral correlates of nontraditional sex-role orientations suggests that (a) on many sex-typed attributes, within-gender differences may be as great as those between males and females; and (b) there may be a number of healthy and satisfying sex-role "stances" for both men and women (Bem, 1976). In compatibility with a life-span perspective, there will be no optimal end state or point of final maturity. Although some current theorizing (Block, 1973a; Rebecca, Hefner, & Olshansky, 1976; Ullian, 1976) proposes that the ideal end state is an androgynous one, or a sex-role "transcendence," this may reflect as much of a sex-role bias as the alternative assumption that traditional sex typing is the desirable outcome (cf. Sampson, 1977). A flexibility theory suggests only the multiple options for change, not the ideological desirability of one outcome over another.

Use of Psychological Constructs That Are Gender-Free

Several traditional theories have been targeted as being "androcentric" (Doherty, 1978; Katz, 1979a). That is, they tend to construct the lives of *persons* according to the developmental lives of *males*. An example of this bias is found in psychoanalytic theory, in which the hypothesized mechanism for identification (and consequently for moral and ethical structures) is rooted in the biopsychology of the male child. Female development is poorly integrated and appears as an afterthought. Such terms as "penis envy" and "castrating female" are examples of androcentric constructs. In contrast, it seems desirable to explain and describe the development of males and females in similar theoretical terms. With the exception of such gender-specific events as pregnancy, lactation, and menstruation (which in themselves are not psychological constructs), there should be no psychological construct that cannot describe both males and females.

How can we describe the development of females and males in similar theoretical terms when there are obvious structural and experiential differences between them? Here, it is certainly possible to separate content of developmental data from constructs devised to explain differences in content. Thus, cognitive concepts such as *expectancy* can remain gender-free, but can be applied to life tasks with differing contents, such as success at verbal and numerical tasks, career development, or commitment to marriage and family. Each of these content areas shows developmental differences between males and females. However, there are also substantial within-gender differences, and these will change with the social and historical time. Therefore, it seems important to construct a theory that allows for gender differences that can change as social history is made and remade.

Regardless of the biological, physical, or experiential differences that may differentiate females from males, a developmental theory should, in this author's view, deal with the psychological meaning of these events for each individual. For example, differences in both anatomy and social power suggest that rape is a more probable event for females than for males. Some writers on female development suggest that the fear of rape acts as a mediator between the developing female and her external environment, and is a possible antecedent to female conciliatory behavior. However, rape is not uncommon for males in situations where they are also caught in powerless, low status positions, such as in prisons. Are the same stages in response to rape that are suggested for women (Frieberg & Bridwell, 1978) also functionally relevant for males caught in similar situations? These comparisons between male and female experience suggest that a satisfactory sex-role development approach will require both gender-free psychological constructs to account for the lives of individuals and a structured life-span model to describe gender-specific developmental events.

Accommodation to Ideographic and Predisposing Experience

It seems important and desirable to keep the personal history of the individual as a focus of development. Recognizing both historical and social normative events as contributors to individual development should not mitigate the continuing relevance of experiences that are specific to an individual. A theory of individual development requires constructs to explain and predict the acquisition, maintenance, and modification of sex-role behaviors (Ahammer, 1973). Theories containing only descriptive or taxonomic constructs appear less useful for dealing with the controlling variables in individual development. Especially, if sex-role acquisition is considered as a complex set of traits, roles, and behaviors that are only partially correlated, then individual learning histories for each of these subsets of sex-role development will be required for understanding the developmental course of any particular person. It is suggested here that this prescription is compatible with a cognitive social learning theory approach. Social learning variables can encompass antecedent and consequent environmental events, and cognitive variables describe the interactions of the phenomenology of the individual with these environmental events.

The foregoing prescriptions for a life-span approach to sex-role development suggest four broad guidelines that appear to be necessary, although not sufficient. The guidelines propose that a satisfactory theory includes a set of multiple life-span considerations, cultural relativism, gender-free psychological constructs, and accommodation to individual histories.

RECENT MODELS

Recent models of sex-role functioning have two important characteristics in common that meet the foregoing prescriptions: They attempt to define a life-span progression in psychological development, and they provide for the possibility of gender-free outcomes. These models generally incorporate an "androgyny is maturity" conception proposing that the end state of sex-role development is the integration of male and female role behaviors. For Block (1973) this is described as "an integration of traits and values, both masculine and feminine self"; Rebecca et al. (1976) refer to "sex-role transcendence . . . in which individuals can feel free to express their human qualities [p. 95]"; and Katz (1979a) has proposed a model based on the development of "sex-role flexibility." Both the Block and Katz models offer preliminary data in support of their conceptions.

A FLEXIBILITY MODEL OF LIFE-SPAN SEX ROLES

The flexibility model incorporates many of the life-span prescriptions just discussed and is worth expanding here. It proposes distinctive but overlapping patterns of lifelong development for males and females. A careful distinction is made between gender and sex roles. The model recognizes that sex roles are complex, and consist of multiple sets of attitudes, values, preferences, behaviors, activities, and aspirations. By definition, then, there can be no single measure of flexibility, and correlations among differing measures may be low. Katz (1979a) points out that this conception of flexibility is broader than the usual definitions of androgyny and is related to more varied aspects of gender-related functioning. A further expansion on previous models suggests that both the content of an individual's sex roles and the sources of influence that shape these role behaviors will vary at differing stages during the life span. Therefore, early and later sex-role orientations may be discontinuous and influenced by the reinforcement and modeling properties of environmental agents other than the same-sex parent. The following scheme outlines the three major levels of development according to this model, and the content and influences contained in each. Each level has several stages that will not be elaborated here.

Level I includes development to the age of 12. The major task for the developing child is to gain knowledge of self and other gender-identity, and to acquire information and skills about what the culture regards as appropriate male and female behaviors during this age span. The direction of development is toward sex typing, with early influences from parents and increasing input from peers, teachers, and the media. Although sex-role socialization is more stringent for boys, external pressures, coupled with the child's cognitive level, encourage high stereotyping and low sex-role flexibility for both boys and girls.

Level II encompasses adolescent behavior and the preparation for adulthood. The major changes include adjustment to biological maturation, the establishment of heterosexual interactions, and future planning for career and marriage. Earlier patterns of behavior may become obsolete and new patterns are established that will form the basis for new directions in adult development. Within this level, significant divergencies may occur between males and females. The earlier maturation of girls provides for increased sources of stress that may extend their influence throughout life in terms of self-esteem, role flexibility, and career development. For girls in contemporary society, there is also a greater noncontinuity than for boys between levels I and II. This discontinuity applies to academic and career expectations, concern with physical attractiveness, and mate selection. Boys will anticipate less marriage–career conflict, and more continuity with previous patterns of interest and activities. Same- and cross-sex peers and media are sources of increasing influence.

Level III ranges from young, through middle, to late adulthood, with differing tasks and influences in each. The three central life tasks of mate selection, parenting, and career, still differ sharply again for males and females. The model provides the possibility for equal participation by both men and women in these roles, but recognizes that contemporary society remains relatively gender differentiated on the timing and importance of these tasks. Katz proposes also that the influence of delayed modeling from one's own parenting experiences encourages the persistence of stereotyped parenting practices in the new generation. These early observational learning influences return to provide a new source of continuity in stereotyped sex roles and tend to attenuate the development of flexibility and change.

Katz (1979b) has reported preliminary results of her research to support the predictions generated by the model. Using a sample of 376 grade-school children and their parents, multiple measures were taken of self, peer, media, parents, and societal influences on development of sex-role flexibility. Specific measures developed for children were: (*a*) Role-model perceptions: Who does household chores; (*b*) Perceived parental influence: parental attitudes and actual parental toy and activity influences; (*c*) Future projections: role anticipations at home and work; (*d*) Choice of future occupation: from traditional to nontraditional; (*e*) Toy and activity preferences: open-ended questions; (*f*) Personality traits: self-rated on dependency and aggression; (*g*) Peer influence: peer gender choices and reactions to nontraditional peer play; (*h*) Opinions on equality; (*i*) Media choices: books, TV, stars, and shows; (*j*) Tolerance for cross-sex activity: rated children and adults engaged in nontraditional tasks. All measures were rated from 0 (most traditional or sex-typed), to 4 (most flexible or non-sex-typed). With a possible range of 0–240, the average score for these kindergarten through third-graders was 77, indicating that this group was quite traditional in its sex-role orientation. These results are not surprising, and support previous findings of strong sex typing in this age range.

More interesting than total flexibility scores were some of the additional analyses, which suggest that gender differences depended on the measures taken. Girls were generally more flexible than boys and their flexibility scores decreased less from kindergarten to Grade 3 than did those of the boys. However, girls were more traditional on certain measures: future domestic roles, household chores, and self-ratings of dependency and aggression. In further support of the model, a multiple regression analysis of influences on children's flexibility scores revealed a combined peer and television contribution of 60% to the variance. Perceived parent influence was eleventh in rank and did not contribute significantly to the prediction of children's flexibility scores.

A similar set of measures was taken on the parents' perceptions of self and children. The findings are complex and do not easily lend themselves to simple statements. Parental flexibility, as with children's, varied with area measured, and with gender of both parent and child. Daughters and sons were treated differentially in some areas but not in others. In overall scores, parents were more flexible than their children, again as predicted by the model. In contrast to their children's perceptions, however, the parents' self-reported behavior showed low but significant correlations with their children's flexibility scores.

The importance of the Katz flexibility model lies not in this discrete set of data, however, but in its promise for a new look at the developmental course of sex-role behavior over the life cycle. The model is testable, and is capable of generating new hypotheses about male and female development. It can assess the utility of cognitive social learning constructs or other intervening variables, for lifelong sex-role adaptation. The hypothesis of delayed modeling as an antecedent to continuity of traditional sex roles in parenting is one of the more interesting of these. The model rejects bipolar measures of sex-role behavior and moves toward multivariate assessment of sex-role orientations across longer periods of the life span. Therefore, we may expect to obtain new information about sex-role development that is only partly commensurate with our present state of knowledge. It is clear from these preliminary data that sex-role flexibility does not follow a straight developmental path (Katz, 1979b).

Acquisition, Continuity, and Change in Life-Span Sex Roles

The major focus in sex-role research has been, until recently, on the acquisition of gender-differentiated patterns of behavior in early and middle childhood. More recently, attention has been redirected toward developmental changes that appear in adolescence, in middle adulthood, and in small samples of older adults. The relevant empirical questions here are these: At what ages or life periods do varying sex-role patterns emerge and become relatively stabilized? Under what conditions do the many separate components of these sex-role patterns remain constant over the life span? And finally, what are the requirements for, and barriers to, individual change? The multivariate nature of the sex-role concept and content suggests that, once certain stereotypic patterns are acquired, both stability and change can be expected in some components of sex-role functioning, in particular situations, and with certain other individuals.

ACQUISITION

Socialization demands for gender-differentiated behavior encourage the early development of many behavioral, cognitive, and attitudinal components of sex roles. Although consensus is far from complete on the timing, patterning, and control mechanisms for this early acquisition, some broad generalizations are possible.

First, it is well established that some aspects of gender and sex-role information and play activities are present as early as ages 2 and 3 (Blakemore, LaRue, & Olejnik, 1977; Kuhn, Nash, & Brucken, 1978; Thompson, 1975). By age 3, boys and girls can identify themselves and others by gender, and can list many common household, play, and interpersonal activities that are culturally sex-role stereotyped. For example, Kuhn *et al.* (1978) found that most 2- and 3-year-olds in their sample agreed that girls like to play with dolls; like to cook dinner, clean house, and help mother; never hit; ask for help; and will be a nurse or teacher when they grow up. In contrast, both girls and boys believe that boys play with cars; build things; threaten to hit; and when they grow up, will be "the boss." Additional elaboration of knowledge, preferences, and refinement of gender-related behaviors continues through middle childhood. By the second or third grade, most boys and girls are strongly sex-typed on many dimensions: preferred activities and friends; personality trait attributions for both children and adults; achievement-related expectancies; anticipated adult occupational roles; and rejection of cross-gender behavior (Emmerich, 1979; Etaugh & Hadley, 1977; Fling & Manosevitz, 1972; Garrett, Ein, & Tremain, 1977; Katz, 1979b; Looft, 1971; Parsons & Ruble, 1977; Rothbaum, 1977; Scheresky, 1976; Schlossberg & Goodman, 1972; Williams, Bennett, & Best, 1975). In addition to increasing peer, teacher, and media influences, the consolidation of sex-role stereotyping in middle childhood may bear a relationship to cognitive development and to the child's elaborated conception of what it means to be a boy or girl (Marcus & Overton, 1978; Slaby & Frey, 1975).

Second, girls are generally more flexible than boys on most of these measures in most studies. Girls appear to have more knowledge of *both* male and female roles, they are less stringently sex-typed in their play preferences than are boys, and they are more tolerant of cross-gender activities for themselves as well as for others (Blakemore *et al.*, 1979; Bryan & Luria, 1978; Edelbrock & Sugawara, 1978; Etaugh & Riley, 1979; Katz, 1979b; Lynch & Cassel, 1979; Urberg, 1979a). Attempts have been made to relate these differences between boys and girls to the greater salience of the male as a role model. Males have a more visible and active physical presence, and they possess more assigned power and higher status. There also appears to be a higher anticipation of punishment by boys for cross-gender behavior.

Finally, the importance of role models other than the same-sex parent has become increasingly evident. Exposure to a variety of social agents is expected to be minimal during the first 2 years of life. It has been seen that between the ages of 2 and 3, children are becoming competent at the process of gender-labeling, and classifying activities accordingly. However, it is also at this period that young children increase their exposure to books, television, peers, and other adults in the environment. Television watching in school children has been reported to range from 5 through 88 hours per week (Stein & Friedrich, 1975). Analysis of role-model portrayals on television suggests that in children's programming, males and females appear in differing frequencies, demonstrate gender-distinctive behaviors, and are reinforced differentially for these behaviors (Sternglantz & Serbin, 1974). Moreover, sex typing increases with increased exposure to television (Frueh & McGhee, 1975; McGhee & Frueh, 1980). Several recent studies on gender effects in modeling found strong influences on imitative behavior of gender-labeling of activities (Masters, Ford, Arend, Grotevant, & Clark, 1979), and of multiple models demonstrating repeated activities consistently (Fehrenbach, Miller, & Thelan, 1979; Franzini, Litrownik, & Blanchard, 1978; Perry & Bussey, 1979). These researchers have suggested that children may engage in sampling practices across multiple examples of observed behaviors that enable them to abstract and generate rules to guide their behavior in subsequent situations.

Reflecting these trends in early development to theoretical considerations, it seems that a satisfactory theory of sex-role acquisition should be able to account for at least three sets of empirical data: the strong stereotyping that develops through middle childhood; the greater flexibility of girls on most measures; and the importance of exposure to multiple sources of role models. Although both cognitive social learning and flexibility theorists have grappled with these diverse findings, a satisfactory theoretical integration has yet to be formulated and cross-validated against new empirical predictions.

TRANSITION FROM CHILDHOOD

It would be appealing to take this apparent stability during middle childhood as a baseline for evaluating later developmental stability and change. In the light of contemporary trends toward revised and more flexible sex-role patterns in adults, the developmental antecedents to current flexibility become of particular interest. It should be informative to compare nontraditional men and women on a variety of earlier childhood measures, to assess similarities in content domains of flexibility in sex-role orientation. For example, a considerable amount of research on achievement patterns supports the extension of individual childhood dispositions into adulthood. In examining the life experiences of nontraditional careers in women, several researchers report some continuities from earlier flexibility of preferences and activities to later achievement strivings (Crandall & Battle, 1970; Hennig, 1974). Although current expectations for women's achievement are undergoing reorientation and change, individual differences in adaptation to social innovation require explanation. As each new generation of cohorts adapts its sex-role patterning to new and differing social norms, researchers may find a continuing source of exploration into the childhood antecedents of later sex-role choices.

With respect to the predictive functions of modeling, it seems important to look more closely at the role models used by adults in maintaining continuity or in implementing change. To what extent, and in what manner, do adults use earlier and recent role models? Does adult role modeling follow principles similar to those that influence the imitative behavior of children? Contemporary increases in the frequency of working mothers, parenting fathers, childless couples, divorcing partners, and revised career patterns in women, suggest that role modeling is an important precessor to developmental change (Douvan, 1976). A careful analysis of the current influence of social role images on the behavior of women and men might be an alternative way to view the cohort effects of "social time."

The limitations of using childhood sex-role functioning as a baseline period become apparent, however, when we consider the introduction of new life tasks to which the school-age child has never been exposed; adapting to biological and social pressures during puberty is an outstanding example. During adolescence, important changes occur in cognitive functioning (Dan, 1979; Fox, Tobin, & Brody, 1979; Nash, 1979; Sherman, 1978), in body image (Dwyer & Mayer, 1968; Peterson, 1979), and in sexuality (Schwartz, 1978). In early adulthood, new situational demands and opportunities provide additional sources of modification in sex-role orientations. The contribution of major changes in life situations to sex-role attitudes and self-descriptions was recently explored by Abrahams, Feldman, and Nash (1979). These researchers compared different sets of heterosexual couples in four life situations: cohabitation, marriage, expecting a first-born, and primaparae parents of a 6–12-month-old child. As predicted, interpersonal trait self-descriptions and androgyny scores on the Bem Sex-Role Inventory (Bem, 1974) varied according to current life situation, as did expressions of masculine and feminine interests. The findings that women situationally adapted their attitudes and self-descriptions more than did the men suggest either that these women were more flexible in response to realistic situational demands, or that they perceived their role to be that of the more adapting one. Despite these adaptations to situational expectations, it is important to note that men and women retained their relative gender-group differences on all measures of masculinity and femininity; within diversity, there was stability. Several other comparisons of androgyny measures across major life-span periods also suggest that life situations may be accompanied by modifications in self-reported sex-role trait descriptions (Eiseman, 1978; Hyde & Phillis, 1979; Urberg, 1979b).

The transition from childhood to adolescent and adult sex-role patterns suggests that the notion of continuity in childhood orientation is only partly useful, and is contraindicated by new, as well as by modified, behavioral trends. The following section will explore the interaction between stability and change in sex-role behaviors and the implications of these conceptions for individual choice.

PATTERNS OF CONTINUITY AND CHANGE

Patterns of continuity and change in sex-role behavior can be viewed within the framework of reciprocal determinism (Bandura, 1977, 1978). The impetus for stability and change comes both from individuals as they interact with their social environments, and from the external environment that provides role models, social expectations, and reciprocal feedback.

Although it would be attractive to view this reciprocal process as a stable spiraling of interactions across time and situations, it has frequently resembled a struggle rather than a transaction. For women in particular, the extensive external and internal barriers to sex-role change have clearly outweighed the personal and societal supports for innovative role behavior. In response to widespread inequalities in the balance of social power, status, and access to opportunities, women have been at the core of pressures for changes in sex-role standards and practices. As a result of their efforts, the social system has yielded on a number of legal and economic fronts that, in turn, enable women to modify their sex-role opportunities still further. Women are now entering the labor force at an unprecedented rate, are delaying marriage, entering professional careers, having fewer or no children, and are returning to productive activities when their children are grown (Hoffman, 1977; Huston-Stein & Higgens-Trenk, 1978; Sales, 1978; Worell, 1979). In accomplishing some elements of social and economic change for themselves, women have inevitably influenced the sex-role behaviors of men. As a result, we now find more men seeking child custody following divorce (DeFrain & Eirick, 1979; Lewis, 1978), exploring the dimensions of male sex roles (David & Brannon, 1976; Farrell, 1974; Pleck & Sawyer, 1974), and participating actively in the care of their infants (Russell, 1978).

The reciprocal effect of men's and women's behavior on their mutual sex-role adaptation has served to support traditional, as well as innovative, sex-role patterns. For example, Frances (1979) found that in dyadic conversational pairs, men took longer speaking in turns than women. In doing so, they created an environment that communicated power. By taking power, they obtained it and further increased their influence. Women, in contrast, spoke less and for shorter periods of time. Women also smiled more and gave longer periods of eye contact. These nonverbal feminine-typed responses may have been construed by males as positive feedback to continue talking. It appears that some well-rehearsed responses brought into the dyadic relationship by both men and women provided the interpersonal cues that maintained these reciprocal stereotypic reactions.

In addressing the issue of stability and change in sex-role behaviors, it seems reasonable to assume that individuals have a part in creating their own environments toward either maintenance or modification. To the extent that persons exhibit their stereotyped interpersonal responses in new situations, the reciprocal exchange hypothesis predicts that they will be agents for supporting stability of sex-role relationships. Thus, stability may be evident because many people are consistent in their expectancies and responses in certain types of situations, and are relatively stable in providing feedback that supports traditional role behaviors.

From a contrasting point of view, stability in behavior is a myth. Gergen (1977) points out that perceptions of past and future may be mediated by the present, so that even individual histories are undergoing constant change. Moreover, it may be that perceived stability is located as much in the person–situation interface as in the person alone. That persons appear similar from one situation to another may reflect similarities in role models, expectancies for behavior, and anticipated outcomes in each situation. From this point of view, situations that are phenotypically dissimilar may be functionally alike in supporting and maintaining sex-typed behaviors. Home, work, and social occasions, for example, may all provide cues for males to be dominant and for women to be submissive and to use indirect means of power assertion (Falbo & Peplau, 1979). It follows from this line of reasoning that modifications in situational cues or supports should modify these traditional response tendencies. This hypothesis has been supported in several recent studies. When situational sex-role cues are modified sufficiently, stereotyped behaviors may change significantly. Two examples follow.

Klein and Willerman (1979) hypothesized that individuals may possess a repertoire of behavioral skills that are not used in situations in which they are perceived to be sex-role inappropriate. In three-person problem-solving groups, women subjects were found to be less dominant with males than with females, as predicted by sex-role expectations. However, when subjects were instructed to "try to be the leader (and to) be as dominant and assertive as you can," female subjects were as dominant in offering opinions and assuming leadership roles with men as they were with women in their groups. In support of the contribution of the individual to her own sex-role development, these authors found that women who scored high in dominance on the California Personality Inventory, or who scored Masculine-typed on the Personality Attributes Questionnaire, were more likely to assert dominance in either triad situation. These findings suggest that both situation and person variables enter into the formula for sex-role stability and variation.

A similar interaction of person and external support variables was demonstrated by Richardson, Bernstein, and Taylor (1979), using aggressive behavior (willingness to administer shock) as the dependent sex-typed variable. Female participants competed against males on a reaction time task under three conditions: alone, with a silent female observer, or with a verbally supportive female. As predicted by sex-role expectations, subjects became increasingly willing to use higher intensities of shock when alone or with a supportive female who verbalized statements such as "I don't think I'd let him step all over me!" In comparison, when performing the task in "public" with a silent observer, these women appeared to be nonagressive even in the face of increasing provocation to retaliate aggression. These results strongly suggest that the participants were capable of demonstrating aggressive behavior but chose not to do so in a situation in which they expected to be evaluated. The facilitating function of a supportive female also highlights the importance of peer support for implementation of nontraditional sex-role behavior.

Implications for Individual Change

In terms of the individual who is moving forward in time, what are the options for behavioral and cognitive control over one's own sex-role adaptations? Do research studies such as these on modifications in traditional sex-typed behaviors imply that individuals can change if only they desire to do so? The reciprocal interaction hypothesis suggests that a change in the balance of mutual expectations for behavior between an individual and the effective environment will create instability and counterreaction. The personal and interpersonal impact of individually initiated change will be greater when the boundaries of important social norms are invaded. Recent research on nontraditional or "deviant" sex-role behaviors by both men and women suggests that in many situations, violations of sex-role expectations may elicit internal conflict and negative feedback from others (Costrich, Feinstein, Kidder, Maracek, & Pascale, 1975; Kelly, Kern, Kirkley, Patterson, & Keene, in press). For women especially, because they have been the primary initiators of change, these aversive effects are most apparent when they are participants in male majority groups (Glenwick, Johansson, & Bondy, 1978; Holahan, 1979; Wolman & Frank, 1975). As a result, the individual who wishes to initiate substantial changes in his or her sex-role behaviors within an otherwise stable environment is at a relative disadvantage and must be willing to risk negative feedback and isolation. The probability that individuals will engage in socially high-risk behaviors is related to their relevant predispositions, such as self-attributions of instrumentality and efficacy, and to their expectations for social support. Such support can come from a social reference group at large (such as the "women's movement"), from legal or institutional advocates that provide the enabling conditions for change, from family and peers who offer approval for nontraditional ventures, or from a single cohort who strengthens situational behavior by means of positive suggestion and direct reinforcement. Again, we have come full circle in relating individual change to some modifications of both self-initiated effort and the response of the effective social environment, verifying the mutual interaction between them.

Summary and Conclusions

The development of life-span sex-role orientations has been considered within a framework of reciprocal determinism, in which overt behavior, internal self-monitoring systems, and external environment variables converge to produce both stability and change. During varying periods of life development, individuals may be influenced more by one or another of these variables as they acquire and personally integrate the complex and changing sex-role expectations of American society. Early to middle childhood was seen as the time of extensive learning of stereotyped categorical expectations for males and females, with concomitant divergencies in gender-typed activities, cognitive and interpersonal skills, and evaluative reactions toward self and others. The concept of sex-roles is viewed as a multivariate one with a variety of measures that evidence only partial, if any, convergence. Consequently, the acquisition and subsequent modification of sex-role functioning shows wide variability both within and between male and female groups. In the context of specific situations, individual opportunities for change are constrained by internal and external barriers that may require personal risk taking and social support. It was proposed that a useful theory to encompass all aspects of sex-role development should include the following: a life-span flexibility model with multiple determinants and multiple opportunities for change; cultural relativism in sex-role prescriptions; equivalent treatment of female and male development; and accommodation to individual differences in sex-role functioning.

Acknowledgments

I would like to extend my appreciation to Nikki Garret-Fulks for her helpful assistance and comments during the completion of this chapter.

References

Abrahams, B., Feldman, S. S., & Nash, S. C. Sex role self-concept and sex role attitudes: Enduring personality characteristics or adaptations to changing life situations? *Developmental Psychology*, 1978, *14*, 393–400.

Ahammer, I. M. Social learning theory as a framework for the study of adult personality development. In P. B. Baltes & K. W. Shaie (Eds.), *Life-span developmental psychology: Personality and socialization.* New York: Academic Press, 1973.

Angrist, S. A. The study of sex roles. *Journal of Social Issues*, 1969, *15*, 215–232.

Baltes, P. B., Reese, H. W., & Lipsett, L. P. Life-span developmental psychology. In M. R. Rosenzweig & L. W. Porter (Eds.), *Annual Review of Psychology*, 1980, *31*, 65–110.

Bandura, A. *Social learning theory.* Englewood Cliffs, N.J.: Prentice-Hall, 1977.

Bandura, A. The self system in reciprocal determinism. *American Psychologist*, 1978, *33*, 344–358.

Barry, H., Bacon, M. K., & Child, I. L. A cross-cultural survey of some sex differences in socialization. *Journal of Abnormal and Social Psychology*, 1957, *55*, 327–332.

Bem, S. L. The measurement of psychological androgyny. *Journal of Consulting and Clinical Psychology*, 1974, *47*, 155–162.

Bem, S. L. Sex-role adaptability: One consequence of psychological androgyny. *Journal of Personality and Social Psychology*, 1975, *31*, 634–643.

Bem, S. L. Probing the promise of androgyny. In A. G. Kaplan & J. P. Bean (Eds.), *Beyond sex-role stereotypes: Readings toward a psychology of androgyny.* Boston: Little, Brown, 1976.

Bem, S. L. Theory and measurement of androgyny: A reply to the Pedhauzer-Tetenbaum and Locksley-Colten critiques. *Journal of Personality and Social Psychology*, 1979, *37*, 1047–1054.

Berzins, J. I., Welling, M. A., & Wetter, R. E. A new measure of psychological androgyny based on the Personality Research Form. *Journal of Consulting and Clinical Psychology*, 1978, *46*, 126–138.

Blakemore, J. E. O., LaRue, A. A., & Olejnik, A. B. Sex-appropriate toy preferences and the ability to conceptualize toys as sex-role related. *Developmental Psychology*, 1979, *15*, 339–340.

Block, J. H. Conceptions of sex roles: Some cross-cultural and longitudinal perspectives. *American Psychologist*, 1973, *28*, 512–526.

Block, J. H. Issues, problems, and pitfalls in assessing sex differences: A critical review of "The psychology of sex differences." *Merrill-Palmer Quarterly*, 1976, *22*, 284–308.

Brown, D. G. Masculinity–femininity development in children. *Journal of Consulting Psychology*, 1957, *21*, 197–202.

Bryan, J. W., & Luria, Z. Sex-role learning: A test of the selective attention hypothesis. *Child Development*, 1978, *49*, 13–23.

Coates, S., Lord, M., & Jakabovics, E. Field dependence–independence, social–nonsocial play, and sex differences in preschool children. *Perceptual and Motor Skills*, 1975, *40*, 195–202.

Connor, J. M., Serbin, L. A., & Schackman, M. Sex differences in children's response to training on a visual–spatial test. *Developmental Psychology*, 1977, *13*, 293–294.

Constantinople, A. Masculinity–femininity: An exception to a famous dictum? *Psychological Bulletin*, 1973, *80*, 389–407.

Costrich, N., Feinstein, J., Kidder, L., Maracek, J., & Pascale, L. When stereotypes hurt: Three studies of penalties for sex-role reversals. *Journal of Experimental Social Psychology*, 1975, *11*, 520–530.

Crandall, V. C., & Battle, E. S. The antecedents and adult correlates of academic and intellectual achievement effort. In J. P. Hill (Ed.), *Minnesota symposia on child psychology* (Vol. 4). Minneapolis: University of Minnesota Press, 1970.

Cytrynbaum, S., & Brandt, L. *Women in authority: Dilemmas for male and female subordinates.* Paper presented at the American Psychological Association, New York, September 1979.

Dan, A. J. The menstrual cycle and sex-related differences in cognitive variability. In M. A. Wittig & A. C. Peterson (Eds.), *Sex-related differences in cognitive functioning: Developmental issues.* New York: Academic Press, 1979.

David, D. S., & Brannon, R. *The forty-nine percent majority: The male sex role.* Reading, Mass.: Addison-Wesley, 1976.

Deaux, K. *The behavior of women and men.* Monterey, Calif.: Brooks/Cole, 1976.

DeFrain, J., & Eirick, R. *A review and study of male and female single parents.* Paper presented at the American Psychological Association, New York, September, 1979.

Doherty, M. A. Sexual bias in personality theory. In L. W. Harmon, J. M. Birk, L. E. Fitzgerald, & M. F. Tanney (Eds.), *Counseling women.* Monterey, Calif.: Brooks/Cole, 1978. Pp. 94–105.

Douvan, E. The role of models in women's professional development. *Psychology of Women Quarterly*, 1976, *2*, 5–20.

Dwyer, J., & Mayer, J. Psychological effects of variations in physical appearance during adolescence. *Adolescence*, 1968, *3*, 353–380.

Edelbrock, C., & Sugawara, A. I. Acquisition of sex-typed preferences in preschool-aged children. *Developmental Psychology*, 1978, *14*, 614–623.

Eiseman, M. F. *Interrelationships among psychological androgyny, moral judgment, and ego development in an adult population.* Unpublished doctoral dissertation, University of Kentucky, 1978.

Emmerich, W. Socialization and sex-role development. In P. B. Baltes & K. W. Schaie (Eds.), *Life-span developmental psychology: Personality and socialization.* New York: Academic Press, 1973.

Emmerich, W. *Developmental trends in sex-stereotyped values.* Paper presented at the Society for Research in Child Development, San Francisco, March 1979.

Erikson, E. H. *Childhood and society* (2nd Ed.). New York: Norton, 1963.

Erikson, E. H. *Identity: Youth, and crisis.* New York: Norton, 1968.

Ernster, V. L. American menstrual expressions. *Sex Roles*, 1975, *1*, 3–13.

Etaugh, C., & Hadley, T. Causal attributions of male and female performance by young children. *Psychology of Women Quarterly*, 1977, *2*, 16–23.

Etaugh, C., & Riley, S. Knowledge of sex stereotypes in preschool children. *Psychological Reports*, 1979, *44*, 1279–1283.

Falbo, T., & Peplau, L. S. *Sex-role self-concept and power in intimate relationships.* Paper presented at the American Psychological Association, New York, September 1979.

Farrell, W. *The liberated male.* New York: Random House, 1974.

Fehrenbach, P. A., Miller, D. J., & Thelan, M. H. The importance of consistency of modeling behavior upon imitation: A comparison of single and multiple models. *Journal of Personality and Social Psychology,* 1979, *37,* 1412–1417.

Fennema, E., & Sherman, J. Sex-related differences in mathematics achievement, spatial visualization and affective factors. *American Educational Research Journal,* 1977, *14,* 51–71.

Fling, S., & Manosevitz, M. Sex typing in nursery school children's play interests. *Developmental Psychology,* 1972, *7,* 146–152.

Fox, L. H., Tobin, D., & Brody, L. Sex-role socialization and achievement in mathematics. In M. A. Wittig & A. C. Peterson (Eds.), *Sex-related differences in cognitive functioning: Developmental issues.* New York: Academic Press, 1979.

Frances, S. J. Sex differences in nonverbal behavior. *Sex Roles,* 1979, *5,* 519–535.

Franzini, L. R., Litrownik, A. J., & Blanchard, F. A. Modeling of sex-typed behaviors: Effects on boys and girls. *Developmental Psychology,* 1978, *14,* 313–314.

Freud, S. *New introductory lectures on psychoanalysis.* New York: Norton, 1965.

Frieberg, P., & Bridwell, M. W. An intervention model for rape and unwanted pregnancy. In L. W. Harmon, J. M. Birk, L. E. Fitzgerald, & M. F. Tanney (Eds.), *Counseling women.* Monterey, Calif.: Brooks/Cole, 1978. Pp. 261–269.

Frieze, I., Fisher, J., Hanusa, M., McHugh, M., & Valle, V. Attributions of the causes of success and failure as internal and external barriers to achievement in women. In J. A. Sherman & F. L. Denmark (Eds.), *The psychology of women: Future directions for research,* pp. 519–552. New York: Psychological Dimensions, 1978.

Frieze, I. H., Parsons, J. E., Johnson, P. B., Ruble, D. N., & Zellman, G. L. *Women and sex roles: A social psychological perspective.* New York: Norton, 1978.

Frodi, A., Macaulay, J., & Thome, P. R. Are women always less aggressive than men? *Psychological Bulletin,* 1977, *84,* 634–660.

Frueh, T., & McGhee, P. E. Traditional sex-role development and amount of time spent watching television. *Developmental Psychology,* 1975, *11,* 109.

Garrett, C. S., Ein, P. L., & Tremaine, L. The development of gender stereotyping of adult occupation in elementary school children. *Child Development,* 1977, *48,* 507–512.

Gergen, K. J. Stability, change, and chance in understanding human development. In N. Datan & H. W. Reese (Eds.), *Life-span developmental psychology: Dialectical perspectives on experimental research.* New York: Academic Press, 1977.

Glenwick, S. L., Johansson, S. L., & Bondy, J. A comparison of the self-images of male and female assistant professors. *Sex Roles,* 1979, *4,* 513–524.

Grady, K. Androgyny reconsidered. In J. H. Williams (Ed.), *Psychology of women: Selected readings.* New York: Norton, 1979.

Gullahorn, J. E. Sex-related factors in cognition and brain lateralization. In J. E. Gullahorn (Ed.), *Psychology and women: In transition.* New York: Wiley, 1979.

Harris, S. Influence of subject and experimenter sex in psychological research. *Journal of Consulting and Clinical Psychology,* 1971, *37,* 291–294.

Helmreich, R. L., Spence, J. T., & Holahan, C. K. Psychological androgyny and sex-role flexibility: A test of two hypotheses. *Journal of Personality and Social Psychology,* 1979, *37,* 1631–1644.

Hennig, M. M. Family dynamics and the successful woman executive. In R. B. Kundsin (Ed.), *Women and success: The anatomy of achievement.* Morrow, 1974.

Hoffman, L. W. Changes in family roles, socialization, and sex differences. *American Psychologist,* 1977, *32,* 644–657.

Holahan, C. K. Stress experiences by women doctoral students, need for support, and occupational sex typing: An interactional view. *Sex Roles,* 1979, *5,* 425–437.

Horrocks, J. E., & Jackson, D. W. *Self and role: A theory of self-process and role behavior*. Boston: Houghton Mifflin, 1972.

Huston-Stein, A., & Higgins-Trenk, A. Development of females from childhood through adulthood: Career and feminine role orientations. In P. B. Baltes (Ed.), *Life-span development and behavior* (Vol. 1). New York: Academic Press, 1978, pp. 258–296.

Hyde, J. S., & Phillis, D. E. Androgyny across the life span. *Developmental Psychology*, 1979, *15*, 334–336.

Kagan, J. Acquisition and significance of sex typing and sex-role identity. In M. L. Hoffman & L. W. Hoffman (Eds.), *Review of child development research*. New York: Russell Sage Foundation, 1964.

Kaplan, A. G. Androgyny as a model of mental health for women: From theory to therapy. In A. G. Kaplan & J. B. Bean (Eds.), *Beyond sex-role stereotypes: Readings toward a psychology of androgyny*. Boston: Little, Brown, 1976.

Katz, P. A. The development of female identity. *Sex Roles*, 1979, *5*, 155–178. (a)

Katz, P. A. *Determinants of sex-role flexibility in children*. Paper presented at the Society for Research in Child Development, San Francisco, March 1979. (b)

Kelly, J. A., Furman, W., & Young, V. Problems associated with the typological measurement of sex roles and androgyny. *Journal of Consulting and Clinical Psychology*, 1978, *46*, 1574–1576.

Kelly, J. A., Kern, J., Kirkley, B. G., Patterson, J. N., & Keane, T. M. Reactions to assertive versus unassertive behavior: Differential effects for males and females and implications for assertive training. *Behavior Therapy*, in press.

Kelly, J. A., & Worell, J. New formulations of sex roles and androgyny: A critical review. *Journal of Consulting and Clinical Psychology*, 1977, *45*, 1101–1115.

Kelly, J. A., & Worell, L. Parent behaviors related to masculine, feminine, and androgynous sex-role orientations. *Journal of Consulting and Clinical Psychology*, 1976, *44*, 443–451.

Klein, H. M., & Willerman, L. Psychological masculinity and femininity and typical and maximal dominance expression in women. *Journal of Personality and Social Psychology*, 1979, *37*, 2059–2070.

Kohlberg, L. A cognitive–developmental analysis of children's sex-role concepts and attitudes. In E. E. Maccoby (Ed.), *The development of sex differences*. Palo Alto: Stanford University Press, 1966, pp. 83–173.

Kohlberg, L. Stages and sequences: The cognitive–developmental approach to socialization. In D. A. Goslin (Ed.), *Handbook of socialization theory and research*. Chicago: Rand McNally, 1969.

Kuhn, D., Nash, S. C., & Brucken, L. Sex role concepts of 2- and 3-year-olds. *Child Development*, 1978, *49*, 445–451.

Larwood, L., O'Neal, E., & Brennan, P. Increasing the physical aggressiveness of women. *Journal of Social Psychology*, 1977, *101*, 97–101.

Laws, J. L. *The second X: Sex roles and social roles*. New York: Elsevier, 1979.

Lenney, E. Women's self-confidence in achievement settings. *Psychological Bulletin*, 1977, *84*, 1–13.

Lenney, E. Androgyny: Some audacious assertions toward its coming of age. *Sex Roles*, 1979, *5*, 703–720.

Lewis, K. *Single-father families: How they come to be and how they fare, according to some recent literature*. Paper presented at the 30th annual meeting of the American Association of Psychiatric Services for Children, Atlanta, January 1978.

Lewis, M., & Weinraub, M. Origins of early sex-role development. *Sex Roles*, 1979, *5*, 135–154.

Locksley, A., & Colton, M. E. Psychological androgyny: A case of mistaken identity? *Journal of Personality and Social Psychology*, 1979, *37*, 1007–1031.

Looft, W. R. Sex differences in the expression of vocational aspirations by elementary schoolchildren. *Developmental Psychology*, 1971, *5*, 366.

Lott, B. *A feminist critique of androgyny: Toward the elimination of gender attribution for learned behavior.* Paper presented at the annual meeting of the American Women in Psychology, Los Angeles, March 1980.

Lynch, K., & Cassel, T. Z. *Children's modeling of sex-role behaviors: Sex of child and model, and family communication styles.* Paper presented at the biennial meeting of the Society for Research in Child Development, San Francisco, March 1979.

Lynn, D. B. *Parental and sex-role identification.* Berkeley, Calif.: McCutchen, 1969.

Maccoby, E. E. Woman's sociobiological heritage: Destiny or free choice? In J. E. Gullahorn, (Ed.), *Psychology and women: In transition.* New York: Wiley, 1979.

Maccoby, E. E., & Jacklin, C. N. *The psychology of sex differences.* Stanford: Stanford University Press, 1974.

Marcus, D. E., & Overton, W. F. The development of cognitive gender constancy and sex-role preferences. *Child Development,* 1978, *49,* 434–444.

Masters, J. D., Ford, M. E., Arend, R., Grotevant, H. D., & Clark, L. V. Modeling and labeling as integrated determinants of children's sex-typed imitative behavior. *Child Development,* 1979, *50,* 364–371.

McGhee, P. E., & Frueh, T. Television viewing and the learning of sex-role stereotypes. *Sex Roles,* 1980, *6,* 179–188.

Mednick, M. T. S. The new psychology of women: A feminist analysis. In J. E. Gullahorn (Ed.), *Psychology and women: In transition.* New York: Wiley, 1979.

Mischel, W. A social learning view of sex differences in behavior. In E. E. Maccoby (Ed.), *The development of sex differences.* Stanford: Stanford University Press, 1966.

Mischel, W. Sex typing and socialization. In P. H. Mussen (Ed.), *Carmichael's handbook of child psychology* (Vol. 2, 3rd ed.). New York: Wiley, 1970.

Mischel, W. Toward a cognitive social learning reconceptualization of personality. *Psychological Review,* 1973, *80,* 252–283.

Mischel, W. On the future of personality measurement. *American Psychologist,* 1977, *32,* 246–254.

Money, J., & Ehrhardt, A. A. *Man and woman, boy and girl.* Baltimore: Johns Hopkins Press, 1972.

Mossip, C. E., & Unger, R. K. The perception of asymmetrical faces: Maturational and environmental factors. Cited in Unger, R. K. *Female and male: Psychological perspectives.* New York: Harper & Row, 1979.

Mussen, P. H. Early sex-role development. In D. A. Goslin (Ed.), *Handbook of socialization theory and research.* Chicago: Rand McNally, 1969.

Nash, S. C. The relationship among sex-role stereotyping, sex-role preference, and sex difference in spatial visualization. *Sex Roles,* 1975, *1,* 15–32.

Nash, S. C. Sex roles as a mediator of intellectual functioning. In M. A. Wittig & A. C. Peterson (Eds.), *Sex-related differences in cognitive functioning: Developmental issues.* New York: Academic Press, 1979.

Neugarten, B. L., & Datan, N. Sociological perspectives on the life cycle. In P. B. Baltes & K. W. Shaie (Eds.), *Life-span developmental psychology: Personality and socialization.* New York: Academic Press, 1973.

Orlofsky, J. L. Parental antecedents of sex-role orientation in college men and women. *Sex Roles,* 1979, *5,* 495–512.

Parsons, J. E., & Ruble, D. N. The development of achievement-related expectancies. *Child Development,* 1977, *48,* 1075–1079.

Pederson, D. M., Shinedling, M. M., & Johnson, D. L. Effects of sex of examiner and subject on children's quantitative test performance. *Journal of Personality and Social Psychology,* 1968, *10,* 251–254.

Perry, D. G., & Bussey, K. The social learning theory of sex differences: Imitation is alive and well. *Journal of Personality and Social Psychology,* 1979, *37,* 1699–1712.

Peterson, A. C. *The psychological significance of pubertal changes to adolescent girls.* Paper presented at the biennial meeting of the Society for Research in Child Development, San Francisco, March 1979.

Pleck, J. H., & Sawyer, J. *Men and masculinity.* Englewood Cliffs, N.J.: Prentice-Hall, 1974.

Rabban, M. Sex-role identification in young children in two diverse social groups. *Genetic Psychology Monographs.* 1950, *42*, 81–158.

Rebecca, M., Hefner, R., & Oleshansky, B. A model of sex-role transcendence. In A. G. Kaplan & J. B. Bean (Eds.), *Beyond sex-role stereotypes: Readings toward a psychology of androgyny.* Boston: Little, Brown, 1976.

Richardson, D. C., Bernstein, S., & Taylor, S. P. The effect of situational contingencies on feminine retaliative behavior. *Journal of Personality and Social Psychology,* 1979, *37,* 2044–2048.

Rosenthal, T. L., & Zimmerman, B. J. *Social learning and cognition.* New York: Academic Press, 1978.

Rothbaum, F. Developmental and gender differences in the sex stereotyping of nurturance and dominance. *Developmental Psychology,* 1977, *13,* 531–532.

Rubin, J. Z., Provenzano, F. J., & Luria, J. The eye of the beholder: Parent's views on sex of newborns. *American Journal of Orthopsychiatry,* 1974, *44,* 512–519.

Rumenik, D. K., Capasso, D. R., & Hendrick, C. Experimenter sex effects in behavioral research. *Psychological Bulletin,* 1977, *84,* 852–877.

Russell, G. The father role and its relation to masculinity, femininity, and androgyny. *Child Development,* 1978, *48,* 1174–1181.

Sales, E. Women's adult development. In I. H. Frieze, J. E. Parsons, P. B. Johnson, D. N. Ruble, & G. L. Zelman (Eds.), *Women and sex roles: A social psychological perspective.* New York: Norton, 1978.

Sampson, E. E. Psychology and the American ideal. *Journal of Personality and Social Psychology,* 1977, *35,* 767–782.

Scheresky, R. The gender factor in six- to ten-year-old children's views of occupational roles. *Psychological Reports,* 1976, *38,* 1207–1210.

Schlossberg, N. K., & Goodman, J. A woman's place: Children's sex stereotyping of occupation. *Vocational Guidance Quarterly,* 1972, *20,* 266–270.

Schwartz, P. The social psychology of female sexuality. In J. Sherman & F. L. Denmark (Eds.), *Psychology of women: Future directions for research.* New York: Psychological Dimensions, 1978.

Seavy, C. A., Katz, P. A., & Zalk, S. R. Baby X: The effect of gender labels on adult responses to infants. *Sex Roles,* 1975, *1,* 103–110.

Sher, M. A., & Lansky, L. M. The It scale for children: Effects of variations in the sex-specificity of the It figure. *Merrill-Palmer Quarterly,* 1968, *14,* 323–330.

Sherman, J. A. *Sex-related cognitive differences: An essay on theory and evidence.* Springfield, Ill.: Charles C Thomas, 1978.

Sistrunk, F., & McDavid, J. Sex variable in conforming behavior. *Journal of Personality and Social Psychology,* 1971, *17,* 200–207.

Slaby, R. G. & Frey, K. S. Development of gender constancy and selective attention to same-sex model. *Child Development,* 1975, *46,* 849–856.

Smith, J. E., Goldman, J. A., & Keller, D. *Sex-role preferences: What are we measuring?* Paper presented at the Society for Research in Child Development, San Francisco, March 1979.

Spence, J. T. Traits, roles, and the concept of androgyny. In J. E. Gullahorn (Ed.), *Psychology and women: In transition.* New York: Wiley, 1979.

Spence, J. T., & Helmreich, R. L. *Masculinity and femininity: Their psychological dimensions, correlates, and antecedents.* Austin: University of Texas Press, 1978.

Spence, J. T., & Helmreich, R. L. On assessing androgyny. *Sex Roles,* 1979, *5,* 721–738.

Spence, J. T., Helmreich, R., & Stapp, J. Ratings of self and peers on sex-role attributes and their relation to self-esteem and conceptions of masculinity and femininity. *Journal of Personality and Social Psychology,* 1975, *32,* 29–39.

Stein, A. H., & Bailey, M. M. The socialization of achievement orientation in females. *Psychological Bulletin*, 1973, *80*, 345–366.

Stein, A. H., & Friedrich, L. K. Impact of television on children and youth. In E. M. Hetherington (Ed.), *Review of child development research* (Vol. 5). Chicago: University of Chicago Press, 1975, pp. 183–258.

Sternglanz, S. H., & Serbin, L. A. Sex-role stereotyping in children's television programs. *Developmental Psychology*, 1974, *10*, 710–715.

Thompson, S. K. Gender labels and early sex-role development. *Child Development*, 1975, *46*, 339–347.

Ullian, D. Z. The development of conceptions of masculinity and femininity. In B. Lloyd & J. Archer (Eds.), *Exploring sex differences*. London: Academic Press, 1976.

Unger, R. K. *Female and male: Psychological perspectives*. New York: Harper & Row, 1979.

Urberg, K. A. *The development of androgynous sex-role concepts in young children*. Paper presented at the Society for Research in Child Development, San Francisco, March 1979. (a)

Urberg, K. A. Sex-role conceptualizations in adolescents and adults. *Developmental Psychology*, 1979, *15*, 90–92. (b)

Waber, D. P. Sex differences in mental abilities, hemispheric lateralization, and rate of physical growth at adolescence. *Developmental Psychology*, 1977, *13*, 29–38.

Waber, D. P. The meaning of sex-related variations in maturation rate. In J. E. Gullahorn (Ed.), *Psychology and women: In transition*. New York: Wiley, 1979.

Weitz, S. *Sex roles: Biological, psychological, and social foundations*. New York: Oxford University Press, 1977.

Whiting, B., & Edwards, C. P. A cross-cultural analysis of sex differences in the behavior of children aged three through eleven. *Journal of Social Psychology*, 1973, *91*, 171–188.

Will, J. A., Self, P. A., & Datan, N. Maternal behavior and perceived sex of infant. *American Journal of Orthopsychiatry*, 1976, *49*, 135–139.

Williams, J. H. *Psychology of Women: Behavior in a biosocial context*. New York: Norton, 1977.

Williams, J. E., Bennett, S. M., & Best, D. L. Awareness and expression of sex stereotypes in young children. *Developmental Psychology*, 1975, *11*, 635–642.

Wittig, M. A., & Peterson, A. C. (Eds.), *Sex-related differences in cognitive functioning: Developmental issues*. New York: Academic Press, 1979.

Wolf, T. M. Effects of live modeled sex-inappropriate play behavior in a naturalistic setting. *Developmental Psychology*, 1973, *9*, 120–123.

Wolman, C., & Frank, H. The solo women in a professional peer group. *Journal of Orthopsychiatry*, 1975, *45*, 164–171.

Worell, J. Sex roles and psychological well-being: Perspectives on methodology. *Journal of Consulting and Clinical Psychology*, 1978, *46*, 777–791.

Worell, J. *Changing sex roles*. Address presented at a meeting of the Southeastern Psychological Association, New Orleans, March 1979. (ERIC Document No. ED 170–066).

Worell, J. Psychological sex roles: Significance and change. In J. Worell (Ed.), *Psychological development in the elementary years*. New York: Academic Press, 1981.

Worell, J., & Stilwell, W. E. *Psychology for teachers and students*. New York: McGraw-Hill, 1981.

Worell, L., & Worell, J. *The parent behavior form*. Unpublished manuscript, University of Kentucky, 1976.

RUSSELL T. JONES
JANELL I. HANEY

13

A Body–Behavior Conceptualization of a Somatopsychological Problem: Race

Introduction

Although the diversity that characterizes people might be said to enhance the quality of human existence, this selfsame characteristic may be
cited as a causal factor in many of the negative facets of humanity, including prejudice, revulsion, unwanted pity, exclusion, and other social
obstacles to the happiness and well-being of the individual. This problem
is, perhaps, most blatantly manifested in the negative social consequences
that individuals with certain variations in physical characteristics have
encountered.

That one's physical attributes play a significant role in others' reactions
to the individual is evident. Indeed, the "tall, dark, and handsome" young
man may become a hit at the box office, the attractive young woman may
be the recipient of whistles and second glances, and the muscular teenager
may attain a position on the football team. However, on the other side
of the coin, obvious variations in physical features, such as cosmetic defect
and physical disability, have, throughout time, resulted in extreme, negative societal reactions, ranging from pity to revulsion. Racial characteristics, although a normal variation in physique that would seem to lack
inherent desirability–undesirability characteristics, may have equally negative consequences for the individual, as witnessed by both historical and

Individuals as Producers of Their Development

current events. Recent research on the effects of physique further points out the importance of variations in appearance.

Both the benefits and problems (whether physical or social) that an individual incurs as a result of his or her physique have been conceptualized as being within the domain of somatopsychology: the study of the body–behavior relationship. However, the present chapter will focus on the negative, rather than positive, side of this relationship. Thus, somatopsychological/body–behavior problems will be examined, with a focus on the problems that may result from racial characteristics–social environment interaction.

Of course, the interaction between one's racial characteristics and his or her social environment need not be and is not always negative. In instances where no negative consequences are incurred as a result of physical characteristics–social environment interaction, there is no need to speak of a body–behavior problem. Unfortunately, the very use of race as a sample case for a chapter on somatopsychological problems points to the fact that racial characteristics, *in interaction with the social environment of twentieth-century America,* can, and often do, result in negative consequences, or body–behavior problems. It is hoped that a body–behavior conceptualization of the negative consequences of racial characteristics–social environment interaction will make this interaction more amenable to interpretation as well as to assessment and intervention.

OVERVIEW

Inasmuch as familiarity with the definition of somatopsychology, the scope of somatopsychology, and the terms involved in somatopsychology will provide an essential foundation for a clear understanding of the current conceptualization of body–behavior problems, this background information will be given at the outset. Following this, a brief chronological account of the historical context from which somatopsychology has grown will be supplied, and issues in the conceptualization of the physique–behavior relationship will be detailed. A discussion concerning the development of body–behavior problems as well as research pertaining to reactions to racial stimuli will then ensue. Next, past intervention techniques will be examined. The chapter will end with a behavioral model, designed to enhance conceptualization, assessment, and amelioration of problems resulting from racial characteristics.

DEFINITION

The term *somatopsychology* is derived from *soma,* meaning 'body,' and *psyche,* meaning 'mind' or 'soul'. Consequently, somatopsychology has been defined as the study of "those variations in physique that affect the psychological situation of a person by influencing the effectiveness of his body as a tool for actions or by serving as a stimulus to himself or to others [Hamilton, 1950, p. 2]," "problems and variables concerned with atypical physique as it relates to psychological status [Barker, Wright, Meyerson, & Gonick, 1953, p. 1]," and "some of the relationships that bind physique and behavior [Meyerson, 1971, p. 2]." In the present chapter, somatopsychology is being conceptualized from a behavioral viewpoint. Thus, the behavioral problems and benefits, rather than psychological problems and benefits, resulting from variations in physical characteristics (such as racial features) are the objects of assessment.

SCOPE

Both the individual and his or her social environment must be examined to ascertain the relevance of the individual's physical characteristics to somatopsychological behavior problems: i.e., (a) Does the physical characteristic necessitate behavioral adjustments that are only indirectly related to it; (b) Does the physical characteristic serve as an indicator of an individual's position in his or her life career; or (c) Is the physical characteristic significant within the individual's societal context (see Barker et al., 1953)? Although characteristics that have been discussed as having somatopsychological effects include size, age, race, sex, cosmetic defect, muscular strength, motor ability, speech defects, visual impairments, auditory impairments, tuberculosis, heart disease, diabetes mellitus, rheumatism, leprosy, cancer, orthopedic disability, and acute illness (Barker et al., 1953), this chapter will focus on body–behavior problems associated with racial characteristics.

In the present conceptualization, physique is being regarded as one factor that influences both (a) the individual's reactions to him- or herself; and (b) others' reactions to the individual. For example, Cyrano's large nose may be both the object of ridicule by others and a source of embarrassment to himself. The nature of the reactions will be viewed as a determinant of the individual's subsequent behavior, consequently affecting future reactions and contributing to the behavioral functioning of the individual. Thus, both physical characteristics (e.g., physical attractiveness, size, age, race, and auditory or visual impairments) and the behavioral characteristics that may develop as a result of physical characteristics, whether directly connected (e.g., a person who is deaf may talk too loud) or indirectly connected (e.g., a person who is physically unattractive may engage in avoidance behaviors) are being considered as factors in the individual's somatopsychological problem.

TERMS

Although the terms *disability* and *handicap* are frequently used interchangeably, professionals concerned with the area of disabilities and handicaps (body–behavior problems) have found this practice to be inhibitory to clear communication. Similarly, terms such as *race, prejudice, discrimi-*

nation, and *racism* are frequently causes of confusion. Inasmuch as the first pair of terms plays an integral role in the understanding of body–behavior problems in general and the latter group is essential to comprehension of those problems specific to race, it is considered expedient to dispel any semantic confusion at this point.

First, it must be remembered that a variation consists of any characteristic that is different from average. Thus, individuals may vary in any number of ways, including hair color and texture, eye color, nose width and length, height, weight, skin color, skin texture, attractiveness, and loss or deformity of bodily parts. However, whether disabilities and handicaps, only handicaps, or no negative consequences accompany variations depends upon the demands of the environment—both physical and social (see Busch-Rossnagel, Chapter 11, this volume, and Susser & Watson, 1962, for further discussion).

Disability has been defined (Smith & Neisworth, 1975) as "an objectively defined deviation in physique or functioning that, through interaction with a specified environment, results in behavioral inadequacies or restrictions for the person [p. 169]"; handicap has been referred to as the "burden imposed upon the individual by the unfortunate product of deviation and environment [p. 169]." Disability may thus refer to physical deviations that result in behavioral restrictions with respect to a certain physical environment. A *handicap*, however, exists when an individual's attainment of either a physical or social goal is hindered by the interaction between a personal characteristic and a particular physical or social environment, disability or not. The handicap is the physical or social hindrance (cf. Busch-Rossnagel; Chapter 11, this volume).

Being deaf is a variation that is a disability if a deaf person is involved in a conversation with people who can hear. The handicap is the inability to hear others' conversation. Being physically unattractive is a variation that is not a disability in that it does not result in a functional, or physical, inadequacy. Physical unattractiveness may, however, result in a social handicap in that the individual may have fewer friends. To reiterate, whereas a person whose legs are paralyzed may incur a disability and a person of a particular race may not, a building with only steps and a group of people with negative opinions about one's race, age, or body build may be equally inaccessible: A physical characteristic that, *in conjunction with the environment*, results in a physical or social hindrance has produced a handicap. Thus, both physical and social handicaps, as negative consequences of a physical characteristic and its possible concomitant behavioral characteristics, are the primary focus of the study of body–behavior problems. Table 13.1 provides two illustrations of the possible consequences of physical variation–environment interaction.

To conceptualize race in terms of body–behavior problems (as a variation that, in interaction with the environment, may result in a handicap), an

TABLE 13.1
Possible Results of Physical Variation–Environment Interaction

Type of variation	A. No body–behavior problem	B. Social handicap	C. Disability + physical handicap	D. Disability + physical and social handicaps
A. Cannot whistle	Nobody can whistle or whistle is unimportant (not a socially valued skill). Whistling is unnecessary to accomplish physical goals.	Whistling is socially valued. Those who cannot whistle are less accepted and even rejected by others.	A person needs a cab and must be able to whistle to hail one.	B + C
B. 5-ft tall	Everyone is 5-ft tall or height is unimportant (not relevant to social desirability). Height has no relevance to ability to accomplish physical goals.	Being taller than 5 ft is socially valued or being shorter than 5 ft is socially valued. Those who are 5 ft tall are less accepted and even rejected by others.	A person who is not over 5-ft tall cannot reach doorknobs, even with the highest heels available.	B + C

objective definition should be sought. However, finding a single, objectively based criterion upon which to categorize by race is difficult because of the ambiguity that has been discussed elsewhere (see Berry & Tischler, 1978; J. M. Jones, 1972).

Initial problems in the search for a definition stem from attempts to ascertain a relevant basis for differentiating people along the racial dimension. Indeed, the term *race* has been applied on at least 10 different bases, including nationality, language, religion, physical characteristics, biology, and culture (Berry & Tischler, 1978). As a result, the *American Heritage Dictionary of the English Language* (1973) lists several definitions of race, including (a) "a local geographic or global human population distinguished as a more or less distinct group by genetically transmitted physical characteristics"; (b) "mankind as a whole"; (c) "any group of people united or classified together on the basis of common history, nationality, or geographic distribution"; (d) "a genealogical line; lineage; family"; and (e) "any group of people more or less distinct from all others [pp. 1074–1075]."

Inasmuch as negative consequences resulting from the interaction of physical characteristics and the environment are a central focus in the study of body–behavior problems, the first definition, concerning "genetically transmitted physical characteristics," is perhaps the most relevant to the current problem. However, biological racial distinctions have been described as difficult, if not impossible to make (Berry & Tischler, 1978; J. M. Jones, 1972). Consequently, this chapter will consider those physical characteristics that socially, rather than biologically, define races. Because negative social consequences are a primary concern in the study of body–behavior problems, this view has the advantage of using the same distinction to define race as is used socially to categorize and react to others. Thus, in the United States, categories such as white, black, Mexican–American, American Indian, and Chinese–American are socially considered to be races.[1] Although an individual's race may vary, in this sense, as a result of who is perceiving him or her, it is the reaction of the perceiver(s) (including the self) to the *supposed* (or perceived) race of the perceived individual that is of concern here.

In discussions of race, the handicaps that may result from the interaction of racial characteristics and environment have traditionally been conceptualized as the results of prejudice, discrimination, and racism. Inasmuch as J. M. Jones (1972) provides an indepth discussion of these three concepts, only definitions and brief descriptions of each will be presented here.

[1] This chapter will focus on relations between the two major groups of individuals in this country (black and white) because extensive work has been done with these two groups. Findings concerning other groups have been reported elsewhere (see Selznick & Steinberg, 1969; Simpson & Yinger, 1958; Williams, 1964).

The first term, *prejudice*, has been defined on both an individual and a social level. Taking both views into account (considering both the feelings of individual group members and the positive reference point that the individual's own group becomes), prejudice may be defined as "*a negative attitude toward a person or group based upon a social comparison process in which the individual's own group is taken as the positive point of reference* [p. 3]." *Discrimination*, however, may be defined as "those actions designed to maintain own-group characteristics and favored position *at the expense of* members of the comparison group [p. 4]." Therefore, some discriminatory acts might be viewed as overt manifestations of prejudice, an attitude.

Racism may exist in three forms: individual, institutional, and cultural. On the individual level, which is closely related to race prejudice, racism has been defined as "any set of beliefs that organic, genetically transmitted differences (whether real or imagined) between human groups are intrinsically associated with the presence or the absence of certain socially relevant abilities or characteristics, hence that such differences are a legitimate basis of invidious distinctions between groups socially defined as races [van den Berghe, 1967, p. 11]." At this level, racists may be divided into two types: (*a*) dominative, who openly try to keep other races in their place (inferior position), through force, if necessary; and (*b*) aversive, who believe in own-race superiority and are quite aware of the superior position that their own racial group holds in the society, but whose behavior is marked more by acts such as avoidance and polite coldness (where contact is unavoidable) than by overt efforts to maintain the superior position (Kovel, 1970, p. 54). On the institutional level, racism may consist of the employment of practices leading to intended or unintended unequal consequences.

Thus, prohibition by white administrators of black individuals' entry into a school (intentional, dominative), permission of entry followed by withdrawal of some white students (intentional, aversive), and use of a standardized achievement test (standardized on white individuals) as an admission requirement (unintentional) are all examples of institutional racism. Cultural racism, which pertains to the individual or institutional expression of cultural superiority, is to be found in beliefs concerning the inferiority of a cultural heritage or, more recently, belief that no distinct heritage (outside of this country) exists.

It must be noted, however, that race, the particular body–behavior problem under discussion, is definitely not a disability, either alone or in interaction with the environment. Additionally, racial characteristics are not a handicap, nor do racial characteristics, alone, ever cause a handicap. Only when an individual encounters negative reactions, including prejudice, discrimination, and racism, as a result of his or her racial characteristics, is he or she faced with a handicap. Thus, this chapter will be concerned only with those situations in which social handicaps, or social body–behavior problems, do occur and with the amelioration of the social (rather than the physical) environment.

Study of the Body–Behavior Relationship

The study of the body–behavior relationship is one that dates back to primitive times. This realm of inquiry has been commonly based on the assumptions that character can be discerned from physical features and that persons can be classified or categorized according to physique.

Around 425 B.C., for example, Hippocrates first delineated two types of physiques, to which he ascribed two different temperaments (Sheldon, 1944). Persons with muscular physiques, he discovered, showed a tendency to develop apoplexy whereas those with delicate physiques tended to be susceptible to tuberculosis.

Physiognomy, phrenology, and other forms of character reading, which flourished during the middle of the nineteenth century, took a different route and attempted to determine character from specific features. Physiognomists studied outer appearance, particularly the face, in the belief that inner character would be reflected in outer characteristics (see Lavater, 1848). Phrenologists investigated the contours of the skull, thinking that personality could be determined from this inner characteristic (see Spurzheim, 1908).

Rostan, Viola, Kretschmer, and Sheldon (among others) followed up on the work of Hippocrates and attempted to classify physique. Sheldon (Sheldon, Stevens, & Tucker, 1940), for example, rated individuals on three components—endomorphy (softness and roundness), mesomorphy (muscularity), and ectomorphy (linearity and fragility)—on a 7-point scale with respect to five bodily areas. Correlations of approximately .80 were found between these components of physique and the three basic types of temperament that he proposed (Sheldon, 1942). Thus, endomorphy was found to be associated with viscerotonia (comfort, sociability, etc.), mesomorphy was discovered to be associated with somatonia (physical activity, risk-taking, etc.), and ectomorphy was found to be associated with cerebrotonia (restraint, secretiveness, etc.).

The establishment of a link between single physical characteristics and personality, as suggested by the early character reading, is not only unlikely in view of the complexity of humans but also tends to be discredited by research (Wright, 1960). Although later efforts have yielded positive, but lower correlations (e.g., Walker, 1962), Sheldon's work in classification has been criticized for its methodology (i.e., subjective determination of physique types, rating of physique and temperament by the same person

[Sheldon], and evidence for two [but not three] physique types; see Humphreys, 1957). The continued interest in this area, however, points to the significance of this earlier work in body–behavior relationships for the current efforts in the area of body–behavior problems.

Issues Surrounding the Body–Behavior Relationship

Several investigators have scrutinized the basic assumptions underlying the search for a body–behavior relationship (Barker *et al.*, 1953; Lindzey, 1965; Meyerson, 1971). A foundation for understanding possible approaches to conceptualization of body–behavior problems is provided through these attempts to explicate the relationship between physique and behavior:

1. "Is there a relationship between physique and behavior?" In some instances, variations in physical characteristics appear to have no corresponding variation in behavior. Such seems to be the case with variations in fingerprints and toe length. Similarly, variations in behavior (many occupations, for example) often have no related variation in physique. A relationship between physique and behavior cannot always be demonstrated.

2. "In situations where there is a relationship between physique and behavior, is the relationship causal?" Whereas behavior may have immediate and/or delayed influence on physique (e.g., giving a speech or weight lifting), physical variations such as height, attractiveness, and vision can limit or facilitate some behaviors directly or indirectly. Additionally, a third variable, such as Down's syndrome, or a past event may simultaneously determine physique and behavior. Thus, causal relationships may exist in either direction, but the relationship is not always causal.

3. "What formulation may be used to describe all situations of relationship or nonrelationship between physique and behavior?" Meyerson (1971) posited that behavior is a function of person–environment interaction. In this explanation physique is simply one factor in determining behavior. Therefore, as noted elsewhere, the individual influences (physical limitations) and the stimulus value (social limitations) of atypical physique function as partial determinants of behavior: This is the somatopsychological aspect of the relationship (see Barker *et al.*, 1953).

APPROACHES TO CONCEPTUALIZATION

From this discussion it is clear that an adequate conceptualization of body–behavior problems must recognize the role of both the individual, who possesses various physical characteristics and behaviors, and the environment. Several current theoretical orientations use this approach, but with variations in their point of focus. Some (dialectically oriented) theorists view development as an active transaction between the individual and the environment (see Riegel, 1975). Other (organismically oriented) developmentalists view the individual as being actively involved in his or her own development (see Lerner, 1976; Schneirla, 1957). Yet other (behaviorally oriented) theorists emphasize environmental action upon the individual (see Bijou & Baer, 1961).

A dialectically oriented theorist such as Riegel (1975) would note that the individual with a variation in physique is experiencing an asynchrony on one or both of two (of the four) levels of development—between his or her own needs and wants and others' reactions (on either the individual–psychological and/or cultural–sociological level) to the particular physical characteristics that he or she possesses. On another level, the individual's problem might be seen as a conflict within the cultural–sociological dimension inasmuch as others' reactions, as a group, may be directed not only toward that individual but toward all individuals with that particular variation. Resolution of such asynchronies are seen to be part of the never-ending (individual, social, and physical) process of change that this view depicts.

Organismic theorists would be inclined to emphasize the role of individuals. From this viewpoint, the individual's physical characteristics would be described as stimuli that cause others in the environment to respond in a particular fashion. The responses of others would be considered as feedback, causing the individual to actively pursue a particular course. Changes in the individual cause others to change their reactions (and cause further changes in the individual), and a "circular function" is created. Development results from this interaction.

From a behavioral point of view, the physical characteristics of the individual might be viewed as stimuli that cause both the person and others to react in a particular fashion. Such reactions may provide reinforcing, punishing, or neutral consequences for the individual. These consequences serve to influence the individual's behavior (and, consequently, future reactions) and thus affect overall development. In an earlier conceptualization of body–behavior problems, Neisworth, R. T. Jones, and Smith (1978) applied this perspective to somatopsychological problems.

Whether one regards the individual, the environment, or both as active in development, it seems evident that certain factors that contribute to body–behavior problems will be attended to: (a) a variation in physical appearance; (b) negative reactions on the part of both the individual and others toward that variation; and (c) negative consequences for the individual's development. Before considering these factors and their relation to body–behavior problems resulting from race, however, it will prove helpful to gain an understanding of both the individual and social origin of the negative attitudes that result in body–behavior problems.

The Development of Somatopsychological/
Body–Behavior Problems

THE INDIVIDUAL

Two determinants of an observer's perception of a characteristic as being "deviant" or different in a negative fashion, are (a) the experience of the observer; and (b) the visibility of the characteristic (Goffman, 1963; Neisworth et al., 1978). These two factors provide a context within which to view negative perception of physical variation.

Thus, for a body–behavior problem to exist, one or more of the physical characteristics of the individual must be viewed by the perceiver (the individual and/or others) as being different. This perception may come about only through past experience of the perceiver: Others can respond only to that to which they have learned to respond. In some situations, this experience might consist of highly specific training, such as medical school. For example, a doctor may recognize signs of a serious illness that would go unnoticed by the lay person. As the "training" becomes more broadly defined, it may refer to the socialization experiences that each child in a given social group or country receives (in varying amounts). However, for these experiences to contribute to a body–behavior problem, the characteristic must be viewed in a negative manner. That is, individuals must have learned to associate particular characteristics with negative attitudes and behaviors. Additionally, in each individual circumstance, the individual's variation must be sufficiently prominent to be observed and reacted to. A physical characteristic that is both capable of being seen and that has negative characteristics associated with it will be perceived negatively by the individual and/or by others. This negative perception is likely to result in negative reactions to the individual that, in turn, may negatively influence the individual's behavior, causing him or her to behave as expected and fulfill a self-fulfilling prophecy (see Merton, 1948; Rosenthal & Jacobson, 1968). Thus, the individual's overall development and the subsequent reactions to him or her may be affected, setting into motion a "circular function" (see Lerner, 1976; Schneirla, 1957).

Consistent with this notion, two studies demonstrated that children rather consistently maintained greater distances from other children with chubby (endomorphic) body types than from children with average (mesomorphic) or skinny (ectomorphic) body types (Lerner, 1973; Lerner, Karabenick, & Meisels, 1975). In addition, a similar study indicated that negative stereotypes toward chubbiness may result in negative body concepts in children, whereas positive stereotypes toward average body types may yield positive body concepts (Lerner & Korn, 1972).

THE SOCIETY

Of course, perception of physical characteristics may vary from situation to situation. One society may perceive certain characteristics in an entirely different manner from another. Subgroups within a society may also differ in their attributions to characteristics. These differing perceptions will determine which characteristics are the recipients of attention and which are perceived in a negative fashion—and, therefore, the categories into which individuals with certain characteristics will be placed.

This categorization is said to develop out of the human need for reduction of the overabundance of stimulus input to manageable proportions (Allport, 1954; Lerner, 1976). Thus, the process of categorization fulfills several needs, including (a) guidance for actions; (b) simplification of the evaluative process; and (c) assistance in quick identification (Allport, 1954). However, overgeneralization eventually leads to social stereotyping and the differential reaction patterns and possible problems of overall development previously mentioned (Lerner, 1976). That is, in attempting to maintain manageability, people who are placed in a particular category are, to some extent, believed to possess the same attributes (stereotyping).

Inasmuch as it is through a stranger's first appearance, as Goffman (1963) has noted, that the stranger is categorized, negative categorizations are sources of potential body–behavior problems. Whereas classification simplifies the complexity of the world by suggesting a stereotypic reaction, the previously cited research on body build indicates that this convenience may, indeed, be costly to individuals possessing certain physical characteristics. The following discussion will focus specifically on somato-psychological/body–behavior problems that the social environment may create in conjunction with racial characteristics.

A Sample Case: Race

SOCIAL CONSEQUENCES OF RACIAL CHARACTERISTICS

Investigations of reactions to racial stimuli have employed numerous modes of assessment, including acceptance, preference, social distance, trait attribution, observational, personality, autonomic, and disguised measures. Findings stemming from the use of these techniques will be detailed in reference to racial acceptance and preference in children, to social distance in adults, to trait attribution in both children and adults, and to the importance of race in relation to other factors. It should be noted at the outset, however, that much of this research has been criticized on a number of points, including conceptualization, methodology, and interpretation. Given the complexity of this domain of inquiry, these efforts may be viewed simply as steps toward methodologically sounder studies. In any case, they provide the best available assessment of the current effect of racial characteristics on interaction. Thus, throughout this chapter, the issues that envelop the findings and the consequently tenuous nature of the subsequent theorizing must be kept in mind.

ACCEPTANCE AND PREFERENCE IN CHILDREN

Investigations designed to assess the influence of a subject's race on his or her acceptance and preference of particular races have generally been conducted with young children. To measure acceptance (defined as willingness to play with children of a particular race), pictures of children of two or more races are typically presented to the experimental subjects, and the experimenter inquires as to whether the subject would like to play with various stimulus children, with no mention of race. Measures of preference (defined as choice of children of a particular race) generally require that the child choose the stimulus child, doll, or puppet with whom he or she would rather play. Williams and Morland (1976) cite several studies that have employed the Morland Picture Inventory (MPI), an assessment device using pictures. The results of their extensive examination of the literature will be briefly described.

On acceptance measures, both black and white experimental subjects have demonstrated acceptance of both black and white stimulus children with this format. However, black children have tended to demonstrate more acceptance of white stimulus children (an average of 95%) than white children have demonstrated toward black stimulus children (an average of 82%). Own-race acceptance, on the other hand, averaged 89% for black children and 93% for white children.

On preference measures, preschool black children (ages 3–6) have more frequently chosen white stimulus children (an average of 58% of the time) than black stimulus children (an average of 30% of the time).[2,3] With in-school black children (Grades 1 through 3, ages 6–9), it was found that white stimulus children were chosen an average of 21% of the time, whereas black stimulus children were chosen an average of 58% of the time. White children, however, were observed to show a high preference for white stimulus children at both in-school and preschool levels, with a preschool average of 74% (and 14% for black stimuli) and an in-school percentage of 79 (and 15% for black stimuli). Whereas doll and puppet studies generally support these findings (e.g., Asher & Allen, 1969; Clark & Clark, 1947; Gregor & McPherson, 1966), some of the more recent studies in this area indicate that black children prefer black stimuli (e.g., Fox & Jordan, 1973; Harris & Braun, 1971; Hraba & Grant, 1970).[4]

[2] Because some children gave no clear indication of preference, percentages do not add up to 100.

[3] It has been noted that the responses of black children on these (preference) measures have generally not been statistically different from chance (see Banks, 1976; Banks, McQuater, & Ross, 1979). However, this interpretation has been challenged (i.e., a comparison of white and black children's responses has been said to be meaningful; Williams & Morland, 1976).

[4] Whereas some authors have attributed this latter finding to recent changes, including the Civil Rights Movement (Hraba & Grant, 1970) and the increased commonness of black dolls (Brand et al., 1974), it has also been noted that the studies showing white preference were also conducted after 1960 (Banks, 1976).

Although the internal and external validity as well as the interpretation of the results of these studies has been questioned (see Banks, 1976; Banks, McQuater, & Ross, 1979; Brand, Ruiz, & Padilla, 1974; J. M. Jones, 1972; Lerner & Knapp, 1976, for example), they do serve as an indication of the influence of racial characteristics on expressed acceptance and preference of racial stimuli on existing measures. That is, both black and white in-school children appear to prefer own-race stimuli, and both black (although not significantly) and white preschool children seem to prefer white stimuli on present preference measures. Although both white and black children seem to accept other-race stimuli, the lesser degree of preference for black stimulus children tentatively suggests, particularly at the preschool level, less frequent interactions and/or more frequent negative interactions for black children.

SOCIAL DISTANCE IN ADULTS

Social distance scales have the added dimension of telling how close, socially, an individual would permit a person of a particular type to be to him- or herself. For example, as in Bogardus' (1925) study, the subject, typically an adult, might be questioned as to whether he or she would permit a person of a particular race to be in his or her family (through marriage), club, neighborhood (same street), occupation, or country (as a citizen or as a visitor) or whether he or she would exclude the person from his or her country.

Using this scale, Bogardus found that native-born Americans of 30 ethnic backgrounds (selected to roughly approximate the proportions found in the population, but favoring the 18 to 35 age bracket) ranked blacks 31 out of 36 groups of individuals in 1926 and 35 out of 36 groups of individuals in 1946, with lower numbers indicating permission of greater closeness (Bogardus, 1947).

Proenza and Strickland (1965) reported that black subjects gave more favorable scores to a "white" cue than white subjects gave to a "Negro" cue. Indeed, in 1960, 77.1% of the variance of a group of white subjects' social distance scores was reported to be attributable to race (Triandis & Triandis, 1960), whereas most of the variance (67.7%) of black subjects' scores in the same study (only nine subjects) was reported to be attributable to interactions of race, social class, religion, and nationality. Although black subjects' scores in a 1960 study did not indicate an alteration in social distance from the early fifties to the early sixties, later white subjects permitted closer relationships with all groups of stimuli except "Cuban" and "Negro," for whom they showed an increase in desired social distance (Fagan & O'Neill, 1965).[5]

[5] This last finding was considered to reflect more realism on the part of the later white subjects, who had a greater likelihood of actually encountering the situation in question (e.g., a black individual in their neighborhood or school) than did earlier white subjects.

Differences in cultural norms (Brand *et al.*, 1974; Triandis & Triandis, 1965) have made it difficult to determine differences in social distance across cultures and times. Additionally, there may be differences in expressed social distance and actual permitted social distance. Although these problems may interfere with the interpretation and generalization of these findings, it appears that, in addition to influencing children's expressed preferences, racial characteristics also have an effect on the amount of social distance that adults prefer to keep between themselves and others. The extremely low ranking of black individuals by white subjects points, again, to potential negative social consequences for this group in actual interaction.

TRAIT ATTRIBUTION IN CHILDREN AND ADULTS

Whereas preference and social distance measures might be employed to indicate positiveness of attitudes, or liking, of individuals of particular races, assessment of trait attribution may indicate how the individual perceives persons of a certain race. Trait attribution measures generally require that the subject assign adjectives or statements (either listed or created) to racial groups or vice versa. For example, the doll, puppet, and picture tests that have been used with young children have included questions that require selection of a doll, puppet, or picture in response to positive and negative adjectives (e.g., good, bad, nice, naughty, smart, or stupid). With older children and adults, the requested responses usually involve selection of a number of traits on a paper and pencil task.

In the investigations that have employed dolls, puppets, and pictures as stimuli, it has been found that both black and white preschool children have assigned more positive adjectives to white stimuli, and that this trend seems to continue through the sixth grade (see Williams & Morland, 1976).[6] However, findings suggest that this positive–negative trend may decrease as the age of the subjects increases. By tenth and eleventh grades, subjects may be more likely to assign both negative and positive stereotypes to blacks (see Blake & Dennis, 1943).

Employment of a series of such investigations may indicate change across time and across race. Indeed, white college students at Princeton University assigned increasingly less favorable traits to the group "American" and increasingly more favorable traits to the group "Negro" from 1933 (D. Katz & Braly, 1933) to 1951 (Gilbert, 1951) to 1969 (Karlins, Coffman, & Walters, 1969). Although the lessening of the distance between the favorability of the terms ("American" and "Negro") and the greater reluctance that the latter two subject groups expressed in making attributions are suggestive of a weakening of stereotypic thought, the continuing uniformity of thought and the continually low "Negro" average

---

[6] However, these findings are subject to the criticisms leveled at preference studies.

favorability rating (near 0 on a scale ranging from -2 to $+2$ in 1967) is indicative of the fact that stereotypes still remain (J. M. Jones, 1972). However, administration of the same (D. Katz & Braly) questionnaire to black college students around 1940 revealed racial stereotyping which was similar to that of the earliest Princeton subjects (Bayton, 1941), and a subsequent study revealed that the class of the stimulus appears to be more important than the race of the stimulus in determining stereotype attribution (Bayton, McAlister, & Hamer, 1956). Indeed, racial influences upon stereotype attribution appear to have their effect through factors that are relevant to social class attributes (Feldman & Hilterman, 1975). Thus, because a larger percentage of black people have been in the lower-class category, both white and black subjects have been likely to use lower-class black individuals as a reference point in studies that provide only race or ethnicity as the stimulus (cf. J. M. Jones, 1972).

Several problems may arise with trait attribution techniques—including forced selection of a stereotype (Brigham, 1971) and employment of particular response sets by subjects (Cook & Sellitz, 1964). In addition, willingness on the part of subjects to stereotype almost any group suggests that stereotyping may occur without prejudice (Brigham, 1971). Nevertheless, the fact that stereotypes exist points to the effect that race may have on perception of groups, if not individuals (through prejudice and discrimination). The fact that stereotyping of blacks, as a group, is negative suggests, in a third way, the potential for body–behavior problems.

THE INFLUENCE OF FACTORS OTHER THAN RACE

As can be seen, race seems to be a factor in acceptance, preference, degree of permitted social closeness, and trait attribution. In addition, race alone has been found to lead to differences in assumed attitude similarity (Byrne & Wong, 1962); immediacy (mainly through personal interaction distance), speech error rate, and interview time (Word, Zanna, & Cooper, 1974); and sociometric choices (Criswell, 1939; Moreno, 1953).

However, the effects of race seem to be mitigated by other variables that hinder interpretation, prediction, and intervention. Indeed, attempts to disguise assessment and to measure autonomic responses (described by Brand *et al.*, 1974) have not succeeded in detecting "true" attitudes. Consequently, several investigators have pointed to the need to consider situational factors in prediction and interpretation of verbal and nonverbal behavior (Bandura, 1969; Baron, Byrne, & Griffith, 1974; Rokeach, 1966; Staats, 1963), and a number of studies have been designed to assess the influences of both the situation and the characteristics of the perceiver and the perceived (in addition to race) on the interaction.

The Situation
Situational factors that may interact with race in affecting social behavior include the presence or absence of the attitude object, the normative

prescriptions of the situation, the alternative behaviors possible, the unforeseen extraneous events, and the expected consequences of the response (Wicker, 1969). Thus, behavior may vary in situations requiring verbal as opposed to motor behavior, in situations requiring different types of motor behaviors, and in situations involving groups of differing composition.

The contradictory nature of results obtained from observation of verbal and overt behavior is not a new phenomenon: LaPiere (1934) found that, of a group of 251 restaurants, cafes, motels, and auto camps in which only one had turned down a Chinese couple who stopped for service, 91.5% stated on a questionnaire that they would not serve members of the "Chinese race" (almost half of the establishments did not reply). Nor is this phenomenon peculiar to particular racial groups: Kutner, Wilkins, and Yarrow (1952) noted similar results with a black confederate. Although a black woman who joined two white women (after they were seated) at 11 restaurants and taverns in a northeastern suburb was never refused admission, only 1 of these establishments replied to a written request for reservations for a racially integrated social group (and this reply came after 19 days). Only 5 (reluctantly) implied acceptance upon receiving a follow-up telephone call (2 confirmed this acceptance with a letter). A similar phone call by the same (white) woman for a "party of friends" resulted in 10 acceptances and 1 invitation to come in and discuss the reservations. However, situational influence is also not limited to entrepreneurs. DeFleur and Westie (1958) found that, although 23 white subjects were unprejudiced by self-report, only 14 agreed to be photographed with a black person of the opposite sex. Although 23 reported being prejudiced, 5 of these agreed to have their picture taken. Similarly, shoppers' attitudes were not correlated with their reaction to black clerks (Saenger & Gilbert, 1950). In fact, Brand et al. (1974) discovered only four major studies that have shown a high correlation between verbal and overt situations, and these have been attributed to a striving, on the part of subjects, to be consistent with publicly stated attitudes (see Brand et al., 1974; Wicker, 1969).

Indeed, this lack of consistency between verbal and overt behavior has also been found in natural settings. Neither racial identification (Goodman, 1952) nor racial preference (Porter, 1971) was an accurate indicator of the actual interaction of children. Although white children evidenced more ethnic identification, white–black interaction was at chance and white–white interaction was below chance (black–black interaction was above chance; Goodman, 1952). Black and white children in one school showed no correlation between doll preference (most chose white) and playmate preference; white children in another school exhibited a negative relation, with those who preferred white dolls more often selecting black playmates in actual interaction than those who preferred black dolls (Porter, 1971).

Together, the numerous studies demonstrating differing results from verbal and overt measures of racial behavior appear to illustrate the influence of the situational factors cited initially. That is, the presence of the attitude object, the social norms, the possible alternatives, the extraneous factors and/or the expected consequences may be expected to affect overt behavior more than verbal behavior. Thus, verbal and overt measures oftentimes do not correlate.

However, overt behavior itself may vary from situation to situation. For example, the social distance studies cited previously, along with other investigations, indicate that race is more significant than other criteria when the social reaction is involved as opposed to uninvolved (i.e., when it entails permanency and intimacy; see, for example, Allen, 1971; Goldstein & Davis, 1972; Minard, 1952; Stein, 1966; Triandis & Davis, 1965; Triandis, Loh, & Levin, 1966; Triandis & Triandis, 1960). Thus, racial factors would decrease in significance as the question changes from one of permitting a person of a particular race to be in the same family or neighborhood to permitting a person of the same race to be a visitor in the same country.

Indeed, racial behavior seems to exist on a continuum, rather than as a dichotomy. That is, the observed "inconsistency" is often attributable to situational threshold differences, as Campbell (1963) notes. Thus, he depicts racial behaviors as abilities to jump over low versus high hurdles, using Minard's (1952) study as an illustration. In this investigation, some miners (20%) could not get over the lowest hurdle; that is, they were not friendly toward black miners either in town or in the mines. There were also those (60%) who could make it over the low hurdle but not the high hurdle: They were friendly in the mines but not in town. Others (20%) could make it over both hurdles: These individuals were friendly both in the mine and in town. Real inconsistency, which would have existed if any could be friendly in town but not in the mines, was not found. Campbell likens these hurdles to the Bogardus social distance scale, described previously. An individual may be consistent, but his or her consistency may lie anywhere on a scale ranging, perhaps, from unwillingness to have an individual of a particular race reside in the same country to willingness to have a member of that race in his or her family (by marriage). Thus, seeming inconsistency in overt behavior may also be explained by some of the factors mentioned previously (i.e., the norms, alternatives, and consequences of the situation).

In addition, it has been noted that the ratio of majority to minority individuals influences sociometric choices, and that girls are more likely to isolate themselves racially when the minority group size increases, whereas boys show the opposite pattern (Brand et al., 1974). Consideration of the perceived social pressure appears to be important in both social distance and belief congruence measurement (Silverman & Cochrane, 1972). Thus, group racial and attitude composition is another situational factor that may confound the effect of racial characteristics, possibly through alteration of social norms.

From these findings, it seems evident that, although racial characteristics may significantly affect interaction, their influence may not be assessed simply: Situational variation, including type of behavior (motor or verbal), type of interaction (e.g., involved or noninvolved), and group composition (e.g., proportion of races) affects responses. Despite this variation, however, it should be noted that, in many instances, race seems to have a significant influence on behavior.

The Perceiver

To further complicate matters, characteristics of the subject, in addition to race, appear to be important in his or her perception of and reaction to a particular stimulus person. For example, it appears that both antiblack (Maykovich, 1975; Selznick & Steinberg, 1969) and antiwhite (Marx, 1969) attitudes are more prevalent among those from the south and among those who have received less education. Although income and age are factors that also appear to influence (white) racial attitudes, this effect has been attributed to the association of these two factors with education (Selznick & Steinberg, 1969). Thus, prejudice encountered in a given situation might be expected to vary with the residence and education of the perceiver.

The prejudiced–unprejudiced dimension appears to be a significant factor affecting the reactions of the subject. For example, given race and attitude information, low prejudice subjects seem more likely to respond similarly to black and white strangers (who possess the same attitudes), whereas high prejudice subjects appear more likely to respond to both the race and attitudes of the stranger (Byrne & McGraw, 1964). As a result, it has been suggested that the prejudiced person requires almost complete attitude similarity to be positively influenced by contact. Indeed, a tentative formula proposed by Byrne (1969) is that being black is equivalent to expressing 10 dissimilar attitudes to the high prejudiced person. However, it has been claimed that there is a "positive prejudice" effect (see Dienstbier, 1970). That is, individuals, in a particular situation, may be even more accepting of black than of white individuals. It has been pointed out that the individual may be attempting to convince others, and perhaps him- or herself more than others, of his or her equalitarianism (see, for example, Allen, 1975; Gaertner, 1974). Whether positive prejudice is attributed to either a general personal attraction to black individuals or an effort to appear equalitarian (see Dienstbier, 1970) or to some other factor, it is important to take both this effect and the effects of high prejudice into consideration in interpretation of findings concerning racial characteristics–social environment interaction. Together, the existence of high prejudiced individuals and "positive prejudice" effects suggest more negative than positive consequences as a result of racial characteristics.

The Perceived

The characteristics of the individual being perceived—in addition to race—also appear to have an influence on reactions. For example, cleanliness (Epstein, Krupat, & Obudho, 1976), physical attractiveness (Langlois & Stephan, 1977), sex (Criswell, 1937; Helgerson, 1943), handicap (Richardson & Royce, 1968), evaluation (of the subject) (Byrne & Ervin, 1969), and attitudes (Rokeach, Smith, & Evans, 1960; Rokeach & Mezei, 1966; Stein, Hardyck, & Smith, 1965) have been found, in some investigations, to influence reactions more than race.

In both interpretation of the results of research and assessment of the effect of race on a given interaction, then, one should be cognizant of the influence of variables that may interact with race. These factors include both contrived and natural variations in situation, perceiver, and perceived. However, it must be noted that, irrespective of this situational and individual variation, it is the large number of instances where race does have an effect that cause it, in association with the social environment, to result in body–behavior problems.

Other Consequences

From the preceding discussion, it is apparent that a host of untoward social consequences may result from the interaction of the social environment with one's racial characteristics. Indeed, these consequences may include lower income and unemployment, residences in areas of higher crime rates, poorer health, exploitation by merchants, and even lynching (Kerner, 1968). Additionally, a number of negative, nonsocial consequences are likely.

Among child populations, these negative consequences may have a large impact on behavioral functioning. Such results might occur in testing and instructional settings. For example, it was found that black children score lower when tested by a white adult than when tested by a black adult (Watson, 1972). Indeed, in the actual learning environment, it has been suggested that teachers, both black and white, generally have negative attitudes toward minority children (Howe, 1971). These children may be perceived as being slower to grasp academic material, more easily distracted, and more often the cause of classroom disruption. Such attitudes may be evidenced in actual teaching behavior. For example, black students may receive less attention than white students in addition to being asked to respond less frequently, praised less, and criticized more as they were in a study conducted in the early 1970s (i.e., Rubovits & Maehr, 1973). Although it was noted that all teachers did not show prejudicial patterns and that the "teachers" were actually inexperienced undergraduates, the results indicate that consideration should be given to assessment and intervention in classroom settings.

On an institutional level, the minority individual seems likely to be at a disadvantage in the areas of labor, economics, housing, education, health, justice, and politics (see J. M. Jones, 1972; Kerner, 1968, for more detail). In addition, however, these disadvantages may have a snowball effect through the "circular function" described earlier. For example, occupational and educational discrimination (e.g., high unemployment rates and inadequate schooling) are, in turn, likely to produce low incomes, high infant mortality rates, and high suicide and arrest rates (Kerner, 1968).

Intervention

RATIONALE

When a physical characteristic interacts with the social environment to affect individuals' employment situations, education, and social interaction (among other areas of their daily lives), the probability that a large number of individuals will encounter body–behavior problems may significantly increase. Racial characteristics appear to result in such an interaction in the United States today. Thus, ameliorative efforts to prevent negative influences are warranted.

However, one's conceptualization of the reason for negative reactions to racial stimuli will have strong implications for the mode of intervention to be employed. Those who emphasize personality variables, such as authoritarianism (e.g., Adorno, Frenkel-Brunswik, Levinson, & Sanford, 1950), might focus on legislation to change only discriminatory behavior (inasmuch as personality might be viewed as resistant to change), whereas those who emphasize factors within one's environment, such as family, school, and mass media (e.g., J. M. Jones, 1972; Williams & Morland, 1976), might employ education, intergroup contact and/or behavior modification in addition to legislation in an effort to change both the discriminatory behavior and the prejudicial attitudes.

Clark (1955) points out that recent research with children has tended to dismiss the earlier beliefs that racial prejudice is an instinctive tendency to dislike the unfamiliar. Indeed, after a thorough review of the literature on the development of racial attitudes, Williams and Morland (1976) conclude that three factors are involved: (a) early experiences with lightness and darkness; (b) cultural messages; and (c) subcultural messages. Similarly, J. M. Jones (1972) states that prejudice is not innate: It comes through direct transmission, observation, and the socialization process. Although the exact nature of the acquisition is unknown, the general consensus that prejudice is not innate brings with it hope of amelioration through intervention. As a result, various types of interventions, developed from the differing conceptualizations, have been employed. A brief overview of these attempts follows.

ATTEMPTED INTERVENTIONS

Investigations in the area of intervention have included the use of coercion, modeling, "punishment," and classical conditioning in the laboratory, and educational–informational approaches, intergroup contact, and reinforcement in applied settings.

One application of coercion and modeling has been to the reduction of aggression (typically electric shock). In this vein, it has been found that most direct aggressive interracial responses (measured by frequency of shocks) may be modified through potential retaliation (Donnerstein & Donnerstein, 1972; Donnerstein, Donnerstein, Simon, & Ditrichs, 1972), potential social censure (Donnerstein & Donnerstein, 1973), and vicarious social censure (Donnerstein & Donnerstein, 1974), but that these methods may result in an increase in indirect aggression (measured by the length of shocks). Observation of either a low aggression or a high reward model was also successful in reducing direct aggression, with a greater reduction when the model exhibited less aggression rather than high reward toward a black person (Donnerstein & Donnerstein, 1977). However, this modeling did not result in increased indirect aggression.

"Punishment," defined by the investigators of the study as the taking away of previously given coins, has been used to decrease prowhite bias in trait attribution. For example, use of this technique for either selection of the white figure in response to any of three positive adjectives, or selection of the black figure in response to any of three negative adjectives, reversed the tendency of white children to respond positively to white figures and negatively to black figures, and generalized to other adjectives of the same evaluative type (e.g., positive if trained on positive) (Edwards & Williams, 1970). Similarly, employment of this procedure plus feedback also resulted in a reversal and, in addition, had an influence on children's responses to the type of evaluative adjective that had not been trained (e.g., positive if trained on negative) (McMurtry & Williams, 1972).

Transference of the effects of training with black and white animals to pictures of white and black children has also been demonstrated, again using children as subjects (Spencer & Horowitz, 1973; Williams & Edwards, 1969). This latter effect has also been achieved through classical conditioning (i.e., pairing of black—but not blue, green, or orange—with spoken positive words that were repeated by the child; Parish & Fleetwood, 1975). However, as noted in the studies of acceptance and preference of children, these findings do not readily permit generalization to preferences of real children in situations where there are real consequences for selections.

In the natural setting, educational–informational approaches may be the simplest methods of affecting change. However, it has been noted that the effectiveness of this method is dependent on the mode of presentation, the presenter, and the circumstances surrounding presentation (see Proshansky, 1966). One of the more creative approaches is role playing (either actual or vicarious), which has shown its effectiveness in altering attitudes toward individuals with physical disabilities (see Clore & Jefferey, 1972). Such an approach may be employed to allow the individual to experience the problems that may result from physical characteristics and discriminatory practices. However, it seems that alteration of belief does not necessarily result in alteration of affective and behavioral responses (Proshansky, 1966).

Intergroup contact is, perhaps, the most direct approach to intervention. The rationale for this method rests on two assumptions: (a) interracial hostilities are partially results of misperception of each other's beliefs and goals; and (b) differences may be shown to be the foundation for interesting, friendly relationships rather than for enmity (J. M. Jones, 1972). In some situations it has been effective: Positive attitudes resulted both from an integrated housing project (Deutsch & Collins, 1951) and from white and black families living near each other in a housing project (Wilner, Walkley, & Cook, 1955).

However, contact alone does not seem to be the answer. Although many classrooms have become integrated physically, social integration is often lacking (Dorr, 1972; Gerard & Miller, 1975). Thus, findings concerning the effects of integration have been positive in some cases, but negative or even mixed in others (e.g., positive effects on white students but negative effects on black students; cf. Amir, 1976; Carithers, 1970; St. John, 1975; Stephan, 1978). This inconsistency is typical not only of nonobservational studies of desegregation but also of observational investigations (see studies by Aronson & Noble, 1966; Schofield & Sagar, 1977; Silverman & Shaw, 1973). On the job, increased acceptance may be exhibited in the integrated work setting, but little of this may be transferred to other social relationships (Harding & Hogrefe, 1952; Palmore, 1955). Moreover, residential immigration by minority groups may result in negative consequences (e.g., moving away by majority group members; Fishman, 1961). Factors that have been found experimentally to lessen respect and liking of both black and white group members include group failure (Blanchard, Adelman, & Cook, 1975) and lack of member participation in decision making (Weigel & Cook, 1975).

Indeed, certain factors are believed to be critical to achieve positive outcomes from contact. Allport (1954) suggested that the following characteristics are essential to the reduction of prejudice in interracial contact situations: (a) equal status; (b) common goals; (c) cooperative dependence; and (d) support by authorities, laws, and customs.

In support of Allport's proposal, several studies have discovered the positive effects of employing multiethnic, cooperative teams whose interaction centers around learning tasks for time periods of at least 6 weeks. In such investigations, results have included increased mutual attraction (Aronson, Blaney, Sikes, Stephen, & Snapp, 1975), increased cross-racial friendship (DeVries, Edwards, & Slavin, 1978), and increased cross-ethnic helping (Weigel, Wiser, & Cook, 1975).

However, in 1972, Cook had less positive results when he implemented similar characteristics with antiblack white coeds who were committed to a month of interaction. This investigation was concerned with the effects of (a) equality of status; (b) mutually interdependent relationships, or cooperation; (c) favorable social norms; (d) possession of nonstereotypic attributes by the black individuals; and (e) promotion of intimate association that encouraged the view of the black person as an individual. As a result of these manipulations, 35 to 40% of the subjects became less prejudiced, 40% remained essentially the same, and 20% became more prejudiced. Examination of personality variables revealed that those who decreased in prejudice (in comparison to those who had not changed) had negative self-concepts and positive attitudes toward people. These results suggest the necessity of not overlooking characteristics of the perceiver as well as characteristics of the social situation.

Additionally, characteristics of the perceived may influence intervention. Thus, one factor in increasing favorable attitudes toward a particular group of people appears to be the group's importance to the subjects. Pairing of slides of Vietnamese and Afro-American individuals with positive words significantly increased attitudes toward only the Vietnamese (Parish, Sharazi, & Lambert, 1976). The authors hypothesized that attitudes toward Afro-Americans were of more importance to the subjects than attitudes toward the Vietnamese. However, this does not mean that the same is necessarily true of contact intervention. It does suggest the importance of consideration of the characteristics of the perceived.

Where contact is ineffective, behavior modification procedures may provide assistance, as they did in a classroom setting for Hauserman, Walen, and Behling (1973). In this study, children were encouraged and subsequently reinforced, both verbally and through receipt of tags (which could be exchanged for a treat during recess), for sitting by a "new friend" at lunch. When pairing the 20 white and 5 black children's names did not succeed in eliciting greater amounts of interracial play during play time (generalization), the teacher encouraged the group, as a whole, to sit with a "new friend." The second approach resulted in less interracial seating patterns at lunch (than the first had) but resulted in significantly higher generalization to free play than had the pairing approach.

In a comparison of techniques of social intervention, P. A. Katz and Zalk (1978) found that, although all four methods resulted in significant short-term reduction of prejudice, approaches that entailed vicarious interracial contact or perceptual differentiation of minority races were more effective than those that employed reinforcement of the color black or increased racial contact (which included common goals and equal status). Whereas caution is warranted, inasmuch as the comparisons pertain to only one study, the success demonstrated with all four methods is consistent with other research and thus attests to the susceptibility of negative racial characteristics–social environment interaction to intervention.

On a larger level, intervention involves elimination of exploitation through compensatory education and alteration of the occupational imbalance (Martin & Poston, 1972). Additionally, employment of the preceding individual and small group methods on a large scale may produce behavior change. Indeed, intergroup contact theory, taken on a nationwide level, suggests the importance of considering equality of status, cooperation, and common goals, legal and social support, and other factors in producing an optimal situation for improved relations. Where these conditions are not met, it is unlikely that behavior will be changed. Thus, these findings provide a beginning point for a much more comprehensive view of racial behavior alteration. It is with this thought in mind that a behavioral model of intervention is being presented.

A BEHAVIORAL APPROACH

Rationale

Judging from the variance in the role that racial characteristics play from situation to situation, it seems unlikely that any single intervention technique will be a panacea. Perhaps the only clear conclusion that may be drawn is that the individual situation must be assessed to determine both (a) whether or not the individual is experiencing a body–behavior problem as a result of his or her racial characteristics; and (b) what type of intervention is likely to be effective.

However, one's mode of assessment and intervention may vary with one's approach to the conceptualization of the development of reactions to racial stimuli. A behavioral approach is being advocated in the present chapter, not only for assistance in sifting out and objectively defining the relationship between body and behavior but also for suggesting alternative and/or more well-defined assessment and intervention strategies. Although many of the previously considered interventions have employed behavioral techniques, the present concern is with an overall approach to the systematic alteration of behavior.

The behavioral approach has proven to be advantageous in several ways. For example, when approaching the topic of racial characteristics–social environment interaction from traditional perspectives, one is often faced with the problem of explaining the causes of such behavior through instincts or personality traits, along with other vaguely defined concepts. A behavioral approach, however, emphasizes the situational and social consequences that affect behavior. That is, both antecedent and consequent events of a given behavior are obtained. A second advantage is that, rather than making assumptions about the behaviors in which individuals will engage, samples of their actual behavior are obtained. Emphasis is not placed solely on indirect modes of assessment (e.g., self-report inventories) but also on direct modes of assessment (e.g., observation). Finally, from this perspective, most behavior is considered to be learned, and is considered to be amenable to change through the application of learning techniques. Thus, the information gained during assessment may be used to develop a variety of methods of controlling the environment and/or helping individuals to modify their own behavior.

Application

The role of learning in the development and maintenance of behavior has been evidenced across numerous settings, populations, and behaviors. However, of the three classifications of learning—classical or respondent conditioning, operant conditioning, and observational learning—the basic principles derived from operant conditioning have proven to be the most beneficial in describing the relationship between one's behavior and the environmental factors affecting it. Indeed, the success of operant conditioning techniques over the past 2 decades is indicative of their potential for assessing and modifying a host of behaviors (see Drabman, 1976; R. T. Jones & Kazdin, 1981; O'Leary & O'Leary, 1976, for reviews).

Several conceptualizations that have used operant principles in explaining how bodily variations may contribute to body–behavior problems have emerged within recent years. For example, the effects of the cuing properties of bodily variations may be explained in terms of differential reinforcement, as detailed by Neisworth *et al.* (1978). Briefly, an individual's physical characteristics may be considered to be cues because they set the occasion for differential reactions. That is, a person's appearance might serve as an S^D (discriminative stimulus) in that it signals that a particular response is likely to be reinforced and occasions that response, or it might serve as an S^Δ in that it signals that a particular response will not be reinforced and does not occasion that response. Staat's 1975 A–R–D paradigm (the letters A–R–D pertain to attitudinal, reinforcer, and directive characteristics of stimuli) suggests a further extension of this theory, naming three ways in which attitude objects (in this case, the individual's variations in physical characteristics) serve as stimuli: (*a*) "the conditioned stimulus function" (i.e., as elicitors of emotion); (*b*) "the reinforcing stimulus function" (i.e., as reinforcers or punishers); and (*c*) "the directive stimulus function" (i.e., as cues for instrumental responses). Returning to Neisworth *et al.*'s (1978) conceptualization, the type of response that a child receives will provide him with feedback that may be either reinforcing or nonreinforcing.

An Illustration

The discriminative stimulus function may be observed in a number of everyday settings. For example, in classroom settings, a teacher may display negative reactions toward black children. That is, she may give them less attention and ignore them more than she does white children. These negative reactions might be assumed to result from the fact that black racial characteristics (*a*) elicit negative emotions (of some sort); (*b*) serve as a discriminative stimulus for punishment (result in thoughts such as "attending to this black child will result in these unpleasant feelings"); and (*c*) cue an instrumental response (i.e., ignoring the black child to avoid unpleasant feelings). White racial characteristics may (*a*) elicit positive emotions (of some sort); (*b*) serve as a discriminative stimulus for reinforcement (result in thoughts such as "attending to this white child will result in these pleasant feelings"); and (*c*) cue an instrumental response (i.e., attending to the white child to receive positive feelings). Thus, the race of the child may cause him or her to receive differential reinforcement in the form of teacher attention. Inasmuch as teacher attention would be expected to serve as a reinforcer, the white children could be expected to increase their academic behavior because of the reinforcement received. The black children, who may be more often nonreinforced as a result of their racial characteristics, might not be expected to increase their academic behavior as much. The increased academic behavior of the white children may result in further reinforcement, whereas the smaller increase in the academic behavior of the black children may result in less reinforcement: A circular function may be created. Although this is merely one example and not necessarily a frequent occurrence, the illustration serves to indicate the seriousness of the body–behavior problems that may result from race–environment interaction.

Behavioral Assessment

As is advocated in behavioral assessment, behavior may be measured with respect to three response systems: cognitive, physiological, and motoric. Thus, cognitive (verbal) measures, including self-report inventories and self-monitoring, may be employed to assess the individual's beliefs concerning his or her racial attitudes. Physiological assessment devices, which include measures of heart rate, galvanic skin response, pupil constriction, and vocal stress, may be used to assess the individual's physiological reaction to racial stimuli. Motoric modes of assessment, including in vivo observation and observation of role-played interaction, may be used to measure more overt manifestations of racial behavior. However, because of low correlations among motoric, cognitive, and physiological measures, no single mode of assessment is completely adequate.

The results presented in the section on the social consequences of racial characteristics are indicative of the inconsistency that pervades measures of reactions to racial stimuli. As a result of the perplexing array of results in this area, investigative attempts have been made to discover the relationships among measures of racial reactions. Contrary to the apparently simplistic nature of the task, the goal is an elusive one.

Theoretically, many plausible contributors to low verbal (cognitive)–motoric and motoric–motoric correlations have been noted. Moreover, it has been cautioned that low correlations are likely to exist when only one motoric measure (Campbell, 1963) or one physiological measure (Hersen, 1976) is taken. The great situational and individual variation makes a single motoric measure an unlikely indicator of overall behavior; individual differences in physiological response preferences (Lacey, 1962; Lacey & Van Lehn, 1952) discredit the generalization of measurement of one physiological response to overall behavior. Practically speaking, the individual's belief that stress is experienced in interracial interaction, the presence of physiological stress and the avoidance of individuals of other races all seem to be significant factors. Additionally, because changes in one area do not necessarily indicate immediate change in the others (Harding & Hogrefe, 1952; Hogrefe & Harding, 1946; Proshansky, 1966), all three modes should receive attention in intervention when possible. Therefore, it seems best to discount none as irrelevant, either in assessment or in intervention.

Behavioral Intervention

In general, intervention to ameliorate body–behavior problems may take two forms: alteration of the individual or alteration of the environment. Direct intervention to remove or modify the discriminative stimuli that cause body–behavior problems may involve the total elimination of the physical characteristics, the teaching of new modes of behavior, and/or the use of artificial devices. Thus, physical deficits may be removed (through surgery, for example) or they may be camouflaged through cosmetic prosthetics. Resultant behavioral deficits may be modified or eliminated through cosmetic and functional (or substitutive) learning or functional prosthetics. Cosmetic and functional learning may be facilitated through manipulation of consequences. Where individual techniques are inappropriate or insufficient, environmental changes may prove useful. Such changes may involve either the physical or social environment. All of these techniques are described in detail by R. T. Jones and Haney (in press), Smith and Neisworth (1975) and Neisworth *et al.* (1978). Manipulation of consequences is more fully dealt with by R. T. Jones and Kazdin (1981).

As previously discussed, racial characteristics are not disabilities and do not result in *physical* handicaps, either alone or in conjunction with the physical environment. However, racial characteristics–social environment interaction *may* result in *social* handicaps. Consequently, outside of (infrequent) instances where an individual may, for social reasons, desire to and be capable of altering his or her racial characteristics, change in this area must, by the nature of the problem, be social rather than physical. Whereas individuals' social handicaps may be overcome by "passing" as nondisabled or physically attractive (or at least not unattractive), or white, or whatever is deemed to provide social benefits in a particular social environment ("passing" is discussed in more detail by Goffman, 1963), such efforts do not eliminate the general problem of physical (e.g., racial) characteristics–social environment *interaction* (i.e., a single individual may eliminate a particular body–behavior problem in this manner, but the broader social problem remains). Thus, alteration of the social environment, rather than the physical characteristics of the individual, is the target for behavioral intervention in this area.

However, social reactions toward racial characteristics tend to have ramifications that extend beyond the boundaries of the social domain and into the realms of education, employment, economics, justice, housing, politics, and other areas, as is illustrated in Table 13.2. In all of these areas, behavioral techniques, such as those employed to alter social interaction in the previously described investigations, may be applied to the amelioration of a wide range of problems.

Beginning with assessment, a functional analysis of behavior in any of the areas may be undertaken through the employment of both verbal–cognitive and motoric measures.[7] In areas such as social interaction in the school, where populations are in an institutional setting, numerous verbal–cognitive measures, including acceptance, preference, attitude, social distance, sociometric choice, and trait attribution may be employed. In addition, motoric measures such as frequency of interaction, length of interaction, and type of interaction may be relatively easy to obtain. However, when teacher–student relationships are the target of assessment, attitude measures and self-reports might be more appropriate verbal–cognitive assessment devices and motoric measures might shift to observation of responses to children, including attention, ignoring, praise, criticism, assistance, and grading. As assessment moves out of the school and into employment, economics, justice, housing, and politics, legal and ethical considerations may require more restraint in assessment options, perhaps limiting the change agent to self-reports and discreet observations of actual practices.

In all situations, intervention techniques may be ranked along a continuum by the negativeness of consequences associated with resistance to change: from informational–educational approaches (minimal conse-

---

[7] A full battery of assessment devices from each of the three areas (verbal–cognitive, motoric, and physiological) should be utilized where possible. However, such multifaceted assessment is seldom feasible for measurement outside of laboratory settings and is thus omitted from this discussion.

TABLE 13.2
Potential Body–Behavior Problems

Source of body–behavior problem	Examples of possible body–behavior problems
	Group:
1. Social (peers)	a. Lessened acceptance of and less likely to be preferred.
	b. More negative traits attributed.
	c. Greater social distance.
	Specific individual and/or group:
	d. Less frequently chosen on sociometric measure.
	e. Less often engaged in interaction.
	f. More often recipient of negative interaction.
	Group:
2. Educational (teachers)	a. Teacher's attitudes, as measured verbally, are negative with respect to a particular race.
	Specific individual and/or group:
	b. Less often recipient of teacher attention.
	c. Less often recipient of positive attention.
	d. More often recipient of negative attention.
	e. Evaluated more negatively by teacher (because of race).
	Group and/or individual:
3. Employment	a. Less often hired.
	b. Less likely to receive promotion.
	c. More often first to be laid off.
	d. Less likely to receive benefits.
	e. More often fired.
4. Economics	a. Less likely to get higher paying jobs.
	b. Less likely to get high status jobs.
	c. Higher assessed value for property (i.e., higher values in black neighborhood).
	d. Less likely to get loan.
5. Justice	a. Fewer police officers of same race.
	b. Less likely to receive assistance.
	c. More likely to have bail set at a higher figure.
	d. Less legal power.
	e. More likely to be arrested.
	f. More likely to be imprisoned.
6. Housing	a. Less likely to be sold house in neighborhood of other race.
	b. Less likely to be rented apartment in neighborhood of other race.
	c. More likely to encounter unfriendly attitudes from neighbors in neighborhood of other race.
7. Political	a. Less likely to be elected.
	b. Less likely to be appointed.

quences) through intergroup contact (social consequences) to legal action (legal consequences). Information, for example, may be disseminated via lecture, discussion, films, tapes, role-playing simulated activities, mass media, and other means. Intergroup contact (discussed in more detail previously) may be used in those situations, such as schools or universities, where the change agent has some control. Legal models of intervention may include laws requiring desegregation of schools and forbidding discriminatory practices in hiring, giving out loans, renting and selling property, and admitting to organizations or institutions.

Again, in school situations, which allow for maximal amounts of change (with administration and public approval), there is a less restricted range of intervention options, and additional techniques may be used. When teachers themselves are the subjects of intervention, the concern might be initially with developing an awareness of any problems that exist, possibly through self-monitoring or videotape or observer feedback. Discussion of problems with other teachers or a consultant and added incentives such as extra benefits might assist in amelioration. When the teacher is the change agent (and the students are the individuals of concern), the teacher might wish to employ reinforcement of positive interaction and to ignore negative interaction. Such reinforcement could be provided in the form of praise or symbols, or perhaps as part of a token economy.

Thus, with the objectives of (a) eliminating discriminatory behaviors; and (b) attaining interracial interaction of a level approximating the level of intraracial interaction, teachers, for example, would (in using a behavioral approach):

1. Assess discriminatory behavior and the interaction patterns of the classroom to determine whether racial characteristics are, in interaction with that particular classroom, resulting in body–behavior problems (e.g., less frequent interaction).
2. Determine which behaviors are most in need of change (e.g., elimination of aggression would be more important than elimination of avoidance, initially).
3. Determine the objective of behavioral change (e.g., an increase of at least 50% over current frequency of interracial "playing" during free play).
4. Define the behavior in operational terms (e.g., interracial "playing" first might be broadly defined as verbalizations directed toward a student of a different race, contact with the same object–toy, and/or participation in the same game and then refined through some initial observation).
5. Measure the occurrence of the behavior (e.g., determine how frequently children engage in interracial play).

6. Intervene (e.g., reinforce children for playing with either a number of different children or a different child than they had the previous day).

7. Fade intervention (e.g., reinforce only every other day and/or praise rather than give tokens and praise). Eventually withdraw intervention. This will enhance the probability of maintenance after program withdrawal.

8. Continue to measure the behavior, on occasion, to ensure that desired behavior is continuing to occur.

Employment of behavioral techniques (of which the present summary has been just a sample) directed at specific behaviors (such as those enumerated in Table 13.2) may assist in alteration of the body–behavior problems that individuals may incur as a result of racial characteristics–social environment interaction. Although success is usually not guaranteed, in any endeavor, it is believed that a focus on specific goals and assessment and intervention strategies directed toward those goals will provide a solid foundation for the future amelioration of racial characteristics–social environment interaction.

Summary and Conclusions

The present chapter has been an attempt to place the problems of behavioral functioning that may result from racial characteristics–social environment interaction within a body–behavior/somatopsychological framework. The focus on race has permitted an in-depth view of social, rather than physical, handicaps that may occur because of physique–environment interaction. These social handicaps have been conceptualized as the effects of discrimination (overt behaviors) that may accompany prejudicial attitudes, aversive and dominative individual racism, and institutional racism.

Attempts to discover the relationship between physique and behavior date back to primitive times. This search has resulted in conceptualizations involving a complex interaction between the individual's characteristics and others' reactions. Indeed, two factors that may be involved in this interaction are (a) the prominence of the individual's characteristics; and (b) the experiences that other people in the individual's environment have had with these characteristics. Thus, the effects of a variation may differ from situation to situation.

It is this situational variation, perhaps, that creates a large portion of the confusion surrounding findings concerning preference, social distance and trait attribution. Indeed, characteristics of the interaction, the perceiver, and the perceived have been shown to influence the obtained results. In spite of the varying results, the potential body–behavior problems are indicative of the necessity for assessment and intervention.

One avenue open to ascertainment of the existence of a body–behavior problem may be direct, objective assessment of the individual(s) and the situation(s). Such assessment should include a thorough analysis of both antecedent and consequent events. Professionals who wish to intervene should use the information gained during this assessment in attempting to control the environment and/or assisting the individual(s) in control of his or her (their) own behavior. Past attempts at intervention have included coercion, modeling, intergroup contact, and behavior modification.

The present chapter has attempted to provide a behavioral model of conceptualization, assessment, and intervention for the body–behavior problems that may result from racial characteristics–social environment interaction. It is believed that such a model, through the directness of its approach, provides the best available foundation upon which to build future efforts in this area.

Acknowledgments

The authors would like to extend special thanks to James Jones and Anthony Hogue for their comments and suggestions on the final draft of this chapter.

References

Adorno, T. W., Frenkel-Brunswik, E., Levinson, D. J., & Sanford, R. N. *The authoritarian personality*. New York: Harper & Row, 1950.

Allen, B. P. Social distance reactions to black and white communicators: A replication of an investigation in support of belief congruence theory. *Psychonomic Science*, 1971, *22*, 344.

Allen, B. P. Social distance and admiration reactions of "unprejudiced" whites. *Journal of Personality*, 1975, *43*, 709–726.

Allport, G. W. *The nature of prejudice*. Reading, Mass.: Addison-Wesley, 1954.

Amir, Y. The role of intergroup contact in change of prejudice and ethnic relations. In P. Katz (Ed.), *Towards the elimination of racism*. New York: Pergamon, 1976.

Aronson, E., Blaney, N., Sikes, J., Stephen, C., & Snapp, M. Busing and racial tension: The jigsaw route to learning and liking. *Psychology Today*, 1975, *8*(4), 43–50.

Aronson, S., & Noble, J. *Urban–suburban school mixing: A feasibility study*. Unpublished manuscript, 1966. (Available from S. Aronson, West Hartford Board of Education, West Hartford, Conn.).

Asher, S. R., & Allen, V. L. Racial preference and social comparison processes. *Journal of Social Issues*, 1969, *25*(1), 157–166.

Bandura, A. *Principles of behavior modification*. New York: Holt, Rinehart & Winston, 1969.

Banks, W. C. White preference in blacks: A paradigm in search of a phenomenon. *Psychological Bulletin*, 1976, *83*, 1179–1186.

Banks, W. C., McQuater, G. V., & Ross, J. A. On the importance of white preference and the comparative difference of blacks and others: Reply to Williams and Morland. *Psychological Bulletin*, 1979, *86*, 33–36.

Barker, R. G., Wright, B. A., Meyerson, L., & Gonick, M. R. *Adjustment to physical handicap and illness: A survey of the social psychology of physique and disability* (2nd ed.). New York: Social Science Research Council, Bulletin 55, 1953.

Baron, R. A., Byrne, D., & Griffith, W. *Social psychology: Understanding human interaction.* Boston: Allyn & Bacon, 1974.

Bayton, J. A. The racial stereotypes of Negro college students. *Journal of Abnormal and Social Psychology*, 1941, *36*, 97–102.

Bayton, J. A., McAlister, L. B., & Hamer, J. Race–class stereotypes. *Journal of Negro Education*, 1956, *25*, 75–78.

Berry, B., & Tischler, H. L. *Race and ethnic relations* (4th ed.). Boston: Houghton Mifflin, 1978.

Bijou, S. W., & Baer, D. M. *Child development I: A systematic and empirical theory.* New York: Appleton-Century-Crofts, 1961.

Blake, R., & Dennis, W. The development of stereotypes concerning the Negro. *Journal of Abnormal and Social Psychology*, 1943, *38*, 525–531.

Blanchard, F. A., Adelman, L., & Cook, S. W. Effect of group success and failure upon interpersonal attraction in cooperating interracial groups. *Journal of Personality and Social Psychology*, 1975, *31*, 1020–1030.

Bogardus, E. S. Measuring social distances. *Journal of Applied Sociology*, 1925, *9*, 299–308.

Bogardus, E. S. Changes in racial distance. *Journal of Opinion and Attitude Research*, 1947, *1*, 55–62.

Brand, E. S., Ruiz, R. A., & Padilla, A. M. Ethnic identification and preference: A review. *Psychological Bulletin*, 1974, *81*, 860–890.

Brigham, J. Ethnic stereotypes. *Psychological Bulletin*, 1971, *76*, 15–38.

Byrne, D. Attitudes and attraction. In L. Berkowitz (Ed.), *Advances in experimental social psychology*. New York: Academic Press, 1969.

Byrne, D., & Ervin, C. R. Attraction toward a Negro stranger as a function of prejudice, attitude similarity, and the stranger's evaluation of the subject. *Human Relations*, 1969, *22*, 397–404.

Byrne, D., & McGraw, C. Interpersonal attraction toward Negroes. *Human Relations*, 1964, *17*, 201–213.

Byrne, D., & Wong, T. J. Racial prejudice, interpersonal attraction, and assumed dissimilarity of attitudes. *Journal of Abnormal and Social Psychology*, 1962, *65*, 246–253.

Campbell, D. T. Social attitudes and other acquired behavioral dispositions. In S. Koch (Ed.), *Psychology: A study of a science.* New York: McGraw-Hill, 1963.

Carithers, M. W. School desegregation and racial cleavage, 1954–1970: A review of the literature. *Journal of Social Issues*, 1970, *26*(4), 25–47.

Clark, K. B. *Prejudice and your child.* Boston: Beacon Press, 1955.

Clark, K. B., & Clark, M. P. Racial identification and preference in Negro children. In E. E. Maccoby, T. M. Newcombe, & E. L. Hartley (Eds.), *Readings in social psychology* (3rd ed.). New York: Holt, 1947.

Clore, G. L., & Jeffery, K. M. Emotional role playing, attitude change, and attraction toward a disabled person. *Journal of Personality and Social Psychology*, 1972, *23*, 105–111.

Cook, S. W. Motives in a conceptual analysis of attitude-related behavior. In J. C. Brigham & T. A. Weissbach (Eds.), *Racial attitudes in America: Analyses and findings of social psychology.* New York: Harper & Row, 1972.

Cook, S. W., & Sellitz, C. A multiple indicator approach to attitude measurement. *Psychological Bulletin*, 1964, *62*, 36–55.

Criswell, J. H. Racial cleavage in Negro–white groups. *Sociometry*, 1937, *1*, 81–89.

Criswell, J. H. A sociometric study of race cleavage in the classroom. *Archives of Psychology*, 1939, No. 235.

DeFleur, M. L., & Westie, F. R. Verbal attitudes and overt acts: An experiment on the salience of attitudes. *American Sociological Review*, 1958, *23*, 667–673.

Deutsch, M., & Collins, M. E. *Interracial housing: A psychological evaluation of a social experiment.* Minneapolis: University of Minnesota Press, 1951.

DeVries, D. L., Edwards, K. J., & Slavin, R. E. Biracial learning teams and race relations in the classroom: Four field experiments using teams–games–tournament. *Journal of Educational Psychology,* 1978, *70,* 356–362.

Dienstbier, R. A. Positive and negative prejudice: Interactions of prejudice with race and social desirability. *Journal of Personality,* 1970, *38,* 198–215.

Donnerstein, E., & Donnerstein, M. White rewarding behavior as a function of the potential for black retaliation. *Journal of Personality and Social Psychology,* 1972, *24,* 327–333.

Donnerstein, E., & Donnerstein, M. Variables in interracial aggression: Potential ingroup censure. *Journal of Personality and Social Psychology,* 1973, *27,* 143–150.

Donnerstein, E., & Donnerstein, M. *Direct and vicarious censure in the control of interracial aggression.* Paper presented at Southeastern Psychological Association, 1974.

Donnerstein, E., Donnerstein, M., Simon, S., & Ditrichs, R. Variables in interracial aggression: Anonymity, expected retaliation, and a riot. *Journal of Personality and Social Psychology,* 1972, *22,* 236–245.

Donnerstein, M., & Donnerstein, E. Modeling in the control of interracial aggression: The problem of generality. *Journal of Personality,* 1977, *45,* 100–116.

Dorr, R. Ordeal by desegregation. *Integrated Education,* 1972, *10*(4), 34–39.

Drabman, R. S. Behavior modification in the classroom. In W. E. Craighead, A. E. Kazdin, & M. J. Mahoney (Eds.), *Behavior modification: Principles, issues, and applications.* Boston: Houghton Mifflin, 1976.

Edwards, C. D., & Williams, J. E. Generalization between evaluative words associated with racial figures in preschool children. *Journal of Experimental Research in Personality,* 1970, *4,* 144–155.

Epstein, Y. M., Krupat, E., & Obudho, C. Clean is beautiful: Identification and preference as a function of race and cleanliness. *Journal of Social Issues,* 1976, *32*(2), 109–118.

Fagan, J., & O'Neill, M. A comparison of social distance scores among college student samples. *Journal of Social Psychology,* 1965, *66,* 281–290.

Feldman, J. M., & Hilterman, R. J. Stereotype attribution revisited: The role of stimulus characteristics, racial attitude, and cognitive differentiation. *Journal of Personality and Social Psychology,* 1975, *31,* 1177–1188.

Fishman, J. A. Some social and psychological determinants of intergroup relations in changing neighborhoods: An introduction to the Bridgeview study. *Social Forces,* 1961, *40,* 42–51.

Fox, D. J., & Jordan, V. B. Racial preference and identification of black, American-Chinese, and white children. *Genetic Psychology Monographs,* 1973, *88,* 229–286.

Gaertner, S. L. *Racial attitudes of liberals.* Paper read at the American Psychological Association Convention, New Orleans, 1974.

Gerard, H. B., & Miller, N. *School desegregation: A long-range study.* New York: Plenum, 1975.

Gilbert, G. M. Stereotype persistence and change among college students. *Journal of Abnormal and Social Psychology,* 1951, *46,* 245–254.

Goffman, E. *Stigma: Notes on the Management of Spoiled Identity.* Englewood Cliffs, N.J.: Prentice-Hall, 1963.

Goldstein, M., & Davis, E. E. Race and belief: A further analysis of the social determinants of behavioral intentions. *Journal of Personality and Social Psychology,* 1972, *22,* 346–355.

Goodman, M. E. *Race Awareness in Young Children.* New York: Collier Macmillan, 1952.

Gregor, A. J., & McPherson, D. A. Racial attitudes among white and Negro children in a deep-south standard metropolitan area. *The Journal of Social Psychology,* 1966, *68,* 95–106.

Hamilton, K. W. *Counseling the handicapped in the rehabilitation process.* New York: Ronald Press, 1950.

Harding, J., & Hogrefe, R. Attitudes of white department store employees toward Negro co-workers. *Journal of Social Issues,* 1952, *8*(1), 18–28.

Harris, S., & Braun, J. R. Self-esteem and racial preference in black children. *Proceedings of the 79th annual convention of the American Psychological Association*, 1971, *6*, 259–260.

Hauserman, N., Walen, S. R., & Behling, M. Reinforced racial integration in the first grade: A study in generalization. *Journal of Applied Behavior Analysis*, 1973, *6*, 193–200.

Helgerson, E. The relative significance of race, sex, and facial expression in choice of playmate by the preschool child. *Journal of Negro Education*, 1943, *12*, 617–622.

Hersen, M. Historical perspectives in behavioral assessment. In M. Hersen & A. S. Bellack (Eds.), *Behavioral assessment: A practical handbook*. Oxford: Pergamon, 1976.

Hogrefe, R., & Harding, J. Club revelation: An experiment with deliquent boys. New York: American Jewish Congress, 1946. (Mimeographed)

Howe, F. C. Teacher perceptions toward the learning ability of students from differing racial and socioeconomic backgrounds. (Doctoral dissertation, Michigan State University, 1970). *Dissertation Abstracts International*, 1971, *31*, 5847A. (University Microfilms No. 71–11, 872)

Hraba, J., & Grant, G. Black is beautiful: A reexamination of racial preference and identification. *Journal of Personality and Social Psychology*, 1970, *16*, 398–402.

Humphreys, L. G. Characteristics of type concepts with special reference to Sheldon's typology. *Psychological Bulletin*, 1957, *54*, 218–228.

Jones, J. M. *Prejudice and racism*. Reading, Mass.: Addison-Wesley, 1972.

Jones, R. T., & Haney, J. I. Cosmetic intervention. In R. M. Smith & J. T. Neisworth (Eds.), *The exceptional child: A functional approach* (2nd ed.). New York: McGraw-Hill, in press.

Jones, R. T., & Kazdin, A. E. Childhood behavior problems in the school. In S. M. Turner, K. Calhoon, & H. E. Adams (Eds.), *The handbook of clinical behavior therapy*. New York: Wiley, 1981.

Karlins, M., Coffman, T. L., & Walters, G. On the fading of social stereotypes: Studies in three generations of college students. *Journal of Personality and Social Psychology*, 1969, *13*, 1–16.

Katz, D., & Braly, K. Racial stereotypes of one hundred college students. *Journal of Abnormal and Social Psychology*, 1933, *28*, 280–290.

Katz, P. A., & Zalk, S. R. Modification of children's racial attitudes. *Developmental Psychology*, 1978, *14*, 447–461.

Kerner, D. (Chairman) *Report of the National Advisory Commission on Civil Disorders. New York Times* (Eds.). New York: Dutton, 1968.

Kovel, J. *White racism: A psychohistory*. New York: Pantheon, 1970.

Kutner, B., Wilkins, C., & Yarrow, P. R. Verbal attitudes and overt behavior involving racial prejudice. *Journal of Abnormal and Social Psychology*, 1952, *47*, 649–652.

Lacey, J. I. Psychophysiological approaches to the evaluation of psychotherapeutic process and outcome. In F. Rubinstein & M. B. Parloff (Eds.), *Research in psychotherapy*. Washington, D.C.: American Psychological Association, 1962.

Lacey, J. I., & Van Lehn, R. Differential emphasis in somatic response to stress: An experimental study. *Psychosomatic Medicine*, 1952, *14*, 71–81.

Langlois, J. H., & Stephan, C. The effects of physical attractiveness and ethnicity on children's behavioral attributions and peer preferences. *Child Development*, 1977, *48*, 1694–1698.

LaPiere, R. T. Attitudes vs. actions. *Social Forces*, 1934, *13*, 230–237.

Lavater, J. C. *Essays on physiognomy: Designed to promote the knowledge and the love of mankind* (T. Holcroft, trans.). London: William Tegg, 1848.

Lerner, R. M. The development of personal space schemata toward body build. *Journal of Psychology*, 1973, *84*, 229–235.

Lerner, R. M. *Concepts and theories of human development*. Reading, Mass.: Addison-Wesley, 1976.

Lerner, R. M., Karabenick, S. A., & Meisels, M. Effects of age and sex on the development of personal space schemata toward body build. *Journal of Genetic Psychology*, 1975, *127*, 91–101.

Lerner, R. M., & Korn, S. J. The development of body-build stereotypes in males. *Child Development*, 1972, *43*, 912–920.

Lerner, R. M., & Knapp, J. R. Structure of racial attitudes in white middle-class adolescents. *Journal of Youth and Adolescence*, 1976, *5*, 283–300.

Lindzey, G. Morphology and behavior. In G. Lindzey & C. S. Hall (Eds.), *Theories of personality: Primary sources and research*. New York: Wiley, 1965.

Martin, W. T., & Poston, D. L. The occupational composition of white females: Sexism, racism, and occupational differentiation. *Social Forces*, 1972, *50*, 349–355.

Marx, G. T. *Protest and prejudice: A study of belief in the black community*. New York: Harper & Row, 1969.

Maykovich, M. K. Correlates of racial prejudice. *Journal of Personality and Social Psychology*, 1975, *32*, 1014–1020.

McMurtry, C. A., & Williams, J. E. Evaluation dimension of the affective meaning system of the preschool child. *Developmental Psychology*, 1972, *6*, 238–246.

Merton, R. K. The self-fulfilling prophecy. *Antioch Review*, 1948, *8*, 193–210.

Meyerson, L. A. Somatopsychology of physical disability. In W. Cruickshank (Ed.), *Psychology of exceptional children and youth*. Englewood Cliffs, N.J.: Prentice-Hall, 1971.

Minard, R. D. Race relationships in the Pocahontas coal field. *Journal of Social Issues*, 1952, *8*, 29–44.

Moreno, J. L. *Who shall survive?:* Foundations of sociometry, group psychotherapy and sociodrama. New York: Beacon House, 1953.

Neisworth, J. T., Jones, R. T., & Smith, R. M. Body–behavior problems: A conceptualization. *Education and Training of the Mentally Retarded*, 1978, *13*, 265–271.

O'Leary, S. G., & O'Leary, K. D. Behavior modification in the school. In H. Leitenberg (Ed.), *Handbook of behavior modification and behavior therapy*. Englewood Cliffs, N.J.: Prentice-Hall, 1976.

Palmore, E. B. The introduction of Negroes into white departments, *Human Organizations*, 1955, *14*, 27–28.

Parish, T. S., & Fleetwood, R. S. Amount of conditioning and subsequent change in racial attitudes of children. *Perceptual and Motor Skills*, 1975, *40*, 79–86.

Parish, T. S., Shirazi, A., & Lambert, F. Conditioning away prejudicial attitudes in children. *Perceptual and Motor Skills*, 1976, *43*, 907–912.

Porter, J. D. R. *Black child, white child: The development of racial attitudes*. Cambridge: Harvard University Press, 1971.

Proenza, L., & Strickland, B. R. A study of prejudice in Negro and white college students. *The Journal of Social Psychology*, 1965, *67*, 273–281.

Proshansky, H. M. The development of intergroup attitudes. In L. W. Hoffman & M. L. Hoffman (Eds.), *Review of child development research* (Vol. 2). New York: Russell Sage Foundation, 1966.

Richardson, S. A., & Royce, J. Race and handicap in children's preference for other children. *Child Development*, 1968, *39*, 467–480.

Riegel, K. F. Toward a dialectical theory of development. *Human Development*, 1975, *18*, 50–64.

Rokeach, M. Attitude change and behavioral change. *Public Opinion Quarterly*, 1966, *30*, 529–550.

Rokeach, M., & Mezei, L. Race and shared belief as factors in social choice. *Science*, 1966, *151*, 167–172.

Rokeach, M., Smith, P. W., & Evans, R. I. Two kinds of prejudice or one? In M. Rokeach (Ed.), *The open and closed mind: Investigations into the nature of belief systems and personality systems*. New York: Basic Books, 1960.

Rosenthal, R., & Jacobson, L. *Pygmalion in the classroom*. New York: Holt, Rinehart & Winston, 1968.

Rubovits, P., & Maehr, M. L. Pygmalion black and white. *Journal of Personality and Social Psychology*, 1973, *25*, 210–218.

Saenger, G., & Gilbert, E. Customer reactions to the integration of Negro sales personnel. *International Journal of Opinion and Attitude Research*, 1950, *4*, 57–76.

Schneirla, T. C. The concept of development in comparative psychology. In D. B. Harris (Ed.), *The concept of development*. Minneapolis: University of Minnesota Press, 1957.

Schofield, J. W., & Sagar, H. A. Peer interaction patterns in an integrated middle school. *Sociometry*, 1977, *40*, 130–138.

Selznick, G. J., & Steinberg, S. *The tenacity of prejudice: Anti-Semitism in contemporary America*. New York: Harper & Row, 1969.

Sheldon, W. H. *The varieties of temperament: A psychology of constitutional differences*. New York: Harper, 1942.

Sheldon, W. H. Constitutional factors in personality. In J. McV. Hunt (Ed.), *Personality and the behavior disorders*. New York: Ronald Press, 1944.

Sheldon, W. H., Stevens, S. S., & Tucker, W. B. *The varieties of human physique: An introduction to constitutional psychology*. New York: Harper, 1940.

Silverman, B. I., & Cochrane, R. Effect of the social context on the principle of belief congruence. *Journal of Personality and Social Psychology*, 1972, *22*, 259–268.

Silverman, I., & Shaw, M. E. Effects of sudden mass school desegregation on interracial interaction and attitudes in one southern city. *Journal of Social Issues*, 1973, *29*(4), 133–142.

Simpson, G. E., & Yinger, J. M. *Racial and cultural minorities: An analysis of prejudice and discrimination* (Rev. ed.). New York: Harper, 1958.

Smith, R. M., & Neisworth, J. T. *The exceptional child: A functional approach*. New York: McGraw-Hill, 1975.

Spencer, M. B., & Horowitz, F. D. Effects of systematic social and token reinforcement on the modification of racial and color concept attitudes in black and white preschool children. *Developmental Psychology*, 1973, *9*, 246–254.

Spurzheim, J. G. *Phrenology: Or the doctrine of the mental phenomena* (Rev. ed.). Philadelphia: Lippincott, 1908.

Staats, A. W. (with contributions by C. K. Staats). *Complex human behavior: A systematic extension of learning principles*. New York: Holt, Rinehart & Winston, 1963.

Staats, A. W. *Social behaviorism*. Homewood, Ill.: Dorsey Press, 1975.

Stein, D. The influence of belief systems on interpersonal preference: A validation study of Rokeach's theory of prejudice. *Psychology Monographs*, 1966, *80*(8, Whole No. 616).

Stein, D. D., Hardyck, J. A., & Smith, M. B. Race *and* belief: An open and shut case. *Journal of Personality and Social Psychology*, 1965, *1*, 281–289.

Stephan, W. G. School desegregation: An evaluation of predictions made in *Brown v. Board of Education*. *Psychological Bulletin*, 1978, *85*, 217–238.

St. John, N. H. *School desegregation: Outcomes for children*. New York: Wiley, 1975.

Susser, M. W., & Watson, W. *Sociology in medicine*. London: Oxford University Press, 1962.

The American heritage dictionary of the English language (W. Morris, Ed.). Boston: American Heritage & Houghton Mifflin, 1973.

Triandis, H. C., & Davis, E. E. Race and belief as determinants of behavioral intentions. *Journal of Personality and Social Psychology*, 1965, *2*, 715–725.

Triandis, H. C., Loh, W. D., & Levin, L. A. Race, status, quality of spoken English, and opinions about civil rights as determinants of interpersonal attitudes. *Journal of Personality and Social Psychology*, 1966, *3*, 468–472.

Triandis, H. C., & Triandis, L. M. Race, social class, religion, and nationality as determinants of social stress. *Journal of Abnormal and Social Psychology*, 1960, *61*, 110–118.

Triandis, H., & Triandis, L. M. Some studies of social distance. In I. D. Steiner & M. Fishbein (Eds.), *Current studies in social psychology*. New York: Holt, Rinehart & Winston, 1965.

van den Berghe, P. L. *Race and racism: A comparative perspective*. New York: Wiley, 1967.

Walker, R. N. Body build and behavior in young children. I: Body build and nursery school teachers' ratings. *Monographs of the Society for Research in Child Development*, 1962, 27, 1–94.

Watson, P. IQ: The racial gap. *Psychology Today*, 1972, 6, 48–52.

Weigel, R. H., & Cook, S. W. Participation in decision making: A determinant of interpersonal attraction in cooperating interracial groups. *International Journal of Group Tensions*, 1975, 5, 179–195.

Weigel, R. H., Wiser, P. L., & Cook, S. W. The impact of cooperative learning experiences on cross-ethnic relations and attitudes. *Journal of Social Issues*, 1975, 31(1), 219–244.

Wicker, A. W. Attitudes versus actions: The relationship of verbal and overt behavioral responses in attitude objects. *Journal of Social Issues*, 1969, 25, 41–78.

Williams, J. E., & Edwards, C. D. An exploratory study of the modification of color and racial concept attitudes in preschool children. *Child Development*, 1969, 40, 737–750.

Williams, J. E., & Morland, J. K. *Race, color, and the young child*. Chapel Hill, N.C.: The University of North Carolina Press, 1976.

Williams, R. M. *Strangers next door: Ethnic relations in American communities*. Englewood Cliffs, N.J.: Prentice-Hall, 1964.

Wilner, D. M., Walkley, R. P., & Cook, S. W. *Human relations in interracial housing: A study of the contact hypothesis*. Minneapolis: University of Minnesota Press, 1955.

Word, C. O., Zanna, M. P., & Cooper, J. The nonverbal mediation of self-fulfilling prophecies in interracial interaction. *Journal of Experimental Social Psychology*, 1974, 10, 109–120.

Wright, B. A. *Physical disability—A psychological approach*. New York: Harper & Row, 1960.

GWENDOLYN T. SORELL
CAROL A. NOWAK

14

The Role of Physical Attractiveness as a Contributor to Individual Development

Introduction

If one thing in life is certain, it is the inevitability of change. Some changes may trigger debate (e.g., see Costa & McCrae, 1979, regarding whether or not personality changes with age, or Baltes & Schaie, 1976, regarding age-related declines in intellectual abilities). Some changes go by practically unnoticed by all but concerned scientists and clinicians (e.g., normal, subtle changes in sensory functioning). But few changes are as stark and as socially meaningful as are those in physical appearance. The appearance of one's body and face is the most immediate, unique, individual characteristic available to others as a basis for impression formation and as a guide for person-to-person interactions in any given social context. Indeed, appearance has been shown to be an important cue in the attribution of age, personality, and social characteristics (e.g., Berscheid & Walster, 1974; Davies & Chown, 1969; Nash, 1958; Nowak, 1975), and to be related to differential social interactions and outcomes (e.g., Benson, Karabenick, & Lerner, 1976; Canning & Mayer, 1966; Elder, 1969; Kurtzberg, Safar, & Cavior, 1968; Langlois & Downs, 1979; Lansdown & Polak, 1975). Appearance is also a source of self-perception, and a stimulus influencing interpersonal contacts, as shown by its association with individual psychological functioning (e.g., Adams, 1977b, 1979, 1980;

389

Jones & Mussen, 1958; Lerner & Karabenick, 1974; Mathes & Kahn, 1975; Mussen & Jones, 1957) and social status (e.g., Berscheid, Dion, Walster, & Walster, 1971; Goldman & Lewis, 1977).

Thus, the way one looks may be seen as related to the quality of one's interactional context, as well as to one's self-perceptions. When both the social and the individual aspects of appearance are recognized, and the changes in appearance over time are noted, a framework for identifying appearance variables as constituting a process contributing to the life-span development of the individual suggests itself. This chapter will seek to elaborate this framework, to examine existing empirical findings in relation to this life-span conceptualization, and to discuss how such an approach may suggest directions for future research regarding physical appearance.

Social psychologists have for some years been interested in the phenomenon of physical appearance, particularly as it relates to the formation of impressions about and attraction toward other individuals. Developmentalists, however, have virtually ignored appearance variables in their empirical research. Yet, where systematic attention has been paid by developmentalists to physical appearance variables, they have consistently been shown to contribute to the impression formations of self and others (e.g., Ames, 1957; Jones & Mussen, 1958; Lerner & Iwawaki, 1975; Lerner & Korn, 1972; Mussen & Jones, 1957; Nowak, 1974, 1975, 1976), and also to have correlates in actual behavior (Langlois & Downs, 1979; Lerner & Lerner, 1977). Many studies have focused only on description of appearance stereotypes. However, recurring trends in the social psychology literature and evidence from developmental studies suggest to us a way to interpret the findings from the two bodies of work that may further our understanding of the functioning of appearance variables.

Before such an approach can be undertaken, however, a mechanism for organizing and integrating the two literatures is needed. The initial section of this chapter will, therefore, set forth a framework within which to conceptualize appearance variables and to organize and interpret the physical appearance literature. The second section of this chapter will discuss the implications of an integrative approach to the study of appearance for research design, and the remaining sections will draw out the possible relevance of extant research findings for understanding the life-span contribution of the individual to his or her own development.

A Dynamic Interaction Model of Development

Harris (1957) has noted that the concept of development is basically biological. It thus follows that biological factors, of which many bodily characteristics and facial attributes are instances, may be seen as fundamental to human developmental processes. Anastasi (1958), however, has pointed out that such biological variables have meaning only within an environmental context and cannot be conceived as making separate and independent contributions to developmental processes. Development conceptualized in this manner may be defined as the ongoing interdependency and interaction of organism and environment (Schneirla, 1957).

Lerner (1976, 1978, 1979) has elaborated this concept of organism–environment relations in his dynamic interaction model of development. This model suggests that individual development is a contextually and historically embedded process of continuously evolving, reciprocal organism–environment influences (Lerner, Skinner, & Sorell, 1980). In other words, biological maturation and history of experience, through their ongoing interrelation and mutual stimulation, give rise to and set the parameters for organism individuality (Lerner, 1979).

The dynamic interaction model seems well-suited to a life-span conceptualization of physical appearance as a contributor to individual development. Specifically, physical appearance is comprised of biological–maturational changes (alterations over time in physical characteristics) and contextual–aesthetic attributes (cultural standards of beauty and associated socialized expectations) that stand in a continually interactive and interdependent relationship to one another. The characteristics of an individual's physical appearance, as they change over time, may thus be associated with appearance-related feedback from others. That is, the behaviors of others toward an individual may accord to some extent with expectations based on appearance stereotypes. An individual's self-perceptions and self-expectations may also involve a personal evaluation of appearance. In other words, when one looks in the mirror and compares the reflected image to an internalized interpretation of cultural, aesthetic standards of beauty and stereotyped expectations for behavior, self-concept and behavioral expectations for the self may be influenced by the "goodness of fit" (Thomas & Chess, Chapter 8, this volume) between appearance and expectation. These self-impression–expectation fits may be translated into observable behavior in an interactional context.

Furthermore, by invoking the well-established appearance stereotypes (Lerner & Korn, 1972; Miller, 1970a) as criteria for imputation of personality and behavioral characteristics, an individual's physical appearance may influence the type of interactions he or she experiences within the environmental context. The nature of these interactions may also influence individual psychological variables, such as social skills or competence, and life-course events, such as mate selection and career. Appearance effects, conceptualized in this manner, may be seen as related to the impressions one's physical characteristics make on oneself and on others, and to the types of interactions one experiences.

It may also be that appearance-related effects that become incorporated into one's history of experience at one point in time are associated with psychological and social outcomes at a later point in time. For example, follow-up studies (Ames, 1957; Jones, 1957; Jones & Mussen, 1958; Mussen & Jones, 1957) of subjects in the Oakland Growth Study investigation of the association between social and psychological characteristics and early or late maturation suggest that appearance-related attributes have long-term effects, at least for males. In their early thirties, those males who had matured later than average had less positive scores than early-maturing males along a number of psychological (e.g., dependence, impulsiveness) and social (e.g., vocational success) dimensions. Although the early- and late-maturing males did not differ in attractiveness in their thirties (Jones, 1957), adolescent maturation rate was found to be a better predictor of adult social behavior than social measures taken at the earlier point in time (Ames, 1957). Thus, appearance, through its affect on self-impressions and/or ongoing life events, such as marriage or career, may continue to have import at a point in time when such physical attributes are not directly and immediately affecting one's development.

Additionally, appearance may have implications for individual adaptation within a sociocultural context. Berscheid and Walster (1974) have pointed out the difficulties in establishing the manner in which physical appearance variables affect an individual's social interactions. They note that appearance has not been found to be orthogonal to attributions along dimensions such as intelligence and socioeconomic status, but rather is confounded with a variety of other factors. Thus, "untangling the complex skein of causal inferences these factors present is likely to prove to be a herculean task, at least with present methodological tools and knowledge [p. 207]." Furthermore, the amount of variance for which appearance variables alone can account is often quite small. From a dynamic interaction perspective, however, the matter of adaptive significance is related less to the identification of causal connections and main effects accounting for large proportions of variance than to the investigation of systematic patterns of covariation over time. It is the interrelatedness and mutually stimulative reciprocal interactions among variables associated with the relationship between the individual and his or her context that form the core of developmental processes. This approach suggests that the adaptiveness of various bodily and facial attributes may be more closely related to their association with other adaptive characteristics than to their isolated impact on individual development.

For example, the Terman longitudinal study of genius (Terman & Oden, 1959) has shown that the subjects' greater intelligence and professional success covaried with greater than average physical attractiveness. It can be argued that those who are high in intelligence and successful in achieving in socially valued undertakings are likely to be able to adapt to the circumstances of a rapidly changing cultural environment. Thus, appearance can be conceptualized as an indirect index of adaptive capacity.

Taking a slightly different perspective on the matter of appearance as adaptively significant, it can be noted that attractiveness, particularly of the body, is an operationalization of characteristics that are indices of physical adaptation. Specifically, it is known that youth, good health, and physical fitness are components of attractiveness stereotypes (Lerner & Korn, 1972). Again, appearance may be seen to be an indirect index of adaptation.

On a more speculative plain, it may also be argued that appearance is adaptive from an evolutionary perspective. In other words, the covariation of body and facial attributes and adaptive characteristics such as intelligence and health may be associated with selective processes. The most adaptive individuals, who may also be the most attractive individuals, may be those selected to carry the cultural structure forward through time. Here it may be noted that Elder (1969) found appearance to be the single most important variable in the upward social mobility of lower-class females. In addition, significant contributions to cultural change, as well as responsibility for perpetuation of social values, have been recognized as attaching to the upper strata of the social structure (Mills, 1956). Appearance, therefore, becomes associated with adaptation of the individual to the evolutionary demands of the sociocultural context.

This conceptualization suggests that five aspects of the functioning of appearance in relation to individual development should be included in an empirical approach deriving from the dynamic interaction model. First, the structure and content of appearance stereotypes, as they apply across the life span, need to be described. That is, the attributions made by persons who are at differing points in the life span to others who are at the same or different points, should be established. Second, self-attributions deriving from appearance, as they vary across the life span, must be discerned. Third, associations between an individual's appearance and social interaction variables across the life span have to be investigated. Fourth, the life-span relationship between appearance and individual behavioral and psychological characteristics must be established. Fifth, the interrelations among the above aspects, as they evolve and differ across the life span, would become the ultimate focus of physical appearance research. That is, any of the first four areas relevant to physical appearance could be studied in independent investigations, either across the life span or during particular developmental periods. However, an understanding of the ongoing interrelations among them would be necessary to clarify empirically the utility of the dynamic interaction conceptualization of appearance variables.

The suggestion that an empirical approach to understanding the relevance of physical appearance to individual development would incorporate the five areas set forth also has implications for the type of research that needs to be done with regard to appearance. The next section of this chapter discusses these implications.

Dimensions for Empirical Investigations of
Physical Appearance

THE NECESSITY FOR
THEORETICALLY BASED RESEARCH

The majority of studies regarding appearance that have appeared to date in the social psychological and developmental literatures have been "single shot," isolated attempts to elaborate one of the five aspects of appearance variables. Attempts have occasionally been made to interpret results within one or another thoretical framework. For example, Barocas and Karoly (1972) and Elder (1969) adopt an exchange theory perspective in looking respectively at social responsiveness and marriage mobility as related to appearance; Murstein and Christy (1976) interpret the association between appearance and marital adjustment in terms of equity theory; Cavior and Dokecki (1971) tested the relationship between physical appearance and self-concept from a symbolic interactionism perspective; and Langlois and Stephan (1981) have suggested a social learning model as appropriate for understanding the relationship between physical appearance and the development of peer relations in childhood. Nevertheless, the majority of studies are atheoretical.

Because the assumptions guiding the conception and design of physical appearance investigations are often unstated, it is difficult to relate such studies to one another and to interpret findings in relation to the overall functioning of appearance variables. This limitation of the extant literature points to the necessity for a theoretical view linking the five areas of appearance-related issues. Adoption of a coherent framework for conceptualization of such variables would permit research to be derived for one or more of the five areas, while also contributing to a common body of related results. For example, research on the nature of physical attractiveness stereotypes held by adults toward young children could be systematically related to the literature that looks at peer relations among young children differing in appearance (cf. Langlois & Stephan, 1981). Were such an approach to prevail, studies could continue to be of a "single shot" nature and also have the virtue of feeding into an overriding framework for incorporating the various facets of the impact of physical appearance on developmental processes.

Recognition of the utility of theoretically based research also raises a second issue in relation to empirical investigations of appearance. To fully explore the various aspects of appearance variables, and the interrelations among them, programmatic research is needed.

THE NECESSITY FOR PROGRAMMATIC RESEARCH

Few studies in the existing body of physical appearance literature represent attempts to contribute to an accumulation of findings systematically elaborating understanding of the area. That is, in addition to standing in atheoretical isolation with respect to one another, most studies are conducted without regard for the methodological consistency necessary to construct an interrelated body of findings that is "greater than the sum of its parts." For example, the relationship between appearance and peer relations has been examined among preschool children using observational measures of behavior (Langlois & Downs, 1979). Among fourth and sixth graders (Lerner & Lerner, 1977), the relationship has been explored through the use of peer popularity nominations, whereas college students' social interactions have been indexed by sociometric ratings of same-sex dorm-mates (Krebs & Adinolfi, 1975) and by self-report journal records of social contacts (Reis, Nezlek, & Wheeler, 1980). Problems of measurement arise in comparing the findings from such studies because of the differential conceptualization and operationalization of peer relations in each of them. Furthermore, there are no studies examining the association between peer relationships and appearance during early and middle adolescence, nor at any points in adulthood and old age. Essentially, the empirical basis for constructing a life-span conceptualization of appearance as a variable relevant to interactions with peers is fragmentary and lacks unity. A similar absence of conceptual and operational comparability and life-span-related completeness characterizes all other areas of physical appearance research, as well.

It must also be pointed out that physical appearance itself has been inconsistently conceptualized and operationalized. Many studies use ratings of facial photographs or slides as an index of attractiveness, whereas others define appearance as variations in body build and employ photographs of whole persons, in which the faces are blacked out, to obtain ratings. On occasion, videotapes, which bring into play many factors not associated with photographic stimuli, such as mobility of expression, have been used as a basis for ratings (e.g., Barocas & Karoly, 1972; Cash, Begley, McCown, & Weise, 1975). Elder (1969) determined his subjects' attractiveness by reviewing observational ratings across a number of facial and body characteristics made by two staff members at the Institute of Human Development at Berkeley. Ratings by experimenters of the overall attractiveness of subjects present in person have also been used (e.g., Cash & Begley, 1976; Cash & Burns, 1977; Curran & Lippold, 1975; Goldman & Lewis, 1977). No attempts have been made to determine whether ratings are affected or influenced by the inclusion or exclusion of body *or* face as a basis for appearance assessments, or whether and how such ratings may relate to composite ratings of body *and* face. In addition, it is not known what, if any, effects are associated with variations in stimulus medium such as those just described.

The conceptualization and operationalization of appearance is muddied to an even greater extent when the manner in which stimulus materials are assembled is considered. Although it is usual to eliminate from consideration persons characterized by physical handicaps or deformities and those wearing eyeglasses, and to attempt standardization of pose and of quality of materials, the ideal is not always achieved. For example, Berscheid, Walster, and Campbell (1972), in studying the relationship between self-reported adulthood happiness and level of attractiveness 20 years earlier, obtained attractiveness ratings for photographic reproductions ranging from enlargements of faces extracted from group pictures to college graduation pictures. These materials differed considerably in pose, as well as in quality of reproduction. Photographic quality is not specified in many reports, and in some cases there are obviously drastic differences. For example, Byrne, London, and Reeves (1968) used Xerox copies of photographs as stimuli to elicit stereotypical expectations attaching to persons differing in level of facial attractiveness, whereas Nowak (1976) used photographs of models who were cosmetically made up to appear as either attractive or unattractive.

Additional complications affecting comparability of findings are encountered in considering variations in the breadth of definitions of appearance. Specifically, in relation to facial attributes, some studies attempt to incorporate a broad range of attractiveness (e.g., Dermer & Thiel, 1975; Stroebe, Insko, Thompson, & Layton, 1971), whereas others include only the range extremes (e.g., Brundage, Derlega, & Cash, 1977) or exclude extremely attractive and/or unattractive individuals (e.g., Bar-Tal & Saxe, 1976a; Byrne et al., 1968; Dion, Berscheid, & Walster, 1972).

Furthermore, the methods of obtaining ratings of such photographs or of persons vary. A few raters may be used, or ratings may be obtained from a large number of persons. As a rule, an attempt is made to include approximately equal numbers of males and females among the raters, although it has been demonstrated that there are not significant or systematic differences along the sex-of-rater dimension (Berscheid et al., 1971; Cavior & Dokecki, 1971; Kopera, Maier, & Johnson, 1971; Murstein, 1972; Reis et al., 1980). There is some evidence of a sex-of-rater by sex-of-target interaction with regard to assessment of appearance (Morse, Reis, Gruzen, & Wolff, 1974; Reis et al., 1980). However, initial findings suggest that males and females may use remarkably similar criteria in evaluating opposite-sex facial and bodily attractiveness and tend to agree both within and across sex groupings as to who is and who is not attractive (Lerner, Karabenick, & Stuart, 1973; Morse, Gruzan, & Reis, 1976; Morse et al., 1974; Reis et al., 1980).

Further investigation is also needed to determine the effects of differences in the methods of collecting data regarding appearance-related attributions. It may be that the results of asking raters to make attributions using a forced-choice checklist format will not fully coincide with those obtained when attributions are made on the basis of the relative degree to which characteristics are typical of individuals who differ in level of attractiveness. Indeed, evidence to this effect has been found in the study of body-build stereotypes (Lerner, Knapp, & Pool, 1974). This type of methodological inconsistency may also be a partial basis for the lack of clarity in studies of facial attractiveness as to whether the attractive are advantaged (as suggested by Landy & Sigall, 1974) or the unattractive disadvantaged (as Dermer & Thiel, 1975, infer from their data).

Whereas most of the practices previously outlined are not, in and of themselves, exceedingly problematic, the variations related to conceptualization and operationalization of appearance do serve to lessen comparability among studies. This is the case primarily because, with the exception of studies showing minimal sex-of-rater effects in controlled situations and slightly lower interrater reliabilities across sex in naturalistic settings, few investigations have been conducted to determine if differential results are obtained when various methods of deriving ratings are employed (e.g., large versus small groups of raters) or when variations in stimuli characteristics exist (e.g., photographs versus videotapes). A programmatic approach to physical appearance research would serve to fill this void and, in addition, would guide researchers in the selection of useful methods and stimulus materials.

It should be noted, however, that other equivalence difficulties of a more serious nature also plague the literature and render a comparative and integrative analysis of findings extremely problematic. Most investigations employ rating scales as the basis for assessment of appearance. In various studies, 5-point to 15-point scales have been used. Although an occasional correlational study uses raw scores as the basis for ascertaining associations between appearance and other variables (e.g., Goldman & Lewis, 1977; Reis et al., 1980), the majority derive dichotomous or trichotomous grouping structures and analyze data in relation to such structures. In other words, stimulus materials (whether photographs, videotapes, or actual persons) are selected for inclusion in groups on the basis of the means and standard deviations of ratings applying to them. However, the range of the rating scale used and the means and standard deviations for the groups are not consistently reported by investigators. When this situation is considered in conjunction with the variability found in the criteria for including or excluding individuals who fall close to the attractiveness continuum extremes, the difficulty in determining what, if any, comparability exists across the literature becomes apparent.

Indeed, many, if not all, of the possible combinations of criteria can be found. For example, Hartnett and Elder (1973) report that for each sex, 10 attractive and 10 unattractive photographs were selected by the experimenter, and subsequently presented to 20 female undergraduates for rating on a 10-point scale. The pictures of two males and two females with the lowest and highest mean ratings were chosen for inclusion in the study. Means and standard deviations are not reported, and thus the definitions of attractive and unattractive remain unknown.

Bar-Tal and Saxe (1976a) obtained physical attractiveness ratings of slides on an undescribed scale from four males and four females, and selected for their dichotomous (attractive versus unattractive) grouping pictures for which there was high interjudge reliability, and which were neither extremely high nor extremely low on the attractiveness continuum. Again, no means or standard deviations for the groups are reported. Thus, the definition of attractiveness level is not specified, but it is known that pictures of markedly beautiful and remarkably ugly persons probably were not used. How the stimulus materials relate to those of Hartnett and Elder (1973) cannot be ascertained.

Stroebe et al. (1971), however, selected pictures of 30 males and 30 females, being careful to include those representing the extreme ends of the attractiveness continuum. Subsequently, an attractiveness trichotomy was derived based on the assessments of 10 opposite-sex raters on an 11-point scale, and photographs of three males and three females were chosen to represent differing level-of-attractiveness by sex categories. Means and standard deviations for each of the photographs selected for inclusion in the study are reported. Here, attractiveness level is clearly defined, but comparisons with the Hartnett and Elder (1973) and Bar-Tal and Saxe (1976a) studies are difficult because of the ambiguity of the operational definitions of attractiveness that they provide. Furthermore, some discrepancies in the composition of the groups of raters, the effects of which have not been investigated, also raise questions. For example, are ratings by four males and four females of an undesignated number of slides of males and females comparable to and consistent with ratings by 20 females of photographs of 20 males and 20 females, or with those by 10 opposite-sex judges of 30 pictures? These factors cloud the operationalizations still further, and useful comparisons among the studies are rendered more difficult. In view of the vagueness in these three studies alone of the criteria used to designate standards of attractiveness and in the design of the stimulus materials, some caution seems in order in assuming that, across the body of physical appearance literature, findings with regard to the functioning of appearance variables are systematically or meaningfully related to one another.

More salient to the present discussion, however, is the suggestion that a programmatic approach to appearance research, conceptualized within a specified theoretical framework, would serve to reduce the lack of comparability among findings. Furthermore, were such an approach to be adopted, research could be derived as an outgrowth of previous work so as to either deepen understanding with regard to one aspect of appearance-related functions (e.g., marital choice) or broaden the range of understanding of such function (e.g., marital choice during different periods of the life span).

In addition, a programmatic approach to the design of research would permit conceptualization and interpretive consideration of the implications of specifically hypothesized interrelations for the totality of appearance-related functions. In this manner, theory concerning the overall interrelational framework encompassing the five areas previously outlined could be refined in light of each new set of findings, and subsequent research guided by the suggestions and implications of such refinements. Ideally, each new project would enhance our conceptualization of appearance-related functions, and the accumulated findings, taken together, would provide a comprehensive and cohesive overview of the interrelations investigated.

The suggestion that a programmatic approach will serve to enhance physical appearance research both with regard to the various aspects of appearance-related phenomena and with respect to the interrelations among them raises a third issue. Useful findings are most likely to be generated in a parsimonious manner if physical appearance research is multivariate.

THE NECESSITY FOR MULTIVARIATE RESEARCH

Although there have been exceptions (e.g., Lerner & Lerner, 1977), the majority of physical appearance studies have been univariate. From the perspective of the dynamic interaction framework that has been suggested herein as a useful vehicle for the conceptualization of appearance functions, this state of affairs is unfortunate. In other words, a univariate approach is inadequate to explore the simultaneous impact of appearance across multiple dimensions. For example, with respect to impression formation in social interaction, the appearance of a kindergarten-aged child would be expected to simultaneously affect relations with peers and with teachers and to provide some basis for differential feedback from each. It may be, however, that it is not the sources of feedback functioning separately but, rather, the pattern of relationships among them that has an impact on individual psychological and behavioral variables. Such a pattern of relationships can be investigated only within a multivariate framework (Baltes, Reese, & Nesselroade, 1977).

Furthermore, as noted previously, a comprehensive understanding of appearance-related functions will require operationalizations of interrelations among appearance stereotypes, self-attributions, social interaction variables, and individual psychological and behavioral characteristics. Whereas hypothetical interrelations can be derived on the basis of uni- variate findings pertaining to the particular aspects of interest to a re- searcher, operationalizations of such linkages must necessarily include at least two dependent variables, one from each of the related domains (Baltes et al., 1977). Again, the necessity for multivariate research is demonstrated.

A multivariate approach to appearance-related phenomena will aid in the operationalization of the reciprocal patterns of relationship suggested by the dynamic interaction model. However, the manner in which such reciprocities evolve across time remains to be addressed. Thus, the issue of longitudinal research designs is raised.

THE NECESSITY FOR LONGITUDINAL RESEARCH

Although an occasional research project has included follow-up mea- surements (e.g., Byrne, Ervin, & Lamberth, 1970; Mathes, 1975), few studies have looked at appearance effects longitudinally. The investiga- tions of early and late maturing individuals (Ames, 1957; Jones, 1957; Jones & Mussen, 1958; Mussen & Jones, 1957) and Elder's (1969) study of female marriage mobility are exceptions. Therefore, data relevant to determination of the manner in which appearance may be associated with developmental processes, and specifically to the contribution appearance may make to individual development across the life span, are almost entirely lacking.

Although cross-sectional studies, such as those comprising the vast majority of extant research regarding physical appearance, can identify interindividual differences, suggest interesting trends, and possibly imply developmental change or differential functioning of appearance variables over time (e.g., Langlois & Downs, 1979; Lerner, 1972), the actual source of such differences and course of change—indeed, the existence of func- tional differences or developmental change—can only be established when the same sample is measured at different points in time. Furthermore, longitudinal studies, when designed to incorporate multivariate opera- tionalizations, would permit detection and empirical elaboration of the evolving reciprocal relations and patterns of interrelations central to the dynamic interaction conceptualization of development.

SUMMARY

The foregoing discussion suggests that useful empirical inquiries con- cerning the functional roles of physical appearance for individual devel- opmental processes will be theory-based, programmatic, multivariate, and, in some instances, longitudinal. This does not imply that any one research project would necessarily be characterized by all of these attri- butes, although the attributes are hierarchically arranged. That is, in our view, all studies should be theory-based. To as great an extent as possible, research should be programmatically derived. Any work involving a multivariate approach should be conceptually and operationally comparable to extant literature. Finally, to meet a criterion of maximal usefulness for the study of change, longitudinal projects should be characterized by the three previously mentioned attributes. Such a body of hierarchically expanding work would be amenable to comparative interpretation on the basis of its unifying theoretical orientation and programmatic execution.

Methodologically, this is not the case in the existing physical appearance literature. Instead, as noted, most studies are essentially atheoretical. Diverse methodologies, ranging from experimental manipulations to paper and pencil self-reports to observational techniques have been employed; and in many instances, the operationalization of variables is problematic. Few studies have (a) systematically hypothesized theoretically suggested relationships among appearance stereotypes, actual appearance, social interaction, and behavioral, psychological, and social functioning; (b) revised theory on the basis of findings; and (c) investigated hypotheses derived from the refined formulations. Furthermore, a minimal number of studies have looked at appearance variables longitudinally, and therefore, the developmental implications of appearance are difficult to specify. Thus, although reviews of selected findings from the physical appearance literature, such as those of Berscheid and Walster (1974), Adams (1977a), and the one undertaken herein, may suggest interesting trends and relationships, the qualification that, in many respects, the studies to which reference is made are lacking in fundamental comparability must be kept in mind.

However, with the existing problems in the literature noted, an examination of findings associated with each of the five roles of appearance-related variables may suggest interesting and useful directions for future research regarding the manner in which appearance provides a basis for individual developmental processes across the life span. Such a review is undertaken in the next section of this chapter.

Physical Appearance Revisited: Directions for Research

Fundamental to an understanding of the functioning of physical appearance variables as contributors to individual development is the elaboration of appearance stereotypes. In other words, it is essential to establish what personality, behavioral, and social attributes are assumed to be typical of persons differing in bodily and facial characteristics. Furthermore, an elaboration of similarities and differences in the stereotypes held by individuals during particular developmental periods—adolescence or middle age, for example—toward peers and toward individuals in other developmental periods is also necessary. Table 14.1 sets forth suggested categories of studies relevant to this area and notes those categories for which findings are reported in the literature.

An assumption that individuals are able to discriminate varying levels of facial and bodily attractiveness underlies the construction of the matrix in Table 14.1. Therefore, before discussing the appearance stereotypes applied by and toward individuals across the life span, it will be useful to examine findings regarding who is considered to be attractive and who is able to make discriminations on the basis of physical appearance.

IDENTIFICATION AND DISCRIMINATION OF VARIATIONS IN PHYSICAL APPEARANCE

Berscheid and Walster (1974) have reviewed the numerous, essentially fruitless, attempts made by social scientists and by others to identify those attributes that serve to make individuals physically attractive. They note that among adolescents and adults, certain factors, such as height in males, and body build, can account for some proportion of the variance in attractiveness ratings. However, the Berscheid and Walster (1974) review concludes that "there exists no compendium of physical characteristics, or configurations of characteristics, which people find attractive in others, even within a single society [p. 186]." Nowak, Karuza, and Namikas (1976), however, have noted the structural congruence of physical appearance and old age stereotypes. "Researchers concerned with interpersonal attraction, but not with attitudes toward aging, have independently discovered a set of characteristics used to describe unattractive people that are remarkably similar to those descriptive of people who are old [p. 1]." Whereas attempts to specifically identify what is and is not beautiful may indeed end in frustration, the findings regarding the relevance of physique and youthfulness to judgments of attractiveness have implications for understanding the significance of certain aspects of appearance as individual developmental variables across the life span.

With respect to physique, the mesomorphic body build, which is muscular, strong, lean, and athletic-looking, has been found to be preferred by children, adolescents, and adults, whereas the ectomorphic (thin, frail) and endomorphic (fat, rounded) body builds are considered unattractive (Iwawaki & Lerner, 1974, 1976; Iwawaki, Lerner, & Chihara, 1977; Lerner, 1969a, b; Lerner & Gellert, 1969; Lerner & Iwawaki, 1975; Lerner, Iwawaki, & Chihara, 1976; Lerner, Karabenick, & Meisels, 1975a, b; Lerner & Korn, 1972; Lerner & Pool, 1972; Lerner, Venning, & Knapp, 1975; Staffieri, 1967, 1972). There are also indications in the literature on aging that firm, smooth, unwrinkled skin is associated with an impression of youthfulness and attractiveness (Kogan & Shelton, 1962a, b; Traxler, 1971). Thus, although the designation of what is attractive may not be possible in a specific sense, the implication of the evidence is that to meet the minimum

TABLE 14.1

Categories of Studies Reporting Appearance-Related Attributions

Attributions by	Infants	Preschoolers	School-aged children	Early and middle adolescents	Late adolescents–young adults	Middle-aged adults	Elderly adults
Attributions to							
Infants							
Preschoolers		X			X		
School-aged children			X	X	X		
Early and middle adolescents			X	X	X		
Late adolescents–young adults			X	X	X	X	
Middle-aged adults					X	X	X
Elderly adults							X

403

or basic criteria for attractiveness, a person should be of average build, be strong and firm-looking, and have skin that is smooth and unwrinkled.

Because both body build and the characteristics associated with visible, biological aging, such as sagging muscles and wrinkled skin, are maturational in nature, it might be expected that judgments regarding level of attractiveness would vary in relation to differences in such attributes. This has indeed been found to be the case with regard to facial characteristics associated with an appearance of youthfulness. In general, adolescents and young adults are judged to be more attractive than children or middle-aged adults (with the exception of middle-aged men, who are believed to be more attractive than young males), and the middle-aged are considered more attractive than the elderly (Cross & Cross, 1971; Nowak, 1975). Furthermore, regardless of their actual age, postchildhood individuals who look young are judged to be more attractive than those whose facial appearance betrays characteristics of aging (Nowak, 1975; Nowak *et al.*, 1976).

Unlike the "youthfulness" aspect of attractiveness, which may be expected to deteriorate unidirectionally after early adulthood, the body-build component of beauty may vary across the life span, depending on personal habits and health, as well as maturational status. One may be fat, thin, or of average size at various times in life, depending on one's eating habits or state of health. Furthermore, during certain periods of biological growth, such as adolescence, body build may be related to maturational status. (The evidence regarding the personality, behavioral, and social variables that have been found to covary with adolescent maturation rate, and hence with body build, will be discussed later in this chapter.) Thus, the situation regarding body build may be somewhat more difficult to disentangle with respect to developmental implications and effects than are facial appearance influences.

It should also be pointed out that, whereas extant findings suggest that, except for middle-aged males, the most attractive people are those who are or appear to be young and who are characterized by mesomorphy, much additional research is needed to corroborate this construction. This is especially pertinent with respect to possible interaction effects between body build and attributes connoting youthfulness. In other words, these two components of beauty are not independent of one another. The appearance of aging may be most obvious to others in the lines, wrinkles, and sagging of the facial muscles and skin, but the skin and muscles of the entire body also age and alter the particulars of one's body build. Furthermore, a person with a fat body may also have a fat, albeit unwrinkled, face. Thus, the facial and bodily attributes suggested to be associated with attractiveness level may interact to convey a holistic impression that is functionally different across developmental periods or that differs qualitatively from the impression formed when the factors are evaluated in isolation from one another.

As was noted earlier, children are not considered as attractive as adolescents and young adults (Cross & Cross, 1971). Although it may be speculated that indications of biological aging contribute to lower attractiveness evaluations among most postchildhood age groupings, few data directly suggest factors associated with the devaluation of children's attractiveness. It may be that children are considered to be less appealing because they have not achieved biological maturity, a suggestion supported, at least with regard to males, by the finding that early-maturing boys are judged to be more attractive than those who mature late in adolescence (Jones & Bayley, 1950; Mussen & Jones, 1957).

Attempts to identify factors relevant to attractiveness evaluations of infants are quite preliminary in nature. Facial variables, such as fatness of cheeks and spacing between the eyes, have been found to contribute to attractiveness ratings (Brooks & Hochberg, 1960; Hildebrandt & Fitzgerald, 1979). It has also been found that maternal behavior toward premature infants varies in relation to the size of the baby (Minde, Trehub, Corter, Boukydis, Celhoffer, & Marton, 1978). However, the manner in which infant size may be associated with judgments of appearance has not been investigated.

In summary, we concur with Berscheid and Walster (1974) that the components of beauty are elusive, at least in their particulars. Hints and trends in the empirical literature are sufficient, however, to suggest that, among all age groups, somatotype is a significant contributor to evaluations of attractiveness. Furthermore, congruence with and deviation from a social ideal of bodily and facial youthfulness associated with adolescence and young adulthood may affect judgments of beauty.

Although specification of what is attractive cannot be made with precision, there is evidence that the standard of facial beauty is reasonably unitary from late childhood through middle adulthood (Cross & Cross, 1971; Morse et al., 1976). A high degree of interrater reliability has been found when judges evaluate who is and who is not attractive (Cavior & Lombardi, 1973; Clifford & Walster, 1973; Dion, 1973; Nowak, 1975; Reis et al., 1980). Furthermore, attractiveness manipulations in research studies reveal significant effects in expected directions. The preferences of younger children may, however, differ from this standard (Udry, 1965). It has also been found that the preferences of older individuals are less uniform than those of other groups and that successive age groups give lower ratings to very young female faces and more positive ratings to mature female faces (Udry, 1965).

In addition, the extent to which familiarity moderates perceptions of attractiveness is not clear. Most studies on attraction, including those designed to determine who is considered to be attractive and what characteristics comprise appearance stereotypes, pit the perceiver and the target in a "kind of subject–object relation that differs considerably from the subject–subject quality of interpersonal relationships [Levinger &

Snoek, 1972, p. 1]." That is, persons are asked to respond to photographic targets and descriptions of people they do not know, in out-of-context situations, and make judgments about how attractive the targets are, what those people are like, and how well they are liked.

The available evidence suggests that, despite the high level of agreement as to the standard of beauty, interpersonal factors may affect judgments of attractiveness, at least among certain age groups. For example, Cavior (1970) found that among fifth and eleventh graders who were evaluated for attractiveness by familiar and unfamiliar peers, being acquainted with the perceived was associated with more positive assessments, particularly for average-looking subjects. Likewise, Corter, Trehub, Boukydis, Ford, Celhoffer, & Minde (1978) found that nurses in a premature nursery tended to upgrade the attractiveness of infants for whom they had cared, as compared to the evaluations given by nurses unfamiliar with the infants. These nurses also rated familiar premature babies as more attractive than unfamiliar premies.

Walster (1971) has reported that college students perceive others with attitudes dissimilar to their own as less attractive, and both males and females have been found to perceive feminists as unattractive (Goldberg, Gottesdiener, & Abramson, 1975). Kopera et al. (1971) found that situational factors, such as making evaluations in a public as opposed to a private setting, and rating a person more than once, tended to result in lowered ratings for individuals of average and low attractiveness. Berman, O'Nan, and Floyd (1978) also suggest that ratings made in private settings differ from those obtained in public and that group composition affects evaluations of the attractiveness of midlife individuals. Specifically, the Berman et al. (1978) findings indicate that the evaluation of middle-aged women as less attractive than middle-aged men may be situational rather than general. Findings by Styczynski and Langlois (1977) suggest that, among preschoolers, familiarity may not affect attractiveness ratings, although knowing the perceived may influence behavioral attributions. There are also data suggesting that appearance evaluations are related to the level of attractiveness of the rater (Dermer & Thiel, 1975; Tennis & Dabbs, 1975). Nowak (1975) found that among middle-aged women, self-evaluations of attractiveness influenced ratings made of others' appearance. Further research to establish the relevance of familiarity, similarity, and other such factors on attractiveness judgments, as well as the manner in which such factors may be differentially applicable to persons at various times across the life span, would seem warranted.

Although empirical evidence in general indicates that most individuals are capable of discriminating attractive from unattractive others, the ability to discriminate along appearance dimensions may not be as fully developed among young children as it is in older age groups. Spiegel (1950) concluded that preadolescents do not have a concept of facial beauty;

however, other data indicate that children as young as 3 years of age attribute characteristics differentially to peers varying in appearance (Dion, 1973; Dion & Berscheid, 1974; Langlois & Styczynski, 1979; Styczynski & Langlois, 1977). Similar results have been found among kindergarten and elementary-school-aged children with regard to discrimination of differences in both the bodily (Lerner, 1973; Lerner & Gellert, 1969; Lerner et al., 1975a, b; Lerner & Korn, 1972; Lerner & Pool, 1972; Lerner et al., 1975; Staffieri, 1967, 1972) and facial attributes (Cavior, 1970; Cavior & Dokecki, 1970, 1971; Cross & Cross, 1971; Dion, 1973; Dion & Berscheid, 1974; Langlois & Stephan, 1977; Lerner & Lerner, 1977; Udry, 1965) of their peers. However, many of the studies indicating the existence of a standard of beauty and the ability to discriminate among individuals on an appearance-related basis have involved peer judgments or judgments by late adolescents or adults of persons younger than themselves. There remains some question as to the ability of preschoolers to discriminate along attractiveness dimensions with regard to persons older than themselves (Cavior & Lombardi, 1973; Dion, 1973). Lerner and Korn (1972) provide evidence that 5- and 6-year-olds use body build as a basis for attributions to adolescents and young adults. Likewise, males in late childhood and adolescence make body-build-related attributions to adult men (Lerner, 1969a). However, no findings have been reported indicating whether young children make appearance-related judgments of individuals younger than themselves. In addition, empirical findings regarding body-build discrimination and preference have involved peer ratings almost exclusively (with the exception of Lerner & Korn, 1972, and Lerner, 1969a, noted earlier), and are particularly limited with regard to adult populations. Beyond childhood, the ability of individuals to discriminate along appearance dimensions is well-established by the numerous studies indicating that adolescents and adults hold appearance stereotypes.

Congruence between attractiveness ratings made by judges during the stimulus preparation phase of investigations and the ratings made by research participants also supports the claim that individuals do perceive others as differing in physical appearance. The differential operation of varying degrees of attractiveness may also be inferred from findings that attributions covary systematically and predictably with differences in appearance. Nevertheless, the literature regarding appearance would be enriched by empirical investigations directed toward both discrimination and attribution effects involving judgments of targets differing from raters with respect to developmental status.

In summary, although there are some areas that remain to be investigated, empirical evidence indicates generally that the ability to discriminate along appearance dimensions probably is present to some extent among fairly young children toward their peers and toward individuals of all ages among postchildhood age groups. Furthermore, preferences with regard to facial and body-build attributes are reasonably uniform across those portions of the life span that have been investigated. Therefore, within the constraints of the evidence cited, the structure and content of appearance stereotypes, as they apply within and across the various developmental periods of the life span, will be examined.

PHYSICAL APPEARANCE STEREOTYPES

For all periods across the life span, in relation to which attempts have been made to ascertain the existence of and to delineate the components of appearance stereotypes, a general statement may be made: Positive personality, behavior, and social characteristics are attributed to beautiful people, and negative traits, intentions, feelings, behaviors, and statuses are associated with low levels of attractiveness. Thus, the evidence indicates that, in the majority of areas, the structure of appearance stereotypes is stable across the life span.

However, due to the variations in context pertaining to successive periods in the life span, the content of the stereotypes might be expected to differ. Furthermore, stereotype content may vary depending on the developmental status of the individual making attributions. This relationship between stereotypical attributions and developmental status is implied in Table 14.1. For example, the characteristics assumed by a middle-aged adult to attach to a 9-year-old child may differ from those attributed by the same middle-aged individual to a college-aged adolescent. Both clusters of attributes may be positive in nature; yet, due to the differences in contextually relevant variables associated with the developmental status of the perceived (i.e., being in elementary school as opposed to making provisional steps toward the assumption of adult social roles), the specific characteristics comprising the appearance stereotypes attaching to each of the two individuals may not be the same. Therefore, insofar as the extant literature permits, stereotype content will be discussed in relation to the developmental period to which it pertains.

There are, however, a number of cells in Table 14.1 with regard to which there is no research. For example, although there is some indication that social interactions with infants covary in relation to appearance (Hildebrandt & Fitzgerald, 1978, 1980; Minde et al., 1978; Parke, Hymel, Power, & Tinsley, 1980; Parke & Sawin, 1975), no studies have been done regarding the attributions made by persons of any age to infants differing in attractiveness. Thus, all the cells on the top line of Table 14.1 are empty.

Likewise, preschoolers and elementary schoolchildren have been evaluated by their peers, their teachers, and by parents. However, no consistent effort has been made to determine attributions made to these groups by middle-aged and older adults except insofar as a teacher or parent falls into these categories. Similarly, our knowledge of appearance-related attributions by elementary-school-aged children to adolescents of all ages and to adults, and by early and middle adolescents to their peers, to children, and to late adolescents and young adults, is limited to that developed by Lerner and Korn (1972) in their somatotype investigation using male subjects and stimuli. Only two studies, again involving body-build variables, have sought to determine the attributions of late adolescents and young adults toward younger adolescents (Lerner, 1969a; Lerner & Korn, 1972).

Thus, although a number of studies have examined the traits, behaviors, and statuses believed to characterize people who differ in level of attractiveness, the majority of this work has been concentrated in a few areas (i.e., within-peer-group stereotypes, and the stereotypes held by college-aged individuals toward others). To the extent that the literature permits, the content of these stereotypes is described in the following section.

PRESCHOOL AND ELEMENTARY SCHOOLCHILDREN

Moderate to strong attractiveness stereotypes seem to operate in relation to the characteristics of children. Teachers, for example, indicate that they believe attractive children have higher educational potential and higher IQs than unattractive children (Adams, 1978; Adams & Cohen, 1976; Clifford & Walster, 1973; Kehle, Bramble, & Mason, 1974; Lerner & Lerner, 1977; Ross & Salvia, 1975); have parents who are interested in their academic achievement; exhibit more prosocial and less aggressive behavior; and have better relationships with their peers (Clifford & Walster, 1973; Kleck, Richardson, & Ronald, 1974; Rich, 1975). Parents perceive physically attractive children as more likely to be elected to class offices, more popular, more likely to possess better personal attitudes, and more assured of high job potential, than their less attractive peers (Adams & LaVoie, 1975). Walker (1963), using parents' ratings of nursery school boys' physiques, found evidence that attractive children are attributed more positive personal characteristics than unattractive children. Young adult women have also been found to attribute the misbehavior of unattractive children to antisocial personality characteristics, whereas attractive children who transgressed were believed to have deviated temporarily from a prosocial dispositional pattern (Dion, 1972). Unattractive children were perceived by the young women in the Dion (1972) study to be less pleasant and more dishonest than the attractive children.

Among pre- and early elementary schoolchildren, Dion (1973) found that children rated pictures of attractive same-aged strangers to be more prosocial and more likely to be their friends than unattractive strangers. Similarly, preschoolers unacquainted with their targets have been found to evaluate unattractive peers negatively and attractive peers positively, with the latter group being better liked (Langlois & Stephan, 1977; Styczynski & Langlois, 1977). When body build has been manipulated, male children, adolescents, and young adults have been found to attribute negative physical, social, and personal characteristics to thin and chubby young males, whereas those of average build were seen as having positively valued attributes (Lerner & Korn, 1972; Staffieri, 1967). This stereotype has been found to become more clearly differentiated in successive age groups (Lerner, 1972).

There is also some evidence that, at least for adults rating unfamiliar children, appearance stereotypes are modified when other information is available. For example, Adams and LaVoie (1974) have reported that physical attractiveness was less salient in teacher expectancy when conduct was taken into consideration. However, no studies appearing to date report data suggesting whether information regarding other aspects of personality and behavior may modify stereotyped expectations among children toward unfamiliar peers.

In essence, preschoolers and elementary-aged children seem to attribute more positive interpersonal characteristics to unfamiliar attractive peers. They evaluate other children primarily in terms of the quality of interactions they expect to have with them. Teachers, parents, and other adults, while making evaluations in terms of interaction variables associated with children's relations with one another, hold additional expectations. The stereotype held by this group also includes attributions regarding school-related abilities and behaviors and future social status potential. In other words, the appearance stereotype attached by young adults to preschoolers and elementary-school-aged children, as reflected in existing research results, is more fully elaborated and incorporates a broader range of variables than does the stereotype held by children toward one another.

The noted differences in stereotype content may, of course, reflect methodological differences in the studies. However, as Langlois and Stephan (1981) point out, cognitive developmental factors may be expected to influence expectations and attributions. The young child's inability to think in terms of abstract concepts, such as attitudes and achievement potential, may explain the tendency of this age group to stereotype peers in terms of interpersonal behaviors.

ADOLESCENTS AND YOUNG ADULTS

The components of appearance stereotypes held by and toward early and middle adolescents have been examined in only one study. Lerner and Korn (1972) asked 15- and 20-year-old males to evaluate pictures of same-aged males and males from the other age group who differed in body build. A cluster of positive physical (e.g., fast, strong, healthy), social (e.g., have many friends, helps others, leader), and personal (e.g., clean, smart, brave, honest) characteristics was found to attach to mesomorphs of both ages, whereas negative attributions along all three dimensions were made toward endomorphs and ectomorphs. As was found to be the case with children (Lerner & Korn, 1972; Staffieri, 1967), the characteristics associated with ectomorphy were different from and fewer than those associated with endomorphy, but all were essentially negative.

The lack of studies regarding the components and functioning of appearance stereotypes in relation to early and middle adolescents is unfortunate with regard to the development of an empirical understanding of appearance. Given the extraordinary concern that people of this age have with their own physical appearance, it seems likely that a strong within-group stereotype would exist. Furthermore, it might be expected that persons of other age groups would be inclined to make characteristic attributions to adolescents on the basis of physical appearance. The extent to which such stereotypes exist, and the specification of their characteristics, must await future empirical elaboration.

The majority of stereotype studies have involved attributions made by late adolescents and young adults—specifically, college students—toward their peers. Within this group, positive evaluations along a number of personality and behavioral dimensions have been found to be associated with high levels of attractiveness. For example, attractive people have been found to be attributed with greater degrees of sensitivity and perceptiveness, calmness, confidence, assertiveness, happiness, sincerity, kindness, amiability, and self-control than less attractive persons (Bar-Tal & Saxe, 1976a; Dermer & Thiel, 1975; Dion et al., 1972; Miller, 1970a, b).

Cash et al. (1975) obtained the perceptions of male and female college students who viewed a videotape of a male professional counselor who was made to appear either attractive or unattractive. In the attractive condition, the counselor was perceived as significantly more competent, intelligent, friendly, warm, likable, trustworthy, and assertive than in the unattractive condition.

Positive evaluations along a number of social dimensions, such as popularity and social success, have also been found to be associated with high levels of attractiveness (Bar-Tal & Saxe, 1976a). With regard to attributions associated with body build, late adolescent and adult females have been found to evaluate adult males differing in somatotype in a manner quite similar to that of male children and adolescents (Lerner, 1969b). That is, the mesomorphic male was seen as having positive physical, social, and personal characteristics, whereas the ectomorphic and endomorphic males were negatively evaluated (Lerner, 1969b).

It has also been found that beautiful women and handsome men are attributed higher levels of traditionally feminine and masculine traits, respectively, than are their unattractive counterparts (Gillen, 1975). However, with respect to sex-role neutral traits, Gillen (1975) reports attractiveness to be associated with positive evaluations for both males and females. In a similar vein, attractive males and females have been attributed with greater success in sex-role traditional task performance than unattractive men and women (Hill & Lando, 1976). It is interesting to note that, despite the attribution of greater sex-role stereotypy to attractive women, they are believed to be less successful mothers than women whose physical appearance is negatively evaluated (Dion et al., 1972). Dermer and Thiel (1975), however, found this effect only with unattractive female raters, in a study in which no male evaluators were included.

Some of the evidence regarding the positively valued attributions made to attractive people has been contradicted. For example, Wiener, Saxe, and Bar-Tal (1975) found that attractive people were evaluated as being less, rather than more, intelligent than the unattractive. In addition, the female judges in this study, but not the male judges, saw attractive individuals as less trustworthy than the unattractive (Wiener et al., 1975). Attractive females have also been evaluated as more conceited and self-centered and less charitable than those possessed of lesser beauty (Dermer & Thiel, 1975).

Evaluation along social dimensions seems to be affected not only by attractiveness level, but also by sex, with more differences found between attractive and unattractive females than between males judged to be attractive and unattractive. For example, Bar-Tal and Saxe (1976a) found that attractive individuals were rated as having higher social success and being more popular than the unattractive, regardless of sex. However, on the dimensions of education, occupational status, and intelligence, a positive attractiveness effect was found for females but not for males. Hill and Lando (1976) found that attractive women were attributed greater happiness and intelligence than the unattractive, but these differential attributions were not made toward males. Thus, as several researchers have suggested (Adams & Crossman, 1978; Bar-Tal & Saxe, 1976b; Cash, Gillen, & Burns, 1977; Miller, 1970b), there is some indication that appearance stereotypes interact with traditional sex-role expectations, and perhaps also with sex (Wiener et al., 1975), and that the effects may be especially strong for females.

An additional complexity of the stereotypes held by and toward the late adolescent–young adult group is implied by findings that attributions associated with appearance are, in certain circumstances, moderated by the appearance of those with whom one is associated. Strane and Watts (1977) report that a female photographed with an attractive male was evaluated more positively than when she appeared with an unattractive male. Bar-Tal and Saxe (1976a), however, did not find this effect. Males have been more favorably evaluated when associated with attractive females (Hartnett & Elder, 1973; Sigall & Landy, 1973), and this effect was particularly strong for unattractive males paired with attractive partners (Bar-Tal & Saxe, 1976a). Unattractive females, however, were negatively evaluated both when associated with attractive males (Bar-Tal & Saxe, 1976a; Hartnett & Elder, 1973) and when evaluated independently (Bar-

Tal & Saxe, 1976a). Again, appearance stereotypes seem to be differentially applicable to males and females.

These findings suggest that it may be useful to direct future research regarding the manner in which attributions are made to late adolescents and young adults to a study of interactions between sex-role and physical appearance stereotypes. Research directed toward establishing the extent to which evaluations and expectations are differentiated along gender lines will not only clarify the content of the period-specific appearance stereotypes, but may also clarify understanding of the manner in which physical appearance is related to self-attributions, social interactions, and individual characteristics. Indeed, the findings with regard to the complexity of appearance stereotypes associated with the late adolescent–young adulthood period suggest that similar investigations for other age groups should be undertaken. Such studies would serve to establish whether this complexity is a structural uniformity characterizing the stereotypes or an aspect of the stereotypes' development that derives from evolving changes in the context of their application across the life span.

MIDDLE-AGED ADULTS

Although the literature is devoid of findings pertaining to appearance stereotypes held toward persons between the earliest phase of young adulthood and middle age, there is some indication that, in midlife, as in prior periods of the life span, attractive individuals are considered to be personally and socially more desirable than are the unattractive (Adams & Huston, 1975). Thus, the structure of appearance stereotypes remains consistent. However, the few findings regarding attributions made to midlife individuals also indicate that appearance stereotypes may undergo elaboration and transformation across the early adulthood years. The changes that are thought to evolve during this period relate directly to changes in appearance associated with aging.

Specifically, to age is to become physically less attractive (Nowak, 1975; Nowak et al., 1976). Thus, it is not surprising to find that, in general, middle-aged individuals are judged by young, midlife, and elderly adults to be less attractive than younger persons, with the exception that young women find middle-aged men more attractive than young men. However, there are now differences in evaluations of males and females with respect to level of attractiveness. In late adolescence and early young adulthood, males and females are usually seen by their peers and by middle-aged and elderly persons, as equally attractive. In midlife, however, males and females are differentially evaluated, in that aging women are seen as less attractive than their male counterparts (Nowak, 1975; Nowak et al., 1976). Furthermore, and in line with what might be expected from the findings regarding appearance stereotypes at other periods, physically unattractive females are evaluated less positively with regard to some personal and social characteristics than are unattractive males or attractive individuals of either sex (Adams & Huston, 1975). This pattern of evaluation of appearance and attribution of characteristics is consistent for both young adult and late adult judges, although along a few dimensions (honesty, pleasantness, social expressiveness), the elderly have been found to be more generous in their evaluations of middle-aged individuals than are the young (Adams & Huston, 1975). In this connection, however, it should be noted that Berman *et al.* (1978) present evidence suggesting that differential evaluations of the attractiveness of midlife men and women may be related to the context in which ratings are made, which is a matter for future empirical clarification.

These findings suggest a number of considerations toward which research regarding midlife appearance stereotypes may be usefully directed. Some of the personal and social attributes comprising midlife appearance stereotypes have been delineated (Adams & Huston, 1975). However, the manner in which the contextual aspects of midlife may interact with such assumed characteristics to yield a period-specific stereotype content has not been investigated. It was suggested earlier, in discussing late adolescence and early adulthood, and has also been argued by Bar-Tal and Saxe (1976b), that sex-role expectations might be related to empirically verified variations in the appearance stereotypes pertinent to males and females. Perhaps for midlife individuals, traditional sex-role expectations continue to be relevant, and an even greater complexity becomes associated with appearance stereotypes as a result of the differential evaluations of male and female attractiveness.

Thus, it may be that a male's signs of biological aging are seen as evidence of years of socially valued, sex-role-related experience, whereas similar biological changes in females symbolize role loss and a lack of traditional social usefulness. In other words, in relation to midlife individuals, traditional sex-role expectations may covary with evaluations of appearance and attributions based on appearance just as has been found with respect to younger adults (Gillen, 1975; Hill & Lando, 1976). Females in midlife, however, are nearing completion of traditional role fulfillment as mothers; males are often at their peak of success. This may be related to differences in the stereotypes for midlife males and females and underlie the adage that middle-aged women look old, whereas middle-aged men have character (Bell, 1970; Moss, 1970).

At least two directions for research are suggested. First, a more complete elaboration of the personality traits, behaviors, and social variables associated with midlife appearance stereotypes, and the manner in which the male and female stereotypes may differ from one another, is necessary. Second, research should focus on possibly relevant contextual aspects of midlife, such as career achievement and the launching of children, that may interact with sex-role-related expectations to give midlife male and female appearance stereotypes distinctive characteristics. As was suggested with regard to late adolescence and early adulthood, this type of research will serve not only to expand understanding of the manner in which appearance may relate to the developmental processes of midlife individuals, but also to specify the evolution of appearance stereotypes.

LATE ADULTHOOD

As stated previously, a comparison of the aging stereotype and those characteristics associated with an unattractive physical appearance for persons ranging from childhood through middle age indicates great similarity between the two sets of attributions (Nowak, 1975, 1976; Nowak et al., 1976). In other words, when taken together, the findings in aging studies and the results of physical appearance research imply that the structure of appearance stereotypes is continuous across all periods of the life span.

This has been shown to be the case with respect to the attributions made by older individuals to others of the same age (Johnson, 1979). Attractive males and females over the age of 60 are assumed to possess high levels of positive personality characteristics (e.g., friendliness, kindness, warmth) and to have positive life experiences (e.g., happily married, high life satisfaction), whereas unattractive older people are attributed negative traits (e.g., stinginess, boringness) and experiences (e.g., financial difficulties) (Johnson, 1979).

Whether similar evaluations would be made by persons in other age groups is not known. Furthermore, no empirical evidence suggests what, if any, contextual variables associated with old age may be relevant to appearance-related evaluations and attributions.

In essence, the appearance stereotypes attaching to the elderly have been explored in only the most general sense. Thus, useful research in this area might be directed toward further elaboration of the stereotypes and any distinguishing characteristics that may attach to them (e.g., sex differences, as are suggested in relation to younger individuals), as well as to investigating contextual influences.

OTHER CONSIDERATIONS IN THE STUDY OF PHYSICAL APPEARANCE STEREOTYPES

It has been suggested that the appearance stereotypes applied to persons at differing points in the life span may vary because of differences in the contextual demands and expectations associated with various developmental periods. Furthermore, it has been noted that there may be variations in the stereotypes held by individuals of different ages. It is necessary to point out that other individual characteristics, such as one's own appearance or personality attributes, may also affect stereotypical beliefs.

For example, there is some evidence indicating that unattractive people may evaluate attractive individuals differently than do those who are attractive (e.g., Dermer & Thiel, 1975). Also, Graham and Perry (1976) found that persons with low self-esteem tended to attribute more enduring negative qualities to the attractive than to the unattractive. However, Lerner and Korn (1972) found that raters' body build did not affect attributions associated with somatotype. In view of these findings, it would seem useful to include assessments of the characteristics of perceivers in future empirical studies designed to describe physical appearance stereotypes.

This discussion has omitted reference to studies bearing on the relationship between stereotyped attributions made toward familiar others. We believe that appearance stereotypes are constructs or ideas that may become modified in the process of specific social interactions with other individuals. In other words, when an association is found between physical appearance and attributions made by preschoolers toward familiar peers, or by teachers toward their own students, the association is not unconfounded by factors other than appearance. The uncovering of associations between appearance and behavior or popularity may reveal in part the manner in which the stereotypes function and the conditions in which the stereotypes have greater or lesser power; but such assessments do not describe the generalized beliefs held by individuals toward unknown but potentially knowable others. Thus, it is our opinion that studies dealing with attributions toward familiar others, as well as those involving components of social interaction rather than beliefs, can be usefully classified separately from descriptions of appearance stereotypes. Such separate classification will allow for an easier specification of the way in which stereotyped beliefs themselves develop and change across time and of how those beliefs are actually modified during interactional processes. In this manner, the power of an individual's appearance, as compared to the power of other personal attributes that become known in the course of interactions, to evoke and maintain differential expectations and behavior on the part of others, may be studied.

Several studies demonstrate the utility of this approach. Gross and Crofton (1977) found that, when male and female undergraduates were presented with either a favorable or unfavorable personality description, then shown a photograph of an attractive, average, or unattractive individual to whom the description supposedly applied, the attractiveness ratings were higher for those with positive personality characteristics. McKelvie and Matthews (1976), using a similar design, found that liking for a photographically presented individual was more closely associated with positive personality characteristics than with an attractive appearance. Also, the effect of attractiveness on teacher expectancy has been found to be reduced or eliminated when information regarding a child's conduct was available (LaVoie & Adams, 1974). Similarly, Solomon and Saxe (1977) made information regarding intelligence as well as appearance available to raters and found that positive attributions were associated with high levels of either characteristic. Because both intelligence and attractiveness affect evaluations of another, the question becomes one of assessing in actual situations the extent to which an initial impression based on appearance affects subsequent evaluations of intelligence or, alternatively, how those initial evaluations may be revised when information regarding intelligence becomes available. Some evidence relevant to this question is presented in other sections of this chapter.

SUMMARY

Although there are numerous omissions in the extant literature, trends in published findings indicate that, across the life span, from childhood through old age, people are able to discriminate among individuals on the basis of physical appearance, and to agree, in general, as to who is attractive and who is not. Furthermore, appearance stereotypes exhibit a life-span structural unity in that attractive individuals of all ages are attributed positive characteristics, whereas the traits, behaviors, intentions, feelings, and statuses associated with an unattractive physical appearance are decidedly negative. The content of appearance stereotypes attached by individuals differing in developmental status to persons at various points across the life span may, however, vary on the basis of contextual variables relevant to specific periods in the life span, as well as characteristics of the persons holding such stereotyped beliefs. Considerable additional research is needed to supplement existing findings and verify the suggested subtleties of period-specific beliefs associated with variations in physical appearance.

Appearance-Related Self-Attributions

Relative to the amount of empirical evidence elaborating the structure and content of physical appearance stereotypes, findings regarding self-attributions associated with appearance variables are sparse. Investigations in this area have focused primarily on the relationship between self-concept or self-esteem and variations in somatotype or in facial attractiveness during adolescence and the earliest phase of young adulthood. A single study has investigated appearance-related self-attributions among midlife individuals. The import of these studies with regard to individual developmental processes across the life span, as well as directions for empirical investigation of the self-attribution aspect suggested by the dynamic interaction framework, are discussed in this section.

Studies involving body-build variables as related to self-attributions are of two types: (a) those relating the self-evaluations of adolescents and young adults to objective or subjective assessments of bodily characteristics; and (b) those relating differential rates of maturation to measures of self-concept among male adolescents. The findings of these investigations indicate that self-attributions among these age groups covary systematically with physical appearance.

Specifically, with regard to the relationship between body build and self-concept, endomorphic late childhood and adolescent males have been found to be characterized by negative self-concepts, whereas mesomorphic late childhood and adolescent males hold positive attitudes toward themselves (Lerner & Korn, 1972). In a similar vein, late adolescents who report being satisfied with the appearance of their bodies, as indexed by subjective assessments of the attractiveness of various body parts and characteristics (e.g., arms, legs, weight, body build) have been found to evaluate themselves more positively than those who are dissatisifed with their bodies' appearance (Lerner et al., 1973; Rosen & Ross, 1968). However, there is some indication that subjective assessments of bodily attractiveness may be of greater significance in relation to self-concept among adolescent females than among adolescent males (Lerner & Karabenick, 1974), and that among the latter group, evaluation of the instrumental effectiveness of bodily characteristics is significantly associated with self-concept (Lerner, Orlos, & Knapp, 1976).

The studies of early- and late-maturing males discussed previously also indicate an association between appearance and self-concept. The early-maturing males, who were for the most part characterized by a mesomorphic somatotype at a relatively young age, were found to hold positive self-concepts (Mussen & Jones, 1957). The late-maturing males, however, who were characterized by ectomorphy during much of their adolescence, had negative self-concepts (Mussen & Jones, 1957).

With respect to facial attractiveness during late adolescence and early adulthood, Walster, Aronson, Abrahams, and Rottman (1966) found no relationship between attractiveness and self-esteem for either males or females, whereas Mathes and Kahn (1975) reported a positive association for females only. Adams (1977b) found a positive relationship between self-concept and appearance for both males and females.

In essence, these findings indicate that, during adolescence and early adulthood, a person's overall self-evaluation is related positively to viewing one's body as attractive and that this association is stronger for females than it is for males. Furthermore, self-concept for males is similarly related to positive assessments of body build by others. However, evidence regarding the relationship between facial attractiveness and self-concept or self-esteem is equivocal. It may be that variables associated with bodily characteristics are of greater relevance in relation to self-evaluation during adolescence than is facial attractiveness. Future research should address this issue in an initial attempt to determine whether, during adolescence, as well as during other portions of the life span, body and face are differentially relevant to self-evaluations.

With regard to the relationship between appearance variables and self-attributions among midlife men and women, no studies in which the self-evaluations of individuals differing in level of attractiveness have been analyzed have come to our attention. However, Nowak (1975; Nowak *et al.*, 1976) found that middle-aged women saw themselves as the least attractive group, when comparing themselves to young and old males and females and to middle-aged men. Midlife men, however, were found to see themselves as less attractive than young people, but more attractive than older individuals. The self-esteem ratings of the subjects in this sample followed a similar pattern. Thus, a relationship between self-perceptions of appearance and self-evaluation is indicated.

Despite differences in the operationalization of self-concept and self-esteem in these studies (for example, Nowak, 1975, used a single-item Likert-type rating scale, whereas Lerner & Karabenick, 1974, and Lerner *et al.*, 1973, used a 16-item 5-point bipolar rating scale), many of the results imply that negative self-evaluations involve the same characteristics as do appearance-related attributions. In other words, the characteristics that comprise the negative pole of the self-concept measures are frequently the same characteristics that are stereotypically attributed to unattractive individuals. Similarly, the characteristic components of a positive self-concept are also components of stereotypes of attractive people. Thus, there is some indication that individuals may internalize appearance stereotypes and use them as a basis for formulating self-evaluations.

The work of Cavior and Dokecki (1971) is interesting in this regard. It was hypothesized that there would be a significant relationship between self-concept, as measured by a person's evaluation of his or her own appearance, and the attractiveness ratings of peers. The hypothesis was not supported, leading the researchers to suggest that self-concept is more closely related to the stereotyped attributions made by strangers than to the evaluations of familiar others, who may modify appearance-related judgments on the basis of additional information developed through interpersonal association. However, it could be that the failure to find any association between self-concept and peer ratings of appearance derived from the operational definition of self-concept, as the association between self-evaluations of attractiveness and appearance ratings made by others has been found to be low (Cavior, 1970; Lerner & Karabenick, 1974; Murstein, 1972; Stroebe *et al.*, 1971).

It is also worthwhile to note that, whereas the few investigations conducted to date with regard to the relationship between physical appearance and self-attributions have focused on somewhat general self-concept and self-esteem constructs, individuals have expectations of themselves in numerous areas. Several studies indicate that associations between appearance and specific self-attributions are stronger when self-ratings of attractiveness are considered than when independent evaluations are used. For example, Adams (1977b) found that self-reported likableness, assertiveness, and intelligence were positively related to self-rated attractiveness, but not to the ratings of others. Although independent attractiveness ratings were not used, an investigation by Berscheid, Walster, and Bohrnstedt (1973) reported similar results. People who had a positive body image considered themselves to be more likable, assertive, conscientious, and intelligent than "the average person."

It would seem useful to broaden the approach to the study of appearance-related self-attributions by incorporating characteristics other than overall self-concept and self-esteem as variables in research undertakings. Those studies describing appearance stereotypes suggest a broad range of personal and social characteristics, such as social competence, popularity, independence, sensitivity, and sincerity, differentially attributed by others to individuals who vary in appearance. Some or all of those characteristics specified by appearance stereotypes may be conceptualized as components of self-concept, and are often included in self-concept measures. However, the convention of reporting only summated scores on such measures precludes defining the association between such components and appearance. Considerable clarification of our understanding of the relationship between physical appearance and self-attributions could derive from ascertaining whether individuals assess themselves in a manner similar or dissimilar to the stereotyped attributions of others, and whether and how such subjective expectations may differ at various periods across the life span.

SUMMARY

In essence, although studies of appearance-related self-attributions indicate that the attractiveness of bodily and facial characteristics covaries with self-concept, self-esteem, and subjective evaluations along specific dimensions, the overall results of these investigations are somewhat equivocal. Furthermore, the studies reported in this area are so few in number and involve such a limited age range of subjects that a life-span conceptualization of individual contributions to developmental processes in this area is not possible. Thus, future research efforts must be directed not only to elaborating the relationship between appearance and self-attributions, but also to clarifying the structure of that association across the life span.

Appearance-Related Social Interactions

The manner in which physical appearance is systematically related to differential social interactions is the third aspect suggested by the dynamic interaction model as relevant to an empirical examination of the individual's contribution to his or her own life-span development. When elaborated to its fullest extent, the model suggests that attributions made on the basis of appearance may guide behavior in interactional situations, and therefore, persons differing in appearance may be exposed to differential experiential milieus and exhibit variations in developmental outcomes. Investigation of the manner in which appearance stereotypes function to affect social interactions across the life span, and the way in which stereotyped attributions are modified by personality and behavioral characteristics outside the appearance domain, falls within the realm of the fifth aspect suggested by the model as relevant to physical appearance variables. Nevertheless, useful steps toward conceptualization of, and hypothesis formation regarding, the interrelations between the stereotypes and social interactions, as well as among the social interactional and self-attributional and personal characteristics aspects of appearance-related phenomena, may be derived from studies that focus directly on covariations of appearance and interpersonal relationships. Therefore, this subsection will concern itself with the implications of the existing research regarding such covariation, and the manner in which the association between appearance and social interactions may be usefully elaborated.

One useful empirical approach to examining this aspect of physical appearance variables, while also providing an empirical basis for formulating hypotheses regarding the interrelations just mentioned, would be based on a matrix such as that in Table 14.1. That is, the dynamic interaction model implies a linkage between one's physical appearance and the type of social interactions one experiences, with appearance stereotypes providing the linkage mechanism. As it has been suggested that position in the life cycle may be related to the structure and/or content of such stereotypes, it would seem useful to explore whether and how differential social interactions based on appearance might also be related to the life-cycle positions of interacting individuals.

Unfortunately, the extant findings are far more limited here than are those regarding description of appearance stereotypes, and therefore, the organization of the existing literature on the basis of such a matrix is not possible. Indeed, most studies bearing on this matter involve interactions of children with their peers and teachers, and of late adolescents and young adults with one another. Thus, an understanding of the association between appearance and social interactions corresponding to the various cells in Table 14.1 must rely on the endeavors of future researchers. The findings to date are presented and discussed in the following subsections.

INFANTS AND CHILDREN

The influence of children on the type and quality of care-giver attention they receive has become an area of increasing interest in recent years (see

Bell & Harper, 1977; Belsky & Tolan, Chapter 4, this volume; Lerner & Spanier, 1978; Sameroff, 1975). Recently, evidence has appeared that not only are care givers influenced by such characteristics as temperament, but also by infant appearance. In two studies designed to assess whether the facial attractiveness of an infant might be related to care-giver attention, Hildebrandt and Fitzgerald (1978, 1980) found that, although mothers looked longest at photographs of their own children, when they were presented with pictures of unfamiliar infants, they, like other adults, spent more time looking at "cute" babies. These findings have led Hildebrandt and Fitzgerald (1978, 1980) to suggest that the type of social interaction experienced by infants may be affected by their appearance, particularly in situations away from their mothers. In other words, cute babies may have more opportunities to engage in interaction and/or may experience more positive exchanges than unattractive babies. Similar implications can be drawn from studies demonstrating that fathers are more likely to interact with attractive than unattractive children (Parke *et al.*, 1980; Parke & Sawin, 1975).

In studies involving social interactions among acquainted preschool and elementary schoolchildren, findings in general indicate that a positive relationship exists between attractiveness and popularity (Cavior & Dokecki, 1971; Kleck *et al.*, 1974; Lerner & Lerner, 1977; Salvia, Sheare, & Algozzine, 1975). However, in samples of very young children, evidence has appeared that suggests there may be sex-related differences in the association between attractiveness and peer popularity during early developmental periods. Styczynski and Langlois (1977) found that attractive males were disliked by peers with whom they were acquainted. Among young females, the unattractive have been found to be preferred to the attractive (Dion & Berscheid, 1974). However, among 5½-year-olds, this trend was reversed, and the attractive girls were more popular and were perceived as better behaved and more self-reliant and independent than unattractive children (Dion & Berscheid, 1974). This distinction seems to be maintained for both males and females at older age levels (Lerner & Lerner, 1977).

However, the extent to which attractive children actually experience more positive or a greater number of peer interactions has not been established. Trnavsky and Bakeman (1976) have reported, on the basis of observational measures, that there were no differences in the number of social contacts of attractive and unattractive preschoolers, although the latter spent more time playing alone. The question of quality and quantity of social contact among young children would seem to be a particularly relevant avenue of study to pursue, in view of findings suggesting that peer group interactions during childhood are related to social adjustment in adulthood (Roff, 1961, 1963). Furthermore, because children seem to rely on physical appearance to a greater extent than other cues, such as attitude or behavior similarity, as a basis of peer relations (Hartup, 1978;

Jacklin & Maccoby, 1978; Langlois, Gottfried, Barnes, & Hendricks, 1978; Langlois, Gottfried, & Seay, 1973; Yarrow & Campbell, 1963), the relationship between peer relations and physical appearance in particular should be given special attention.

With regard to interactions between children and their teachers, evidence indicates that, when the students are known to the teacher, other characteristics seem to moderate or eliminate the attractiveness effects in the teachers' assessments (Adams & Cohen, 1974; Adams & LaVoie, 1974, 1976; LaVoie & Adams, 1974). A stronger relationship has been found between teachers' perceptions of students' academic abilities and the students' actual performance than between attractiveness and either teachers' perceptions or actual performance (although the latter relationships were significant; Lerner & Lerner, 1977). However, teachers' ratings of students' adjustment have been found to bear little relationship to social skills and school relations scores on a standard personality measure, although the teachers' ratings were correlated with attractiveness (Lerner & Lerner, 1977). Furthermore, Barocas and Black (1974) found that teachers of elementary-aged children were more likely to refer attractive than unattractive students for remedial instruction, suggesting that the difficulties encountered by members of the better-looking group may be viewed as learning problems and those of the less attractive children as behavior problems.

These findings, which are suggestive of a linkage between appearance and student–teacher relations at the preschool and elementary school levels, do not lend themselves to simplistic or clear-cut interpretation. As noted by several researchers (e.g., Berscheid & Walster, 1974; Lerner & Lerner, 1977), findings regarding the positive relationship between teacher attitudes and student performance suggest the manner in which appearance is associated with student–teacher interactions deserves serious consideration. However, the only finding with which we are familiar that approaches the matter directly is that of Adams and Cohen (1974), indicating that attractive children have a greater number of positive verbal interactions with their teachers than do unattractive children.

With regard to the appearance-related social interactions of children outside school settings, Dion (1974) found that female college students who viewed a videotape of young children performing a task penalized attractive girls to a greater extent than they did attractive boys, but did not discriminate on the basis of sex in penalizing the performance of unattractive children. Male students, on the other hand, were not influenced by either sex or attractiveness, but related their penalties to the adequacy of the children's task performance. This finding may be seen as contradicting to some extent those of Rich (1975) indicating that teachers evaluated the misbehavior of unattractive girls as less undesirable than that of other students, whereas that of unattractive boys was seen as the most undesirable. It may be that appearance variables have differing relevance for teachers than they do for adults who do not stand in this type of relationship to children. Given the increasing use of day care and other types of caretaking services for the preschool and elementary-aged children of working parents, the lack of research regarding the appearance-related social interactions of children outside school settings seems unfortunate.

It is also to be hoped that greater attention will be given in the future to examining intrafamilial effects of children's attractiveness. Some evidence suggests that abused children are perceived by their parents to be more attractive than they are judged to be by independent raters (Boinski-McConnell, 1977). However, the meaning and significance of these findings is not known, and the extent to which appearance may be related to other aspects of family interaction is also unknown.

In essence, enough data regarding differential social interactions pertaining to children who vary in attractiveness has appeared to suggest that it is worthwhile to investigate appearance effects in naturalistic settings. Useful elaboration of this area will include parent–child interactions, as well as peer and adult–child interactions in school and nonschool settings.

ADOLESCENTS AND YOUNG ADULTS

With regard to social relations among late adolescents and young adults, many of the findings involve self-report, observational, or simulation assessments of actual interactional behaviors. Thus, although these studies may not fully represent the dynamics of ongoing interpersonal contacts, they more closely approximate actual social relations than do studies that involve the responses of unfamiliar others to photographic stimuli.

Many of the existing findings in the appearance literature relate attractiveness to the social interactions associated with mate selection processes. With respect to dating, attractive individuals are preferred as dates (Crouse & Mehrabian, 1977; Huston, 1973). Furthermore, attractive individuals are better liked in actual first date situations, and a linear relationship between a date's appraisal of his or her partner's attractiveness and liking for the partner has been found in several studies to account for over 50% of the variance (Brislin & Lewis, 1968; Curran, 1973; Curran & Lippold, 1975; Tesser & Brodie, 1971; Walster et al., 1966). Physical appearance is also significantly related to dating experience and popularity (Berscheid et al., 1971; Curran & Lippold, 1975; Krebs & Adinolfi, 1975; Reis et al., 1980; Walster et al., 1966) and to sexual experience for both males (Curran & Lippold, 1975) and females (Kaats & Davis, 1970). Furthermore, it has been shown that attributes imputed to another on the basis of appearance continue to be associated with an individual over a series of five encounters, even in the face of contradicting evidence (Mathes, 1975). It would, therefore, seem useful to direct some effort toward investigating whether physical attractiveness is relevant primarily to the early phases of relationship formation, as suggested by self-report data (Levinger, 1964), or if the belief that appearance is irrelevant to or declines in importance as relationships become deeper may be a reflection of the reluctance people feel to acknowledge they are concerned with how others look (Hudson & Henze, 1969; Miller & Rivenbark, 1970; Perrin, 1921).

It was noted in an earlier section of this chapter that attractive males and females are believed to be more masculine and feminine, respectively, than their unattractive counterparts (Gillen, 1975). Nida and Williams (1977) found that, not only were attractive people uniformly preferred as co-workers and spouses, but persons displaying high levels of traditionally appropriate sex-related traits were more highly valued, particularly within the context of marriage. Taken together, these data imply that the association of socially valued sex-role characteristics with an appealing appearance may amount to an attractiveness advantage insofar as romantic relationships are concerned.

The evidence is not unconfounded, however, nor are the implications of such findings clear. For example, as pointed out in the discussion of appearance stereotypes, differential attributions are made to males and to females on the basis of their own attractiveness and that of the cross-sex partner with whom they are associated. Highly valued characteristics are attributed to unattractive males associated with attractive females (Bar-Tal & Saxe, 1976a; Hartnett & Elder, 1973; Sigall & Landy, 1973), whereas unattractive males are not positively evaluated without the presence of an attractive partner (Bar-Tal & Saxe, 1976a). An unattractive female does not benefit similarly from association with an attractive male, and, in addition, a negative evaluation is attached to an attractive male paired with an unattractive female (Bar-Tal & Saxe, 1976a). In general, the findings imply that the attractive woman may be of greater benefit to her mate along those dimensions relevant to physical appearance than is the man, regardless of his level of attractiveness, to his female partner. These findings must, however, be considered in conjunction with those indicating that persons who are similar in attractiveness tend to affiliate with one another on both romantic (Murstein, 1972; Murstein & Christy, 1976; Silverman, 1971) and friendship (Cash & Derlega, 1978; Nagy, 1980) bases.

Some evidence has been interpreted as indicating appearance is more important in determining the reactions of males to females than is the case with females' responses to males (Adams & Crossman, 1978; Bar-Tal & Saxe, 1976b; Berscheid et al., 1971; McKelvie & Matthews, 1976; Stroebe et al., 1971; Walster et al., 1966). However, studies do not uniformly support this conclusion (Byrne et al., 1970; Crouse & Mehrabian, 1977; Lerner et al., 1973; Reis et al., 1980). Furthermore, many of the studies designed to measure cross-sex interactions use female stimuli and male respondents. In view of the lack of clarity regarding the relative importance of appearance to males and females, the inclusion of both among the stimuli and respondents in studies designed to assess cross-sex social interactions seems warranted.

The issue of the relative significance of an attractiveness advantage to males and to females also raises again the matter of the extent to which sex-role considerations are relevant to appearance-related phenomena. It has been suggested in this chapter and by others (e.g., Bar-Tal & Saxe, 1976b) that attractiveness effects might be related to traditional conceptions of sex roles, particularly during the late adolescent and adult years, and that contextual variables associated with life-cycle position could be relevant to stereotype content. Because the link between appearance and differential social relations may be composed to some extent of attributions based on appearance stereotypes, sex-role and life-cycle position considerations should also be included in an empirical approach to appearance-related social interactions. Indeed, there are sufficient theoretical grounds, as well as some empirical bases in the existing literature, to suggest that the omission of such considerations from physical appearance research would impair the usefulness and interpretability of results.

For example, many theorists (e.g., Erikson, 1964, 1968; Havighurst, 1951; Levinson, 1978) agree that mate selection and occupational choice are focal tasks during late adolescence and early adulthood. However, mate selection and career establishment do not appear to be similarly significant for males and females. Traditional sex-role prescriptions are such that women may choose to have a career, but for men, the only choice is what that career will be (Bailyn, 1964). In other words, the personal and social foci of evaluation of a male's adulthood experience have been suggested to be related to his occupational choice and opportunities and the degree of success associated with his career pursuits (Fasteau, 1974). A female, however, is believed to evaluate herself and to be evaluated by society primarily on the basis of her success as a wife and mother, regardless of any occupational undertakings in which she may engage (Rubin, 1979; Strong, Reynolds, Suid, & Dabagian, 1979; Weitz, 1977). Thus, the mate selection process appears to be crucial for females to a greater extent, perhaps, than for males.

Again, it is worth noting in this regard that Elder (1969) found, that among lower class females, the attractive were far more likely to marry "up"—to marry men whose social class was higher than their own—than were the unattractive poor. Comparable data for males, however, do not appear in the literature; and again the importance of including both male and female subjects in appearance studies is emphasized. In any event, researchers concerned with attractiveness effects might well turn their attention to clarifying whether good looks are more advantageous to females in relation to marriage than is the case with males.

With respect to the matter of occupational opportunities, Dipboye, Fromkin, and Wiback (1975) found that an attractive individual was evaluated more positively as a job applicant than was an unattractive one. However, it has also been found that in leadership situations, sex (i.e., being male) determines effectiveness in such settings, and level of attractiveness is inconsequential (Altemeyer & Jones, 1974). Furthermore, evidence has been presented indicating that, although attractive co-workers are preferred, the unattractive are considered less objectionable in a work setting than in a marital context (Nida & Williams, 1977). These findings with regard to the occupational domain again imply that attractiveness advantages interact with traditional sex-role prescriptions, and also that, in a work context, sex-role considerations may override those of appearance. Indeed, this was shown to be the case in a study of evaluations by professional personnel consultants regarding opportunities, alternatives, and success probabilities for males and females differing in appearance (Cash et al., 1977).

Attractiveness considerations cannot be entirely discounted in relation to occupational undertakings, however. In the discussion of appearance stereotypes, the negative traits attributed to an unattractive male counselor were described (Cash et al., 1975). In following up on those results, Cash and Kehr (1978) found that not only did female college-aged raters negatively stereotype unattractive peer counselors, but they also felt these people would be less helpful with respect to a number of problem areas than would the attractive counselors. The women raters also expressed less willingness to be involved in a counseling situation with an unattractive peer. Furthermore, sex of counselor had no effect on attributions, outcome expectations, or motivation (Cash & Kehr, 1978). Another study in this series by Cash and his colleagues produced evidence that, in a counseling situation, the debilitating effects of an unattractive appearance can be mitigated by self-disclosure (Cash & Salzbach, 1978).

The extent to which appearance is related to social interactions has been studied in a number of areas besides the domains of mate selection and career or occupation. The overwhelming import of these findings is that both the quality and quantity of the social experience of attractive people differs from that of unattractive individuals. Adams (1980) has recently presented evidence that attractive females are visited more frequently than are the unattractive. However, Reis et al. (1980) found that attractive males had more opposite-sex and fewer same-sex social interactions than their less attractive peers, whereas there was no systematic relationship between appearance and number of social contacts for females. Nevertheless, attractive individuals of both sexes report being more satisfied with the quality of their social interactions than are the less attractive (Herold, 1979; Reis et al., 1980). Such satisfaction has been found to increase over an eight month period (Reis et al., 1980).

Along the majority of those dimensions that have been studied, the interactions of attractive people are of a more positive, socially valued, or advantageous nature than those of the less attractive. For example, it has been found that people are more likely to be honest with an attractive than an unattractive female (Sroufe, Chaikin, Cook, & Freeman, 1977) and that greater amounts of social responsiveness are directed toward the former than the latter (Barocas & Karoly, 1972). Cash and Burns (1977) found evidence that both males and females who are attractive experience greater amounts of social reinforcement than do unattractive persons. Opposite-sex social exchanges in general seem to be more positively affected by attractiveness than same-sex exchanges (Mathes & Edwards, 1978). However, there is some indication that women who are aware that they are perceived as attractive may find it more difficult to accept positive evaluations of their task performance as deriving from actual success rather than representing a response to their appearance (Sigall & Michela, 1976). In view of the Landy and Sigall (1974) finding that performance evaluations for attractive women are inflated, the reactions of the participants in the Sigall and Michela (1976) study may be warranted.

Attractive individuals have also been found to receive a greater number of self-disclosures in both same-sex and opposite-sex dyads (Brundage et al., 1977; Cash, 1978). In addition, it appears that people have a greater desire to please attractive than unattractive females (Sigall & Aronson, 1969), and will expend more effort when in a subordinate position to an attractive person (Sigall, Page, & Brown, 1971). Mills and Aronson (1965) found that an attractive woman who openly announced her desire to influence male participants was more successful than when she did not declare her intention. However, when the female persuader was unattractive, making her intentions known had no effect on her effectiveness.

Helping behavior is more likely to be exhibited toward attractive than unattractive people (Benson et al., 1976). It has also been found that attractive, self-disclosing females are most likely and unattractive self-disclosers least likely to receive help (Harrell, 1978), a finding that contrasts interestingly with that of Cash and Salzbach (1978) that self-disclosure may counteract the negative effects of unattractiveness in a counseling situation. Finally, it even seems that the physically attractive candidate stands a better chance at the polls than does a less attractive contender for public office (Efran & Patterson, 1974).

In addition to bearing some relationship to the quality of interpersonal contact, physical appearance in late adolescence and early adulthood has also been found to be associated with social events of a broader nature. For example, Efran (1974) has shown that in situations involving infractions of the law, unattractive transgressors are assessed more severe punishment than are attractive individuals. Sigall and Ostrove (1975) elaborated Efran's (1974) findings by demonstrating that severity of judgment may be mediated by the nature of the crime. That is, an attractive woman was treated leniently as compared to an unattractive woman only if the crime did not involve an exploitation of her beauty. When the offense was attractiveness-related (e.g., swindling), the attractive defendant received more severe punishment than the unattractive defendant. In a similar vein, attractive offenders have been found to be more harshly punished for serious infractions, such as involvement in a fatal accident (Piehl, 1977).

The performance of attractive women on an essay composition task has also been found to receive a more positive evaluation than that of unattractive women when the quality of performance is low (Landy & Sigall, 1974). The evaluations of the unattractive women's writings were associated with the quality of their performance. In other words, they were not penalized for being unattractive. However, Canning and Mayer (1966) found evidence that, among equally qualified college applicants, overweight females were less likely to be accepted for admission than were girls of average stature.

Approaching the matter of the quality of social interaction experienced by attractive and unattractive persons from a slightly different angle, Hobfoll and Penner (1978) examined the relationship between subjects' physical appearance and therapists' judgments regarding self-concept. Attractive subjects were evaluated as having higher self-concepts than unattractive subjects when an audiotaped interview was presented. When the presentation was augmented by videotape, the therapists' ratings of attractive subjects' self-concepts increased, whereas the ratings for unattractive subjects did not change. The effect was especially pronounced for female subjects.

Similarly, Barocas and Vance (1974) found that the adjustment and prognosis for attractive clients were evaluated more positively by therapists than was the case for unattractive clients. Likewise, in relation to peer judgments of psychological disturbance, college students have been found to attribute high maladjustment and poor prognosis to unattractive females disclosing minor problems, whereas the reverse was the case for attractive females disclosing major difficulties (Cash, Kehr, Polyson, & Freeman, 1977).

Finally, in relation to quality of social interaction, attractive women have been seen as bearing more responsibility for achieving a positive outcome than was attributed to unattractive women. The latter, however, were judged as being more responsible than the former in situations having a negative outcome (Seligman, Paschall, & Takata, 1974). Similarly, Wiener et al. (1975) found that the successes of unattractive people were seen as indicative of high ability and motivation, whereas their failures indicated low levels of these traits. These effects were particularly strong for females. The successes of attractive individuals were also seen as due to high ability and motivation, but no systematic effects were found when the attractive were unsuccessful. Subtly related to the findings regarding attribution of responsibility are those of Thornton (1977) indicating that the credibility and responsibility of a female rape victim were not affected by her physical appearance. However, the sentence pronounced on the rapist was more severe when the victim was attractive than when she was unattractive.

In summary, there is considerable support for the contention that during the late adolescent and early adulthood portion of the life span, people who differ in appearance will also experience different types of social interactions. Furthermore, considerable evidence suggests that the quality of contact, on both interpersonal and broader social levels, may vary in relation to appearance. Overall, the unattractive person, and particularly the unattractive female, may be less likely to be exposed to a variety of interpersonal and social situations, than an attractive individual.

MIDDLE AGE AND LATE ADULTHOOD

Empirical findings regarding the link between appearance and social interaction in the years beyond early adulthood do not exist. Future researchers should seek to fill this void by designing studies to ascertain whether the attractiveness effects found in samples of younger individuals are maintained across the life cycle and whether the structure and/or content of appearance-related social interactions covary with period-specific contextual variables or differential sex-role prescriptions.

SUMMARY

The existing literature suggests that, for the age groups studied, appearance-related social interactions follow a structure similar in many, but not all, ways to that implied by the appearance stereotype. However, such interactions are modified by other variables, such as familiarity and sex, thus indicating that the nature of appearance functions in this area may be quite complex. Indeed, it may be the case that appearance becomes so confounded with age-, sex-, or context-related variables in social interaction situations evolving across the life span that the specification of its contribution to individual developmental processes may present a major challenge to researchers.

It has been suggested that a first step in meeting this challenge would be an empirical approach paralleling that set forth in the subsection regarding appearance stereotypes. Such an approach will generate findings intrinsically useful in the elucidation of appearance-related phenomena during specific periods of the life cycle and across the life span. In addition, studies programmatically designed in this manner will provide a basis for hypotheses regarding the interrelations between appearance stereotypes and differential social interactions.

Appearance-Related Personal Characteristics

The conceptualizations and empirical findings discussed thus far indicate that physical appearance is associated with stereotypes, with self-attributions, and with social interactions. However, the extent to which physical appearance may be seen as contributing to individual developmental processes is also dependent on assessing whether variations in appearance are associated with differences in personal characteristics, such as personality attributes, interactional behavior, and task performance. This subsection will examine the empirical evidence and suggest future research directions regarding this fourth potential role of appearance-related variables.

Empirical findings regarding the relationship between appearance and self-concept and self-esteem were presented in the subsection discussing appearance-related self-attributions. Those findings, which are contradictory and far from conclusive, will not be repeated here. However, it should be noted that we do not consider an individual's self-evaluations and self-image as separate from a conceptualization of personal characteristics. Indeed, self-concept and self-esteem are integral components of an individual's personality, representing the subjective assessment of a person's attributes and typical patterns of behavior. However, the formulation within which this chapter is framed suggests that, for the purpose of empirical investigation of appearance-related developmental functions, self-attributions may be considered apart from, as well as in conjunction with, data relevant to personal characteristics. Thus, those findings previously reviewed with regard to self-concept and self-esteem should also be considered as relevant to the present discussion.

One logical entry point for examination of possible variations in personal characteristics associated with appearance would be to assess the extent to which stereotyped attributions are actually manifested in measurements of personality and behavior. Ideally, such studies would be derived for each of the life-span periods designated by one axis of the matrix in Table 14.1. This would provide a basis for precise multivariate investigation of the interrelations between appearance stereotypes and personal attributes. The dearth of research designed from this perspective may be seen as a fundamental weakness in the appearance literature.

In the section regarding appearance stereotypes, it was noted that attractive children are believed to have higher IQs and are expected to show greater achievement than unattractive preschoolers and elementary-aged children. However, Clifford (1975) found that, among second, fourth, and sixth graders, no systematic relationship between appearance and IQ or achievement existed. Styczynski (1976) also failed to find any association between IQ and attractiveness in a sample of fourth graders. However, the Styczynski (1976) data indicated that, in this sample, the achievement scores of unattractive children declined from the second to the fourth grades. The possibility that an appearance-related self-fulfilling prophesy, such as is suggested by Langlois and Stephan (1981) and by Lerner and Lerner (1977), may be functioning with respect to children's school performance should be an area of serious concern to researchers designing physical attractiveness studies.

Extant findings also indicate appearance-related variations along certain personality trait dimensions, and support predictions based on descriptions of appearance stereotypes. For example, attractive 5-year-olds have been found to exhibit fewer aggressive behaviors in play interactions than do their unattractive peers (Langlois & Downs, 1979). In samples of college undergraduates, attractive women have been found to be happier and less neurotic than unattractive women; however, these associations were not found to be significant among males (Mathes & Kahn, 1975). Adams (1977b) reports that attractive women have greater self-confidence, and attractive men, a greater sense of internal control, than do their unattractive counterparts, whereas Cash and Begley (1979) confirm an internal locus of control for attractive males and females alike. Attractive women have also been found to be more assertive and secure than unattractive females (Jackson & Huston, 1975; Rokeach, 1943). In addition, there is an indication that attractive undergraduates are more socially skillful (Goldman & Lewis, 1977) and resistant to peer pressure (Adams, 1977b) than are the unattractive.

However, data reported by Shea, Crossman, and Adams (1978) do not support the contention that differences in attractiveness are associated with personality differences. Specifically, college-aged men and women who were evaluated with regard to both body build and facial beauty were found to display no systematic appearance-related differences on measures of ego identity, ego development, or locus of control. These findings suggest that the extent to which stereotyped attributions are associated with actual differences in personality and behavior is a fertile area for future investigation.

Other findings relevant to differences in personal characteristics associated with appearance have been derived from the studies of early and late maturers. In the Oakland Growth Study, to which reference has previously been made, evidence was derived from two sources: (a) peer judgments; and (b) projective personality tests. The unattractive, late-maturing males were judged by their peers to be more restless, bossy, attention-seeking, less assured, and less likely to have a sense of humor about themselves than the attractive early-maturing males (Mussen & Jones, 1957). With regard to the projective testing, late-maturing males indicated feelings of inadequacy, weakness, rejection, rebelliousness toward their families, and disapproval from parents and authorities (Mussen & Jones, 1957). The early-maturing males, however, were found to have feelings of self-confidence, independence, and interpersonal maturity, and to lack rebelliousness toward parents (Mussen & Jones, 1957). This group also scored high on an assessment of aggressiveness. The implications of this latter finding will be discussed in greater detail in what follows.

Congruent with the depiction of early-maturing males as possessing more positive personal characteristics than late maturers are the findings of Kinsey, Pomeroy, and Martin (1948) that the former were alert, energetic, spontaneous, active, extroverted, and aggressive. The latter were found to be slow, quiet, mild, unforceful, reserved, timid, introverted, and socially inept. Likewise, Weatherly (1964) found late maturers to have greater feelings of guilt, inferiority, depression, rebelliousness, and unconventionality, and to be less oriented toward leadership, control, and domination than were average and early maturers.

A reverse trend of that for males has been found among early- and late-maturing females (Jones, 1939). In other words, early-maturing females were more likely to be characterized by negatively valued personal attributes than were late-maturing females. However, males and females have been found to be differentiated not only on this basis, but also on the basis of long-term effects. The appearance-related differences in personal characteristics between early- and late-maturing females diminished in late adolescence (Jones & Mussen, 1958). Among the males, the differences were present at the age of 33, when the late maturers were also found to be more insightful and assertive than were the early maturers (Jones, 1957). However, by the time these male groups were in their 40s, the differences between them had diminished (Jones, 1965).

Thus, it appears that with regard to the relationship between personality and physique, the effects of appearance for males and females may differ, as has been implied previously in relation to facial beauty and other aspects of appearance-related variables. Here, however, the impact may be greater with respect to males. In other words, it may be that facial attractiveness is more salient to female developmental processes and bodily attractiveness more salient to developmental processes in males. This suggestion is not intended to imply that the two classes of appearance variables are not related to one another. As was pointed out previously, the extent and manner in which facial and bodily characteristics interact has not been investigated. However, it may be that if certain baseline levels along one dimension are present, the importance of characteristics along the other dimension varies disproportionately or nonlinearly on a sex-related basis. This possibility should be empirically examined not only with regard to personal characteristics and attributes, but also with respect to the other functional aspects of appearance-related phenomena.

The findings with regard to early and late maturers, although indicative of both concurrent differences and differential adult outcomes, would not necessarily derive from predictions based on the presently existing description of appearance stereotypes. Other findings, too, suggest that, if there is a link between the stereotypes and personal characteristics and behavior, it is neither simple nor direct. For example, in a sample of 3- and 5-year-olds differentiated on the basis of appearance, unattractive children were found to exhibit higher activity levels and to have a greater preference for stereotypically masculine toys when compared to attractive children (Langlois & Downs, 1979). Furthermore, in contradiction of what would be predicted on the basis of empirically verified stereotyped attributions, Langlois and Downs (1979) did not find differences between the groups in affiliative behaviors.

It was noted earlier that Langlois and Downs (1979) found attractiveness-related differences in aggressiveness among their 5-year-old subjects. This difference was not found among the 3-year-olds studied, leading the researchers to suggest that appearance-related stereotyped behavior (i.e., that unattractive children are more aggressive than attractive children) may develop as a result of a self-fulfilling prophesy. That is, unattractive children internalize the appearance stereotypes. As they come to recognize themselves as being unattractive, they label themselves and are labeled by others, and thus behave in accordance with stereotyped expectations. Evidence in support of this conceptualization has been reported by Snyder, Tanke, and Berscheid (1977). In this study, it was found that, when interacting with an unseen female who was presumed, on the basis of a photograph, to be either attractive or unattractive, males were able to elicit from the female responses according with the stereotypical expectations. Although this suggestion is intriguing and is theoretically compatible with the dynamic interaction model, it must be noted that the data in the studies cited are cross-sectional. Empirical verification of developmental progressions is dependent on longitudinal research strategies capable of differentiating interindividual differences from ontogenetic changes. In addition, the extent to which the operationalization of aggressive behavior in the Langlois and Downs (1979) study is comparable to that in stereotype studies must be made specific before the self-fulfilling prophesy interpretation can be accepted as a general interrelational pattern regarding appearance-related variables. Nevertheless, these findings are extremely provocative and provide an excellent basis for interrelational hypotheses to be tested using the type of developmental research designs described earlier in this chapter.

An even greater complexity to the manner in which aggressiveness and appearance may be associated is suggested by the previously noted finding that, with regard to rate of maturation, the more attractive early-maturing males were more aggressive than the late-maturing, unattractive males. This suggests that aggressiveness may be differentially associated with appearance during successive periods of development. However, it must also be pointed out that in the Langlois and Downs (1979) study, attractiveness was operationalized on the basis of facial characteristics, whereas in the Mussen and Jones (1957) study, physique was used to operationalize attractiveness. Thus, the suggestions derived from comparing findings regarding the association between aggressiveness and appearance may reflect differences in research design, and in the conceptualization of variables and their relationships to one another, rather than developmental processes.

In summary, those findings that have appeared in the literature tend to confirm that with respect to the few personal attributes examined, physically attractive individuals exhibit positively valued, socially adaptive characteristics to a greater extent than do unattractive persons. However, the findings are not entirely consistent and do not uniformly support those predictions that might be derived from descriptions of appearance stereotypes. Furthermore, studies have been limited with respect to the number of age groups involved, and relatively few variables have been examined. Those variables that have been studied have tended to be ambiguously operationalized. In addition, because research in this area has been sporadic and cross-sectional, it is not permissible to draw empirical links between appearance and individual development from a lifespan perspective. Nevertheless, extant findings suggest not only that individual developmental processes may be influenced by appearance, but also point to hypotheses that may serve to elucidate the nature and structure of such influence. In other words, several findings serve the useful and necessary end of describing how attractive and unattractive individuals differ or do not differ from one another with regard to personal attributes. In addition to providing descriptive information, these findings provide a basis for the type of interrelational studies relevant to the fifth role of appearance-related phenomena.

Interrelations between and
among the Roles of Physical Appearance

As was stated in the introductory section of this chapter, the ultimate goal of physical appearance research, conceptualized within a dynamic interaction framework, would be the investigation of interrelations among stereotypes, self-attributions, social interactions, and individual personality and behavioral characteristics, as each relates to variations in facial and bodily attributes. The complexity of studying such interrelations no doubt explains why no empirical findings in this area are to be found in the literature. Indeed, it may be that the direct empirical verification of the nature of interrelational links among the aspects of physical appearance affecting individual development across the life span will remain an ideal. However, this aspect of the developmental significance of appearance can be approached through a theoretical integration of the findings outlined in the previous sections of this chapter.

One such attempt has recently appeared in the literature. Langlois and Stephan (1981) have suggested a model based on the principles of social learning theory, representing the development of appearance-related differences in the social behavior of young children. This model incorporates interrelations among the various aspects of appearance-related phenomena discussed in this chapter. That is, Langlois and Stephan (1981) suggest that stereotyped expectations, interacting with characteristics of the situation, the perceiver, and the perceived, lead to reinforcement of expected behaviors. The behaviors, in turn, serve to reinforce the stereotyped expectations. Over time, unattractive and attractive children come to exhibit differential social behaviors that accord with and further substantiate appearance stereotypes.

Although physical appearance variables have been incorporated in other theoretical models (e.g., Duck, 1973; Huston & Levinger, 1978; Lerner, 1979; Levinger & Snoek, 1972), none of these models focuses primarily or exclusively on the contribution of physical appearance variables to individual developmental processes. Thus, the most useful step for researchers to pursue in this regard would seem to be the theoretical elaboration of linkages suggested by findings in physical appearance research projects, as they pertain to individual development across the life span.

Summary

The preceding discussion suggests that, because of its ready noticeability to both self and others, and thus its availability as a basis for the formulation of stereotyped attributions and expectations, physical appearance may be related to individual psychological and social status. Furthermore, the changes in physical appearance associated with aging, considered in conjunction with age-role-related contextual variables, permit conceptualization of appearance variables as contributors to individual developmental processes across the life span. Empirical evidence relevant to such a conceptualization has appeared in both the social psychological and the developmental literatures. However, due to variations in the theoretical frameworks, research designs, and operational methods employed by physical appearance researchers, many findings lack empirical and interpretive comparability, clarity, and continuity.

To correct existing difficulties in physical appearance research, and to render future research useful as a basis for understanding the import and function of appearance variables as developmental phenomena, an integrative conceptual framework is necessary. The dynamic interaction model is suggested as an appropriate conceptual vehicle for organizing and critiquing existing findings, as well as for guiding future empirical undertakings. This model suggests that many of the problems identified in the existing literature could be corrected by the adoption of certain criteria for research projects. Specifically, useful empirical inquiries involving physical appearance variables should be (a) theoretically based; (b) programmatic; (c) multivariate; and (d) longitudinal. It is also suggested that these criteria are hierarchical in nature, such that all projects need not be characterized by all four attributes. Rather, the adoption of a theory-based, programmatic approach will permit "single shot," univariate, cross-sectional studies to contribute systematically to a body of findings serving as a basis for the formulation of hypotheses to be tested using multivariate, and in some instances, longitudinal, research designs.

The dynamic interaction model also suggests that appearance-related phenomena can be conceptualized as involving five functional categories or types of variables: (a) appearance stereotypes; (b) self-attributions associated with appearance; (c) appearance-related social interactions; (d) personal characteristics related to appearance; and (e) interrelations between and among the stereotypes, self-attributions, social interactions, and personal characteristics associated with appearance. The developmental structure of appearance-related phenomena can be investigated by examining each functional aspect and their interrelations across the life span.

The appearance literature is incomplete and is theoretically and methodologically inadequate in many respects. However, an examination of extant findings as they relate to the conceptually derived roles of appearance-related phenomena supports the usefulness of the dynamic interaction model as a vehicle for organizing such results. Furthermore, the dynamic interaction framework is shown to provide not only a basis for critiquing existing findings and for identifying trends in the literature, but also a basis for conceptualizing and designing empirical inquiries aimed at elucidating the contribution of physical appearance to individual development across the life span.

References

Adams, G. R. Physical attractiveness research: Toward a developmental social psychology of beauty. *Human Development*, 1977, *20*, 217–239. (a)

Adams, G. R. Physical attractiveness, personality, and social reactions to peer pressures. *Journal of Psychology*, 1977, *96*, 287–296. (b)

Adams, G. R. Racial membership and physical attractiveness effects on preschool teachers' expectations. *Child Study Journal*, 1978, *8*, 29–41.

Adams, G. R. *Beautiful is good: A test of the "kernel of truth" hypothesis.* Unpublished manuscript, Utah State University, 1979.

Adams, G. R. Social psychology of beauty: Effects of age, height, and weight on self-reported personality traits and social behavior. *Journal of Social Psychology*, 1980, *112*, 287–293.

Adams, G. R., & Cohen, A. S. Children's physical and interpersonal characteristics that affect student–teacher interactions. *Journal of Experimental Education*, 1974, *43*, 1–5.

Adams, G. R., & Cohen, A. S. Characteristics of children and teacher expectancy: An extension to the child's social and family life. *Journal of Educational Research,* 1976, *70,* 87–90.

Adams, G. R., & Crossman, S. M. *Physical attractiveness: A cultural imperative.* Roslyn Heights, N.Y.: Libra, 1978.

Adams, G. R., & Huston, T. L. Social perception of middle-aged persons varying in physical attractiveness. *Developmental Psychology,* 1975, *11,* 657–658.

Adams, G. R., & LaVoie, J. C. The effects of student sex, conduct, and facial attractiveness on teacher expectancy. *Education,* 1974, *95,* 76–83.

Adams, G. R., & LaVoie, J. C. Parental expectations of educational and personal–social performance and child-rearing patterns as a function of attractiveness, sex, and conduct of the child. *Child Study Journal,* 1975, *5,* 125–142.

Altemeyer, R. A., & Jones, K. Sexual identity, physical attractiveness and seating position as determinants of influence in discussion groups. *Canadian Journal of Behavioral Science,* 1974, *6,* 357–375.

Ames, R. Physical maturing among boys as related to adult social behavior: A longitudinal study. *California Journal of Educational Research,* 1957, *8,* 69–75.

Anastasi, A. Heredity, environment, and the question "how"? *Psychological Review,* 1958, *65,* 197–208.

Bailyn, L. Notes on the role of choice in the psychology of professional women. In R. J. Lifton (Ed.), *The woman in America.* Boston: Beacon, 1964.

Baltes, P. B., Reese, H. W., & Nesselroade, J. R. *Life-span developmental psychology: Introduction to research methods.* Monterey, California: Brooks/Cole, 1977.

Baltes, P. B., & Schaie, K. W. On the plasticity of intelligence in adulthood and old age: Where Horn and Donaldson fail. *American Psychologist,* 1976, *31,* 720–725.

Barocas, R., & Black, H. K. Referral rate and physical attractiveness in third-grade children. *Perceptual and Motor Skills,* 1974, *39,* 731–734.

Barocas, R., & Karoly, P. Effects of physical appearance on social responsiveness. *Psychological Reports,* 1972, *31,* 495–500.

Barocas, R., & Vance, F. L. Physical appearance and personal adjustment counseling. *Journal of Counseling Psychology,* 1974, *21,* 96–100.

Bar-Tal, D., & Saxe, L. Perceptions of similarly attractive couples and individuals. *Journal of Personality and Social Psychology,* 1976, *33,* 772–781. (a)

Bar-Tal, D., & Saxe, L. Physical attractiveness and its relationship to sex-role stereotyping. *Sex Roles,* 1976, *2,* 123–133. (b)

Bell, I. P. The double standard. *Trans-Action,* 1970, *8,* 75–80.

Bell, R. Q., & Harper, L. V. *Child effects on adults.* New York: Wiley, 1977.

Benson, P. L., Karabenick, S. A., & Lerner, R. M. Pretty pleases: The effects of physical attractiveness, race, and sex on receiving help. *Journal of Experimental Social Psychology,* 1976, *12,* 409–415.

Berman, P. W., O'Nan, B. A., & Floyd, W. *The double standard of aging and the social situation: Judgments of attractiveness of the middle-aged woman.* Unpublished manuscript, Florida State University, 1978.

Berscheid, E., Dion, K., Walster, E., & Walster, G. W. Physical attractiveness and dating choice: A test of the matching hypothesis. *Journal of Experimental Social Psychology,* 1971, *7,* 173–189.

Berscheid, E., & Walster, E. Physical attractiveness. In L. Berkowitz (Ed.), *Advances in experimental social psychology* (Vol. 7). New York: Academic Press, 1974.

Berscheid, E., Walster, E., & Bohrnstedt, G. W. *Body image, physical appearance, and self-esteem.* Paper presented at the Meetings of the American Sociological Association, New York City, 1973.

Berscheid, E., Walster, E., & Campbell, R. *Grow old along with me.* Unpublished manuscript, University of Minnesota, 1972.

Boinski-McConnell, H. *The effect of physical attractiveness on family interaction patterns in problem and nonproblem families.* Unpublished master's thesis, The Pennsylvania State University, 1977.

Brislin, R. W., & Lewis, S. A. Dating and physical attractiveness: Replication. *Psychological Reports,* 1968, *22,* 976.

Brooks, V., & Hochberg, J. A psychophysical study of "cuteness." *Perceptual and Motor Skills,* 1960, *11,* 205.

Brundage, L. E., Derlega, V. J., & Cash, T. F. The effects of physical attractiveness and need for approval on self-disclosure. *Personality and Social Psychology Bulletin,* 1977, *3,* 63–66.

Byrne, D., Ervin, C. R., & Lamberth, J. Continuity between the experimental study of attraction and real-life computer dating. *Journal of Personality and Social Psychology,* 1970, *16,* 157–165.

Byrne, D., London, O., & Reeves, K. The effects of physical attractiveness, sex, and attitude similarity on interpersonal attraction. *Journal of Personality,* 1968, *36,* 259–271.

Canning, H., & Mayer, J. Obesity—its possible effect on college acceptance. *New England Journal of Medicine,* 1966, *275,* 1172–1174.

Cash, T. F. Self-disclosure in initial acquaintanceship: Effects of sex, approval motivation, and physical attractiveness. *Catalog of Selected Documents in Psychology,* 1978, *8,* 11.

Cash, T. F., & Begley, P. J. Internal–external control, achievement orientation, and physical attractiveness of college students. *Psychological Reports,* 1976, *38,* 1205–1206.

Cash, T. F., Begley, P. J., McCown, D. A., & Weise, B. C. When counselors are heard but not seen: Initial impact of physical attractiveness. *Journal of Counseling Psychology,* 1975, *22,* 273–279.

Cash, T. F., & Burns, D. S. The occurrence of reinforcing activities in relation to locus of control, success–failure expectancies, and physical attractiveness. *Journal of Personality Assessment,* 1977, *41,* 387–391.

Cash, T. F., & Derlega, V. J. The matching hypothesis: Physical attractiveness among same-sexed friends. *Personality and Social Psychology Bulletin,* 1978, *4,* 240–243.

Cash, T. F., Gillen, B., & Burns, D. S. Sexism and "beautyism" in personnel consultant decision making. *Journal of Applied Psychology,* 1977, *62,* 301–310.

Cash, T. F., & Kehr, J. A. Influence of nonprofessional counselors' physical attractiveness and sex on perceptions of counselor behavior. *Journal of Counseling Psychology,* 1978, *25,* 336–342.

Cash, T. F., Kehr, J. A., Polyson, J., & Freeman, V. Role of physical attractiveness in peer attribution of psychological disturbance. *Journal of Consulting and Clinical Psychology,* 1977, *45,* 987–993.

Cash, T. F., & Salzbach, R. F. The beauty of counseling: Effects of counselor physical attractiveness and self-disclosures on perceptions of counselor behavior. *Journal of Counseling Psychology,* 1978, *25,* 283–291.

Cash, T. F., & Soloway, D. Self-disclosure correlates of physical attractiveness: An exploratory study. *Psychological Reports,* 1975, *36,* 579–586.

Cavior, N. *Physical attractiveness, perceived attitude similarity, and interpersonal attraction among fifth- and eleventh-grade boys and girls.* Unpublished doctoral dissertation, University of Houston, 1970.

Cavior, N., & Dokecki, P. R. *Physical attractiveness and interpersonal attraction among fifth-grade boys: A replication with Mexican children.* Paper presented at the Meeting of the Southwestern Psychological Association, St. Louis, 1970.

Cavior, N., & Dokecki, P. R. Physical attractiveness self-concept: A test of Mead's hypothesis. *Proceedings of the 79th Annual Convention, American Psychological Association,* 1971, *6,* 319–320.

Cavior, N., & Lombardi, P. A. Developmental aspects of judgments of physical attractiveness. *Developmental Psychology,* 1973, *8,* 67–71.

Clifford, M. M. Physical attractiveness and academic performance. *Child Study Journal*, 1975, 5, 201–209.

Clifford, M. M., & Walster, E. Research note: The effect of physical attractiveness on teacher expectations. *Sociology of Education*, 1973, 46, 248–258.

Corter, C., Trehub, S., Boukydis, C., Ford, L., Celhoffer, L., & Minde, K. Nurses' judgments of the attractiveness of premature infants. *Infant Behavior and Development*, 1978, 1, 373–380.

Costa, P. T., & McCrae, R. R. Still stable after all these years: Personality as a key to some issues in aging. In P. B. Baltes & O. G. Brim (Eds.), *Life-span development and behavior* (Vol. 2). New York: Academic Press, 1979.

Cross, J. F., & Cross, J. Age, sex, race, and perception of facial beauty. *Developmental Psychology*, 1971, 5, 433–439.

Crouse, B. B., & Mehrabian, A. Affiliation of opposite-sexed strangers. *Journal of Research in Personality*, 1977, 11, 38–47.

Curran, J. P. Examination of various interpersonal attraction principles in the dating dyad. *Journal of Experimental Research in Personality*, 1973, 6, 347–356.

Curran, J. P., & Lippold, S. The effects of physical attraction and attitude similarity on attraction in dating dyads. *Journal of Personality*, 1975, 43, 528–539.

Davies, A. D. M., & Chown, S. M. The perception of another's age. *Proceedings, Eighth International Congress on Gerontology*, Washington, D. C., 1969.

Dermer, M., & Thiel, D. L. When beauty may fail. *Journal of Personality and Social Psychology*, 1975, 31, 1168–1176.

Dion, K. K. Physical attractiveness and evaluations of children's transgressions. *Journal of Personality and Social Psychology*, 1972, 24, 207–213.

Dion, K. K. Young children's stereotyping of facial attractiveness. *Developmental Psychology*, 1973, 9, 183–188.

Dion, K. K. Children's physical attractiveness and sex as determinants of adult punitiveness. *Developmental Psychology*, 1974, 10, 772–778.

Dion, K. K., & Berscheid, E. Physical attractiveness and peer perception among children. *Sociometry*, 1974, 37, 1–12.

Dion, K. K., Berscheid, E., & Walster, E. What is beautiful is good. *Journal of Personality and Social Psychology*, 1972, 24, 285–290.

Dipboye, R. L., Fromkin, H. L., & Wiback, K. Relative importance of applicant sex, attractiveness, and scholastic standing in evaluation of job applicant resumés. *Journal of Applied Psychology*, 1975, 60, 39–43.

Duck, S. W. *Personal relationships and personal constructs: A study of friendship formation.* New York: Wiley, 1973.

Efran, M. G. Effect of physical appearance on the judgment of guilt, interpersonal attraction, and severity of recommended punishment in a simulated jury task. *Journal of Research in Personality*, 1974, 8, 45–54.

Efran, M. G., & Patterson, E. W. J. Voters vote beautiful: The effect of physical appearance on a national election. *Canadian Journal of Behavioral Science*, 1974, 6, 352–356.

Elder, G. H., Jr. Appearance and education in marriage mobility. *American Sociological Review*, 1969, 34, 519–533.

Erikson, E. H. Inner and outer space: Reflections on womanhood. In R. J. Lifton (Ed.), *The woman in America*. Boston: Beacon, 1964.

Erikson, E. H. *Identity, youth, and crisis*. New York: Norton, 1968.

Fasteau, M. F. *The male machine*. New York: McGraw-Hill, 1974.

Gillen, B. *Physical attractiveness as a determinant of perceived sex-role appropriateness.* Paper presented at the Meeting of the Southeastern Psychological Association, Atlanta, 1975.

Goldberg, P. A., Gottesdiener, M., & Abramson, P. R. Another put-down of women?: Perceived attractiveness as a function of support for the feminist movement. *Journal of Personality and Social Psychology*, 1975, 32, 113–115.

Goldman, W., & Lewis, P. Beautiful is good: Evidence that the physically attractive are more socially skillful. *Journal of Experimental Social Psychology*, 1977, *13*, 125–130.

Graham, D., & Perry, R. Limitations in generalizability of the physical attractiveness stereotype: The self-esteem exception. *Canadian Journal of Behavioral Science*, 1976, *8*, 263–273.

Gross, A. E., & Crofton, C. What is good is beautiful. *Sociometry*, 1977, *40*, 85–90.

Harrell, W. A. Physical attractiveness, self-disclosure, and helping behavior. *Journal of Social Psychology*, 1978, *104*, 15–17.

Harris, D. B. Problems in formulating a scientific concept of development. In D. B. Harris (Ed.), *The concept of development*. Minneapolis: University of Minnesota Press, 1957.

Hartnett, J., & Elder, D. The princess and the nice frog: Study in person perception. *Perceptual and Motor Skills*, 1973, *37*, 863–866.

Hartup, W. W. Children and their friends. In H. McGurk (Ed.), *Child social development*. London: Methuen, 1978.

Havighurst, R. J. *Developmental tasks and education*. New York: McKay, 1951.

Herold, E. S. Variables influencing the dating adjustment of university students. *Journal of Youth and Adolescence*, 1979, *8*, 73–79.

Hildebrandt, K., & Fitzgerald, H. Adults' responses to infants varying in perceived cuteness. *Behavioral Processes*, 1978, *3*, 159–172.

Hildebrandt, K., & Fitzgerald, H. Facial feature determinants of perceived infant attractiveness. *Infant Behavior and Development*, 1979, *2*, 329–339.

Hildebrandt, K., & Fitzgerald, H. Mothers' responses to infant physical appearance. *Infant Mental Health Journal*, 1980.

Hill, M. K., & Lando, H. A. Physical attractiveness and sex-role stereotypes in impression formation. *Perceptual and Motor Skills*, 1976, *43*, 1251–1255.

Hobfoll, S. E., & Penner, L. A. Effect of physical attractiveness on therapists' initial judgments of a person's self-concept. *Journal of Consulting and Clinical Psychology*, 1978, *46*, 200–201.

Hudson, J. W., & Henze, L. S. Campus values in mate selection: A replication. *Journal of Marriage and the Family*, 1969, *31*, 772–775.

Huston, T. L. Ambiguity of acceptance, social desirability, and dating choice. *Journal of Experimental Social Psychology*, 1973, *9*, 32–42.

Huston, T. L., & Levinger, G. Interpersonal attraction and relationships. *Annual Review of Psychology*, 1978, *29*, 115–156.

Iwawaki, S., & Lerner, R. M. Cross-cultural analyses of body–behavior relations: I. A comparison of body-build stereotypes of Japanese and American males and females. *Psychologia*, 1974, *17*, 75–81.

Iwawaki, S., & Lerner, R. M. Cross-cultural analyses of body–behavior relations: III. Developmental intra- and intercultural factor congruence in the body-build stereotypes of Japanese and American males and females. *Psychologia*, 1976, *19*, 67–76.

Iwawaki, S., Lerner, R. M., & Chihara, T. Development of personal space schemata among Japanese in late childhood. *Psychologia*, 1977, *20*, 89–97.

Jacklin, C. N., & Maccoby, E. E. Social behavior at 33 months in same-sex and mixed-sex dyads. *Child Development*, 1978, *49*, 557–569.

Jackson, D. J., & Huston, T. L. Physical attractiveness and assertiveness. *Journal of Social Psychology*, 1975, *96*, 79–86.

Johnson, D. F. *Physical attractiveness and attribution in the elderly*. Paper presented at the Annual Meeting of the Gerontological Society, Washington, D. C., 1979.

Jones, H. E. The adolescent growth study. *Journal of Consulting Psychology*, 1939, *3*, 157–159, 177–180.

Jones, M. C. The later careers of boys who were early or late maturing. *Child Development*, 1957, *28*, 113–128.

Jones, M. C. Psychological correlates of somatic development. *Child Development*, 1965, *36*, 899–911.

Jones, M. C., & Bayley, N. Physical maturing among boys as related to behavior. *Journal of Educational Psychology*, 1950, *41*, 129–148.

Jones, M. C., & Mussen, P. H. Self-conceptions, motivations, and interpersonal attitudes of late and early maturing girls. *Child Development*, 1958, *29*, 491–501.

Kaats, G. R., & Davis, K. E. The dynamics of sexual behavior of college students. *Journal of Marriage and the Family*, 1970, *32*, 390–399.

Kehle, T. J., Bramble, W. J., & Mason, J. Teachers' expectations. Ratings of student performance as biased by student characteristics. *Journal of Experimental Education*, 1974, *43*, 54–60.

Kinsey, A. C., Pomeroy, W. B., & Martin, C. E. *Sexual behavior in the human male*. Philadelphia: Saunders, 1948.

Kleck, R., Richardson, S., & Ronald, L. Physical appearance cues and interpersonal attraction in children. *Child Development*, 1974, *45*, 305–310.

Kogan, N., & Shelton, F. Images of "old people" and "people in general" in an older sample. *Journal of Genetic Psychology*, 1962, *100*, 3–21. (a)

Kogan, N., & Shelton, F. Beliefs about "old people"; a comparative study of older and younger samples. *Journal of Genetic Psychology*, 1962, *100*, 93–111. (b)

Kopera, A. A., Maier, R. A., & Johnson, J. E. Perception of physical attractiveness: The influence of group interaction and group coaction on ratings of the attractiveness of photographs of women. *Proceedings of the 79th Annual Convention of the American Psychological Association*, 1971, *6*, 317–318.

Krebs, D., & Adinolfi, A. A. Physical attractiveness, social relations, and personality style. *Journal of Personality and Social Psychology*, 1975, *31*, 245–253.

Kurtzberg, R. L., Safar, H., & Cavior, N. Surgical and social rehabilitation of adult offenders. *Proceedings of the 76th Annual Convention of the American Psychological Association*, 1968, *3*, 649–650.

Landy, D., & Sigall, H. Beauty is talent: Task evaluation as a function of the performer's physical attractiveness. *Journal of Personality and Social Psychology*, 1974, *29*, 299–304.

Langlois, J. H., & Downs, A. C. Peer relations as a function of physical attractiveness: The eye of the beholder or behavioral reality. *Child Development*, 1979, *50*, 409–418.

Langlois, J. H., Gottfried, N. W., Barnes, B. M., & Hendricks, D. The effect of peer age on the social behavior of preschool children. *Journal of Genetic Psychology*, 1978, *132*, 11–19.

Langlois, J. H., Gottfried, N. W., & Seay, B. The influence of sex of peer on the social behavior of preschool children. *Developmental Psychology*, 1973, *8*, 93–98.

Langlois, J. H., & Stephan, C. The effects of physical attractiveness and ethnicity on children's behavioral attribution and peer preferences. *Child Development*, 1977, *48*, 1694–1698.

Langlois, J. H., & Stephan, C. Beauty and the beast: The role of physical attractiveness in the development of peer relations and social behavior. In S. S. Brehm, S. M. Kassin, & F. X. Gibbons (Eds.), *Developmental social psychology: Theory and Research*. New York: Oxford University Press, 1981.

Langlois, J. H., & Styczynski, L. E. The effects of physical attractiveness on the behavioral attributions and peer preferences in acquainted children. *International Journal of Behavioral Development*, 1979, *2*, 325–341.

Lansdown, R., & Polak, L. A study of the psychological effects of facial deformity in children. *Child: Care, Health and Development*, 1975, *1*, 85–91.

LaVoie, J., & Adams, G. R. Teacher expectancy and its relation to physical and interpersonal characteristics of the child. *The Alberta Journal of Educational Research*, 1974, *20*, 122–131.

Lerner, R. M. The development of stereotyped expectancies of body-build–behavior relations. *Child Development*, 1969, *40*, 137–141. (a)

Lerner, R. M. Some female stereotypes of male body-build–behavior relations. *Perceptual and Motor Skills*, 1969, *28*, 363–366. (b)

Lerner, R. M. "Richness" analyses of body-build stereotype development. *Developmental Psychology*, 1972, *7*, 219.

Lerner, R. M. The development of personal space schemata toward body build. *Journal of Psychology*, 1973, *84*, 229–235.

Lerner, R. M. *Concepts and theories of human development.* Reading, Mass.: Addison-Wesley, 1976.

Lerner, R. M. Nature, nurture, and dynamic interactionism. *Human Development*, 1978, *21*, 1–20.

Lerner, R. M. A dynamic interactional concept of individual and social relationship development. In R. L. Burgess & T. L. Huston (Eds.), *Social exchange in developing relationships.* New York: Academic Press, 1979.

Lerner, R. M., & Gellert, E. Body build identification, preference, and aversion in children. *Developmental Psychology*, 1969, *1*, 456–462.

Lerner, R. M., & Iwawaki, S. Cross-cultural analyses of body–behavior relations: II. Factor structure of body-build stereotypes of Japanese and American adolescents. *Psychologia*, 1975, *18*, 83–91.

Lerner, R. M., Iwawaki, S., & Chihara, T. Development of personal space schemata among Japanese children. *Developmental Psychology*, 1976, *12*, 466–467.

Lerner, R. M., & Karabenick, S. A. Physical attractiveness, body attitudes, and self-concept in late adolescents. *Journal of Youth and Adolescence*, 1974, *3*, 307–316.

Lerner, R. M., Karabenick, S. A., & Meisels, M. Effects of age and sex on the development of personal space schemata towards body build. *Journal of Genetic Psychology*, 1975, *127*, 91–101. (a)

Lerner, R. M., Karabenick, S. A., & Meisels, M. One-year stability of children's personal space schemata towards body build. *Journal of Genetic Psychology*, 1975, *127*, 151–152. (b)

Lerner, R. M., Karabenick, S. A., & Stuart, J. L. Relations among physical attractiveness, body attitudes, and self-concept in male and female college students. *Journal of Psychology*, 1973, *85*, 119–129.

Lerner, R. M., Knapp, J. R., & Pool, K. B. Structure of body-build stereotypes: A methodological analysis. *Perceptual and Motor Skills*, 1974, *39*, 719–729.

Lerner, R. M., & Korn, S. J. The development of body-build stereotypes in males. *Child Development*, 1972, *43*, 912–920.

Lerner, R. M., & Lerner, J. V. Effects of age, sex, and physical attractiveness on child–peer relations, academic performance, and elementary school adjustment. *Developmental Psychology*, 1977, *13*, 585–590.

Lerner, R. M., Orlos, J. B., & Knapp, J. R. Physical attractiveness, physical effectiveness, and self-concept in late adolescents. *Adolescence*, 1976, *11*, 313–326.

Lerner, R. M., & Pool, K. B. Body-build stereotypes: A cross-cultural comparison. *Psychological Reports*, 1972, *31*, 527–532.

Lerner, R. M., Skinner, E. A., & Sorell, G. T. Methodological implications of contextual/dialectical theories of development. *Human Development*, 1980, *23*, 225–235.

Lerner, R. M., & Spanier, G. B. A dynamic interactional view of child and family development. In R. M. Lerner & G. B. Spanier (Eds.), *Child influences on marital and family interaction: A life-span perspective.* New York: Academic Press, 1978.

Lerner, R. M., Venning, J., & Knapp, J. R. Age and sex effects on personal space schemata towards body build in late childhood. *Developmental Psychology*, 1975, *11*, 855–856.

Levinger, G. *Stage effects on "complementarity" in the sequence of relationship formation.* Unpublished manuscript, Western Reserve University, 1964.

Levinger, G., & Snoek, J. D. *Attraction in relationship: A new look at interpersonal attraction.* New York: General Learning Press, 1972.

Levinson, D. J. *The seasons of a man's life.* New York: Knopf, 1978.

Mathes, E. W. The effects of physical attractiveness and anxiety on heterosexual attraction over a series of five encounters. *Journal of Marriage and the Family*, 1975, *37*, 769–781.

Mathes, E. W., & Edwards, L. L. Physical attractiveness as an input in social exchanges. *Journal of Psychology*, 1978, *98*, 267–275.

Mathes, E. W., & Kahn, A. Physical attractiveness, happiness, neuroticism, and self-esteem. *Journal of Psychology*, 1975, *90*, 27–30.

McKelvie, S., & Matthews, S. Effects of physical attractiveness and favorableness of character on liking. *Psychological Reports*, 1976, *38*, 1223–1230.

Miller, A. G. Role of physical attractiveness in impression formation. *Psychonomic Science*, 1970, *19*, 241–243. (a)

Miller, A. G. Social perception of internal–external control. *Perceptual and Motor Skills*, 1970, *30*, 103–109. (b)

Miller, H. L., & Rivenbark, W. H. Sexual differences in physical attractiveness as a determinant of heterosexual likings. *Psychological Reports*, 1970, *27*, 701–702.

Mills, C. Wright. *The power elite.* New York: Oxford University Press, 1956.

Mills, J., & Aronson, E. Opinion change as a function of the communicator's attractiveness and desire to influence. *Journal of Personality and Social Psychology*, 1965, *1*, 173–177.

Minde, K., Trehub, S., Corter, C., Boukydis, C., Celhoffer, L., & Marton, P. Mother–child relationships in the premature nursery: An observational study. *Pediatrics*, 1978, *61*, 373–379.

Morse, S. J., Gruzan, J., & Reis, H. The "eye of the beholder": A neglected variable in the study of physical attractiveness? *Journal of Personality*, 1976, *44*, 209–225.

Morse, S. J., Reis, H. T., Gruzen, J., & Wolff, E. The "eye of the beholder": Determinants of physical attractiveness judgments in the U.S. and South Africa. *Journal of Personality*, 1974, *42*, 528–542.

Moss, Z. It hurts to be alive and obsolete: The aging woman. In R. Morgan (Ed.), *Sisterhood is powerful.* New York: Vintage Books, 1970.

Murstein, B. I. Physical attraction and marital choice. *Journal of Personality and Social Psychology*, 1972, *22*, 8–12.

Murstein, B. I., & Christy, P. Physical attractiveness and marriage adjustment in middle-aged couples. *Journal of Personality and Social Psychology*, 1976, *34*, 537–542.

Mussen, P. H., & Jones, M. C. Self-conceptions, motivations, and interpersonal attitudes of late and early maturing boys. *Child Development*, 1957, *28*, 242–256.

Nagy, B. A. Similarity of physical attractiveness in same-sex pairs. Paper presented at the Annual Meeting of the Eastern Psychological Association, Hartford, Conn., 1980.

Nash, F. A. Observation of real age and apparent age. *Journal of the American Geriatric Society*, 1958, *6*, 515–521.

Nida, S. A., & Williams, J. E. Sex-stereotyped traits, physical attractiveness, and interpersonal attraction. *Psychological Reports*, 1977, *41*, 1311–1322.

Nowak, C. A. *Age-concept in women: An analysis of concern with attractiveness, youthfulness, and self-esteem relative to self-perceived age.* Unpublished master's thesis, Wayne State University, Detroit, 1974.

Nowak, C. A. *The appearance signal in adult development.* Unpublished doctoral dissertation, Wayne State University, Detroit, 1975.

Nowak, C. A. *Youthfulness, attractiveness, and the midlife woman: An analysis of the appearance signal in adult development.* Paper presented at the Annual Meeting of the Midwestern Psychological Association, Chicago, 1976.

Nowak, C. A., Karuza, J., & Namikas, J. *Youth, beauty, and the midlife woman: The double whammy strikes again.* Paper presented at Conference on Women in Midlife Crisis, Cornell University, Ithica, 1976.

Parke, R. D., Hymel, S., Power, T., & Tinsley, B. Fathers and risk: A hospital based model of intervention. In D. B. Sawin & R. C. Hawkins (Eds.), *Exceptional infant: Psychosocial risks in infant-environment transactions* (Vol. 4). Brunner-Mazel, 1980.

Parke, R. D., & Sawin, D. B. *Infant characteristics and behavior as elicitors of maternal and paternal responsivity in the newborn period.* Paper presented at the Meeting of the Society for Research in Child Development, Denver, 1975.

Perrin, F. S. C. Physical attractiveness and repulsiveness. *Journal of Experimental Psychology*, 1921, *4*, 203–217.

Piehl, J. Integration of information in the courts: Influence of physical attractiveness on amount of punishment for traffic offender. *Psychological Reports*, 1977, *41*, 551–556.

Reis, H. T., Nezlek, J., & Wheeler, L. Physical attractiveness in social interaction. *Journal of Personality and Social Psychology*, 1980, *38*, 604–617.

Rich, J. Effects of children's physical attractiveness on teacher's evaluations. *Journal of Educational Psychology*, 1975, *67*, 599–609.

Roff, M. Childhood social interactions and young adult bad conduct. *Journal of Abnormal and Social Psychology*, 1961, *63*, 333–337.

Roff, M. Childhood social interaction and young adult psychosis. *Journal of Clinical Psychology*, 1963, *19*, 152–157.

Rokeach, M. Studies in beauty: I. The relationship between beauty in women, dominance, and security. *Journal of Social Psychology*, 1943, *17*, 181–189.

Rosen, G. M., & Ross, A. O. Relationship of body image to self-concept. *Journal of Consulting and Clinical Psychology*, 1968, *32*, 100.

Ross, M. B., & Salvia, J. Attractiveness as biasing factor in teacher judgment. *American Journal of Mental Deficiency*, 1975, *80*, 96–98.

Rubin, L. *Women of a certain age*. New York: Harper & Row, 1979.

Salvia, J., Sheare, J. B., & Algozzine, B. Facial attractiveness and personal–social development. *Journal of Abnormal Child Psychology*, 1975, *3*, 171–178.

Sameroff, A. Transactional models in early social relations. *Human Development*, 1975, *18*, 65–79.

Schneirla, T. C. The concept of development in comparative psychology. In D. B. Harris (Ed.), *The concept of development*. Minneapolis: University of Minnesota Press, 1957.

Seligman, C., Paschall, N., & Takata, G. Effects of physical attractiveness on attribution of responsibility. *Canadian Journal of Behavioral Science*, 1974, *6*, 290–296.

Shea, J., Crossman, S., & Adams, G. R. Physical attractiveness and personality development. *Journal of Psychology*, 1978, *99*, 59–62.

Sigall, H., & Aronson, E. Liking for an evaluator as a function of her physical attractiveness and nature of the evaluations. *Journal of Experimental Social Psychology*, 1969, *5*, 93–100.

Sigall, H., & Landy, D. Radiating beauty: Effects of having a physically attractive partner on perception. *Journal of Personality and Social Psychology*, 1973, *28*, 218–224.

Sigall, H., & Michela, J. I'll bet you say that to all the girls: Physical attractiveness and reactions to praise. *Journal of Personality*, 1976, *44*, 611–626.

Sigall, H., & Ostrove, N. Beautiful but dangerous: Effects of offender attractiveness and nature of the crime on juridic judgment. *Journal of Personality and Social Psychology*, 1975, *31*, 410–414.

Sigall, H., Page, R., & Brown, A. C. Effort expenditure as a function of evaluation and evaluator attractiveness. *Representative Research in Social Psychology*, 1971, *2*, 19–25.

Silverman, J. Physical attractiveness and courtship. *Sexual Behavior*, 1971, *1*, 22–25.

Snyder, M., Tanke, E., & Berscheid, E. Social perception and interpersonal behavior: On the self-fulfilling nature of social stereotypes. *Journal of Personality and Social Psychology*, 1977, *35*, 656–666.

Solomon, S., & Saxe, L. What is intelligent, as well as attractive, is good. *Personality and Social Psychology Bulletin*, 1977, *3*, 670–673.

Spiegel, L. A. The child's concept of beauty: A study in concept formation. *Journal of Genetic Psychology*, 1950, *77*, 11–23.

Sroufe, R., Chaikin, A., Cook, R., & Freeman, V. The effects of physical attractiveness on honesty: A socially desirable response. *Personality and Social Psychology Bulletin*, 1977, *3*, 59–62.

Staffieri, J. R. A study of social stereotype of body image in children. *Journal of Personality and Social Psychology,* 1967, *7,* 101–104.

Staffieri, J. R. Body build and behavioral expectancies in young females. *Developmental Psychology,* 1972, *6,* 125–127.

Strane, K., & Watts, C. Females judged by attractiveness of partner. *Perceptual and Motor Skills,* 1977, *45,* 225–226.

Stroebe, W., Insko, C. A., Thompson, V. D., & Layton, B. D. Effects of physical attractiveness, attitude similarity, and sex on various aspects of interpersonal attraction. *Journal of Personality and Social Psychology,* 1971, *18,* 79–91.

Strong, B., Reynolds, R., Suid, M., & Dabagian, J. *The marriage and family experience.* New York: West, 1979.

Styczynski, L. E. *Effects of physical characteristics on the social, emotional, and intellectual development of early school-age children.* Unpublished doctoral dissertation, The University of Texas at Austin, 1976.

Styczynski, L. E., & Langlois, J. H. The effects of familiarity on behavioral stereotypes associated with physical attractiveness in young children. *Child Development,* 1977, *48,* 1137–1141.

Tennis, G. H., & Dabbs, J. M. Judging physical attractiveness: Effects of judges' own attractiveness. *Personality and Social Psychology Bulletin,* 1975, *1,* 513–516.

Terman, L. M., & Oden, M. H. *Genetic studies of genius, V: The gifted group at midlife.* Palo Alto, Calif.: Stanford University Press, 1959.

Tesser, A., & Brodie, M. A note on the evaluation of a "computer date." *Psychonomic Science,* 1971, *23,* 300.

Thornton, B. Effect of rape victim's attractiveness in a jury simulation. *Personality and Social Psychology Bulletin,* 1977, *3,* 666–669.

Traxler, A. *Intergenerational differences in attitudes toward old people.* Paper presented at the Annual Meeting of the Gerontological Society, Houston, 1971.

Trnavsky, P. A., & Bakeman, R. *Physical attractiveness: Stereotype and social behavior in preschool children.* Paper presented at the Annual Meeting of the American Psychological Association, Washington, D. C., 1976.

Udry, R. Structural correlates of feminine beauty preferences in Britain and the United States: A comparison. *Sociology and Social Research,* 1965, *49,* 330–342.

Walker, R. Body build and behavior in young children: II. Body build and parents' ratings. *Child Development,* 1963, *34,* 1–23.

Walster, E. *Did you ever see a beautiful conservative? A note.* Unpublished manuscript, University of Wisconsin, 1971.

Walster, E., Aronson, V., Abrahams, D., & Rottman, L. Importance of physical attractiveness in dating behavior. *Journal of Personality and Social Psychology,* 1966, *65,* 246–253.

Weatherly, D. Self-perceived rate of physical maturation and personality in late adolescents. *Child Development,* 1964, *35,* 1197–1210.

Weitz, S. *Sex roles: Biological, psychological, and social foundations.* New York: Oxford University Press, 1977.

Wiener, S., Saxe, L., & Bar-Tal, D. *The effects of physical attractiveness on attributions of causality for success and failure.* Paper presented at the Annual Meeting of the Midwestern Psychological Association, Chicago, 1975.

Yarrow, M. R., & Campbell, J. D. Person perception in children. *Merrill-Palmer Quarterly,* 1963, *9,* 57–72.

JOHN A. MEACHAM **15**

Political Values, Conceptual Models, and Research

Determinants of Individual Development: Where Have We Been?

The thesis that individuals are producers of their own development is presented and evaluated in diverse ways in the chapters in the present volume. In the majority of the chapters, it is employed as a conceptual tool for the presentation, integration, and elaboration of a particular set of findings on the course of individual development. In contrast, I will endeavor to evaluate this thesis, not by applying it, but by considering the context within which the thesis itself has been developed. Certainly the thesis that individuals are producers of their own development has arisen in contradiction to some alternative, perhaps earlier thesis. What is that alternative? If individuals are not producers of their own development, then who or what, as an alternative, is thought to bring about the development of individuals? What are the social and historical contexts within which these alternative theses have arisen, and to what extent do the theses remain consistent with both their original and contemporary contexts? Can we expect the thesis that individuals are producers of their own development to some day be incorporated within a more radical and encompassing synthesis?

These questions may be considered by inquiring more generally into the multiple potential determinants of individual development, including

447

heredity and environment. The thrust of the present chapter will be to conclude that the thesis that individuals are producers of their own development ultimately implies a rejection of the simplistic input–output model of individual development, and acceptance of a model that I will characterize by the term *interpenetration.* The validation of either of these models is to be found in the extent to which there is a correspondence of the models with the political values and ideas of particular developmental psychologists, and with the social and historical contexts within which they work.

On the assumption that what is presented in our basic textbooks is a good indication of commonly accepted knowledge regarding the determinants of development, I recently surveyed eight developmental psychology textbooks. Each included, either as a section of a chapter or by division of the material into two chapters, a discussion of the "causes," "determinants," "factors," or "influences" in human development. In each case, only two major categories were mentioned: heredity, biology, dispositional, or internal influences, on the one hand, and environmental, situational, or external influences, on the other. Bee's (1975) *The Developing Child* stood out among this sample in identifying not only internal and external influences on development but also, as a separate and equal category, interaction effects that, as she cautions the reader, include not merely additive effects of internal and external influences but, instead, complex combinations. In none of the books sampled were individuals identified as the producers of their own development, and so the thesis of the present volume does indeed represent a new and significant conceptual model within the discipline of developmental psychology.

At the risk of belaboring what has been said by others, both in the present volume and elsewhere, it may be helpful to summarize the difficulties that arise when one adopts as a framework, as these textbook authors have for their students and for the general public, merely heredity and environment as causes of individual development. The first difficulty is the incorrect assumption that the nature of these causes is one of stability and lack of change. In contrast, individual development must be considered within the context of continual changes both in genetics and in the environment. The potential contribution of heredity—the structure of the genes—changes through mutations caused by radiation and various chemicals, natural selection, the mixing of gene pools, and so on; but more important is that the operation of any particular gene and so its realized effect upon the course of individual development is variable as a result of changes in the intrauterine environment, food additives, water and airborne pollution, diet, educational opportunities, stress, technology, and so forth that alter the likelihood or nature of expression of that gene. The environment can change in equally dramatic ways. Boocock (1976) and Elder (1977), among others, have provided evidence that developmental research in the past quarter century has been carried out under rather unusual environmental conditions, that is, a high birth rate, strong familial orientations, and economic affluence following World War II. The next quarter century may yield a quite different environment for individual development.

The second difficulty, once heredity and environment have been misunderstood as stable and unchanging entities, is that they are incorrectly considered as causes that can act independently of one another. Yet certainly heredity can have no impact upon individual development in the absence of an environment (cellular material, etc.), nor can the environment produce meaningful changes without heredity (Carmichael, 1925, p. 257, 260; Lerner, 1978). In short, there can be little disagreement that heredity and environment must be related or "interact" in a common process. Nevertheless, insufficient attention has been given to the precise manner in which these two factors interact. Because of the assumption that they exist as stable, independent causes, it is easy to infer that they interact in an additive manner. For example, "good" heredity plus a "good" environment are said to yield good individual development; "good" heredity plus a "poor" environment yield less good development. Such an interpretation is too simplistic: The quality of a genetic background cannot be evaluated without simultaneous specification of the environment within which the genetic structure operates. A "good" heredity within one environment may be quite poor in another environment; a "good" environment for one individual may be quite poor for another individual with a different genetic background.

For example, the Pima Indians carry a group of genes that is "good" in an environment that includes periodic episodes of drought and famine. The genes encourage the storage of calories as body fat that is then used during famines. However, in the current environment that provides ample food, the same genes are "bad," for they are associated with obesity and diabetes (Brody, 1980). (Alternatively, for these Indians, a "good" environment is one without a regular and adequate supply of food.) As a second illustration that heredity and environment cannot be evaluated independently, one can note that a quarter of European Caucasians inherit a white blood cell antigen of type B8. This antigen provides protection against bacteria commonly found in Europe. However, these individuals are *more* susceptible to some kinds of arthritis, myasthenia gravis, Addison's disease, Hodgkin's disease, acute lymphatic leukemia, and other diseases. An environmental triggering event appears to disrupt the immune system, leading to the disease to which the individual is susceptible (Douglas, 1979). As a third example, the co-occurrence of sickle cell anemia and resistance to malaria can be mentioned. In this case the particular gene is "good" in an environment where exposure to malaria is frequent, but "bad" otherwise.

A corollary to the assumption that heredity and environment can act as independent causes is the belief—widespread among students and the general public—that intelligence is determined 80% by heredity and 20% by environment. Once heredity and environment are assumed to be independent causes in individual development, it is difficult to conceive of their interaction in a manner that is inconsistent with this incorrect belief. Carmichael (1925), Elias (1973, p. 125), Furth (1973), Hirsch (1970/1972), and Overton (1973), among others, have argued effectively against this additive model. Efforts to improve upon the additive model include the concept of norm of reaction, according to which heredity provides the upper and lower limits on a range of potential outcomes or reactions, and the particular outcome within those limits is determined by the specific environment of the developing individual. The norm of reaction concept is difficult to distinguish from the additive model—heredity plus a "poor" environment yield the lower boundary of development, and heredity plus a "good" environment yield the upper boundary. Dobzhansky (1973), Hirsch (1970), and Lerner (1976), among others, have argued against the utility of the norm of reaction concept, because of our inability to assess norms of reaction given the wide range of existing and potential environments within which development might take place. In short, a conceptual answer to Anastasi's (1958) question regarding *how* heredity and environment come together to determine development has yet to be provided, because of the incorrect assumptions of lack of change and of independence of heredity and environment.

A third difficulty in considering only heredity and environment as causes is the common inference that, if heredity plays a major role in development, modification of the course of development is relatively difficult. This confusion no doubt arises from the previous two difficulties; that is, if heredity is stable and unchanging, and if heredity can act independently of environment (or is merely added together with the effects of environment), it would seem to follow that in instances in which heredity is thought to play a major role in development it must be difficult to modify the course of development. The error at this point is not merely one of inappropriately inferring from high heritability estimates that heredity is a more important factor in development than is environment (Anastasi, 1971; Hebb, 1970; Hirsch, 1970/1972; Lawler, 1978, p. 138). Even if one were to grant that, for a given instance, heredity plays a more direct role than environment, one can still not know the extent of modifiability of the course of development. For example, in the case of phenylketonuria (PKU) syndrome, in which the genes fail to direct the production of an enzyme necessary for the metabolism of phenylalanine, development can still proceed normally if the child's environment is changed to include a diet low in phenylalanine (Jarvik, 1975). Similarly, inherited susceptibility to allergies may be counteracted by living in an environment free of the particular allergen or through treatment with antihistamines. As a third example, women who develop male secondary sex characteristics because of a gene that directs an excesssive production of androgen may develop normally with appropriate cortisone therapy (Money & Ehrhardt, 1972). In all three examples, despite the direct role that heredity plays in development, the potential for modification of the course of development through change in the environment is not limited.

The acceptance of the view that heredity and environment are un-changing and independently acting causes of individual development is facilitated by our tendency to analyze problems in terms of input–output models. Input–output models suggest that output may be understood and predicted by describing the proportional amounts of various inde-pendent inputs. Large increments in input are expected to lead directly to large increments in output. Although this model may be an accurate description of many processes, for example, increasing the number of workers to produce more units of a particular product, or adding more wood to a fire to produce more heat, it may not hold for some important developmental processes. Even the nonsocial sciences, such as chemistry, have moved beyond a consideration of merely the nature and concentra-tion of the reactants, that is, those elements that are incorporated and changed from one time to the next. By focusing, instead, on the processes involved, chemists have come to appreciate that a very minute amount of a particular reactant, or even an input that itself remains unchanged during the course of the reaction, may change the final product dramat-ically, through the processes of seeding and catalysis, respectively. We need to be more open to the likelihood that, in the course of individual development as well, apparently minor inputs can lead to rather major differences in outcomes (see Riegel & Meacham, 1978, for further dis-cussion and examples). There are also processes—for example, individuals producing their own development, or autocatalysis—that make the rela-tionship between input and output nonlinear.

The fourth difficulty in adopting as a framework merely heredity and environment as causes of development is that this leads to a miscatego-rization and misunderstanding of Piaget's theory of structural develop-ment. As Kohlberg (1968) and Liben (Chapter 5, this volume) have noted, even those who are otherwise enthusiastic about Piaget's ideas have as-similated these to a framework that is quite different from Piaget's own. Piaget (e.g., 1964, 1970) identifies four main factors that are required for an explanation of structural development. Three of these factors are similar to those found in many other developmental theories and are consistent with the heredity–environment framework: maturation; physical experi-ence (including logicomathematical experience that derives from actions performed upon objects); and social experiences (including the transmis-sion of cultural information). The principal factor in Piaget's theory, however, and one that plays a fundamental role in regulating the other three factors, is equilibration (see Chapter 5 by Liben). The categorization of Piaget's theory has been a source of difficulty for those who recognize only two major categories: biological theories, on the one hand, and environmental or learning theories, on the other. Although either choice is a misrepresentation of Piaget's theory, it has generally been categorized and approached as a biological theory, and consequently has been widely misunderstood.

Where Are We Now? The Active Role of the Individual in Development

The fifth difficulty in adopting merely heredity and environment as a causal framework for individual development is presented within the chapters of the present volume. Among the constructs that have been introduced or are receiving renewed attention in recent years, in addition to Piaget's equilibration, are self-regulation, interpretation of stimulus events, mediation between environmental inputs and behavior, formulation of goals and plans, reflective thought, constructivism, and so on. These constructs may be grouped into several categories, depending on the specific role that is attributed to the individual: First and most basic are those processes that maintain the comprehensive functioning of the individual as a whole, such as Piaget's equilibration process (Furth, 1969; Labouvie-Vief, Chapter 8, this volume; Liben, Chapter 5, this volume; Piaget, 1964, 1970), which serves to maintain the balance between the processes of assimilation and accommodation and between biological and environmental disturbances to the individual, as well as to promote movement toward more stable structures of organization. Similarly, Sameroff (1979) has recently called attention to self-righting tendencies within the child, which serve to promote development even in high-risk cases through the coordination of whatever inputs may be available. In addition, Tobach (Chapter 2, this volume) has described the most fundamental activity of the organism as adjustment to internal and external change.

Both Piaget's and Sameroff's views are similar to Waddington's (1962) notion of homeorhesis, according to which development may be thought of as proceeding along certain canals or chreodes. Each canal may be described in terms of the relative height of its banks, that is, in terms of the difficulty of bringing about a change in development from any particular canal or course. The general appeal of Waddington's epigenetic landscape for developmental psychologists may derive from the fact that it represents not hereditary constraints, but whether a minor or a major force is required to modify the course of development of the *phenotype* (Carter-Saltzman, 1978, p. 187). In other words, the epigenetic landscape provides a means of moving beyond the interaction of heredity and environment and conceptualizing directly the question of modifiability. A reasonable question for developmental psychologists to pursue within this model is what minimal force is required at a particular point in time to modify or to restore the normal or desired course of development.

A second category includes the individual's impact on behavior as mediated by actions on the environment. Kvale (1977) has called attention to Skinner's (1974) radical behaviorist view of the relationship between the individual and the environment, that is, that the individual acts upon the environment in order that something will happen that in turn will change the individual. This second category also includes the Soviet perspective on the development of the individual, according to which the individual through activity and participation in social interactions is able to change the social–historical milieu and thus the environmental context within which further development takes place (see Meacham, 1972, 1977a, 1977c). Payne (1968) has summarized the views of the Soviet theoretician S. L. Rubenstein: "By his labour man changes and so creates a new environment in which further individual development can take place. It is in this sense that man can be said to create himself by his own labour— by transforming nature to transform himself [p. 90]." This second category appears consistent with Schneirla's (1957) view that traces within the individual of earlier experiences may affect later experiences, especially as this view is elaborated by Lerner (1976, p. 102): The actions of the individual upon the environment (and the consequent actions back upon the individual) constitute a "third source" of development as important as any other source of the individual's behavior (also see Chapters 4, 7, and 9 by Belsky & Tolan, Rodeheaver & Datan, and Thomas & Chess, respectively, in this volume and, in particular, the discussion of reactions by animals to abiotic aspects of the environment, in Tobach's Chapter 2, this volume).

A third category includes the individual's impact on behavior and development through setting goals, forming plans, making commitments to engage in particular behaviors, and so on. Although this category is similar to the previous one, it may be distinguished by the greater extent to which the individual is assumed to anticipate the consequences of his or her actions. For example, a variety of techniques for self-control, self-improvement, and modification of behavior toward desired ends (e.g., cessation of smoking, weight loss, etc.) is based upon the individual's deliberate arrangement of the environment so as to inhibit or promote the occurrence or development of particular behaviors (e.g., Thoreson & Mahoney, 1974). Current cognitive social learning theory perspectives (e.g., Bandura, 1978; Mischel, 1973; Chapter 11 by Worell, this volume) appear to fall within this category, although they tend to portray the individual's role as one of cognitively *mediating* between environmental forces and behavior. Cognition and behavior have been distinguished (another perspective is to regard cognitions *as* behaviors; see Meacham, 1972), but as long as the role of cognition is mediational it seems implicit that a greater or primary role has been attributed to the environment rather than to the individual as a causal factor in behavior and development (Rychlak, 1979).

Elsewhere (Meacham, 1979), I have provided evidence consistent with the idea that the ability of preschoolers to plan and guide the course of their behavior (Stage 4) derives from the use of language and cognition to facilitate the remembering of anticipated goals of actions (Stage 3). Memory of the anticipated goals of actions is important for comparison with actual outcomes, so that corrective action may subsequently be engaged in if the outcomes do not match the anticipated goals. Remembering of the anticipated goals (Stage 3) derives from the use of language for describing and reflecting upon the completed outcomes of actions (Stage 2; in Stage 1, language and action are independent). In short, the role of the individual in guiding his or her own behavior, as considered in this third category, may change during the course of development within particular domains from a stage of no impact to a stage of considerable impact.

A fourth category includes the role of the individual in constructing the psychological environment. This category may be distinguished from the third by the emphasis upon perception and the attribution of meaning. Numerous theories in psychology provide a role for the individual in interpreting environmental events within the framework provided by cognitive structures, past experiences, current motivational states, and so on. For example, in Piaget's theory (see Liben's Chapter 5, this volume) a rattle may have a variety of meanings for an infant, according to whether it is assimilated to schemas for listening, sucking, throwing, hitting, looking, or others. Similarly, whether a child interprets a particular parental action in terms of its consequences or the inferred intentions of the parent may have a far-reaching impact upon the development of parent–child relations and the subsequent personality development of the child. Fein's Chapter 10 in this volume on the child's representation of the environment during play provides further examples.

A fifth category includes those processes of the individual involved in the construction of the self. These constructive processes may be similar to those in the previous category, but by being applied reflectively by individuals to their own thoughts and experiences, and indeed to the self-concept itself, successive transformations in one's sense of identity may occur, and so individuals may be said to have brought about their own development (see Chapter 6 by Haan, this volume). For example, Butler (1963), Lewis (1973), and others (see Meacham, 1977a) have suggested that it is through reviewing, evaluating, and integrating experiences over one's life that individuals are able to achieve satisfactory adjustment in old age, or ego integrity as it is described by Erikson (1950). Sorell and Nowak (Chapter 14, this volume) discuss the construction by individuals of self-attributions based on physical experience. Many psychological therapies have as a goal the reinterpretation and acceptance by individuals of earlier experiences; the therapist guides and facilitates the individuals' efforts in restructuring their views of themselves.

The preceding list of categories—including general organizational processes, actions by individuals upon the environment, actions planned and carried out to achieve anticipated goals, construction and interpretation of the environment, and construction and understanding of the self—is no doubt not exhaustive; it is intended merely to illustrate the wide range of constructs that are consistent with the view that heredity and environment do not provide a sufficient causal framework for understanding human development. Certainly there are a number of substantial differences between these various constructs. One is whether the active role of the individual can be adequately understood by *reducing* it to some product of the interaction of heredity and environment. From an organismic perspective, the active role of the individual's cognitive structures is a primary and unquestionable assumption; this activity does not depend upon a prior causal action of heredity or environment (Overton, 1975, 1976). However, from a behaviorist perspective, the activity of the individual is not a primary cause, but is derivable from the interaction of heredity and environment (e.g., White, 1976). Although the distinction is an interesting and important one, it is not easily resolvable, as different world views are involved (Overton & Reese, 1973; Reese, 1976; Rychlak, 1979).

For the purposes to follow, it is important merely to agree that, *at some point* in the course of development, the active role of the individual becomes at least as important a causal factor in psychological development as heredity and environment, if not more so. (A comparison may be made with the achievement motive that, although derived from more basic needs and drives, may, for some individuals, become one of the most compelling sources of motivation.) In short, for many developmental psychologists, it is no longer the question of whether the individual has an active role to play that is in dispute, but rather the nature of that role—equilibration, mediation, language, use of tools, symbol formation, self-concept, consciousness, and so on—and the point in development at which that role becomes effective in determining the further course of behavior and development.

The conceptual leap that is taken, in acknowledging that the individual can be a source of his or her own development, is radical. The leap would not have been nearly as significant if a new cause had been introduced on the input side, parallel with heredity and environment (for example, it is not radical to distinguish the physical and the social environments as separate causes in the development of the individual). In contrast, the output—the individual—has now been given status simultaneously as an input, and so the input–output model of previous perspectives on development must be substantially modified. The inadequate input–output model may be contrasted with the concept of reciprocal causality or strong interaction (versus unidirectional causality), according to which heredity, environment, and the individual both affect and are affected by each other (Overton & Reese, 1973). The assumption of reciprocal causality is inconsistent with the notions reviewed earlier that heredity and environment may act as stable and independent causes.

Alternatives to the Input–Output Model

The long-term significance of the perspective of this volume, that individuals are producers of their own development, may rest in the recognition of the need for alternatives to the input–output, heredity–environment model of individual development. Currently, there is widespread interest in developmental psychology in models that can provide such an alternative and that can, in particular, provide tools for research on issues involving reciprocal causality or strong interaction. In addition to Piaget's (1964, 1970) theory, attention can be directed to transactional models, contextual models, the use of nonsocial science metaphors, and dialectical models. Transactional models (Lazarus & Launier, 1978; Meacham, 1977a; Pervin, 1968; Sameroff, 1979) are based on a distinction introduced by Dewey and Bentley (1949/1960) between processes of interaction and transaction. Interaction assumes elements that can be located and described independently of one another (as some have attempted to do with heredity and environment). Inquiries are then made into the relationship between these elements. In transactional models, activities or relations are assumed to be primary, and elements are derived as secondary categories within the transactional system. A concrete example of such elements is buyer and seller, which depend for their definition upon a prior understanding of the activity of exchange.

Sameroff and Chandler (1975) have documented the inadequacy, in predicting the consequences of trauma in infancy, of both main effects models, in which either constitution or environment is a factor, and of interactional models, in which each unique combination of constitution and environment has a specified developmental outcome. In their transactional model, both the infant and the caretaking environment are continually changed as a result of their mutual activity. Elsewhere (Meacham, 1977a), I have outlined a transactional model of remembering, in which memories, the remembering individual, and the social context are all

regarded as continually changeable events, derived from more basic activities. Not only are the memories constructed by the individual, but the
identity of the individual depends upon his or her memories. The social
context or psychological environment is interpreted within the framework
of the individual's memories, and memories are always constructed within
a social context. In short, the relationship between the individual, his or
her memories, and the social context is one of reciprocal causality. Despite
the construction of transactional models in a number of areas of developmental psychology, however, the search for causes or determinants by
means of traditional research procedures, which tend to abstract a stable
and timeless snapshot from the flux of activity, continues not to provide
substantial changes in our understanding of individual development.

Contextual models (Chapters 11, 8, and 1 by Busch-Rossnagel, Labouvie-Vief, and Lerner & Busch-Rossnagel, respectively, this volume; Lerner,
Skinner, & Sorell, 1978; Pepper, 1942; Reese, 1977), in contrast to mechanistic and organismic models, are based on the metaphor of the historical
event. Change is assumed to be a constant, as each event alters the context
for all future events. Recently, a variety of writers has begun to describe
the course of individual development in terms that are consistent with
the contextual model. Jenkins (1974) and Reese (1977) have referred explicitly to contextualism in discussing processes of remembering and learning. Reese has also noted that Soviet theories of individual development
(see, e.g., Meacham, 1977c) are also consistent with the contextual model,
because of their emphasis on the importance of the social and historical
environment, and the existence of reciprocal causality between the individual and the social context. Lipsitt (1979) has called attention to the
unavailability to developmental researchers of knowledge of specific
events that may determine the later course of an individual's development,
for example, a specific locker room experience that may determine the
subsequent course of sex-role development in one of two identical twins.
Lipsitt suggests looking at the processes by which such events are given
meaning and integrated within the individual's life course (e.g., coping
style) rather than studying presumably stable traits (e.g., passivity, dependency) as we have done in the past. Lipsitt's suggestion is consistent
with contextualism and with reciprocal causality, in that the event has no
meaning aside from the individual's interpretation of it, and the individual
has no qualities aside from the relationship between processes and specific
events.

Gergen (1977) has proposed an aleatory (chance) change model, according to which all relationships are fashioned in part by historically
specific conditions. Sarbin (1977) has described G. A. Kelley's psychology
of personal constructs as an effort to break away from mechanism and
to adopt the contextualist metaphor, and illustrates the use of contextual
models in schizophrenia, hypnosis, and imagination. Mancuso (1977) ar-

gues that contextualixm is "pushing mechanism into a sideline position" in experimental psychology, and provides examples from the areas of motivation, attention, and moral judgment. For the most part, however, all these writers have merely described existing research from the perspective of contextualism. An important question is whether contextualism implies a new research methodology that is compatible with existing research traditions. Sarbin (1977, p. 37) suggests that researchers might examine the world of literature for evidence of the importance of contexts in behavior and development. Although this approach certainly has merit, it raises the issue of idiographic versus nomothetic methods in psychology.

A third approach that has been pursued to have a conceptual model for reciprocal causality, in addition to transactionalism and contextualism, has been to turn to the nonsocial sciences for new metaphors. This dependence of the social sciences upon the nonsocial sciences is not new—one can point to Freud's metaphors of the flow and conservation of energy, and to models of learning and remembering based upon telephone switchboards, or, more recently, information processing in computers. The processes of chemistry, in particular, often appear attractive as possible metaphors for enriching social science concepts: Sameroff (1979) has referred to the process of buffering, and psychological processes have been described as analogous to the chemical processes of seeding and catalysis (Riegel & Meacham, 1978). The analogy is especially apt in the case of autocatalysis or self-catalysis, in which a product of the reaction serves as a catalyst to further speed the subsequent reaction. For example, in the reaction of permanganate and oxalic acid, the production of manganese ions permits the reaction to take place at an increasing rate. Autocatalysis is illustrated in psychological development by the production of concepts, tools, signs, and so on.

Brent (1978b) notes that this dependence of the social sciences upon the nonsocial sciences for metaphors may be turned around through the Nobel prize-winning work of Prigogine (1978; Nicolis & Prigogine, 1977) on self-organization in biological, psychological, and social systems. Such open systems maintain their organization only by discharging entropy (disorder) into the surrounding environment, or by taking in negative entropy (order) from the environment. Classical thermodynamics (nonsocial science) is thus reduced to a description of special cases (i.e., isolated, closed systems). Although Prigogine's conceptions are rich in potential applications for developmental psychology (see especially Brent, 1978b), it remains the case that for the most part the social sciences have drawn metaphors from the nonsocial sciences, rather than having constructed metaphors that are uniquely suited to the social and psychological phenomena for which understanding is sought.

One uniquely social metaphor is that of communication or exchange (see, e.g., Tamir, 1979; Wilden, 1972, 1975; the metaphor of communication is also implicit within the transactional models noted earlier). Riegel (1976, 1978, 1979) has made explicit use of the communication or dialogue metaphor in advancing a dialectical psychology, in which change and development may be understood as a result of contradictions between events occurring in different progressions, such as the biological, psychological, or cultural–sociological progressions (also see Chapter 7 by Rodeheaver & Datan, this volume). Dialogues may be understood in terms of dialogical units, each of which includes a thesis, antithesis, and synthesis. The relationships within each dialogue, and between events in the different progressions, are those of reciprocal causality (Overton & Reese, 1973, p. 86). Riegel has provided many examples of the application of the dialectical metaphor, in parent–child relations, language acquisition, Piaget's theory, and so on.

Riegel's dialectical psychology may be subject, however, to some of the same criticisms that can be advanced against the heredity–environment framework for understanding individual development. Tolman (1981) has argued that the biological, psychological, and cultural–sociological progressions in Riegel's theory may be conceived of as existing independently *before* the question of their being in a relationship of contradiction, crisis, or conflict, on the one hand, or synchrony, on the other, is considered. If so, then the problem of change and development, which Riegel's dialectical theory attempts to address, is reduced to matters of external relations among stable things, and the problem of movement and development *within* these progressions (i.e., how they exist independently) is not addressed. Tolman characterizes Riegel's theory as not dialectical, but as a metaphysic of relations.

Riegel's dialectical psychology has much in common with the metaphors of transaction and contextualism. In contrast to the transactional metaphor, dialectics is a more general world view and philosophy. The dialectical approach has drawn attention to and provided a framework for incorporating the impact of social and historical contexts upon individual development. It also emphasizes the participation of scientists themselves in a relationship of reciprocal causality with the objects of study and with the products of scientific activity. Scientists construct and change their subject matter by acting upon it, and their interpretations, once constructed, act back upon and change the scientists and the social and historical context within which they work. Thus the dialectical metaphor is not merely a lens that *mediates* between scientists and that which they seek to understand, but a metaphor that *includes* the scientist as well (Meacham, 1977b/1978; 1978/1980). Because of the seriousness with which reciprocal causality is considered, the dialectical approach is unique in recognizing and indeed in predicting its own continual transformation into new, more encompassing, and contextually more appropriate forms. Indeed, if the dialectical approach were to be formalized into a rigid orthodoxy, it would have lost its utility in terms of its appropriateness to contemporary social and historical contexts and in terms of its meaningfulness in the lives of developmental psychologists and of the individuals whose development is being studied.

Where Are We Going?

BOUNDARIES THAT SHOULD NOT BE

The attempt to understand individual development within the framework of heredity and environment as causes of development has foundered on the assumptions that heredity and environment are stable and independent causes and that a strong role for heredity implies lack of modifiability, and on reliance on an input–output model of development, according to which the output (individual) has no substantial impact on the input (heredity and environment). Efforts to move beyond the input–output model, such as transactionalism, contextualism, and dialectics, although representing conceptual advances, have not in practice led to substantial changes in research or in our understanding of individual development. This may be because the false assumptions regarding heredity and environment continue to bias these new models of reciprocal causality. What is needed is to extend the transactional, contextual, and dialectical models forcefully toward a resolution of the issues of heredity and environment, to construct an interpretation of individual development that is consistent throughout with the principle of reciprocal causality. How can the direct role of heredity in development be reconciled with plasticity (Lerner & Busch-Rossnagel, Chapter 1, this volume) and the potential for modification of the course of individual development? How can this reconciliation be presented so as to be readily comprehensible to students and to the general public? Can a model of the course of human development be constructed that acknowledges that heredity has a direct, determining role in individual development, without at the same time providing a facile justification for existing racial, sexual, and class differences?

Can one, in practice, identify the boundary between heredity and environment, that is, the point at which heredity ends and environment begins? The action of any gene may be initiated or inhibited by other nearby genes (regulators) on the same chromosome; that is, the genes themselves may constitute an environment for genes. Furthermore, as Brent (1978a) notes, the ability of a particular gene to produce proteins is limited by the availability of essential chemicals in the immediate environment of the gene. This chemical environment is controlled by membranes surrounding the cell nucleus, by the cytoplasm of the cell, by the cell wall, by the surrounding cells, tissues, and organs, and so on. Each of these in turn is guided in its structure and functioning by the genes themselves. Brent comments that "at this structural level of analysis we are not dealing with a question of heredity *or* environment, but rather with biochemical information and biochemical processes embedded within layer upon layer of protective environment [p. 27]." Tobach (Chapter 2, this volume) emphasizes the embeddedness of the biological processes within layers of social processes: ". . . the societal processes of which [the mother] is a part are preeminent in determining what shall be the biochemical and biophysical factors in the developing embryo." Certainly, there is little support for a mutually exclusive, two-category framework. One might counter that the genes nevertheless represent a fixed set of instructions prepared to guide one set of processes (e.g., to produce a mouse) and not another (an elephant; but see the false assumption of stability discussed in the first section of this chapter). Nevertheless, from the very moment that the fertilized egg begins to develop, it is no longer the range of potential instructions that is of interest, but rather the realized effect of those instructions as they operate within a specific environment. From this moment onward, no distinction can be made between developmental outcomes based on heredity versus those based on environment (Carmichael, 1925).

Confusion brought about by the attempt to create boundaries between categories that are overlapping exists in other areas of psychology as well. The problems of mind and body, individual and society, form and content, quality and quantity may all be understood as futile efforts to bring together that which should not have been conceived as separate. The problem of the individual and society (or person versus environment, or traits versus situations, etc.) may be taken as an example (also see Chapters 8 and 1 by Labouvie-Vief and Lerner & Busch-Rossnagel, this volume): Endler (1973, p. 289) has described the dichotomy between individuals and environmental contexts as a pseudoissue and has made explicit the parallel between questions asked regarding the impact of persons and situations upon behavior and questions (Which one? How much? How?) regarding heredity and environment as outlined by Anastasi (1958). The mutual interdependence of social and psychological processes is most explicit within Soviet developmental psychology (Meacham, 1977c). Wertsch (1979) has provided a clarification of L. S. Vygotsky's general theoretical framework for the development of higher psychological processes in the context of adult–child social interactions.

There are no doubt a number of additional boundaries that would be found, upon close examination, to be not as clearly defined as we might at first imagine, for example, between nuclear and extended families, between families and neighborhoods, between male and female, between cohorts, social classes, ethnic and religious groups, and many more. These boundaries are merely abstractions that, although perhaps having utility in limited social, historical, conceptual, or research contexts, have unfortunately been permitted to define categories as though they had a mutually exclusive, concrete, material existence. The question of why the boundaries are placed and the categories defined as they are cannot be answered at the level of the category system itself, but—by analogy with Gödel's Theorem—can only be answered at a higher level, that is, by considering the context within which the boundaries and the category system have been set forth. This consideration is discussed in a following section (also see Gadlin & Rubin, 1979; Sampson, 1977); first, however, an alternative to the input–output, heredity–environment model will be set forth.

THE INTERPENETRATION MODEL

What initial statement can be made about the causes of individual development, without at the same time making assumptions, regarding the location of boundaries between categories, that may eventually impede our understanding of individual development? If the initial assumptions are incorrect (e.g., that heredity and environment are independent categories), then unnecessary and unsolvable problems are introduced (How do these categories interact?). Let me suggest as an initial statement that the relationship among the categories, causes, structures, and processes that may play roles in the course of individual development is one of *interpenetration*. Such a statement makes no commitment regarding the existence of boundaries between categories or causes, or whether they might be hierarchically ordered, or what the causal relationships might be. In a relationship of interpenetration, as one aspect changes, all the others necessarily change simultaneously. (Lerner & Busch-Rossnagel, Chapter 1, this volume, refer to the same notion as embeddedness.)

The interpenetration model may be made more clear by making explicit a parallel with S. L. Rubinstein's (Payne, 1968) resolution of the conflict between the introspectionist notion of consciousness (mind) and the behaviorist notion of human activity (body). For Rubinstein, consciousness and behavior are not isolated entities, so that the question of how they interact must then be considered. Instead, Rubinstein suggested as a starting point the principle of the unity—an interpenetration, not an identity—of consciousness and behavior (Meacham, 1977c, p. 275; Payne, 1968, pp. 84–94). To return to the causes of individual development (e.g., heredity, the environment, the individual, or whatever other categories), these too can be conceived of as neither isolated nor identical, but as existing in a relationship of interpenetration.

At a conceptual level, the metaphors of interpenetration and transaction appear consistent, because, in transaction, entities are derived from more basic activities. For students and the general public, however, transaction may be a less successful metaphor, as it suggests the idea of "between" or "from one place to another," that is, it may be taken casually and inappropriately to imply entities existing separately and prior to the process of communication or exchange. As Overton (1976) suggests, however, metaphors are of vital importance in guiding theory construction, the questions raised, and the methods used, as well as how our students and the general public assimilate developmental psychology, and so it is well worth trying and discarding a variety of metaphors to find a good one. (The "goodness" of a metaphor will depend upon its appropriateness within specific social and historical contexts; I will turn to this question in the next section.) The metaphors of interpenetration and dialectics also appear consistent, at least as dialectics is set forth in Riegel's (1976, 1978, 1979) dialectical theory of human development. Riegel's theory is based to a large extent in the work of Rubinstein, and one may assume that Riegel thought of the biological, psychological, and cultural–sociological progressions not as independent entities but as being in a relationship like that of interpenetration.

The interpenetration model is also consistent with numerous other commentaries on heredity, environment, and individual development: Lerner (1978, 1980; Lerner & Busch-Rossnagel, Chapter 1, this volume) notes that all variables (e.g., heredity and environment) in a bidirectional, dialectical interaction must be simultaneously products and producers of each other. Deutsch (1968, p. 61) has used the term interpenetration to emphasize that the environment and nature do more than merely interact in the production of the person, and to emphasize the modifiability of nature as well as nurture. Furth (1973) notes that physiological maturation, the acquisition of information from the environment, and developmental experience "are not separately existing processes or behaviors. Rather, they are three interrelated aspects of one concrete reality, namely, the growing child in his cognitive activity [p. 63]." Overton (1973), in discussing the reciprocal causality or strong interactions between heredity and environment, notes that "over the course of development it becomes impossible to distinguish in any meaningful way the individual components [p. 78]." Finally, Tobach (Chapter 2, this volume) has emphasized the "inseparable interconnectedness of genetic processes with ecological change and with the activities of the individual; all these processes are interpenetrating and causal."

HEREDITY, ENVIRONMENT, AND THE QUESTION "WHY?"

Anastasi's (1958) framework of questions on the relationship of heredity and environment—"Which one?" "How much?" and "How?"—may be extended to a fourth question, "Why?" Why are the first three questions phrased in terms of heredity and environment as the principal categories whose interaction must then be considered? Although the answer can certainly be found in part in the history of science, especially biology and the work of G. Mendel, the answer can also be sought through an examination of the usefulness of this particular two-category, input–output model within its social and historical context. What political values and ideas are consistent with a conceptual framework that conceives of heredity and environment as stable and independent and that neglects individuals as a source of input into their own development? This category system appears consistent with political values and ideas that emphasize maintaining inqualitiies, especially differences associated with class, sex, race, ethnic background, and so on, and inconsistent with views that emphasize change and the overcoming of differences in education, income, and employment opportunities between these and other groups.

The continuing interest among students, the general public, and developmental psychologists in the heredity–environment controversy reflects an underlying and yet paramount concern with the question of the plasticity or modifiability of the course of individual development. The theme of people against nature, including their own, is an ancient one that still reverberates through our culture (see Leiss, 1972): Can people's behavior be improved, or does nature set limits against which it is futile to strive? Certainly questions regarding the extent of modifiability of people's behavior may properly be answered through seeking to understand more fully the processes of individual development, including the roles played by both heredity and environment. Nevertheless, the assumption that the stable and independent categories of heredity and environment, in conjunction with an input–output model, provide a sufficient framework for understanding individual development continues to be readily assimilable to political views that it is difficult to change people's behavior and futile to expend money and effort attempting to change social conditions. I will illustrate this linkage for the cases of heredity, environment, and individuals as producers of their own development. As a preface, however, I should note that my intended audience is not necessarily those developmental psychologists who are aware of the complexities of what is known about individual development and so are able to avoid—although perhaps only by means of some rather complex verbal and conceptual acrobatics—the simplistic conclusions suggested here. Rather, my concern is with students, the general public, and those in policymaking positions for whom these simplistic conclusions may unfortunately seem altogether reasonable.

Heredity

Many persons interested in modifiability of the course of individual development have sought to know merely whether a particular developmental outcome—schizophrenia, sociopathology, retardation, racial differences, class differences—is caused by heredity or by the environment (parents, schools, culture, etc.). The answer that heredity is the cause (or that heritability is high) has served to free society from its responsibilities for both prevention and treatment. Legal and ethical reasons are cited in the case of prevention, and the presumed difficulty or impossibility of modification is cited in the case of treatment (note that neither prevention nor treatment are necessarily unethical or difficult within the interpenetration model; see discussion of modification in the first section of this chapter). Evidence that heredity plays a role in individual development—as of course it does in all development—has been used too often as a rationale for racism, sexism, colonialism, restrictive immigration laws, eugenics, and other political views that depend upon or encourage maintenance of inequalities (Elias, 1973, p. 121; Gould, 1976/1978; Looft, 1973, p. 29). What is needed, as suggested by Eisenberg (1972/1978), is to distinguish clearly the issue of a role for heredity in development from the issue of modifiability of the course of development: Although behavior is always under genetic control, this does not warrant the assumption of a lack of modifiability or plasticity, that is, a lack of susceptibility to environmental influences.

Environment

It would be too easy and incorrect to say that to place the emphasis upon environment rather than on heredity is necessarily consistent with change-oriented political values and ideas. Overemphasis of environment to the neglect of heredity can unfortunately be consistent with the political view that might—when it comes to changing the environment—makes right. Chomsky (1975) notes that if indeed people are "malleable and plastic beings with no essential psychological nature, then why should they not be controlled and coerced by those who claim authority, special knowledge, and a unique insight into what is best for those less enlightened? [p. 132]." Chomsky credits the rationalist model for providing the foundation for Rousseau's opposition to tyranny, Kant's defense of freedom, and Marx's critique that alienated labor deprives men of their character. At another level, arguments over the precise statistic for the heritability of intelligence have served only to reaffirm the validity of the input–output, heredity–environment model, and so reinforce those who base their rationalization of existing inequality upon this model. As Looft (1973) has noted, the simplistic environmental thesis serves merely as a negation of the heredity thesis: "Unfortunately, to end the analysis only at negation leads to an implicit affirmation of the original thesis. The next—and most necessary—step is to move beyond both thesis and antithesis and work toward developing an acceptable synthesis [p. 19]." Hebb (1970) agrees with the need to continue to consider openly and to criticize the heredity thesis; by preventing such a consideration, the racist would be convinced that the truth was being suppressed. In summary, although often environmentalism and political values oriented toward change have gone hand-in-hand (Pastore, 1949), this is not a necessary liaison. Those seeking a conceptual model as a justification for change would be on firmer ground with a model such as that of interpenetration.

Individuals

It would be satisfying within the context of the present volume to be able to assert that the perspective that individuals are producers of their own development is necessarily consistent with political views emphasizing change away from inequality. It ought to be the case that, if individuals can play a substantial role in their own development, one could be optimistic that individuals could pull themselves up by their bootstraps, overcome adversity, better their condition, and so on. Ample examples of such positive changes are provided throughout the present volume. Nevertheless, unless this perspective is grounded in a framework other than the heredity–environment, input–output model, it too may be used to provide a rationalization for maintaining inequalities.

Levine and Levine (1970) have documented two major modes in the history of the provision of clinic and community services, the situational, which assumes that a basically good person has been influenced by poor social conditions that can be changed through reform (1890–1914); and the intrapsychic, which assumes that inner weaknesses and failings can account for the individual's difficulties (1920s). This latter, conservative view was derived from Social Darwinism, and reflected the emphasis in the 1920s on self-development, on heroes such as Lindbergh and Babe Ruth, and on competition and prosperity in business, that is, on individuals producing their own development. Those who did not succeed lacked something inside themselves (Levine & Levine, 1960, p. 233); they were individuals who had failed to produce their own development.

Similarly, Ryan (1976) has distinguished two social ideologies: the first understands social problems as a function of the structure of the community and the larger society, and the second Ryan terms "blaming the victim." In the latter case, although environmental causes (e.g., living in poverty) of social problems are acknowledged, the emphasis is upon differences (e.g., between the poor and the middle class) that are seen as located *within* the individual. Thus the blaming the victim ideology leads to attempts to change individuals through compensatory education rather than to change the structure of the schools, to "strengthen" families rather than to increase employment opportunities, to provide information to overcome ignorance regarding health care rather than to eliminate inequities in the health care delivery system. The ideology of blaming the victim calls for conducting and interpreting research to show that the poor, minorities, slum tenants, and so on "think in different forms, act in different patterns, cling to different values, seek different goals, and learn different truths [p. 8]." In other words, the "explanation" for the social problems is that these individuals do not (are not able? do not choose to?) produce their own development, and so the larger or more powerful part of society bears little or no responsibility for their condition and need not consider changes away from existing inequalities.

A similar argument has been made by Lane (1976), who suggests that the interdependence of societal structures "militates against the possibilities of individuals determining to any real extent their own daily behaviors or destiny [p. 1056]," so that the individual is an inappropriate unit of analysis of human behavior. Lane indicts psychologists for perpetuating the "cult of individualism" and accepting explanations of problems that blame the individual for the problem. Lane suggests the need for a systems analysis, that is, avoiding simplistic input–output models (also see Sampson, 1977).

The input–output model assumes that individuals as products may be understood in terms of some combination of independent inputs. Nevertheless, this model itself is the obstacle to a fair consideration of various social problems. Within the input–output model, when the output is not successful, one turns to the various categories of input to discover the "cause" of the lack of success. When only heredity and environment are recognized as possible inputs, and the output is faulty, blame is assigned to one or the other, or to some additive combination of the two. The reconceptualization of the status of the individual as both output and input is radical, but not radical enough, for it can be consistent with political views that maintain existing inequalities. As Ryan (1976) has pointed out, blame can be shifted from heredity and environment to the individuals themselves as inputs. Political values and ideas that emphasize change away from inequality are generally inconsistent with input–output models, regardless of whether these models emphasize heredity, the environment, or individuals as producers of their own development.

Within the interpenetration model, however, the conflict between people and nature is a false one, for the categories of people and nature are not mutually exclusive. Rather, people are a part of nature. If a change is made from any one perspective within the model—for example, a gene, one's self-concept, the cultural milieu—then changes simultaneously occur within each of the other perspectives. What political values are consistent with the interpenetration model? This model is readily consistent with notions of change: Not only does a change within any one perspective make itself apparent within all others, but also changes may be introduced within any of the perspectives indirectly, by introducing change within any other. To be specific: One may bring about changes in the biological perspective on individual development (e.g., PKU syndrome) by introducing a change in the environment (e.g., diet); or one may change the impact of a particular body-build type through intervention directed at improving self-concept or destroying social stereotypes (Lerner, 1976; Sorell & Nowak, Chapter 14, this volume); or, as Jones and Haney (Chapter

13, this volume) outline, one may reduce negative reactions to racial characteristics through behavioral programs that increase social contact between groups, and so on. In summary, the thesis that individuals are producers of their own development is best understood within the context of change oriented models such as transaction, contextualism, or dialectics, that emphasize relationships of strong interaction, reciprocal causality, or interpenetration.

Conclusion: Taking the Next Steps

The discipline of developmental psychology is concerned with the description, explanation, and modification (optimization) of changes in behavior across the life span (Baltes, Reese, & Nesselroade, 1977). The perspective that individuals are producers of their own development is significant in calling attention to the need—especially when the concern is with modification—for alternatives to the heredity–environment, input–output model, a model that can too easily be incorrectly understood as providing a justification for maintaining existing social inequalities. Transactional, contextual, and dialectical models, on the other hand, are consistent with political values and ideas that emphasize the need for and the possibility of change.

Implicit within this brief summary, and indeed throughout this entire chapter, is that conceptual models are not value free. Whether one assumes an input–output model or a model based on reciprocal causality has important implications for the direction that one's research program will take, for the understanding that is achieved, and for the use that can be made, both by oneself and by others, of the products of one's thought, research activity, and scholarship. (The input–output model can be used, as a heuristic simplification, for investigating aspects of what one acknowledges to be complex processes involving reciprocal causality. It is important, however, to be able to specify precisely the dimensions and the assumptions underlying the simplification, and the consequences—in terms of possible limits on the generalizability and application of one's conclusions—of working solely within an input–output model.)

That there is a correspondence between the political values of researchers and the social and historical contexts within which they work, on the one hand, and the course and products of their research activity, on the other, is gaining increasing recognition (see, e.g., Buss, 1975; Gergen, 1973; Haan, Chapter 6, this volume; Habermas, 1971; Labouvie-Vief & Chandler, 1978; Meacham, 1977b/1978, 1977d, 1978/1980; Samelson, 1975). There are no absolute, objective "facts" or truths to be revealed regarding individual development. Instead, "analyses mean something only in terms of their utilities for some purpose [Jenkins, 1974, p. 789]." Gergen (1977) notes that "No investigation is without implicit valuational implications. What the theorist singles out for study, the terms in which it is described, . . . and the very attempt to avoid value statements may all have significant effects on one's conception of the good, the moral, or the desirable [p. 139]."

In this context, however, it may be useful to call attention to the despair occasionally felt by those who become aware, for the first time, of the social and historical relativity of research in developmental psychology. In short, these people feel that nothing can be known for certain and there can be no cumulation of understanding, because all knowledge is relative and must be evaluated according to its particular social and historical context, the implicit assumptions and values of the researcher, the specific methods of investigation, and so on. There are some typical but inadequate responses to this despair: One might, for example, randomly choose a particular research framework (e.g., as a result of some opportunities that arise during graduate training) and naively plod ahead, ignoring the question of values. One might also strive to achieve an abstract, integrative knowledge through bringing together the conclusions from a variety of research perspectives. These inadequate solutions, however, assume that there can be objective "facts" that have meaning apart from the context within which they are constructed (Meacham, 1977b/1978).

The more appropriate solution is to recognize that, from the perspective of transaction, contextualism, and dialectics, research methodology is of utmost importance (Meacham, 1978/1980). Knowing depends upon a specification of the relationship of presumed "facts" to the methodology employed by the researcher, and to the social and historical context within which the researcher has labored. To be more concrete, the significance of a presumed "fact" cannot be appreciated without considering the context within which that "fact" has been constructed (see also Labouvie-Vief, Chapter 8, this volume): What influenced the decision of the researcher to invest time and energy in exploring a particular hypothesis? What implicit assumptions or simplifications have been made to make the topic amenable to research? What was the social and historical context within which the data were gathered, interpreted, and prepared for communication to the general public?

To raise such questions is not to say that the social–historical context determines the activities of researchers. Rather, there is a consistency or complementarity between the themes and issues important to each (Meacham, 1977b/1978). The concern of developmental psychologists with particular issues—for example, the heredity–environment issue—reflects the fact that these issues—including the question of modifiability—are sources of tension in the larger society. At the same time, the work of developmental psychologists provides grist for efforts by the society to understand and to transform basic issues. The social and historical milieu provides the context, therefore, within which the input–output model and the interpenetration model may be evaluated. Neither model has intrinsic value on its own, but one may consider the extent to which each is consistent with the values and goals of researchers and of the larger society. It is in the superordinate social and cultural context (cf. Gödel's Theorem) that answers are found to questions as to the choice of a particular model, the definitions of boundaries and categories, and so on (Samelson, 1975). In short, researchers themselves living within a personal and societal context must be included within the framework of research methodology (Meacham, 1978/1980).

The stage is now set for an evaluation of the thesis that individuals are producers of their own development. That evaluation, however, depends upon the political values of the audience—primarily researchers and students—that will read this volume. They must face the challenge that is implicit within the thesis that individuals are producers of their own development: Can they take firm command of the course of their own professional development, and the course of their own research programs, and lead both in a direction consistent with their political values and ideas?

References

Anastasi, A. Heredity, environment, and the question "How?" *Psychological Review*, 1958, 65, 197–208.

Anastasi, A. More on heritability: Addendum to the Hebb and Jensen exchange. *American Psychologist*, 1971, 26, 1036–1037.

Baltes, P. B., Reese, H. W., & Nesselroade, J. B. *Life-span developmental psychology: Introduction to research methods.* Montery: Brooks/Cole, 1977.

Bandura, A. The self-system in reciprocal determinism. *American Psychologist*, 1978, 33, 344–358.

Bee, H. *The developing child.* New York: Harper & Row, 1975.

Boocock, S. S. Children in contemporary society. In A. Skolnick (Ed.), *Rethinking childhood: Perspectives on development and society.* Boston: Little, Brown, 1976.

Brent, S. B. Individual specialization, collective adaptation, and rate of environmental change. *Human Development*, 1978, 21, 21–33. (a)

Brent, S. B. Prigogine's model for self-organization in nonequilibrium systems: Its relevance for developmental psychology. *Human Development*, 1978, 21, 374–387. (b)

Brody, J. E. Tending to obesity, inbred tribe aids diabetes study. *The New York Times*, February 5, 1980, pp. C1, C5.

Buss, A. R. The emerging field of the sociology of psychological knowledge. *American Psychologist*, 1975, 30, 988–1002.

Butler, R. The life review: An interpretation of reminiscence in the aged. *Psychiatry*, 1963, 26, 65–76.

Carmichael, L. Heredity and environment: Are they antithetical? *Journal of Abnormal and Social Psychology*, 1925, 20, 245–260.

Carter-Saltzman, L. Behavior genetics from an interactional point of view. In L. A. Pervin & M. Lewis (Eds.), *Perspectives in interactional psychology.* New York: Plenum, 1978.

Chomsky, N. *Reflections on language.* New York: Pantheon, 1975.

Deutsch, C. P. Environment and perception. In M. Deutsch, I. Katz, & A. R. Jensen (Eds.), *Social class, race, and psychological development.* New York: Holt, Rhinehart & Winston, 1968.

Dewey, J., and Bentley, A. F. *Knowing and the known.* Boston: Beacon, 1960. (Originally published, 1949.)

Dobzhansky, T. Differences are not deficits. *Psychology Today,* 1973, *7* (December), 97–101.

Douglas, J. H. Genetic susceptibility to disease. *Science News,* 1979, *116*(22), 337.

Eisenburg, L. The "human" nature of human nature. *Science,* 1972, *176* (Apr. 14), 123–128. (Also in A. L. Caplan (Ed.), *The sociobiology debate.* New York: Harper & Row, 1978.)

Elder, G. H., Jr. Family history and the life course. *Journal of Family History,* 1977, *2,* 279–304.

Elias, M. F. Disciplinary barriers to progress in behavior genetics: Defensive reactions to bits and pieces. *Human Development,* 1973, *16,* 119–132. (Also in K. F. Riegel (Ed.), *Intelligence: Alternative views of a paradigm.* Basel: Karger, 1973.)

Endler, N. S. The person versus the situation—a pseudo issue? A response to Alker. *Journal of Personality,* 1973, *41,* 287–303.

Erikson, E. H. *Childhood and society.* New York: Norton, 1950.

Furth, H. G. *Piaget and knowledge.* Englewood Cliffs, N. J.: Prentice-Hall, 1969.

Furth, H. G. Piaget, IQ, and the nature–nurture controversy. *Human Development,* 1973, *16,* 61–73. (Also in K. F. Riegel (Ed.), *Intelligence: Alternative views of a paradigm.* Basel: Karger, 1973.)

Gadlin, H., & Rubin, I. "Interaction" in social theory. In A. Buss (Ed.), *The sociology of psychological knowledge.* New York: Irvington, 1979.

Gergen, K. J. Social psychology as history. *Journal of Personality and Social Psychology,* 1973, *26,* 309–320.

Gergen, K. J. Stability, change, and chance in understanding human development. In N. Datan & H. W. Reese (Eds.), *Life-span developmental psychology: Dialectical perspectives on experimental research.* New York: Academic Press, 1977.

Gould, S. J. Biological potential vs. biological determinism. *Natural History,* 1976, *85*(5), 12–22. (Also in A. L. Caplan (Ed.), *The sociobiology debate.* New York: Harper & Row, 1978.)

Habermas, J. *Knowledge and human interests.* Boston: Beacon, 1971.

Hebb, D. O. A return to Jensen and his social science critics. *American Psychologist,* 1970, *25,* 568.

Hirsch, J. Behavior–genetic analysis and its biological consequences. *Seminars in Psychiatry,* 1970, *2,* 89–105. (Also in W. R. Looft (Ed.), *Developmental psychology.* Hinsdale, Ill.: Dryden, 1972.)

Jarvik, L. Thoughts on the psychobiology of aging. *American Psychologist,* 1975, *30,* 576–583.

Jenkins, J. J. Remember that old theory of memory? Well, forget it! *American Psychologist,* 1974, *29,* 785–795.

Kohlberg, L. Early education: A cognitive–developmental view. *Child Development,* 1968, *39,* 1013–1062.

Kvale, S. Dialectics and research on remembering. In N. Datan and H. W. Reese (Eds.), *Life-span developmental psychology: Dialectical perspectives on experimental research.* New York: Academic Press, 1977.

Labouvie-Vief, G., & Chandler, M. J. Cognitive development and life-span developmental theory: Idealistic versus contextual perspectives. In P. B. Baltes (Ed.), *Life-span development and behavior* (Vol. 1). New York: Academic Press, 1978.

Lane, M. K. A reconsideration of context: Perspectives on prediction—mote in the eye. *American Psychologist,* 1977, *32,* 1056–1059.

Lawler, J. M. *IQ, heritability, and racism.* New York: International, 1978.

Lazarus, R. S., & Launier, R. Stress-related transactions between persons and environment. In L. A. Pervin & M. Lewis (Eds.), *Perspectives in interactional psychology.* New York: Plenum, 1978.

Leiss, W. *The domination of nature*. New York: Braziller, 1972.

Lerner, R. M. *Concepts and theories of human development*. Reading, Mass.: Addison-Wesley, 1976.

Lerner, R. M. Nature, nurture, and dynamic interactionism. *Human Development*, 1978, *21*, 1–20.

Lerner, R. M. Concepts of epigenesis: Descriptive and explanatory issues. *Human Development*, 1980, *23*, 63–72.

Lerner, R. M., Skinner, E. A., & Sorell, G. T. Methodological implications of contextual–dialectic theories of development. In D. F. Hultsch (Chair), *Implications of a dialectical perspective for research methodology*. Symposium presented at the meeting of the American Psychological Association, Toronto, August, 1978. (Also in *Human Development*, 1980, *23*, 225–235.)

Levine, M., & Levine, A. *A social history of helping services*. New York: Appleton-Century-Crofts, 1970.

Lewis, C. N. The adaptive value of reminiscing in old age. *Journal of Geriatric Psychiatry*, 1973, *6*, 117–121.

Lipsitt, L. P. Infancy and life-span development. In R. M. Lerner (Chair), *Child development in life-span perspective*. Symposium presented at the meeting of the Society for Research in Child Development, San Francisco, March, 1979. (Also in *Human Development*, 1981, *24*, in press.)

Looft, W. R. Conceptions of human nature, educational practice, and individual development. *Human Development*, 1973, *16*, 21–32. (Also in K. F. Riegel (Ed.), *Intelligence: Alternative views of a paradigm*. Basel: Karger, 1973.)

Mancuso, J. C. Current motivational models in the elaboration of personal construct theory. In J. K. Cole & A. W. Landfield (Eds.), *Nebraska Symposium on Motivation 1976* (Vol. 24). Lincoln: University of Nebraska Press, 1977.

Meacham, J. A. The development of memory abilities in the individual and society. *Human Development*, 1972, *15*, 205–228. (Also in J. G. Seamon (Ed.), *Recent contributions in memory and cognition*. Oxford: Oxford University Press, 1980.)

Meacham, J. A. A transactional model of remembering. In N. Datan & H. W. Reese (Eds.), *Life-span developmental psychology: Dialectical perspectives on experimental research*. New York: Academic Press, 1977. (a)

Meacham, J. A. History and developmental psychology. In F. P. Hardesty & P. B. Baltes (Chairs), *The contributions of Klaus F. Riegel (1925–1977)*. Symposium presented at the meeting of the American Psychological Association, San Francisco, August, 1977. (b) (Also in *Human Development*, 1978, *21*, 363–369.)

Meacham, J. A. Soviet investigations of memory development. In R. V. Kail, Jr., & J. W. Hagen (Eds.), *Perspectives on the development of memory and cognition*. Hillsdale, N. J.: Erlbaum, 1977. (c)

Meacham, J. A. The decentration of developmental psychology. *Merrill-Palmer Quarterly*, 1977, *23*, 287–295. (d)

Meacham, J. A. Research on remembering: Interrogation or conversation, monologue or dialogue? In D. F. Hultsch (Chair), *Implications of a dialectical perspective for research methodology*. Symposium presented at the meeting of the American Psychological Association, Toronto, August, 1978. (Also in *Human Development*, 1980, *23*, 236–245.)

Meacham, J. A. The role of verbal activity in remembering the goals of actions. In G. L Zivin (Ed.), *Development of self-regulation through private speech*. New York: Wiley, 1979.

Mischel, W. Toward a cognitive social learning reconceptualization of personality. *Psychological Review*, 1973, *80*, 252–283.

Money, J., & Ehrhardt, A. A. *Man and woman, boy and girl*. Baltimore: Johns Hopkins University Press, 1972.

Nicolis, G., & Prigogine, I. *Self-organization in nonequilibrium systems*. New York: Wiley, 1977.

Overton, W. F. On the assumptive base of the nature–nurture controversy: Additive versus interactive conceptions. *Human Development*, 1973, *16*, 74–89. (Also in K. F. Riegel (Ed.), *Intelligence: Alternative views of a paradigm*. Basel: Karger, 1973.)

Overton, W. F. General systems, structure, and development. In K. F. Riegel & G. C. Rosenwald (Eds.), *Structure and transformation: Developmental and historical aspects*. New York: Wiley, 1975.

Overton, W. F. The active organism in structuralism. *Human Development*, 1976, *19*, 71–86.

Overton, W. F., & Reese, H. W. Models of development: Methodological implications. In J. R. Nesselroade & H. W. Reese (Eds.), *Life-span developmental psychology: Methodological issues*. New York: Academic Press, 1973.

Pastore, N. *The nature–nurture controversy*. New York: Kings Crown Press, 1949.

Payne, T. R. *S. L. Rubinstein and the philosophical foundations of Soviet psychology*. New York: Humanities Press, 1968.

Pepper, S. C. *World hypotheses*. Berkeley: University of California Press, 1942.

Pervin, L. A. Performance and satisfaction as a function of individual–environment fit. *Psychological Bulletin*, 1968, *69*, 56–68.

Piaget, J. Development and learning. In R. Ripple & V. Rockcastle (Eds.), *Piaget rediscovered*. Ithaca: Cornell University Press, 1964. Also in C. S. Lavatelli & F. Stendler (Eds.), *Readings in child behavior and development* (3rd ed.). New York: Harcourt Brace Jovanovich, 1972.

Piaget, J. Piaget's theory. In P. H. Mussen (Ed.), *Carmichael's manual of child psychology* (Vol. 1). New York: Wiley, 1970.

Prigogine, I. Time, structure, and fluctuation. *Science*, 1978, *201*, 777–785.

Reese, H. W. Conceptions of the active organism: Discussion. *Human Development*, 1976, *19*, 108–119.

Reese, H. W. Discriminative learning and transfer: Dialectical perspectives. In N. Datan & H. W. Reese, (Eds.), *Life-span developmental psychology: Dialectical perspectives on experimental research*. New York: Academic Press, 1977.

Riegel, K. F. The dialectics of human development. *American Psychologist*, 1976, *31*, 689–700.

Riegel, K. F. *Psychology, mon amour: A countertext*. Boston: Houghton Mifflin, 1978.

Riegel, K. F. *Foundations of dialectical psychology*. New York: Academic Press, 1979. (Stuttgart: Klett-Cotta Verlag, 1980.)

Riegel, K. F., & Meacham, J. A. Dialectics, transactions, and Piaget's theory. In L. A. Pervin & M. Lewis (Eds.), *Perspectives in interactional psychology*. New York: Plenum, 1978.

Ryan, W. *Blaming the victim*. New York: Vintage, 1976.

Rychlak, J. F. A nontelic teleology? *American Psychologist*, 1979, *34*, 435–438.

Samelson, F. On the science and politics of IQ. *Social Research*, 1975,*42*, 467–488.

Sameroff, A. J. *Theoretical and empirical issues in the operationalization of transactional research*. Paper presented at the meeting of the Society for Research in Child Development, San Francisco, March, 1979.

Sameroff, A. J., & Chandler, M. J. Reproductive risk and the continuum of caretaking casualty. In F. D. Horowitz (Ed.), *Review of child development research* (Vol. 4). Chicago: University of Chicago Press, 1975.

Sampson, E. E. Psychology and the American ideal. *Journal of Personality and Social Psychology*, 1977, *35*, 767–782.

Sarbin, T. R. Contextualism: A world view for modern psychology. In J. K. Cole & A. W. Landfield (Eds.), *Nebraska Symposium on Motivation 1976* (Vol. 24). Lincoln: University of Nebraska Press, 1977.

Schneirla, T. C. The concept of development in comparative psychology. In D. B. Harris (Ed.), *The concept of development*. Minneapolis: University of Minnesota Press, 1957.

Skinner, B. F. *About behaviorism*. New York: Knopf, 1974.

Tamir, L. *Communication and the aging process: Interaction throughout the life cycle*. New York: Pergamon, 1979.

Thoreson, C. E. & Mahoney, M. J. *Behavioral self-control*. New York: Holt, Rinehart & Winston, 1974.

Tolman, C. The metaphysic of relations in Klaus Riegel's "dialectics" of human development. *Human Development*, 1981, *24*, 33–51.

Waddington, C. H. *New patterns in genetics and development.* New York: Columbia University Press, 1962.

Wertsch, J. V. From social interaction to higher psychological processes: A clarification of Vygotsky's theory. *Human Development*, 1979, *22*, 1–22.

White, S. H. The active organism in theoretical behaviorism. *Human Development*, 1976, *19*, 99–107.

Wilden, A. *System and structure: Essays in communication and exchange.* London: Tavistock, 1972.

Wilden, A. Piaget and the structure as law and order. In K. F. Riegel & G. C. Rosenwald (Eds.), *Structure and transformation: developmental aspects.* New York: Wiley, 1975.

Author Index

Numbers in italics refer to the pages on which the complete references are listed.

A

Abeson, A., 297, *307*
Abrahams, B., 336, *341*
Abrahams, D., 418, 424, 425, *446*
Abramson, P. R., 406, *440*
Abravanel, E., 21, 23, 29, *31*
Achenbach, T. M., 205, *226*
Adams, G. R., 389, 401, 409, 410, 412, 413, 414, 417, 418, 420, 423, 425, 427, 432, *437*, *438*, *442*, *445*
Adelman, L., 371, *382*
Adelson, R., 299, 300, *310*
Adinolfi, A. A., 395, 425, *442*
Adlerstein, A., 293, 295, *311*
Adorno, T. W., 369, *381*
Ahammer, I. M., 217, 218, *226*, 330, *341*
Ainsworth, M. D. S., 104, 107, 109, *111*, *112*
Alcorn, D., 305, *312*
Alessi, D. F., 299, *307*
Alexander, G., 59, *65*
Algozzine, B., 422, *445*
Allen, B. P., 367, *381*
Allen, P. M., 24, 25, *35*

Allen, T. W., 143, *148*
Allen, V. L., 361, *381*
Allport, G. W., 360, 371, *381*
Altemeir, W., 94, *112*
Altemeyer, R. A., 427, *438*
Alvy, K. T., 248, *254*
Ames, R., 390, 392, 400, *438*
Amir, Y., 371, *381*
Anastasi, A., 391, *438*, 450, 461, 463, *470*
Anderson, C. O., 41, 48, *65*
Angrist, S. A., 317, *341*
Anthony, W. A., 299, *307*
Apfel, N., 259, 263, 266, 267, *277*
Aquilino, W., 242, *255*
Arend, R., 109, *112*, 335, *345*
Aries, P., 177, *180*
Arlin, P. K., 171, *180*
Arndt, C., 301, *310*
Aronson, E., 371, 372, *381*, 428, *444*, *445*
Aronson, L. R., 47, *65*
Aronson, V., 418, 424, 425, *446*
Asher, S. R., 361, *381*
Atchley, R. C., 186, 188, *196*

Subject Index